MW00657742

THE DATA SCIENCE WORKSHOP

SECOND EDITION

Learn how you can build machine learning models and create your own real-world data science projects

Anthony So, Thomas V. Joseph, Robert Thas John, Andrew Worsley, and Dr. Samuel Asare

Packt

THE DATA SCIENCE WORKSHOP

SECOND EDITION

Authors: Anthony So, Thomas V. Joseph, Robert Thas John, Andrew Worsley, and Dr. Samuel Asare

Reviewers: Tianxiang Liu, Tiffany Ford, and Pritesh Tiwari

Managing Editor: Snehal Tambe

Acquisitions Editor: Sarah Lawton

Production Editor: Salma Patel

First published: January 2020

Second edition: August 2020

Production reference: 1280820

ISBN: 978-1-80056-692-7
Published by Packt Publishing Ltd.
Livery Place, 35 Livery Street
Birmingham B3 2PB, UK

EXPERIENCE THE WORKSHOP ONLINE

Thank you for purchasing the print edition of *The Data Science Workshop, Second Edition*. Every physical print copy includes free online access to the premium interactive edition. There are no extra costs or hidden charges.

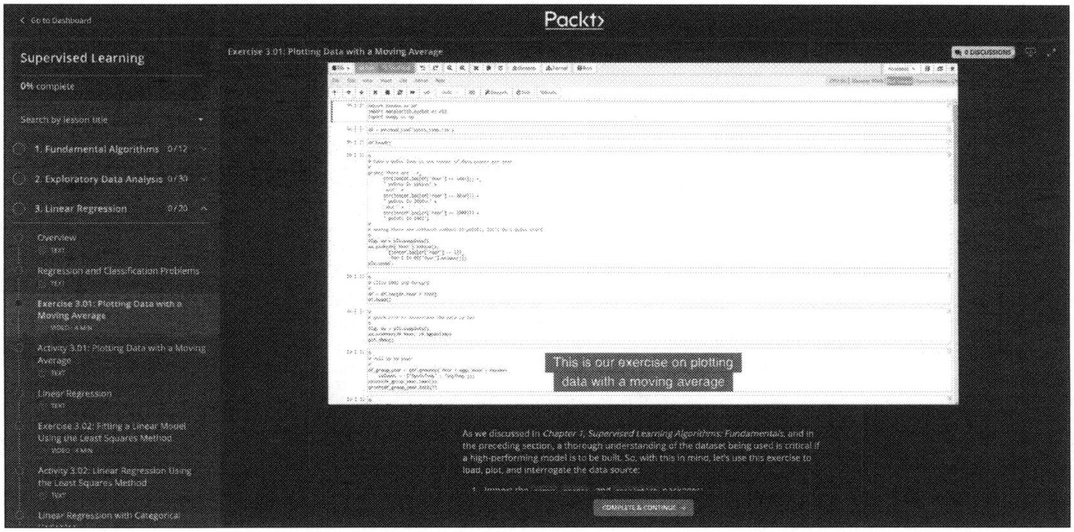

Figure A: An example of the companion video in the Workshop course player (dark mode)

With the interactive edition you'll unlock:

- **Screencasts**: Supercharge your progress with screencasts of all exercises and activities.
- **Built-In Discussions**: Engage in discussions where you can ask questions, share notes and interact. Tap straight into insight from expert instructors and editorial teams.
- **Skill Verification**: Complete the course online to earn a Packt credential that is easy to share and unique to you. All authenticated on the public Bitcoin blockchain.
- **Download PDF and EPUB**: Download a digital version of the course to read offline. Available as PDF or EPUB, and always DRM-free.

To redeem your free digital copy of *The Data Science Workshop, Second Edition,* you'll need to follow these simple steps:

1. Visit us at https://courses.packtpub.com/pages/redeem.
2. Login with your Packt account, or register as a new Packt user.
3. Select your course from the list, making a note of the three page numbers for your product. Your unique redemption code needs to match the order of the pages specified.
4. Open up your print copy and find the codes at the bottom of the pages specified. They'll always be in the same place:

EXERCISE 4.02: PERFORMING MISSING VALUE ANALYSIS FOR THE DATAFRAMES

In this section, we will be implementing a missing value analysis on the first DataFrame to find the missing values. This exercise is a continuation of *Exercise 4.01, Importing Data into DataFrames*. Follow these steps to complete this exercise:

1. Import the **missingno** package:

```
# To analyze the missing data
!pip install missingno
import missingno as msno
```

2. Find the missing values in the first DataFrame and visualize the missing values in a plot:

```
# Missing Values in the first DataFrame
msno.bar(dataframes[0],color='red',labels=True,sort="ascending")
```

A B 2 1 C

Figure B: Example code in the bottom-right corner, to be used for free digital redemption of a print workshop

5. Merge the codes together (without spaces), ensuring they are in the correct order.
6. At checkout, click **`Have a redemption code?`** and enter your unique product string. Click **`Apply`**, and the price should be free!

Finally, we'd like to thank you for purchasing the print edition of *The Data Science Workshop, Second Edition*! We hope that you finish the course feeling capable of tackling challenges in the real world. Remember that we're here to help if you ever feel like you're not making progress.

If you run into issues during redemption (or have any other feedback) you can reach us at workshops@packt.com.

Table of Contents

Preface i

Chapter 1: Introduction to Data Science in Python 1

Introduction 2
Application of Data Science 3
What Is Machine Learning? 4
Supervised Learning 4
Unsupervised Learning 6
Reinforcement Learning 7
Overview of Python 7
Types of Variable 7
Numeric Variables 7
Text Variables 8
Python List 9
Python Dictionary 11
Exercise 1.01: Creating a Dictionary That Will Contain Machine Learning Algorithms 14
Python for Data Science 18
The pandas Package 18
DataFrame and Series 18
CSV Files 20
Excel Spreadsheets 22
JSON 23

Exercise 1.02: Loading Data of Different Formats into a pandas DataFrame 24
Scikit-Learn 28
What Is a Model? 28
Model Hyperparameters 31
The sklearn API 31
Exercise 1.03: Predicting Breast Cancer from a Dataset Using sklearn 34
Activity 1.01: Train a Spam Detector Algorithm 38
Summary 39
Chapter 2: Regression 41
Introduction 42
Simple Linear Regression 44
The Method of Least Squares 46
Multiple Linear Regression 47
Estimating the Regression Coefficients (β_0, β_1, β_2 and β_3) 47
Logarithmic Transformations of Variables 47
Correlation Matrices 48
Conducting Regression Analysis Using Python 48
Exercise 2.01: Loading and Preparing the Data for Analysis 49
The Correlation Coefficient 57
Exercise 2.02: Graphical Investigation of Linear Relationships Using Python 59
Exercise 2.03: Examining a Possible Log-Linear Relationship Using Python 62
The Statsmodels formula API 65
Exercise 2.04: Fitting a Simple Linear Regression Model Using the Statsmodels formula API 65

Analyzing the Model Summary 67
The Model Formula Language 68
Intercept Handling 70
Activity 2.01: Fitting a Log-Linear Model Using the Statsmodels Formula API 70
Multiple Regression Analysis 71
Exercise 2.05: Fitting a Multiple Linear Regression Model Using the Statsmodels Formula API 72
Assumptions of Regression Analysis 74
Activity 2.02: Fitting a Multiple Log-Linear Regression Model 76
Explaining the Results of Regression Analysis 77
Regression Analysis Checks and Balances 78
The F-test 80
The t-test 80
Summary 81
Chapter 3: Binary Classification 83
Introduction 84
Understanding the Business Context 85
Business Discovery 85
Exercise 3.01: Loading and Exploring the Data from the Dataset 86
Testing Business Hypotheses Using Exploratory Data Analysis 89
Visualization for Exploratory Data Analysis 89
Exercise 3.02: Business Hypothesis Testing for Age versus Propensity for a Term Loan 94
Intuitions from the Exploratory Analysis 100
Activity 3.01: Business Hypothesis Testing to Find Employment Status versus Propensity for Term Deposits 100

Feature Engineering 102
Business-Driven Feature Engineering 102
Exercise 3.03: Feature Engineering – Exploration of Individual Features 103
Exercise 3.04: Feature Engineering – Creating New Features from Existing Ones 109
Data-Driven Feature Engineering 115
A Quick Peek at Data Types and a Descriptive Summary 115
Correlation Matrix and Visualization 118
Exercise 3.05: Finding the Correlation in Data to Generate a Correlation Plot Using Bank Data 118
Skewness of Data 121
Histograms 122
Density Plots 123
Other Feature Engineering Methods 124
Summarizing Feature Engineering 127
Building a Binary Classification Model Using the Logistic Regression Function 128
Logistic Regression Demystified 131
Metrics for Evaluating Model Performance 132
Confusion Matrix 133
Accuracy 134
Classification Report 135
Data Preprocessing 135
Exercise 3.06: A Logistic Regression Model for Predicting the Propensity of Term Deposit Purchases in a Bank 136
Activity 3.02: Model Iteration 2 – Logistic Regression Model with Feature Engineered Variables 142

Next Steps 144
Summary 145

Chapter 4: Multiclass Classification with RandomForest 147

Introduction 148
Training a Random Forest Classifier 148
Evaluating the Model's Performance 152
Exercise 4.01: Building a Model for Classifying Animal Type and Assessing Its Performance 154
Number of Trees Estimator 158
Exercise 4.02: Tuning n_estimators to Reduce Overfitting 162
Maximum Depth 166
Exercise 4.03: Tuning max_depth to Reduce Overfitting 168
Minimum Sample in Leaf 171
Exercise 4.04: Tuning min_samples_leaf 174
Maximum Features 178
Exercise 4.05: Tuning max_features 181
Activity 4.01: Train a Random Forest Classifier on the ISOLET Dataset 184
Summary 186

Chapter 5: Performing Your First Cluster Analysis 189

Introduction 190
Clustering with k-means 192
Exercise 5.01: Performing Your First Clustering Analysis on the ATO Dataset 194
Interpreting k-means Results 199

Exercise 5.02: Clustering Australian Postcodes by Business Income and Expenses 204
Choosing the Number of Clusters 210
Exercise 5.03: Finding the Optimal Number of Clusters 215
Initializing Clusters 221
Exercise 5.04: Using Different Initialization Parameters to Achieve a Suitable Outcome 225
Calculating the Distance to the Centroid 230
Exercise 5.05: Finding the Closest Centroids in Our Dataset 235
Standardizing Data 244
Exercise 5.06: Standardizing the Data from Our Dataset 250
Activity 5.01: Perform Customer Segmentation Analysis in a Bank Using k-means 254
Summary 256

Chapter 6: How to Assess Performance 259

Introduction 260
Splitting Data 260
Exercise 6.01: Importing and Splitting Data 261
Assessing Model Performance for Regression Models 266
Data Structures – Vectors and Matrices 268
Scalars 268
Vectors 268
Matrices 270
R^2 Score 272
Exercise 6.02: Computing the R^2 Score of a Linear Regression Model 272
Mean Absolute Error 277

Exercise 6.03: Computing the MAE of a Model 277
Exercise 6.04: Computing the Mean Absolute Error of a Second Model 281
Other Evaluation Metrics 285
Assessing Model Performance for Classification Models 286
Exercise 6.05: Creating a Classification Model for Computing Evaluation Metrics 287
The Confusion Matrix 291
Exercise 6.06: Generating a Confusion Matrix for the Classification Model 292
More on the Confusion Matrix 293
Precision 294
Exercise 6.07: Computing Precision for the Classification Model 295
Recall 296
Exercise 6.08: Computing Recall for the Classification Model 297
F1 Score 298
Exercise 6.09: Computing the F1 Score for the Classification Model 299
Accuracy 300
Exercise 6.10: Computing Model Accuracy for the Classification Model 300
Logarithmic Loss 301
Exercise 6.11: Computing the Log Loss for the Classification Model 302
Receiver Operating Characteristic Curve 303
Exercise 6.12: Computing and Plotting ROC Curve for a Binary Classification Problem 303
Area Under the ROC Curve 310
Exercise 6.13: Computing the ROC AUC for the Caesarian Dataset .. 311

Saving and Loading Models 312
Exercise 6.14: Saving and Loading a Model 313
Activity 6.01: Train Three Different Models and Use Evaluation Metrics to Pick the Best Performing Model 316
Summary 318

Chapter 7: The Generalization of Machine Learning Models 321

Introduction 322
Overfitting 322
Training on Too Many Features 322
Training for Too Long 323
Underfitting 324
Data 324
The Ratio for Dataset Splits 324
Creating Dataset Splits 325
Exercise 7.01: Importing and Splitting Data 326
Random State 331
Exercise 7.02: Setting a Random State When Splitting Data 332
Cross-Validation 334
KFold 335
Exercise 7.03: Creating a Five-Fold Cross-Validation Dataset 335
Exercise 7.04: Creating a Five-Fold Cross-Validation Dataset Using a Loop for Calls 338
cross_val_score 342
Exercise 7.05: Getting the Scores from Five-Fold Cross-Validation ... 343
Understanding Estimators That Implement CV 346

LogisticRegressionCV 347

Exercise 7.06: Training a Logistic Regression Model Using Cross-Validation 347

Hyperparameter Tuning with GridSearchCV 351

Decision Trees 351

Exercise 7.07: Using Grid Search with Cross-Validation to Find the Best Parameters for a Model 357

Hyperparameter Tuning with RandomizedSearchCV 363

Exercise 7.08: Using Randomized Search for Hyperparameter Tuning 363

Model Regularization with Lasso Regression 368

Exercise 7.09: Fixing Model Overfitting Using Lasso Regression 368

Ridge Regression 379

Exercise 7.10: Fixing Model Overfitting Using Ridge Regression 379

Activity 7.01: Find an Optimal Model for Predicting the Critical Temperatures of Superconductors 389

Summary 391

Chapter 8: Hyperparameter Tuning 393

Introduction 394

What Are Hyperparameters? 394

Difference between Hyperparameters and Statistical Model Parameters 395

Setting Hyperparameters 396

A Note on Defaults 398

Finding the Best Hyperparameterization 399

Exercise 8.01: Manual Hyperparameter Tuning for a k-NN Classifier 399

Advantages and Disadvantages of a Manual Search 403

Tuning Using Grid Search 403
Simple Demonstration of the Grid Search Strategy 404
GridSearchCV 409
Tuning using GridSearchCV 409
Support Vector Machine (SVM) Classifiers..413
Exercise 8.02: Grid Search Hyperparameter Tuning for an SVM 414
Advantages and Disadvantages of Grid Search 418
Random Search 418
Random Variables and Their Distributions 419
Simple Demonstration of the Random Search Process 424
Tuning Using RandomizedSearchCV 430
Exercise 8.03: Random Search Hyperparameter Tuning for a Random Forest Classifier 432
Advantages and Disadvantages of a Random Search 437
Activity 8.01: Is the Mushroom Poisonous? 438
Summary 440

Chapter 9: Interpreting a Machine Learning Model 443

Introduction 444
Linear Model Coefficients 445
Exercise 9.01: Extracting the Linear Regression Coefficient 447
RandomForest Variable Importance 454
Exercise 9.02: Extracting RandomForest Feature Importance 458
Variable Importance via Permutation 463
Exercise 9.03: Extracting Feature Importance via Permutation 467
Partial Dependence Plots 471
Exercise 9.04: Plotting Partial Dependence 474

Local Interpretation with LIME 478
Exercise 9.05: Local Interpretation with LIME 482
Activity 9.01: Train and Analyze a Network Intrusion Detection Model 486
Summary 487

Chapter 10: Analyzing a Dataset 491

Introduction 492
Exploring Your Data 493
Analyzing Your Dataset 497
Exercise 10.01: Exploring the Ames Housing Dataset with Descriptive Statistics 500
Analyzing the Content of a Categorical Variable 504
Exercise 10.02: Analyzing the Categorical Variables from the Ames Housing Dataset 506
Summarizing Numerical Variables 510
Exercise 10.03: Analyzing Numerical Variables from the Ames Housing Dataset 514
Visualizing Your Data 517
Using the Altair API 518
Histogram for Numerical Variables 524
Bar Chart for Categorical Variables 527
Boxplots 530
Exercise 10.04: Visualizing the Ames Housing Dataset with Altair 533
Activity 10.01: Analyzing Churn Data Using Visual Data Analysis Techniques 543
Summary 546

Chapter 11: Data Preparation 549

Introduction 550

Handling Row Duplication 550

Exercise 11.01: Handling Duplicates in a Breast Cancer Dataset 558

Converting Data Types 562

Exercise 11.02: Converting Data Types for the Ames Housing Dataset 566

Handling Incorrect Values 572

Exercise 11.03: Fixing Incorrect Values in the State Column 575

Handling Missing Values 582

Exercise 11.04: Fixing Missing Values for the Horse Colic Dataset 587

Activity 11.01: Preparing the Speed Dating Dataset 592

Summary 597

Chapter 12: Feature Engineering 599

Introduction 600

Merging Datasets 601

The Left Join 604

The Right Join 606

Exercise 12.01: Merging the ATO Dataset with the Postcode Data 609

Binning Variables 614

Exercise 12.02: Binning the YearBuilt Variable from the AMES Housing Dataset 617

Manipulating Dates 621

Exercise 12.03: Date Manipulation on Financial Services Consumer Complaints 626

Performing Data Aggregation 632

Exercise 12.04: Feature Engineering Using Data Aggregation on the AMES Housing Dataset 638

Activity 12.01: Feature Engineering on a Financial Dataset 643

Summary 645

Chapter 13: Imbalanced Datasets 647

Introduction 648

Understanding the Business Context 648

Exercise 13.01: Benchmarking the Logistic Regression Model on the Dataset 649

Analysis of the Result 654

Challenges of Imbalanced Datasets 656

Strategies for Dealing with Imbalanced Datasets 658

Collecting More Data 658

Resampling Data 659

Exercise 13.02: Implementing Random Undersampling and Classification on Our Banking Dataset to Find the Optimal Result ... 660

Analysis 666

Generating Synthetic Samples 667

Implementation of SMOTE and MSMOTE 668

Exercise 13.03: Implementing SMOTE on Our Banking Dataset to Find the Optimal Result 669

Exercise 13.04: Implementing MSMOTE on Our Banking Dataset to Find the Optimal Result 673

Applying Balancing Techniques on a Telecom Dataset 676

Activity 13.01: Finding the Best Balancing Technique by Fitting a Classifier on the Telecom Churn Dataset 677

Summary 680

Chapter 14: Dimensionality Reduction 683

Introduction 684

Business Context 685

Exercise 14.01: Loading and Cleaning the Dataset 685

Creating a High-Dimensional Dataset 693

Activity 14.01: Fitting a Logistic Regression Model on a HighDimensional Dataset 694

Strategies for Addressing High-Dimensional Datasets 697

Backward Feature Elimination (Recursive Feature Elimination) 698

Exercise 14.02: Dimensionality Reduction Using Backward Feature Elimination 699

Forward Feature Selection 706

Exercise 14.03: Dimensionality Reduction Using Forward Feature Selection 707

Principal Component Analysis (PCA) 712

Exercise 14.04: Dimensionality Reduction Using PCA 716

Independent Component Analysis (ICA) 723

Exercise 14.05: Dimensionality Reduction Using Independent Component Analysis 723

Factor Analysis 728

Exercise 14.06: Dimensionality Reduction Using Factor Analysis 729

Comparing Different Dimensionality Reduction Techniques 735

Activity 14.02: Comparison of Dimensionality Reduction Techniques on the Enhanced Ads Dataset 737

Summary 740

Chapter 15: Ensemble Learning 743

Introduction 744

Ensemble Learning 744

Variance 745
Bias 745
Business Context 746
Exercise 15.01: Loading, Exploring, and Cleaning the Data 746
Activity 15.01: Fitting a Logistic Regression Model on Credit Card Data 753
Simple Methods for Ensemble Learning 754
Averaging 755
Exercise 15.02: Ensemble Model Using the Averaging Technique 756
Weighted Averaging 760
Exercise 15.03: Ensemble Model Using the Weighted Averaging Technique 760
Iteration 2 with Different Weights 763
Max Voting 765
Exercise 15.04: Ensemble Model Using Max Voting 766
Advanced Techniques for Ensemble Learning 768
Bagging 769
Exercise 15.05: Ensemble Learning Using Bagging 771
Boosting 773
Exercise 15.06: Ensemble Learning Using Boosting 774
Stacking 776
Exercise 15.07: Ensemble Learning Using Stacking 778
Activity 15.02: Comparison of Advanced Ensemble Techniques 780
Summary 783
Index 787

PREFACE

ABOUT THE BOOK

Where there's data, there's insight. With so much data being generated, there is immense scope to extract meaningful information that'll boost business productivity and profitability. By learning to convert raw data into game-changing insights, you'll open new career paths and opportunities.

The Data Science Workshop, Second Edition, begins by introducing different types of projects and showing you how to incorporate machine learning algorithms in them. You'll learn to select a relevant metric and even assess the performance of your model. To tune the hyperparameters of an algorithm and improve its accuracy, you'll get hands-on with approaches such as grid search and random search.

Finally, you'll learn dimensionality reduction techniques to easily handle many variables at once, before exploring how to use model ensembling techniques and create new features to enhance model performance.

By the end of this book, you'll have the skills to start working on data science projects confidently.

AUDIENCE

This is one of the most useful data science books for aspiring data analysts, data scientists, database engineers, and business analysts. It is aimed at those who want to kick-start their careers in data science by quickly learning data science techniques without going through all the mathematics behind machine learning algorithms. Basic knowledge of the Python programming language will help you easily grasp the concepts explained in this book.

ABOUT THE CHAPTERS

Chapter 1, Introduction to Data Science in Python, will introduce you to the field of data science and walk you through an overview of Python's core concepts and their application in the world of data science.

Chapter 2, Regression, will acquaint you with linear regression analysis and its application to practical problem solving in data science.

Chapter 3, Binary Classification, will teach you a supervised learning technique called classification to generate business outcomes.

Chapter 4, Multiclass Classification with RandomForest, will show you how to train a multiclass classifier using the Random Forest algorithm.

Chapter 5, Performing Your First Cluster Analysis, will introduce you to unsupervised learning tasks, where algorithms have to automatically learn patterns from data by themselves as no target variables are defined beforehand.

Chapter 6, How to Assess Performance, will teach you to evaluate a model and assess its performance before you decide to put it into production.

Chapter 7, The Generalization of Machine Learning Models, will teach you how to make best use of your data to train better models, by either splitting the data or making use of cross-validation.

Chapter 8, Hyperparameter Tuning, will guide you to find further predictive performance improvements via the systematic evaluation of estimators with different hyperparameters.

Chapter 9, Interpreting a Machine Learning Model, will show you how to interpret a machine learning model's results and get deeper insights into the patterns it found.

Chapter 10, Analyzing a Dataset, will introduce you to the art of performing exploratory data analysis and visualizing the data in order to identify quality issues, potential data transformations, and interesting patterns.

Chapter 11, Data Preparation, will present the main techniques you can use to handle data issues in order to ensure your data is of a high enough quality for successful modeling.

Chapter 12, Feature Engineering, will teach you some of the key techniques for creating new variables on an existing dataset.

Chapter 13, Imbalanced Datasets, will equip you to identify use cases where datasets are likely to be imbalanced, and formulate strategies for dealing with imbalanced datasets.

Chapter 14, Dimensionality Reduction, will show how to analyze datasets with high dimensions and deal with the challenges posed by these datasets.

Chapter 15, *Ensemble Learning*, will teach you to apply different ensemble learning techniques to your dataset.

> **NOTE**
>
> There are also three bonus chapters, *Chapter 16*, *Machine Learning Pipelines*, *Chapter 17*, *Automated Feature Engineering*, and *Chapter 18*, *Model as a Service with Flask*, which you can find as part of the interactive online edition at https://packt.live/2sSKX3D.
>
> You can also find the solutions for all of the Activities in this Workshop in the online edition and on GitHub at https://packt.live/3jd1iog.

CONVENTIONS

Code words in text, database table names, folder names, filenames, file extensions, path names, dummy URLs, user input, and Twitter handles are shown as follows:

"**`sklearn`** has a class called **`train_test_split`**, which provides the functionality for splitting data."

Words that you see on the screen, for example, in menus or dialog boxes, also appear in the same format.

A block of code is set as follows:

```
import pandas as pd
from sklearn.model_selection import train_test_split
```

New terms and important words are shown like this:

"A dictionary contains multiple elements, like a **list**, but each element is organized as a key-value pair."

CODE PRESENTATION

Lines of code that span multiple lines are split using a backslash (\ ). When the code is executed, Python will ignore the backslash, and treat the code on the next line as a direct continuation of the current line.

For example:

```
history = model.fit(X, y, epochs=100, batch_size=5, verbose=1, \
                    validation_split=0.2, shuffle=False)
```

Comments are added into code to help explain specific bits of logic. Single-line comments are denoted using the # symbol, as follows:

```
# Print the sizes of the datasets
print("Number of Examples in the Dataset = ", X.shape[0])
print("Number of Features for each example = ", X.shape[1])
```

Multi-line comments are enclosed by triple quotes, as shown below:

```
"""
Define a seed for the random number generator to ensure the
result will be reproducible
"""
seed = 1
np.random.seed(seed)
random.set_seed(seed)
```

SETTING UP YOUR ENVIRONMENT

Before we explore the book in detail, we need to set up specific software and tools. In the following section, we shall see how to do that.

HOW TO SET UP GOOGLE COLAB

There are many **integrated development environments** (**IDE**) for Python. The most popular one for running data science projects is Jupyter Notebook from Anaconda but this is not the one we are recommending for this book. As you are starting your journey into data science, rather than asking you to setup a Python environment from scratch, we think it is better for you to use a plug-and-play solution so that you can fully focus on learning the concepts we are presenting in this book. We want to remove as many difficulties as we can and ensure your first step into data science is as straightforward as possible.

Luckily such a tool does exist, and it is called **Google Colab**. It is a free tool provided by Google that is run on the cloud, so you don't need to buy a new laptop or computer or upgrade its specs. The other benefit of using Colab is most of the Python packages we are using in this book are already installed so you can use them straight away. The only thing you need is a Google account. If you don't have one, you can create one here: https://packt.live/37mea5X.

Then, you will need to subscribe to the Colab service:

1. First, log into Google Drive: https://packt.live/2TM1v8w
2. Then, go to the following url: https://packt.live/2NKaAuP

   You should see the following screen:

Figure 0.1: Google Colab Introduction page

3. Then, you can click on **`NEW PYTHON 3 NOTEBOOK`** and you should see a new Colab notebook

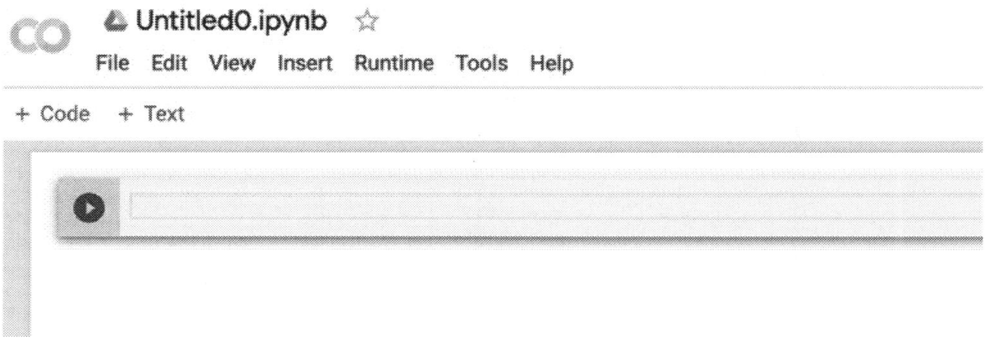

Figure 0.2: New Colab notebook

You just added Google Colab to your Google account and now you are ready to write and execute your own Python code.

HOW TO USE GOOGLE COLAB

Now that you have added Google Colab to your account, let's see how to use it. Google Colab is very similar to Jupyter Notebook. It is actually based on Jupyter, but run on Google servers with additional integrations with their services such as Google Drive.

To open a new Colab notebook, you need to login into your Google Drive account and then click on **+ New** icon:

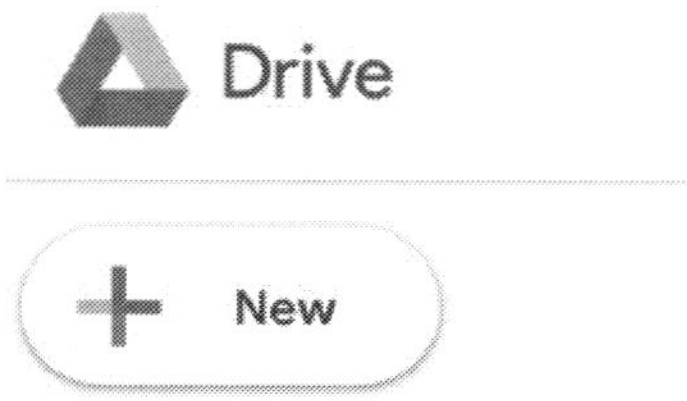

Figure 0.3: Option to open new notebook

On the menu displayed, select **More** and then **Google Colaboratory**

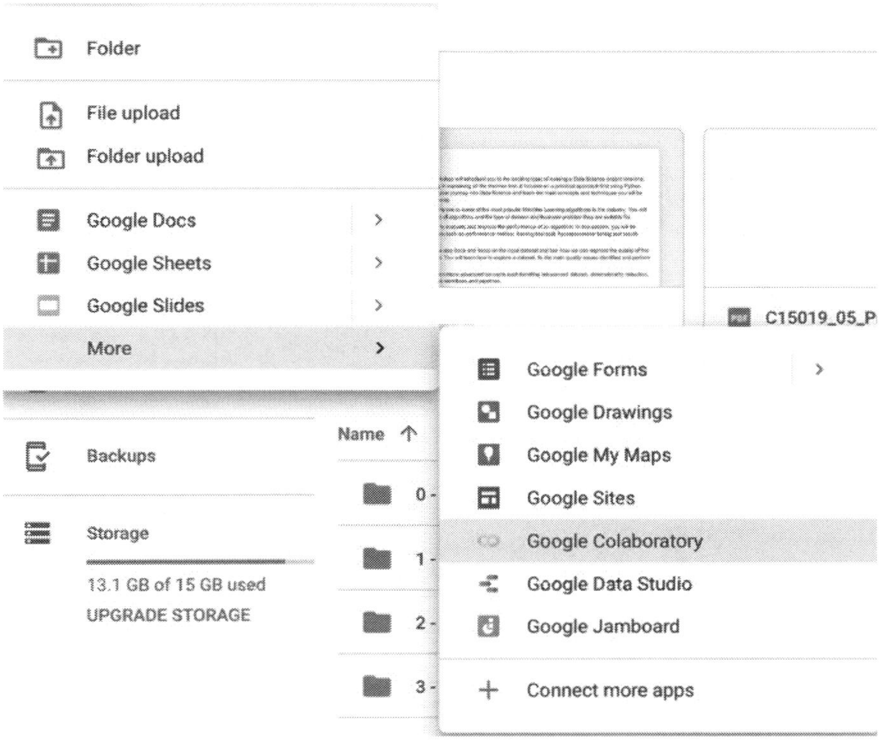

Figure 0.4: Option to open Colab notebook from Google Drive

A new Colab notebook will be created.

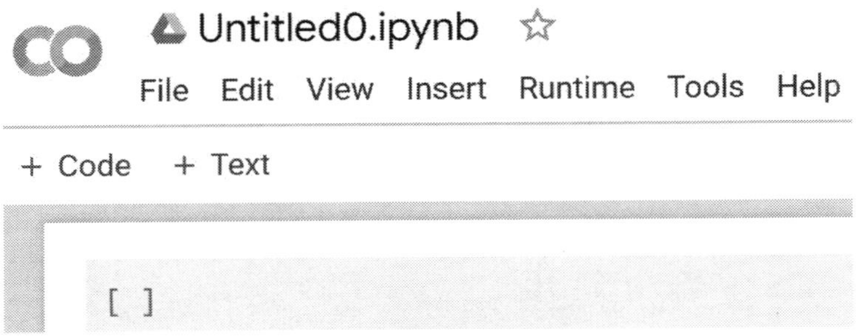

Figure 0.5: New Colab notebook

A Colab notebook is an interactive IDE where you can run Python code or add text using cells. A cell is a container where you will add your lines of code or any text information related to your project. In each cell, you can put as many lines of code or text as you want. A cell can display the output of your code after running it, so it is a very powerful way of testing and checking the results of your work. It is a good practice to not overload each cell with tons of code. Try to split it into multiple cells so you will be able to run them independently and check step by step if your code is working.

Let us now see how we can write some Python code in a cell and run it. A cell is composed of 4 main parts:

1. The text box where you will write your code
2. The **Run** button for running your code
3. The options menu that will provide additional functionalities
4. The output display

Figure 0.6: Parts of the Colab notebook cell

In this preceding example, we just wrote a simple line of code that adds 2 to 3. Now, we either need to click on the `Run` button or use the shortcut **Ctrl + Enter** to run the code. The result will then be displayed below the cell. If your code breaks (when there is an error), the error message will be displayed below the cell:

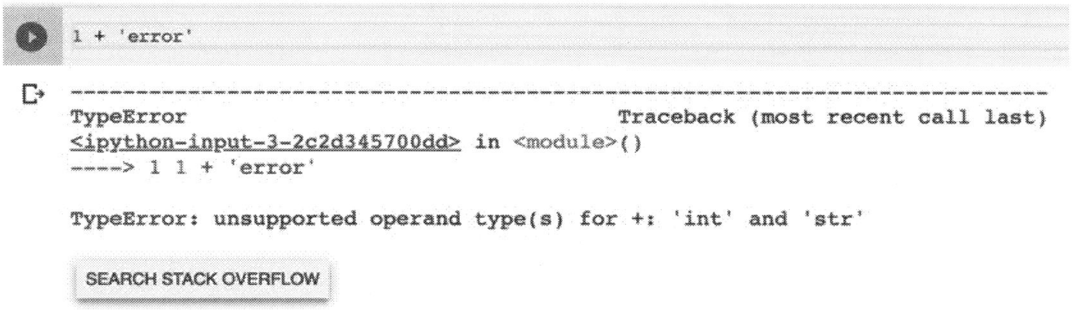

Figure 0.7: Error message on Google Colab

As you can see, we tried to add an integer to a string which is not possible as their data types are not compatible and this is exactly what this error message is telling us.

To add a new cell, you just need to click on either `+ Code` or `+ Text` on the option bar at the top:

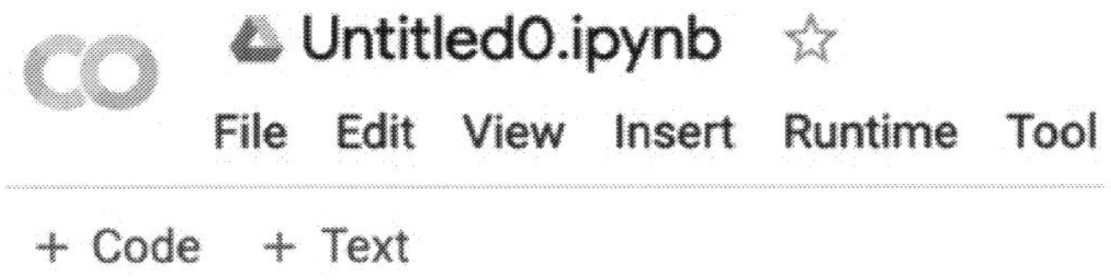

Figure 0.8: New cell button

If you add a new `Text` cell, you have access to specific options for editing your text such as bold, italic, and hypertext links and so on:

Figure 0.9: Different options on cell

This type of cell is actually Markdown compatible. So, you can easily create a title, sub-title, bullet points and so on. Here is a link for learning more about the Markdown options: https://packt.live/2NVgVDT.

With the cell option menu, you can delete a cell or move it up or down in the notebook:

Figure 0.10: Cell options

If you need to install a specific Python package that is not available in Google Colab, you just need to run a cell with the following syntax:

```
!pip install <package_name>
```

> **NOTE**
>
> The '!' is a magic command to run shell commands.

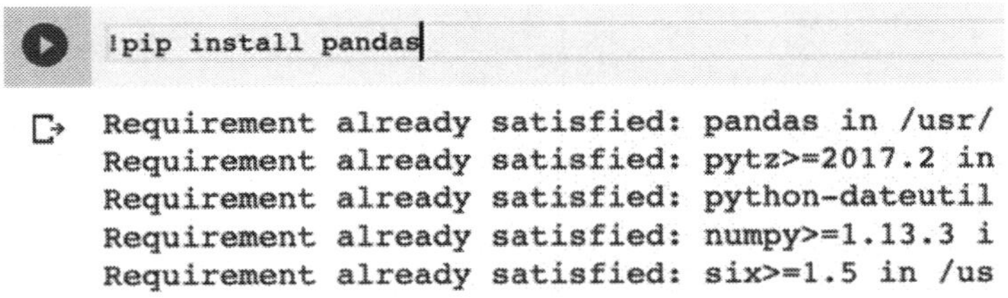

Figure 0.11: Using "!" command

You just learnt the main functionalities provided by Google Colab for running Python code. There are many more functionalities available, but you now know enough for going through the contents of this book.

ACCESSING THE CODE FILES

You can find the complete code files of this book at https://packt.live/2ucwsId. You can also run many activities and exercises directly in your web browser by using the interactive lab environment at https://packt.live/3gfsH76.

We've tried to support interactive versions of all activities and exercises, but we recommend executing the code on Google Colab as well for instances where this support isn't available.

The high-quality color images used in book can be found at https://packt.live/30O91Bd.

If you have any issues or questions about installation, please email us at **workshops@packt.com**.

1

INTRODUCTION TO DATA SCIENCE IN PYTHON

OVERVIEW

This very first chapter will introduce you to the field of data science and walk you through an overview of Python's core concepts and their application in the world of data science.

By the end of this chapter, you will be able to explain what data science is and distinguish between supervised and unsupervised learning. You will also be able to explain what machine learning is and distinguish between regression, classification, and clustering problems. You'll have learnt to create and manipulate different types of Python variable, including core variables, lists, and dictionaries. You'll be able to build a `for` loop, print results using f-strings, define functions, import Python packages and load data in different formats using `pandas`. You will also have had your first taste of training a model using scikit-learn.

INTRODUCTION

Welcome to the fascinating world of data science! We are sure you must be pretty excited to start your journey and learn interesting and exciting techniques and algorithms. This is exactly what this book is intended for.

But before diving into it, let's define what data science is: it is a combination of multiple disciplines, including business, statistics, and programming, that intends to extract meaningful insights from data by running controlled experiments similar to scientific research.

The objective of any data science project is to derive valuable knowledge for the business from data in order to make better decisions. It is the responsibility of data scientists to define the goals to be achieved for a project. This requires business knowledge and expertise. In this book, you will be exposed to some examples of data science tasks from real-world datasets.

Statistics is a mathematical field used for analyzing and finding patterns from data. A lot of the newest and most advanced techniques still rely on core statistical approaches. This book will present to you the basic techniques required to understand the concepts we will be covering.

With an exponential increase in data generation, more computational power is required for processing it efficiently. This is the reason why programming is a required skill for data scientists. You may wonder why we chose Python for this Workshop. That's because Python is one of the most popular programming languages for data science. It is extremely easy to learn how to code in Python thanks to its simple and easily readable syntax. It also has an incredible number of packages available to anyone for free, such as pandas, scikit-learn, TensorFlow, and PyTorch. Its community is expanding at an incredible rate, adding more and more new functionalities and improving its performance and reliability. It's no wonder companies such as Facebook, Airbnb, and Google are using it as one of their main stacks. No prior knowledge of Python is required for this book. If you do have some experience with Python or other programming languages, then this will be an advantage, but all concepts will be fully explained, so don't worry if you are new to programming.

APPLICATION OF DATA SCIENCE

As mentioned in the introduction, data science is a multidisciplinary approach to analyzing and identifying complex patterns and extracting valuable insights from data. Running a data science project usually involves multiple steps, including the following:

1. Defining the business problem to be solved
2. Collecting or extracting existing data
3. Analyzing, visualizing, and preparing data
4. Training a model to spot patterns in data and make predictions
5. Assessing a model's performance and making improvements
6. Communicating and presenting findings and gained insights
7. Deploying and maintaining a model

As its name implies, data science projects require data, but it is actually more important to have defined a clear business problem to solve first. If it's not framed correctly, a project may lead to incorrect results as you may have used the wrong information, not prepared the data properly, or led a model to learn the wrong patterns. So, it is absolutely critical to properly define the scope and objective of a data science project with your stakeholders.

There are a lot of data science applications in real-world situations or in business environments. For example, healthcare providers may train a model for predicting a medical outcome or its severity based on medical measurements, or a high school may want to predict which students are at risk of dropping out within a year's time based on their historical grades and past behaviors. Corporations may be interested to know the likelihood of a customer buying a certain product based on his or her past purchases. They may also need to better understand which customers are more likely to stop using existing services and churn. These are examples where data science can be used to achieve a clearly defined goal, such as increasing the number of patients detected with a heart condition at an early stage or reducing the number of customers canceling their subscriptions after six months. That sounds exciting, right? Soon enough, you will be working on such interesting projects.

WHAT IS MACHINE LEARNING?

When we mention data science, we usually think about machine learning, and some people may not understand the difference between them. Machine learning is the field of building algorithms that can learn patterns by themselves without being programmed explicitly. So machine learning is a family of techniques that can be used at the modeling stage of a data science project.

Machine learning is composed of three different types of learning:

- Supervised learning
- Unsupervised learning
- Reinforcement learning

SUPERVISED LEARNING

Supervised learning refers to a type of task where an algorithm is trained to learn patterns based on prior knowledge. That means this kind of learning requires the labeling of the outcome (also called the response variable, dependent variable, or target variable) to be predicted beforehand. For instance, if you want to train a model that will predict whether a customer will cancel their subscription, you will need a dataset with a column (or variable) that already contains the churn outcome (cancel or not cancel) for past or existing customers. This outcome has to be labeled by someone prior to the training of a model. If this dataset contains 5,000 observations, then all of them need to have the outcome being populated. The objective of the model is to learn the relationship between this outcome column and the other features (also called independent variables or predictor variables). Following is an example of such a dataset:

Target | Features

Cancel	Months since first subscription	Monthly average spent	Average number of phone calls made last month	Average number of phone calls made last quarter	Additional options
Yes	13	$70	56	63	Yes
No	2	$35	35	34	Yes
No	6	$40	46	50	Yes
Yes	16	$110	53	75	No

Figure 1.1: Example of customer churn dataset

The `Cancel` column is the response variable. This is the column you are interested in, and you want the model to predict accurately the outcome for new input data (in this case, new customers). All the other columns are the predictor variables.

The model, after being trained, may find the following pattern: a customer is more likely to cancel their subscription after 12 months and if their average monthly spent is over `$50`. So, if a new customer has gone through 15 months of subscription and is spending $85 per month, the model will predict this customer will cancel their contract in the future.

When the response variable contains a limited number of possible values (or classes), it is a classification problem (you will learn more about this in *Chapter 3, Binary Classification*, and *Chapter 4, Multiclass Classification with RandomForest*). The model will learn how to predict the right class given the values of the independent variables. The churn example we just mentioned is a classification problem as the response variable can only take two different values: `yes` or `no`.

On the other hand, if the response variable can have a value from an infinite number of possibilities, it is called a regression problem.

An example of a regression problem is where you are trying to predict the exact number of mobile phones produced every day for some manufacturing plants. This value can potentially range from 0 to an infinite number (or a number big enough to have a large range of potential values), as shown in *Figure 1.2*.

Daily output	Plant ID	Number of staff	Stock of screens	Stock of 5G chip
53003	A	124	102432	0
21342	N	54	30132	0
42032	C	103	125312	0
15234	E	84	42232	50234

Figure 1.2: Example of a mobile phone production dataset

In the preceding figure, you can see that the values for `Daily output` can take any value from `15000` to more than `50000`. This is a regression problem, which we will look at in *Chapter 2, Regression*.

UNSUPERVISED LEARNING

Unsupervised learning is a type of algorithm that doesn't require any response variables at all. In this case, the model will learn patterns from the data by itself. You may ask what kind of pattern it can find if there is no target specified beforehand.

This type of algorithm usually can detect similarities between variables or records, so it will try to group those that are very close to each other. This kind of algorithm can be used for clustering (grouping records) or dimensionality reduction (reducing the number of variables). Clustering is very popular for performing customer segmentation, where the algorithm will look to group customers with similar behaviors together from the data. *Chapter 5, Performing Your First Cluster Analysis*, will walk you through an example of clustering analysis.

REINFORCEMENT LEARNING

Reinforcement learning is another type of algorithm that learns how to act in a specific environment based on the feedback it receives. You may have seen some videos where algorithms are trained to play Atari games by themselves. Reinforcement learning techniques are being used to teach the agent how to act in the game based on the rewards or penalties it receives from the game.

For instance, in the game Pong, the agent will learn to not let the ball drop after multiple rounds of training in which it receives high penalties every time the ball drops.

> **NOTE**
>
> Reinforcement learning algorithms are out of scope and will not be covered in this book.

OVERVIEW OF PYTHON

As mentioned earlier, Python is one of the most popular programming languages for data science. But before diving into Python's data science applications, let's have a quick introduction to some core Python concepts.

TYPES OF VARIABLE

In Python, you can handle and manipulate different types of variables. Each has its own specificities and benefits. We will not go through every single one of them but rather focus on the main ones that you will have to use in this book. For each of the following code examples, you can run the code in Google Colab to view the given output.

NUMERIC VARIABLES

The most basic variable type is numeric. This can contain integer or decimal (or float) numbers, and some mathematical operations can be performed on top of them.

Let's use an integer variable called **var1** that will take the value **8** and another one called **var2** with the value **160.88**, and add them together with the **+** operator, as shown here:

```
var1 = 8
var2 = 160.88
var1 + var2
```

You should get the following output:

```
168.88
```

Figure 1.3: Output of the addition of two variables

In Python, you can perform other mathematical operations on numerical variables, such as multiplication (with the ***** operator) and division (with **/**).

TEXT VARIABLES

Another interesting type of variable is **string**, which contains textual information. You can create a variable with some specific text using the single or double quote, as shown in the following example:

```
var3 = 'Hello, '
var4 = 'World'
```

In order to display the content of a variable, you can call the **print()** function:

```
print(var3)
print(var4)
```

You should get the following output:

```
Hello,
World
```

Figure 1.4: Printing the two text variables

Python also provides an interface called f-strings for printing text with the value of defined variables. It is very handy when you want to print results with additional text to make it more readable and interpret results. It is also quite common to use f-strings to print logs. You will need to add **f** before the quotes (or double quotes) to specify that the text will be an f-string. Then you can add an existing variable inside the quotes and display the text with the value of this variable. You need to wrap the variable with curly brackets, **{}**.

For instance, if we want to print **Text:** before the values of **var3** and **var4**, we will write the following code:

```
print(f"Text: {var3} {var4}!")
```

You should get the following output:

```
Text: Hello,  World!
```

Figure 1.5: Printing with f-strings

You can also perform some text-related transformations with string variables, such as capitalizing or replacing characters. For instance, you can concatenate the two variables together with the **+** operator:

```
var3 + var4
```

You should get the following output:

```
'Hello, World'
```

Figure 1.6: Concatenation of the two text variables

PYTHON LIST

Another very useful type of variable is the list. It is a collection of items that can be changed (you can add, update, or remove items). To declare a list, you will need to use square brackets, **[]**, like this:

```
var5 = ['I', 'love', 'data', 'science']
print(var5)
```

You should get the following output:

```
['I', 'love', 'data', 'science']
```

Figure 1.7: List containing only string items

A list can have different item types, so you can mix numerical and text variables in it:

```
var6 = ['Packt', 15019, 2020, 'Data Science']
print(var6)
```

You should get the following output:

```
['Packt', 15019, 2020, 'Data Science']
```

Figure 1.8: List containing numeric and string items

An item in a list can be accessed by its index (its position in the list). To access the first (index 0) and third elements (index 2) of a list, you do the following:

```
print(var6[0])
print(var6[2])
```

> **NOTE**
>
> In Python, all indexes start at `0`.

You should get the following output:

```
Packt
2020
```

Figure 1.9: The first and third items in the var6 list

Python provides an API to access a range of items using the `:` operator. You just need to specify the starting index on the left side of the operator and the ending index on the right side. The ending index is always excluded from the range. So, if you want to get the first three items (index 0 to 2), you should do as follows:

```
print(var6[0:3])
```

You should get the following output:

```
['Packt', 15019, 2020]
```

Figure 1.10: The first three items of var6

You can also iterate through every item of a list using a **`for`** loop. If you want to print every item of the **`var6`** list, you should do this:

```
for item in var6:
    print(item)
```

You should get the following output:

```
Packt
15019
2020
Data Science
```

Figure 1.11: Output of the for loop

You can add an item at the end of the list using the `.append()` method:

```
var6.append('Python')
print(var6)
```

You should get the following output:

```
['Packt', 15019, 2020, 'Data Science', 'Python']
```

Figure 1.12: Output of var6 after inserting the 'Python' item

To delete an item from the list, you use the `.remove()` method:

```
var6.remove(15019)
print(var6)
```

You should get the following output:

```
['Packt', 2020, 'Data Science', 'Python']
```

Figure 1.13: Output of var6 after removing the '15019' item

PYTHON DICTIONARY

Another very popular Python variable used by data scientists is the dictionary type. For example, it can be used to load JSON data into Python so that it can then be converted into a DataFrame (you will learn more about the JSON format and DataFrames in the following sections). A dictionary contains multiple elements, like a **list**, but each element is organized as a key-value pair. A dictionary is not indexed by numbers but by keys. So, to access a specific value, you will have to call the item by its corresponding key. To define a dictionary in Python, you will use curly brackets, `{}`, and specify the keys and values separated by `:`, as shown here:

```
var7 = {'Topic': 'Data Science', 'Language': 'Python'}
print(var7)
```

You should get the following output:

```
{'Topic': 'Data Science', 'Language': 'Python'}
```

Figure 1.14: Output of var7

To access a specific value, you need to provide the corresponding key name. For instance, if you want to get the value **Python**, you do this:

```
var7['Language']
```

You should get the following output:

```
'Python'
```

Figure 1.15: Value for the 'Language' key

> **NOTE**
>
> Each key-value pair in a dictionary needs to be unique.

Python provides a method to access all the key names from a dictionary, **.keys()**, which is used as shown in the following code snippet:

```
var7.keys()
```

You should get the following output:

```
dict_keys(['Topic', 'Language'])
```

Figure 1.16: List of key names

There is also a method called **.values()**, which is used to access all the values of a dictionary:

```
var7.values()
```

You should get the following output:

```
dict_values(['Data Science', 'Python'])
```

Figure 1.17: List of values

You can iterate through all items from a dictionary using a **for** loop and the **.items()** method, as shown in the following code snippet:

```
for key, value in var7.items():
    print(key)
    print(value)
```

You should get the following output:

```
Topic
Data Science
Language
Python
```

Figure 1.18: Output after iterating through the items of a dictionary

You can add a new element in a dictionary by providing the key name like this:

```
var7['Publisher'] = 'Packt'
print(var7)
```

You should get the following output:

```
{'Topic': 'Data Science', 'Language': 'Python', 'Publisher': 'Packt'}
```

Figure 1.19: Output of a dictionary after adding an item

You can delete an item from a dictionary with the **del** command:

```
del var7['Publisher']
print(var7)
```

You should get the following output:

```
{'Topic': 'Data Science', 'Language': 'Python'}
```

Figure 1.20: Output of a dictionary after removing an item

In *Exercise 1.01*, *Creating a Dictionary That Will Contain Machine Learning Algorithms*, we will be looking to use these concepts that we've just looked at.

> **NOTE**
>
> If you are interested in exploring Python in more depth, head over to our website (https://packt.live/2FcXpOp) to get yourself the Python Workshop.

EXERCISE 1.01: CREATING A DICTIONARY THAT WILL CONTAIN MACHINE LEARNING ALGORITHMS

In this exercise, we will create a dictionary using Python that will contain a collection of different machine learning algorithms that will be covered in this book.

The following steps will help you complete the exercise:

> **NOTE**
>
> Every exercise and activity in this book is to be executed on Google Colab.

1. Open on a new Colab notebook.
2. Create a list called **algorithm** that will contain the following elements: **Linear Regression**, **Logistic Regression**, **RandomForest**, and **a3c**:

```
algorithm = ['Linear Regression', 'Logistic Regression', \
             'RandomForest', 'a3c']
```

> **NOTE**
>
> The code snippet shown above uses a backslash (\ ) to split the logic across multiple lines. When the code is executed, Python will ignore the backslash, and treat the code on the next line as a direct continuation of the current line.

3. Now, create a list called **learning** that will contain the following elements: **Supervised**, **Supervised**, **Supervised**, and **Reinforcement**:

```
learning = ['Supervised', 'Supervised', 'Supervised', \
            'Reinforcement']
```

4. Create a list called **algorithm_type** that will contain the following elements: **Regression**, **Classification**, **Regression or Classification**, and **Game AI**:

```
algorithm_type = ['Regression', 'Classification', \
                  'Regression or Classification', 'Game AI']
```

5. Add an item called **k-means** into the **algorithm** list using the **.append()** method:

```
algorithm.append('k-means')
```

6. Display the content of **algorithm** using the **print()** function:

```
print(algorithm)
```

You should get the following output:

```
['Linear Regression', 'Logistic Regression', 'RandomForest', 'a3c', 'k-means']
```

Figure 1.21: Output of 'algorithm'

From the preceding output, we can see that we added the **k-means** item to the list.

7. Now, add the **Unsupervised** item into the **learning** list using the **.append()** method:

```
learning.append('Unsupervised')
```

8. Display the content of **learning** using the **print()** function:

```
print(learning)
```

You should get the following output:

```
['Supervised', 'Supervised', 'Supervised', 'Reinforcement', 'Unsupervised']
```

Figure 1.22: Output of 'learning'

From the preceding output, we can see that we added the **Unsupervised** item into the list.

9. Add the **Clustering** item into the **algorithm_type** list using the **.append()** method:

```
algorithm_type.append('Clustering')
```

10. Display the content of **algorithm_type** using the **print()** function:

```
print(algorithm_type)
```

You should get the following output:

```
['Regression', 'Classification', 'Regression or Classification', 'Game AI', 'Clustering']
```

Figure 1.23: Output of 'algorithm_type'

From the preceding output, we can see that we added the **Clustering** item into the list.

11. Create an empty dictionary called **machine_learning** using curly brackets, **{}**:

```
machine_learning = {}
```

12. Create a new item in **machine_learning** with the key as **algorithm** and the value as all the items from the **algorithm** list:

```
machine_learning['algorithm'] = algorithm
```

13. Display the content of **machine_learning** using the **print()** function.

```
print(machine_learning)
```

You should get the following output:

```
{'algorithm': ['Linear Regression', 'Logistic Regression', 'RandomForest', 'a3c', 'k-means']}
```

Figure 1.24: Output of 'machine_learning'

From the preceding output, we notice that we have created a dictionary from the **algorithm** list.

14. Create a new item in **machine_learning** with the key as **learning** and the value as all the items from the **learning** list:

```
machine_learning['learning'] = learning
```

15. Now, create a new item in **machine_learning** with the key as **algorithm_type** and the value as all the items from the algorithm_type list:

```
machine_learning['algorithm_type'] = algorithm_type
```

16. Display the content of **machine_learning** using the **print()** function.

```
print(machine_learning)
```

You should get the following output:

```
{'algorithm': ['Linear Regression', 'Logistic Regression', 'RandomForest', 'a3
c', 'k-means'], 'learning': ['Supervised', 'Supervised', 'Supervised', 'Reinfor
cement', 'Unsupervised'], 'algorithm_type': ['Regression', 'Classification', 'R
egression or Classification', 'Game AI', 'Clustering']}
```

Figure 1.25: Output of 'machine_learning'

17. Remove the **a3c** item from the **algorithm** key using the **.remove()** method:

```
machine_learning['algorithm'].remove('a3c')
```

18. Display the content of the **algorithm** item from the **machine_learning** dictionary using the **print()** function:

```
print(machine_learning['algorithm'])
```

You should get the following output:

```
['Linear Regression', 'Logistic Regression', 'RandomForest', 'k-means']
```

Figure 1.26: Output of 'algorithm' from 'machine_learning'

19. Remove the **Reinforcement** item from the **learning** key using the **.remove()** method:

```
machine_learning['learning'].remove('Reinforcement')
```

20. Remove the **Game AI** item from the **algorithm_type** key using the **.remove()** method:

```
machine_learning['algorithm_type'].remove('Game AI')
```

21. Display the content of **machine_learning** using the **print()** function:

```
print(machine_learning)
```

You should get the following output:

```
{'algorithm': ['Linear Regression', 'Logistic Regression', 'RandomForest', 'k-means'], 'learning': ['Supervised'
```

Figure 1.27: Output of 'machine_learning'

You have successfully created a dictionary containing the machine learning algorithms that you will come across in this book. You learned how to create and manipulate Python lists and dictionaries.

> **NOTE**
>
> To access the source code for this specific section, please refer to https://packt.live/315EmRP.
>
> You can also run this example online at https://packt.live/3ay1tYg.

In the next section, you will learn more about the two main Python packages used for data science:

- **`pandas`**
- **`scikit-learn`**

PYTHON FOR DATA SCIENCE

Python offers an incredible number of packages for data science. A package is a collection of prebuilt functions and classes shared publicly by its author(s). These packages extend the core functionalities of Python. The Python Package Index (https://packt.live/37iTRXc) lists all the packages available in Python.

In this section, we will present to you two of the most popular ones: **`pandas`** and **`scikit-learn`**.

THE PANDAS PACKAGE

The pandas package provides an incredible amount of APIs for manipulating data structures. The two main data structures defined in the **`pandas`** package are **`DataFrame`** and **`Series`**.

DATAFRAME AND SERIES

A **`DataFrame`** is a tabular data structure that is represented as a two-dimensional table. It is composed of rows, columns, indexes, and cells. It is very similar to a sheet in Excel or a table in a database:

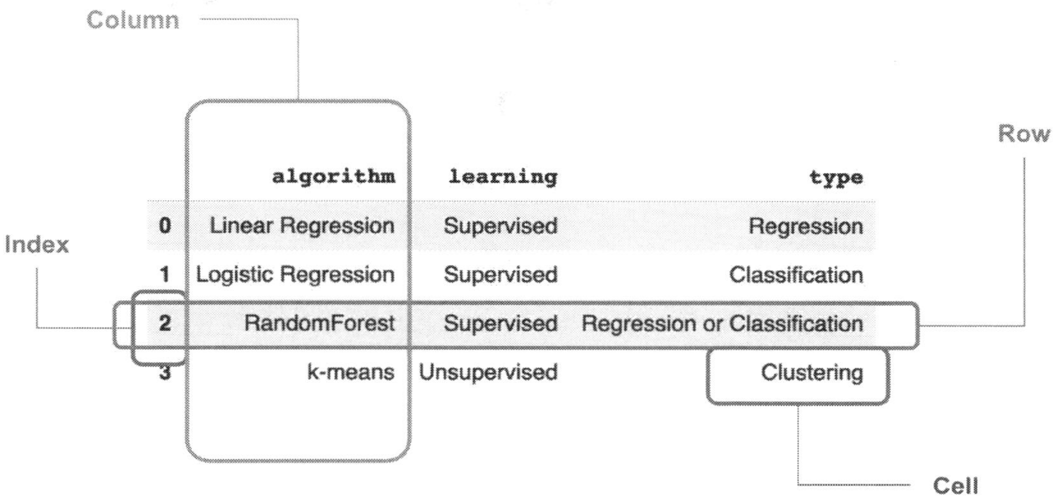

Figure 1.28: Components of a DataFrame

In *Figure 1.28*, there are three different columns: **algorithm**, **learning**, and **type**. Each of these columns (also called variables) contains a specific type of information. For instance, the **algorithm** variable lists the names of different machine learning algorithms.

A row stores the information related to a record (also called an observation). For instance, row number **2** (index number **2**) refers to the **RandomForest** record and all its attributes are stored in the different columns.

Finally, a cell is the value of a given row and column. For example, **Clustering** is the value of the cell of the row index **2** and the **type** column. You can see it as the intersection of a specified row and column.

So, a DataFrame is a structured representation of some data organized by rows and columns. A row represents an observation and each column contains the value of its attributes. This is the most common data structure used in data science.

In pandas, a DataFrame is represented by the **DataFrame** class. A **pandas** DataFrame is composed of **pandas** Series, which are 1-dimensional arrays. A **pandas** Series is basically a single column in a DataFrame.

Data is usually classified into two groups: *structured* and *unstructured*. Think of structured data as database tables or Excel spreadsheets where each column and row has a predefined structure. For example, in a table or spreadsheet that lists all the employees of a company, every record will follow the same pattern, such as the first column containing the date of birth, the second and third ones being for first and last names, and so on.

On the other hand, unstructured data is not organized with predefined and static patterns. Text and images are good examples of unstructured data. If you read a book and look at each sentence, it will not be possible for you to say that the second word of a sentence is always a verb or a person's name; it can be anything depending on how the author wanted to convey the information they wanted to share. Each sentence has its own structure and will be different from the last. Similarly, for a group of images, you can't say that pixels 20 to 30 will always represent the eye of a person or the wheel of a car: it will be different for each image.

Data can come from different data sources: there could be flat files, data storage, or Application Programming Interface (API) feeds, for example. In this book, we will work with flat files such as CSVs, Excel spreadsheets, or JSON. All these types of files are storing information with their own format and structure.

We'll have a look at the CSV file first.

CSV FILES

CSV files use the comma character—`,`—to separate columns and newlines for a new row. The previous example of a DataFrame would look like this in a CSV file:

```
algorithm,learning,type
Linear Regression,Supervised,Regression
Logistic Regression,Supervised,Classification
RandomForest,Supervised,Regression or Classification
k-means,Unsupervised,Clustering
```

In Python, you need to first import the packages you require before being able to use them. To do so, you will have to use the **`import`** command. You can create an alias of each imported package using the **`as`** keyword. It is quite common to import the **`pandas`** package with the alias **`pd`**:

```
import pandas as pd
```

pandas provides a **.read_csv()** method to easily load a CSV file directly into a DataFrame. You just need to provide the path or the URL to the CSV file, as shown below.

> **NOTE**
>
> Watch out for the slashes in the string below. Remember that the backslashes (\ ) are used to split the code across multiple lines, while the forward slashes (/) are part of the URL.

```
pd.read_csv('https://raw.githubusercontent.com/PacktWorkshops'\
            '/The-Data-Science-Workshop/master/Chapter01/'\
            'Dataset/csv_example.csv')
```

You should get the following output:

	algorithm	learning	type
0	Linear Regression	Supervised	Regression
1	Logistic Regression	Supervised	Classification
2	RandomForest	Supervised	Regression or Classification
3	k-means	Unsupervised	Clustering

Figure 1.29: DataFrame after loading a CSV file

> **NOTE**
>
> In this book, we will be loading datasets stored in the Packt GitHub repository: https://packt.live/2ucwsld.

GitHub wraps stored data into its own specific format. To load the original version of a dataset, you will need to load the raw version of it by clicking on the **Raw** button and copying the URL provided on your browser.

Have a look at *Figure 1.30*:

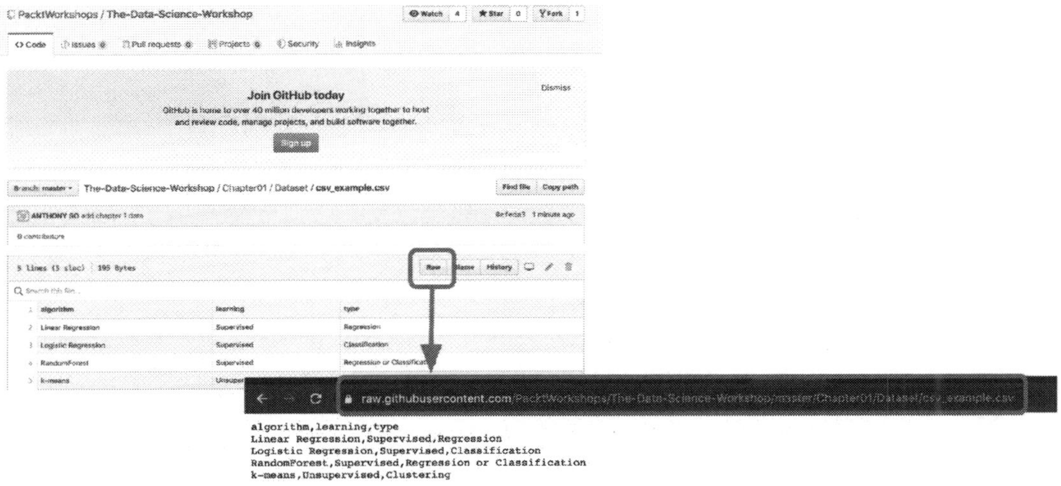

Figure 1.30: Getting the URL of a raw dataset on GitHub

EXCEL SPREADSHEETS

Excel is a Microsoft tool and is very popular in the industry. It has its own internal structure for recording additional information, such as the data type of each cell or even Excel formulas. There is a specific method in **pandas** to load Excel spreadsheets called **.read_excel()**:

```
pd.read_excel('https://github.com/PacktWorkshops'\
              '/The-Data-Science-Workshop/blob/master'\
              '/Chapter01/Dataset/excel_example.xlsx?raw=true')
```

You should get the following output:

	algorithm	learning	type
0	Linear Regression	Supervised	Regression
1	Logistic Regression	Supervised	Classification
2	RandomForest	Supervised	Regression or Classification
3	k-means	Unsupervised	Clustering

Figure 1.31: Dataframe after loading an Excel spreadsheet

JSON

JSON is a very popular file format, mainly used for transferring data from web APIs. Its structure is very similar to that of a Python dictionary with key-value pairs. The example DataFrame we used before would look like this in JSON format:

```
{
  "algorithm":{
     "0":"Linear Regression",
     "1":"Logistic Regression",
     "2":"RandomForest",
     "3":"k-means"
  },
  "learning":{
     "0":"Supervised",
     "1":"Supervised",
     "2":"Supervised",
     "3":"Unsupervised"
  },
  "type":{
     "0":"Regression",
     "1":"Classification",
     "2":"Regression or Classification",
     "3":"Clustering"
  }
}
```

As you may have guessed, there is a **pandas** method for reading JSON data as well, and it is called **.read_json()**:

```
pd.read_json('https://raw.githubusercontent.com/PacktWorkshops'\
             '/The-Data-Science-Workshop/master/Chapter01'\
             '/Dataset/json_example.json')
```

You should get the following output:

	algorithm	learning	type
0	Linear Regression	Supervised	Regression
1	Logistic Regression	Supervised	Classification
2	RandomForest	Supervised	Regression or Classification
3	k-means	Unsupervised	Clustering

Figure 1.32: Dataframe after loading JSON data

`pandas` provides more methods to load other types of files. The full list can be found in the following documentation: https://packt.live/2FiYB2O.

pandas is not limited to only loading data into DataFrames; it also provides a lot of other APIs for creating, analyzing, or transforming DataFrames. You will be introduced to some of its most useful methods in the following chapters.

EXERCISE 1.02: LOADING DATA OF DIFFERENT FORMATS INTO A PANDAS DATAFRAME

In this exercise, we will practice loading different data formats, such as CSV, TSV, and XLSX, into pandas DataFrames. The dataset we will use is the Top 10 Postcodes for the First Home Owner Grants dataset (this is a grant provided by the Australian government to help first-time real estate buyers). It lists the 10 postcodes (also known as zip codes) with the highest number of First Home Owner grants.

In this dataset, you will find the number of First Home Owner grant applications for each postcode and the corresponding suburb.

> **NOTE**
>
> This dataset can be found on our GitHub repository at https://packt.live/2FgAT7d.
>
> Also, it is publicly available here: https://packt.live/2ZJBYhi.

The following steps will help you complete the exercise:

1. Open a new Colab notebook.
2. Import the pandas package, as shown in the following code snippet:

```
import pandas as pd
```

3. Create a new variable called **csv_url** containing the URL to the raw CSV file:

```
csv_url = 'https://raw.githubusercontent.com/PacktWorkshops'\
          '/The-Data-Science-Workshop/master/Chapter01'\
          '/Dataset/overall_topten_2012-2013.csv'
```

4. Load the CSV file into a DataFrame using the pandas **.read_csv()** method. The first row of this CSV file contains the name of the file, which you can see if you open the file directly. You will need to exclude this row by using the **skiprows=1** parameter. Save the result in a variable called **csv_df** and print it:

```
csv_df = pd.read_csv(csv_url, skiprows=1)
csv_df
```

You should get the following output:

	Number	Postcode	Suburbs	Number of Applications
0	1	3029	Hoppers Crossing, Tarneit	1069
1	2	3977	Cranbourne, Devon Meadows, Skye	1037
2	3	3064	Craigieburn, Donnybrook, Roxburgh Park, Mickleham	821
3	4	3030	Point Cook, Werribee, Derrimut	816
4	5	3754	Doreen, Mernda	530
5	6	3810	Pakenham, Rythdale	479
6	7	3350	Alfredton, Ballarat, Canadian, Invermay Park, ...	383
7	8	3216	Belmont, Grovedale, Highton, Marshall, Waurn P...	351
8	9	3136	Croydon, Croydon Hills, Croydon North, Croydon...	344
9	10	3805	Fountain Gate, Narre Warren, Narre Warren South	335

Figure 1.33: The DataFrame after loading the CSV file

5. Create a new variable called **tsv_url** containing the URL to the raw TSV file:

```
tsv_url = 'https://raw.githubusercontent.com/PacktWorkshops'\
          '/The-Data-Science-Workshop/master/Chapter01'\
          '/Dataset/overall_topten_2012-2013.tsv'
```

> **NOTE**
>
> A TSV file is similar to a CSV file but instead of using the comma character (**,**) as a separator, it uses the tab character (**\t**).

6. Load the TSV file into a DataFrame using the pandas **.read_csv()** method and specify the **skiprows=1** and **sep='\t'** parameters. Save the result in a variable called **tsv_df** and print it:

```
tsv_df = pd.read_csv(tsv_url, skiprows=1, sep='\t')
tsv_df
```

You should get the following output:

	Number	Postcode	Suburbs	Number of Applications
0	1	3029	Hoppers Crossing, Tarneit	1069
1	2	3977	Cranbourne, Devon Meadows, Skye	1037
2	3	3064	Craigieburn, Donnybrook, Roxburgh Park, Mickleham	821
3	4	3030	Point Cook, Werribee, Derrimut	816
4	5	3754	Doreen, Mernda	530
5	6	3810	Pakenham, Rythdale	479
6	7	3350	Alfredton, Ballarat, Canadian, Invermay Park, ...	383
7	8	3216	Belmont, Grovedale, Highton, Marshall, Waurn P...	351
8	9	3136	Croydon, Croydon Hills, Croydon North, Croydon...	344
9	10	3805	Fountain Gate, Narre Warren, Narre Warren South	335

Figure 1.34: The DataFrame after loading the TSV file

7. Create a new variable called **xlsx_url** containing the URL to the raw Excel spreadsheet:

```
xlsx_url = 'https://github.com/PacktWorkshops'\
           '/The-Data-Science-Workshop/blob/master/'\
           'Chapter01/Dataset'\
           '/overall_topten_2012-2013.xlsx?raw=true'
```

8. Load the Excel spreadsheet into a DataFrame using the pandas **.read_excel()** method. Save the result in a variable called **xlsx_df** and print it:

```
xlsx_df = pd.read_excel(xlsx_url)
xlsx_df
```

You should get the following output:

This tab doesn't contain the data we are looking for

Figure 1.35: Display of the DataFrame after loading the Excel spreadsheet

By default, **.read_excel()** loads the first sheet of an Excel spreadsheet. In this example, the data we're looking for is actually stored in the second sheet.

9. Load the Excel spreadsheet into a Dataframe using the pandas **.read_excel()** method and specify the **skiprows=1** and **sheet_name=1** parameters. (Note that the **sheet_name** parameter is zero-indexed, so **sheet_name=0** returns the first sheet, while **sheet_name=1** returns the second sheet.) Save the result in a variable called **xlsx_df1** and print it:

```
xlsx_df1 = pd.read_excel(xlsx_url, skiprows=1, sheet_name=1)
xlsx_df1
```

You should get the following output:

	Number	Postcode	Suburbs	Number of Applications
0	1	3029	Hoppers Crossing, Tarneit	1069
1	2	3977	Cranbourne, Devon Meadows, Skye	1037
2	3	3064	Craigieburn, Donnybrook, Roxburgh Park, Mickleham	821
3	4	3030	Point Cook, Werribee, Derrimut	816
4	5	3754	Doreen, Mernda	530
5	6	3810	Pakenham, Rythdale	479
6	7	3350	Alfredton, Ballarat, Canadian, Invermay Park, ...	383
7	8	3216	Belmont, Grovedale, Highton, Marshall, Waurn P...	351
8	9	3136	Croydon, Croydon Hills, Croydon North, Croydon...	344
9	10	3805	Fountain Gate, Narre Warren, Narre Warren South	335

Figure 1.36: The DataFrame after loading the second sheet of the Excel spreadsheet

> **NOTE**
>
> To access the source code for this specific section, please refer to https://packt.live/2Yajzuq.
>
> You can also run this example online at https://packt.live/2Q4dThe.

In this exercise, we learned how to load the Top 10 Postcodes for First Home Buyer Grants dataset from different file formats.

In the next section, we will be introduced to scikit-learn.

SCIKIT-LEARN

Scikit-learn (also referred to as **sklearn**) is another extremely popular package used by data scientists. The main purpose of **sklearn** is to provide APIs for processing data and training machine learning algorithms. But before moving ahead, we need to know what a model is.

WHAT IS A MODEL?

A machine learning model learns patterns from data and creates a mathematical function to generate predictions. A supervised learning algorithm will try to find the relationship between a response variable and the given features.

Have a look at the following example.

A mathematical function can be represented as a function, ƒ(), that is applied to some input variables, X (which is composed of multiple features), and will calculate an output (or prediction), ŷ:

$$\hat{y} = f(X) = f(x_1, x_2, \ldots, x_n)$$

Figure 1.37: Function f(X)

The function, ƒ(), can be quite complex and have different numbers of parameters. If we take a linear regression (this will be presented in more detail in *Chapter 2, Regression*) as an example, the model parameters can be represented as W=(w_1, w_2, ... , w_n). So, the function we saw earlier will become as follows:

$$f(X) = f(x_1, x_2, \ldots, x_n) = w_0 + w_1 * x_1 + w_2 * x_2 + \ldots + w_n * x_n = \hat{y}$$

Figure 1.38: Function for linear regression

A machine learning algorithm will receive some examples of input *X* with the relevant output, *y*, and its goal will be to find the values of (w_1, w_2, ... , w_n) that will minimize the difference between its prediction, $\hat{y}$ and the true output, *y*.

The previous formulas can be a bit intimidating, but this is actually quite simple. Let's say we have a dataset composed of only one target variable y and one feature X, such as the following one:

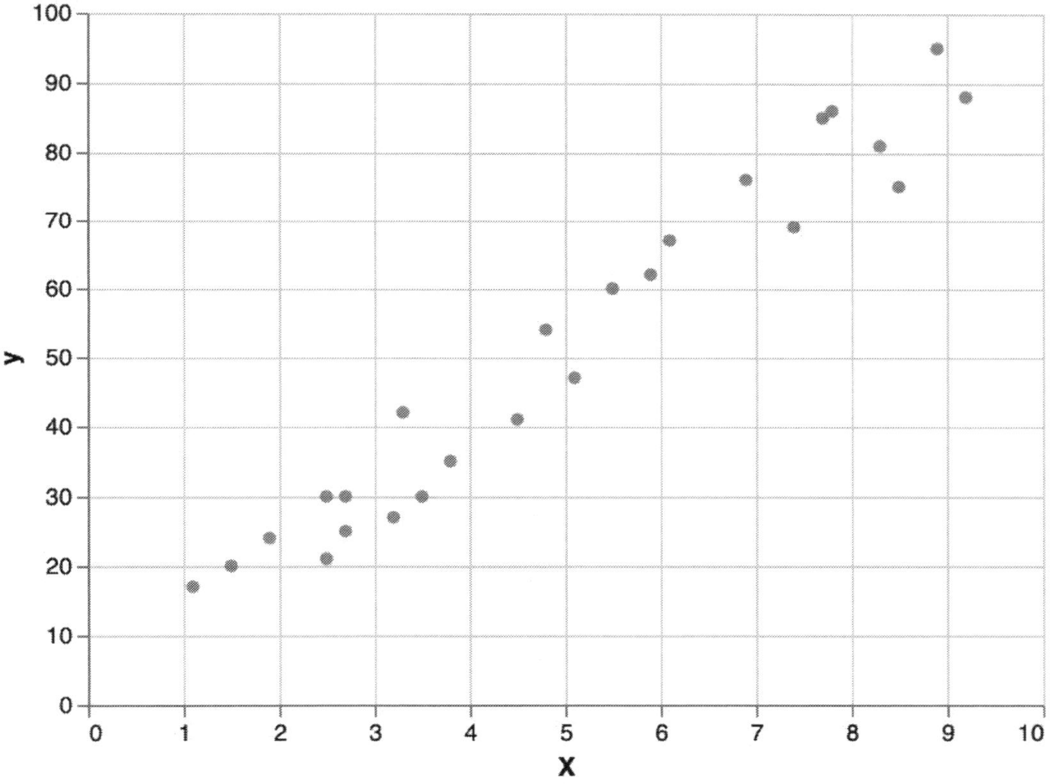

Figure 1.39: Example of a dataset with one target variable and one feature

If we fit a linear regression on this dataset, the algorithm will try to find a solution for the following equation:

$$f(X) = w_0 + w_1 * x_1$$

Figure 1.40: Function f(x) for linear regression fitting on a dataset

o, it just needs to find the values of the **w0** and w_1 parameters that will approximate the data as closely as possible. In this case, the algorithm may come up with **wo = 0** and **w1 = 10**. So, the function the model learns will be as follows:

$$f(X) = 0 + 10 * x_1 = 10 * x_1$$

Figure 1.41: Function f(x) using estimated values

We can visualize this on the same graph as for the data:

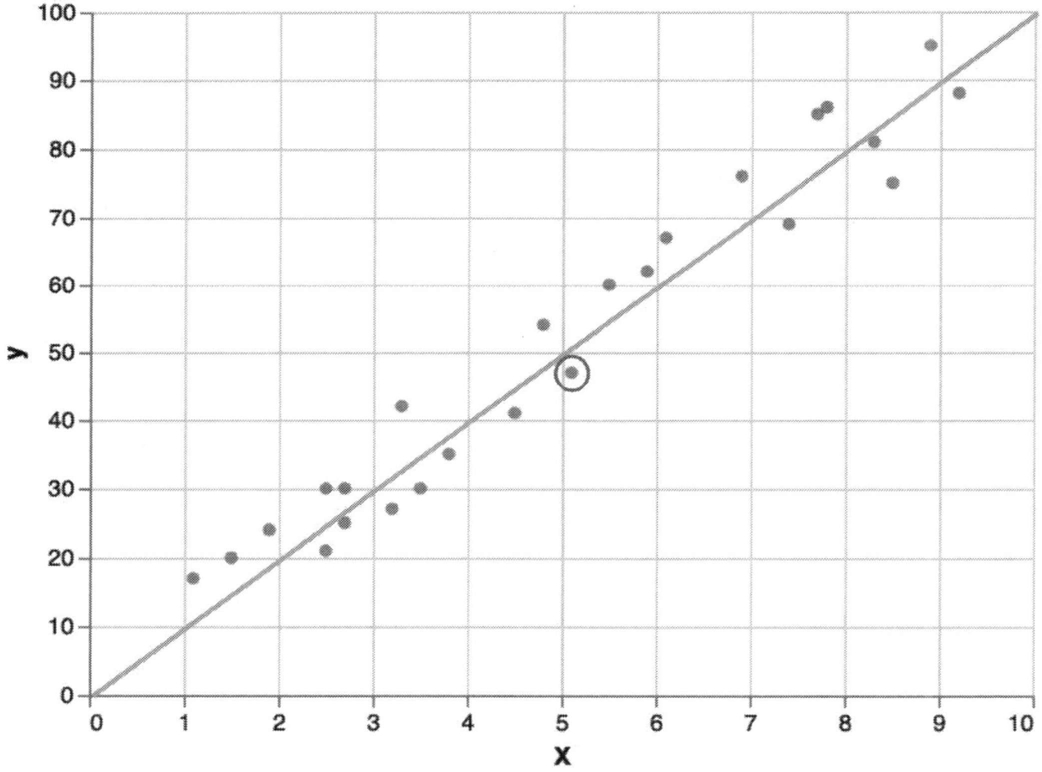

Figure 1.42: Fitted linear model on the example dataset

We can see that the fitted model (the orange line) is approximating the original data quite closely. So, if we predict the outcome for a new data point, it will be very close to the true value. For example, if we take a point that is close to 5 (let's say its values are **x = 5.1** and **y = 48**), the model will predict the following:

$$\hat{y} = 10 * x = 10 * 5.1 = 51$$

Figure 1.43: Model prediction

This value is actually very close to the ground truth, 48 (red circle). So, our model prediction is quite accurate.

This is it. It is quite simple, right? In general, a dataset will have more than one feature, but the logic will be the same: the trained model will try to find the best parameters for each variable to get predictions as close as possible to the true values.

We just saw an example of linear models, but there are actually other types of machine learning algorithms, such as tree-based or neural networks, that can find more complex patterns from data.

MODEL HYPERPARAMETERS

On top of the model parameters that are learned automatically by the algorithm (now you understand why we call it machine learning), there is also another type of parameter called the hyperparameter. Hyperparameters cannot be learned by the model. They are set by data scientists in order to define some specific conditions for the algorithm learning process. These hyperparameters are different for each family of algorithms and they can, for instance, help fast-track the learning process or limit the risk of overfitting. In this book, you will learn how to tune some of these machine learning hyperparameters.

THE SKLEARN API

As mentioned before, the scikit-learn (or **`sklearn`**) package has implemented an incredible amount of machine learning algorithms, such as logistic regression, k-nearest neighbors, k-means, and random forest.

> **NOTE**
>
> Do not worry about these terms—you are not expected to know what these algorithms involve just yet. You will see a simple random forest example in this chapter, but all of these algorithms will be explained in detail in later chapters of the book.

`sklearn` groups algorithms by family. For instance, **`RandomForest`** and **`GradientBoosting`** are part of the **`ensemble`** module. In order to make use of an algorithm, you will need to import it first like this:

```
from sklearn.ensemble import RandomForestClassifier
```

Another reason why **sklearn** is so popular is that all the algorithms follow the exact same API structure. So, once you have learned how to train one algorithm, it is extremely easy to train another one with very minimal code changes. With **sklearn**, there are four main steps to train a machine learning model:

1. Instantiate a model with specified hyperparameters: this will configure the machine learning model you want to train.
2. Train the model with training data: during this step, the model will learn the best parameters to get predictions as close as possible to the actual values of the target.
3. Predict the outcome from input data: using the learned parameter, the model will predict the outcome for new data.
4. Assess the performance of the model predictions: for checking whether the model learned the right patterns to get accurate predictions.

> **NOTE**
>
> In a real project, there might be more steps depending on the situation, but for simplicity, we will stick with these four for now. You will learn the remaining ones in the following chapters.

As mentioned before, each algorithm will have its own specific hyperparameters that can be tuned. To instantiate a model, you just need to create a new variable from the class you imported previously and specify the values of the hyperparameters. If you leave the hyperparameters blank, the model will use the default values specified by **sklearn**.

It is recommended to at least set the **random_state** hyperparameter in order to get reproducible results every time that you have to run the same code:

```
rf_model = RandomForestClassifier(random_state=1)
```

The second step is to train the model with some data. In this example, we will use a simple dataset that classifies 178 instances of Italian wines into 3 categories based on 13 features. This dataset is part of the few examples that **sklearn** provides within its API. We need to load the data first:

```
from sklearn.datasets import load_wine
features, target = load_wine(return_X_y=True)
```

Then using the **`.fit()`** method to train the model, you will provide the features and the target variable as input:

```
rf_model.fit(features, target)
```

You should get the following output:

```
RandomForestClassifier(bootstrap=True, class_weight=None, criterion='gini',
                       max_depth=None, max_features='auto', max_leaf_nodes=None,
                       min_impurity_decrease=0.0, min_impurity_split=None,
                       min_samples_leaf=1, min_samples_split=2,
                       min_weight_fraction_leaf=0.0, n_estimators=10,
                       n_jobs=None, oob_score=False, random_state=1, verbose=0,
                       warm_start=False)
```

Figure 1.44: Logs of the trained Random Forest model

In the preceding output, we can see a Random Forest model with the default hyperparameters. You will be introduced to some of them in *Chapter 4, Multiclass Classification with RandomForest.*

Once trained, we can use the **`.predict()`** method to predict the target for one or more observations. Here we will use the same data as for the training step:

```
preds = rf_model.predict(features)
preds
```

You should get the following output:

```
array([0, 0, 0, 0, 0, 0, 0, 0, 0, 0, 0, 0, 0, 0, 0, 0, 0, 0, 0, 0, 0, 0,
       0, 0, 0, 0, 0, 0, 0, 0, 0, 0, 0, 0, 0, 0, 0, 0, 0, 0, 0, 0, 0, 0,
       0, 0, 0, 0, 0, 0, 0, 0, 0, 0, 0, 0, 0, 0, 0, 1, 1, 1, 1, 1, 1, 1,
       1, 1, 1, 1, 1, 1, 1, 1, 1, 1, 1, 1, 1, 1, 1, 1, 1, 1, 1, 1, 1, 1,
       1, 1, 1, 1, 1, 1, 1, 1, 1, 1, 1, 1, 1, 1, 1, 1, 1, 1, 1, 1, 1, 1,
       1, 1, 1, 1, 1, 1, 1, 1, 1, 1, 1, 1, 1, 1, 1, 1, 1, 1, 1, 1, 2, 2,
       2, 2, 2, 2, 2, 2, 2, 2, 2, 2, 2, 2, 2, 2, 2, 2, 2, 2, 2, 2, 2, 2,
       2, 2, 2, 2, 2, 2, 2, 2, 2, 2, 2, 2, 2, 2, 2, 2, 2, 2, 2, 2, 2, 2,
       2, 2])
```

Figure 1.45: Predictions of the trained Random Forest model

From the preceding output, you can see that the 178 different wines in the dataset have been classified into one of the three different wine categories. The first lot of wines have been classified as being in category 0, the second lot are category 1, and the last lot are category 2. At this point, we do not know what classes 0, 1, or 2 represent (in the context of the "type" of wine in each category), but finding this out would form part of the larger data science project.

Finally, we want to assess the model's performance by comparing its predictions to the actual values of the target variable. There are a lot of different metrics that can be used for assessing model performance, and you will learn more about them later in this book. For now, though, we will just use a metric called **accuracy**. This metric calculates the ratio of correct predictions to the total number of observations:

```
from sklearn.metrics import accuracy_score
accuracy_score(target, preds)
```

You should get the following output

```
1.0
```

Figure 1.46: Accuracy of the trained Random Forest model

In this example, the Random Forest model learned to predict correctly all the observations from this dataset; it achieves an accuracy score of `1` (that is, 100% of the predictions matched the actual true values).

It's as simple as that! This may be too good to be true. In the following chapters, you will learn how to check whether the trained models are able to accurately predict unseen or future data points or if they have only learned the specific patterns of this input data (also called overfitting).

EXERCISE 1.03: PREDICTING BREAST CANCER FROM A DATASET USING SKLEARN

In this exercise, we will build a machine learning classifier using **`RandomForest`** from **`sklearn`** to predict whether the breast cancer of a patient is malignant (harmful) or benign (not harmful).

The dataset we will use is the Breast Cancer Wisconsin (Diagnostic) dataset, which is available directly from the **`sklearn`** package at https://packt.live/2FcOTim.

The following steps will help you complete the exercise:

1. Open a new Colab notebook.
2. Import the **`load_breast_cancer`** function from **`sklearn.datasets`**:

```
from sklearn.datasets import load_breast_cancer
```

3. Load the dataset from the **load_breast_cancer** function with the **return_X_y=True** parameter to return the features and response variable only:

```
features, target = load_breast_cancer(return_X_y=True)
```

4. Print the variable features:

```
print(features)
```

You should get the following output:

```
[[1.799e+01 1.038e+01 1.228e+02 ... 2.654e-01 4.601e-01 1.189e-01]
 [2.057e+01 1.777e+01 1.329e+02 ... 1.860e-01 2.750e-01 8.902e-02]
 [1.969e+01 2.125e+01 1.300e+02 ... 2.430e-01 3.613e-01 8.758e-02]
 ...
 [1.660e+01 2.808e+01 1.083e+02 ... 1.418e-01 2.218e-01 7.820e-02]
 [2.060e+01 2.933e+01 1.401e+02 ... 2.650e-01 4.087e-01 1.240e-01]
 [7.760e+00 2.454e+01 4.792e+01 ... 0.000e+00 2.871e-01 7.039e-02]]
```

Figure 1.47: Output of the variable features

The preceding output shows the values of the features. (You can learn more about the features from the link given previously.)

5. Print the **target** variable:

```
print(target)
```

You should get the following output:

```
[0 0 0 0 0 0 0 0 0 0 0 0 0 0 0 0 0 0 0 1 1 1 0 0 0 0 0 0 0 0 0 0 0 0 0 0 0
 1 0 0 0 0 0 0 0 0 1 0 1 1 1 1 1 0 0 1 0 0 1 1 1 1 0 1 0 0 1 1 1 1 0 1 0 0
 1 0 1 0 0 1 1 1 0 0 1 0 0 0 1 1 1 0 1 1 0 0 1 1 1 0 0 1 1 1 1 0 1 1 0 1 1
 1 1 1 1 1 1 0 0 0 1 0 0 1 1 1 0 0 1 0 1 0 0 1 0 0 1 1 0 1 1 0 1 1 1 1 0 1
 1 1 1 1 1 1 1 1 0 1 1 1 1 0 0 1 0 1 1 0 0 1 1 0 0 1 1 1 1 0 1 1 0 0 0 1 0
 1 0 1 1 1 0 1 1 0 0 1 0 0 0 0 1 0 0 0 1 0 1 0 1 1 0 1 0 0 0 0 1 1 0 0 1 1
 1 0 1 1 1 1 1 0 0 1 1 0 1 1 0 0 1 0 1 1 1 1 0 1 1 1 1 1 0 1 0 0 0 0 0 0 0
 0 0 0 0 0 0 0 1 1 1 1 1 1 0 1 0 1 1 0 1 1 0 1 0 0 1 1 1 1 1 1 1 1 1 1 1 1
 1 0 1 1 0 1 0 1 1 1 1 1 1 1 1 1 1 1 1 1 1 0 1 1 1 0 1 0 1 1 1 1 0 0 0 1 1
 1 1 0 1 0 1 0 1 1 1 0 1 1 1 1 1 1 1 0 0 0 1 1 1 1 1 1 1 1 1 1 1 0 0 1 0 0
 0 1 0 0 1 1 1 1 1 0 1 1 1 1 1 0 1 1 1 0 1 1 0 0 1 1 1 1 1 1 0 1 1 1 1 1 1
 1 0 1 1 1 1 1 0 1 1 0 1 1 1 1 1 1 1 1 1 1 1 1 0 1 0 0 1 0 1 1 1 1 1 0 1 1
 0 1 0 1 1 0 1 0 1 1 1 1 1 1 1 1 0 0 1 1 1 1 1 1 0 1 1 1 1 1 1 1 1 1 1 0 1
 1 1 1 1 1 1 0 1 0 1 1 0 1 1 1 1 1 0 0 1 0 1 0 1 1 1 1 1 0 1 1 0 1 0 1 0 0
 1 1 1 0 1 1 1 1 1 1 1 1 1 1 1 0 1 0 0 1 1 1 1 1 1 1 1 1 1 1 1 1 1 1 1 1 1
 1 1 1 1 1 1 1 0 0 0 0 0 0 1]
```

Figure 1.48: Output of the variable target

The preceding output shows the values of the target variable. There are two classes shown for each instance in the dataset. These classes are **0** and **1**, representing whether the cancer is malignant or benign.

6. Import the **RandomForestClassifier** class from **sklearn.ensemble**:

```
from sklearn.ensemble import RandomForestClassifier
```

7. Create a new variable called **seed**, which will take the value **888** (chosen arbitrarily):

```
seed = 888
```

8. Instantiate **RandomForestClassifier** with the **random_state=seed** parameter and save it into a variable called **rf_model**:

```
rf_model = RandomForestClassifier(random_state=seed)
```

9. Train the model with the **.fit()** method with **features** and **target** as parameters:

```
rf_model.fit(features, target)
```

You should get the following output:

```
RandomForestClassifier(bootstrap=True, class_weight=None, criterion='gini',
                       max_depth=None, max_features='auto', max_leaf_nodes=None,
                       min_impurity_decrease=0.0, min_impurity_split=None,
                       min_samples_leaf=1, min_samples_split=2,
                       min_weight_fraction_leaf=0.0, n_estimators=10,
                       n_jobs=None, oob_score=False, random_state=888,
                       verbose=0, warm_start=False)
```

Figure 1.49: Logs of RandomForestClassifier

10. Make predictions with the trained model using the **.predict()** method and **features** as a parameter and save the results into a variable called **preds**:

```
preds = rf_model.predict(features)
```

11. Print the **preds** variable:

```
print(preds)
```

You should get the following output:

```
[0 0 0 0 0 0 0 0 0 0 0 0 0 0 0 0 0 0 0 1 1 1 0 0 0 0 0 0 0 0 0 0 0 0 0 0 0
 1 0 0 0 0 0 0 0 0 1 0 1 1 1 1 1 0 0 1 0 0 1 1 1 1 0 1 0 0 1 1 1 1 0 1 0 0
 1 0 1 0 0 1 1 1 0 0 1 0 0 0 1 1 1 0 1 1 0 0 1 1 1 0 0 1 1 1 1 0 1 1 0 1 1
 1 1 1 1 1 1 0 0 0 1 0 0 1 1 1 0 0 1 0 1 0 0 1 0 0 1 1 0 1 1 0 1 1 1 1 0 1
 1 1 1 1 1 1 1 1 0 1 1 1 1 0 0 1 0 1 1 0 0 1 1 0 0 1 1 1 1 0 1 1 0 0 0 1 0
 1 0 1 1 1 0 1 1 0 0 1 0 0 0 0 1 0 0 0 1 0 1 0 1 1 0 1 0 0 0 0 1 1 0 0 1 1
 1 0 1 1 1 1 1 0 0 1 1 0 1 1 0 0 1 0 1 1 1 1 0 1 1 1 1 1 0 1 0 0 0 0 0 0 0
 0 0 0 0 0 0 0 1 1 1 1 1 1 0 1 0 1 1 0 1 1 0 1 0 0 1 1 1 1 1 1 1 1 1 1 1 1
 1 0 1 1 0 1 0 1 1 1 1 1 1 1 1 1 1 1 1 1 1 0 1 1 1 0 1 0 1 1 1 1 0 0 0 1 1
 1 1 0 1 0 1 0 1 1 1 0 1 1 1 1 1 1 1 0 0 0 1 1 1 1 1 1 1 1 1 1 1 0 0 1 0 0
 0 1 0 0 1 1 1 1 1 0 1 1 1 1 1 0 1 1 1 0 1 1 0 0 1 1 1 1 1 1 0 1 1 1 1 1 1
 1 0 1 1 1 1 1 0 1 1 0 1 1 1 1 1 1 1 1 1 1 1 1 0 1 0 0 1 0 1 1 1 1 1 0 1 1
 0 1 0 1 1 0 1 0 1 1 1 1 1 1 1 1 0 0 1 1 1 1 1 1 0 1 1 1 1 1 1 1 1 1 1 0 1
 1 1 1 1 1 1 0 1 0 1 1 0 1 1 1 1 1 0 0 1 0 1 0 1 1 1 1 1 0 1 1 0 1 0 1 0 0
 1 1 1 0 1 1 1 1 1 1 1 1 1 1 1 0 1 0 0 1 1 1 1 1 1 1 1 1 1 1 1 1 1 1 1 1 1
 1 1 1 1 1 1 1 0 0 0 0 0 0 1]
```

Figure 1.50: Predictions of the Random Forest model

The preceding output shows the predictions for the training set. You can compare this with the actual target variable values shown in *Figure 1.48*.

12. Import the **accuracy_score** method from **sklearn.metrics**:

```
from sklearn.metrics import accuracy_score
```

13. Calculate **accuracy_score()** with **target** and **preds** as parameters:

```
accuracy_score(target, preds)
```

You should get the following output:

```
1.0
```

Figure 1.51: Accuracy of the model

> **NOTE**
>
> To access the source code for this specific section, please refer to https://packt.live/3aBso5i.
>
> You can also run this example online at https://packt.live/316OiKA.

You just trained a Random Forest model using **sklearn** APIs and achieved an accuracy score of **1** in classifying breast cancer observations.

ACTIVITY 1.01: TRAIN A SPAM DETECTOR ALGORITHM

You are working for an email service provider and have been tasked with training an algorithm that recognizes whether an email is spam or not from a given dataset and checking its performance.

In this dataset, the authors have already created 57 different features based on some statistics for relevant keywords in order to classify whether an email is spam or not.

> **NOTE**
>
> The dataset was originally shared by Mark Hopkins, Erik Reeber, George Forman, and Jaap Suermondt: https://packt.live/35fdUUA.
>
> You can download it from the Packt GitHub at https://packt.live/2MPmnrl.

The following steps will help you to complete this activity:

1. Import the required libraries.
2. Load the dataset using **.pd.read_csv()**.
3. Extract the response variable using **.pop()** from **pandas**. This method will extract the column provided as a parameter from the DataFrame. You can then assign it a variable name, for example, **target = df.pop('class')**.
4. Instantiate **RandomForestClassifier**.
5. Train a Random Forest model to predict the outcome with **.fit()**.
6. Predict the outcomes from the input data using **.predict()**.

7. Calculate the accuracy score using **accuracy_score**.

   The output will be similar to the following:

```
0.9958704629428385
```

Figure 1.52: Accuracy score for spam detector

> **NOTE**
>
> The solution to this activity can be found at the following address: https://packt.live/2GbJloz.

SUMMARY

This chapter provided you with an overview of what data science is in general. We also learned the different types of machine learning algorithms, including supervised and unsupervised, as well as regression and classification. We had a quick introduction to Python and how to manipulate the main data structures (lists and dictionaries) that will be used in this book.

Then we walked you through what a DataFrame is and how to create one by loading data from different file formats using the famous pandas package. Finally, we learned how to use the sklearn package to train a machine learning model and make predictions with it.

This was just a quick glimpse into the fascinating world of data science. In this book, you will learn much more and discover new techniques for handling data science projects from end to end.

The next chapter will show you how to perform a regression task on a real-world dataset.

2

REGRESSION

OVERVIEW

This chapter is an introduction to linear regression analysis and its application to practical problem-solving in data science. You will learn how to use Python, a versatile programming language, to carry out regression analysis and examine the results. The use of the logarithm function to transform inherently non-linear relationships between variables and to enable the application of the linear regression method of analysis will also be introduced.

By the end of this chapter, you will be able to identify and import the Python modules required for regression analysis; use the **`pandas`** module to load a dataset and prepare it for regression analysis; create a scatter plot of bivariate data and fit a regression line through it; use the methods available in the Python **`statsmodels`** module to fit a regression model to a dataset; explain the results of simple and multiple linear regression analysis; assess the goodness of fit of a linear regression model; and apply linear regression analysis as a tool for practical problem-solving.

INTRODUCTION

The previous chapter provided a primer to Python programming and an overview of the data science field. Data science is a relatively young multidisciplinary field of study. It draws its concepts and methods from the traditional fields of statistics, computer science, and the broad field of artificial intelligence (AI), especially the subfield of AI called machine learning:

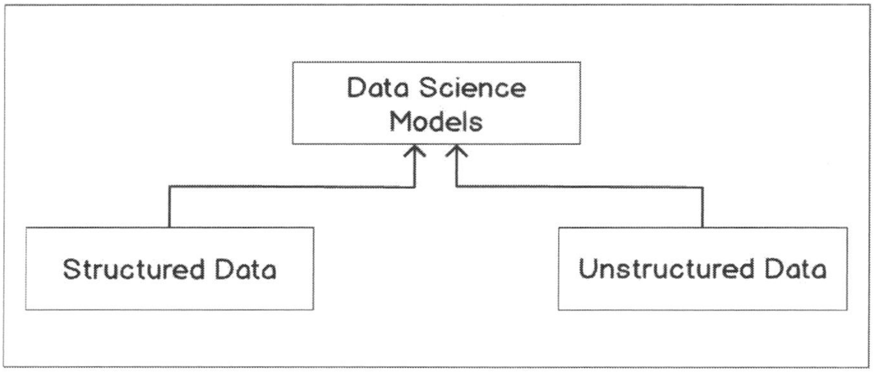

Figure 2.1: The data science models

As you can see in *Figure 2.1*, data science aims to make use of both **structured** and **unstructured** data, develop models that can be effectively used, make predictions, and also derive insights for decision making.

A loose description of structured data will be any set of data that can be conveniently arranged into a table that consists of rows and columns. This kind of data is normally stored in database management systems.

Unstructured data, however, cannot be conveniently stored in tabular form – an example of such a dataset is a text document. To achieve the objectives of data science, a flexible programming language that effectively combines interactivity with computing power and speed is necessary. This is where the Python programming language meets the needs of data science and, as mentioned in *Chapter 1, Introduction to Data Science in Python*, we will be using Python in this book.

The need to develop models to make predictions and to gain insights for decisionmaking cuts across many industries. Data science is, therefore, finding uses in many industries, including healthcare, manufacturing and the process industries in general, the banking and finance sectors, marketing and e-commerce, the government, and education.

In this chapter, we will be specifically be looking at regression, which is one of the key methods that is used regularly in data science, in order to model relationships between variables, where the **target variable** (that is, the value you're looking for) is a real number.

Consider a situation where a real estate business wants to understand and, if possible, model the relationship between the prices of property in a city and knowing the key attributes of the properties. This is a data science problem and it can be tackled using regression.

This is because the target variable of interest, which is the price of a property, is a real number. Examples of the key attributes of a property that can be used to predict its value are as follows:

- The age of the property
- The number of bedrooms in a property
- Whether the property has a pool or not
- The area of land the property covers
- The distance of the property from facilities such as railway stations and schools

Regression analysis can be employed to study this scenario, in which you have to create a function that maps the key attributes of a property to the target variable, which, in this case, is the price of a property.

Regression analysis is part of a family of machine learning techniques called **supervised machine learning**. It is called supervised because the machine learning algorithm that learns the model is provided a kind of *question* and *answer* dataset to learn from. The *question* here is the key attribute and the *answer* is the property price for each property that is used in the study, as shown in the following figure:

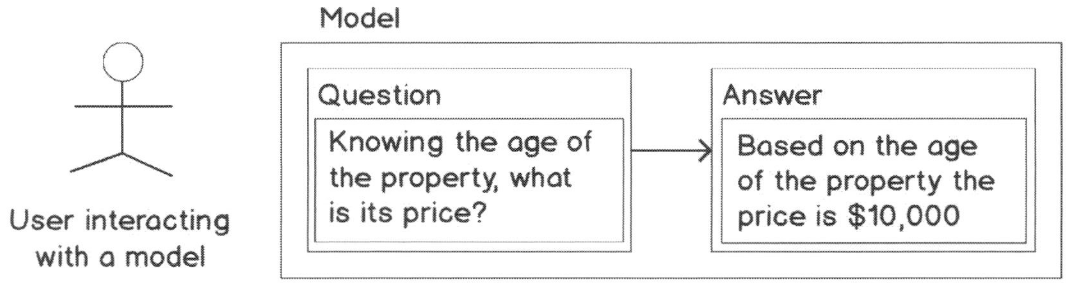

Figure 2.2: Example of a supervised learning technique

Once a model has been learned by the algorithm, we can provide the model with a question (that is, a set of attributes for a property whose price we want to find) for it to tell us what the answer (that is, the price) of that property will be.

This chapter is an introduction to linear regression and how it can be applied to solve practical problems like the one described previously in data science. Python provides a rich set of modules (libraries) that can be used to conduct rigorous regression analysis of various kinds. In this chapter, we will make use of the following Python modules, among others: **`pandas`**, **`statsmodels`**, **`seaborn`**, **`matplotlib`**, and **`scikit-learn`**.

SIMPLE LINEAR REGRESSION

In *Figure 2.3*, you can see the crime rate per capita and the median value of owner-occupied homes for the city of Boston, which is the largest city of the Commonwealth of Massachusetts. We seek to use regression analysis to gain an insight into what drives crime rates in the city.

Such analysis is useful to policy makers and society in general because it can help with decision-making directed toward the reduction of the crime rate, and hopefully the eradication of crime across communities. This can make communities safer and increase the quality of life in society.

This is a data science problem and is of the supervised machine learning type. There is a dependent variable named **`crime rate`** (let's denote it *Y*), whose variation we seek to understand in terms of an independent variable, named **`Median value of owner-occupied homes`** (let's denote it *X*).

In other words, we are trying to understand the variation in crime rate based on different neighborhoods.

Regression analysis is about finding a function, under a given set of assumptions, that best describes the relationship between the dependent variable (*Y* in this case) and the independent variable (*X* in this case).

When the number of independent variables is only one, and the relationship between the dependent and the independent variable is assumed to be a straight line, as shown in *Figure 2.3*, this type of regression analysis is called **simple linear regression**. The straight-line relationship is called the regression line or the line of **best fit**:

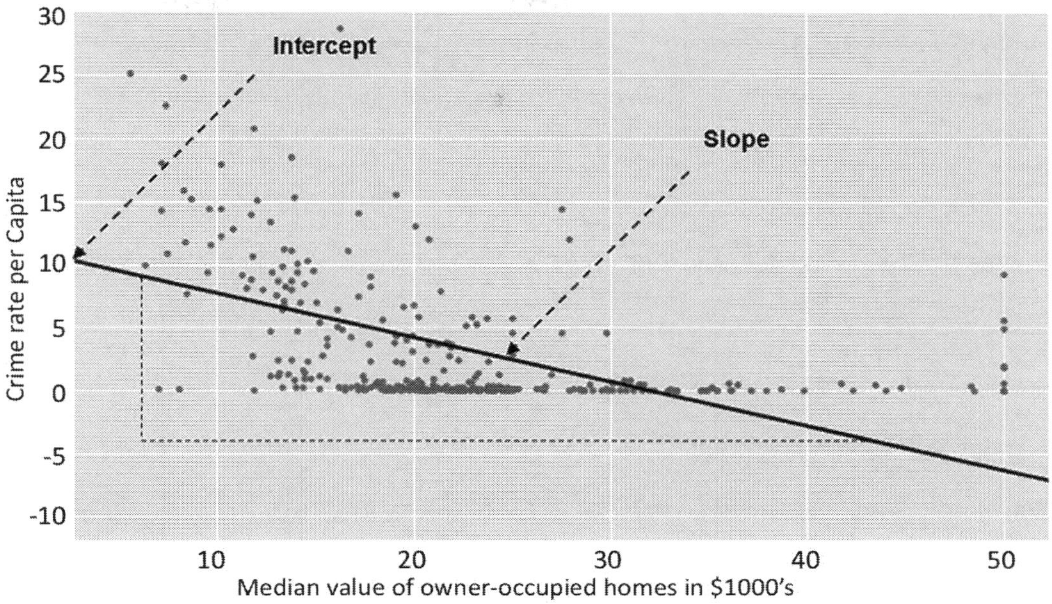

Figure 2.3: A scatter plot of the crime rate against the median value of owner-occupied homes

In *Figure 2.3*, the regression line is shown as a solid black line. Ignoring the poor quality of the fit of the regression line to the data in the figure, we can see a decline in crime rate per capita as the median value of owner-occupied homes increases.

From a data science point of view, this observation may pose lots of questions. For instance, what is driving the decline in crime rate per capita as the median value of owner-occupier homes increases? Are richer suburbs and towns receiving more policing resources than less fortunate suburbs and towns? Unfortunately, these questions cannot be answered with such a simple plot as we find in *Figure 2.3*. But the observed trend may serve as a starting point for a discussion to review the distribution of police and community-wide security resources.

Returning to the question of how well the regression line fits the data, it is evident that almost one-third of the regression line has no data points scattered around it at all. Many data points are simply clustered on the horizontal axis around the zero (**0**) crime rate mark. This is not what you expect of a good regression line that fits the data well. A good regression line that fits the data well must sit amidst a *cloud* of data points.

It appears that the relationship between the crime rate per capita and the median value of owner-occupied homes is not as linear as you may have thought initially.

In this chapter, we will learn how to use the logarithm function (a mathematical function for transforming values) to linearize the relationship between the crime rate per capita and the median value of owner-occupied homes, in order to improve the fit of the regression line to the data points on the scatter graph.

We have ignored a very important question thus far. That is, *how can you determine the regression line for a given set of data?*

A common method used to determine the regression line is called the method of least squares, which is covered in the next section.

THE METHOD OF LEAST SQUARES

The simple linear regression line is generally of the form shown in *Figure 2.4*, where β_0 and β_1 are unknown constants, representing the intercept and the slope of the regression line, respectively.

The intercept is the value of the dependent variable (Y) when the independent variable (X) has a value of zero (0). The slope is a measure of the rate at which the dependent variable (Y) changes when the independent variable (X) changes by one (1). The unknown constants are called the **model coefficients** or **parameters**. This form of the regression line is sometimes known as the population regression line, and, as a probabilistic model, it fits the dataset approximately, hence the use of the symbol (≈) in *Figure 2.4*. The model is called probabilistic because it does not model all the variability in the dependent variable (Y) :

$$Y \approx \beta_0 + \beta_1 X$$

Figure 2.4: Simple linear regression equation

Calculating the difference between the actual dependent variable value and the predicted dependent variable value gives an error that is commonly termed as the residual (ϵ_i).

Repeating this calculation for every data point in the sample, the residual (ϵ_i) for every data point can be squared, to eliminate algebraic signs, and added together to obtain the **error sum of squares (ESS)**.

The least squares method seeks to minimize the ESS.

MULTIPLE LINEAR REGRESSION

In the simple linear regression discussed previously, we only have one independent variable. If we include multiple independent variables in our analysis, we get a multiple linear regression model. Multiple linear regression is represented in a way that's similar to simple linear regression.

Let's consider a case where we want to fit a linear regression model that has three independent variables, X_1, X_2, and X_3. The formula for the multiple linear regression equation will look like *Figure 2.5*:

$$Y \approx \beta_0 + \beta_1 X_1 + \beta_2 X_2 + \beta_3 X_3$$

Figure 2.5: Multiple linear regression equation

Each independent variable will have its own coefficient or parameter (that is, β_1 β_2 or β_3). The β_s coefficient tells us how a change in their respective independent variable influences the dependent variable if all other independent variables are unchanged.

ESTIMATING THE REGRESSION COEFFICIENTS ($\beta_{0,}$ $\beta_{1,}$ β_2 AND β_3)

The regression coefficients in *Figure 2.5* are estimated using the same least squares approach that was discussed when simple linear regression was introduced. To satisfy the least squares method, the chosen coefficients must minimize the sum of squared residuals.

Later in the chapter, we will make use of the Python programming language to compute these coefficient estimates practically.

LOGARITHMIC TRANSFORMATIONS OF VARIABLES

As has been mentioned already, sometimes the relationship between the dependent and independent variables is not linear. This limits the use of linear regression. To get around this, depending on the nature of the relationship, the logarithm function can be used to transform the variable of interest. What happens then is that the transformed variable tends to have a linear relationship with the other untransformed variables, enabling the use of linear regression to fit the data. This will be illustrated in practice on the dataset being analyzed later in the exercises of the book.

CORRELATION MATRICES

In *Figure 2.3*, we saw how a linear relationship between two variables can be analyzed using a straight-line graph. Another way of visualizing the linear relationship between variables is with a correlation matrix. A correlation matrix is a kind of cross-table of numbers showing the correlation between pairs of variables, that is, how strongly the two variables are connected (this can be thought of as how a change in one variable will cause a change in the other variable). It is not easy analyzing raw figures in a table. A correlation matrix can, therefore, be converted to a form of "heatmap" so that the correlation between variables can easily be observed using different colors. An example of this is shown in *Exercise 2.01, Loading and Preparing the Data for Analysis*.

CONDUCTING REGRESSION ANALYSIS USING PYTHON

Having discussed the basics of regression analysis, it is now time to get our hands dirty and actually do some regression analysis using Python.

To begin with our analysis, we need to start a session in Python and load the relevant modules and dataset required.

All of the regression analysis we will do in this chapter will be based on the Boston Housing dataset. The dataset is good for teaching and is suitable for linear regression analysis. It presents the level of challenge that necessitates the use of the logarithm function to transform variables in order to achieve a better level of model fit to the data. The dataset contains information on a collection of properties in the Boston area and can be used to determine how the different housing attributes of a specific property affect the property's value.

The column headings of the Boston Housing dataset CSV file can be explained as follows:

- CRIM – per capita crime rate by town
- ZN – proportion of residential land zoned for lots over 25,000 sq.ft.
- INDUS – proportion of non-retail business acres per town
- CHAS – Charles River dummy variable (= 1 if tract bounds river; 0 otherwise)
- NOX – nitric oxide concentration (parts per 10 million)
- RM – average number of rooms per dwelling
- AGE – proportion of owner-occupied units built prior to 1940

- DIS – weighted distances to five Boston employment centers
- RAD – index of accessibility to radial highways
- TAX – full-value property-tax rate per $10,000
- PTRATIO – pupil-teacher ratio by town
- LSTAT – % of lower status of the population
- MEDV – median value of owner-occupied homes in $1,000s

The dataset we're using is a slightly modified version of the original and was sourced from https://packt.live/39IN8Y6.

EXERCISE 2.01: LOADING AND PREPARING THE DATA FOR ANALYSIS

In this exercise, we will learn how to load Python modules, and the dataset we need for analysis, into our Python session and prepare the data for analysis.

> **NOTE**
>
> We will be using the Boston Housing dataset in this chapter, which can be found on our GitHub repository at https://packt.live/2QCCbQB.

The following steps will help you to complete this exercise:

1. Open a new Colab notebook file.
2. Load the necessary Python modules by entering the following code snippet into a single Colab notebook cell. Press the **Shift** and **Enter** keys together to run the block of code:

```
%matplotlib inline
import matplotlib as mpl
import seaborn as sns
import matplotlib.pyplot as plt
import statsmodels.formula.api as smf
import statsmodels.graphics.api as smg
import pandas as pd
import numpy as np
import patsy
```

```
from statsmodels.graphics.correlation import plot_corr
from sklearn.model_selection import train_test_split
plt.style.use('seaborn')
```

The first line of the preceding code enables **matplotlib** to display the graphical output of the code in the notebook environment. The lines of code that follow use the **import** keyword to load various Python modules into our programming environment. This includes **patsy**, which is a Python module. Some of the modules are given aliases for easy referencing, such as the **seaborn** module being given the alias **sns**. Therefore, whenever we refer to **seaborn** in subsequent code, we use the alias **sns**. The **patsy** module is imported without an alias. We, therefore, use the full name of the **patsy** module in our code where needed.

The **plot_corr** and **train_test_split** functions are imported from the **statsmodels.graphics.correlation** and **sklearn.model_selection** modules respectively. The last statement is used to set the aesthetic look of the graphs that **matplotlib** generates to the type displayed by the **seaborn** module.

3. Next, load the **Boston.CSV** file and assign the variable name **rawBostonData** to it by running the following code:

```
rawBostonData = pd.read_csv\
                ('https://raw.githubusercontent.com/'\
                 'PacktWorkshops/The-Data-Science-'\
                 'Workshop/master/Chapter02/'\
                 'Dataset/Boston.csv')
```

4. Inspect the first five records in the DataFrame:

```
rawBostonData.head()
```

You should get the following output:

	CRIM	ZN	INDUS	CHAS	NOX	RM	AGE	DIS	RAD	TAX	PTRATIO	LSTAT	MEDV
0	0.00632	18.0	2.31	0	0.538	6.575	65.2	4.0900	1	296	15.3	4.98	24.0
1	0.02731	0.0	7.07	0	0.469	6.421	78.9	4.9671	2	242	17.8	9.14	21.6
2	0.02729	0.0	7.07	0	0.469	7.185	61.1	4.9671	2	242	17.8	4.03	34.7
3	0.03237	0.0	2.18	0	0.458	6.998	45.8	6.0622	3	222	18.7	2.94	33.4
4	0.06905	0.0	2.18	0	0.458	7.147	54.2	6.0622	3	222	18.7	5.33	36.2

Figure 2.6: First five rows of the dataset

5. Check for missing values (*null* values) in the DataFrame and then drop them in order to get a clean dataset Use the pandas method **dropna()** to find and remove these missing values:

```
rawBostonData = rawBostonData.dropna()
```

6. Check for duplicate records in the DataFrame and then drop them in order to get a clean dataset. Use the **drop_duplicates()** method from pandas:

```
rawBostonData = rawBostonData.drop_duplicates()
```

7. List the column names of the DataFrame so that you can examine the fields in your dataset, and modify the names, if necessary, to names that are meaningful:

```
list(rawBostonData.columns)
```

You should get the following output:

```
['CRIM',
 ' ZN ',
 'INDUS ',
 'CHAS',
 'NOX',
 'RM',
 'AGE',
 'DIS',
 'RAD',
 'TAX',
 'PTRATIO',
 'LSTAT',
 'MEDV']
```

Figure 2.7: Listing all the column names

8. Rename the DataFrame columns so that they are meaningful. Be mindful to match the column names exactly as leaving out even white spaces in the name strings will result in an error. For example, this string, **ZN**, has a white space before and after and it is different from **ZN**. After renaming, print the head of the new DataFrame as follows:

```
renamedBostonData = rawBostonData.rename\
                    (columns = {\
                     'CRIM':'crimeRatePerCapita',\
                     ' ZN ':'landOver25K_sqft',\
```

```
                        'INDUS ':'non-retailLandProptn',\
                        'CHAS':'riverDummy',\
                        'NOX':'nitrixOxide_pp10m',\
                        'RM':'AvgNo.RoomsPerDwelling',\
                        'AGE':'ProptnOwnerOccupied',\
                        'DIS':'weightedDist',\
                        'RAD':'radialHighwaysAccess',\
                        'TAX':'propTaxRate_per10K',\
                        'PTRATIO':'pupilTeacherRatio',\
                        'LSTAT':'pctLowerStatus',\
                        'MEDV':'medianValue_Ks'})
renamedBostonData.head()
```

You should get the following output:

	crimeRatePerCapita	landOver25K_sqft	non-retailLandProptn	riverDummy
0	0.00632	18.0	2.31	0
1	0.02731	0.0	7.07	0
2	0.02729	0.0	7.07	0
3	0.03237	0.0	2.18	0
4	0.06905	0.0	2.18	0

Figure 2.8: DataFrames being renamed

> **NOTE**
>
> The preceding output is truncated. Please head to the GitHub repository to find the entire output.

9. Inspect the data types of the columns in your DataFrame using the **.info()** function:

```
renamedBostonData.info()
```

You should get the following output:

```
<class 'pandas.core.frame.DataFrame'>
Int64Index: 506 entries, 0 to 505
Data columns (total 13 columns):
crimeRatePerCapita         506 non-null float64
landOver25K_sqft           506 non-null float64
non-retailLandProptn       506 non-null float64
riverDummy                 506 non-null int64
nitrixOxide_pp10m          506 non-null float64
AvgNo.RoomsPerDwelling     506 non-null float64
ProptnOwnerOccupied        506 non-null float64
weightedDist               506 non-null float64
radialHighwaysAccess       506 non-null int64
propTaxRate_per10K         506 non-null int64
pupilTeacherRatio          506 non-null float64
pctLowerStatus             506 non-null float64
medianValue_Ks             506 non-null float64
dtypes: float64(10), int64(3)
memory usage: 55.3 KB
```

Figure 2.9: The different data types in the dataset

The output shows that there are **506** rows (**Int64Index: 506 entries**) in the dataset. There are also **13** columns in total (**Data columns**). None of the **13** columns has a row with a missing value (all **506** rows are *non-null*). 10 of the columns have floating-point (decimal) type data and three have integer type data.

10. Now, calculate basic statistics for the numeric columns in the DataFrame:

```
renamedBostonData.describe(include=[np.number]).T
```

We used the pandas function, **describe**, called on the DataFrame to calculate simple statistics for numeric fields (this includes any field with a **numpy** number data type) in the DataFrame. The statistics include the minimum, the maximum, the count of rows in each column, the average of each column (mean), the 25th percentile, the 50th percentile, and the 75th percentile. We transpose (using the **.T** function) the output of the **describe** function to get a better layout.

You should get the following output:

	count	mean	std	min	25%	50%	75%	max
crimeRatePerCapita	506.0	3.613524	8.601545	0.00632	0.082045	0.25651	3.677082	88.9762
landOver25K_sqft	506.0	11.363636	23.322453	0.00000	0.000000	0.00000	12.500000	100.0000
non-retailLandProptn	506.0	11.136779	6.860353	0.46000	5.190000	9.69000	18.100000	27.7400
riverDummy	506.0	0.069170	0.253994	0.00000	0.000000	0.00000	0.000000	1.0000
nitrixOxide_pp10m	506.0	0.554695	0.115878	0.38500	0.449000	0.53800	0.624000	0.8710
avgNo.RoomsPerDwelling	506.0	6.284634	0.702617	3.56100	5.885500	6.20850	6.623500	8.7800
proptnOwnerOccupied	506.0	68.574901	28.148861	2.90000	45.025000	77.50000	94.075000	100.0000
weightedDist	506.0	3.795043	2.105710	1.12960	2.100175	3.20745	5.188425	12.1265
radialHighwaysAccess	506.0	9.549407	8.707259	1.00000	4.000000	5.00000	24.000000	24.0000
propTaxRate_per10K	506.0	408.237154	168.537116	187.00000	279.000000	330.00000	666.000000	711.0000
pupilTeacherRatio	506.0	18.455534	2.164946	12.60000	17.400000	19.05000	20.200000	22.0000
pctLowerStatus	506.0	12.653063	7.141062	1.73000	6.950000	11.36000	16.955000	37.9700
medianValue_Ks	506.0	22.532806	9.197104	5.00000	17.025000	21.20000	25.000000	50.0000

Figure 2.10: Basic statistics of the numeric column

11. Divide the DataFrame into training and test sets, as shown in the following code snippet:

```
X = renamedBostonData.drop('crimeRatePerCapita', axis = 1)
y = renamedBostonData[['crimeRatePerCapita']]
seed = 10
test_data_size = 0.3
X_train, X_test, \
y_train, y_test = train_test_split(X, y, \
                                   test_size = test_data_size, \
                                   random_state = seed)
train_data = pd.concat([X_train, y_train], axis = 1)
test_data = pd.concat([X_test, y_test], axis = 1)
```

We choose a test data size of 30%, which is **0.3**. The **train_test_split** function is used to achieve this. We set the seed of the random number generator so that we can obtain a reproducible split each time we run this code. An arbitrary value of **10** is used here. It is good model-building practice to divide a dataset being used to develop a model into at least two parts. One part is used to develop the model and it is called a training set (**X_train** and **y_train** combined).

> **NOTE**
>
> Splitting your data into training and test subsets allows you to use some of the data to train your model (that is, it lets you build a model that learns the relationships between the variables), and the rest of the data to test your model (that is, to see how well your new model can make predictions when given new data). You will use train-test splits throughout this book, and the concept will be explained in more detail in *Chapter 7, The Generalization Of Machine Learning Models*.

12. Calculate and plot a correlation matrix for the **train_data** set:

```
corrMatrix = train_data.corr(method = 'pearson')
xnames=list(train_data.columns)
ynames=list(train_data.columns)
plot_corr(corrMatrix, xnames=xnames, ynames=ynames,\
          title=None, normcolor=False, cmap='RdYlBu_r')
```

The use of the backslash character, ****, on *line 4* in the preceding code snippet is to enforce the continuation of code on to a new line in Python. The **** character is not required if you are entering the full line of code into a single line in your notebook.

You should get the following output:

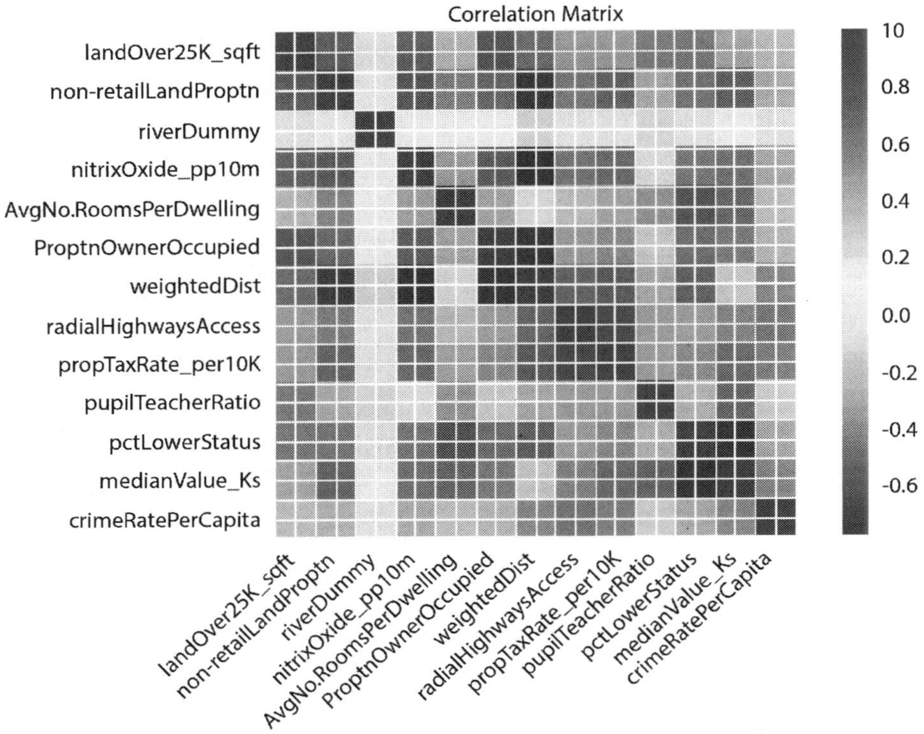

Figure 2.11: Output with the expected heatmap

In the preceding heatmap, we can see that there is a strong positive correlation (an increase in one causes an increase in the other) between variables that have orange or red squares. There is a strong negative correlation (an increase in one causes a decrease in the other) between variables with blue squares. There is little or no correlation between variables with pale-colored squares. For example, there appears to be a relatively strong correlation between **`nitrixOxide_pp10m`** and **`non-retailLandProptn`**, but a low correlation between **`riverDummy`** and any other variable.

> **NOTE**
>
> To access the source code for this specific section, please refer to https://packt.live/320HLAH.
>
> You can also run this example online at https://packt.live/34baJAA.

We can use the findings from the correlation matrix as the starting point for further regression analysis. The heatmap gives us a good overview of relationships in the data and can show us which variables to target in our investigation.

THE CORRELATION COEFFICIENT

In the previous exercise, we have seen how a correlation matrix heatmap can be used to visualize the relationships between pairs of variables. We can also see these same relationships in numerical form using the raw correlation coefficient numbers. These are values between -1 and 1, which represent how closely two variables are linked.

Pandas provides a **`corr`** function, which when called on DataFrame provides a matrix (table) of the correlation of all numeric data types. In our case, running the code, **`train_data.corr (method = 'pearson')`**, in the Colab notebook provides the results in *Figure 2.12*.

> **NOTE**
>
> Pearson is the standard correlation coefficient for measuring the relationship between variables.

It is important to note that *Figure 2.12* is symmetric along the left diagonal. The left diagonal values are correlation coefficients for features against themselves (and so all of them have a value of one (1)), and therefore are not relevant to our analysis. The data in *Figure 2.12* is what is presented as a plot in the output of *Step 12* in *Exercise 2.01*, *Loading and Preparing the Data for Analysis*.

You should get the following output:

	landOver25K_sqft	non-retailLandProptn	riverDummy	nitrixOxide_pp10m	avgNo.RoomsPerDwelling
landOver25K_sqft	1.000000	-0.540095	-0.059189	-0.520305	0.355346
non-retailLandProptn	-0.540095	1.000000	0.065271	0.758178	-0.399166
riverDummy	-0.059189	0.065271	1.000000	0.091469	0.107996
nitrixOxide_pp10m	-0.520305	0.758178	0.091469	1.000000	-0.306510
avgNo.RoomsPerDwelling	0.355346	-0.399166	0.107996	-0.306510	1.000000
proptnOwnerOccupied	-0.577457	0.667887	0.106329	0.742016	-0.263085
weightedDist	0.659340	-0.728968	-0.098551	-0.776311	0.215439
radialHighwaysAccess	-0.311920	0.580813	0.022731	0.606721	-0.183000
propTaxRate_per10K	-0.324172	0.702973	-0.007864	0.662164	-0.280341

Figure 2.12: A correlation matrix of the training dataset

> **NOTE**
>
> The preceding output is truncated.

Data scientists use the correlation coefficient as a statistic in order to measure the linear relationship between two numeric variables, X and Y. The correlation coefficient for a sample of bivariate data is commonly represented by r. In statistics, the common method to measure the correlation between two numeric variables is by using the Pearson correlation coefficient. Going forward in this chapter, therefore, any reference to the correlation coefficient means the Pearson correlation coefficient.

To practically calculate the correlation coefficient statistic for the variables in our dataset in this course, we use a Python function. What is important to this discussion is the meaning of the values the correlation coefficient we calculate takes. The correlation coefficient (r) takes values between +1 and -1.

When r is equal to +1, the relationship between X and Y is such that both X and Y increase or decrease in the same direction perfectly. When r is equal to -1, the relationship between X and Y is such that an increase in X is associated with a decrease in Y perfectly and vice versa. When r is equal to zero (0), there is no linear relationship between X and Y.

Having no linear relationship between X and Y does not mean that X and Y are not related; instead, it means that if there is any relationship, it cannot be described by a straight line. In practice, correlation coefficient values around 0.6 or higher (or -0.6 or lower) is a sign of a potentially exciting linear relationship between two variables, X and Y.

The last column of the output of *Exercise 2.01*, *Loading and Preparing the Data for Analysis*, *Step 12*, provides r values for crime rate per capita against other features in color shades. Using the color bar, it is obvious that **`radialHighwaysAccess`**, **`propTaxRate_per10K`**, **`nitrixOxide_pp10m`**, and **`pctLowerStatus`** have the strongest correlation with crime rate per capita. This indicates that a possible linear relationship, between crime rate per capita and any of these independent variables, may be worth looking into.

EXERCISE 2.02: GRAPHICAL INVESTIGATION OF LINEAR RELATIONSHIPS USING PYTHON

Scatter graphs fitted with a regression line are a quick way by which a data scientist can visualize a possible correlation between a dependent variable and an independent variable.

The goal of the exercise is to use this technique to investigate any linear relationship that may exist between crime rate per capita and the median value of owner-occupied homes in towns in the city of Boston.

The following steps will help you complete the exercise:

1. Open a new Colab notebook file and execute the steps up to and including *Step 11* from *Exercise 2.01, Loading and Preparing the Data for Analysis*. This is shown in the code blocks below, starting with the import statements:

```
%matplotlib inline
import matplotlib as mpl
import seaborn as sns
import matplotlib.pyplot as plt
import statsmodels.formula.api as smf
import statsmodels.graphics.api as smg
import pandas as pd
import numpy as np
import patsy
from statsmodels.graphics.correlation import plot_corr
from sklearn.model_selection import train_test_split
plt.style.use('seaborn')
```

Loading and preprocessing the data:

```
rawBostonData = pd.read_csv\
                ('https://raw.githubusercontent.com/'\
                 'PacktWorkshops/The-Data-Science-'\
                 'Workshop/master/Chapter02/'
                 'Dataset/Boston.csv')

rawBostonData = rawBostonData.dropna()
rawBostonData = rawBostonData.drop_duplicates()

renamedBostonData = rawBostonData.rename\
                    (columns = {\
                     'CRIM':'crimeRatePerCapita',\
```

```
                          ' ZN ':'landOver25K_sqft',\
                          'INDUS ':'non-retailLandProptn',\
                          'CHAS':'riverDummy',\
                          'NOX':'nitrixOxide_pp10m',\
                          'RM':'AvgNo.RoomsPerDwelling',\
                          'AGE':'ProptnOwnerOccupied',\
                          'DIS':'weightedDist',\
                          'RAD':'radialHighwaysAccess',\
                          'TAX':'propTaxRate_per10K',\
                          'PTRATIO':'pupilTeacherRatio',\
                          'LSTAT':'pctLowerStatus',\
                          'MEDV':'medianValue_Ks'})
```

Setting up the test and train data:

```
X = renamedBostonData.drop('crimeRatePerCapita', axis = 1)
y = renamedBostonData[['crimeRatePerCapita']]
seed = 10
test_data_size = 0.3
X_train, X_test, y_train, y_test = train_test_split\
                                   (X, y, \
                                    test_size = test_data_size,\
                                    random_state = seed)


train_data = pd.concat([X_train, y_train], axis = 1)
test_data = pd.concat([X_test, y_test], axis = 1)
```

2. Now use the **subplots** function in **matplotlib** to define a canvas (assigned the variable name **fig** in the following code) and a graph object (assigned the variable name **ax** in the following code) in Python. You can set the size of the graph by setting the **figsize** (width = **10**, height = **6**) argument of the function:

```
fig, ax = plt.subplots(figsize=(10, 6))
```

Do not execute the code yet.

3. Use the **seaborn** function **regplot** to create the scatter plot. Do not execute this code cell yet; we will add more code to style the plot in the next step:

```
sns.regplot(x='medianValue_Ks', y='crimeRatePerCapita', \
            ci=None, data=train_data, ax=ax, color='k', \
            scatter_kws={"s": 20,"color": "royalblue", \
            "alpha":1})
```

The function accepts arguments for the independent variable (**x**), the dependent variable (**y**), the confidence interval of the regression parameters (**ci**), which takes values from 0 to 100, the DataFrame that has **x** and **y** (**data**), a matplotlib graph object (**ax**), and others to control the aesthetics of the points on the graph. (In this case, the confidence interval is set to **None** – we will see more on confidence intervals later in the chapter.)

4. In the same cell as step 3, set the **x** and **y** labels, the **fontsize** and **name** labels, the **x** and **y** limits, and the **tick** parameters of the matplotlib graph object (**ax**). Also, set the layout of the canvas to **tight**:

```
ax.set_ylabel('Crime rate per Capita', fontsize=15, \
              fontname='DejaVu Sans')
ax.set_xlabel("Median value of owner-occupied homes "\
             "in $1000's", fontsize=15, \
             fontname='DejaVu Sans')
ax.set_xlim(left=None, right=None)
ax.set_ylim(bottom=None, top=30)
ax.tick_params(axis='both', which='major', labelsize=12)
fig.tight_layout()
```

Now execute the cell. You should get the following output:

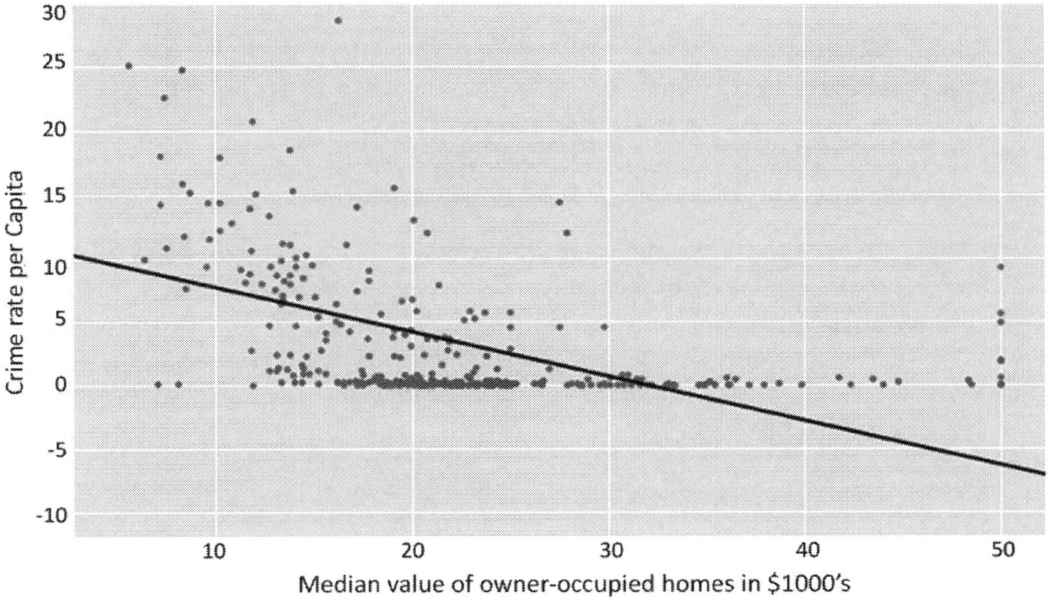

Figure 2.13: Scatter graph with a regression line using Python

If the exercise was followed correctly, the output must be the same as the graph in *Figure 2.3*. In *Figure 2.3*, this output was presented and used to introduce linear regression without showing how it was created. What this exercise has taught us is how to create a scatter graph and fit a regression line through it using Python.

> **NOTE**
>
> To access the source code for this specific section, please refer to https://packt.live/34clTnk.
>
> You can also run this example online at https://packt.live/2CA4NFG.

EXERCISE 2.03: EXAMINING A POSSIBLE LOG-LINEAR RELATIONSHIP USING PYTHON

In this exercise, we will use the logarithm function to transform variables and investigate whether this helps provide a better fit of the regression line to the data. We will also look at how to use confidence intervals by including a 95% confidence interval of the regression coefficients on the plot.

The following steps will help you to complete this exercise:

1. Open a new Colab notebook file and execute all the steps up to *Step 11* from *Exercise 2.01*, *Loading and Preparing the Data for Analysis*.
2. Use the **`subplots`** function in **`matplotlib`** to define a canvas and a graph object in Python:

```
fig, ax = plt.subplots(figsize=(10, 6))
```

   Do not execute this code yet.

3. In the same code cell, use the logarithm function in **`numpy`** (**`np.log`**) to transform the dependent variable (**`y`**). This essentially creates a new variable, **`log(y)`**:

```
y = np.log(train_data['crimeRatePerCapita'])
```

   Do not execute this code yet.

4. Use the seaborn **`regplot`** function to create the scatter plot. Set the **`regplot`** function confidence interval argument (**`ci`**) to **`95%`**. This will calculate a **`95%`** confidence interval for the regression coefficients and have them plotted on the graph as a shaded area along the regression line.

> **NOTE**
>
> A confidence interval gives an estimated range that is likely to contain the true value that you're looking for. So, a **95%** confidence interval indicates we can be **95%** certain that the true regression coefficients lie in that shaded area.

Parse the **y** argument with the new variable we defined in the preceding step. The **x** argument is the original variable from the DataFrame without any transformation. Continue in the same code cell. Do not execute this cell yet; we will add in more styling code in the next step.

```
sns.regplot(x='medianValue_Ks', y=y, ci=95, \
            data=train_data, ax=ax, color='k', \
            scatter_kws={"s": 20,"color": "royalblue", \
            "alpha":1})
```

5. Continuing in the same cell, set the **x** and **y** labels, the **fontsize** and **name** labels, the **x** and **y** limits, and the **tick** parameters of the **matplotlib** graph object (**ax**). Also, set the layout of the canvas to **tight**:

```
ax.set_ylabel('log of Crime rate per Capita', \
              fontsize=15, fontname='DejaVu Sans')
ax.set_xlabel("Median value of owner-occupied homes "\
              "in $1000's", fontsize=15, \
              fontname='DejaVu Sans')
ax.set_xlim(left=None, right=None)
ax.set_ylim(bottom=None, top=None)
ax.tick_params(axis='both', which='major', labelsize=12)
fig.tight_layout()
```

Now execute this cell. The output is as follows:

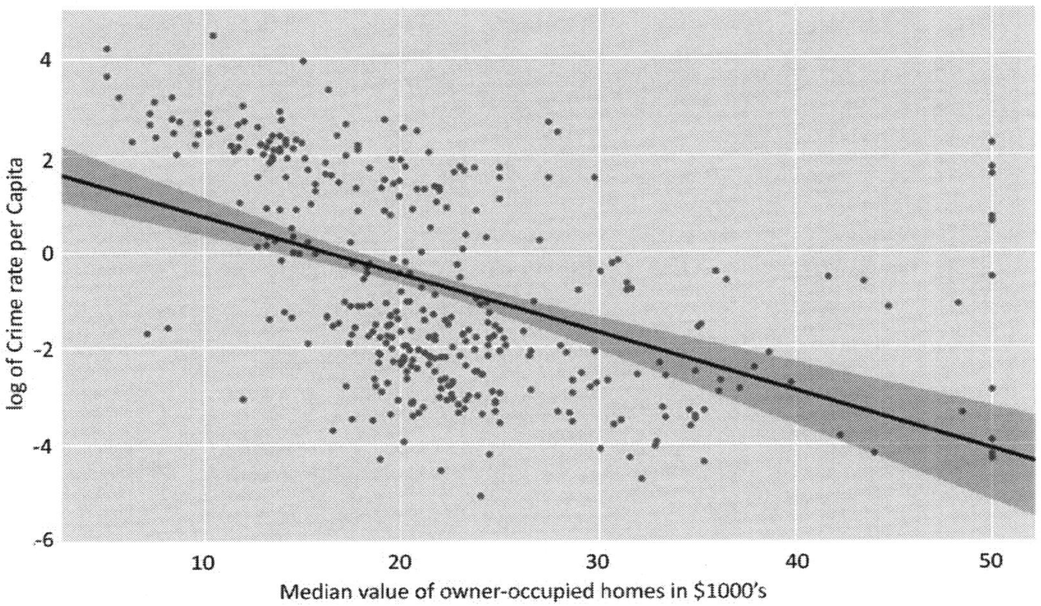

Figure 2.14: Expected scatter plot with an improved linear regression line

By completing this exercise, we have successfully improved our scatter plot. The regression line created in this activity fits the data better than what was created in *Exercise 2.02, Graphical Investigation of Linear Relationships Using Python*. You can see by comparing the two graphs, the regression line in the log graph more clearly matches the spread of the data points. We have solved the issue where the bottom third of the line had no points clustered around it. This was achieved by transforming the dependent variable with the logarithm function. The transformed dependent variable (log of crime rate per capita) has an improved linear relationship with the median value of owner-occupied homes than the untransformed variable.

> **NOTE**
>
> To access the source code for this specific section, please refer to https://packt.live/3ay4aZS.
>
> You can also run this example online at https://packt.live/324nN7R.

THE STATSMODELS FORMULA API

In *Figure 2.3*, a solid line represents the relationship between the crime rate per capita and the median value of owner-occupied homes. But how can we obtain the equation that describes this line? In other words, how can we find the intercept and the slope of the straight-line relationship?

Python provides a rich **Application Programming Interface (API)** for doing this easily. The statsmodels formula API enables the data scientist to use the formula language to define regression models that can be found in statistics literature and many dedicated statistical computer packages.

EXERCISE 2.04: FITTING A SIMPLE LINEAR REGRESSION MODEL USING THE STATSMODELS FORMULA API

In this exercise, we examine a simple linear regression model where the crime rate per capita is the dependent variable and the median value of owner-occupied homes is the independent variable. We use the statsmodels formula API to create a linear regression model for Python to analyze.

The following steps will help you complete this exercise:

1. Open a new Colab notebook file and import the required packages.

```
import pandas as pd
import statsmodels.formula.api as smf
from sklearn.model_selection import train_test_split
```

2. Execute *Step 2* to *11* from *Exercise 2.01*, *Loading and Preparing the Data for Analysis*.

3. Define a linear regression model and assign it to a variable named **linearModel**:

```
linearModel = smf.ols\
              (formula='crimeRatePerCapita ~ medianValue_Ks',\
               data=train_data)
```

As you can see, we call the **ols** function of the statsmodels API and set its formula argument by defining a **patsy** formula string that uses the tilde (**~**) symbol to relate the dependent variable to the independent variable. Tell the function where to find the variables named, in the string, by assigning the data argument of the **ols** function to the DataFrame that contains your variables (**train_data**).

4. Call the **`.fit`** method of the model instance and assign the results of the method to a **`linearModelResult`** variable, as shown in the following code snippet:

```
linearModelResult = linearModel.fit()
```

5. Print a summary of the results stored the **`linearModelResult`** variable by running the following code:

```
print(linearModelResult.summary())
```

You should get the following output:

```
                            OLS Regression Results
==============================================================================
Dep. Variable:      crimeRatePerCapita   R-squared:                       0.144
Model:                             OLS   Adj. R-squared:                  0.141
Method:                  Least Squares   F-statistic:                     59.02
Date:                 Sun, 13 Oct 2019   Prob (F-statistic):           1.56e-13
Time:                         20:57:35   Log-Likelihood:                -1217.4
No. Observations:                  354   AIC:                             2439.
Df Residuals:                      352   BIC:          Section 1          2447.
Df Model:                            1
Covariance Type:             nonrobust
==================================================================================
  Section 2           coef    std err          t      P>|t|      [0.025      0.975]
----------------------------------------------------------------------------------
Intercept          11.2094      1.079     10.386      0.000       9.087      13.332
medianValue_Ks     -0.3502      0.046     -7.683      0.000      -0.440      -0.261
==============================================================================
Omnibus:                      447.354   Durbin-Watson:                   1.928
Prob(Omnibus):                  0.000   Jarque-Bera (JB):            39791.431
Skew:                           5.897   Prob(JB):         Section 3       0.00
Kurtosis:                      53.583   Cond. No.                         63.7
==============================================================================

Warnings:
[1] Standard Errors assume that the covariance matrix of the errors is correctly specified.
```

Figure 2.15: A summary of the simple linear regression analysis results

If the exercise was correctly followed, then a model has been created with the **statsmodels** formula API. The **fit** method (**.fit()**) of the model object was called to fit the linear regression model to the data. What fitting here means is to estimate the regression coefficients (parameters) using the ordinary least squares method.

> **NOTE**
>
> To access the source code for this specific section, please refer to https://packt.live/3iJXXge.
>
> You can also run this example online at https://packt.live/2YbZ54v.

ANALYZING THE MODEL SUMMARY

The **.fit** method provides many functions to explore its output. These include the **conf_int()**, **pvalues**, **tvalues**, and **summary()** parameters. With these functions, the parameters of the model, the confidence intervals, and the p-values and t-values for the analysis can be retrieved from the results. (The concept of p-values and t-values will be explained later in the chapter.)

The syntax simply involves following the dot notation, after the variable name containing the results, with the relevant function name – for example, **linearModelResult.conf_int()** will output the confidence interval values. The handiest of them all is the **summary()** function, which presents a table of all relevant results from the analysis.

In *Figure 2.15*, the output of the summary function used in *Exercise 2.04, Fitting a Simple Linear Regression Model Using the Statsmodels formula API,* is presented. The output of the summary function is divided, using double dashed lines, into three main sections.

In *Chapter 9, Interpreting a Machine Learning Model*, the results of the three sections will be treated in detail. However, it is important to comment on a few points here.

In the top-left corner of *Section 1* in *Figure 2.15*, we find the dependent variable in the model (**`Dep. Variable`**) printed and **`crimeRatePerCapita`** is the value for *Exercise 2.04, Fitting a Simple Linear Regression Model Using the Statsmodels formula API*. A statistic named R-squared with a value of **`0.144`** for our model is also provided in *Section 1*. The R-squared value is calculated by Python as a fraction (**`0.144`**) but it is to be reported in percentages so the value for our model is **`14.4%`** The R-squared statistic provides a measure of how much of the variability in the dependent variable (**`crimeRatePerCapita`**), our model is able to explain. It can be interpreted as a measure of how well our model fits the dataset. In *Section 2* of *Figure 2.15*, the intercept and the independent variable in our model is reported. The independent variable in our model is the median value of owner-occupied homes (**`medianValue_Ks`**).

In this same *Section 2*, just next to the intercept and the independent variable, is a column that reports the model coefficients (**`coef`**). The intercept and the coefficient of the independent variable are printed under the column labeled **`coef`** in the summary report that Python prints out. The intercept has a value of **`11.2094`** with the coefficient of the independent variable having a value of negative **`0.3502`** (**`-0.3502`**). If we choose to denote the dependent variable in our model (**`crimeRatePerCapita`**) as y and the independent variable (the median value of owner-occupied homes) as *x*, we have
all the ingredients to write out the equation that defines our model.

Thus, $y \approx 11.2094 - 0.3502\ x$, is the equation for our model. In *Chapter 9, Interpreting a Machine Learning Model*, what this model means and how it can be used will be discussed in full.

THE MODEL FORMULA LANGUAGE

Python is a very powerful language liked by many developers. Since the release of version 0.5.0 of statsmodels, Python now provides a very competitive option for statistical analysis and modeling rivaling R and SAS.

This includes what is commonly referred to as the R-style formula language, by which statistical models can be easily defined. Statsmodels implements the R-style formula language by using the **`Patsy`** Python library internally to convert formulas and data to the matrices that are used in model fitting.

Figure 2.16 summarizes the operators used to construct the **`Patsy`** formula strings and what they mean:

Operator Symbol	Meaning	Example
~	Separates the left-hand side and the right-hand side of a formula.	Y~X will define the model $Y = \beta_0 + \beta X$.
+	This is used to include an independent variable in the model (not arithmetic addition). It computes a set union of terms given on its left and those given on its right.	$Y \sim X_1 + X_2$ will define the model $Y = \beta_0 + \beta_1 X_1 + \beta_2 X_2$.
-	This is used to delete an independent variable from the model (not arithmetic subtraction). It computes a set difference by removing terms given on its right from terms given on its left.	Y~X-1 will define the model $Y = \beta X$. The intercept is defined as 1, hence the minus operator (-) deletes it from this model. This model, therefore, goes through the origin. See more on intercept handling after this table.
*	This is used to include independent variables on its left and right and their interactions in a model (not arithmetic multiplication).	$Y \sim X_1 * X_2$ will define the model $Y = \beta_0 + \beta_1 X_1 + \beta_2 X_2 + \beta_3 X_1 X_2$.
/	This indicates nesting of independent variables in the model (not arithmetic division). Intended to be useful in cases where one wants to fit a standard analysis of variance (ANOVA) model but one term is nested in another term.	$Y \sim X_1 / X_2$ will define the model $Y = \beta_0 + \beta_1 X_1 + \beta_2 X_1 X_2$. Here, X_2. is a term nested within X_1.
:	The colon operator includes a pure interaction term of the variables to its left and right in a model.	$Y \sim X_1 : X_2$ will define the model $Y = \beta_0 + \beta_1 X_1 X_2$.
**	Use this operator to define a model that includes the nth order of its interaction terms. *n* here is an integer. See the example for details.	$Y \sim (X_1 + X_2 + X_3)**2$ will define the model $Y = \beta_0 + \beta_1 X_1 + \beta_2 X_2 + \beta_3 X_3 + \beta_4 X_1 X_2 + \beta_5 X_1 X_3 + \beta_6 X_2 X_3$.
f(expr)	This denotes the possibility to include an arbitrary Python function f(expr) in a Patsy formula string.	$Y \sim X_1 +$ np.log(X_2) will define the model $Y = \beta_0 + \beta_1 X_1 +$ $\beta_2$np.log(X_2). Note that f(expr) is equal to np.log(X_2).
I(expr)	Use this to escape operators in an expression f(expr) so that they have arithmetic meaning rather than the set operator meaning used by the Patsy formula parser.	$Y \sim X_1 +$ np.log(I($X_2 + X_3$)) will define a model where the plus operator in ($X_2 + X_3$) is treated as an arithmetic plus sign by the Patsy formula parser because of the identity operator (denoted as I()), and NOT as a set union of X_2 and X_3.
C(var)	Use this to define a variable (var) in a Patsy formula string as a categorical variable type.	Defining C(X) in a formula will tell the formula parser to treat the values of the term as categorical,

Figure 2.16: A summary of the Patsy formula syntax and examples

INTERCEPT HANDLING

In patsy formula strings, **`string 1`** is used to define the intercept of a model. Because the intercept is needed most of the time, **`string 1`** is automatically included in every formula string definition. You don't have to include it in your string to specify the intercept. It is there invisibly. If you want to delete the intercept from your model, however, then you can subtract one (-1) from the formula string and that will define a model that passes through the origin. For compatibility with other statistical software, **`Patsy`** also allows the use of the string zero (0) and negative one (-1) to be used to exclude the intercept from a model. What this means is that, if you include 0 or -1 on the right-hand side of your formula string, your model will have no intercept.

ACTIVITY 2.01: FITTING A LOG-LINEAR MODEL USING THE STATSMODELS FORMULA API

You have seen how to use the statsmodels API to fit a linear regression model. In this activity, you are asked to fit a log-linear model. Your model should represent the relationship between the log-transformed dependent variable (log of crime rate per capita) and the median value of owner-occupied homes.

The steps to complete this activity are as follows:

1. Define a linear regression model and assign it to a variable. Remember to use the **`log`** function to transform the dependent variable in the formula string.
2. Call the **`fit`** method of the log-linear model instance and assign the results of the method to a variable.
3. Print a summary of the results and analyze the output.

Your output should look like the following figure:

```
                            OLS Regression Results
==============================================================================
Dep. Variable:     np.log(crimeRatePerCapita)   R-squared:                       0.238
Model:                                    OLS   Adj. R-squared:                  0.236
Method:                         Least Squares   F-statistic:                     109.9
Date:                        Mon, 14 Oct 2019   Prob (F-statistic):           1.48e-22
Time:                                04:08:39   Log-Likelihood:                -727.67
No. Observations:                         354   AIC:                             1459.
Df Residuals:                             352   BIC:                             1467.
Df Model:                                   1
Covariance Type:                    nonrobust
==================================================================================
                     coef    std err          t      P>|t|      [0.025      0.975]
----------------------------------------------------------------------------------
Intercept          1.9107      0.271      7.062      0.000       1.379       2.443
medianValue_Ks    -0.1198      0.011    -10.482      0.000      -0.142      -0.097
==============================================================================
Omnibus:                       11.420   Durbin-Watson:                   1.907
Prob(Omnibus):                  0.003   Jarque-Bera (JB):               10.764
Skew:                           0.376   Prob(JB):                      0.00460
Kurtosis:                       2.594   Cond. No.                         63.7
==============================================================================

Warnings:
[1] Standard Errors assume that the covariance matrix of the errors is correctly specified.
```

Figure 2.17: A log-linear regression of crime rate per capita on the median value of owner-occupied homes

> **NOTE**
>
> The solution to this activity can be found here: https://packt.live/2GbJloz.

MULTIPLE REGRESSION ANALYSIS

In the exercises and activity so far, we have used only one independent variable in our regression analysis. In practice, as we have seen with the Boston Housing dataset, processes and phenomena of analytic interest are rarely influenced by only one feature. To be able to model the variability to a higher level of accuracy, therefore, it is necessary to investigate all the independent variables that may contribute significantly toward explaining the variability in the dependent variable. Multiple regression analysis is the method that is used to achieve this.

EXERCISE 2.05: FITTING A MULTIPLE LINEAR REGRESSION MODEL USING THE STATSMODELS FORMULA API

In this exercise, we will be using the plus operator (+) in the **patsy** formula string to define a linear regression model that includes more than one independent variable.

To complete this activity, run the code in the following steps in your Colab notebook:

1. Open a new Colab notebook file and import the required packages.

```
import statsmodels.formula.api as smf
import pandas as pd
from sklearn.model_selection import train_test_split
```

2. Execute *Step 2* to *11* from *Exercise 2.01, Loading and Preparing the Data for Analysis*.

3. Use the plus operator (+) of the Patsy formula language to define a linear model that regresses **crimeRatePerCapita** on **pctLowerStatus**, **radialHighwaysAccess**, **medianValue_Ks**, and **nitrixOxide_pp10m** and assign it to a variable named **multiLinearModel**. Use the Python line continuation symbol (\) to continue your code on a new line should you run out of space:

```
multiLinearModel = smf.ols\
                   (formula = 'crimeRatePerCapita \
                              ~ pctLowerStatus \
                              + radialHighwaysAccess \
                              + medianValue_Ks \
                              + nitrixOxide_pp10m', \
                              data=train_data)
```

4. Call the **fit** method of the model instance and assign the results of the method to a variable:

```
multiLinearModResult = multiLinearModel.fit()
```

5. Print a summary of the results stored the variable created in *Step 3*:

```
print(multiLinearModResult.summary())
```

The output is as follows:

```
                            OLS Regression Results
==============================================================================
Dep. Variable:      crimeRatePerCapita   R-squared:                       0.398
Model:                             OLS   Adj. R-squared:                  0.391
Method:                  Least Squares   F-statistic:                     57.77
Date:                 Thu, 12 Sep 2019   Prob (F-statistic):           2.19e-37
Time:                         15:00:55   Log-Likelihood:                -1154.9
No. Observations:                  354   AIC:                             2320.
Df Residuals:                      349   BIC:          Section 1          2339.
Df Model:                            4
Covariance Type:             nonrobust
=========================================================================================
                          coef    std err          t      P>|t|      [0.025      0.975]
----------   Section 2  -----------------------------------------------------------------
Intercept                0.8912      2.670      0.334      0.739      -4.360       6.142
pctLowerStatus           0.1028      0.080      1.277      0.202      -0.055       0.261
radialHighwaysAccess     0.4948      0.048     10.216      0.000       0.400       0.590
medianValue_Ks          -0.1103      0.058     -1.916      0.056      -0.224       0.003
nitrixOxide_pp10m       -2.1039      4.131     -0.509      0.611     -10.229       6.021
==============================================================================
Omnibus:                       534.476   Durbin-Watson:                   1.999
Prob(Omnibus):                   0.000   Jarque-Bera (JB):           100129.789
Skew:              Section 3     7.866   Prob(JB):                         0.00
Kurtosis:                       83.876   Cond. No.                         374.
==============================================================================

Warnings:
[1] Standard Errors assume that the covariance matrix of the errors is correctly specified.
```

Figure 2.18: A summary of multiple linear regression results

> **NOTE**
>
> To access the source code for this specific section, please refer to https://packt.live/34cJgOK.
>
> You can also run this example online at https://packt.live/3h1CKOt.

If the exercise was correctly followed, *Figure 2.18* will be the result of the analysis. In *Activity 2.01*, the R-squared statistic was used to assess the model for goodness of fit. When multiple independent variables are involved, the goodness of fit of the model created is assessed using the adjusted R-squared statistic.

The adjusted R-squared statistic considers the presence of the extra independent variables in the model and corrects for inflation of the goodness of fit measure of the model, which is just caused by the fact that more independent variables are being used to create the model.

The lesson we learn from this exercise is the improvement in the adjusted R-squared value in *Section 1* of *Figure 2.18*. When only one independent variable was used to create a model that seeks to explain the variability in **`crimeRatePerCapita`** in *Exercise 2.04, Fitting a Simple Linear Regression Model Using the Statsmodels formula API*, the R-squared value calculated was only **`14.4`** percent. In this exercise, we used four independent variables. The model that was created improved the adjusted R-squared statistic to **`39.1`** percent, an increase of **`24.7`** percent.

We learn that the presence of independent variables that are correlated to a dependent variable can help explain the variability in the independent variable in a model. But it is clear that a considerable amount of variability, about **`60.9`** percent, in the dependent variable is still not explained by our model.

There is still room for improvement if we want a model that does a good job of explaining the variability we see in **`crimeRatePerCapita`**. In *Section 2* of *Figure 2.18*, the intercept and all the independent variables in our model are listed together with their coefficients. If we denote **`pctLowerStatus`** by x_1, **`radialHighwaysAccess`** by x_2, **`medianValue_Ks`** by x_3 , and **`nitrixOxide_pp10m`** by x_4, a mathematical expression for the model created can be written as $y \approx 0.8912+0.1028x_1+0.4948x_2-0.1103x_3-2.1039x_4$.

The expression just stated defines the model created in this exercise, and it is comparable to the expression for multiple linear regression provided in *Figure 2.5* earlier.

ASSUMPTIONS OF REGRESSION ANALYSIS

Due to the parametric nature of linear regression analysis, the method makes certain assumptions about the data it analyzes. When these assumptions are not met, the results of the regression analysis may be misleading to say the least. It is, therefore, necessary to check any analysis work to ensure the regression assumptions are not violated.

Let's review the main assumptions of linear regression analysis that we must ensure are met in order to develop a good model:

1. The relationship between the dependent and independent variables must be linear and additive.

This means that the relationship must be of the straight-line type, and if there are many independent variables involved, thus multiple linear regression, the weighted sum of these independent variables must be able to explain the variability in the dependent variable.

2. The residual terms (ϵ_i) must be normally distributed. This is so that the standard error of estimate is calculated correctly. This standard error of estimate statistic is used to calculate t-values, which, in turn, are used to make statistical significance decisions. So, if the standard error of estimate is wrong, the t-values will be wrong and so are the statistical significance decisions that follow on from the p-values. The t-values that are calculated using the standard error of estimate are also used to construct confidence intervals for the population regression parameters. If the standard error is wrong, then the confidence intervals will be wrong as well.
3. The residual terms (ϵ_i) must have constant variance (homoskedasticity). When this is not the case, we have the heteroskedasticity problem. This point refers to the variance of the residual terms. It is assumed to be constant. We assume that each data point in our regression analysis contributes equal explanation to the variability we are seeking to model. If some data points contribute more explanation than others, our regression line will be pulled toward the points with more information. The data points will not be equally scattered around our regression line. The error (variance) about the regression line, in that case, will not be constant.
4. The residual terms (ϵ_i) must not be correlated. When there is correlation in the residual terms, we have the problem known as autocorrelation. Knowing one residual term, must not give us any information about what the next residual term will be. Residual terms that are autocorrelated are unlikely to have a normal distribution.
5. There must not be correlation among the independent variables. When the independent variables are correlated among themselves, we have a problem called multicollinearity. This would lead to developing a model with coefficients that have values that depend on the presence of other independent variables. In other words, we will have a model that will change drastically should a particular independent variable be dropped from the model for example. A model like that will be inaccurate.

ACTIVITY 2.02: FITTING A MULTIPLE LOG-LINEAR REGRESSION MODEL

A log-linear regression model you developed earlier was able to explain about 24% of the variability in the transformed crime rate per capita variable (see the values in *Figure 2.17*). You are now asked to develop a log-linear multiple regression model that will likely explain 80% or more of the variability in the transformed dependent variable. You should use independent variables from the Boston Housing dataset that have a correlation coefficient of 0.4 or more.

You are also encouraged to include the interaction of these variables to order two in your model. You should produce graphs and data that show that your model satisfies the assumptions of linear regression.

The steps are as follows:

1. Define a linear regression model and assign it to a variable. Remember to use the **`log`** function to transform the dependent variable in the formula string, and also include more than one independent variable in your analysis.

2. Call the **`fit`** method of the model instance and assign the results of the method to a new variable.

3. Print a summary of the results and analyze your model.

   Your output should appear as shown:

```
                            OLS Regression Results
==============================================================================
Dep. Variable:     np.log(crimeRatePerCapita)   R-squared:                       0.884
Model:                                    OLS   Adj. R-squared:                  0.881
Method:                         Least Squares   F-statistic:                     261.5
Date:                        Fri, 13 Sep 2019   Prob (F-statistic):          7.79e-154
Time:                                05:01:38   Log-Likelihood:                -394.39
No. Observations:                         354   AIC:                             810.8
Df Residuals:                             343   BIC:                             853.3
Df Model:                                  10
Covariance Type:                    nonrobust
=========================================================================================================
                                            coef    std err          t      P>|t|      [0.025      0.975]
---------------------------------------------------------------------------------------------------------
Intercept                                -5.4707      1.490     -3.671      0.000      -8.402      -2.540
pctLowerStatus                            0.1541      0.049      3.161      0.002       0.058       0.250
radialHighwaysAccess                      0.4697      0.052      9.070      0.000       0.368       0.572
medianValue_Ks                           -0.1457      0.044     -3.325      0.001      -0.232      -0.059
nitrixOxide_pp10m                         3.4509      3.000      1.150      0.251      -2.450       9.352
pctLowerStatus:radialHighwaysAccess      -0.0006      0.001     -0.576      0.565      -0.003       0.002
pctLowerStatus:medianValue_Ks            -0.0041      0.001     -4.159      0.000      -0.006      -0.002
pctLowerStatus:nitrixOxide_pp10m         -0.0783      0.081     -0.964      0.336      -0.238       0.082
radialHighwaysAccess:medianValue_Ks      -0.0027      0.001     -2.694      0.007      -0.005      -0.001
radialHighwaysAccess:nitrixOxide_pp10m   -0.4234      0.066     -6.404      0.000      -0.553      -0.293
medianValue_Ks:nitrixOxide_pp10m          0.3552      0.092      3.869      0.000       0.175       0.536
==============================================================================
Omnibus:                        4.124   Durbin-Watson:                   1.966
Prob(Omnibus):                  0.127   Jarque-Bera (JB):                4.107
Skew:                           0.175   Prob(JB):                        0.128
Kurtosis:                       3.395   Cond. No.                     3.29e+04
==============================================================================

Warnings:
[1] Standard Errors assume that the covariance matrix of the errors is correctly specified.
[2] The condition number is large, 3.29e+04. This might indicate that there are
strong multicollinearity or other numerical problems.
```

Figure 2.19: Expected OLS results

> **NOTE**
>
> The solution to this activity can be found here: https://packt.live/2GbJloz.

EXPLAINING THE RESULTS OF REGRESSION ANALYSIS

A primary objective of regression analysis is to find a model that explains the variability observed in a dependent variable of interest. It is, therefore, very important to have a quantity that measures how well a regression model explains this variability. The statistic that does this is called R-squared (R^2). Sometimes, it is also called the coefficient of determination. To understand what it actually measures, we need to take a look at some other definitions.

The first of these is called the **Total Sum of Squares** (**TSS**). TSS gives us a measure of the total variance found in the dependent variable from its mean value.

The next quantity is called the **Regression sum of squares** (**RSS**). This gives us a measure of the amount of variability in the dependent variable that our model explains. If you imagine us creating a perfect model with no errors in prediction, then TSS will be equal to RSS. Our hypothetically perfect model will provide an explanation for all the variability we see in the dependent variable with respect to the mean value. In practice, this rarely happens. Instead, we create models that are not perfect, so RSS is less than TSS. The missing amount by which RSS falls short of TSS is the amount of variability in the dependent variable that our regression model is not able to explain. That quantity is the **Error Sum of Squares** (**ESS**), which is essentially the sum of the residual terms of our model.

R-squared is the ratio of RSS to TSS. This, therefore, gives us a percentage measure of how much variability our regression model is able to explain compared to the total variability in the dependent variable with respect to the mean. R^2 will become smaller when RSS grows smaller and vice versa. In the case of simple linear regression where the independent variable is one, R^2 is enough to decide the overall fit of the model to the data.

There is a problem, however, when it comes to multiple linear regression. The R^2 is known to be sensitive to the addition of extra independent variables to the model, even if the independent variable is only slightly correlated to the dependent variable. Its addition will increase R^2. Depending on R^2 alone to make a decision between models defined for the same dependent variable will lead to chasing a complex model that has many independent variables in it. This complexity is not helpful practically. In fact, it may lead to a problem in modeling called overfitting.

To overcome this problem, the Adjusted R^2 (denoted *Adj. R-Squared* on the output of statsmodels) is used to select between models defined for the same dependent variable. Adjusted R^2 will increase only when the addition of an independent variable to the model contributes to explaining the variability in the dependent variable in a meaningful way.

In *Activity 2.02, Fitting a Multiple Log-Linear Regression Model*, our model explained 88 percent of the variability in the transformed dependent variable, which is really good. We started with simple models and worked to improve the fit of the models using different techniques. All the exercises and activities done in this chapter have pointed out that the regression analysis workflow is iterative. You start by plotting to get a visual picture and follow from there to improve upon the model you finally develop by using different techniques. Once a good model has been developed, the next step is to validate the model statistically before it can be used for making a prediction or acquiring insight for decision making. Next, let's discuss what validating the model statistically means.

REGRESSION ANALYSIS CHECKS AND BALANCES

In the preceding discussions, we used the R-squared and the Adjusted R-squared statistics to assess the goodness of fit of our models. While the R-squared statistic provides an estimate of the strength of the relationship between a model and the dependent variable(s), it does not provide a formal statistical hypothesis test for this relationship.

What do we mean by a formal statistical hypothesis test for a relationship between a dependent variable and some independent variable(s) in a model?

We must recall that, to say an independent variable has a relationship with a dependent variable in a model, the coefficient (β) of that independent variable in the regression model must *not* be zero (0). It is well and good to conduct a regression analysis with our Boston Housing dataset and find an independent variable (say the median value of owner-occupied homes) in our model to have a nonzero coefficient (β).

The question is will we (or someone else) find the median value of owner-occupied homes as having a nonzero coefficient (β), if we repeat this analysis using a different sample of Boston Housing dataset taken at different locations or times? Is the nonzero coefficient for the median value of owner-occupied homes, found in our analysis, specific to our sample dataset and zero for any other Boston Housing data sample that may be collected? Did we find the nonzero coefficient for the median value of owner-occupied homes by chance? These questions are what hypothesis tests seek to clarify. We cannot be a hundred percent sure that the nonzero coefficient (β) of an independent variable is by chance or not. But hypothesis testing gives a framework by which we can calculate the level of confidence where we can say that the nonzero coefficient (β) found in our analysis is not by chance. This is how it works.

We first agree a level of risk (α-value or α-risk or Type I error) that may exist that the nonzero coefficient (β) may have been found by chance. The idea is that we are happy to live with this level of risk of making the error or mistake of claiming that the coefficient (β) is nonzero when in fact it is zero.

In most practical analyses, the α-value is set at 0.05, which is 5 in percentage terms. When we subtract the α-risk from one (1-α) we have a measure of the level of confidence that we have that the nonzero coefficient (β) found in our analysis did not come about by chance. So, our confidence level is 95% at 5% α-value.

We then go ahead to calculate a probability value (usually called the p-value), which gives us a measure of the α-risk related to the coefficient (β) of interest in our model. We compare the p-value to our chosen α-risk, and if the p-value is less than the agreed α-risk, we reject the idea that the nonzero coefficient (β) was found by chance. This is because the risk of making a mistake of claiming the coefficient (β) is nonzero is within the acceptable limit we set for ourselves earlier.

Another way of stating that the nonzero coefficient (β) was NOT found by chance is to say that the coefficient (β) is statistically significant or that we reject the null hypothesis (the null hypothesis being that there is no relationship between the variables being studied). We apply these ideas of statistical significance to our models in two stages:

1. In stage one, we validate the model as a whole statistically.
2. In stage two, we validate the independent variables in our model individually for statistical significance.

THE F-TEST

The F-test is what validates the overall statistical significance of the strength of the relationship between a model and its dependent variables. If the p-value for the F-test is less than the chosen α-level (0.05, in our case), we reject the null hypothesis and conclude that the model is statistically significant overall.

When we fit a regression model, we generate an F-value. This value can be used to determine whether the test is statistically significant. In general, an increase in R^2 increases the F-value. This means that the larger the F-value, the better the chances of the overall statistical significance of a model.

A good F-value is expected to be larger than **one**. The model in *Figure 2.19* has an F-statistic value of 261.5, which is larger than one, and a p-value (Prob (F-statistic)) of approximately zero. The risk of making a mistake and rejecting the null hypothesis when we should not (known as a Type I error in hypothesis testing), is less than the 5% limit we chose to live with at the beginning of the hypothesis test. Because the p-value is less than 0.05, we reject the null hypothesis about our model in *Figure 2.19*. Therefore, we state that the model is statistically significant at the chosen 95% confidence level.

THE T-TEST

Once a model has been determined to be statistically significant globally, we can proceed to examine the significance of individual independent variables in the model. In *Figure 2.19*, the p-values (denoted `p>|t|` in *Section 2*) for the independent variables are provided. The p-values were calculated using the t-values also given on the summary results. The process is not different from what was just discussed for the global case. We compare the p-values to the 0.05 α-level. If an independent variable has a p-value of less than 0.05, the independent variable is statistically significant in our model in explaining the variability in the dependent variable. If the p-value is 0.05 or higher, the particular independent variable (or term) in our model is not statistically significant. What this means is that that term in our model does not contribute toward explaining the variability in our dependent variable statistically. A close inspection of *Figure 2.19* shows that some of the terms have p-values larger than 0.05. These terms don't contribute in a statistically significant way of explaining the variability in our transformed dependent variable. To improve this model, those terms will have to be dropped and a new model tried. It is clear by this point that the process of building a regression model is truly iterative.

SUMMARY

This chapter introduced the topic of linear regression analysis using Python. We learned that regression analysis, in general, is a supervised machine learning or data science problem. We learned about the fundamentals of linear regression analysis, including the ideas behind the method of least squares. We also learned about how to use the pandas Python module to load and prepare data for exploration and analysis.

We explored how to create scatter graphs of bivariate data and how to fit a line of best fit through them. Along the way, we discovered the power of the statsmodels module in Python. We explored how to use it to define simple linear regression models and to solve the model for the relevant parameters. We also learned how to extend that to situations where the number of independent variables is more than one – multiple linear regressions. We investigated approaches by which we can transform a non-linear relation between a dependent and independent variable so that a non-linear problem can be handled using linear regression, introduced because of the transformation. We took a closer look at the statsmodels formula language. We learned how to use it to define a variety of linear models and to solve for their respective model parameters.

We continued to learn about the ideas underpinning model goodness of fit. We discussed the R-squared statistic as a measure of the goodness of fit for regression models. We followed our discussions with the basic concepts of statistical significance. We learned about how to validate a regression model globally using the F-statistic, which Python calculates for us. We also examined how to check for the statistical significance of individual model coefficients using t-tests and their associated p-values. We reviewed the assumptions of linear regression analysis and how they impact on the validity of any regression analysis work.

We will now move on from regression analysis, and *Chapter 3, Binary Classification*, and *Chapter 4, Multiclass Classification with RandomForest*, will discuss binary and multi-label classification, respectively. These chapters will introduce the techniques needed to handle supervised data science problems where the dependent variable is of the categorical data type.

Regression analysis will be revisited when the important topics of model performance improvement and interpretation are given a closer look later in the book. In *Chapter 8, Hyperparameter Tuning*, we will see how to use k-nearest neighbors and as another method for carrying out regression analysis. We will also be introduced to ridge regression, a linear regression method that is useful for situations where there are a large number of parameters.

3

BINARY CLASSIFICATION

OVERVIEW

In this chapter, we will be using a real-world dataset and a supervised learning technique called classification to generate business outcomes.

By the end of this chapter, you will be able to formulate a data science problem statement from a business perspective; build hypotheses from various business drivers influencing a use case and verify the hypotheses using exploratory data analysis; derive features based on intuitions that are derived from exploratory analysis through feature engineering; build binary classification models using a logistic regression function and analyze classification metrics and formulate action plans for the improvement of the model.

INTRODUCTION

In previous chapters, where an introduction to machine learning was covered, you were introduced to two broad categories of machine learning; supervised learning and unsupervised learning. Supervised learning can be further divided into two types of problem cases, regression and classification. In the last chapter, we covered regression problems. In this chapter, we will peek into the world of classification problems.

Take a look at the following *Figure 3.1*:

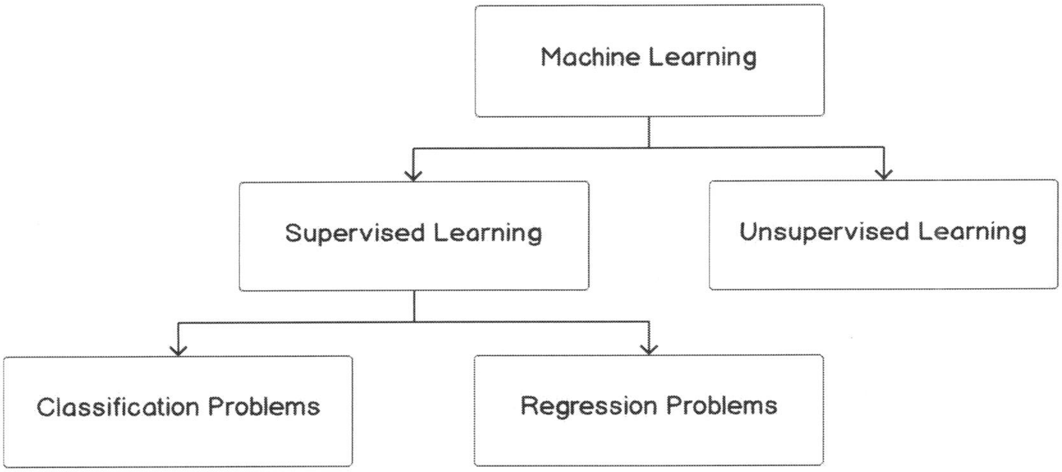

Figure 3.1: Overview of machine learning algorithms

Classification problems are the most prevalent use cases you will encounter in the real world. Unlike regression problems, where a real numbered value is predicted, classification problems deal with associating an example to a category. Classification use cases will take forms such as the following:

- Predicting whether a customer will buy the recommended product
- Identifying whether a credit transaction is fraudulent
- Determining whether a patient has a disease
- Analyzing images of animals and predicting whether the image is of a dog, cat, or panda
- Analyzing text reviews and capturing the underlying emotion such as happiness, anger, sorrow, or sarcasm

If you observe the preceding examples, there is a subtle difference between the first three and the last two. The first three revolve around binary decisions:

- Customers can either buy the product or not.
- Credit card transactions can be fraudulent or legitimate.
- Patients can be diagnosed as positive or negative for a disease.

Use cases that align with the preceding three genres where a binary decision is made are called binary classification problems. Unlike the first three, the last two associate an example with multiple classes or categories. Such problems are called multiclass classification problems. This chapter will deal with binary classification problems. Multiclass classification will be covered next in *Chapter 4, Multiclass Classification with RandomForest*.

UNDERSTANDING THE BUSINESS CONTEXT

The best way to work using a concept is with an example you can relate to. To understand the business context, let's, for instance, consider the following example.

The marketing head of the bank where you are a data scientist approaches you with a problem they would like to be addressed. The marketing team recently completed a marketing campaign where they have collated a lot of information on existing customers. They require your help to identify which of these customers are likely to buy a term deposit plan. Based on your assessment of the customer base, the marketing team will chalk out strategies for target marketing. The marketing team has provided access to historical data of past campaigns and their outcomes—that is, whether the targeted customers really bought the term deposits or not. Equipped with the historical data, you have set out on the task to identify the customers with the highest propensity (an inclination) to buy term deposits.

BUSINESS DISCOVERY

The first process when embarking on a data science problem like the preceding is the business discovery process. This entails understanding various drivers influencing the business problem. Getting to know the business drivers is important as it will help in formulating hypotheses about the business problem, which can be verified during the **exploratory data analysis** (**EDA**). The verification of hypotheses will help in formulating intuitions for feature engineering, which will be critical for the veracity of the models that we build.

Let's understand this process in detail from the context of our use case. The problem statement is to identify those customers who have a propensity to buy term deposits. As you might be aware, term deposits are bank instruments where your money will be locked for a certain period, assuring higher interest rates than saving accounts or interest-bearing checking accounts. From an investment propensity perspective, term deposits are generally popular among risk-averse customers. Equipped with the business context, let's look at some questions on business factors influencing a propensity to buy term deposits:

- Would age be a factor, with more propensity shown by the elderly?
- Is there any relationship between employment status and the propensity to buy term deposits?
- Would the asset portfolio of a customer—that is, house, loan, or higher bank balance—influence the propensity to buy?
- Will demographics such as marital status and education influence the propensity to buy term deposits? If so, how are demographics correlated to a propensity to buy?

Formulating questions on the business context is critical as this will help in arriving at various trails that we can take when we do exploratory analysis. We will deal with that in the next section. First, let's explore the data related to the preceding business problem.

EXERCISE 3.01: LOADING AND EXPLORING THE DATA FROM THE DATASET

In this exercise, we will load the dataset in our Colab notebook and do some basic explorations such as printing the dimensions of the dataset using the **`.shape()`** function and generating summary statistics of the dataset using the **`.describe()`** function.

> **NOTE**
>
> The dataset for this exercise is the bank dataset, courtesy of S. Moro, P. Cortez and P. Rita: A Data-Driven Approach to Predict the Success of Bank Telemarketing.
>
> It is from the UCI Machine Learning Repository: https://packt.live/2MItXEl and can be downloaded from our GitHub at: https://packt.live/2Wav1nJ.

The following steps will help you to complete this exercise:

1. Open a new Colab notebook.
2. Now, **import pandas** as **pd** in your Colab notebook:

```
import pandas as pd
```

3. Assign the link to the dataset to a variable called **file_url**

```
file_url = 'https://raw.githubusercontent.com/PacktWorkshops'\
           '/The-Data-Science-Workshop/master/Chapter03'\
           '/bank-full.csv'
```

4. Now, read the file using the **pd.read_csv()** function from the pandas DataFrame:

```
# Loading the data using pandas
bankData = pd.read_csv(file_url, sep=";")
bankData.head()
```

> **NOTE**
>
> The **#** symbol in the code snippet above denotes a code comment. Comments are added into code to help explain specific bits of logic.

The **pd.read_csv()** function's arguments are the filename as a string and the limit separator of a CSV, which is **";"**. After reading the file, the DataFrame is printed using the **.head()** function. Note that the **#** symbol in the code above denotes a comment. Comments are added into code to help explain specific bits of logic.

You should get the following output:

	age	job	marital	education	default	balance	housing	loan	contact	day	month	duration	campaign	pdays	previous	poutcome	y
0	58	management	married	tertiary	no	2143	yes	no	unknown	5	may	261	1	-1	0	unknown	no
1	44	technician	single	secondary	no	29	yes	no	unknown	5	may	151	1	-1	0	unknown	no
2	33	entrepreneur	married	secondary	no	2	yes	yes	unknown	5	may	76	1	-1	0	unknown	no
3	47	blue-collar	married	unknown	no	1506	yes	no	unknown	5	may	92	1	-1	0	unknown	no
4	33	unknown	single	unknown	no	1	no	no	unknown	5	may	198	1	-1	0	unknown	no

Figure 3.2: Loading data into a Colab notebook

Here, we loaded the **CSV** file and then stored it as a pandas DataFrame for further analysis.

5. Next, print the shape of the dataset, as mentioned in the following code snippet:

```
# Printing the shape of the data
print(bankData.shape)
```

The **.shape** function is used to find the overall shape of the dataset.

You should get the following output:

```
(45211, 17)
```

6. Now, find the summary of the numerical raw data as a table output using the **.describe()** function in pandas, as mentioned in the following code snippet:

```
# Summarizing the statistics of the numerical raw data
bankData.describe()
```

You should get the following output:

	age	balance	day	duration	campaign	pdays	previous
count	45211.000000	45211.000000	45211.000000	45211.000000	45211.000000	45211.000000	45211.000000
mean	40.936210	1362.272058	15.806419	258.163080	2.763841	40.197828	0.580323
std	10.618762	3044.765829	8.322476	257.527812	3.098021	100.128746	2.303441
min	18.000000	-8019.000000	1.000000	0.000000	1.000000	-1.000000	0.000000
25%	33.000000	72.000000	8.000000	103.000000	1.000000	-1.000000	0.000000
50%	39.000000	448.000000	16.000000	180.000000	2.000000	-1.000000	0.000000
75%	48.000000	1428.000000	21.000000	319.000000	3.000000	-1.000000	0.000000
max	95.000000	102127.000000	31.000000	4918.000000	63.000000	871.000000	275.000000

Figure 3.3: Loading data into a Colab notebook

As seen from the shape of the data, the dataset has **45211** examples with **17** variables. The variable set has both categorical and numerical variables. The preceding summary statistics are derived only for the numerical data.

> **NOTE**
>
> To access the source code for this specific section, please refer to https://packt.live/31UQhAU.
>
> You can also run this example online at https://packt.live/2YdiSAF.

You have completed the first tasks that are required before embarking on our journey. In this exercise, you have learned how to load data and to derive basic statistics, such as the summary statistics, from the dataset. In the subsequent dataset, we will take a deep dive into the loaded dataset.

Testing Business Hypotheses Using Exploratory Data Analysis

In the previous section, you approached the problem statement from a domain perspective, thereby identifying some of the business drivers. Once business drivers are identified, the next step is to evolve some hypotheses about the relationship of these business drivers and the business outcome you have set out to achieve. These hypotheses need to be verified using the data you have. This is where **exploratory data analysis** (**EDA**) plays a big part in the data science life cycle.

Let's return to the problem statement we are trying to analyze. From the previous section, we identified some business drivers such as age, demographics, employment status, and asset portfolio, which we feel will influence the propensity for buying a term deposit. Let's go ahead and formulate our hypotheses on some of these business drivers and then verify them using EDA.

Visualization for Exploratory Data Analysis

Visualization is imperative for EDA. Effective visualization helps in deriving business intuitions from the data. In this section, we will introduce some of the visualization techniques that will be used for EDA:

- **Line graphs**: Line graphs are one of the simplest forms of visualization. Line graphs are the preferred method for revealing trends in the data. These types of graphs are mostly used for continuous data. We will be generating this graph in *Exercise 3.02, Business Hypothesis Testing for Age versus Propensity for a Term Loan*.

Here is what a line graph looks like:

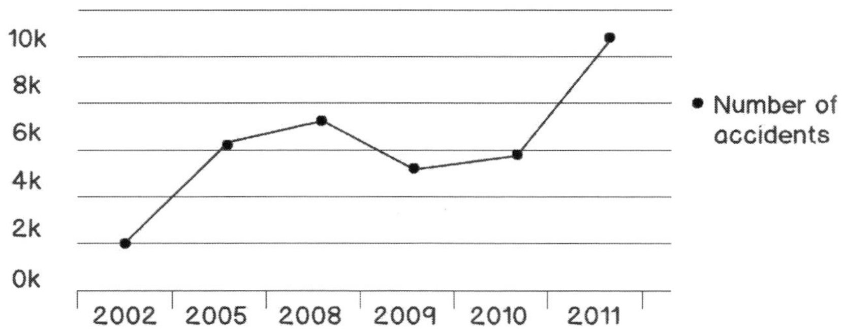

Figure 3.4: Example of a line graph

- **Histograms**: Histograms are plots of the proportion of data along with some specified intervals. They are mostly used for visualizing the distribution of data. Histograms are very effective for identifying whether data distribution is symmetric and for identifying outliers in data. We will be looking at histograms in much more detail later in this chapter.

  Here is what a histogram looks like:

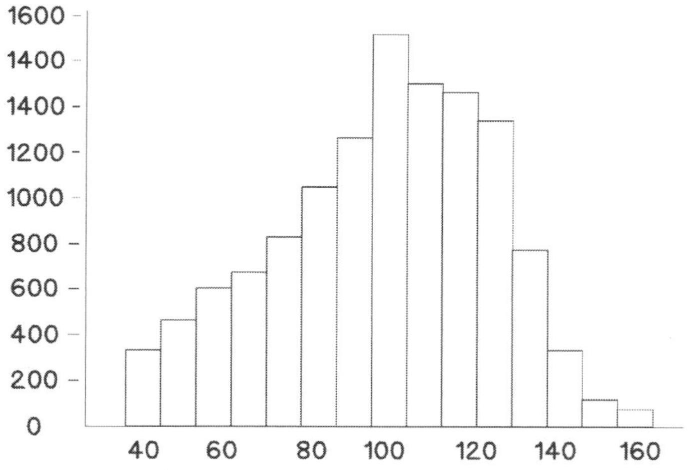

Figure 3.5: Example of a histogram

- **Density plots**: Like histograms, density plots are also used for visualizing the distribution of data. However, density plots give a smoother representation of the distribution. We will be looking at this later in this chapter.

Here is what a density plot looks like:

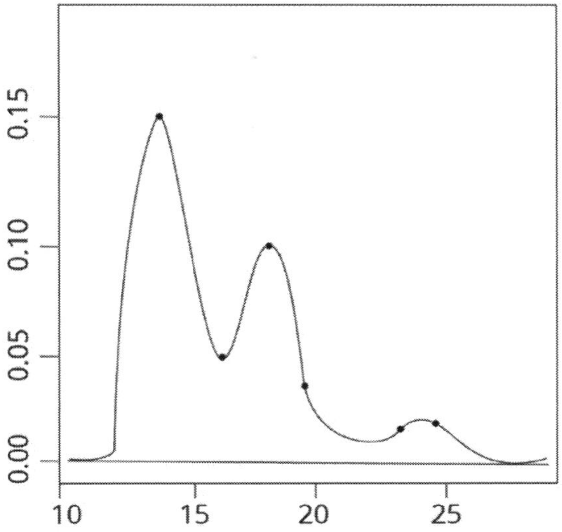

Figure 3.6: Example of a density plot

- **Stacked bar charts**: A stacked bar chart helps you to visualize the various categories of data, one on top of the other, in order to give you a sense of proportion of the categories; for instance, if you want to plot a bar chart showing the values, **`Yes`** and **`No`**, on a single bar. This can be done using the stacked bar chart, which cannot be done on the other charts.

  Let's create some dummy data and generate a stacked bar chart to check the proportion of jobs in different sectors.

> **NOTE**
>
> Do not execute any of the following code snippets until the final step. Enter all the code in the same cell.

Import the library files required for the task:

```
# Importing library files
import matplotlib.pyplot as plt
import numpy as np
```

Next, create some sample data detailing a list of jobs:

```
# Create a simple list of categories
jobList = ['admin','scientist','doctor','management']
```

Each job will have two categories to be plotted, **yes** and **No**, with some proportion between **yes** and **No**. These are detailed as follows:

```
# Getting two categories ( 'yes','No') for each of jobs
jobYes = [20,60,70,40]
jobNo = [80,40,30,60]
```

In the next steps, the length of the job list is taken for plotting **xlabels** and then they are arranged using the **np.arange()** function:

```
# Get the length of x axis labels and arranging its indexes
xlabels = len(jobList)

ind = np.arange(xlabels)
```

Next, let's define the width of each bar and do the plotting. In the plot, **p2**, we define that when stacking, **yes** will be at the bottom and **No** at top:

```
# Get width of each bar
width = 0.35

# Getting the plots
p1 = plt.bar(ind, jobYes, width)
p2 = plt.bar(ind, jobNo, width, bottom=jobYes)
```

Define the labels for the *Y* axis and the title of the plot:

```
# Getting the labels for the plots
plt.ylabel('Proportion of Jobs')
plt.title('Job')
```

The indexes for the *X* and *Y* axes are defined next. For the *X* axis, the list of jobs are given, and, for the *Y* axis, the indices are in proportion from **0** to **100** with an increment of **10** (0, 10, 20, 30, and so on):

```
# Defining the x label indexes and y label indexes
plt.xticks(ind, jobList)
plt.yticks(np.arange(0, 100, 10))
```

The last step is to define the legends and to rotate the axis labels to **90** degrees. The plot is finally displayed:

```
# Defining the legends
plt.legend((p1[0], p2[0]), ('Yes', 'No'))

# To rotate the axis labels
plt.xticks(rotation=90)
plt.show()
```

Here is what a stacked bar chart looks like based on the preceding example:

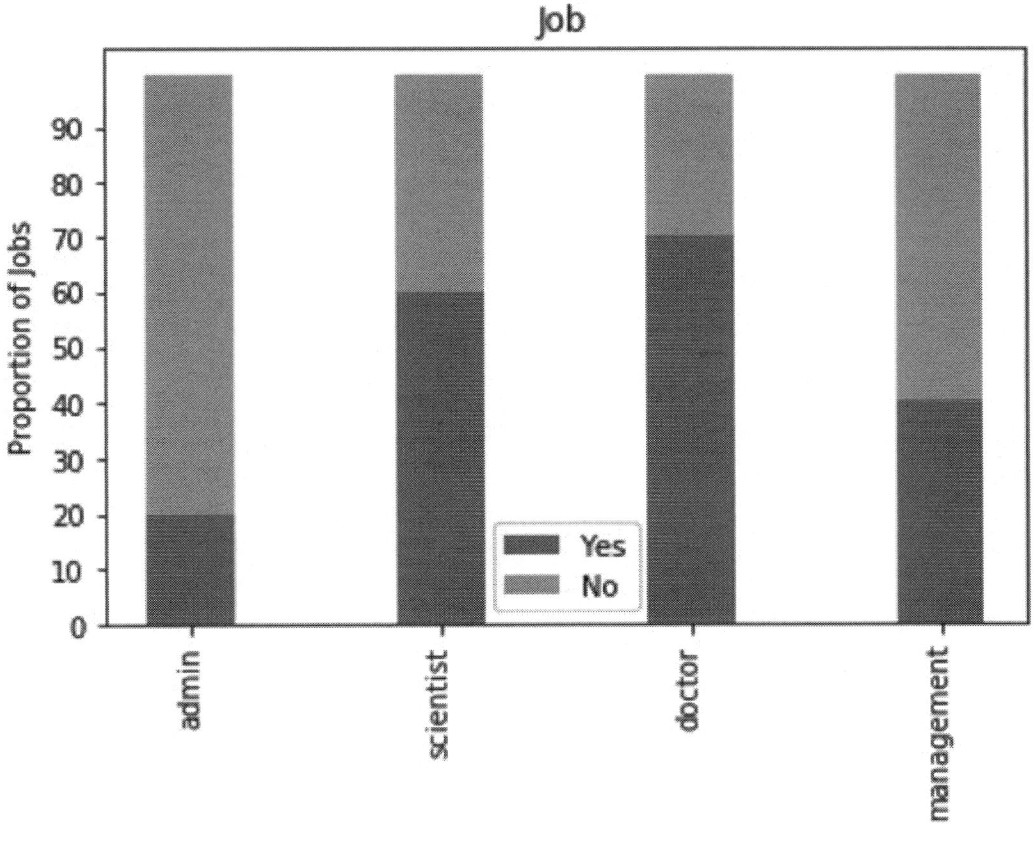

Figure 3.7: Example of a stacked bar plot

Let's use these graphs in the following exercises and activities.

EXERCISE 3.02: BUSINESS HYPOTHESIS TESTING FOR AGE VERSUS PROPENSITY FOR A TERM LOAN

The goal of this exercise is to define a hypothesis to check the propensity for an individual to purchase a term deposit plan against their age. We will be using a line graph for this exercise.

The following steps will help you to complete this exercise:

1. Begin by defining the hypothesis.

   The first step in the verification process will be to define a hypothesis about the relationship. A hypothesis can be based on your experiences, domain knowledge, some published pieces of knowledge, or your business intuitions.

   Let's first define our hypothesis on age and propensity to buy term deposits:

   The propensity to buy term deposits is more with elderly customers compared to younger ones. This is our hypothesis.

   Now that we have defined our hypothesis, it is time to verify its veracity with the data. One of the best ways to get business intuitions from data is by taking cross-sections of our data and visualizing them.

2. Import the pandas and altair packages:

```
import pandas as pd
import altair as alt
```

3. Next, you need to load the dataset, just like you loaded the dataset in *Exercise 3.01, Loading and Exploring the Data from the Dataset*:

```
file_url = 'https://raw.githubusercontent.com/'\
           'PacktWorkshops/The-Data-Science-Workshop/'\
           'master/Chapter03/bank-full.csv'

bankData = pd.read_csv(file_url, sep=";")
```

> **NOTE**
>
> *Steps 2-3* will be repeated in the following exercises for this chapter.

We will be verifying how the purchased term deposits are distributed by age.

4. Next, we will count the number of records for each age group. We will be using the combination of **.groupby()**, **.agg()**, **.reset_index()** methods from **pandas**.

> **NOTE**
>
> You will see further details of these methods in *Chapter 12, Feature Engineering*.

```
filter_mask = bankData['y'] == 'yes'
bankSub1 = bankData[filter_mask]\
            .groupby('age')['y'].agg(agegrp='count')\
            .reset_index()
```

We first take the pandas **DataFrame**, **bankData**, which we loaded in *Exercise 3.01, Loading and Exploring the Data from the Dataset* and then filter it for all cases where the term deposit is yes using the mask **bankData['y'] == 'yes'**. These cases are grouped through the **groupby()** method and then aggregated according to age through the **agg()** method. Finally we need to use **.reset_index()** to get a well-structure DataFrame that will be stored in a new **DataFrame** called **bankSub1**.

5. Now, plot a line chart using altair and the **.Chart().mark_line().encode()** methods and we will define the **x** and **y** variables, as shown in the following code snippet:

```
# Visualising the relationship using altair
alt.Chart(bankSub1).mark_line().encode(x='age', y='agegrp')
```

You should get the following output:

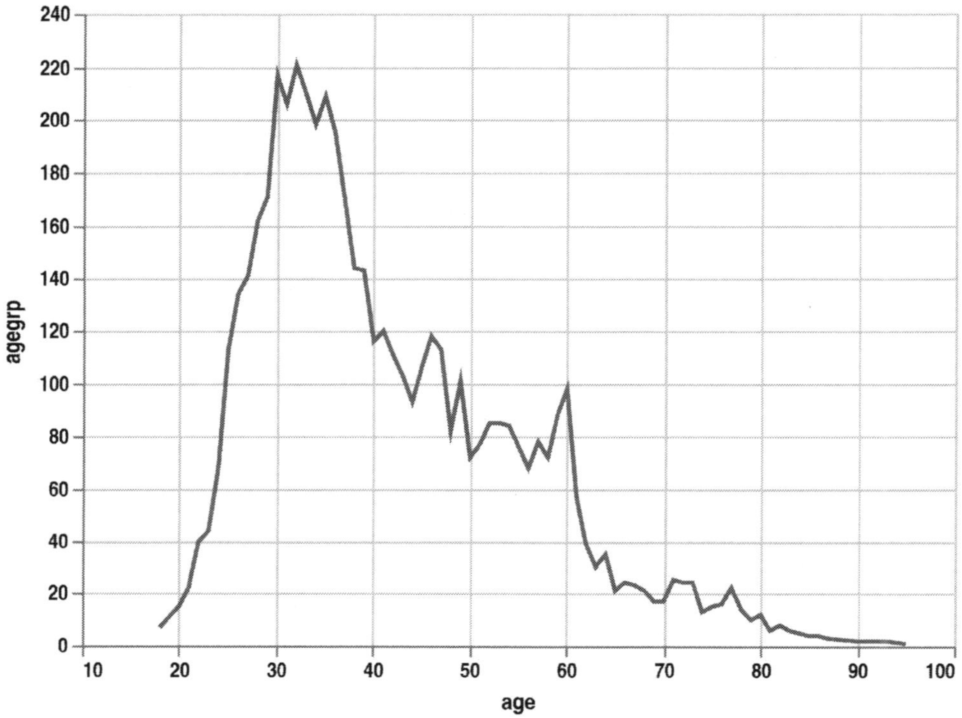

Figure 3.8: Relationship between age and propensity to purchase

From the plot, we can see that the highest number of term deposit purchases are done by customers within an age range between 25 and 40, with the propensity to buy tapering off with age.

This relationship is quite counterintuitive from our assumptions in the hypothesis, right? But, wait a minute, aren't we missing an important point here? We are taking the data based on the absolute count of customers in each age range. If the proportion of banking customers is higher within the age range of 25 to 40, then we are very likely to get a plot like the one that we have got. What we really should plot is the proportion of customers, within each age group, who buy a term deposit.

Let's look at how we can represent the data by taking the proportion of customers. Just like you did in the earlier steps, we will aggregate the customer propensity with respect to age, and then divide each category of buying propensity by the total number of customers in that age group to get the proportion.

6. Group the data per age using the **groupby()** method and find the total number of customers under each age group using the **agg()** method:

```
# Getting another perspective
ageTot = bankData.groupby('age')['y']\
         .agg(ageTot='count').reset_index()
ageTot.head()
```

The output is as follows:

	age	ageTot
0	18	12
1	19	35
2	20	50
3	21	79
4	22	129

Figure 3.9: Customers per age group

7. Now, group the data by both age and propensity of purchase and find the total counts under each category of propensity, which are **yes** and **no**:

```
# Getting all the details in one place
ageProp = bankData.groupby(['age','y'])['y']\
         .agg(ageCat='count').reset_index()
ageProp.head()
```

The output is as follows:

	age	y	ageCat
0	18	no	5
1	18	yes	7
2	19	no	24
3	19	yes	11
4	20	no	35

Figure 3.10: Propensity by age group

8. Merge both of these DataFrames based on the **age** variable using the **pd.merge()** function, and then divide each category of propensity within each age group by the total customers in the respective age group to get the proportion of customers, as shown in the following code snippet:

```
# Merging both the data frames
ageComb = pd.merge(ageProp, ageTot,left_on = ['age'], \
                   right_on = ['age'])
ageComb['catProp'] = (ageComb.ageCat/ageComb.ageTot)*100
ageComb.head()
```

The output is as follows:

	age	y	ageCat	ageTot	catProp
0	18	no	5	12	41.666667
1	18	yes	7	12	58.333333
2	19	no	24	35	68.571429
3	19	yes	11	35	31.428571
4	20	no	35	50	70.000000

Figure 3.11: Merged DataFrames with proportion of customers by age group

9. Now, display the proportion where you plot both categories (yes and no) as separate plots. This can be achieved through a method within **altair** called **facet()**:

```
# Visualising the relationship using altair
alt.Chart(ageComb).mark_line()\
    .encode(x='age', y='catProp').facet(column='y')
```

This function makes as many plots as there are categories within the variable. Here, we give the **'y'** variable, which is the variable name for the **yes** and **no** categories to the **facet()** function, and we get two different plots: one for **yes** and another for **no**.

You should get the following output:

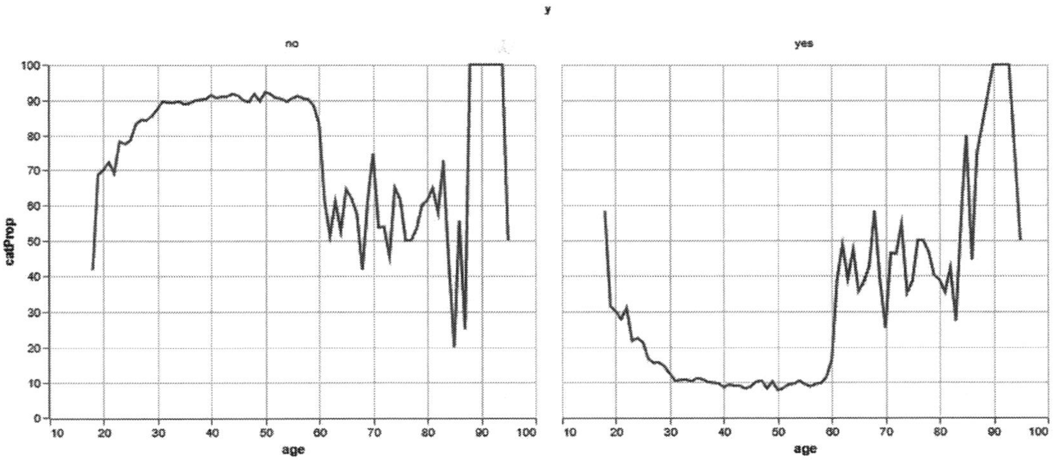

Figure 3.12: Visualizing normalized relationships

By the end of this exercise, you were able to get two meaningful plots showing the propensity of people to buy term deposit plans. The final output for this exercise shows two graphs in which the left graph shows the proportion of people who do not buy term deposits and the right one shows those customers who buy term deposits.

We can see, in the first graph, with the age group beginning from **22** to **60**, individuals would not be inclined to purchase the term deposit. However, in the second graph, we see the opposite, where the age group of **60** and over are much more inclined to purchase the term deposit plan.

> **NOTE**
>
> To access the source code for this specific section, please refer to https://packt.live/3iOw7Q4.
>
> This section does not currently have an online interactive example, but can be run as usual on Google Colab.

In the following section, we will begin to analyze our plots based on our intuitions.

INTUITIONS FROM THE EXPLORATORY ANALYSIS

What are the intuitions we can take out of the exercise that we have done so far? We have seen two contrasting plots by taking the proportion of users and without taking the proportions. As you can see, taking the proportion of users is the right approach to get the right perspective in which we must view data. This is more in line with the hypothesis that we have evolved. We can see from the plots that the propensity to buy term deposits is low for age groups from **22** to around **60**.

After **60**, we see a rising trend in the demand for term deposits. Another interesting fact we can observe is the higher proportion of term deposit purchases for ages younger than **20**.

In *Exercise 3.02, Business Hypothesis Testing for Age versus Propensity for a Term Loan* we discovered how to develop our hypothesis and then verify the hypothesis using EDA. After the following activity, we will delve into another important step in the journey, Feature Engineering.

ACTIVITY 3.01: BUSINESS HYPOTHESIS TESTING TO FIND EMPLOYMENT STATUS VERSUS PROPENSITY FOR TERM DEPOSITS

You are working as a data scientist for a bank. You are provided with historical data from the management of the bank and are asked to try to formulate a hypothesis between employment status and the propensity to buy term deposits.

In *Exercise 3.02, Business Hypothesis Testing for Age versus Propensity for a Term Loan* we worked on a problem to find the relationship between age and the propensity to buy term deposits. In this activity, we will use a similar route and verify the relationship between employment status and term deposit purchase propensity.

The steps are as follows:

1. Formulate the hypothesis between employment status and the propensity for term deposits. Let the hypothesis be as follows: *High paying employees prefer term deposits than other categories of employees.*

2. Open a Colab notebook file similar to what was used in *Exercise 3.02, Business Hypothesis Testing for Age versus Propensity for a Term Loan* and install and import the necessary libraries such as **pandas** and **altair**.

3. From the banking DataFrame, **bankData**, find the distribution of employment status using the **.groupby()**, **.agg()** and **.reset_index()** methods.

Group the data with respect to employment status using the **`.groupby()`** method and find the total count of propensities for each employment status using the **`.agg()`** method.

4. Now, merge both DataFrames using the **`pd.merge()`** function and then find the propensity count by calculating the proportion of propensity for each type of employment status. When creating the new variable for finding the propensity proportion.
5. Plot the data and summarize intuitions from the plot using **`matplotlib`**. Use the stacked bar chart for this activity.

> **NOTE**
>
> The **`bank-full.csv`** dataset to be used in this activity can be found at https://packt.live/2Wav1nJ.

Expected output: The final plot of the propensity to buy with respect to employment status will be similar to the following plot:

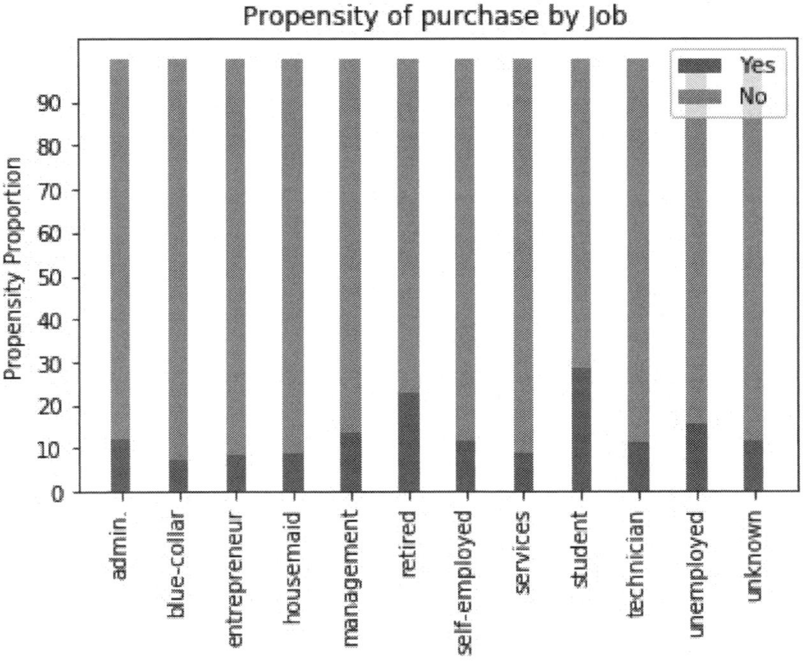

Figure 3.13: Visualizing propensity of purchase by job

> **NOTE**
>
> The solution to this activity can be found at the following address: https://packt.live/2GbJloz.

Now that we have seen EDA, let's dive into feature engineering.

FEATURE ENGINEERING

In the previous section, we traversed the process of EDA. As part of the earlier process, we tested our business hypotheses by slicing and dicing the data and through visualizations. You might be wondering where we will use the intuitions that we derived from all of the analysis we did. The answer to that question will be addressed in this section.

Feature engineering is the process of transforming raw variables to create new variables and this will be covered later in the chapter. Feature engineering is one of the most important steps that influence the accuracy of the models that we build.

There are two broad types of feature engineering:

1. Here, we transform raw variables based on intuitions from a business perspective. These intuitions are what we build during the exploratory analysis.
2. The transformation of raw variables is done from a statistical and data normalization perspective.

We will look into each type of feature engineering next.

> **NOTE**
>
> Feature engineering will be covered in much more detail in *Chapter 12, Feature Engineering*. In this section you will see the purpose of learning about classification.

BUSINESS-DRIVEN FEATURE ENGINEERING

Business-driven feature engineering is the process of transforming raw variables based on business intuitions that were derived during the exploratory analysis. It entails transforming data and creating new variables based on business factors or drivers that influence a business problem.

In the previous exercises on exploratory analysis, we explored the relationship of a single variable with the dependent variable. In this exercise, we will combine multiple variables and then derive new features. We will explore the relationship between an asset portfolio and the propensity for term deposit purchases. An asset portfolio is the combination of all assets and liabilities the customer has with the bank. We will combine assets and liabilities such as bank balance, home ownership, and loans to get a new feature called an **asset** index.

These feature engineering steps will be split into two exercises. In *Exercise 3.03, Feature Engineering – Exploration of Individual Features*, we explore individual variables such as balance, housing, and loans to understand their relationship to a propensity for term deposits.

In *Exercise 3.04, Feature Engineering – Creating New Features from Existing Ones,* we will transform individual variables and then combine them to form a new feature.

EXERCISE 3.03: FEATURE ENGINEERING – EXPLORATION OF INDIVIDUAL FEATURES

In this exercise, we will explore the relationship between two variables, which are whether an individual owns a house and whether an individual has a loan, to the propensity for term deposit purchases by these individuals.

The following steps will help you to complete this exercise:

1. Open a new Colab notebook.
2. Import the **pandas** package.

```
import pandas as pd
```

3. Assign the link to the dataset to a variable called **file_url**:

```
file_url = 'https://raw.githubusercontent.com'\
           '/PacktWorkshops/The-Data-Science-Workshop'\
           '/master/Chapter03/bank-full.csv'
```

4. Read the banking dataset using the **.read_csv()** function:

```
# Reading the banking data
bankData = pd.read_csv(file_url, sep=";")
```

5. Next, we will find a relationship between housing and the propensity for term deposits, as mentioned in the following code snippet:

```
# Relationship between housing and propensity for term deposits
bankData.groupby(['housing', 'y'])['y']\
          .agg(houseTot='count').reset_index()
```

You should get the following output:

	housing	y	houseTot
0	no	no	16727
1	no	yes	3354
2	yes	no	23195
3	yes	yes	1935

Figure 3.14: Housing status versus propensity to buy term deposits

The first part of the code is to group customers based on whether they own a house or not. The count of customers under each category is calculated with the **.agg()** method. From the values, we can see that the propensity to buy term deposits is much higher for people who do not own a house compared with those who do own one: **(3354 / (3354 + 16727) = 17% to 1935 / (1935 + 23195) = 8%)**.

6. Explore the **'loan'** variable to find its relationship with the propensity for a term deposit, as mentioned in the following code snippet:

```
"""
Relationship between having a loan and propensity for term
deposits
"""
bankData.groupby(['loan', 'y'])['y']\
          .agg(loanTot='count').reset_index()
```

> **NOTE**
>
> The triple-quotes (**"""**) shown in the code snippet above are used to denote the start and end points of a multi-line code comment. This is an alternative to using the **#** symbol.

You should get the following output:

	loan	y	loanTot
0	no	no	33162
1	no	yes	4805
2	yes	no	6760
3	yes	yes	484

Figure 3.15: Loan versus term deposit propensity

In the case of loan portfolios, the propensity to buy term deposits is higher for customers without loans: **(4805 / (4805 + 33162) = 12 % to 484/ (484 + 6760) = 6%)**.

Housing and loans were categorical data and finding a relationship was straightforward. However, bank balance data is numerical and to analyze it, we need to have a different strategy. One common strategy is to convert the continuous numerical data into ordinal data and look at how the propensity varies across each category.

7. To convert numerical values into ordinal values, we first find the quantile values and take them as threshold values. The quantiles are obtained using the following code snippet:

```
#Taking the quantiles for 25%, 50% and 75% of the balance data
import numpy as np
np.quantile(bankData['balance'],[0.25,0.5,0.75])
```

You should get the following output:

```
array([  72.,  448., 1428.])
```

Figure 3.16: Quantiles for bank balance data

Quantile values represent certain threshold values for data distribution. For example, when we say the 25th quantile percentile, we are talking about a value below which **25%** of the data exists. The quantile can be calculated using the **np.quantile()** function in NumPy. In the code snippet of *Step 4*, we calculated the 25th, 50th, and 75th percentiles, which resulted in **72**, **448**, and **1428**.

8. Now, convert the numerical values of bank balances into categorical values, as mentioned in the following code snippet:

```
bankData['balanceClass'] = 'Quant1'
bankData.loc[(bankData['balance'] > 72) \
              & (bankData['balance'] < 448), \
              'balanceClass'] = 'Quant2'
bankData.loc[(bankData['balance'] > 448) \
              & (bankData['balance'] < 1428), \
              'balanceClass'] = 'Quant3'
bankData.loc[bankData['balance'] > 1428, \
             'balanceClass'] = 'Quant4'
bankData.head()
```

You should get the following output:

	age	job	marital	education	default	balance	housing	loan	contact	day	month	duration	campaign	pdays	previous	poutcome	y	balanceClass
0	58	management	married	tertiary	no	2143	yes	no	unknown	5	may	261	1	-1	0	unknown	no	Quant4
1	44	technician	single	secondary	no	29	yes	no	unknown	5	may	151	1	-1	0	unknown	no	Quant1
2	33	entrepreneur	married	secondary	no	2	yes	yes	unknown	5	may	76	1	-1	0	unknown	no	Quant1
3	47	blue-collar	married	unknown	no	1506	yes	no	unknown	5	may	92	1	-1	0	unknown	no	Quant4
4	33	unknown	single	unknown	no	1	no	no	unknown	5	may	198	1	-1	0	unknown	no	Quant1

Figure 3.17: New features from bank balance data

We did this is by looking at the quantile thresholds we took in the *Step 4*, and categorizing the numerical data into the corresponding quantile class. For example, all values lower than the 25th quantile value, 72, were classified as **`Quant1`**, values between 72 and 448 were classified as **`Quant2`**, and so on. To store the quantile categories, we created a new feature in the bank dataset called **`balanceClass`** and set its default value to **`Quan1`**. After this, based on each value threshold, the data points were classified to the respective quantile class.

9. Next, we need to find the propensity of term deposit purchases based on each quantile the customers fall into. This task is similar to what we did in *Exercise 3.02, Business Hypothesis Testing for Age versus Propensity for a Term Loan*:

```
# Calculating the customers under each quantile
balanceTot = bankData.groupby(['balanceClass'])['y']\
                     .agg(balanceTot='count').reset_index()
balanceTot
```

You should get the following output:

	balanceClass	balanceTot
0	Quant1	11340
1	Quant2	11275
2	Quant3	11299
3	Quant4	11297

Figure 3:18: Classification based on quantiles

10. Calculate the total number of customers categorized by quantile and propensity classification, as mentioned in the following code snippet:

```
"""
Calculating the total customers categorised as per quantile
and propensity classification
"""
balanceProp = bankData.groupby(['balanceClass', 'y'])['y']\
                      .agg(balanceCat='count').reset_index()
balanceProp
```

You should get the following output:

	balanceClass	y	balanceCat
0	Quant1	no	10517
1	Quant1	yes	823
2	Quant2	no	10049
3	Quant2	yes	1226
4	Quant3	no	9884
5	Quant3	yes	1415
6	Quant4	no	9472
7	Quant4	yes	1825

Figure 3.19: Total number of customers categorized by quantile and propensity classification

11. Now, **merge** both DataFrames:

```
# Merging both the data frames
balanceComb = pd.merge(balanceProp, balanceTot, \
                       on = ['balanceClass'])
balanceComb['catProp'] = (balanceComb.balanceCat \
                          / balanceComb.balanceTot)*100
balanceComb
```

You should get the following output:

	balanceClass	y	balanceCat	balanceTot	catProp
0	Quant1	no	10517	11340	92.742504
1	Quant1	yes	823	11340	7.257496
2	Quant2	no	10049	11275	89.126386
3	Quant2	yes	1226	11275	10.873614
4	Quant3	no	9884	11299	87.476768
5	Quant3	yes	1415	11299	12.523232
6	Quant4	no	9472	11297	83.845269
7	Quant4	yes	1825	11297	16.154731

Figure 3.20: Propensity versus balance category

From the distribution of data, we can see that, as we move from Quantile 1 to Quantile 4, the proportion of customers who buy term deposits keeps on increasing. For instance, of all of the customers who belong to **Quant 1**, 7.25% have bought term deposits (we get this percentage from **catProp**). This proportion increases to 10.87 % for **Quant 2** and thereafter to 12.52 % and 16.15% for **Quant 3** and **Quant4**, respectively. From this trend, we can conclude that individuals with higher balances have more propensity for term deposits.

In this exercise, we explored the relationship of each variable to the propensity for term deposit purchases. The overall trend that we can observe is that people with more cash in hand (no loans and a higher balance) have a higher propensity to buy term deposits.

> **NOTE**
>
> To access the source code for this specific section, please refer to https://packt.live/3g7rK0w.
>
> You can also run this example online at https://packt.live/2PZbcNV.

In the next exercise, we will use these intuitions to derive a new feature.

EXERCISE 3.04: FEATURE ENGINEERING – CREATING NEW FEATURES FROM EXISTING ONES

In this exercise, we will combine the individual variables we analyzed in *Exercise 3.03, Feature Engineering - Exploration of Individual Features* to derive a new feature called an asset index. One methodology to create an asset index is by assigning weights based on the asset or liability of the customer.

For instance, a higher bank balance or home ownership will have a positive bearing on the overall asset index and, therefore, will be assigned a higher weight. In contrast, the presence of a loan will be a liability and, therefore, will have to have a lower weight. Let's give a weight of 5 if the customer has a house and 1 in its absence. Similarly, we can give a weight of 1 if the customer has a loan and 5 in case of no loans:

1. Open a new Colab notebook.
2. Import the pandas and numpy package:

```
import pandas as pd
import numpy as np
```

3. Assign the link to the dataset to a variable called 'file_url'.

```
file_url = 'https://raw.githubusercontent.com'\
           '/PacktWorkshops/The-Data-Science-Workshop'\
           '/master/Chapter03/bank-full.csv'
```

4. Read the banking dataset using the **.read_csv()** function:

```
# Reading the banking data
bankData = pd.read_csv(file_url,sep=";")
```

5. The first step we will follow is to normalize the numerical variables. This is implemented using the following code snippet:

```
# Normalizing data
from sklearn import preprocessing
x = bankData[['balance']].values.astype(float)
```

6. As the bank balance dataset contains numerical values, we need to first normalize the data. The purpose of normalization is to bring all of the variables that we are using to create the new feature into a common scale. One effective method we can use here for the normalizing function is called **`MinMaxScaler()`**, which converts all of the numerical data between a scaled range of 0 to 1. The **`MinMaxScaler`** function is available within the **`preprocessing`** method in **`sklearn`**:

```
minmaxScaler = preprocessing.MinMaxScaler()
```

7. Transform the balance data by normalizing it with **`minmaxScaler`**:

```
bankData['balanceTran'] = minmaxScaler.fit_transform(x)
```

In this step, we created a new feature called **`'balanceTran'`** to store the normalized bank balance values.

8. Print the head of the data using the **`.head()`** function:

```
bankData.head()
```

You should get the following output:

	age	job	marital	education	default	balance	housing	loan	contact	day	month	duration	campaign	pdays	previous	poutcome	y	balanceTran
0	58	management	married	tertiary	no	2143	yes	no	unknown	5	may	261	1	-1	0	unknown	no	0.092259
1	44	technician	single	secondary	no	29	yes	no	unknown	5	may	151	1	-1	0	unknown	no	0.073067
2	33	entrepreneur	married	secondary	no	2	yes	yes	unknown	5	may	76	1	-1	0	unknown	no	0.072822
3	47	blue-collar	married	unknown	no	1506	yes	no	unknown	5	may	92	1	-1	0	unknown	no	0.086476
4	33	unknown	single	unknown	no	1	no	no	unknown	5	may	198	1	-1	0	unknown	no	0.072812

Figure 3.21: Normalizing the bank balance data

9. After creating the normalized variable, add a small value of **`0.001`** so as to eliminate the 0 values in the variable. This is mentioned in the following code snippet:

```
# Adding a small numerical constant to eliminate 0 values
bankData['balanceTran'] = bankData['balanceTran'] + 0.00001
```

The purpose of adding this small value is because, in the subsequent steps, we will be multiplying three transformed variables together to form a composite index. The small value is added to avoid the variable values becoming 0 during the multiplying operation.

10. Now, add two additional columns for introducing the transformed variables for loans and housing, as per the weighting approach discussed at the start of this exercise:

```
# Let us transform values for loan data
bankData['loanTran'] = 1
# Giving a weight of 5 if there is no loan
bankData.loc[bankData['loan'] == 'no', 'loanTran'] = 5
bankData.head()
```

You should get the following output:

age	job	marital	education	default	balance	housing	loan	contact	day	month	duration	campaign	pdays	previous	poutcome	y	balanceTran	loanTran
58	management	married	tertiary	no	2143	yes	no	unknown	5	may	261	1	-1	0	unknown	no	0.092269	5
44	technician	single	secondary	no	29	yes	no	unknown	5	may	151	1	-1	0	unknown	no	0.073077	5
33	entrepreneur	married	secondary	no	2	yes	yes	unknown	5	may	76	1	-1	0	unknown	no	0.072832	1
47	blue-collar	married	unknown	no	1506	yes	no	unknown	5	may	92	1	-1	0	unknown	no	0.086486	5
33	unknown	single	unknown	no	1	no	no	unknown	5	may	198	1	-1	0	unknown	no	0.072822	5

Figure 3.22: Additional columns with the transformed variables

We transformed values for the loan data as per the weighting approach. When a customer has a loan, it is given a weight of **`1`**, and when there's no loan, the weight assigned is **`5`**. The value of **`1`** and **`5`** are intuitive weights we are assigning. What values we assign can vary based on the business context you may be provided with.

11. Now, transform values for the **`Housing data`**, as mentioned here:

```
# Let us transform values for Housing data
bankData['houseTran'] = 5
```

12. Give a weight of **`1`** if the customer has a house and print the results, as mentioned in the following code snippet:

```
bankData.loc[bankData['housing'] == 'no', 'houseTran'] = 1
print(bankData.head())
```

You should get the following output:

	age	job	marital	education	...	y	balanceTran	loanTran	houseTran
0	58	management	married	tertiary	...	no	0.092269	5	5
1	44	technician	single	secondary	...	no	0.073077	5	5
2	33	entrepreneur	married	secondary	...	no	0.072832	1	5
3	47	blue-collar	married	unknown	...	no	0.086486	5	5
4	33	unknown	single	unknown	...	no	0.072822	5	1

Figure 3.23: Transforming loan and housing data

Once all the transformed variables are created, we can multiply all of the transformed variables together to create a new index called **`assetIndex`**. This is a composite index that represents the combined effect of all three variables.

13. Now, create a new variable, which is the product of all of the transformed variables:

```
"""
Let us now create the new variable which is a product of all
these
"""
bankData['assetIndex'] = bankData['balanceTran'] \
                         * bankData['loanTran'] \
                         * bankData['houseTran']
bankData.head()
```

You should get the following output:

	age	job	marital	education	default	balance	housing	loan	contact	day	month	duration	campaign	pdays	previous	poutcome	y	balanceTran	loanTran	houseTran	assetIndex
0	58	management	married	tertiary	no	2143	yes	no	unknown	5	may	261	1	-1	0	unknown	no	0.092269	5	5	2.306734
1	44	technician	single	secondary	no	29	yes	no	unknown	5	may	151	1	-1	0	unknown	no	0.073077	5	5	1.826916
2	33	entrepreneur	married	secondary	no	2	yes	yes	unknown	5	may	76	1	-1	0	unknown	no	0.072832	1	5	0.364158
3	47	blue-collar	married	unknown	no	1506	yes	no	unknown	5	may	92	1	-1	0	unknown	no	0.086486	5	5	2.162153
4	33	unknown	single	unknown	no	1	no	no	unknown	5	may	198	1	-1	0	unknown	no	0.072822	5	1	0.364112

Figure 3.24: Creating a composite index

14. Explore the propensity with respect to the composite index.

We observe the relationship between the asset index and the propensity of term deposit purchases. We adopt a similar strategy of converting the numerical values of the asset index into ordinal values by taking the quantiles and then mapping the quantiles to the propensity of term deposit purchases, as mentioned in *Exercise 3.03, Feature Engineering – Exploration of Individual Features*:

```
# Finding the quantile
np.quantile(bankData['assetIndex'],[0.25,0.5,0.75])
```

You should get the following output:

```
array([0.37668646, 0.56920367, 1.9027249 ])
```

Figure 3.25: Conversion of numerical values into ordinal values

15. Next, create quantiles from the **assetindex** data, as mentioned in the following code snippet:

```
bankData['assetClass'] = 'Quant1'
bankData.loc[(bankData['assetIndex'] > 0.38) \
             & (bankData['assetIndex'] < 0.57), \
             'assetClass'] = 'Quant2'
bankData.loc[(bankData['assetIndex'] > 0.57) \
             & (bankData['assetIndex'] < 1.9), \
             'assetClass'] = 'Quant3'
bankData.loc[bankData['assetIndex'] > 1.9, \
            'assetClass'] = 'Quant4'
bankData.head()
bankData.assetClass[bankData['assetIndex'] > 1.9] = 'Quant4'
bankData.head()
```

You should get the following output:

	age	job	marital	education	default	balance	housing	loan	contact	day	month	duration	campaign	pdays	previous	poutcome	y	balanceTran	loanTran	houseTran	assetIndex	assetClass
0	58	management	married	tertiary	no	2143	yes	no	unknown	5	may	261	1	-1	0	unknown	no	0.092269	5	5	2.306734	Quant4
1	44	technician	single	secondary	no	29	yes	no	unknown	5	may	151	1	-1	0	unknown	no	0.073077	5	5	1.826916	Quant3
2	33	entrepreneur	married	secondary	no	2	yes	yes	unknown	5	may	76	1	-1	0	unknown	no	0.072832	1	5	0.364158	Quant1
3	47	blue-collar	married	unknown	no	1506	yes	no	unknown	5	may	92	1	-1	0	unknown	no	0.086486	5	5	2.162153	Quant4
4	33	unknown	single	unknown	no	1	no	no	unknown	5	may	198	1	-1	0	unknown	no	0.072822	5	1	0.364112	Quant1

Figure 3.26: Quantiles for the asset index

16. Calculate the total of each asset class and the category-wise counts, as mentioned in the following code snippet:

```
# Calculating total of each asset class
assetTot = bankData.groupby('assetClass')['y']\
                   .agg(assetTot='count').reset_index()
# Calculating the category wise counts
assetProp = bankData.groupby(['assetClass', 'y'])['y']\
                    .agg(assetCat='count').reset_index()
```

17. Next, merge both DataFrames:

```
# Merging both the data frames
assetComb = pd.merge(assetProp, assetTot, on = ['assetClass'])
assetComb['catProp'] = (assetComb.assetCat \
                        / assetComb.assetTot)*100
assetComb
```

You should get the following output:

	assetClass	y	assetCat	assetTot	catProp
0	Quant1	no	10921	12212	89.428431
1	Quant1	yes	1291	12212	10.571569
2	Quant2	no	8436	10400	81.115385
3	Quant2	yes	1964	10400	18.884615
4	Quant3	no	10144	11121	91.214819
5	Quant3	yes	977	11121	8.785181
6	Quant4	no	10421	11478	90.791079
7	Quant4	yes	1057	11478	9.208921

Figure 3.27: Composite index relationship mapping

From the new feature we created, we can see that 18.88% (we get this percentage from **catProp**) of customers who are in **Quant2** have bought term deposits compared to 10.57 % for **Quant1**, 8.78% for **Quant3**, and 9.28% for **Quant4**. Since **Quant2** has the highest proportion of customers who have bought term deposits, we can conclude that customers in **Quant2** have higher propensity to purchase the term deposits than all other customers.

> **NOTE**
>
> To access the source code for this specific section, please refer to https://packt.live/316hUrO.
>
> You can also run this example online at https://packt.live/3kVc7Ny.

Similar to the exercise that we just completed, you should think of new variables that can be created from the existing variables based on business intuitions. Creating new features based on business intuitions is the essence of business-driven feature engineering. In the next section, we will look at another type of feature engineering called data-driven feature engineering.

DATA-DRIVEN FEATURE ENGINEERING

The previous section dealt with business-driven feature engineering. In addition to features we can derive from the business perspective, it would also be imperative to transform data through feature engineering from the perspective of data structures. We will look into different methods of identifying data structures and take a peek into some data transformation techniques.

A QUICK PEEK AT DATA TYPES AND A DESCRIPTIVE SUMMARY

Looking at the data types such as categorical or numeric and then deriving summary statistics is a good way to take a quick peek into data before you do some of the downstream feature engineering steps. Let's take a look at an example from our dataset:

```
# Looking at Data types
print(bankData.dtypes)
# Looking at descriptive statistics
print(bankData.describe())
```

You should get the following output:

```
age                 int64
job                object
marital            object
education          object
default            object
balance             int64
housing            object
loan               object
contact            object
day                 int64
month              object
duration            int64
campaign            int64
pdays               int64
previous            int64
poutcome           object
y                  object
balanceClass       object
balanceTran       float64
loanTran            int64
houseTran           int64
assetIndex        float64
assetClass         object
```

Figure 3.28: Output showing the different data types in the dataset

In the preceding output, you see the different types of information in the dataset and its corresponding data types. For instance, **age** is an integer and so is **day**.

The following output is that of a descriptive summary statistic, which displays some of the basic measures such as **`mean`**, **`standard deviation`**, **`count`**, and the **`quantile values`** of the respective features:

```
                age        balance           day      duration      campaign  \
count  45211.000000   45211.000000  45211.000000  45211.000000  45211.000000
mean      40.936210    1362.272058     15.806419    258.163080      2.763841
std       10.618762    3044.765829      8.322476    257.527812      3.098021
min       18.000000   -8019.000000      1.000000      0.000000      1.000000
25%       33.000000      72.000000      8.000000    103.000000      1.000000
50%       39.000000     448.000000     16.000000    180.000000      2.000000
75%       48.000000    1428.000000     21.000000    319.000000      3.000000
max       95.000000  102127.000000     31.000000   4918.000000     63.000000

              pdays      previous   balanceTran      loanTran     houseTran  \
count  45211.000000  45211.000000  45211.000000  45211.000000  45211.000000
mean      40.197828      0.580323      0.085171      4.359094      3.223353
std      100.128746      2.303441      0.027643      1.467280      1.987511
min       -1.000000      0.000000      0.000000      1.000000      1.000000
25%       -1.000000      0.000000      0.073457      5.000000      1.000000
50%       -1.000000      0.000000      0.076871      5.000000      5.000000
75%       -1.000000      0.000000      0.085768      5.000000      5.000000
max      871.000000    275.000000      1.000000      5.000000      5.000000

         assetIndex
count  45211.000000
mean       1.179050
std        0.951987
min        0.000000
25%        0.376636
50%        0.569154
75%        1.902475
max       15.107902
```

Figure 3.29: Data types and a descriptive summary

The purpose of a descriptive summary is to get a quick feel of the data with respect to the distribution and some basic statistics such as mean and standard deviation. Getting a perspective on the summary statistics is critical for thinking about what kind of transformations are required for each variable.

For instance, in the earlier exercises, we converted the numerical data into categorical variables based on the quantile values. Intuitions for transforming variables would come from the quick summary statistics that we can derive from the dataset.

In the following sections, we will be looking at the correlation matrix and visualization.

CORRELATION MATRIX AND VISUALIZATION

Correlation, as you know, is a measure that indicates how two variables fluctuate together. Any correlation value of 1, or near 1, indicates that those variables are highly correlated. Highly correlated variables can sometimes be damaging for the veracity of models and, in many circumstances, we make the decision to eliminate such variables or to combine them to form composite or interactive variables.

Let's look at how data correlation can be generated and then visualized in the following exercise.

EXERCISE 3.05: FINDING THE CORRELATION IN DATA TO GENERATE A CORRELATION PLOT USING BANK DATA

In this exercise, we will be creating a correlation plot and analyzing the results of the bank dataset.

The following steps will help you to complete the exercise:

1. Open a new Colab notebook, install the **pandas** packages and load the banking data:

```
import pandas as pd
file_url = 'https://raw.githubusercontent.com'\
           '/PacktWorkshops/The-Data-Science-Workshop'\
           '/master/Chapter03/bank-full.csv'
bankData = pd.read_csv(file_url, sep=";")
```

2. Now, **import** the **set_option** library from **pandas**, as mentioned here:

```
from pandas import set_option
```

   The **set_option** function is used to define the display options for many operations.

3. Next, create a variable that would store numerical variables such as **'age'**, **'balance'**, **'day'**, **'duration'**, **'campaign'**, **'pdays'**, **'previous'**, as mentioned in the following code snippet. A correlation plot can be extracted only with numerical data. This is why the numerical data has to be extracted separately:

```
bankNumeric = bankData[['age','balance','day','duration',\
                        'campaign','pdays','previous']]
```

4. Now, use the **.corr()** function to find the correlation matrix for the dataset:

```
set_option('display.width',150)
set_option('precision',3)
bankCorr = bankNumeric.corr(method = 'pearson')
bankCorr
```

You should get the following output:

	age	balance	day	duration	campaign	pdays	previous
age	1.000	0.098	-0.009	-0.005	0.005	-0.024	0.001
balance	0.098	1.000	0.005	0.022	-0.015	0.003	0.017
day	-0.009	0.005	1.000	-0.030	0.162	-0.093	-0.052
duration	-0.005	0.022	-0.030	1.000	-0.085	-0.002	0.001
campaign	0.005	-0.015	0.162	-0.085	1.000	-0.089	-0.033
pdays	-0.024	0.003	-0.093	-0.002	-0.089	1.000	0.455
previous	0.001	0.017	-0.052	0.001	-0.033	0.455	1.000

Figure 3.30: Correlation matrix

The method we use for correlation is the **Pearson** correlation coefficient. We can see from the correlation matrix that the diagonal elements have a correlation of 1. This is because the diagonals are a correlation of a variable with itself, which will always be 1. This is the Pearson correlation coefficient.

5. Now, plot the data:

```
from matplotlib import pyplot
corFig = pyplot.figure()
figAxis = corFig.add_subplot(111)
corAx = figAxis.matshow(bankCorr,vmin=-1,vmax=1)
corFig.colorbar(corAx)
pyplot.show()
```

You should get the following output:

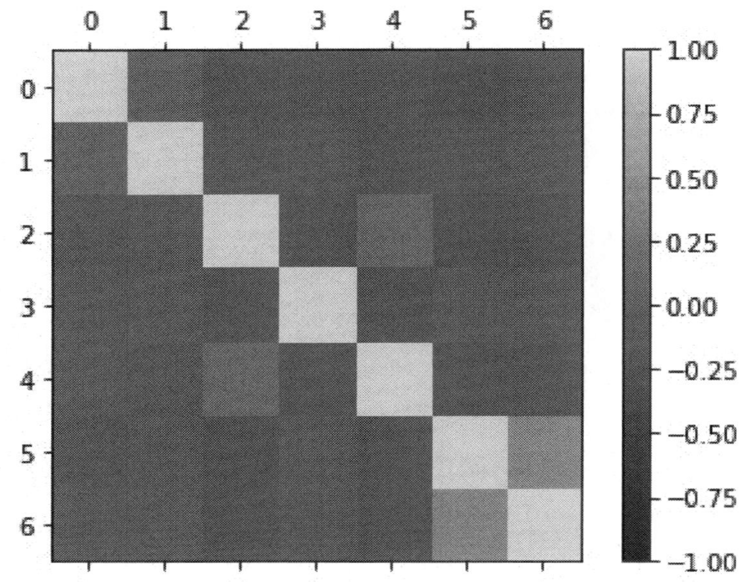

Figure 3.31: Correlation plot

We used many plotting parameters in this code block. **`pyplot.figure()`** is the plotting class that is instantiated. **`.add_subplot()`** is a grid parameter for the plotting. For example, 111 means a 1 x 1 grid for the first subplot. The **`.matshow()`** function is to display the plot, and the **`vmin`** and **`vmax`** arguments are for normalizing the data in the plot.

Let's look at the plot of the correlation matrix to visualize the matrix for quicker identification of correlated variables. Some obvious candidates are the high correlation between **`'balance'`** and **`'balanceTran'`** and the **`'asset index'`** with many of the transformed variables that we created in the earlier exercise. Other than that, there aren't many variables that are highly correlated.

> **NOTE**
>
> To access the source code for this specific section, please refer to https://packt.live/3kXr9SK.
>
> You can also run this example online at https://packt.live/3gbfbkR.

In this exercise, we developed a correlation plot that allows us to visualize the correlation between variables.

SKEWNESS OF DATA

Another area for feature engineering is skewness. Skewed data means data that is shifted in one direction or the other. Skewness can cause machine learning models to underperform. Many machine learning models assume normally distributed data or data structures to follow the Gaussian structure. Any deviation from the assumed Gaussian structure, which is the popular bell curve, can affect model performance. A very effective area where we can apply feature engineering is by looking at the skewness of data and then correcting the skewness through normalization of the data. Skewness can be visualized by plotting the data using histograms and density plots. We will investigate each of these techniques.

Let's take a look at the following example. Here, we use the **`.skew()`** function to find the skewness in data. For instance, to find the skewness of data in our **`bank-full.csv`** dataset, we perform the following:

```
# Skewness of numeric attributes
bankNumeric.skew()
```

> **NOTE**
>
> This code refers to the **`bankNumeric`** data, so you should ensure you are working in the same notebook as the previous exercise.

You should get the following output:

```
age          0.685
balance      8.360
day          0.093
duration     3.144
campaign     4.899
pdays        2.616
previous    41.846
dtype: float64
```

Figure 3.32: Degree of skewness

The preceding matrix is the skewness index. Any value closer to 0 indicates a low degree of skewness. Positive values indicate right skew and negative values, left skew. Variables that show higher values of right skew and left skew are candidates for further feature engineering by normalization. Let's now visualize the skewness by plotting histograms and density plots.

HISTOGRAMS

Histograms are an effective way to plot the distribution of data and to identify skewness in data, if any. The histogram outputs of two columns of **bankData** are listed here. The histogram is plotted with the **pyplot** package from **matplotlib** using the **.hist()** function. The number of subplots we want to include is controlled by the **.subplots()** function. **(1,2)** in subplots would mean one row and two columns. The titles are set by the **set_title()** function:

```
# Histograms
from matplotlib import pyplot as plt

fig, axs = plt.subplots(1,2)

axs[0].hist(bankNumeric['age'])
axs[0].set_title('Distribution of age')

axs[1].hist(bankNumeric['balance'])
axs[1].set_title('Distribution of Balance')

# Ensure plots do not overlap
plt.tight_layout()
```

You should get the following output:

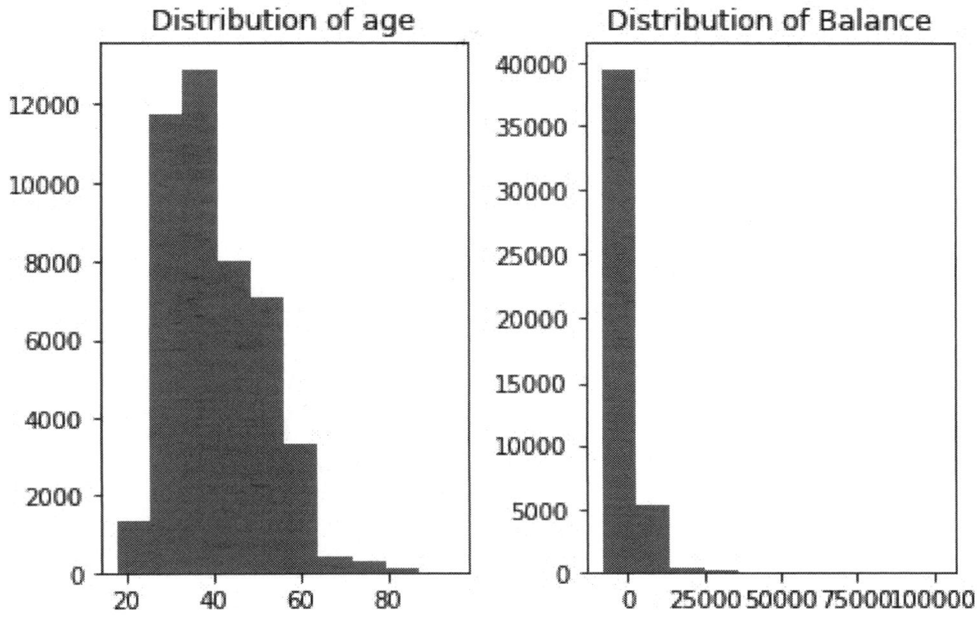

Figure 3.33: Code showing the generation of histograms

From the histogram, we can see that the **age** variable has a distribution closer to the bell curve with a lower degree of skewness. In contrast, the asset index shows a relatively higher right skew, which makes it a more probable candidate for normalization.

DENSITY PLOTS

Density plots help in visualizing the distribution of data. A density plot can be created using the **kind = 'density'** parameter:

```
from matplotlib import pyplot as plt
# Density plots
bankNumeric['age'].plot(kind = 'density', subplots = False, \
                        layout = (1,1))
plt.title('Age Distribution')
plt.xlabel('Age')
plt.ylabel('Normalised age distribution')

pyplot.show()
```

You should get the following output:

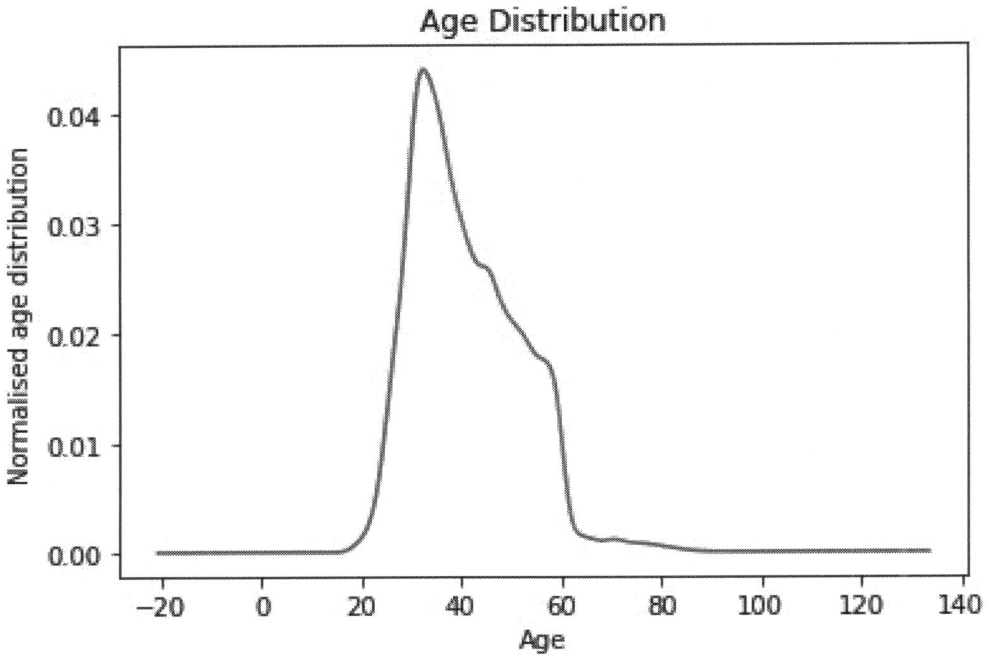

Figure 3.34: Code showing the generation of a density plot

Density plots help in getting a smoother visualization of the distribution of the data. From the density plot of Age, we can see that it has a distribution similar to a bell curve.

OTHER FEATURE ENGINEERING METHODS

So far, we were looking at various descriptive statistics and visualizations that are precursors for applying many feature engineering techniques on data structures. We investigated one such feature engineering technique in *Exercise 3.02, Business Hypothesis Testing for Age versus Propensity for a Term Loan* where we applied the **min max** scaler for normalizing data.

We will now look into two other similar data transformation techniques, namely, standard scaler and normalizer. Standard scaler standardizes data to a mean of 0 and standard deviation of 1. The mean is the average of the data and the standard deviation is a measure of the spread of data. By standardizing to the same mean and standard deviation, comparison across different distributions of data is enabled.

The normalizer function normalizes the length of data. This means that each value in a row is divided by the normalization of the row vector to normalize the row. The normalizer function is applied on the rows while standard scaler is applied columnwise. The normalizer and standard scaler functions are important feature engineering steps that are applied to the data before downstream modeling steps. Let's look at both of these techniques:

```
# Standardize data (0 mean, 1 stdev)
from sklearn.preprocessing import StandardScaler
from numpy import set_printoptions

scaling = StandardScaler().fit(bankNumeric)
rescaledNum = scaling.transform(bankNumeric)

set_printoptions(precision = 3)
print(rescaledNum)
```

You should get the following output:

```
[[ 1.607  0.256 -1.298 ...  0.437  0.894  1.184]
 [ 0.289 -0.438 -1.298 ...  0.437  0.894  0.68 ]
 [-0.747 -0.447 -1.298 ... -2.289  0.894 -0.856]
 ...
 [ 2.925  1.43   0.143 ...  0.437 -1.119 -0.584]
 [ 1.513 -0.228  0.143 ...  0.437 -1.119 -0.824]
 [-0.371  0.528  0.143 ...  0.437 -1.119 -0.714]]
```

Figure 3.35: Output from standardizing the data

The following code uses the normalizer data transmission techniques:

```
# Normalizing Data (Length of 1)
from sklearn.preprocessing import Normalizer
normaliser = Normalizer().fit(bankNumeric)
normalisedNum = normaliser.transform(bankNumeric)

set_printoptions(precision = 3)
print(normalisedNum)
```

You should get the following output:

```
[[2.686e-02 9.923e-01 2.315e-03 ... 2.315e-03 2.315e-03 1.068e-03]
 [2.747e-01 1.810e-01 3.121e-02 ... 3.121e-02 3.121e-02 1.140e-02]
 [3.966e-01 2.404e-02 6.010e-02 ... 1.202e-02 6.010e-02 4.376e-03]
 ...
 [1.235e-02 9.805e-01 2.917e-03 ... 8.579e-04 1.716e-04 1.070e-04]
 [6.775e-02 7.940e-01 2.021e-02 ... 5.943e-03 1.189e-03 4.687e-04]
 [1.234e-02 9.906e-01 5.668e-03 ... 1.667e-03 3.334e-04 1.663e-04]]
```

Figure 3.36 Output by the normalizer

The output from standard scaler is normalized along the columns. The output would have 11 columns corresponding to 11 numeric columns (age, balance, day, duration, and so on). If we observe the output, we can see that each value along a column is normalized so as to have a mean of 0 and standard deviation of 1. By transforming data in this way, we can easily compare across columns.

For instance, in the **age** variable, we have data ranging from 18 up to 95. In contrast, for the balance data, we have data ranging from -8,019 to 102,127. We can see that both of these variables have different ranges of data that cannot be compared. The standard scaler function converts these data points at very different scales into a common scale so as to compare the distribution of data. Normalizer rescales each row so as to have a vector with a length of 1.

The big question we have to think about is why do we have to standardize or normalize data? Many machine learning algorithms converge faster when the features are of a similar scale or are normally distributed. Standardizing is more useful in algorithms that assume input variables to have a Gaussian structure. Algorithms such as linear regression, logistic regression, and linear discriminate analysis fall under this genre. Normalization techniques would be more congenial for sparse datasets (datasets with lots of zeros) when using algorithms such as k-nearest neighbor or neural networks.

SUMMARIZING FEATURE ENGINEERING

In this section, we investigated the process of feature engineering from a business perspective and data structure perspective. Feature engineering is a very important step in the life cycle of a data science project and helps determine the veracity of the models that we build. As seen in *Exercise 3.02, Business Hypothesis Testing for Age versus Propensity for a Term Loan* we translated our understanding of the domain and our intuitions to build intelligent features. Let's summarize the processes that we followed:

1. We obtain intuitions from a business perspective through EDA
2. Based on the business intuitions, we devised a new feature that is a combination of three other variables.
3. We verified the influence of constituent variables of the new feature and devised an approach for weights to be applied.
4. Converted ordinal data into corresponding weights.
5. Transformed numerical data by normalizing them using an appropriate normalizer.
6. Combined all three variables into a new feature.
7. Observed the relationship between the composite index and the propensity to purchase term deposits and derived our intuitions.
8. Explored techniques for visualizing and extracting summary statistics from data.
9. Identified techniques for transforming data into feature engineered data structures.

Now that we have completed the feature engineering step, the next question is where do we go from here and what is the relevance of the new feature we created? As you will see in the subsequent sections, the new features that we created will be used for the modeling process. The preceding exercises are an example of a trail we can follow in creating new features. There will be multiple trails like these, which should be thought of as based on more domain knowledge and understanding. The veracity of the models that we build will be dependent on all such intelligent features we can build by translating business knowledge into data.

BUILDING A BINARY CLASSIFICATION MODEL USING THE LOGISTIC REGRESSION FUNCTION

The essence of data science is about mapping a business problem into its data elements and then transforming those data elements to get our desired business outcomes. In the previous sections, we discussed how we do the necessary transformation on the data elements. The right transformation of the data elements can highly influence the generation of the right business outcomes by the downstream modeling process.

Let's look at the business outcome generation process from the perspective of our use case. The desired business outcome, in our use case, is to identify those customers who are likely to buy a term deposit. To correctly identify which customers are likely to buy a term deposit, we first need to learn the traits or features that, when present in a customer, helps in the identification process. This learning of traits is what is achieved through machine learning.

By now, you may have realized that the goal of machine learning is to estimate a mapping function (*f*) between an output variable and input variables. In mathematical form, this can be written as follows:

$$Y = f(X)$$

Figure 3.37: A mapping function in mathematical form

Let's look at this equation from the perspective of our use case.

Y is the dependent variable, which is our prediction as to whether a customer has the probability to buy a term deposit or not.

X is the independent variable(s), which are those attributes such as age, education, and marital status and are part of the dataset.

f() is a function that connects various attributes of the data to the probability or whether a customer will buy a term deposit or not. This function is learned during the machine learning process. This function is a combination of different coefficients or parameters applied to each of the attributes to get the probability of term deposit purchases. Let's unravel this concept using a simple example of our bank data use case.

For simplicity, let's assume that we have only two attributes, age and bank balance. Using these, we have to predict whether a customer is likely to buy a term deposit or not. Let the age be 40 years and the balance $1,000. With all of these attribute values, let's assume that the mapping equation is as follows:

$$Y = M_0 + M_1 age * Age + M_2 balance * balance$$

Figure 3.38: Updated mapping equation

Using the preceding equation, we get the following:

*Y = 0.1 + 0.4 * 40 + 0.002 * 1000*

Y = 18.1

Now, you might be wondering, we are getting a real number and how does this represent a decision of whether a customer will buy a term deposit or not? This is where the concept of a decision boundary comes in. Let's also assume that, on analyzing the data, we have also identified that if the value of *Y* goes above 15 (an assumed value in this case), then the customer is likely to buy the term deposit, otherwise they will not buy a term deposit. This means that, as per this example, the customer is likely to buy a term deposit.

Let's now look at the dynamics in this example and try to decipher the concepts. The values such as 0.1, 0.4, and 0.002, which are applied to each of the attributes, are the coefficients. These coefficients, along with the equation connecting the coefficients and the variables, are the functions that we are learning from the data. The essence of machine learning is to learn all of these from the provided data. All of these coefficients along with the functions can also be called by another common name called the **model**. A model is an approximation of the data generation process. During machine learning, we are trying to get as close to the real model that has generated the data we are analyzing. To learn or estimate the data generating models, we use different machine learning algorithms.

Machine learning models can be broadly classified into two types, parametric models and non-parametric models. Parametric models are where we assume the form of the function we are trying to learn and then learn the coefficients from the training data. By assuming a form for the function, we simplify the learning process.

To understand the concept better, let's take the example of a linear model. For a linear model, the mapping function takes the following form:

$$Y = C_0 + M_1 * X_1 + M_2 * X_2$$

Figure 3.39: Linear model mapping function

The terms C_0, M_1, and M_2 are the coefficients of the line that influences the intercept and slope of the line. X_1 and X_2 are the input variables. What we are doing here is that we assume that the data generating model is a linear model and then, using the data, we estimate the coefficients, which will enable the generation of the predictions. By assuming the data generating model, we have simplified the whole learning process. However, these simple processes also come with their pitfalls. Only if the underlying function is linear or similar to linear will we get good results. If the assumptions about the form are wrong, we are bound to get bad results.

Some examples of parametric models include:

- Linear and logistic regression
- Naïve Bayes
- Linear support vector machines
- Perceptron

Machine learning models that do not make strong assumptions on the function are called non-parametric models. In the absence of an assumed form, non-parametric models are free to learn any functional form from the data. Non-parametric models generally require a lot of training data to estimate the underlying function. Some examples of non-parametric models include the following:

- Decision trees
- K –nearest neighbors
- Neural networks
- Support vector machines with Gaussian kernels

LOGISTIC REGRESSION DEMYSTIFIED

Logistic regression is a linear model similar to the linear regression that was covered in the previous chapter. At the core of logistic regression is the sigmoid function, which quashes any real-valued number to a value between 0 and 1, which renders this function ideal for predicting probabilities. The mathematical equation for a logistic regression function can be written as follows:

$$Y = \frac{e^{(C_0 + M_1 * X_1 + M_2 * X_2)}}{(1 + e^{(C_0 + M_1 * X_1 + M_2 * X_2)})}$$

Figure 3.40: Logistic regression function

Here, *Y* is the probability of whether a customer is likely to buy a term deposit or not.

The terms *C0 + M1 * X1 + M2 * X2* are very similar to the ones we have seen in the linear regression function, covered in an earlier chapter. As you would have learned by now, a linear regression function gives a real-valued output. To transform the real-valued output into a probability, we use the logistic function, which has the following form:

$$\frac{e^{X}}{(1 + e^{X})}$$

Figure 3.41: An expression to transform the real-valued output to a probability

Here, *e* is the natural logarithm. We will not dive deep into the math behind this; however, let's realize that, using the logistic function, we can transform the real-valued output into a probability function.

Let's now look at the logistic regression function from the business problem that we are trying to solve. In the business problem, we are trying to predict the probability of whether a customer would buy a term deposit or not. To do that, let's return to the example we derived from the problem statement:

$$Y = M_0 + M_{1age} * Age + M_{2balance} * balance$$

Figure 3.42: The logistic regression function updated with the business problem statement

Adding the following values, we get *Y = 0.1 + 0.4 * 40 + 0.002 * 100.*

To get the probability, we must transform this problem statement using the logistic function, as follows:

$$Y = \frac{e^{(0.1 + 0.4 \times 40 + 0.002 \times 1000)}}{(1 + e^{(0.1 + 0.4 \times 40 + 0.002 \times 1000)})}$$

Figure 3.43: Transformed problem statement to find the probability of using the logistic function

In applying this, we get a value of *Y = 1*, which is a 100% probability that the customer will buy the term deposit. As discussed in the previous example, the coefficients of the model such as 0.1, 0.4, and 0.002 are what we learn using the logistic regression algorithm during the training process.

METRICS FOR EVALUATING MODEL PERFORMANCE

As a data scientist, you always have to make decisions on the models you build. These evaluations are done based on various metrics on the predictions. In this section, we introduce some of the important metrics that are used for evaluating the performance of models.

> **NOTE**
>
> Model performance will be covered in much more detail in *Chapter 6, How to Assess Performance*. This section provides you with an introduction to work with classification models.

CONFUSION MATRIX

As you will have learned, we evaluate a model based on its performance on a test set. A test set will have its labels, which we call the ground truth, and, using the model, we also generate predictions for the test set. The evaluation of model performance is all about comparison of the ground truth and the predictions. Let's see this in action with a dummy test set:

Test Examples	Ground Truth	Predictions	Evaluation
Example 1	Yes	Yes	Correct
Example 2	Yes	No	Misclassified
Example 3	Yes	Yes	Correct
Example 4	No	No	Correct
Example 5	Yes	Yes	Correct
Example 6	No	Yes	Misclassified
Example 7	Yes	No	Misclassified

Figure 3.44: Confusion matrix generation

The preceding table shows a dummy dataset with seven examples. The second column is the ground truth, which are the actual labels, and the third column contains the results of our predictions. From the data, we can see that four have been correctly classified and three were misclassified.

A confusion matrix generates the resultant comparison between prediction and ground truth, as represented in the following table:

	Predicted	
Ground truth	Yes	No
Yes	True positive (TP) = 3	False negative (FN) = 2
No	False positive (FP) = 1	True negative (TN) = 1

Figure 3.45: Confusion matrix

As you can see from the table, there are five examples whose labels (ground truth) are **`Yes`** and the balance is two examples that have the labels of **`No`**.

The first row of the confusion matrix is the evaluation of the label **`Yes`**. **`True positive`** shows those examples whose ground truth and predictions are **`Yes`** (examples 1, 3, and 5). **`False negative`** shows those examples whose ground truth is **`Yes`** and who have been wrongly predicted as **`No`** (examples 2 and 7).

Similarly, the second row of the confusion matrix evaluates the performance of the label **`No`**. **`False positive`** are those examples whose ground truth is **`No`** and who have been wrongly classified as **`Yes`** (example 6). **`True negative`** examples are those examples whose ground truth and predictions are both **`No`** (example 4).

The generation of a confusion matrix is used for calculating many of the matrices such as accuracy and classification reports, which are explained later. It is based on metrics such as accuracy or other detailed metrics shown in the classification report such as precision or recall the models for testing. We generally pick models where these metrics are the highest.

ACCURACY

Accuracy is the first level of evaluation, which we will resort to in order to have a quick check on model performance. Referring to the preceding table, accuracy can be represented as follows:

$$Accuracy = \frac{TP + TN}{TP + FP + TN + FN}$$

Figure 3.46: A function that represents accuracy

Accuracy is the proportion of correct predictions out of all of the predictions.

CLASSIFICATION REPORT

A classification report outputs three key metrics: **precision**, **recall**, and the **F1 score**.

Precision is the ratio of true positives to the sum of true positives and false positives:

$$\frac{tp}{(tp + fp)}$$

Figure 3.47: The precision ratio

Precision is the indicator that tells you, out of all of the positives that were predicted, how many were true positives.

Recall is the ratio of true positives to the sum of true positives and false negatives:

$$\frac{tp}{(tp + fn)}$$

Figure 3.48: The recall ratio

Recall manifests the ability of the model to identify all true positives.

The F1 score is a weighted score of both precision and recall. An F1 score of 1 indicates the best performance and 0 indicates the worst performance.

In the next section, let's take a look at data preprocessing, which is an important process to work with data and come to conclusions in data analysis.

DATA PREPROCESSING

Data preprocessing has an important role to play in the life cycle of data science projects. These processes are often the most time-consuming part of the data science life cycle. Careful implementation of the preprocessing steps is critical and will have a strong bearing on the results of the data science project.

The various preprocessing steps include the following:

- **Data loading**: This involves loading the data from different sources into the notebook.
- **Data cleaning**: Data cleaning process entails removing anomalies, for instance, special characters, duplicate data, and identification of missing data from the available dataset. Data cleaning is one of the most time-consuming steps in the data science process.

- **Data imputation**: Data imputation is filling missing data with new data points.
- **Converting data types**: Datasets will have different types of data such as numerical data, categorical data, and character data. Running models will necessitate the transformation of data types.

> **NOTE**
>
> Data processing will be covered in depth in the following chapters of this book.

We will implement some of these preprocessing steps in the subsequent sections and in *Exercise 3.06, A Logistic Regression Model for Predicting the Propensity of Term Deposit Purchases in a Bank*.

EXERCISE 3.06: A LOGISTIC REGRESSION MODEL FOR PREDICTING THE PROPENSITY OF TERM DEPOSIT PURCHASES IN A BANK

In this exercise, we will build a logistic regression model, which will be used for predicting the propensity of term deposit purchases. This exercise will have three parts. The first part will be the preprocessing of the data, the second part will deal with the training process, and the last part will be spent on prediction, analysis of metrics, and deriving strategies for further improvement of the model.

You begin with data preprocessing.

In this part, we will first load the data, convert the ordinal data into dummy data, and then split the data into training and test sets for the subsequent training phase:

1. Open a Colab notebook, mount the drives, install necessary packages, and load the data, as in previous exercises:

```
import pandas as pd
import altair as alt
file_url = 'https://raw.githubusercontent.com'\
           '/PacktWorkshops/The-Data-Science-Workshop'\
           '/master/Chapter03/bank-full.csv'
bankData = pd.read_csv(file_url, sep=";")
```

2. Now, load the library functions and data:

```
from sklearn.linear_model import LogisticRegression
from sklearn.model_selection import train_test_split
```

3. Now, find the data types:

```
bankData.dtypes
```

You should get the following output:

```
age            int64
job           object
marital       object
education     object
default       object
balance        int64
housing       object
loan          object
contact       object
day            int64
month         object
duration       int64
campaign       int64
pdays          int64
previous       int64
poutcome      object
y             object
dtype: object
```

Figure 3.49: Data types

4. Convert the ordinal data into dummy data.

As you can see in the dataset, we have two types of data: the numerical data and the ordinal data. Machine learning algorithms need numerical representation of data and, therefore, we must convert the ordinal data into a numerical form by creating dummy variables. The dummy variable will have values of either 1 or 0 corresponding to whether that category is present or not. The function we use for converting ordinal data into numerical form is **pd.get_dummies()**. This function converts the data structure into a long form or horizontal form. So, if there are three categories in a variable, there will be three new variables created as dummy variables corresponding to each of the categories.

The value against each variable would be either 1 or 0, depending on whether that category was present in the variable as an example. Let's look at the code for doing that:

```
"""
Converting all the categorical variables to dummy variables
"""
bankCat = pd.get_dummies\
          (bankData[['job','marital',\
                     'education','default','housing',\
                     'loan','contact','month','poutcome']])
bankCat.shape
```

You should get the following output:

```
(45211, 44)
```

We now have a new subset of the data corresponding to the categorical data that was converted into numerical form. Also, we had some numerical variables in the original dataset, which did not need any transformation. The transformed categorical data and the original numerical data have to be combined to get all of the original features. To combine both, let's first extract the numerical data from the original DataFrame.

5. Now, separate the numerical variables:

```
bankNum = bankData[['age','balance','day','duration',\
                    'campaign','pdays','previous']]
bankNum.shape
```

You should get the following output:

```
(45211, 7)
```

6. Now, prepare the **X** and **Y** variables and print the **Y** shape. The **X** variable is the concatenation of the transformed categorical variable and the separated numerical data:

```
# Preparing the X variables
X = pd.concat([bankCat, bankNum], axis=1)
print(X.shape)
# Preparing the Y variable
Y = bankData['y']
print(Y.shape)
X.head()
```

The output shown below is truncated:

```
(45211, 51)
(45211,)
```

	job_admin.	job_blue-collar	job_entrepreneur	job_housemaid	job_management	job_retired	job_self-employed	job_services
0	0	0	0	0	1	0	0	0
1	0	0	0	0	0	0	0	0
2	0	0	1	0	0	0	0	0
3	0	1	0	0	0	0	0	0
4	0	0	0	0	0	0	0	0

Figure 3.50 Combining categorical and numerical DataFrames

Once the DataFrame is created, we can split the data into training and test sets. We specify the proportion in which the DataFrame must be split into training and test sets.

7. Split the data into training and test sets:

```
# Splitting the data into train and test sets
X_train, X_test, y_train, y_test = train_test_split\
                                   (X, Y, test_size=0.3, \
                                    random_state=123)
```

Now, the data is all prepared for the modeling task. Next, we begin with modeling.

In this part, we will train the model using the training set we created in the earlier step. First, we call the **`logistic regression`** function and then fit the model with the training set data.

8. Define the **`LogisticRegression`** function:

```
bankModel = LogisticRegression()
bankModel.fit(X_train, y_train)
```

You should get the following output:

```
LogisticRegression(C=1.0, class_weight=None, dual=False, fit_intercept=True,
          intercept_scaling=1, max_iter=100, multi_class='warn',
          n_jobs=None, penalty='l2', random_state=None, solver='warn',
          tol=0.0001, verbose=0, warm_start=False)
```

Figure 3.51: Parameters of the model that fits

9. Now, that the model is created, use it for predicting on the test sets and then getting the accuracy level of the predictions:

```
pred = bankModel.predict(X_test)
print('Accuracy of Logistic regression model' \
       'prediction on test set: {:.2f}'\
       .format(bankModel.score(X_test, y_test)))
```

You should get the following output:

```
Accuracy of Logistic regression model prediction on test set: 0.89
```

Figure 3.52: Prediction with the model

10. From an initial look, an accuracy metric of 90% gives us the impression that the model has done a decent job of approximating the data generating process. Or is it otherwise? Let's take a closer look at the details of the prediction by generating the metrics for the model. We will use two metric-generating functions, the confusion matrix and classification report:

```
# Confusion Matrix for the model
from sklearn.metrics import confusion_matrix
confusionMatrix = confusion_matrix(y_test, pred)
print(confusionMatrix)
```

You should get the following output in the following format; however, the values can vary as the modeling task will involve variability:

```
[[11754   244]
 [ 1242   324]]
```

Figure 3.53: Generation of the confusion matrix

> **NOTE**
>
> The end results that you get will be different from what you see here as it depends on the system you are using. This is because the modeling part is stochastic in nature and there will always be differences.

11. Next, let's generate a **classification_report**:

```
from sklearn.metrics import classification_report
print(classification_report(y_test, pred))
```

You should get a similar output; however, with different values due to variability in the modeling process:

```
              precision    recall  f1-score   support

          no       0.90      0.98      0.94     11998
         yes       0.57      0.21      0.30      1566

    accuracy                           0.89     13564
   macro avg       0.74      0.59      0.62     13564
weighted avg       0.87      0.89      0.87     13564
```

Figure 3.54: Confusion matrix and classification report

> **NOTE**
>
> To access the source code for this specific section, please refer to https://packt.live/2CGFYYU.
>
> You can also run this example online at https://packt.live/3aDq8KX.

From the metrics, we can see that, out of the total 11,998 examples of **no**, 11,754 were correctly classified as **no** and the balance, 244, were classified as **yes**. This gives a recall value of *11,754/11,998*, which is nearly 98%. From a precision perspective, out of the total 12,996 examples that were predicted as **no**, only 11,754 of them were really **no**, which takes our precision to 11,754/12,996 or 90%.

However, the metrics for **yes** give a different picture. Out of the total 1,566 cases of **yes**, only 324 were correctly identified as **yes**. This gives us a recall of *324/1,566 = 21%*. The precision is *324 / (324 + 244) = 57%*.

From an overall accuracy level, this can be calculated as follows: correctly classified *examples / total examples = (11754 + 324) / 13564 = 89%*.

The metrics might seem good when you look only at the accuracy level. However, looking at the details, we can see that the classifier, in fact, is doing a poor job of classifying the **`yes`** cases. The classifier has been trained to predict mostly **`no`** values, which from a business perspective is useless. From a business perspective, we predominantly want the **`yes`** estimates, so that we can target those cases for focused marketing to try to sell term deposits. However, with the results we have, we don't seem to have done a good job in helping the business to increase revenue from term deposit sales.

In this exercise, we have preprocessed data, then we performed the training process, and finally, we found useful prediction, analysis of metrics, and deriving strategies for further improvement of the model.

What we have now built is the first model or a benchmark model. The next step is to try to improve on the benchmark model through different strategies. One such strategy is to feature engineer variables and build new models with new features. Let's achieve that in the next activity.

ACTIVITY 3.02: MODEL ITERATION 2 – LOGISTIC REGRESSION MODEL WITH FEATURE ENGINEERED VARIABLES

As the data scientist of the bank, you created a benchmark model to predict which customers are likely to buy a term deposit. However, management wants to improve the results you got in the benchmark model. In *Exercise 3.04, Feature Engineering – Creating New Features from Existing Ones,* you discussed the business scenario with the marketing and operations teams and created a new variable, **`assetIndex`**, by feature engineering three raw variables. You are now fitting another logistic regression model on the feature engineered variables and are trying to improve the results.

In this activity, you will be feature engineering some of the variables to verify their effects on the predictions.

The steps are as follows:

1. Open the Colab notebook used for the feature engineering in *Exercise 3.04, Feature Engineering – Creating New Features from Existing Ones,* and execute all of the steps from that exercise.
2. Create dummy variables for the categorical variables using the **`pd.get_dummies()`** function. Exclude original raw variables such as loan and housing, which were used to create the new variable, **`assetIndex`**.

3. Select the numerical variables including the new feature engineered variable, **assetIndex**, that was created.
4. Transform some of the numerical variables by normalizing them using the **MinMaxScaler()** function.
5. Concatenate the numerical variables and categorical variables using the **pd.concat()** function and then create **X** and **Y** variables.
6. Split the dataset using the **train_test_split()** function and then fit a new model using the **LogisticRegression()** model on the new features.
7. Analyze the results after generating the confusion matrix and classification report.

   You should get the following output:

```
              precision    recall  f1-score   support

          no       0.91      0.98      0.94     11969
         yes       0.64      0.32      0.42      1595

   micro avg       0.90      0.90      0.90     13564
   macro avg       0.78      0.65      0.68     13564
weighted avg       0.88      0.90      0.88     13564
```

Figure 3.55: Expected output with the classification report

The classification report will be similar to the one shown here. However, the values can differ due to the variability in the modeling process.

> **NOTE**
>
> The solution to this activity can be found at the following address: https://packt.live/2GbJloz.

Let's now discuss the next steps that need to be adopted in order to improve upon the metrics we got from our two iterations.

NEXT STEPS

The next obvious question we can ask is where do we go from all of the processes that we have implemented in this chapter? Let's discuss strategies that we can adopt for further improvement:

- **Class imbalance**: Class imbalance implies use cases where one class outnumbers the other class(es) in the dataset. In the dataset that we used for training, out of the total 31,647 examples, 27,953 or 88% of them belonged to the `no` class. When there are class imbalances, there is a high likelihood that the classifier overfits to the majority class. This is what we have seen in our example. This is also the reason why we shouldn't draw our conclusions on the performance of our classifier by only looking at the accuracy values.

  Class imbalance is very prevalent in many use cases such as fraud detection, medical diagnostics, and customer churn, to name a few. There are different strategies for addressing use cases where there are class imbalances. We will deal with class imbalance scenarios in *Chapter 13*, *Imbalanced Datasets*.

- **Feature engineering**: Data science is an iterative science. Getting the desired outcome will depend on the variety of experiments we undertake. One big area to make improvements in the initial model is to make changes to the raw variables through feature engineering. We dealt with feature engineering and built a model using feature engineered variables. In building the new features, we followed a trail of creating a new feature related to the asset portfolio. Similarly, there would be other trails that we could follow from a business perspective, which have the potential to yield more features similar to what we created. Identification of such trails would depend on extending the business knowledge we apply through the hypotheses we formulate and the exploratory analysis we do to validate those business hypotheses. A very potent way to improve the veracity of the models is to identify more business trails and then build models through innovative feature engineering.

- **Model selection strategy**: When we discussed parametric and non-parametric models, we touched upon the point that if the real data generation process is not similar to the model that we have assumed, we will get poor results. In our case, we assumed linearity and, therefore, adopted a linear model. What if the real data generation process is not linear? Or, what if there are other parametric or non-parametric models that are much more suitable for this use case? These are all considerations when we try to analyze results and try to improve the model. We must adopt a strategy called model spot checking, which entails working out the use case with different models and checking the initial metrics before adopting a model for the use case. In subsequent chapters, we will discuss other modeling techniques and it will be advisable to try out this use case with other types of models to spot check which modeling technique is more apt for this use case.

SUMMARY

In this chapter, we learned about binary classification using logistic regression from the perspective of solving a use case. Let's summarize our learnings in this chapter. We were introduced to classification problems and specifically binary classification problems. We also looked at the classification problem from the perspective of predicting term deposit propensity through a business discovery process. In the business discovery process, we identified different business drivers that influence business outcomes.

Intuitions derived from the exploratory analysis were used to create new features from the raw variables. A benchmark logistic regression model was built, and the metrics were analyzed to identify a future course of action, and we iterated on the benchmark model by building a second model by incorporating the feature engineered variables.

Having equipped yourselves to solve binary classification problems, it is time to take the next step forward. In the next chapter, you will deal with multiclass classification, where you will be introduced to different techniques for solving such problems.

4

MULTICLASS CLASSIFICATION WITH RANDOMFOREST

OVERVIEW

This chapter will show you how to train a multiclass classifier using the Random Forest algorithm. You will also see how to evaluate the performance of multiclass models.

By the end of the chapter, you will be able to implement a Random Forest classifier, as well as tune hyperparameters in order to improve model performance.

INTRODUCTION

In the previous chapter, you saw how to build a binary classifier using the famous **Logistic Regression** algorithm. A binary classifier can only take two different values for its response variables, such as 0 and 1 or yes and no. A multiclass classification task is just an extension. Its response variable can have more than two different values.

In the data science industry, quite often you will face multiclass classification problems. For example, if you were working for Netflix or any other streaming platform, you would have to build a model that could predict the user rating for a movie based on key attributes such as genre, duration, or cast. A potential list of rating values may be: *Hate it*, *Dislike it*, *Neutral*, *Like it*, *Love it*. The objective of the model would be to predict the right rating from those five possible values.

Multiclass classification doesn't always mean the response variable will be text. In some datasets, the target variable may be encoded into a numerical form. Taking the same example as discussed, the rating may be coded from 1 to 5: 1 for *Hate it*, 2 for *Dislike it*, 3 for *Neutral*, and so on. So, it is important to understand the meaning of this response variable first before jumping to the conclusion that this is a regression problem.

In the next section, we will be looking at training our first Random Forest classifier.

TRAINING A RANDOM FOREST CLASSIFIER

In this chapter, we will use the Random Forest algorithm for multiclass classification. There are other algorithms on the market, but Random Forest is probably one of the most popular for such types of projects.

The Random Forest methodology was first proposed in 1995 by Tin Kam Ho but it was first developed by Leo Breiman in 2001.

So Random Forest is not really a recent algorithm per se. It has been in use for almost two decades already. But its popularity hasn't faded, thanks to its performance and simplicity.

For the examples in this chapter, we will be using a dataset called "Activity Recognition system based on Multisensor data." It was originally shared by *F. Palumbo, C. Gallicchio, R. Pucci, and A. Micheli, Human activity recognition using multisensor data fusion based on Reservoir Computing, Journal of Ambient Intelligence and Smart Environments, 2016, 8 (2), pp. 87-107.*

> **NOTE**
>
> The complete dataset can be found here: https://packt.live/3a5Fl1s

Let's see how we can train a Random Forest classifier on this dataset. First, we need to load the data from the GitHub repository using **pandas** and then we will print its first five rows using the **head()** method.

> **NOTE**
>
> All the example code given outside of Exercises in this chapter relates to this Activity Recognition dataset. It is recommended that all code from these examples is entered and run in a single Google Colab Notebook, and kept separate from your Exercise Notebooks.

```
import pandas as pd

file_url = 'https://raw.githubusercontent.com/PacktWorkshops'\
           '/The-Data-Science-Workshop/master/Chapter04/'\
           'Dataset/activity.csv'

df = pd.read_csv(file_url)
df.head()
```

The output will be as follows:

	avg_rss12	var_rss12	avg_rss13	var_rss13	avg_rss23	var_rss23	Activity
0	42.00	0.00	18.50	0.50	12.00	0.00	bending1
1	42.00	0.00	18.00	0.00	11.33	0.94	bending1
2	42.75	0.43	16.75	1.79	18.25	0.43	bending1
3	42.50	0.50	16.75	0.83	19.00	1.22	bending1
4	43.00	0.82	16.25	0.83	18.00	0.00	bending1

Figure 4.1: First five rows of the dataset

Each row represents an activity that was performed by a person and the name of the activity is stored in the **Activity** column. There are seven different activities in this variable: **bending1**, **bending2**, **cycling**, **lying**, **sitting**, **standing**, and **Walking**. The other six columns are different measurements taken from sensor data.

In this example, you will accurately predict the target variable (**'Activity'**) from the features (the six other columns) using Random Forest. For example, for the first row of the preceding example, the model will receive the following features as input and will predict the **'bending1'** class:

	avg_rss12	var_rss12	avg_rss13	var_rss13	avg_rss23	var_rss23	Activity
0	42.00	0.00	18.50	0.50	12.00	0.00	bending1

Figure 4.2: Features for the first row of the dataset

But before that, we need to do a bit of data preparation. The **sklearn** package (we will use it to train Random Forest model) requires the target variable and the features to be separated. So, we need to extract the response variable using the **.pop()** method from **pandas**. The **.pop()** method extracts the specified column and removes it from the DataFrame:

```
target = df.pop('Activity')
```

Now the response variable is contained in the variable called **target** and all the features are in the DataFrame called **df**.

Now we are going to split the dataset into training and testing sets. The model uses the training set to learn relevant parameters in predicting the response variable. The test set is used to check whether a model can accurately predict unseen data. We say the model is overfitting when it has learned the patterns relevant only to the training set and makes incorrect predictions about the testing set. In this case, the model performance will be much higher for the training set compared to the testing one. Ideally, we want to have a very similar level of performance for the training and testing sets. This topic will be covered in more depth in *Chapter 7, The Generalization of Machine Learning Models*.

The **sklearn** package provides a function called **train_test_split()** to randomly split the dataset into two different sets. We need to specify the following parameters for this function: the feature and target variables, the ratio of the testing set (**test_size**), and **random_state** in order to get reproducible results if we have to run the code again:

```
from sklearn.model_selection import train_test_split
X_train, X_test, y_train, y_test = train_test_split\
                                   (df, target, test_size=0.33, \
                                    random_state=42)
```

There are four different outputs to the **train_test_split()** function: the features for the training set, the target variable for the training set, the features for the testing set, and its target variable.

Now that we have got our training and testing sets, we are ready for modeling. Let's first import the **RandomForestClassifier** class from **sklearn.ensemble**:

```
from sklearn.ensemble import RandomForestClassifier
```

Now we can instantiate the Random Forest classifier with some hyperparameters. Remember from *Chapter 1, Introduction to Data Science in Python*, a hyperparameter is a type of parameter the model can't learn but is set by data scientists to tune the model's learning process. This topic will be covered more in depth in *Chapter 8, Hyperparameter Tuning*. For now, we will just specify the **random_state** value. We will walk you through some of the key hyperparameters in the following sections:

```
rf_model = RandomForestClassifier(random_state=1, \
                                  n_estimators=10)
```

The next step is to train (also called fit) the model with the training data. During this step, the model will try to learn the relationship between the response variable and the independent variables and save the parameters learned. We need to specify the features and target variables as parameters:

```
rf_model.fit(X_train, y_train)
```

The output will be as follows:

```
RandomForestClassifier(bootstrap=True, class_weight=None, criterion='gini',
                       max_depth=None, max_features='auto', max_leaf_nodes=None,
                       min_impurity_decrease=0.0, min_impurity_split=None,
                       min_samples_leaf=1, min_samples_split=2,
                       min_weight_fraction_leaf=0.0, n_estimators=10,
                       n_jobs=None, oob_score=False, random_state=1, verbose=0,
                       warm_start=False)
```

Figure 4.3: Logs of the trained RandomForest

Now that the model has completed its training, we can use the parameters it learned to make predictions on the input data we will provide. In the following example, we are using the features from the training set:

```
preds = rf_model.predict(X_train)
```

Now we can print these predictions:

```
preds
```

The output will be as follows:

```
array(['lying', 'bending1', 'cycling', ..., 'cycling', 'bending1',
       'standing'], dtype=object)
```

Figure 4.4: Predictions of the RandomForest algorithm on the training set

This output shows us the model predicted, respectively, the values **`lying`**, **`bending1`**, and **`cycling`** for the first three observations and **`cycling`**, **`bending1`**, and **`standing`** for the last three observations. Python, by default, truncates the output for a long list of values. This is why it shows only six values here.

These are basically the key steps required for training a Random Forest classifier. This was quite straightforward, right? Training a machine learning model is incredibly easy but getting meaningful and accurate results is where the challenges lie. In the next section, we will learn how to assess the performance of a trained model.

EVALUATING THE MODEL'S PERFORMANCE

Now that we know how to train a Random Forest classifier, it is time to check whether we did a good job or not. What we want is to get a model that makes extremely accurate predictions, so we need to assess its performance using some kind of metric.

For a classification problem, multiple metrics can be used to assess the model's predictive power, such as F1 score, precision, recall, or ROC AUC. Each of them has its own specificity and depending on the projects and datasets, you may use one or another.

In this chapter, we will use a metric called **accuracy score**. It calculates the ratio between the number of correct predictions and the total number of predictions made by the model:

$$accuracy = \frac{number\ of\ correct\ predictions}{total\ number\ of\ predictions}$$

Figure 4.5: Formula for accuracy score

For instance, if your model made 950 correct predictions out of 1,000 cases, then the accuracy score would be 950/1000 = 0.95. This would mean that your model was 95% accurate on that dataset. The **sklearn** package provides a function to calculate this score automatically and it is called **accuracy_score()**. We need to import it first:

```
from sklearn.metrics import accuracy_score
```

Then, we just need to provide the list of predictions for some observations and the corresponding true value for the target variable. Using the previous example, we will use the **y_train** and **preds** variables, which respectively contain the response variable (also known as the target) for the training set and the corresponding predictions made by the Random Forest model. We will reuse the predictions from the previous section – **preds**:

```
accuracy_score(y_train, preds)
```

The output will be as follows:

```
0.9876688826935449
```

Figure 4.6: Accuracy score on the training set

We achieved an accuracy score of 0.988 on our training data. This means we accurately predicted more than **98%** of these cases. Unfortunately, this doesn't mean you will be able to achieve such a high score for new, unseen data. Your model may have just learned the patterns that are only relevant to this training set, and in that case, the model will overfit.

If we take the analogy of a student learning a subject for a semester, they could memorize by heart all the textbook exercises but when given a similar but unseen exercise, they wouldn't be able to solve it. Ideally, the student should understand the underlying concepts of the subject and be able to apply that learning to any similar exercises. This is exactly the same for our model: we want it to learn the generic patterns that will help it to make accurate predictions even on unseen data.

But how can we assess the performance of a model for unseen data? Is there a way to get that kind of assessment? The answer to these questions is yes.

Remember, in the last section, we split the dataset into training and testing sets. We used the training set to fit the model and assess its predictive power on it. But it hasn't seen the observations from the testing set at all, so we can use it to assess whether our model is capable of generalizing unseen data. Let's calculate the accuracy score for the testing set:

```
test_preds = rf_model.predict(X_test)
accuracy_score(y_test, test_preds)
```

The output will be as follows:

```
0.767868804876279
```

Figure 4.7: Accuracy score on the testing set

OK. Now the accuracy has dropped drastically to **0.77**. The difference between the training and testing sets is quite big. This tells us our model is actually overfitting and learned only the patterns relevant to the training set. In an ideal case, the performance of your model should be equal or very close to equal for those two sets.

In the next sections, we will look at tuning some Random Forest hyperparameters in order to reduce overfitting.

EXERCISE 4.01: BUILDING A MODEL FOR CLASSIFYING ANIMAL TYPE AND ASSESSING ITS PERFORMANCE

In this exercise, we will train a Random Forest classifier to predict the type of an animal based on its attributes and check its accuracy score:

> **NOTE**
>
> The dataset we will be using is the Zoo Data Set shared by Richard S. Forsyth: https://packt.live/36DpRVK. The CSV version of this dataset can be found here: https://packt.live/37RWGhF.

1. Open a new Colab notebook.
2. Import the **pandas** package:

```
import pandas as pd
```

3. Create a variable called **file_url** that contains the URL of the dataset:

```
file_url = 'https://raw.githubusercontent.com'\
           '/PacktWorkshops/The-Data-Science-Workshop'\
           '/master/Chapter04/Dataset'\
           '/openml_phpZNNasq.csv'
```

4. Load the dataset into a DataFrame using the **.read_csv()** method from pandas:

```
df = pd.read_csv(file_url)
```

5. Print the first five rows of the DataFrame:

```
df.head()
```

You should get the following output:

	animal	hair	feathers	eggs	milk	airborne	aquatic	predator	toothed	backbone	breathes	venomous	fins	legs	tail	domestic	catsize	type
0	aardvark	True	False	False	True	False	False	True	True	True	True	False	False	4	False	False	True	mammal
1	antelope	True	False	False	True	False	False	False	True	True	True	False	False	4	True	False	True	mammal
2	bass	False	False	True	False	False	True	True	True	True	False	False	True	0	True	False	False	fish
3	bear	True	False	False	True	False	False	True	True	True	True	False	False	4	False	False	True	mammal
4	boar	True	False	False	True	False	False	True	True	True	True	False	False	4	True	False	True	mammal

Figure 4.8: First five rows of the DataFrame

We will be using the **type** column as our target variable. We will need to remove the **animal** column from the DataFrame and only use the remaining columns as features.

6. Remove the **'animal'** column using the **.drop()** method from **pandas** and specify the **columns='animal'** and **inplace=True** parameters (to directly update the original DataFrame):

```
df.drop(columns='animal', inplace=True)
```

7. Extract the **'type'** column using the **.pop()** method from **pandas**:

```
y = df.pop('type')
```

8. Print the first five rows of the updated DataFrame:

```
df.head()
```

You should get the following output:

	hair	feathers	eggs	milk	airborne	aquatic	predator	toothed	backbone	breathes	venomous	fins	legs	tail	domestic	catsize
0	True	False	False	True	False	False	True	True	True	True	False	False	4	False	False	True
1	True	False	False	True	False	False	False	True	True	True	False	False	4	True	False	True
2	False	False	True	False	False	True	True	True	True	False	False	True	0	True	False	False
3	True	False	False	True	False	False	True	True	True	True	False	False	4	False	False	True
4	True	False	False	True	False	False	True	True	True	True	False	False	4	True	False	True

Figure 4.9: First five rows of the DataFrame

9. Import the **train_test_split** function from **sklearn.model_selection**:

```
from sklearn.model_selection import train_test_split
```

10. Split the dataset into training and testing sets with the **df**, **y**, **test_size=0.4**, and **random_state=188** parameters:

```
X_train, X_test, y_train, y_test = train_test_split\
                                   (df, y, test_size=0.4, \
                                    random_state=188)
```

11. Import **RandomForestClassifier** from **sklearn.ensemble**:

```
from sklearn.ensemble import RandomForestClassifier
```

12. Instantiate the **RandomForestClassifier** object with **random_state** equal to **42**. Set the **n-estimators** value to an initial default value of **10**. We'll discuss later how changing this value affects the result.

```
rf_model = RandomForestClassifier(random_state=42, \
                                  n_estimators=10)
```

13. Fit **RandomForestClassifier** with the training set:

```
rf_model.fit(X_train, y_train)
```

You should get the following output:

```
RandomForestClassifier(bootstrap=True, class_weight=None, criterion='gini',
                       max_depth=None, max_features='auto', max_leaf_nodes=None,
                       min_impurity_decrease=0.0, min_impurity_split=None,
                       min_samples_leaf=1, min_samples_split=2,
                       min_weight_fraction_leaf=0.0, n_estimators=10,
                       n_jobs=None, oob_score=False, random_state=42, verbose=0,
                       warm_start=False)
```

Figure 4.10: Logs of RandomForestClassifier

14. Predict the outcome of the training set with the **.predict()** method, save the results in a variable called '**train_preds**', and print its value:

```
train_preds = rf_model.predict(X_train)
train_preds
```

You should get the following output:

```
array(['mammal', 'mammal', 'mammal', 'fish', 'mammal', 'insect', 'fish',
       'bird', 'mammal', 'mammal', 'fish', 'bird', 'reptile', 'bird',
       'fish', 'mammal', 'mammal', 'bird', 'bird', 'mammal', 'bird',
       'bird', 'mammal', 'invertebrate', 'reptile', 'invertebrate',
       'fish', 'bird', 'mammal', 'mammal', 'amphibian', 'mammal',
       'invertebrate', 'mammal', 'mammal', 'insect', 'mammal', 'fish',
       'invertebrate', 'mammal', 'invertebrate', 'invertebrate', 'insect',
       'amphibian', 'mammal', 'reptile', 'amphibian', 'invertebrate',
       'mammal', 'fish', 'bird', 'mammal', 'mammal', 'bird', 'mammal',
       'mammal', 'fish', 'mammal', 'bird', 'fish'], dtype=object)
```

Figure 4.11: Predictions on the training set

15. Import the **accuracy_score** function from **sklearn.metrics**:

```
from sklearn.metrics import accuracy_score
```

16. Calculate the accuracy score on the training set, save the result in a variable called **train_acc**, and print its value:

```
train_acc = accuracy_score(y_train, train_preds)
print(train_acc)
```

You should get the following output:

```
1.0
```

Figure 4.12: Accuracy score on the training set

Our model achieved an accuracy of **1** on the training set, which means it perfectly predicted the target variable on all of those observations. Let's check the performance on the testing set.

17. Predict the outcome of the testing set with the **.predict()** method and save the results into a variable called **test_preds**:

```
test_preds = rf_model.predict(X_test)
```

18. Calculate the accuracy score on the testing set, save the result in a variable called **test_acc**, and print its value:

```
test_acc = accuracy_score(y_test, test_preds)
print(test_acc)
```

You should get the following output:

```
0.8780487804878049
```

Figure 4.13: Accuracy score on the testing set

In this exercise, we trained a RandomForest to predict the type of animals based on their key attributes. Our model achieved a perfect accuracy score of **1** on the training set but only **0.88** on the testing set. This means our model is overfitting and is not general enough. The ideal situation would be for the model to achieve a very similar, high-accuracy score on both the training and testing sets.

> **NOTE**
>
> To access the source code for this specific section, please refer to https://packt.live/2Q4jpQK.
>
> You can also run this example online at https://packt.live/3h6JieL.

NUMBER OF TREES ESTIMATOR

Now that we know how to fit a Random Forest classifier and assess its performance, it is time to dig into the details. In the coming sections, we will learn how to tune some of the most important hyperparameters for this algorithm. As mentioned in *Chapter 1, Introduction to Data Science in Python*, hyperparameters are parameters that are not learned automatically by machine learning algorithms. Their values have to be set by data scientists. These hyperparameters can have a huge impact on the performance of a model, its ability to generalize to unseen data, and the time taken to learn patterns from the data.

The first hyperparameter you will look at in this section is called **n_estimators**. This hyperparameter is responsible for defining the number of trees that will be trained by the **RandomForest** algorithm.

Before looking at how to tune this hyperparameter, we need to understand what a tree is and why it is so important for the **RandomForest** algorithm.

A tree is a logical graph that maps a decision and its outcomes at each of its nodes. Simply speaking, it is a series of yes/no (or true/false) questions that lead to different outcomes.

A leaf is a special type of node where the model will make a prediction. There will be no split after a leaf. A single node split of a tree may look like this:

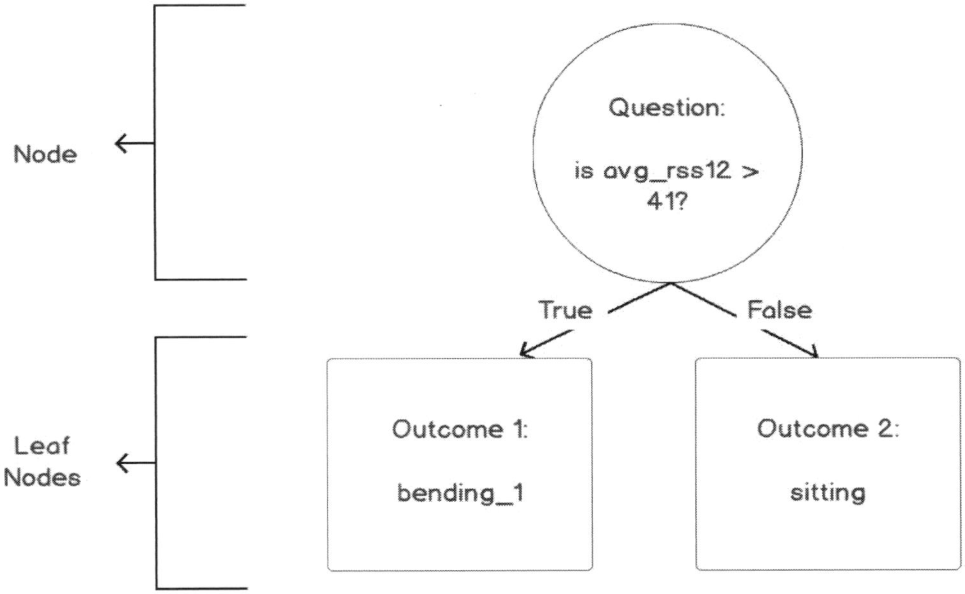

Figure 4.14: Example of a single tree node

A tree node is composed of a question and two outcomes depending on whether the condition defined by the question is met or not. In the preceding example, the question is **is avg_rss12 > 41?** If the answer is yes, the outcome is the **bending_1** leaf and if not, it will be the **sitting** leaf.

A tree is just a series of nodes and leaves combined together:

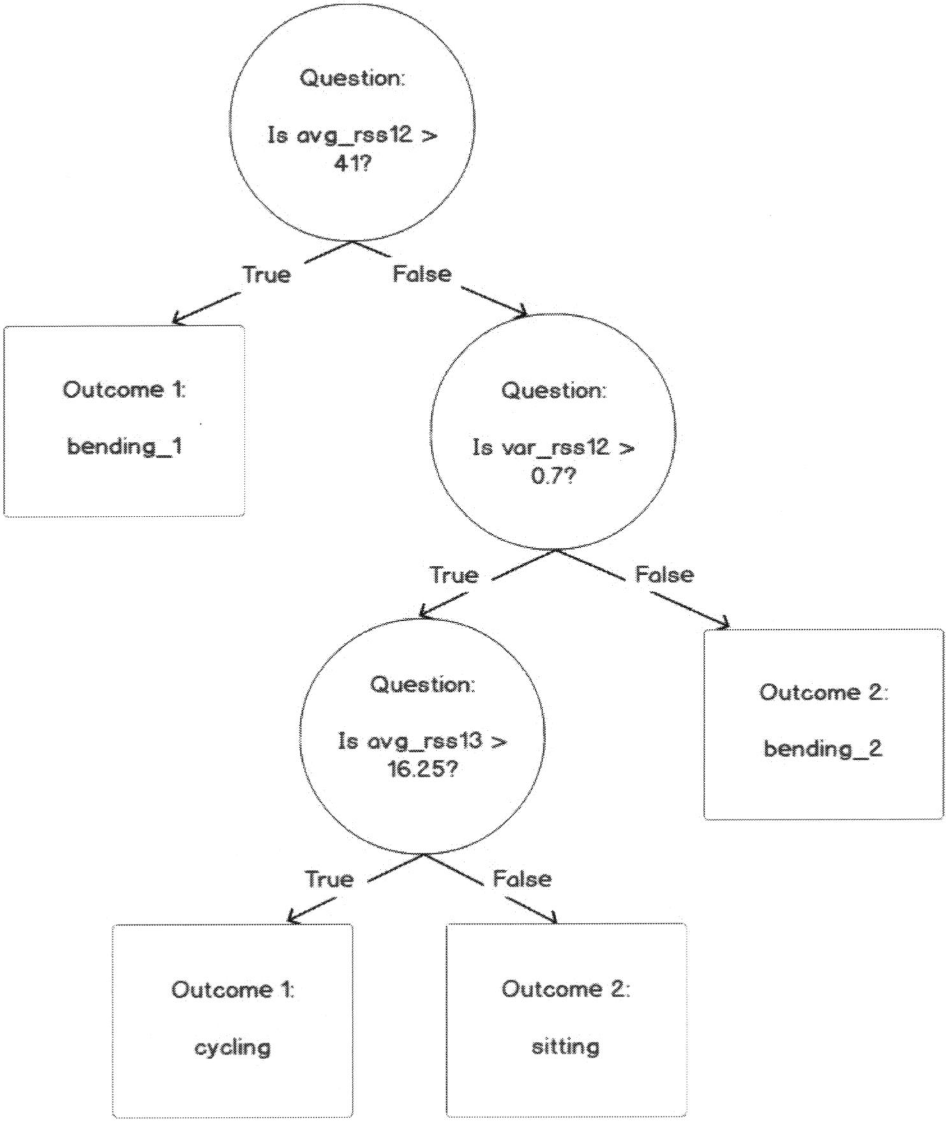

Figure 4.15: Example of a tree

In the preceding example, the tree is composed of three nodes with different questions. Now, for an observation to be predicted as **`sitting`**, it will need to meet the conditions: **`avg_rss13 <= 41`**, **`var_rss > 0.7`**, and **`avg_rss13 <= 16.25`**.

The **RandomForest** algorithm will build this kind of tree based on the training data it sees. We will not go through the mathematical details about how it defines the split for each node but, basically, it will go through every column of the dataset and see which split value will best help to separate the data into two groups of similar classes. Taking the preceding example, the first node with the **avg_rss13 > 41** condition will help to get the group of data on the left-hand side with mostly the **bending_1** class. The **RandomForest** algorithm usually builds several of this kind of tree and this is the reason why it is called a forest.

As you may have guessed now, the **n_estimators** hyperparameter is used to specify the number of trees the **RandomForest** algorithm will build. For example (as in the previous exercise), say we ask it to build 10 trees. For a given observation, it will ask each tree to make a prediction. Then, it will average those predictions and use the result as the final prediction for this input. For instance, if, out of 10 trees, 8 of them predict the outcome **sitting**, then the **RandomForest** algorithm will use this outcome as the final prediction.

> **NOTE**
>
> If you don't pass in a specific **n_estimators** hyperparameter, it will use the default value. The default depends on the version of scikit-learn you're using. In early versions, the default value is 10. From version 0.22 onwards, the default is 100. You can find out which version you are using by executing the following code:
>
> **import sklearn**
>
> **sklearn.__version__**
>
> For more information, see here: https://scikit-learn.org/stable/modules/generated/sklearn.ensemble.RandomForestClassifier.html

In general, the higher the number of trees is, the better the performance you will get. Let's see what happens with **n_estimators = 2** on the Activity Recognition dataset:

```
rf_model2 = RandomForestClassifier(random_state=1, \
                                   n_estimators=2)
rf_model2.fit(X_train, y_train)
preds2 = rf_model2.predict(X_train)
test_preds2 = rf_model2.predict(X_test)
```

```
print(accuracy_score(y_train, preds2))
print(accuracy_score(y_test, test_preds2))
```

The output will be as follows:

```
0.8881978697548073
0.6971917857920326
```

Figure 4.16: Accuracy of RandomForest with n_estimators = 2

As expected, the accuracy is significantly lower than the previous example with **`n_estimators = 10`**. Let's now try with **`50`** trees:

```
rf_model3 = RandomForestClassifier(random_state=1, \
                                   n_estimators=50)
rf_model3.fit(X_train, y_train)
preds3 = rf_model3.predict(X_train)
test_preds3 = rf_model3.predict(X_test)
print(accuracy_score(y_train, preds3))
print(accuracy_score(y_test, test_preds3))
```

The output will be as follows:

```
0.9969618986346415
0.7897830346128728
```

Figure 4.17: Accuracy of RandomForest with n_estimators = 50

With **`n_estimators = 50`**, we respectively gained **`1%`** and **`2%`** on the accuracy scored for the training and testing sets, which is great. But the main drawback of increasing the number of trees is that it requires more computational power. So, it will take more time to train a model. In a real project, you will need to find the right balance between performance and training duration.

EXERCISE 4.02: TUNING N_ESTIMATORS TO REDUCE OVERFITTING

In this exercise, we will train a Random Forest classifier to predict the type of an animal based on its attributes and will try two different values for the **`n_estimators`** hyperparameter:

We will be using the same zoo dataset as in the previous exercise.

1. Open a new Colab notebook.

2. Import the **pandas** package, **train_test_split**, **RandomForestClassifier**, and **accuracy_score** from **sklearn**:

```
import pandas as pd
from sklearn.model_selection import train_test_split
from sklearn.ensemble import RandomForestClassifier
from sklearn.metrics import accuracy_score
```

3. Create a variable called **file_url** that contains the URL to the dataset:

```
file_url = 'https://raw.githubusercontent.com'\
           '/PacktWorkshops/The-Data-Science-Workshop'\
           '/master/Chapter04/Dataset'\
           '/openml_phpZNNasq.csv'
```

4. Load the dataset into a DataFrame using the **.read_csv()** method from **pandas**:

```
df = pd.read_csv(file_url)
```

5. Remove the **animal** column using **.drop()** and then extract the **type** target variable into a new variable called **y** using **.pop()**:

```
df.drop(columns='animal', inplace=True)
y = df.pop('type')
```

6. Split the data into training and testing sets with **train_test_split()** and the **test_size=0.4** and **random_state=188** parameters:

```
X_train, X_test, y_train, y_test = train_test_split\
                                   (df, y, test_size=0.4, \
                                    random_state=188)
```

7. Instantiate **RandomForestClassifier** with **random_state=42** and **n_estimators=1**, and then fit the model with the training set:

```
rf_model = RandomForestClassifier(random_state=42, \
                                  n_estimators=1)
rf_model.fit(X_train, y_train)
```

You should get the following output:

```
RandomForestClassifier(bootstrap=True, class_weight=None, criterion='gini',
                       max_depth=None, max_features='auto', max_leaf_nodes=None,
                       min_impurity_decrease=0.0, min_impurity_split=None,
                       min_samples_leaf=1, min_samples_split=2,
                       min_weight_fraction_leaf=0.0, n_estimators=1,
                       n_jobs=None, oob_score=False, random_state=42, verbose=0,
                       warm_start=False)
```

Figure 4.18: Logs of RandomForestClassifier

8. Make predictions on the training and testing sets with **.predict()** and save the results into two new variables called **train_preds** and **test_preds**:

```
train_preds = rf_model.predict(X_train)
test_preds = rf_model.predict(X_test)
```

9. Calculate the accuracy score for the training and testing sets and save the results in two new variables called **train_acc** and **test_acc**:

```
train_acc = accuracy_score(y_train, train_preds)
test_acc = accuracy_score(y_test, test_preds)
```

10. Print the accuracy scores: **train_acc** and **test_acc**:

```
print(train_acc)
print(test_acc)
```

You should get the following output:

```
0.9166666666666666
0.8048780487804879
```

Figure 4.19: Accuracy scores for the training and testing sets

The accuracy score decreased for both the training and testing sets. But now the difference is smaller compared to the results from *Exercise 4.01, Building a Model for Classifying Animal Type and Assessing Its Performance*.

11. Instantiate another **RandomForestClassifier** with **random_state=42** and **n_estimators=30**, and then fit the model with the training set:

```
rf_model2 = RandomForestClassifier(random_state=42, \
                                   n_estimators=30)
rf_model2.fit(X_train, y_train)
```

You should get the following output:

```
RandomForestClassifier(bootstrap=True, class_weight=None, criterion='gini',
                       max_depth=None, max_features='auto', max_leaf_nodes=None,
                       min_impurity_decrease=0.0, min_impurity_split=None,
                       min_samples_leaf=1, min_samples_split=2,
                       min_weight_fraction_leaf=0.0, n_estimators=30,
                       n_jobs=None, oob_score=False, random_state=42, verbose=0,
                       warm_start=False)
```

Figure 4.20: Logs of RandomForest with n_estimators = 30

12. Make predictions on the training and testing sets with **.predict()** and save the results into two new variables called **train_preds2** and **test_preds2**:

```
train_preds2 = rf_model2.predict(X_train)
test_preds2 = rf_model2.predict(X_test)
```

13. Calculate the accuracy score for the training and testing sets and save the results in two new variables called **train_acc2** and **test_acc2**:

```
train_acc2 = accuracy_score(y_train, train_preds2)
test_acc2 = accuracy_score(y_test, test_preds2)
```

14. Print the accuracy scores: **train_acc** and **test_acc**:

```
print(train_acc2)
print(test_acc2)
```

You should get the following output:

```
1.0
0.9024390243902439
```

Figure 4.21: Accuracy scores for the training and testing sets

This output shows us the model is overfitting less compared to the results from the previous step and still has a very high-performance level for the training set.

In the previous exercise, we achieved an accuracy score of **1** for the training set and **0.88** for the testing one. In this exercise, we trained two additional Random Forest models with **n_estimators = 1** and **30**. The model with the lowest number of trees has the lowest accuracy: **0.92** (training) and **0.8** (testing). On the other hand, increasing the number of trees to **30**, we achieved a higher accuracy: **1** and **0.9**. Our model is overfitting slightly less now. It is not perfect, but it is a good start.

> **NOTE**
>
> To access the source code for this specific section, please refer to https://packt.live/322x8gz.
>
> You can also run this example online at https://packt.live/313gUV8.

MAXIMUM DEPTH

In the previous section, we learned how Random Forest builds multiple trees to make predictions. Increasing the number of trees does improve model performance but it usually doesn't help much to decrease the risk of overfitting. Our model in the previous example is still performing much better on the training set (data it has already seen) than on the testing set (unseen data).

So, we are not confident enough yet to say the model will perform well in production. There are different hyperparameters that can help to lower the risk of overfitting for Random Forest and one of them is called **max_depth**.

This hyperparameter defines the depth of the trees built by Random Forest. Basically, it tells Random Forest model, how many nodes (questions) it can create before making predictions. But how will that help to reduce overfitting, you may ask. Well, let's say you built a single tree and set the **max_depth** hyperparameter to **50**. This would mean that there would be some cases where you could ask 49 different questions (the value **c** includes the final leaf node) before making a prediction. So, the logic would be **IF X1 > value1 AND X2 > value2 AND X1 <= value3 AND … AND X3 > value49 THEN predict class A**.

As you can imagine, this is a very specific rule. In the end, it may apply to only a few observations in the training set, with this case appearing very infrequently. Therefore, your model would be overfitting. By default, the value of this **max_depth** parameter is **None**, which means there is no limit set for the depth of the trees.

What you really want is to find some rules that are generic enough to be applied to bigger groups of observations. This is why it is recommended to not create deep trees with Random Forest. Let's try several values for this hyperparameter on the Activity Recognition dataset: **3**, **10**, and **50**:

```
rf_model4 = RandomForestClassifier(random_state=1, \
                                   n_estimators=50, max_depth=3)
rf_model4.fit(X_train, y_train)
preds4 = rf_model4.predict(X_train)
```

```
test_preds4 = rf_model4.predict(X_test)
print(accuracy_score(y_train, preds4))
print(accuracy_score(y_test, test_preds4))
```

You should get the following output:

```
0.6133747944813782
0.6122922864813874
```

Figure 4.22: Accuracy scores for the training and testing sets and a max_depth of 3

For a **max_depth** of **3**, we got extremely similar results for the training and testing sets but the overall performance decreased drastically to **0.61**. Our model is not overfitting anymore, but it is now underfitting; that is, it is not predicting the target variable very well (only in **61%** of cases). Let's increase **max_depth** to **10**:

```
rf_model5 = RandomForestClassifier(random_state=1, \
                                   n_estimators=50, \
                                   max_depth=10)
rf_model5.fit(X_train, y_train)
preds5 = rf_model5.predict(X_train)
test_preds5 = rf_model5.predict(X_test)
print(accuracy_score(y_train, preds5))
print(accuracy_score(y_test, test_preds5))
```

```
0.811423261133748
0.7637326754226834
```

Figure 4.23: Accuracy scores for the training and testing sets and a max_depth of 10

The accuracy of the training set increased and is relatively close to the testing set. We are starting to get some good results, but the model is still slightly overfitting. Now we will see the results for **max_depth = 50**:

```
rf_model6 = RandomForestClassifier(random_state=1, \
                                   n_estimators=50, \
                                   max_depth=50)
rf_model6.fit(X_train, y_train)
preds6 = rf_model6.predict(X_train)
test_preds6 = rf_model6.predict(X_test)
print(accuracy_score(y_train, preds6))
print(accuracy_score(y_test, test_preds6))
```

The output will be as follows:

```
0.9969618986346415
0.7897830346128728
```

Figure 4.24: Accuracy scores for the training and testing sets and a max_depth of 50

The accuracy jumped to **0.99** for the training set but it didn't improve much for the testing set. So, the model is overfitting with **max_depth = 50**. It seems the sweet spot to get good predictions and not much overfitting is around **10** for the **max_depth** hyperparameter in this dataset.

EXERCISE 4.03: TUNING MAX_DEPTH TO REDUCE OVERFITTING

In this exercise, we will keep tuning our RandomForest classifier that predicts animal type by trying two different values for the **max_depth** hyperparameter:

We will be using the same zoo dataset as in the previous exercise.

1. Open a new Colab notebook.
2. Import the **pandas** package, **train_test_split**, **RandomForestClassifier**, and **accuracy_score** from **sklearn**:

```
import pandas as pd
from sklearn.model_selection import train_test_split
from sklearn.ensemble import RandomForestClassifier
from sklearn.metrics import accuracy_score
```

3. Create a variable called **file_url** that contains the URL to the dataset:

```
file_url = 'https://raw.githubusercontent.com'\
           'PacktWorkshops/The-Data-Science-Workshop'\
           '/master/Chapter04/Dataset'\
           '/openml_phpZNNasq.csv'
```

4. Load the dataset into a DataFrame using the **.read_csv()** method from **pandas**:

```
df = pd.read_csv(file_url)
```

5. Remove the **animal** column using **.drop()** and then extract the **type** target variable into a new variable called **y** using **.pop()**:

```
df.drop(columns='animal', inplace=True)
y = df.pop('type')
```

6. Split the data into training and testing sets with **train_test_split()** and the parameters **test_size=0.4** and **random_state=188**:

```
X_train, X_test, y_train, y_test = train_test_split\
                                   (df, y, test_size=0.4, \
                                    random_state=188)
```

7. Instantiate **RandomForestClassifier** with **random_state=42**, **n_estimators=30**, and **max_depth=5**, and then fit the model with the training set:

```
rf_model = RandomForestClassifier(random_state=42, \
                                  n_estimators=30, \
                                  max_depth=5)
rf_model.fit(X_train, y_train)
```

You should get the following output:

```
RandomForestClassifier(bootstrap=True, class_weight=None, criterion='gini',
                       max_depth=5, max_features='auto', max_leaf_nodes=None,
                       min_impurity_decrease=0.0, min_impurity_split=None,
                       min_samples_leaf=1, min_samples_split=2,
                       min_weight_fraction_leaf=0.0, n_estimators=30,
                       n_jobs=None, oob_score=False, random_state=42, verbose=0,
                       warm_start=False)
```

Figure 4.25: Logs of RandomForest

8. Make predictions on the training and testing sets with **.predict()** and save the results into two new variables called **train_preds** and **test_preds**:

```
train_preds = rf_model.predict(X_train)
test_preds = rf_model.predict(X_test)
```

9. Calculate the accuracy score for the training and testing sets and save the results in two new variables called **train_acc** and **test_acc**:

```
train_acc = accuracy_score(y_train, train_preds)
test_acc = accuracy_score(y_test, test_preds)
```

10. Print the accuracy scores: **train_acc** and **test_acc**:

```
print(train_acc)
print(test_acc)
```

You should get the following output:

```
1.0
0.9024390243902439
```

Figure 4.26: Accuracy scores for the training and testing sets

We got the exact same accuracy scores as for the best result we obtained in the previous exercise. This value for the **max_depth** hyperparameter hasn't impacted the model's performance.

11. Instantiate another **RandomForestClassifier** with **random_state=42**, **n_estimators=30**, and **max_depth=2**, and then fit the model with the training set:

```
rf_model2 = RandomForestClassifier(random_state=42, \
                                   n_estimators=30, \
                                   max_depth=2)
rf_model2.fit(X_train, y_train)
```

You should get the following output:

```
RandomForestClassifier(bootstrap=True, class_weight=None, criterion='gini',
                       max_depth=2, max_features='auto', max_leaf_nodes=None,
                       min_impurity_decrease=0.0, min_impurity_split=None,
                       min_samples_leaf=1, min_samples_split=2,
                       min_weight_fraction_leaf=0.0, n_estimators=30,
                       n_jobs=None, oob_score=False, random_state=42, verbose=0,
                       warm_start=False)
```

Figure 4.27: Logs of RandomForestClassifier with max_depth = 2

12. Make predictions on the training and testing sets with **.predict()** and save the results into two new variables called **train_preds2** and **test_preds2**:

```
train_preds2 = rf_model2.predict(X_train)
test_preds2 = rf_model2.predict(X_test)
```

13. Calculate the accuracy scores for the training and testing sets and save the results in two new variables called **train_acc2** and **test_acc2**:

```
train_acc2 = accuracy_score(y_train, train_preds2)
test_acc2 = accuracy_score(y_test, test_preds2)
```

14. Print the accuracy scores: **train_acc** and **test_acc**:

```
print(train_acc2)
print(test_acc2)
```

You should get the following output:

```
0.9
0.8292682926829268
```

Figure 4.28: Accuracy scores for training and testing sets

You learned how to tune the **`max_depth`** hyperparameter in this exercise. Reducing its value to **2** decreased the accuracy score for the training set to 0.9 but it also helped to reduce the overfitting for the training and testing set (0.83), so we will keep this value as the optimal one and proceed to the next step.

> **NOTE**
>
> To access the source code for this specific section, please refer to https://packt.live/31YXkIY.
>
> You can also run this example online at https://packt.live/2CCkxYX.

MINIMUM SAMPLE IN LEAF

Previously, we learned how to reduce or increase the depth of trees in Random Forest and saw how it can affect its performance and tendency to overfit or not. Now we will go through another important hyperparameter: **`min_samples_leaf`**.

This hyperparameter, as its name implies, is related to the leaf nodes of the trees. We saw earlier that the **`RandomForest`** algorithm builds nodes that will clearly separate observations into two different groups. If we look at the tree example in *Figure 4.15*, the top node is splitting data into two groups: the left-hand group contains mainly observations for the **`bending_1`** class and the right-hand group can be from any class. This sounds like a reasonable split but are we sure it is not increasing the risk of overfitting? For instance, what if this split leads to only one observation falling on the left-hand side? This rule would be very specific (applying to only one single case) and we can't say it is generic enough for unseen data. It may be an edge case in the training set that will never happen again.

It would be great if we could let the model know to not create such specific rules that happen quite infrequently. Luckily, **RandomForest** has such a hyperparameter and, you guessed it, it is **min_samples_leaf**. This hyperparameter will specify the minimum number of observations (or samples) that will have to fall under a leaf node to be considered in the tree. For instance, if we set **min_samples_leaf** to **3**, then **RandomForest** will only consider a split that leads to at least three observations on both the left and right leaf nodes. If this condition is not met for a split, the model will not consider it and will exclude it from the tree. The default value in **sklearn** for this hyperparameter is **1**. Let's try to find the optimal value for **min_samples_leaf** for the Activity Recognition dataset:

```
rf_model7 = RandomForestClassifier(random_state=1, \
                                   n_estimators=50, \
                                   max_depth=10, \
                                   min_samples_leaf=3)
rf_model7.fit(X_train, y_train)
preds7 = rf_model7.predict(X_train)
test_preds7 = rf_model7.predict(X_test)
print(accuracy_score(y_train, preds7))
print(accuracy_score(y_test, test_preds7))
```

The output will be as follows:

```
0.8037029094288369
0.7611929468108265
```

Figure 4.29: Accuracy scores for the training and testing sets for min_samples_leaf=3

With **min_samples_leaf=3**, the accuracy for both the training and testing sets didn't change much compared to the best model we found in the previous section. Let's try increasing it to **10**:

```
rf_model8 = RandomForestClassifier(random_state=1, \
                                   n_estimators=50, \
                                   max_depth=10, \
                                   min_samples_leaf=10)
rf_model8.fit(X_train, y_train)
preds8 = rf_model8.predict(X_train)
test_preds8 = rf_model8.predict(X_test)
print(accuracy_score(y_train, preds8))
print(accuracy_score(y_test, test_preds8))
```

The output will be as follows:

```
0.7930159410965759
0.7623539656048183
```

Figure 4.30: Accuracy scores for the training and testing sets for min_samples_leaf=10

Now the accuracy of the training set dropped a bit but increased for the testing set and their difference is smaller now. So, our model is overfitting less. Let's try another value for this hyperparameter – **25**:

```
rf_model9 = RandomForestClassifier(random_state=1, \
                                   n_estimators=50, \
                                   max_depth=10, \
                                   min_samples_leaf=25)
rf_model9.fit(X_train, y_train)
preds9 = rf_model9.predict(X_train)
test_preds9 = rf_model9.predict(X_test)
print(accuracy_score(y_train, preds9))
print(accuracy_score(y_test, test_preds9))
```

The output will be as follows:

```
0.7810422474801629
0.7593062912705899
```

Figure 4.31: Accuracy scores for the training and testing sets for min_samples_leaf=25

Both accuracies for the training and testing sets decreased but they are quite close to each other now. So, we will keep this value (**25**) as the optimal one for this dataset as the performance is still OK and we are not overfitting too much.

When choosing the optimal value for this hyperparameter, you need to be careful: a value that's too low will increase the chance of the model overfitting, but on the other hand, setting a very high value will lead to underfitting (the model will not accurately predict the right outcome).

For instance, if you have a dataset of **1000** rows, if you set **min_samples_leaf** to **400**, then the model will not be able to find good splits to predict **5** different classes. In this case, the model can only create one single split and the model will only be able to predict two different classes instead of **5**. It is good practice to start with low values first and then progressively increase them until you reach satisfactory performance.

EXERCISE 4.04: TUNING MIN_SAMPLES_LEAF

In this exercise, we will keep tuning our Random Forest classifier that predicts animal type by trying two different values for the **min_samples_leaf** hyperparameter:

We will be using the same zoo dataset as in the previous exercise.

1. Open a new Colab notebook.
2. Import the **pandas** package, **train_test_split**, **RandomForestClassifier**, and **accuracy_score** from **sklearn**:

```
import pandas as pd
from sklearn.model_selection import train_test_split
from sklearn.ensemble import RandomForestClassifier
from sklearn.metrics import accuracy_score
```

3. Create a variable called **file_url** that contains the URL to the dataset:

```
file_url = 'https://raw.githubusercontent.com'\
           '/PacktWorkshops/The-Data-Science-Workshop'\
           '/master/Chapter04/Dataset/openml_phpZNNasq.csv'
```

4. Load the dataset into a DataFrame using the **.read_csv()** method from **pandas**:

```
df = pd.read_csv(file_url)
```

5. Remove the **animal** column using **.drop()** and then extract the **type** target variable into a new variable called **y** using **.pop()**:

```
df.drop(columns='animal', inplace=True)
y = df.pop('type')
```

6. Split the data into training and testing sets with **train_test_split()** and the parameters **test_size=0.4** and **random_state=188**:

```
X_train, X_test, \
y_train, y_test = train_test_split(df, y, test_size=0.4, \
                                   random_state=188)
```

7. Instantiate **RandomForestClassifier** with **random_state=42**, **n_estimators=30**, **max_depth=2**, and **min_samples_leaf=3**, and then fit the model with the training set:

```
rf_model = RandomForestClassifier(random_state=42, \
                                  n_estimators=30, \
                                  max_depth=2, \
                                  min_samples_leaf=3)
rf_model.fit(X_train, y_train)
```

You should get the following output:

```
RandomForestClassifier(bootstrap=True, class_weight=None, criterion='gini',
                       max_depth=2, max_features='auto', max_leaf_nodes=None,
                       min_impurity_decrease=0.0, min_impurity_split=None,
                       min_samples_leaf=3, min_samples_split=2,
                       min_weight_fraction_leaf=0.0, n_estimators=30,
                       n_jobs=None, oob_score=False, random_state=42, verbose=0,
                       warm_start=False)
```

Figure 4.32: Logs of RandomForest

8. Make predictions on the training and testing sets with **.predict()** and save the results into two new variables called **train_preds** and **test_preds**:

```
train_preds = rf_model.predict(X_train)
test_preds = rf_model.predict(X_test)
```

9. Calculate the accuracy score for the training and testing sets and save the results in two new variables called **train_acc** and **test_acc**:

```
train_acc = accuracy_score(y_train, train_preds)
test_acc = accuracy_score(y_test, test_preds)
```

10. Print the accuracy score – **train_acc** and **test_acc**:

```
print(train_acc)
print(test_acc)
```

You should get the following output:

```
0.8333333333333334
0.8048780487804879
```

Figure 4.33: Accuracy scores for the training and testing sets

The accuracy score decreased for both the training and testing sets compared to the best result we got in the previous exercise. Now the difference between the training and testing sets' accuracy scores is much smaller so our model is overfitting less.

11. Instantiate another **RandomForestClassifier** with **random_state=42**, **n_estimators=30**, **max_depth=2**, and **min_samples_leaf=7**, and then fit the model with the training set:

```
rf_model2 = RandomForestClassifier(random_state=42, \
                                   n_estimators=30, \
                                   max_depth=2, \
                                   min_samples_leaf=7)
rf_model2.fit(X_train, y_train)
```

You should get the following output:

```
RandomForestClassifier(bootstrap=True, class_weight=None, criterion='gini',
                       max_depth=2, max_features='auto', max_leaf_nodes=None,
                       min_impurity_decrease=0.0, min_impurity_split=None,
                       min_samples_leaf=7, min_samples_split=2,
                       min_weight_fraction_leaf=0.0, n_estimators=30,
                       n_jobs=None, oob_score=False, random_state=42, verbose=0,
                       warm_start=False)
```

Figure 4.34: Logs of RandomForest with max_depth=2

12. Make predictions on the training and testing sets with **.predict()** and save the results into two new variables called **train_preds2** and **test_preds2**:

```
train_preds2 = rf_model2.predict(X_train)
test_preds2 = rf_model2.predict(X_test)
```

13. Calculate the accuracy score for the training and testing sets and save the results in two new variables called **train_acc2** and **test_acc2**:

```
train_acc2 = accuracy_score(y_train, train_preds2)
test_acc2 = accuracy_score(y_test, test_preds2)
```

14. Print the accuracy scores: **train_acc** and **test_acc**:

```
print(train_acc2)
print(test_acc2)
```

You should get the following output:

```
0.8
0.8048780487804879
```

Figure 4.35: Accuracy scores for the training and testing sets

Increasing the value of **min_samples_leaf** to **7** has led the model to not overfit anymore. We got extremely similar accuracy scores for the training and testing sets, at around **0.8**. We will choose this value as the optimal one for **min_samples_leaf** for this dataset.

> **NOTE**
>
> To access the source code for this specific section, please refer to https://packt.live/3kUYVZa.
>
> You can also run this example online at https://packt.live/348bv0W.

MAXIMUM FEATURES

We are getting close to the end of this chapter. You have already learned how to tune several of the most important hyperparameters for RandomForest. In this section, we will present you with another extremely important one: **`max_features`**.

Earlier, we learned that **`RandomForest`** builds multiple trees and takes the average to make predictions. This is why it is called a forest, but we haven't really discussed the "random" part yet. Going through this chapter, you may have asked yourself: how does building multiple trees help to get better predictions, and won't all the trees look the same given that the input data is the same?

Before answering these questions, let's use the analogy of a court trial. In some countries, the final decision of a trial is either made by a judge or a jury. A judge is a person who knows the law in detail and can decide whether a person has broken the law or not. On the other hand, a jury is composed of people from different backgrounds who don't know each other or any of the parties involved in the trial and have limited knowledge of the legal system. In this case, we are asking random people who are not expert in the law to decide the outcome of a case. This sounds very risky at first. The risk of one person making the wrong decision is very high. But in fact, the risk of 10 or 20 people all making the wrong decision is relatively low.

But there is one condition that needs to be met for this to work: randomness. If all the people in the jury come from the same background, work in the same industry, or live in the same area, they may share the same way of thinking and make similar decisions. For instance, if a group of people were raised in a community where you only drink hot chocolate at breakfast and one day you ask them if it is OK to drink coffee at breakfast, they would all say no.

On the other hand, say you got another group of people from different backgrounds with different habits: some drink coffee, others tea, a few drink orange juice, and so on. If you asked them the same question, you would end up with the majority of them saying yes. Because we randomly picked these people, they have less bias as a group, and this therefore lowers the risk of them making a wrong decision.

RandomForest actually applies the same logic: it builds a number of trees independently of each other by randomly sampling the data. A tree may see **`60%`** of the training data, another one **`70%`**, and so on. By doing so, there is a high chance that the trees are absolutely different from each other and don't share the same bias. This is the secret of RandomForest: building multiple random trees leads to higher accuracy.

But it is not the only way RandomForest creates randomness. It does so also by randomly sampling columns. Each tree will only see a subset of the features rather than all of them. And this is exactly what the **max_features** hyperparameter is for: it will set the maximum number of features a tree is allowed to see.

In **sklearn**, you can specify the value of this hyperparameter as:

- The maximum number of features, as an integer.
- A ratio, as the percentage of allowed features.
- The **sqrt** function (the default value in **sklearn**, which stands for square root), which will use the square root of the number of features as the maximum value. If, for a dataset, there are **25** features, its square root will be **5** and this will be the value for **max_features**.
- The **log2** function, which will use the log base, **2**, of the number of features as the maximum value. If, for a dataset, there are eight features, its **log2** will be **3** and this will be the value for **max_features**.
- The **None** value, which means Random Forest will use all the features available.

Let's try three different values on the activity dataset. First, we will specify the maximum number of features as two:

```
rf_model10 = RandomForestClassifier(random_state=1, \
                                    n_estimators=50, \
                                    max_depth=10, \
                                    min_samples_leaf=25, \
                                    max_features=2)
rf_model10.fit(X_train, y_train)
preds10 = rf_model10.predict(X_train)
test_preds10 = rf_model10.predict(X_test)
print(accuracy_score(y_train, preds10))
print(accuracy_score(y_test, test_preds10))
```

The output will be as follows:

```
0.7810422474801629
0.7593062912705899
```

Figure 4.36: Accuracy scores for the training and testing sets for max_features=2

We got results similar to those of the best model we trained in the previous section. This is not really surprising as we were using the default value of **max_features** at that time, which is **sqrt**. The square root of **2** equals **1.45**, which is quite close to **2**. This time, let's try with the ratio **0.7**:

```
rf_model11 = RandomForestClassifier(random_state=1, \
                                    n_estimators=50, \
                                    max_depth=10, \
                                    min_samples_leaf=25, \
                                    max_features=0.7)
rf_model11.fit(X_train, y_train)
preds11 = rf_model11.predict(X_train)
test_preds11 = rf_model11.predict(X_test)
print(accuracy_score(y_train, preds11))
print(accuracy_score(y_test, test_preds11))
```

The output will be as follows:

```
0.792229608978483
0.7654016399390465
```

Figure 4.37: Accuracy scores for the training and testing sets for max_features=0.7

With this ratio, both accuracy scores increased for the training and testing sets and the difference between them is less. Our model is overfitting less now and has slightly improved its predictive power. Let's give it a shot with the **log2** option:

```
rf_model12 = RandomForestClassifier(random_state=1, \
                                    n_estimators=50, \
                                    max_depth=10, \
                                    min_samples_leaf=25, \
                                    max_features='log2')
rf_model12.fit(X_train, y_train)
preds12 = rf_model12.predict(X_train)
test_preds12 = rf_model12.predict(X_test)
print(accuracy_score(y_train, preds12))
print(accuracy_score(y_test, test_preds12))
```

The output will be as follows:

```
0.7810422474801629
0.7593062912705899
```

Figure 4.38: Accuracy scores for the training and testing sets for max_features='log2'

We got similar results as for the default value (**sqrt**) and **2**. Again, this is normal as the **log2** of **6** equals **2.58**. So, the optimal value we found for the **max_features** hyperparameter is **0.7** for this dataset.

EXERCISE 4.05: TUNING MAX_FEATURES

In this exercise, we will keep tuning our RandomForest classifier that predicts animal type by trying two different values for the **max_features** hyperparameter:

We will be using the same zoo dataset as in the previous exercise.

1. Open a new Colab notebook.
2. Import the **pandas** package, **train_test_split**, **RandomForestClassifier**, and **accuracy_score** from **sklearn**:

```
import pandas as pd
from sklearn.model_selection import train_test_split
from sklearn.ensemble import RandomForestClassifier
from sklearn.metrics import accuracy_score
```

3. Create a variable called **file_url** that contains the URL to the dataset:

```
file_url = 'https://raw.githubusercontent.com'\
           '/PacktWorkshops/The-Data-Science-Workshop'\
           '/master/Chapter04/Dataset/openml_phpZNNasq.csv'
```

4. Load the dataset into a DataFrame using the **.read_csv()** method from **pandas**:

```
df = pd.read_csv(file_url)
```

5. Remove the **animal** column using **.drop()** and then extract the **type** target variable into a new variable called **y** using **.pop()**:

```
df.drop(columns='animal', inplace=True)
y = df.pop('type')
```

6. Split the data into training and testing sets with **train_test_split()** and the parameters **test_size=0.4** and **random_state=188**:

```
X_train, X_test, \
y_train, y_test = train_test_split(df, y, test_size=0.4, \
                                   random_state=188)
```

7. Instantiate **RandomForestClassifier** with **random_state=42**, **n_estimators=30**, **max_depth=2**, **min_samples_leaf=7**, and **max_features=10**, and then fit the model with the training set:

```
rf_model = RandomForestClassifier(random_state=42, \
                                  n_estimators=30, \
                                  max_depth=2, \
                                  min_samples_leaf=7, \
                                  max_features=10)
rf_model.fit(X_train, y_train)
```

You should get the following output:

```
RandomForestClassifier(bootstrap=True, class_weight=None, criterion='gini',
                       max_depth=2, max_features=10, max_leaf_nodes=None,
                       min_impurity_decrease=0.0, min_impurity_split=None,
                       min_samples_leaf=7, min_samples_split=2,
                       min_weight_fraction_leaf=0.0, n_estimators=30,
                       n_jobs=None, oob_score=False, random_state=42, verbose=0,
                       warm_start=False)
```

Figure 4.39: Logs of RandomForest

8. Make predictions on the training and testing sets with **.predict()** and save the results into two new variables called **train_preds** and **test_preds**:

```
train_preds = rf_model.predict(X_train)
test_preds = rf_model.predict(X_test)
```

9. Calculate the accuracy scores for the training and testing sets and save the results in two new variables called **train_acc** and **test_acc**:

```
train_acc = accuracy_score(y_train, train_preds)
test_acc = accuracy_score(y_test, test_preds)
```

10. Print the accuracy scores: **train_acc** and **test_acc**:

```
print(train_acc)
print(test_acc)
```

You should get the following output:

```
0.85
0.8048780487804879
```

Figure 4.40: Accuracy scores for the training and testing sets

11. Instantiate another **RandomForestClassifier** with **random_state=42**, **n_estimators=30**, **max_depth=2**, **min_samples_leaf=7**, and **max_features=0.2**, and then fit the model with the training set:

```
rf_model2 = RandomForestClassifier(random_state=42, \
                                   n_estimators=30, \
                                   max_depth=2, \
                                   min_samples_leaf=7, \
                                   max_features=0.2)
rf_model2.fit(X_train, y_train)
```

You should get the following output:

```
RandomForestClassifier(bootstrap=True, class_weight=None, criterion='gini',
                       max_depth=2, max_features=0.2, max_leaf_nodes=None,
                       min_impurity_decrease=0.0, min_impurity_split=None,
                       min_samples_leaf=7, min_samples_split=2,
                       min_weight_fraction_leaf=0.0, n_estimators=30,
                       n_jobs=None, oob_score=False, random_state=42, verbose=0,
                       warm_start=False)
```

Figure 4.41: Logs of RandomForest with max_features = 0.2

12. Make predictions on the training and testing sets with **.predict()** and save the results into two new variables called **train_preds2** and **test_preds2**:

```
train_preds2 = rf_model2.predict(X_train)
test_preds2 = rf_model2.predict(X_test)
```

13. Calculate the accuracy score for the training and testing sets and save the results in two new variables called **train_acc2** and **test_acc2**:

```
train_acc2 = accuracy_score(y_train, train_preds2)
test_acc2 = accuracy_score(y_test, test_preds2)
```

14. Print the accuracy scores: **train_acc** and **test_acc**:

```
print(train_acc2)
print(test_acc2)
```

You should get the following output:

```
0.8333333333333334
0.8048780487804879
```

Figure 4.42: Accuracy scores for the training and testing sets

The values **`10`** and **`0.2`**, which we tried in this exercise for the **`max_features`** hyperparameter, did improve the accuracy of the training set but not the testing set. With these values, the model starts to overfit again. The optimal value for **`max_features`** is the default value (**`sqrt`**) for this dataset. In the end, we succeeded in building a model with a 0.8 accuracy score that is not overfitting. This is a pretty good result given the fact the dataset wasn't big: we got only **`6`** features and **`41759`** observations.

> **NOTE**
>
> To access the source code for this specific section, please refer to https://packt.live/3g8nTk7.
>
> You can also run this example online at https://packt.live/324quGv.

ACTIVITY 4.01: TRAIN A RANDOM FOREST CLASSIFIER ON THE ISOLET DATASET

You are working for a technology company and they are planning to launch a new voice assistant product. You have been tasked with building a classification model that will recognize the letters spelled out by a user based on the signal frequencies captured. Each sound can be captured and represented as a signal composed of multiple frequencies.

> **NOTE**
>
> This activity uses the ISOLET dataset, taken from the UCI Machine Learning Repository from the following link: https://packt.live/2QFOawy.
>
> The CSV version of this dataset can be found here: https://packt.live/36DWHpi.

The following steps will help you to complete this activity:

1. Download and load the dataset using **.read_csv()** from **pandas**.
2. Extract the response variable using **.pop()** from **pandas**.
3. Split the dataset into training and test sets using **train_test_split()** from **sklearn.model_selection**.
4. Create a function that will instantiate and fit a **RandomForestClassifier** using **.fit()** from **sklearn.ensemble**.
5. Create a function that will predict the outcome for the training and testing sets using **.predict()**.
6. Create a function that will print the accuracy score for the training and testing sets using **accuracy_score()** from **sklearn.metrics**.
7. Train and get the accuracy score for a range of different hyperparameters. Here are some options you can try:

- **n_estimators = 20** and **50**
- **max_depth = 5** and **10**
- **min_samples_leaf = 10** and **50**
- **max_features = 0.5** and **0.3**

8. Select the best hyperparameter value.

These are the accuracy scores for the best model we trained:

```
0.9184533626534725
0.8940170940170941
```

Figure 4.43: Accuracy scores for the Random Forest classifier

> **NOTE**
>
> The solution to the activity can be found here: https://packt.live/2GbJloz.

SUMMARY

We have finally reached the end of this chapter on multiclass classification with Random Forest. We learned that multiclass classification is an extension of binary classification: instead of predicting only two classes, target variables can have many more values. We saw how we can train a Random Forest model in just a few lines of code and assess its performance by calculating the accuracy score for the training and testing sets. Finally, we learned how to tune some of its most important hyperparameters: **`n_estimators`**, **`max_depth`**, **`min_samples_leaf`**, and **`max_features`**. We also saw how their values can have a significant impact on the predictive power of a model but also on its ability to generalize to unseen data.

In real projects, it is extremely important to choose a valid testing set. This is your final proxy before putting a model into production so you really want it to reflect the types of data you think it will receive in the future. For instance, if your dataset has a date field, you can use the last few weeks or months as your testing set and everything before that date as the training set. If you don't choose the testing set properly, you may end up with a very good model that seems to not overfit but once in production, it will generate incorrect results. The problem doesn't come from the model but from the fact the testing set was chosen poorly.

In some projects, you may see that the dataset is split into three different sets: training, validation, and testing. The validation set can be used to tune the hyperparameters and once you are confident enough, you can test your model on the testing set. As mentioned earlier, we don't want the model to see too much of the testing set but hyperparameter tuning requires you to run a model several times until you find the optimal values. This is the reason why most data scientists create a validation set for this purpose and only use the testing set a handful of times. This will be explained in more depth in *Chapter 7, The Generalization of Machine Learning Models*.

In the next chapter, you will be introduced to unsupervised learning and will learn how to build a clustering model with the k-means algorithm.

5

PERFORMING YOUR FIRST CLUSTER ANALYSIS

OVERVIEW

This chapter will introduce you to unsupervised learning tasks, where algorithms have to automatically learn patterns from data by themselves as no target variables are defined beforehand. We will focus specifically on the k-means algorithm, and see how to standardize and process data for use in cluster analysis.

By the end of this chapter, you will be able to load and visualize data and clusters with scatter plots; prepare data for cluster analysis; perform centroid clustering with k-means; interpret clustering results and determine the optimal number of clusters for a given dataset.

INTRODUCTION

The previous chapters introduced you to very popular and extremely powerful machine learning algorithms. They all have one thing in common, which is that they belong to the same category of algorithms: supervised learning. This kind of algorithm tries to learn patterns based on a specified outcome column (target variable) such as sales, employee churn, or class of customer.

But what if you don't have such a variable in your dataset or you don't want to specify a target variable? Will you still be able to run some machine learning algorithms on it and find interesting patterns? The answer is yes, with the use of clustering algorithms that belong to the unsupervised learning category.

Clustering algorithms are very popular in the data science industry for grouping similar data points and detecting outliers. For instance, clustering algorithms can be used by banks for fraud detection by identifying unusual clusters from the data. They can also be used by e-commerce companies to identify groups of users with similar browsing behaviors, as in the following figures:

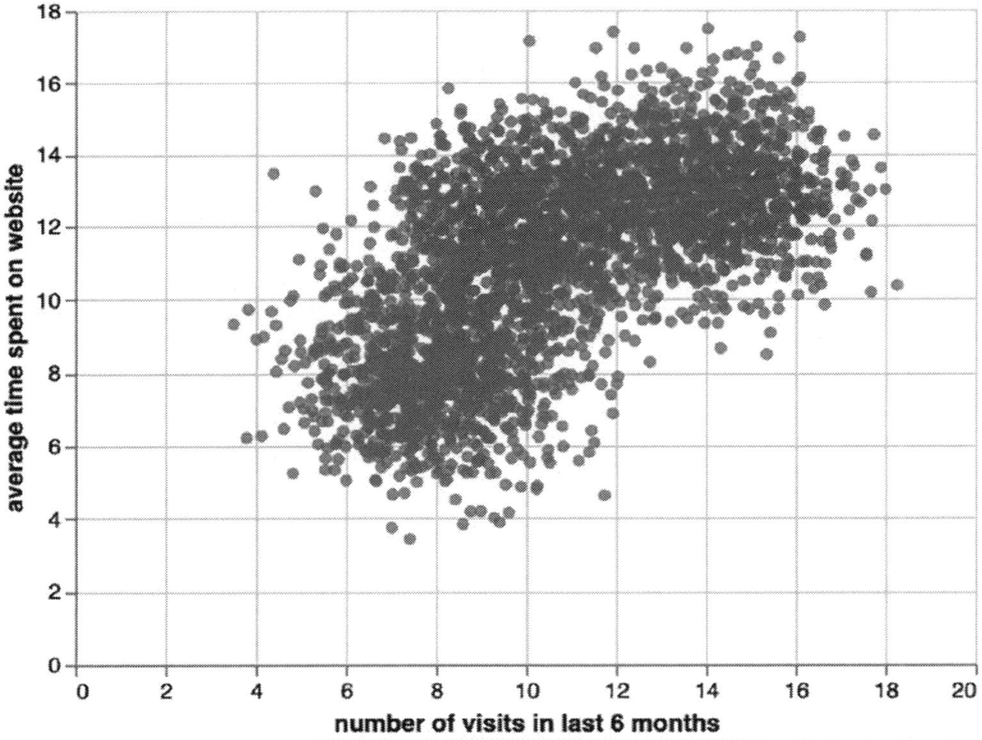

Figure 5.1: Example of data on customers with similar browsing behaviors without clustering analysis performed

Clustering analysis performed on this data would uncover natural patterns by grouping similar data points such that you may get the following result:

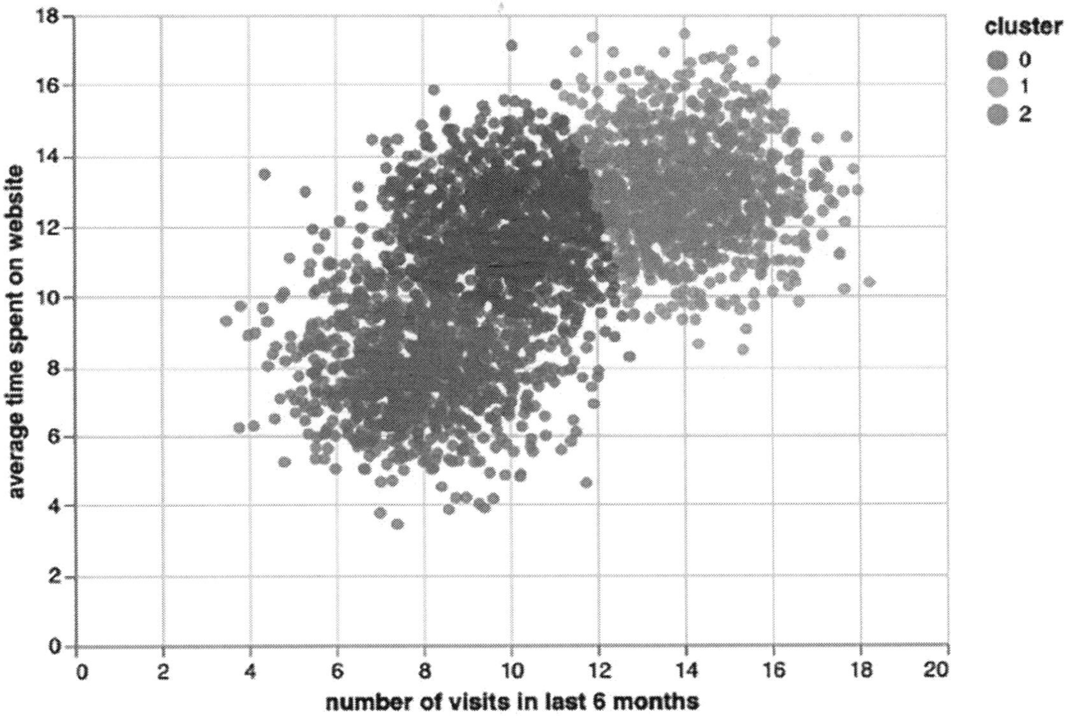

Figure 5.2: Clustering analysis performed on the data on customers with similar browsing behaviors

The data is now segmented into three customer groups depending on their recurring visits and time spent on the website, and different marketing plans can then be used for each of these groups in order to maximize sales.

In this chapter, you will learn how to perform such analysis using a very famous clustering algorithm called k-means.

CLUSTERING WITH K-MEANS

k-means is one of the most popular clustering algorithms (if not the most popular) among data scientists due to its simplicity and high performance. Its origins date back as early as 1956, when a famous mathematician named Hugo Steinhaus laid its foundations, but it was a decade later that another researcher called James MacQueen named this approach k-means.

The objective of k-means is to group similar data points (or observations) together that will form a cluster. Think of it as grouping elements close to each other (we will define how to measure closeness later in this chapter). For example, if you were manually analyzing user behavior on a mobile app, you might end up grouping customers who log in quite frequently, or users who make bigger in-app purchases, together. This is the kind of grouping that clustering algorithms such as k-means will automatically find for you from the data.

In this chapter, we will be working with an open source dataset shared publicly by the **Australian Taxation Office** (**ATO**). The dataset contains statistics about each postcode (*also known as a zip code, which is an identification code used for sorting mail by area*) in Australia during the financial year of 2014-15.

> **NOTE**
>
> The Australian Taxation Office (ATO) dataset can be found in the Packt GitHub repository here: https://packt.live/340xO5t.
>
> The source of the dataset can be found here: https://packt.live/361i1p3.

We will perform cluster analysis on this dataset for two specific variables (or columns): `Average net tax` and `Average total deductions`. Our objective is to find groups (or clusters) of postcodes sharing similar patterns in terms of tax received and money deducted. Here is a scatter plot of these two variables:

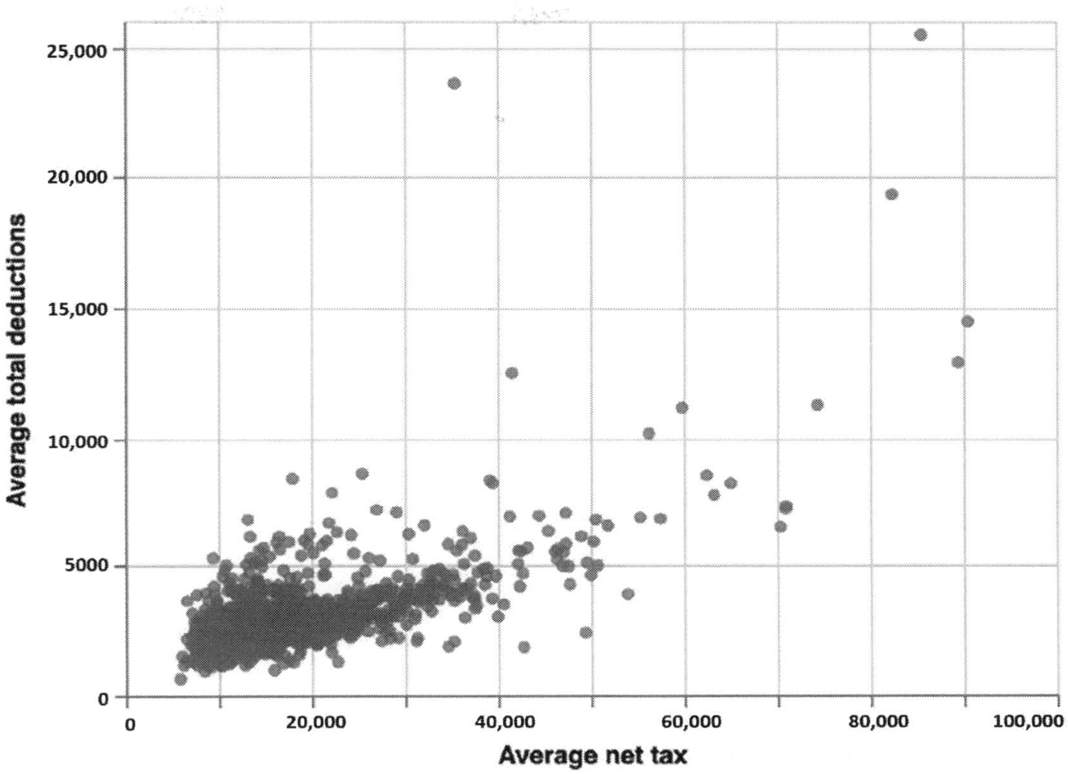

Figure 5.3: Scatter plot of the ATO dataset

As part of being a data scientist, you need to analyze the graphs achieved from this dataset and come to conclusions. Let's say you have to analyze manually potential groupings of observations from this dataset. One potential result could be as follows:

- All the data points in the bottom-left corner could be grouped together (average net tax from 0 to 40,000).
- A second group could be all the data points in the center area (average net tax from 40,000 to 60,000 and average total deductions below 10,000).
- Finally, all the remaining data points could be grouped together.

But rather having you to manually guess these groupings, it will be better if we can use an algorithm to do it for us. This is what we are going to see in practice in the following exercise, where we'll perform clustering analysis on this dataset.

EXERCISE 5.01: PERFORMING YOUR FIRST CLUSTERING ANALYSIS ON THE ATO DATASET

In this exercise, we will be using k-means clustering on the ATO dataset and observing the different clusters that the dataset divides itself into, after which we will conclude by analyzing the output:

1. Open a new Colab notebook.
2. Next, load the required Python packages: **pandas** and **KMeans** from **sklearn.cluster**.

   We will be using the **import** function from Python:

   > **NOTE**
   >
   > You can create short aliases for the packages you will be calling quite often in your script with the function mentioned in the following code snippet.

```
import pandas as pd
from sklearn.cluster import KMeans
```

   > **NOTE**
   >
   > We will be looking into **KMeans** (from **sklearn.cluster**), which you have used in the code here, later in the chapter for a more detailed explanation of it.

3. Next, create a variable containing the link to the file. We will call this variable **file_url**:

```
file_url = 'https://raw.githubusercontent.com'\
           '/PacktWorkshops/The-Data-Science-Workshop'\
           '/master/Chapter05/DataSet/taxstats2015.csv'
```

In the next step, we will use the **pandas** package to load our data into a DataFrame (think of it as a table, like on an Excel spreadsheet, with a row index and column names).

Our input file is in **CSV** format, and **pandas** has a method that can directly read this format, which is **.read_csv()**.

4. Use the **usecols** parameter to subset only the columns we need rather than loading the entire dataset. We just need to provide a list of the column names we are interested in, which are mentioned in the following code snippet:

```
df = pd.read_csv(file_url, \
                 usecols=['Postcode', \
                          'Average net tax', \
                          'Average total deductions'])
```

Now we have loaded the data into a **pandas** DataFrame.

5. Next, let's display the first 5 rows of this DataFrame , using the method **.head()**:

```
df.head()
```

You should get the following output:

	Postcode	Average total deductions	Average net tax
0	2000	2071	27555
1	2006	3804	28142
2	2007	1740	15649
3	2008	3917	53976
4	2009	3433	32430

Figure 5.4: The first five rows of the ATO DataFrame

6. Now, to output the last 5 rows, we use **.tail()**:

```
df.tail()
```

You should get the following output:

	Postcode	Average total deductions	Average net tax
2468	870	2377	14788
2469	872	1218	9017
2470	880	2309	16574
2471	885	3039	28795
2472	886	2191	18141

Figure 5.5: The last five rows of the ATO DataFrame

Now that we have our data, let's jump straight to what we want to do: find clusters.

As you saw in the previous chapters, **sklearn** provides the exact same APIs for training different machine learning algorithms, such as:

- Instantiate an algorithm with the specified hyperparameters (here it will be KMeans(hyperparameters)).
- Fit the model with the training data with the method **.fit()**.
- Predict the result with the given input data with the method **.predict()**.

> **NOTE**
>
> Here, we will use all the default values for the k-means hyperparameters except for the **random_state** one. Specifying a fixed random state (also called a **seed**) will help us to get reproducible results every time we have to rerun our code.

7. Instantiate k-means with a random state of **42** and save it into a variable called **kmeans**:

```
kmeans = KMeans(random_state=42)
```

8. Now feed k-means with our training data. To do so, we need to get only the variables (or columns) used for fitting the model. In our case, the variables are **'Average net tax'** and **'Average total deductions'**, and they are saved in a new variable called **X**:

```
X = df[['Average net tax', 'Average total deductions']]
```

9. Now fit **kmeans** with this training data:

```
kmeans.fit(X)
```

You should get the following output:

```
KMeans(algorithm='auto', copy_x=True, init='k-means++', max_iter=300,
       n_clusters=8, n_init=10, n_jobs=None, precompute_distances='auto',
       random_state=42, tol=0.0001, verbose=0)
```

Figure 5.6: Summary of the fitted kmeans and its hyperparameters

We just ran our first clustering algorithm in just a few lines of code.

10. See which cluster each data point belongs to by using the **.predict()** method:

```
y_preds = kmeans.predict(X)
y_preds
```

You should get the following output:

```
array([6, 6, 5, ..., 5, 6, 5], dtype=int32)
```

Figure 5.7: Output of the k-means predictions

> **NOTE**
>
> Although we set a **random_state** value, you may still get an output with different cluster numbers than the one shown above. This will depend on the version of scikit-learn you are using. The output above was generated using version 0.22.2. You can find out which version you are using by executing the following code:
>
> ```
> import sklearn
> sklearn.__version__
> ```

11. Now, add these predictions into the original DataFrame and take a look at the first five postcodes:

```
df['cluster'] = y_preds
df.head()
```

> **NOTE**
>
> The predictions from the sklearn **predict()** method are in the exact same order as the input data. So, the first prediction will correspond to the first row of your DataFrame.

You should get the following output:

	Postcode	Average total deductions	Average net tax	cluster
0	2000	2071	27555	6
1	2006	3804	28142	6
2	2007	1740	15649	5
3	2008	3917	53976	7
4	2009	3433	32430	2

Figure 5.8: Cluster number assigned to the first five postcodes

Our k-means model has grouped the first two rows into the same cluster, **6**. We can see these two observations both have average net tax values around 28,000. The last three data points have been assigned to different clusters (**5**, **7**, and **2**, respectively) and we can see their values for both average total deductions and average net tax are very different from each other. It seems that lower values are grouped into cluster **5** while higher values are classified into cluster **7**. We are starting to build our understanding of how k-means has decided to group the observations from this dataset.

> **NOTE**
>
> To access the source code for this specific section, please refer to https://packt.live/2DUCWAZ.
>
> You can also run this example online at https://packt.live/2EgduFS.

This is a great start. You have learned how to train (or fit) a k-means model in a few lines of code. Now we can start diving deeper into the magic behind k-means.

INTERPRETING K-MEANS RESULTS

After training our k-means algorithm, we will likely be interested in analyzing its results in more detail. Remember, the objective of cluster analysis is to group observations with similar patterns together. But how can we see whether the groupings found by the algorithm are meaningful? We will be looking at this in this section by using the dataset results we just generated.

One way of investigating this is to analyze the dataset row by row with the assigned cluster for each observation. This can be quite tedious, especially if the size of your dataset is quite big, so it would be better to have a kind of summary of the cluster results.

If you are familiar with Excel spreadsheets, you are probably thinking about using a pivot table to get the average of the variables for each cluster. In SQL, you would have probably used a **`GROUP BY`** statement. If you are not familiar with either of these, you may think of grouping each cluster together and then calculating the average for each of them. The good news is that this can be easily achieved with the **`pandas`** package in Python. Let's see how this can be done with an example.

To create a pivot table similar to an Excel one, we will be using the **`pivot_table()`** method from **`pandas`**. We need to specify the following parameters for this method:

- **`values`**: This parameter corresponds to the numerical columns you want to calculate summaries for (or aggregations), such as getting averages or counts. In an Excel pivot table, it is also called **`values`**. In our dataset, we will use the **`Average net tax`** and **`Average total deductions`** variables.
- **`index`**: This parameter is used to specify the columns you want to see summaries for. In our case, it will be the **`cluster`** column. In a pivot table in Excel, this corresponds with the **`Rows`** field.

- **aggfunc**: This is where you will specify the aggregation functions you want to summarize the data with, such as getting averages or counts. In Excel, this is the **Summarize by** option in the **values** field. An example of how to use the **aggfunc** method is shown below.

> **NOTE**
>
> Run the code below in the same notebook as you used for the previous exercise.

```
import numpy as np
df.pivot_table(values=['Average net tax', \
                       'Average total deductions'], \
               index='cluster', aggfunc=np.mean)
```

> **NOTE**
>
> We will be using the **numpy** implementation of **mean()** as it is more optimized for pandas DataFrames.

cluster	Average net tax	Average total deductions
0	10126.249641	2176.045911
1	20474.671096	2909.352159
2	36197.407895	4789.328947
3	13016.528477	2480.054305
4	77733.111111	12523.111111
5	16391.342495	2657.048626
6	26765.963235	3498.676471
7	50887.692308	6156.961538

Figure 5.9: Output of the pivot_table function

In this summary, we can see that the algorithm has grouped the data into eight clusters (clusters 0 to 7). Cluster 0 has the lowest average net tax and total deductions amounts among all the clusters, while cluster 4 has the highest values. With this pivot table, we are able to compare clusters between them using their summarized values.

Using an aggregated view of clusters is a good way of seeing the difference between them, but it is not the only way. Another possibility is to visualize clusters in a graph. This is exactly what we are going to do now.

You may have heard of different visualization packages, such as **matplotlib**, **seaborn**, and **bokeh**, but in this chapter, we will be using the **altair** package because it is quite simple to use (its API is very similar to **sklearn**). Let's import it first:

```
import altair as alt
```

Then, we will instantiate a **Chart()** object with our DataFrame and save it into a variable called **chart**:

```
chart = alt.Chart(df)
```

Now we will specify the type of graph we want, a scatter plot, with the **.mark_circle()** method and will save it into a new variable called **scatter_plot**:

```
scatter_plot = chart.mark_circle()
```

Finally, we need to configure our scatter plot by specifying the names of the columns that will be our **x**- and **y**-axes on the graph. We also tell the scatter plot to color each point according to its cluster value with the **color** option:

```
scatter_plot.encode(x='Average net tax', \
                    y='Average total deductions', \
                    color='cluster:N')
```

> **NOTE**
>
> You may have noticed that we added **:N** at the end of the **cluster** column name. This extra parameter is used in **altair** to specify the type of value for this column. **:N** means the information contained in this column is categorical. **altair** automatically defines the color scheme to be used depending on the type of a column.

You should get the following output:

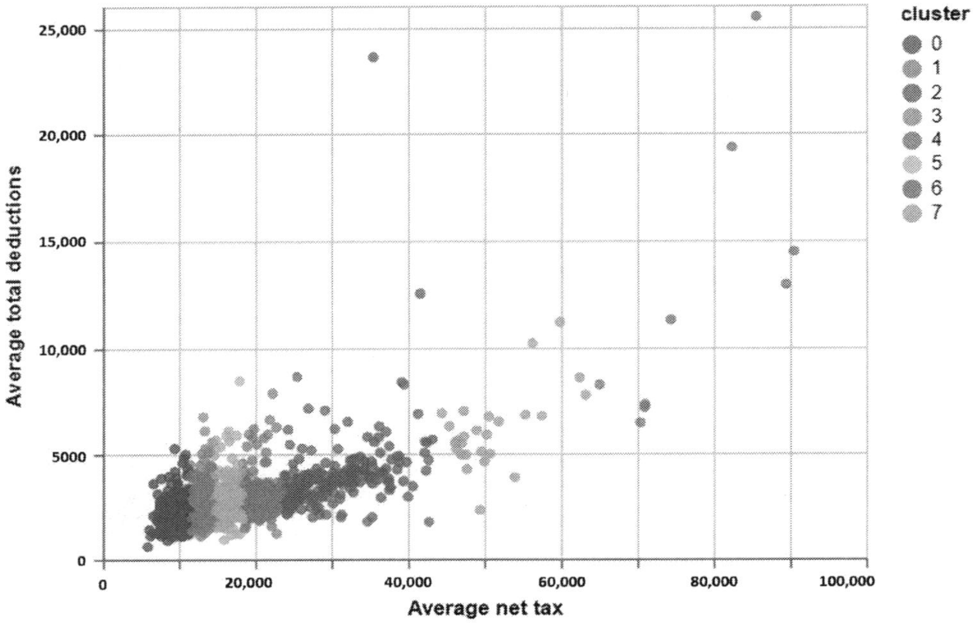

Figure 5.10: Scatter plot of the clusters

We can now easily see what the clusters in this graph are and how they differ from each other. We can clearly see that k-means assigned data points to each cluster mainly based on the x-axis variable, which is `Average net tax`. The boundaries of the clusters are vertical straight lines. For instance, the boundary separating the yellow and orange clusters is roughly around 18,000. Observations below this limit are assigned to the red cluster (2) and those above to the purple cluster (6).

> **NOTE**
>
> You can see the high quality color images for this Workshop at: https://packt.live/30O91Bd

If you have used visualization tools such as **Tableau** or **Power BI**, you might feel a bit frustrated as this graph is static, you can't hover over each data point to get more information and find, for instance, what is the limit separating the orange cluster from the pink one. But this can be easily achieved with altair and this is one of the reasons we chose to use it We can add some interactions to your chart with minimal code changes.

Let's say we want to add a tooltip that will display the values for the two columns of interest: the postcode and the assigned cluster. With **altair**, we just need to add a parameter called **tooltip** in the **encode()** method with a list of corresponding column names and call the **interactive()** method just after, as seen in the following code snippet:

```
scatter_plot.encode(x='Average net tax', \
                    y='Average total deductions', \
                    color='cluster:N', \
                    tooltip=['Postcode', \
                             'cluster', 'Average net tax', \
                             'Average total deductions'])\
                    .interactive()
```

You should get the following output:

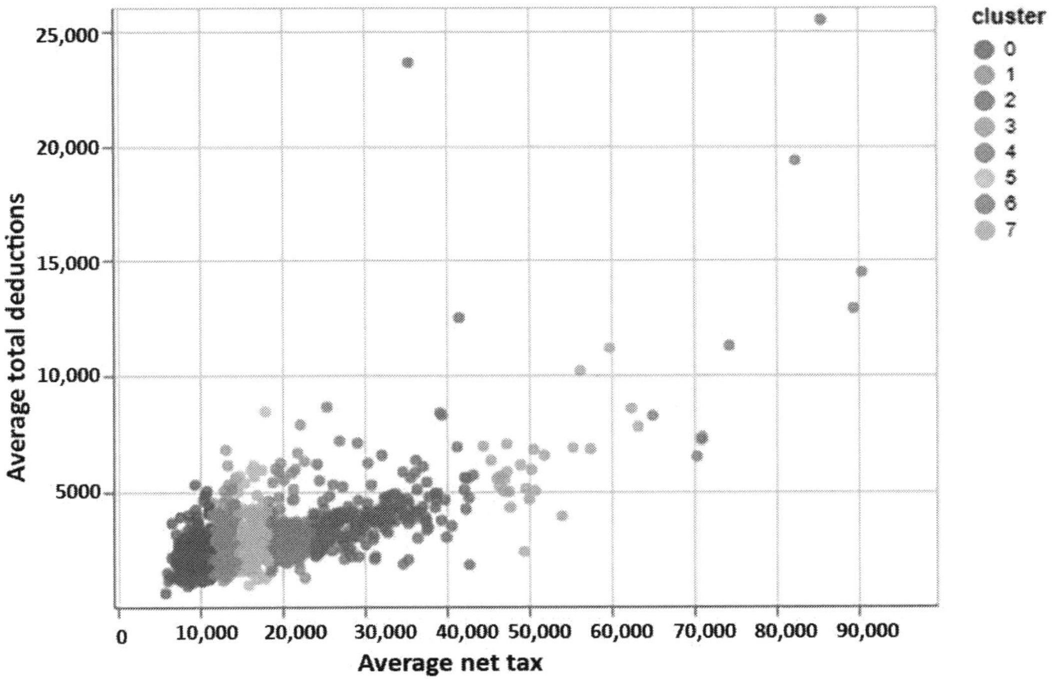

Figure 5.11: Interactive scatter plot of the clusters with tooltip

Now we can easily hover over and inspect the data points near the cluster boundaries and find out that the threshold used to differentiate the purple cluster (6) from the red one (2) is close to 32,000 in **'Average Net Tax'**.

EXERCISE 5.02: CLUSTERING AUSTRALIAN POSTCODES BY BUSINESS INCOME AND EXPENSES

In this exercise, we will learn how to perform clustering analysis with k-means and visualize its results based on postcode values sorted by business income and expenses. The following steps will help you complete this exercise:

1. Open a new Colab notebook for this exercise.
2. Now **import** the required packages (**pandas**, **sklearn**, **altair**, and **numpy**):

```
import pandas as pd
from sklearn.cluster import KMeans
import altair as alt
import numpy as np
```

3. Assign the link to the ATO dataset to a variable called **file_url**:

```
file_url = 'https://raw.githubusercontent.com'\
           '/PacktWorkshops/The-Data-Science-Workshop'\
           '/master/Chapter05/DataSet/taxstats2015.csv'
```

4. Using the **read_csv** method from the pandas package, load the dataset with only the following columns with the **use_cols** parameter: **'Postcode'**, **'Average total business income'**, and **'Average total business expenses'**:

```
df = pd.read_csv(file_url, \
                 usecols=['Postcode', \
                          'Average total business income', \
                          'Average total business expenses'])
```

5. Display the last 10 rows from the ATO dataset using the **.tail()** method from pandas:

```
df.tail(10)
```

You should get the following output:

	Postcode	Average total business income	Average total business expenses
2463	852	95299	79526
2464	853	21186	15336
2465	854	49303	29720
2466	860	63190	55802
2467	862	134224	144254
2468	870	62793	44687
2469	872	53025	45670
2470	880	45603	28700
2471	885	53148	39850
2472	886	121057	90120

Figure 5.12: The last 10 rows of the ATO dataset

6. Extract the **'Average total business income'** and **'Average total business expenses'** columns using the following pandas column subsetting syntax: **dataframe_name[<list_of_columns>]**. Then, save them into a new variable called **X**:

```
X = df[['Average total business income', \
        'Average total business expenses']]
```

7. Now fit **kmeans** with this new variable using a value of **8** for the **random_state** hyperparameter:

```
kmeans = KMeans(random_state=8)
kmeans.fit(X)
```

You should get the following output:

```
KMeans(algorithm='auto', copy_x=True, init='k-means++', max_iter=300,
       n_clusters=8, n_init=10, n_jobs=None, precompute_distances='auto',
       random_state=8, tol=0.0001, verbose=0)
```

Figure 5.13: Summary of the fitted kmeans and its hyperparameters

8. Using the **predict** method from the **sklearn** package, predict the clustering assignment from the input variable, **(X)**, save the results into a new variable called **y_preds**, and display the last **10** predictions:

```
y_preds = kmeans.predict(X)
y_preds[-10:]
```

You should get the following output:

```
array([3, 0, 0, 1, 6, 0, 0, 0, 0, 3], dtype=int32)
```

Figure 5.14: Results of the clusters assigned to the last 10 observations

9. Save the predicted clusters back to the DataFrame by creating a new column called **'cluster'** and print the last **10** rows of the DataFrame using the **.tail()** method from the **pandas** package:

```
df['cluster'] = y_preds
df.tail(10)
```

You should get the following output:

	Postcode	Average total business income	Average total business expenses	cluster
2463	852	95299	79526	3
2464	853	21186	15336	0
2465	854	49303	29720	0
2466	860	63190	55802	1
2467	862	134224	144254	6
2468	870	62793	44687	0
2469	872	53025	45670	0
2470	880	45603	28700	0
2471	885	53148	39850	0
2472	886	121057	90120	3

Figure 5.15: The last 10 rows of the ATO dataset with the added cluster column

10. Generate a pivot table with the averages of the two columns for each cluster value using the **pivot_table** method from the **pandas** package with the following parameters:

    Provide the names of the columns to be aggregated, **'Average total business income'** and **'Average total business expenses'**, to the parameter values.

    Provide the name of the column to be grouped, **'cluster'**, to the parameter index.

    Use the **.mean** method from NumPy (**np**) as the aggregation function for the **aggfunc** parameter:

```
df.pivot_table(values=['Average total business income', \
                       'Average total business expenses'], \
               index='cluster', aggfunc=np.mean)
```

    You should get the following output:

	Average total business expenses	Average total business income
cluster		
0	38130.124827	53608.097087
1	58310.891111	76449.391111
2	250410.190476	301417.809524
3	82319.305970	104102.712687
4	812481.333333	837920.333333
5	173350.259740	208767.740260
6	118572.299517	145933.570048
7	449722.500000	488551.625000

Figure 5.16: Output of the pivot_table function

11. Now let's plot the clusters using an interactive scatter plot. First, use **Chart()** and **mark_circle()** from the **altair** package to instantiate a scatter plot graph:

```
scatter_plot = alt.Chart(df).mark_circle()
```

12. Use the **encode** and **interactive** methods from **altair** to specify the display of the scatter plot and its interactivity options with the following parameters:

    Provide the name of the **'Average total business income'** column to the **x** parameter (the x-axis).

    Provide the name of the **'Average total business expenses'** column to the **y** parameter (the y-axis).

    Provide the name of the **cluster:N** column to the **color** parameter (providing a different color for each group).

    Provide these column names – **'Postcode'**, **'cluster'**, **'Average total business income'**, and **'Average total business expenses'** – to the **'tooltip'** parameter (this being the information displayed by the tooltip):

```
scatter_plot.encode(x='Average total business income', \
                    y='Average total business expenses', \
                    color='cluster:N', tooltip = ['Postcode', \
                                                  'cluster', \
                    'Average total business income', \
                    'Average total business expenses'])\
                    .interactive()
```

You should get the following output:

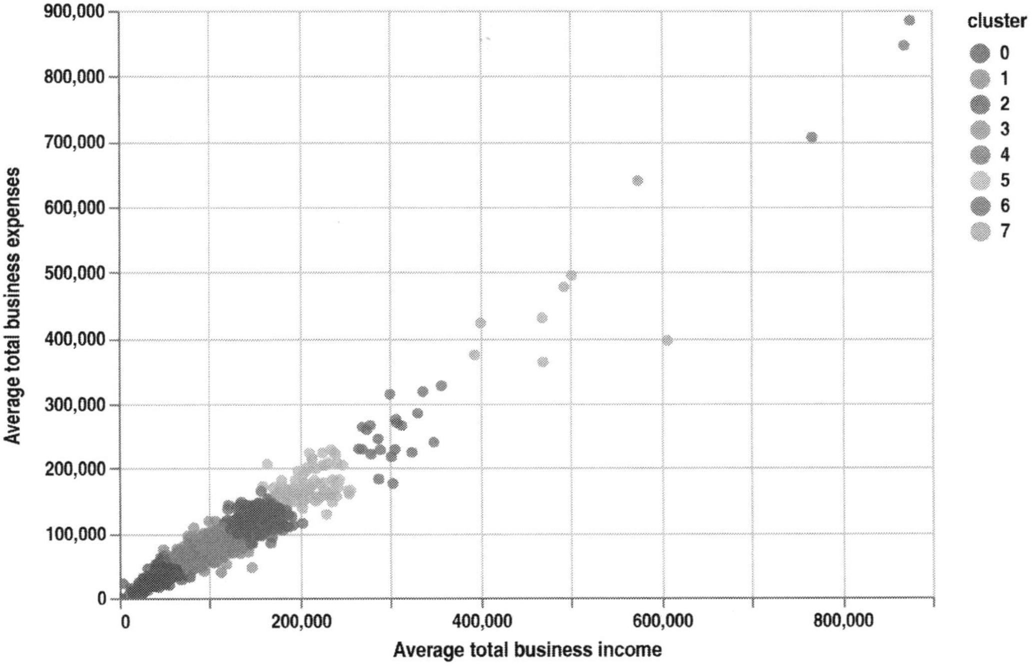

Figure 5.17: Interactive scatter plot of the clusters

> **NOTE**
>
> To access the source code for this specific section, please refer to https://packt.live/3hacbXA.
>
> This section does not currently have an online interactive example, but can be run as usual on Google Colab.

We can see that k-means has grouped the observations into eight different clusters based on the value of the two variables (`'Average total business income'` and `'Average total business expense'`). For instance, all the low-value data points have been assigned to cluster 0, while the ones with extremely high values belong to cluster 4. So, k-means has grouped the data points that share similar behaviors.

You just successfully completed a cluster analysis and visualized its results. You learned how to load a real-world dataset, fit k-means, and display a scatter plot. This is a great start, and we will be delving into more details on how to improve the performance of your model in the sections to come in this chapter.

CHOOSING THE NUMBER OF CLUSTERS

In the previous sections, we saw how easy it is to fit the k-means algorithm on a given dataset. In our ATO dataset, we found 8 different clusters that were mainly defined by the values of the **`Average net tax`** variable.

But you may have asked yourself: "*Why 8 clusters? Why not 3 or 15 clusters?*" These are indeed excellent questions. The short answer is that we used k-means' default value for the hyperparameter **`n_cluster`**, defining the number of clusters to be found, as 8.

As you will recall from *Chapter 2, Regression*, and *Chapter 4, Multiclass Classification with RandomForest*, the value of a hyperparameter isn't learned by the algorithm but has to be set arbitrarily by you prior to training. For k-means, **`n_cluster`** is one of the most important hyperparameters you will have to tune. Choosing a low value will lead k-means to group many data points together, even though they are very different from each other. On the other hand, choosing a high value may force the algorithm to split close observations into multiple ones, even though they are very similar.

Looking at the scatter plot from the ATO dataset, eight clusters seems to be a lot. On the graph, some of the clusters look very close to each other and have similar values. Intuitively, just by looking at the plot, you could have said that there were between two and four different clusters. As you can see, this is quite suggestive, and it would be great if there was a function that could help us to define the right number of clusters for a dataset. Such a method does indeed exist, and it is called the **Elbow** method.

This method assesses the compactness of clusters, the objective being to minimize a value known as **inertia**. More details and an explanation about this will be provided later in this chapter. For now, think of inertia as a value that says, for a group of data points, how far from each other or how close to each other they are.

Let's apply this method to our ATO dataset. First, we will define the range of cluster numbers we want to evaluate (between 1 and 10) and save them in a DataFrame called **`clusters`**. We will also create an empty list called **`inertia`**, where we will store our calculated values.

> **NOTE**
>
> Open the notebook you were using for *Exercise 5.01*, *Performing Your First Clustering Analysis on the ATO Dataset*, execute the code you already entered, and then continue at the end of the notebook with the following code.

```
clusters = pd.DataFrame()
clusters['cluster_range'] = range(1, 10)
inertia = []
```

Next, we will create a **for** loop that will iterate over the range, fit a k-means model with the specified number of **clusters**, extract the **inertia** value, and store it in our list, as in the following code snippet:

```
for k in clusters['cluster_range']:
    kmeans = KMeans(n_clusters=k, random_state=8).fit(X)
    inertia.append(kmeans.inertia_)
```

Now we can use our list of **inertia** values in the **clusters** DataFrame:

```
clusters['inertia'] = inertia
clusters
```

You should get the following output:

	cluster_range	inertia
0	1	1.586459e+11
1	2	6.655056e+10
2	3	3.708115e+10
3	4	2.253973e+10
4	5	1.575012e+10
5	6	1.154406e+10
6	7	8.776361e+09
7	8	7.285696e+09
8	9	6.000036e+09

Figure 5.18: Dataframe containing inertia values for our clusters

Then, we need to plot a line chart using **altair** with the **mark_line()** method. We will specify the **'cluster_range'** column as our x-axis and **'inertia'** as our y-axis, as in the following code snippet:

```
alt.Chart(clusters).mark_line()\
                  .encode(x='cluster_range', y='inertia')
```

You should get the following output:

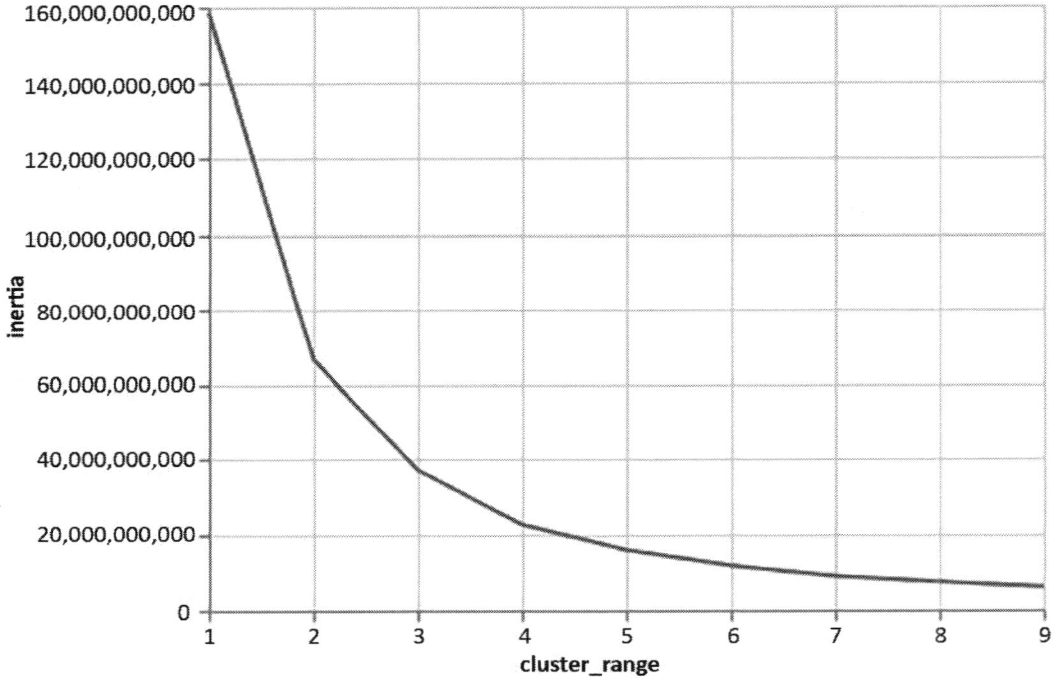

Figure 5.19: Plotting the Elbow method

> **NOTE**
>
> You don't have to save each of the **altair** objects in a separate variable; you can just append the methods one after the other with "**.**".

Now that we have plotted the inertia value against the number of clusters, we need to find the optimal number of clusters. What we need to do is to find the inflection point in the graph, where the inertia value starts to decrease more slowly (that is, where the slope of the line almost reaches a 45-degree angle). Finding the right **inflection point** can be a bit tricky. If you picture this line chart as an arm, what we want is to find the center of the Elbow (now you know where the name for this method comes from). So, looking at our example, we will say that the optimal number of clusters is three. If we kept adding more clusters, the inertia would not decrease drastically and add any value. This is the reason why we want to find the middle of the Elbow as the inflection point.

Now let's retrain our **`Kmeans`** with this hyperparameter and plot the clusters as shown in the following code snippet:

```
kmeans = KMeans(random_state=42, n_clusters=3)
kmeans.fit(X)
df['cluster2'] = kmeans.predict(X)
scatter_plot.encode(x='Average net tax', \
                    y='Average total deductions', \
                    color='cluster2:N', \
                    tooltip=['Postcode', 'cluster', \
                             'Average net tax', \
                             'Average total deductions'])\
                    .interactive()
```

You should get the following output:

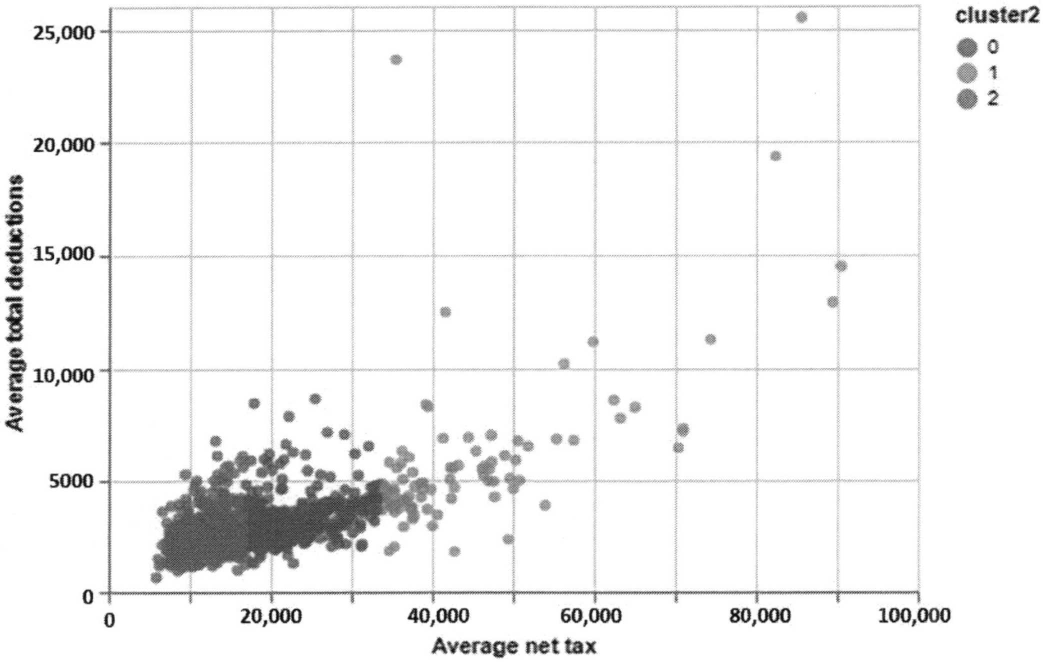

Figure 5.20: Scatter plot of the three clusters

This is very different compared to our initial results. Looking at the three clusters, we can see that:

- The first cluster (red) represents postcodes with low values for both average net tax and total deductions.
- The second cluster (blue) is for medium average net tax and low average total deductions.
- The third cluster (orange) is grouping all postcodes with average net tax values above 35,000.

> **NOTE**
>
> It is worth noticing that the data points are more spread in the third cluster; this may indicate that there are some outliers in this group.

This example showed us how important it is to define the right number of clusters before training a k-means algorithm if we want to get meaningful groups from data. We used a method called the Elbow method to find this optimal number.

EXERCISE 5.03: FINDING THE OPTIMAL NUMBER OF CLUSTERS

In this exercise, we will apply the Elbow method to the same data as in *Exercise 5.02, Clustering Australian Postcodes by Business Income and Expenses*, to find the optimal number of clusters, before fitting a k-means model:

1. Open a new Colab notebook for this exercise.
2. Now **import** the required packages (**pandas**, **sklearn**, and **altair**):

```
import pandas as pd
from sklearn.cluster import KMeans
import altair as alt
```

   Next, we will load the dataset and select the same columns as in *Exercise 5.02, Clustering Australian Postcodes by Business Income and Expenses*, and print the first five rows.

3. Assign the link to the ATO dataset to a variable called **file_url**:

```
file_url = 'https://raw.githubusercontent.com'\
           '/PacktWorkshops/The-Data-Science-Workshop'\
           '/master/Chapter05/DataSet/taxstats2015.csv'
```

4. Using the **.read_csv()** method from the pandas package, load the dataset with only the following columns using the **use_cols** parameter: **'Postcode'**, **'Average total business income'**, and **'Average total business expenses'**:

```
df = pd.read_csv(file_url, \
                 usecols=['Postcode', \
                          'Average total business income', \
                          'Average total business expenses'])
```

5. Display the first five rows of the DataFrame with the **.head()** method from the pandas package:

```
df.head()
```

You should get the following output:

	Postcode	Average total business income	Average total business expenses
0	2000	210901	222191
1	2006	69983	48971
2	2007	575099	639499
3	2008	53329	32173
4	2009	237539	222993

Figure 5.21: The first five rows of the ATO DataFrame

6. Assign the **'Average total business income'** and **'Average total business expenses'** columns to a new variable called **X**:

```
X = df[['Average total business income', \
        'Average total business expenses']]
```

7. Create an empty pandas DataFrame called **clusters** and an empty list called **inertia**:

```
clusters = pd.DataFrame()
inertia = []
```

Now, use the **range** function to generate a list containing the range of cluster numbers, from **1** to **15**, and assign it to a new column called **'cluster_range'** from the **'clusters'** DataFrame:

```
clusters['cluster_range'] = range(1, 15)
```

8. Create a **for** loop to go through each cluster number and fit a k-means model accordingly, then append the **inertia** values using the **'inertia_'** parameter with the **'inertia'** list:

```
for k in clusters['cluster_range']:
    kmeans = KMeans(n_clusters=k).fit(X)
    inertia.append(kmeans.inertia_)
```

9. Assign the **inertia** list to a new column called **'inertia'** from the **clusters** DataFrame and display its content:

```
clusters['inertia'] = inertia
clusters
```

You should get the following output:

	cluster_range	inertia
0	1	1.333516e+13
1	2	7.063097e+12
2	3	3.718740e+12
3	4	2.342332e+12
4	5	1.714920e+12
5	6	1.224488e+12
6	7	9.420108e+11
7	8	7.489221e+11
8	9	6.347024e+11
9	10	5.786862e+11
10	11	5.100297e+11
11	12	4.579617e+11
12	13	4.208861e+11
13	14	3.982078e+11

Figure 5.22: Plotting the Elbow method

10. Now use **mark_line()** and **encode()** from the **altair** package to plot the Elbow graph with **'cluster_range'** as the x-axis and **'inertia'** as the y-axis:

```
alt.Chart(clusters).mark_line()\
    .encode(alt.X('cluster_range'), alt.Y('inertia'))
```

You should get the following output:

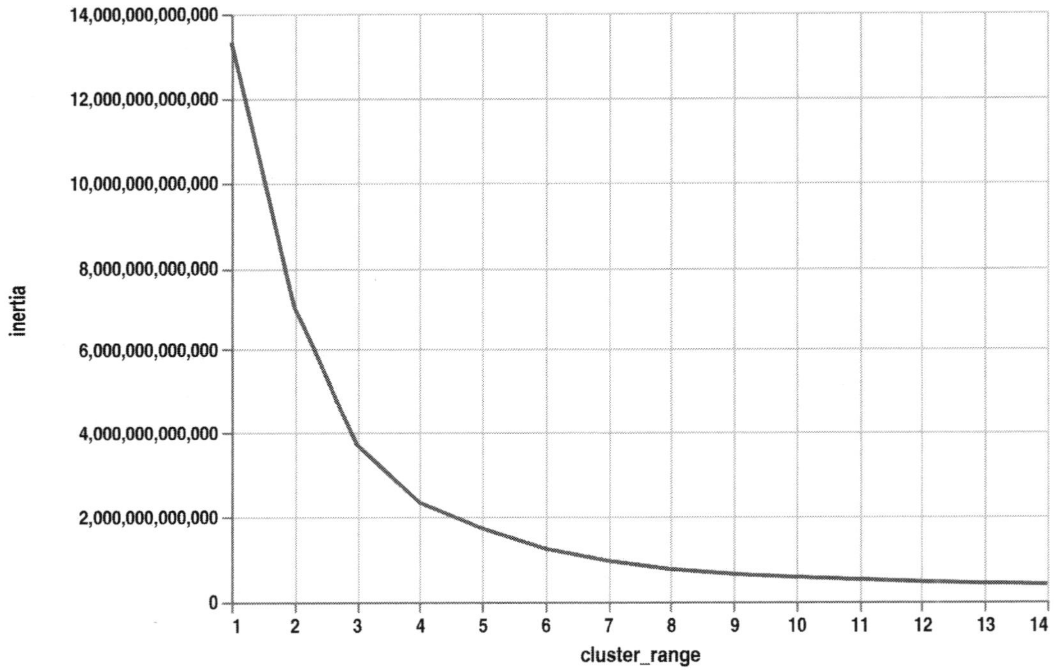

Figure 5.23: Plotting the Elbow method

11. Looking at the Elbow plot, identify the optimal number of clusters, and assign this value to a variable called **optim_cluster**:

```
optim_cluster = 4
```

12. Train a k-means model with this number of clusters and a **random_state** value of **42** using the **fit** method from **sklearn**:

```
kmeans = KMeans(random_state=42, n_clusters=optim_cluster)
kmeans.fit(X)
```

13. Now, using the **predict** method from **sklearn**, get the predicted assigned cluster for each data point contained in the **X** variable and save the results into a new column called **'cluster2'** from the **df** DataFrame:

```
df['cluster2'] = kmeans.predict(X)
```

14. Display the first five rows of the **df** DataFrame using the **head** method from the **pandas** package:

```
df.head()
```

You should get the following output:

	Postcode	Average total business income	Average total business expenses	cluster2
0	2000	210901	222191	3
1	2006	69983	48971	0
2	2007	575099	639499	2
3	2008	53329	32173	0
4	2009	237539	222993	3

Figure 5.24: The first five rows with the cluster predictions

15. Now plot the scatter plot using the **mark_circle()** and **encode()** methods from the **altair** package. Also, to add interactiveness, use the **tooltip** parameter and the **interactive()** method from the **altair** package as shown in the following code snippet:

```
alt.Chart(df).mark_circle()\
             .encode\
              (x='Average total business income', \
               y='Average total business expenses', \
               color='cluster2:N', \
               tooltip=['Postcode', 'cluster2', \
                        'Average total business income',\
                        'Average total business expenses'])\
             .interactive()
```

You should get the following output:

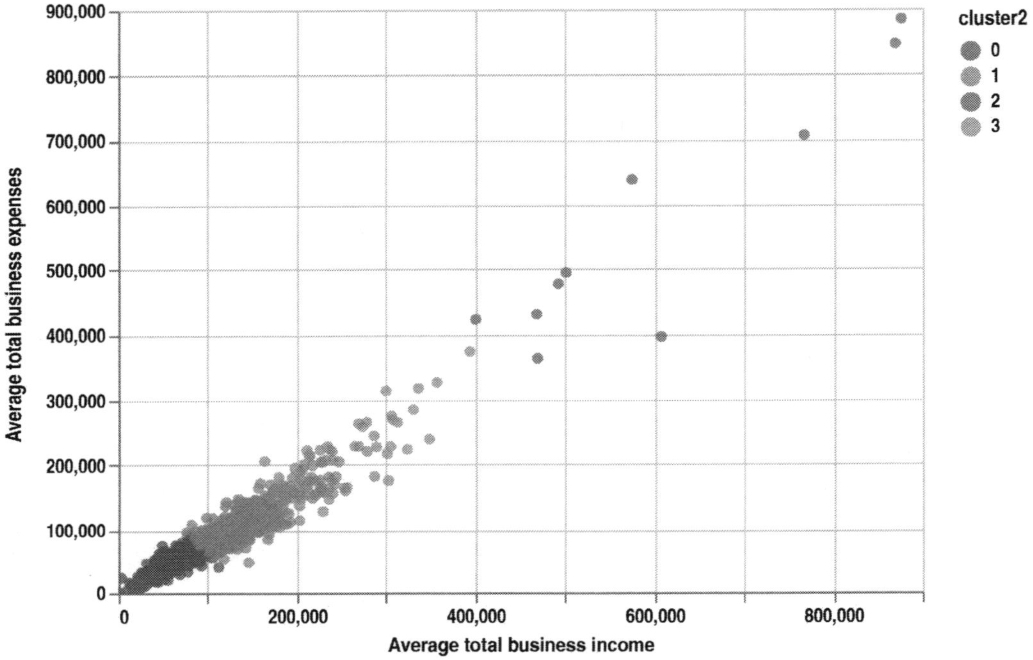

Figure 5.25: Scatter plot of the four clusters

> **NOTE**
>
> To access the source code for this specific section, please refer to https://packt.live/3iK1rPQ.
>
> This section does not currently have an online interactive example, but can be run as usual on Google Colab.

You just learned how to find the optimal number of clusters before fitting a k-means model. The data points are grouped into four different clusters in our output here:

- Cluster 0 (blue) is for all the observations with average total business income values lower than 100,000 and average total business expense values lower than 80,000.
- Cluster 1 (orange) is grouping data points that have an average total business income value lower than 180,000 and average total business expense values lower than 160,000.
- Cluster 3 (cyan) is for data points that have an average total business income value lower than 370,000 and average total business expense values lower than 330,000.
- Cluster 2 (red) is for data points with extreme values – those with average total business income values higher than 370,000 and average total business expense values higher than 330,000.

The results from *Exercise 5.02, Clustering Australian Postcodes by Business Income and Expenses*, have eight different clusters, and some of them are very similar to each other. Here, you saw that having the optimal number of clusters provides better differentiation between the groups, and this is why it is one of the most important hyperparameters to be tuned for k-means. In the next section, we will look at two other important hyperparameters for initializing k-means.

INITIALIZING CLUSTERS

Since the beginning of this chapter, we've been referring to k-means every time we've fitted our clustering algorithms. But you may have noticed in each model summary that there was a hyperparameter called **`init`** with the default value as k-means++. We were, in fact, using k-means++ all this time.

The difference between k-means and k-means++ is in how they initialize clusters at the start of the training. k-means randomly chooses the center of each cluster (called the **centroid**) and then assigns each data point to its nearest cluster. If this cluster initialization is chosen incorrectly, this may lead to non-optimal grouping at the end of the training process. For example, in the following graph, we can clearly see the three natural groupings of the data, but the algorithm didn't succeed in identifying them properly:

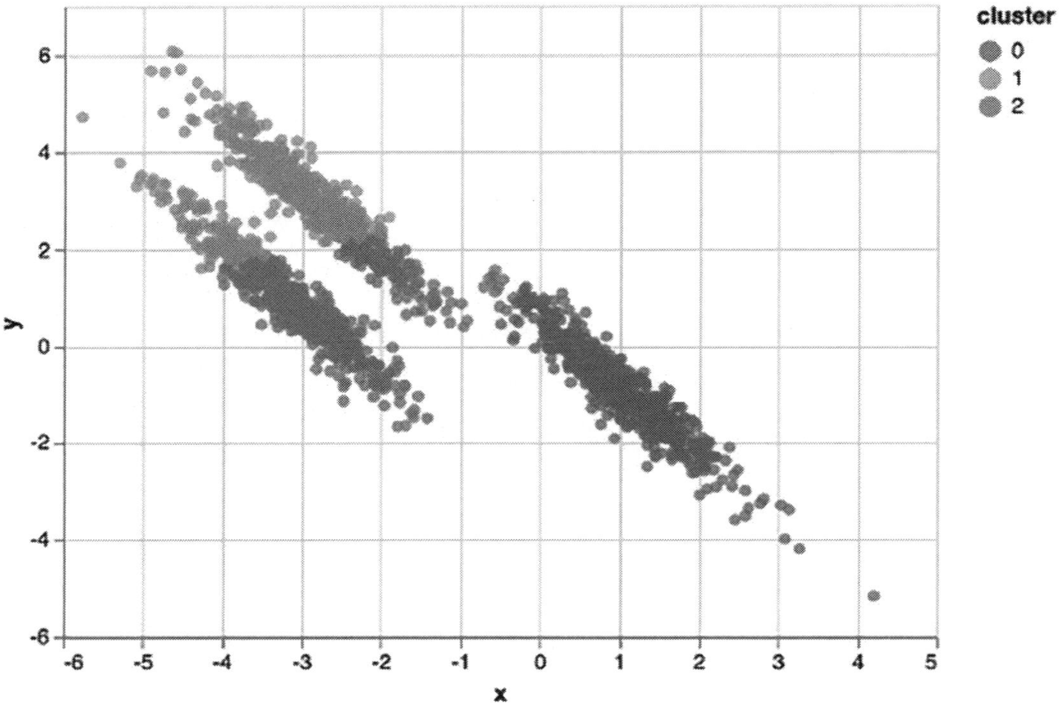

Figure 5.26: Example of non-optimal clusters being found

k-means++ is an attempt to find better clusters at initialization time. The idea behind it is to choose the first cluster randomly and then pick the next ones, those further away, using a probability distribution from the remaining data points. Even though k-means++ tends to get better results compared to the original k-means, in some cases, it can still lead to non-optimal clustering.

Another hyperparameter data scientists can use to lower the risk of incorrect clusters is **`n_init`**. This corresponds to the number of times k-means is run with different initializations, the final model being the best run. So, if you have a high number for this hyperparameter, you will have a higher chance of finding the optimal clusters, but the downside is that the training time will be longer. So, you have to choose this value carefully, especially if you have a large dataset.

Let's try this out on our ATO dataset by having a look at the following example.

> **NOTE**
>
> Open the notebook you were using for *Exercise 5.01*, *Performing Your First Clustering Analysis on the ATO Dataset,* and earlier examples. Execute the code you already entered, and then continue at the end of the notebook with the following code.

First, let's run only one iteration using random initialization:

```
kmeans = KMeans(random_state=14, n_clusters=3, \
                init='random', n_init=1)
kmeans.fit(X)
```

As usual, we want to visualize our clusters with a scatter plot, as defined in the following code snippet:

```
df['cluster3'] = kmeans.predict(X)
alt.Chart(df).mark_circle()\
             .encode(x='Average net tax', \
                     y='Average total deductions', \
                     color='cluster3:N', \
                     tooltip=['Postcode', 'cluster', \
                              'Average net tax', \
                              'Average total deductions']) \
             .interactive()
```

You should get the following output:

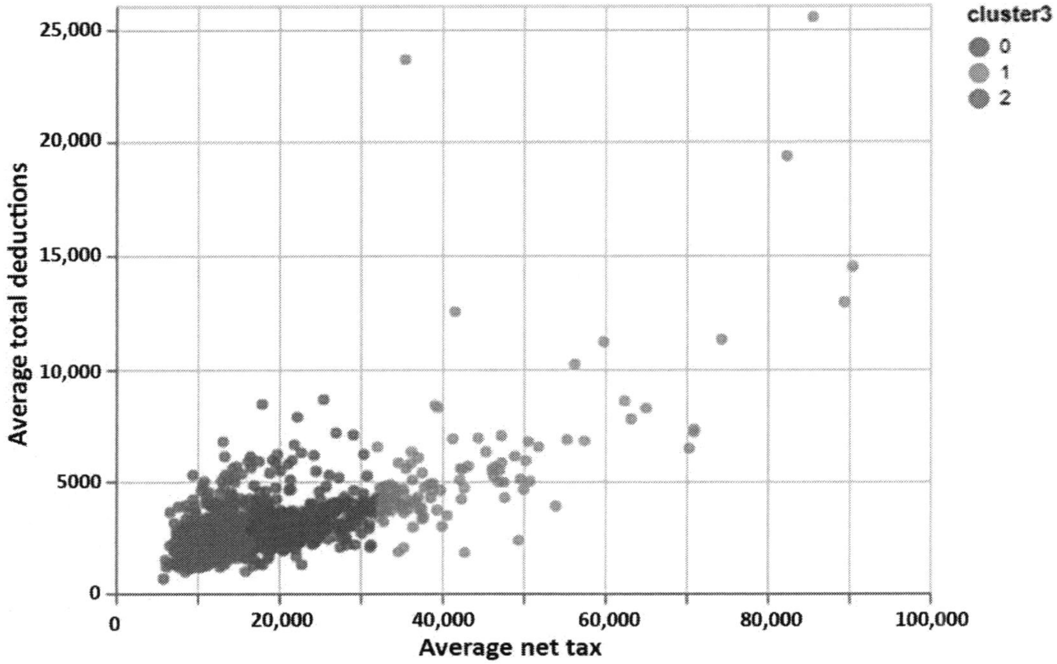

Figure 5.27: Clustering results with n_init as 1 and init as random

Overall, the result is very close to that of our previous run. It is worth noticing that the boundaries between the clusters are slightly different.

Now let's try with five iterations (using the **`n_init`** hyperparameter) and k-means++ initialization (using the **`init`** hyperparameter):

```
kmeans = KMeans(random_state=14, n_clusters=3, \
                init='k-means++', n_init=5)
kmeans.fit(X)
df['cluster4'] = kmeans.predict(X)
alt.Chart(df).mark_circle()\
                .encode(x='Average net tax', \
                        y='Average total deductions', \
                        color='cluster4:N', \
                        tooltip=['Postcode', 'cluster', \
                                 'Average net tax', \
                                 'Average total deductions'])\
                .interactive()
```

You should get the following output:

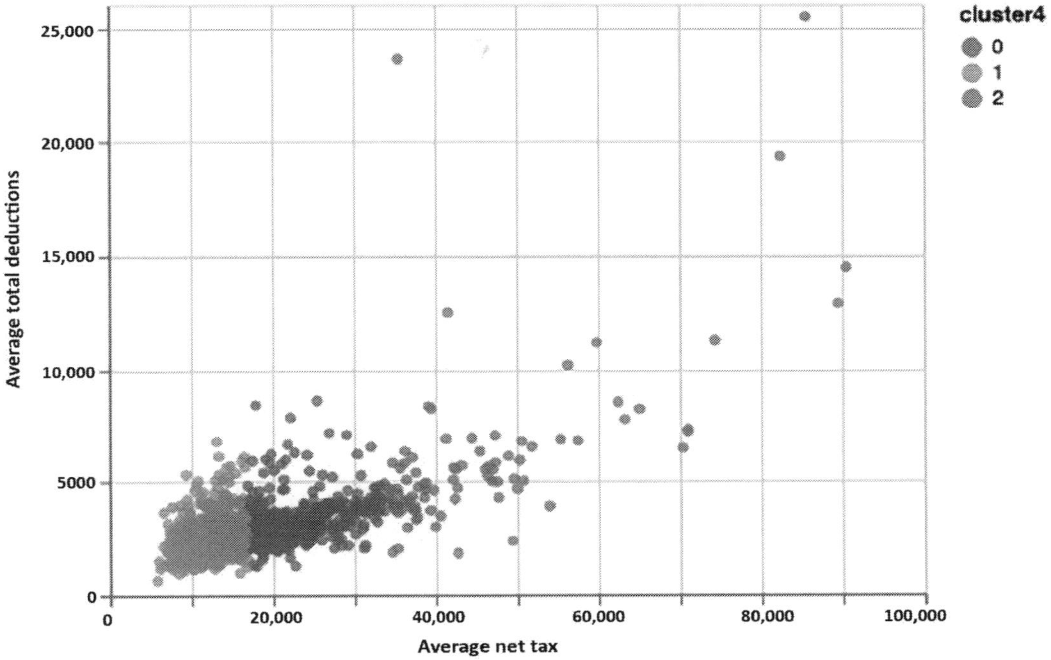

Figure 5.28: Clustering results with n_init as 5 and init as k-means++

Here, the results are very close to the original run with 10 iterations. This means that we didn't have to run so many iterations for k-means to converge and could have saved some time with a lower number.

EXERCISE 5.04: USING DIFFERENT INITIALIZATION PARAMETERS TO ACHIEVE A SUITABLE OUTCOME

In this exercise, we will use the same data as in *Exercise 5.02, Clustering Australian Postcodes by Business Income and Expenses*, and try different values for the **init** and **n_init** hyperparameters and see how they affect the final clustering result:

1. Open a new Colab notebook.
2. Import the required packages, which are **pandas**, **sklearn**, and **altair**:

```
import pandas as pd
from sklearn.cluster import KMeans
import altair as alt
```

3. Assign the link to the ATO dataset to a variable called **file_url**:

```
file_url = 'https://raw.githubusercontent.com'\
           '/PacktWorkshops/The-Data-Science-Workshop'\
           '/master/Chapter05/DataSet/taxstats2015.csv'
```

4. Load the dataset and select the same columns as in *Exercise 5.02, Clustering Australian Postcodes by Business Income and Expenses*, and *Exercise 5.03, Finding the Optimal Number of Clusters*, using the **read_csv()** method from the **pandas** package:

```
df = pd.read_csv(file_url, \
                 usecols=['Postcode', \
                          'Average total business income', \
                          'Average total business expenses'])
```

5. Assign the **'Average total business income'** and **'Average total business expenses'** columns to a new variable called **X**:

```
X = df[['Average total business income', \
        'Average total business expenses']]
```

6. Fit a k-means model with **n_init** equal to **1** and a random **init**:

```
kmeans = KMeans(random_state=1, n_clusters=4, \
                init='random', n_init=1)
kmeans.fit(X)
```

7. Using the **predict** method from the **sklearn** package, predict the clustering assignment from the input variable, **(X)**, and save the results into a new column called **'cluster3'** in the DataFrame:

```
df['cluster3'] = kmeans.predict(X)
```

8. Plot the clusters using an interactive scatter plot. First, use **Chart()** and **mark_circle()** from the **altair** package to instantiate a scatter plot graph, as shown in the following code snippet:

```
scatter_plot = alt.Chart(df).mark_circle()
```

9. Use the **encode** and **interactive** methods from **altair** to specify the display of the scatter plot and its interactivity options with the following parameters:

   Provide the name of the **'Average total business income'** column to the **x** parameter (x-axis).

Provide the name of the **'Average total business expenses'** column to the **y** parameter (y-axis).

Provide the name of the **'cluster3:N'** column to the **color** parameter (which defines the different colors for each group).

Provide these column names – **'Postcode'**, **'cluster3'**, **'Average total business income'**, and **'Average total business expenses'** – to the **tooltip** parameter:

```
scatter_plot.encode(x='Average total business income', \
                    y='Average total business expenses', \
                    color='cluster3:N', \
                    tooltip=['Postcode', 'cluster3', \
                             'Average total business income', \
                             'Average total business expenses'])\
                   .interactive()
```

You should get the following output:

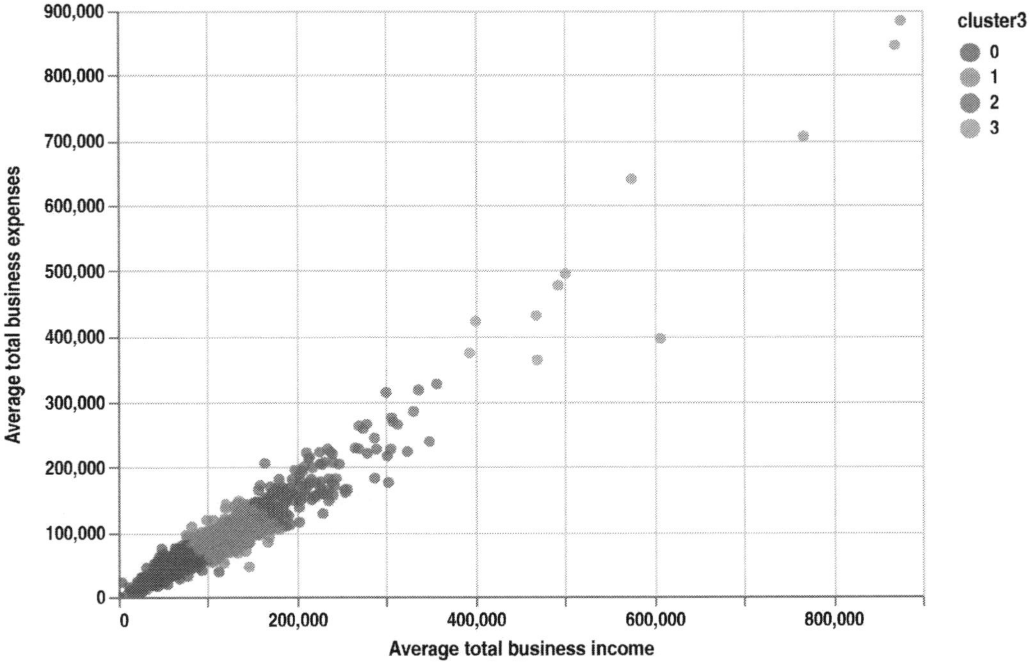

Figure 5.29: Clustering results with n_init as 1 and init as random

10. Repeat *Steps 5* to *8* but with different k-means hyperparameters, **`n_init=10`** and random **`init`**, as shown in the following code snippet:

```
kmeans = KMeans(random_state=1, n_clusters=4, \
                init='random', n_init=10)
kmeans.fit(X)
df['cluster4'] = kmeans.predict(X)
scatter_plot = alt.Chart(df).mark_circle()
scatter_plot.encode(x='Average total business income', \
                    y='Average total business expenses', \
                    color='cluster4:N',
                    tooltip=['Postcode', 'cluster4', \
                             'Average total business income', \
                             'Average total business expenses'])\
                   .interactive()
```

You should get the following output:

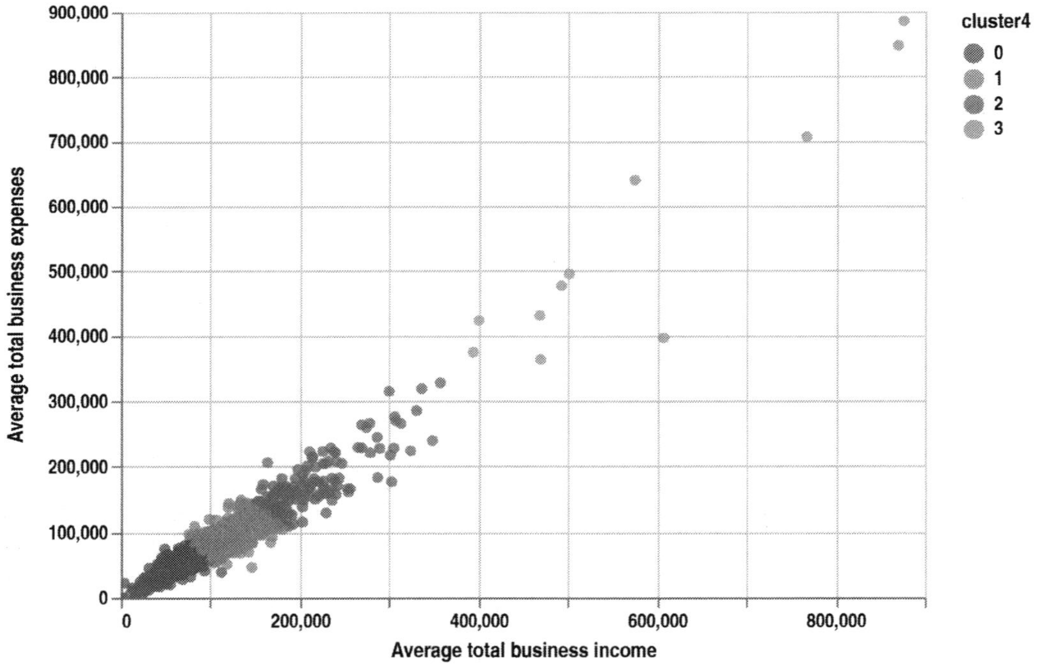

Figure 5.30: Clustering results with n_init as 10 and init as random

11. Again, repeat *Steps 5* to *8* but with different k-means hyperparameters – **`n_init=100`** and random **`init`**:

```
kmeans = KMeans(random_state=1, n_clusters=4, \
                init='random', n_init=100)
kmeans.fit(X)
df['cluster5'] = kmeans.predict(X)
scatter_plot = alt.Chart(df).mark_circle()
scatter_plot.encode(x='Average total business income', \
                    y='Average total business expenses', \
                    color='cluster5:N', \
                    tooltip=['Postcode', 'cluster5', \
                    'Average total business income', \
                    'Average total business expenses'])\
            .interactive()
```

You should get the following output:

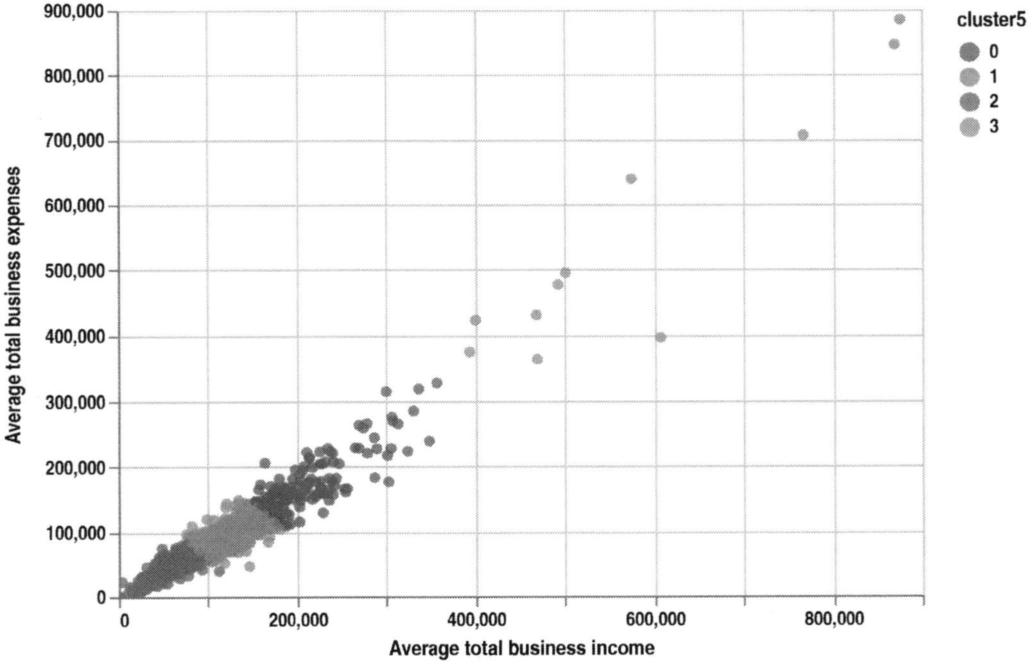

Figure 5.31: Clustering results with n_init as 10 and init as random

> **NOTE**
>
> To access the source code for this specific section, please refer to https://packt.live/315yGqP.
>
> This section does not currently have an online interactive example, but can be run as usual on Google Colab.

You just learned how to tune the two main hyperparameters responsible for initializing k-means clusters. You have seen in this exercise that increasing the number of iterations with **`n_init`** didn't have much impact on the clustering result for this dataset.

In this case, it is better to use a lower value for this hyperparameter as it will speed up the training time. But for a different dataset, you may face a case where the results differ drastically depending on the **`n_init`** value. In such a case, you will have to find a value of **`n_init`** that is not too small but also not too big. You want to find the sweet spot where the results do not change much compared to the last result obtained with a different value.

CALCULATING THE DISTANCE TO THE CENTROID

We've talked a lot about similarities between data points in the previous sections, but we haven't really defined what this means. You have probably guessed that it has something to do with how close or how far observations are from each other. You are heading in the right direction. It has to do with some sort of distance measure between two points. The one used by k-means is called **squared Euclidean distance** and its formula is:

$$d(x, y)^2 = \sum_{i=1}^{n} (x_i - y_i)^2$$

Figure 5.32: The squared Euclidean distance formula

If you don't have a statistical background, this formula may look intimidating, but it is actually very simple. It is the sum of the squared difference between the data coordinates. Here, *x* and *y* are two data points and the index, *i*, represents the number of coordinates. If the data has two dimensions, *i* equals 2. Similarly, if there are three dimensions, then *i* will be 3.

Let's apply this formula to the ATO dataset.

First, we will grab the values needed – that is, the coordinates from the first two observations – and print them:

> **NOTE**
>
> Open the notebook you were using for *Exercise 5.01*, *Performing Your First Clustering Analysis on the ATO Dataset*, and earlier examples. Execute the code you already entered, and then continue at the end of the notebook with the following code.

```
x = X.iloc[0,].values
y = X.iloc[1,].values
print(x)
print(y)
```

You should get the following output:

```
[27555  2071]
[28142  3804]
```

Figure 5.33: Extracting the first two observations from the ATO dataset

> **NOTE**
>
> In pandas, the **`iloc`** method is used to subset the rows or columns of a DataFrame by index. For instance, if we wanted to grab row number 888 and column number 6, we would use the following syntax: **`dataframe.iloc[888, 6]`**.

The coordinates for **`x`** are **`(27555, 2071)`** and the coordinates for **`y`** are **`(28142, 3804)`**. Here, the formula is telling us to calculate the squared difference between each axis of the two data points and sum them:

```
squared_euclidean = (x[0] - y[0])**2 + (x[1] - y[1])**2
print(squared_euclidean)
```

You should get the following output:

```
3347858
```

k-means uses this metric to calculate the distance between each data point and the center of its assigned cluster (also called the centroid). Here is the basic logic behind this algorithm:

1. Choose the centers of the clusters (the centroids) randomly.
2. Assign each data point to the nearest centroid using the squared Euclidean distance.
3. Update each centroid's coordinates to the newly calculated center of the data points assigned to it.
4. Repeat *Steps 2* and *3* until the clusters converge (that is, until the cluster assignment doesn't change anymore) or until the maximum number of iterations has been reached.

That's it. The k-means algorithm is as simple as that. We can extract the centroids after fitting a k-means model with **`cluster_centers_`**.

Let's see how we can plot the centroids in an example.

First, we fit a k-means model as shown in the following code snippet:

```
kmeans = KMeans(random_state=42, n_clusters=3, \
                init='k-means++', n_init=5)
kmeans.fit(X)
df['cluster6'] = kmeans.predict(X)
```

Now extract the **`centroids`** into a DataFrame and print them:

```
centroids = kmeans.cluster_centers_
centroids = pd.DataFrame(centroids, \
                         columns=['Average net tax', \
                                  'Average total deductions'])
print(centroids)
```

You should get the following output:

	Average net tax	Average total deductions
0	21645.622924	3054.901993
1	12395.607303	2383.760674
2	45279.802198	6067.000000

Figure 5.34: Coordinates of the three centroids

We will plot the usual scatter plot but will assign it to a variable called **chart1**:

```
chart1 = alt.Chart(df).mark_circle()\
            .encode(x='Average net tax', \
                    y='Average total deductions', \
                    color='cluster6:N', \
                    tooltip=['Postcode', 'cluster6', \
                             'Average net tax', \
                             'Average total deductions'])\
                   .interactive()
chart1
```

You should get the following output:

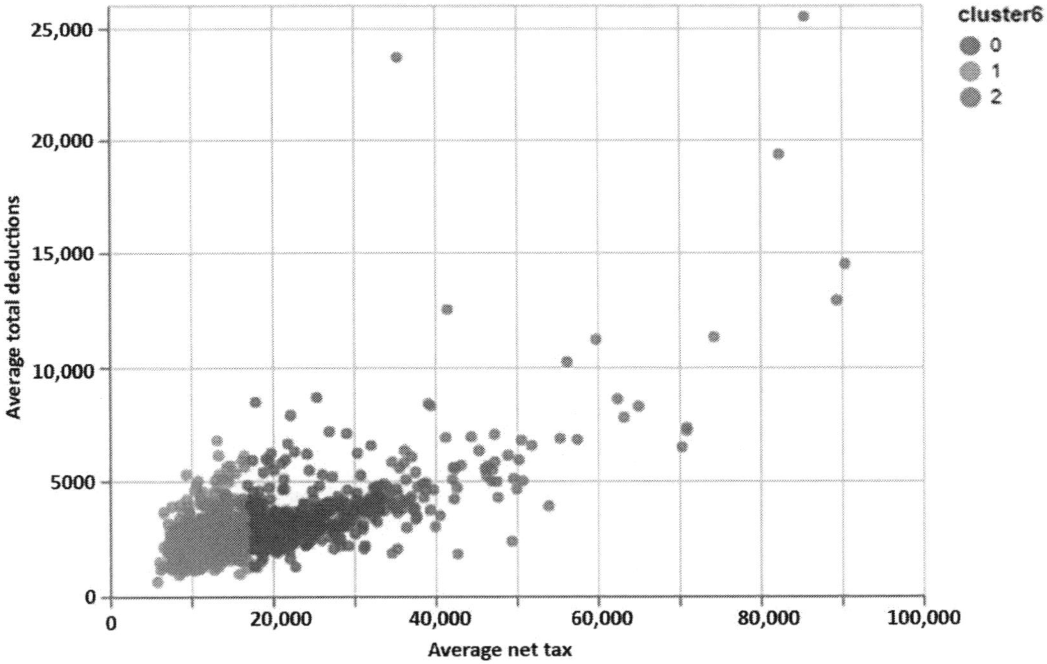

Figure 5.35: Scatter plot of the clusters

Now, to create a second scatter plot only for the centroids called **`chart2`**:

```
chart2 = alt.Chart(centroids).mark_circle(size=100)\
           .encode(x='Average net tax', \
                   y='Average total deductions', \
                   color=alt.value('black'), \
                   tooltip=['Average net tax', \
                            'Average total deductions'])\
                  .interactive()
chart2
```

You should get the following output:

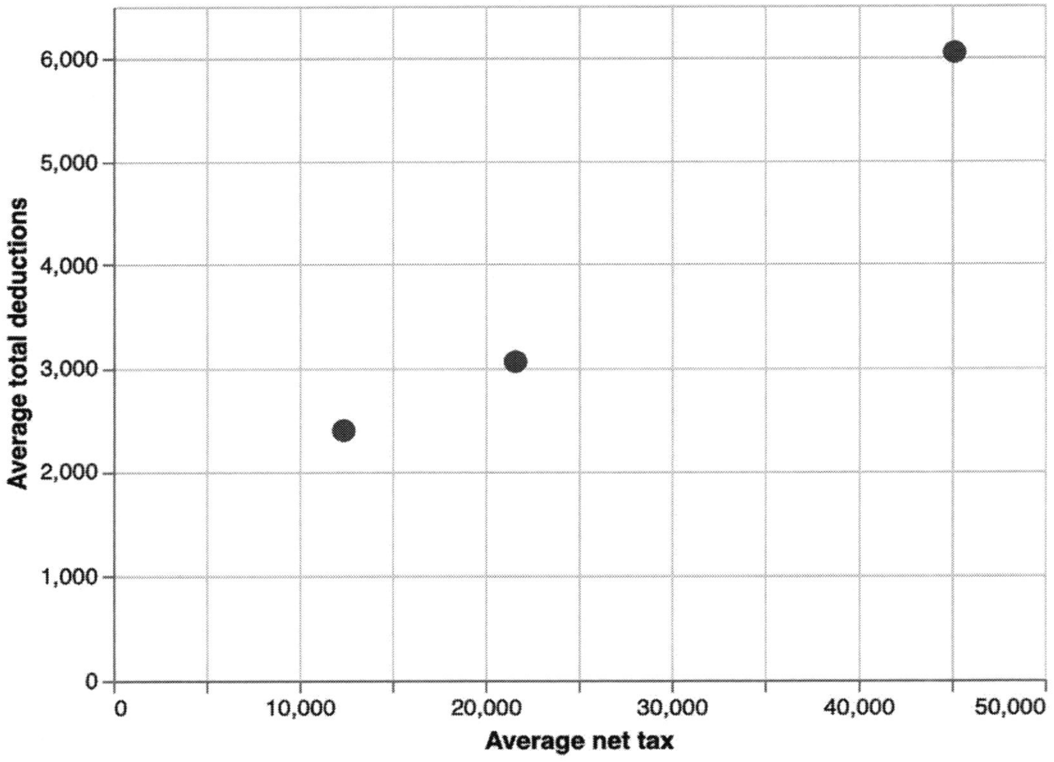

Figure 5.36: Scatter plot of the centroids

And now we combine the two charts, which is extremely easy with **`altair`**:

```
chart1 + chart2
```

You should get the following output:

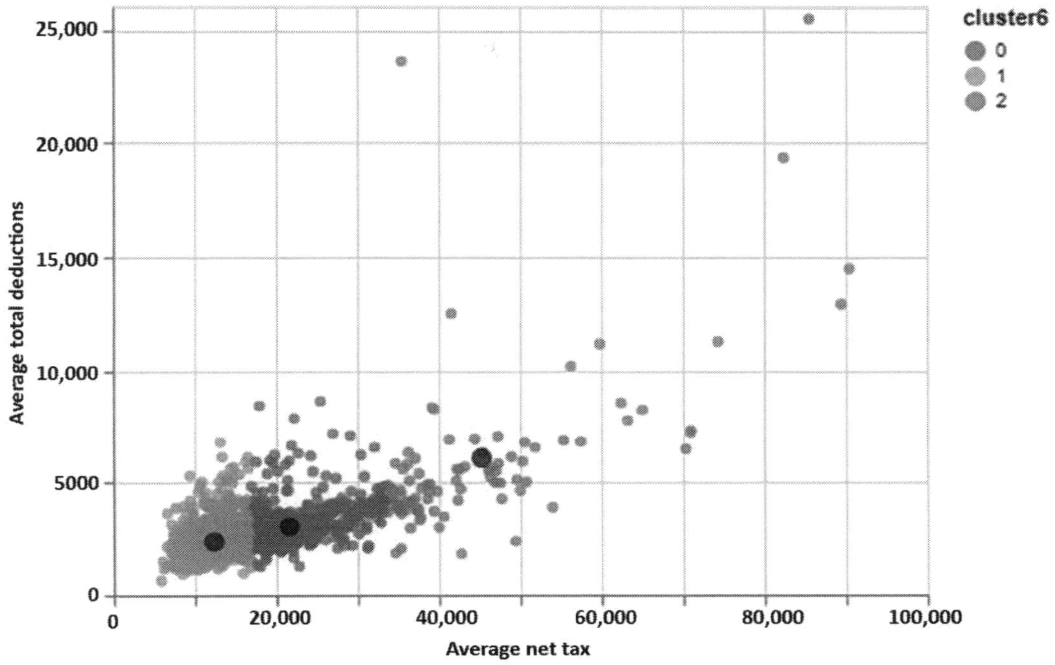

Figure 5.37: Scatter plot of the clusters and their centroids

Now we can easily see which centroids the observations are closest to.

EXERCISE 5.05: FINDING THE CLOSEST CENTROIDS IN OUR DATASET

In this exercise, we will be coding the first iteration of k-means in order to assign data points to their closest cluster centroids. The following steps will help you complete the exercise:

1. Open a new Colab notebook.
2. Now **`import`** the required packages, which are **`pandas`**, **`sklearn`**, and **`altair`**:

```
import pandas as pd
from sklearn.cluster import KMeans
import altair as alt
```

3. Load the dataset and select the same columns as in *Exercise 5.02, Clustering Australian Postcodes by Business Income and Expenses*, using the **read_csv()** method from the **pandas** package:

```
file_url = 'https://raw.githubusercontent.com/'\
           'PacktWorkshops/The-Data-Science-Workshop/'\
           'master/Chapter05/DataSet/taxstats2015.csv'
df = pd.read_csv(file_url, \
                 usecols=['Postcode', \
                          'Average total business income', \
                          'Average total business expenses'])
```

4. Assign the **'Average total business income'** and **'Average total business expenses'** columns to a new variable called **X**:

```
X = df[['Average total business income', \
        'Average total business expenses']]
```

5. Now, calculate the minimum and maximum using the **min()** and **max()** values of the **'Average total business income'** and **'Average total business income'** variables, as shown in the following code snippet:

```
business_income_min = df['Average total business income'].min()
business_income_max = df['Average total business income'].max()

business_expenses_min = df['Average total business expenses']\
                        .min()
business_expenses_max = df['Average total business expenses']\
                        .max()
```

6. Print the values of these four variables, which are the minimum and maximum values of the two variables:

```
print(business_income_min)
print(business_income_max)
print(business_expenses_min)
print(business_expenses_max)
```

You should get the following output:

```
0
876324
0
884659
```

7. Now import the **random** package and use the **seed()** method to set a seed of **42**, as shown in the following code snippet:

```
import random
random.seed(42)
```

8. Create an empty pandas DataFrame and assign it to a variable called **centroids**:

```
centroids = pd.DataFrame()
```

9. Generate four random values using the **sample()** method from the **random** package with possible values between the minimum and maximum values of the **'Average total business expenses'** column using **range()** and store the results in a new column called **'Average total business income'** from the **centroids** DataFrame:

```
centroids\
['Average total business income'] = random.sample\
                                    (range\
                                    (business_income_min, \
                                     business_income_max), 4)
```

10. Repeat the same process to generate **4** random values for **'Average total business expenses'**:

```
centroids\
['Average total business expenses'] = random.sample\
                                      (range\
                                      (business_expenses_min,\
                                       business_expenses_max), 4)
```

11. Create a new column called **'cluster'** from the **centroids** DataFrame using the **.index** attributes from the pandas package and print this DataFrame:

```
centroids['cluster'] = centroids.index
centroids
```

You should get the following output:

	Average total business income	Average total business expenses	cluster
0	670487	288389	0
1	116739	256787	1
2	26225	234053	2
3	777572	146316	3

Figure 5.38: Coordinates of the four random centroids

12. Create a scatter plot with the **altair** package to display the data contained in the **df** DataFrame and save it in a variable called **'chart1'**:

```
chart1 = alt.Chart(df.head()).mark_circle()\
              .encode(x='Average total business income', \
                      y='Average total business expenses', \
                      color=alt.value('orange'), \
                      tooltip=['Postcode', \
                               'Average total business income', \
                               'Average total business expenses'])\
                 .interactive()
```

13. Now create a second scatter plot using the **altair** package to display the centroids and save it in a variable called **'chart2'**:

```
chart2 = alt.Chart(centroids).mark_circle(size=100)\
              .encode(x='Average total business income', \
                      y='Average total business expenses', \
                      color=alt.value('black'), \
                      tooltip=['cluster', \
                               'Average total business income',\
                               'Average total business expenses'])\
                 .interactive()
```

14. Display the two charts together using the altair syntax: **<chart> + <chart>**:

```
chart1 + chart2
```

You should get the following output:

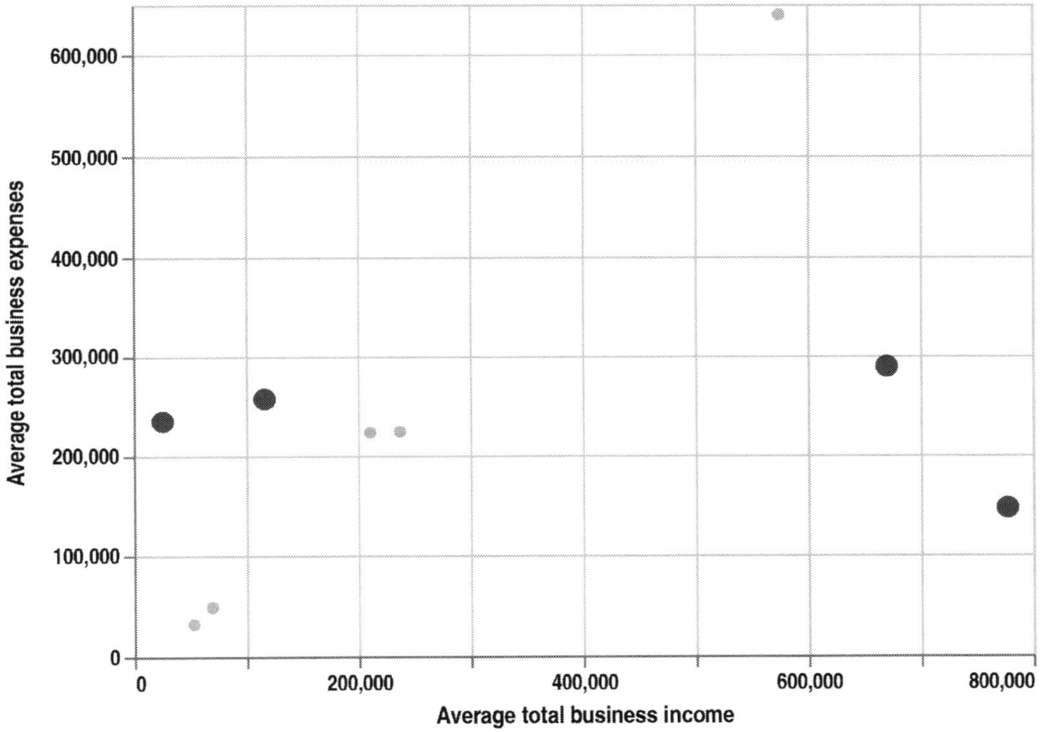

Figure 5.39: Scatter plot of the random centroids and the first five observations

15. Define a function that will calculate the **squared_euclidean** distance and return its value. This function will take the **x** and **y** coordinates of a data point and a centroid:

```
def squared_euclidean(data_x, data_y, \
                      centroid_x, centroid_y, ):
    return (data_x - centroid_x)**2 + (data_y - centroid_y)**2
```

16. Using the **.at** method from the pandas package, extract the first row's **x** and **y** coordinates and save them in two variables called **data_x** and **data_y**:

```
data_x = df.at[0, 'Average total business income']
data_y = df.at[0, 'Average total business expenses']
```

17. Using a **for** loop or list comprehension, calculate the **squared_euclidean** distance of the first observation (using its **data_x** and **data_y** coordinates) against the **4** different centroids contained in **centroids**, save the result in a variable called **distance**, and display it:

```
distances = [squared_euclidean\
             (data_x, data_y, centroids.at\
              [i, 'Average total business income'], \
              centroids.at[i, \
              'Average total business expenses']) \
              for i in range(4)]
distances
```

You should get the following output:

```
[215601466600, 10063365460, 34245932020, 326873037866]
```

18. Use the **index** method from the list containing the **squared_euclidean** distances to find the cluster with the shortest distance, as shown in the following code snippet:

```
cluster_index = distances.index(min(distances))
```

19. Save the **cluster** index in a column called **'cluster'** from the **df** DataFrame for the first observation using the **.at** method from the pandas package:

```
df.at[0, 'cluster'] = cluster_index
```

20. Display the first five rows of **df** using the **head()** method from the **pandas** package:

```
df.head()
```

You should get the following output:

	Postcode	Average total business income	Average total business expenses	cluster
0	2000	210901	222191	1.0
1	2006	69983	48971	NaN
2	2007	575099	639499	NaN
3	2008	53329	32173	NaN
4	2009	237539	222993	NaN

Figure 5.40: The first five rows of the ATO DataFrame with the assigned cluster number for the first row

21. Repeat *Steps 15* to *19* for the next **4** rows to calculate their distances from the centroids and find the cluster with the smallest distance value:

```
distances = [squared_euclidean\
             (df.at[1, 'Average total business income'], \
              df.at[1, 'Average total business expenses'], \
              centroids.at[i, 'Average total business income'],\
              centroids.at[i, \
                           'Average total business expenses'])\
             for i in range(4)]
df.at[1, 'cluster'] = distances.index(min(distances))

distances = [squared_euclidean\
             (df.at[2, 'Average total business income'], \
              df.at[2, 'Average total business expenses'], \
              centroids.at[i, 'Average total business income'],\
              centroids.at[i, \
                           'Average total business expenses'])\
             for i in range(4)]
df.at[2, 'cluster'] = distances.index(min(distances))

distances = [squared_euclidean\
             (df.at[3, 'Average total business income'], \
              df.at[3, 'Average total business expenses'], \
              centroids.at[i, 'Average total business income'],\
              centroids.at[i, \
                           'Average total business expenses'])\
             for i in range(4)]
df.at[3, 'cluster'] = distances.index(min(distances))

distances = [squared_euclidean\
             (df.at[4, 'Average total business income'], \
              df.at[4, 'Average total business expenses'], \
              centroids.at[i, \
              'Average total business income'], \
              centroids.at[i, \
              'Average total business expenses']) \
             for i in range(4)]
```

```
df.at[4, 'cluster'] = distances.index(min(distances))

df.head()
```

You should get the following output:

	Postcode	Average total business income	Average total business expenses	cluster
0	2000	210901	222191	1.0
1	2006	69983	48971	2.0
2	2007	575099	639499	0.0
3	2008	53329	32173	2.0
4	2009	237539	222993	1.0

Figure 5.41: The first five rows of the ATO DataFrame and their assigned clusters

22. Finally, plot the centroids and the first **5** rows of the dataset using the **altair** package as in *Steps 12* to *13*:

```
chart1 = alt.Chart(df.head()).mark_circle()\
              .encode(x='Average total business income', \
                      y='Average total business expenses', \
                      color='cluster:N', \
                      tooltip=['Postcode', 'cluster', \
                               'Average total business income', \
                               'Average total business expenses'])\
                      .interactive()

chart2 = alt.Chart(centroids).mark_circle(size=100)\
              .encode(x='Average total business income', \
                      y='Average total business expenses', \
                      color=alt.value('black'), \
                      tooltip=['cluster', \
                               'Average total business income',\
                               'Average total business expenses'])\
                      .interactive()
chart1 + chart2
```

UJQ95

You should get the following output:

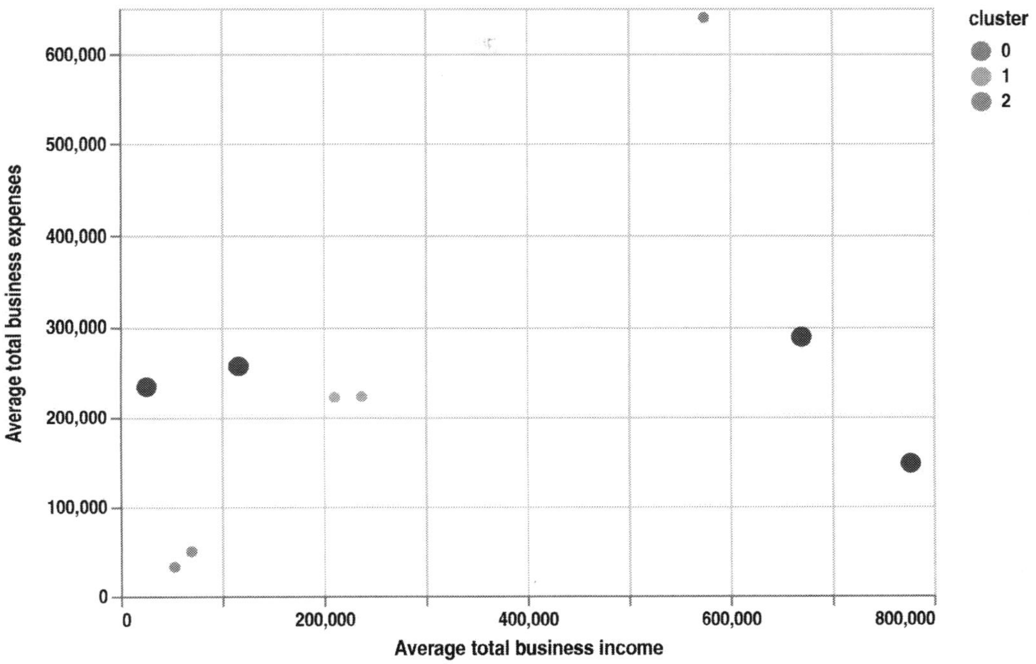

Figure 5.42: Scatter plot of the random centroids and the first five observations

> **NOTE**
>
> To access the source code for this specific section, please refer to https://packt.live/3iPQo7L.
>
> This section does not currently have an online interactive example, but can be run as usual on Google Colab.

In this final result, we can see where the four clusters have been placed in the graph and which cluster the five data points have been assigned to:

- The two data points in the bottom-left corner have been assigned to cluster 2, which corresponds to the one with a centroid of coordinates of 26,000 (average total business income) and 234,000 (average total business expense). It is the closest centroid for these two points.
- The two observations in the middle are very close to the centroid with coordinates of 116,000 (average total business income) and 256,000 (average total business expense), which corresponds to cluster 1.
- The observation at the top has been assigned to cluster 0, whose centroid has coordinates of 670,000 (average total business income) and 288,000 (average total business expense).

You just re-implemented a big part of the k-means algorithm from scratch. You went through how to randomly initialize centroids (cluster centers), calculate the squared Euclidean distance for some data points, find their closest centroid, and assign them to the corresponding cluster. This wasn't easy, but you made it.

STANDARDIZING DATA

You've already learned a lot about the k-means algorithm, and we are close to the end of this chapter. In this final section, we will not talk about another hyperparameter (you've already been through the main ones) but a very important topic: **data processing**.

Fitting a k-means algorithm is extremely easy. The trickiest part is making sure the resulting clusters are meaningful for your project, and we have seen how we can tune some hyperparameters to ensure this. But handling input data is as important as all the steps you have learned about so far. If your dataset is not well prepared, even if you find the best hyperparameters, you will still get some bad results.

Let's have another look at our ATO dataset. In the previous section, *Calculating the Distance to the Centroid*, we found three different clusters, and they were mainly defined by the `'Average net tax'` variable. It was as if k-means didn't take into account the second variable, `'Average total deductions'`, at all. This is in fact due to these two variables having very different ranges of values and the way that squared Euclidean distance is calculated.

Squared Euclidean distance is weighted more toward high-value variables. Let's take an example to illustrate this point with two data points called A and B with respective x and y coordinates of (1, 50000) and (100, 100000). The squared Euclidean distance between A and B will be (100000 - 50000)^2 + (100 - 1)^2. We can clearly see that the result will be mainly driven by the difference between 100,000 and 50,000: 50,000^2. The difference of 100 minus 1 (99^2) will account for very little in the final result.

But if you look at the ratio between 100,000 and 50,000, it is a factor of 2 (100,000 / 50,000 = 2), while the ratio between 100 and 1 is a factor of 100 (100 / 1 = 100). Does it make sense for the higher-value variable to "dominate" the clustering result? It really depends on your project, and this situation may be intended. But if you want things to be fair between the different axes, it's preferable to bring them all into a similar range of values before fitting a k-means model. This is the reason why you should always consider standardizing your data before running your k-means algorithm.

There are multiple ways to standardize data, and we will have a look at the two most popular ones: **min-max scaling** and **z-score**. Luckily for us, the **`sklearn`** package has an implementation for both methods.

The formula for min-max scaling is very simple: on each axis, you need to remove the minimum value for each data point and divide the result by the difference between the maximum and minimum values. The scaled data will have values ranging between 0 and 1:

$$X_{sc} = \frac{X - X_{min}}{X_{max} - X_{min}}.$$

Figure 5.43: Min-max scaling formula

Let's look at min-max scaling with **`sklearn`** in the following example.

> **NOTE**
>
> Open the notebook you were using for *Exercise 5.01, Performing Your First Clustering Analysis on the ATO Dataset*, and earlier examples. Execute the code you already entered, and then continue at the end of the notebook with the following code.

First, we import the relevant class and instantiate an object:

```
from sklearn.preprocessing import MinMaxScaler
min_max_scaler = MinMaxScaler()
```

Then, we fit it to our dataset:

```
min_max_scaler.fit(X)
```

You should get the following output:

```
MinMaxScaler(copy=True, feature_range=(0, 1))
```

Figure 5.44: Min-max scaling summary

And finally, call the **transform()** method to standardize the data:

```
X_min_max = min_max_scaler.transform(X)
X_min_max
```

You should get the following output:

```
array([[0.25619932, 0.05804452],
       [0.26313737, 0.1278026 ],
       [0.11547644, 0.04472085],
       ...,
       [0.12640947, 0.06762468],
       [0.27085549, 0.09700922],
       [0.14493062, 0.06287485]])
```

Figure 5.45: Min-max-scaled data

Now we print the minimum and maximum values of the min-max-scaled data for both axes:

```
X_min_max[:,0].min(), X_min_max[:,0].max(), \
X_min_max[:,1].min(), X_min_max[:,1].max()
```

You should get the following output:

```
(0.0, 1.0000000000000002, 0.0, 1.0)
```

Figure 5.46: Minimum and maximum values of the min-max-scaled data

We can see that both axes now have their values sitting between 0 and 1.

The **z-score** is calculated by removing the overall average from the data point and dividing the result by the standard deviation for each axis. The distribution of the standardized data will have a mean of 0 and a standard deviation of 1:

$$z_i = \frac{x_i - \bar{x}}{s}$$

Figure 5.47: Z-score formula

To apply it with **sklearn**, first, we have to import the relevant **StandardScaler** class and instantiate an object:

```
from sklearn.preprocessing import StandardScaler
standard_scaler = StandardScaler()
```

This time, instead of calling **fit()** and then **transform()**, we use the **fit_transform()** method:

```
X_scaled = standard_scaler.fit_transform(X)
X_scaled
```

You should get the following output:

```
array([[ 1.47818338, -0.49490091],
       [ 1.55236034,  0.90726658],
       [-0.02633256, -0.76271247],
       ...,
       [ 0.09055617, -0.30233549],
       [ 1.63487747,  0.28830632],
       [ 0.288572  , -0.3978091 ]])
```

Figure 5.48: Z-score-standardized data

Now we'll look at the minimum and maximum values for each axis:

```
X_scaled[:,0].min(), X_scaled[:,0].max(), \
X_scaled[:,1].min(), X_scaled[:,1].max()
```

You should get the following output:

```
(-1.2609303032180148,
 9.430408155273339,
 -1.6616207628956663,
 18.438810177350547)
```

Figure 5.49: Minimum and maximum values of the z-score-standardized data

The value ranges for both axes are much lower now and we can see that their maximum values are around 9 and 18, which indicates that there are some extreme outliers in the data.

Now, to fit a k-means model and plot a scatter plot on the z-score-standardized data with the following code snippet:

```
kmeans = KMeans(random_state=42, n_clusters=3, \
                init='k-means++', n_init=5)
kmeans.fit(X_scaled)
df['cluster7'] = kmeans.predict(X_scaled)
alt.Chart(df).mark_circle()\
             .encode(x='Average net tax', \
                     y='Average total deductions', \
                     color='cluster7:N', \
                     tooltip=['Postcode', 'cluster7', \
                              'Average net tax', \
                              'Average total deductions'])\
                    .interactive()
```

You should get the following output:

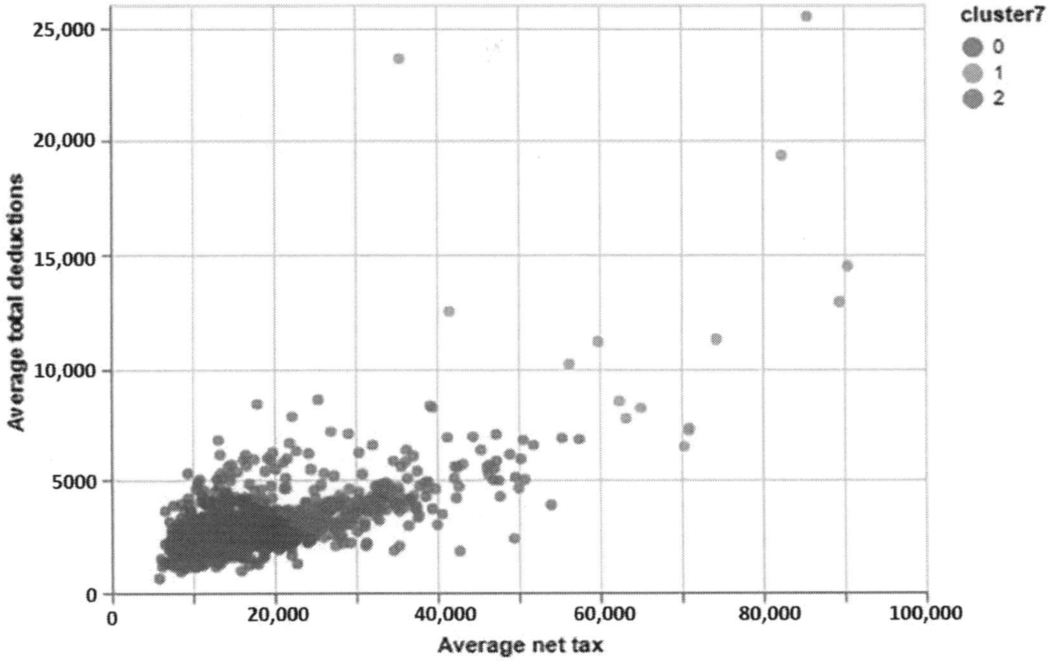

Figure 5.50: Scatter plot of the standardized data

k-means results are very different from the standardized data. Now we can see that there are two main clusters (blue and red) and their boundaries are not straight vertical lines anymore but diagonal. So, k-means is actually taking into consideration both axes now. The orange cluster contains much fewer data points compared to previous iterations, and it seems it is grouping all the extreme outliers with high values together. If your project was about detecting anomalies, you would have found a way here to easily separate outliers from "normal" observations.

EXERCISE 5.06: STANDARDIZING THE DATA FROM OUR DATASET

In this final exercise, we will standardize the data using min-max scaling and the z-score and fit a k-means model for each method and see their impact on k-means:

1. Open a new Colab notebook.
2. Now import the required **pandas**, **sklearn**, and **altair** packages:

```
import pandas as pd
from sklearn.cluster import KMeans
import altair as alt
```

3. Load the dataset and select the same columns as in *Exercise 5.02, Clustering Australian Postcodes by Business Income and Expenses*, using the **read_csv()** method from the **pandas** package:

```
file_url = 'https://raw.githubusercontent.com'\
           '/PacktWorkshops/The-Data-Science-Workshop'\
           '/master/Chapter05/DataSet/taxstats2015.csv'
df = pd.read_csv(file_url, \
                 usecols=['Postcode', \
                          'Average total business income', \
                          'Average total business expenses'])
```

4. Assign the **'Average total business income'** and **'Average total business expenses'** columns to a new variable called **X**:

```
X = df[['Average total business income', \
        'Average total business expenses']]
```

5. Import the **MinMaxScaler** and **StandardScaler** classes from **sklearn**:

```
from sklearn.preprocessing import MinMaxScaler
from sklearn.preprocessing import StandardScaler
```

6. Instantiate and fit **MinMaxScaler** with the data:

```
min_max_scaler = MinMaxScaler()
min_max_scaler.fit(X)
```

You should get the following output:

```
MinMaxScaler(copy=True, feature_range=(0,1))
```

Figure 5.51: Summary of the min-max scaler

7. Perform the min-max scaling transformation and save the data into a new variable called **X_min_max**:

```
X_min_max = min_max_scaler.transform(X)
X_min_max
```

You should get the following output:

```
array([[0.24066555, 0.25116005],
       [0.07985973, 0.05535579],
       [0.65626298, 0.72287627],
       ...,
       [0.05203897, 0.03244188],
       [0.0606488 , 0.04504561],
       [0.13814183, 0.10186976]])
```

Figure 5.52: Min-max-scaled data

8. Fit a k-means model on the scaled data with the following hyperparameters: **random_state=1**, **n_clusters=4, init='k-means++', n_init=5**, as shown in the following code snippet:

```
kmeans = KMeans(random_state=1, n_clusters=4, \
                init='k-means++', n_init=5)
kmeans.fit(X_min_max)
```

9. Assign the k-means predictions of each value of **X** in a new column called **'cluster8'** in the **df** DataFrame:

```
df['cluster8'] = kmeans.predict(X_min_max)
```

10. Plot the k-means results into a scatter plot using the **altair** package:

```
scatter_plot = alt.Chart(df).mark_circle()
scatter_plot.encode(x='Average total business income', \
                    y='Average total business expenses',\
                    color='cluster8:N',\
                    tooltip=['Postcode', 'cluster8', \
                             'Average total business income',\
                             'Average total business expenses'])\
                   .interactive()
```

You should get the following output:

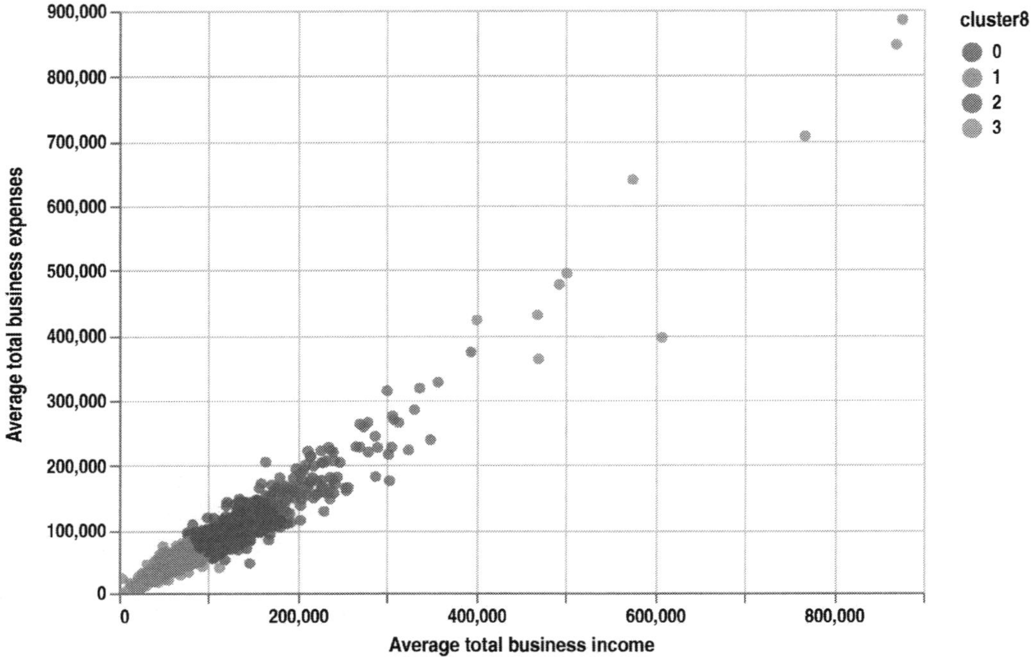

Figure 5.53: Scatter plot of k-means results using the min-max-scaled data

11. Re-train the k-means model but on the z-score-standardized data with the same hyperparameter values, **`random_state=1, n_clusters=4, init='k-means++', n_init=5`**:

```
standard_scaler = StandardScaler()
X_scaled = standard_scaler.fit_transform(X)
kmeans = KMeans(random_state=1, n_clusters=4, \
                init='k-means++', n_init=5)
kmeans.fit(X_scaled)
```

12. Assign the k-means predictions of each value of **`X_scaled`** in a new column called **`'cluster9'`** in the **`df`** DataFrame:

```
df['cluster9'] = kmeans.predict(X_scaled)
```

13. Plot the k-means results in a scatter plot using the **altair** package:

```
scatter_plot = alt.Chart(df).mark_circle()
scatter_plot.encode(x='Average total business income', \
                    y='Average total business expenses', \
                    color='cluster9:N', \
                    tooltip=['Postcode', 'cluster9', \
                             'Average total business income',\
                             'Average total business expenses'])\
                   .interactive()
```

You should get the following output:

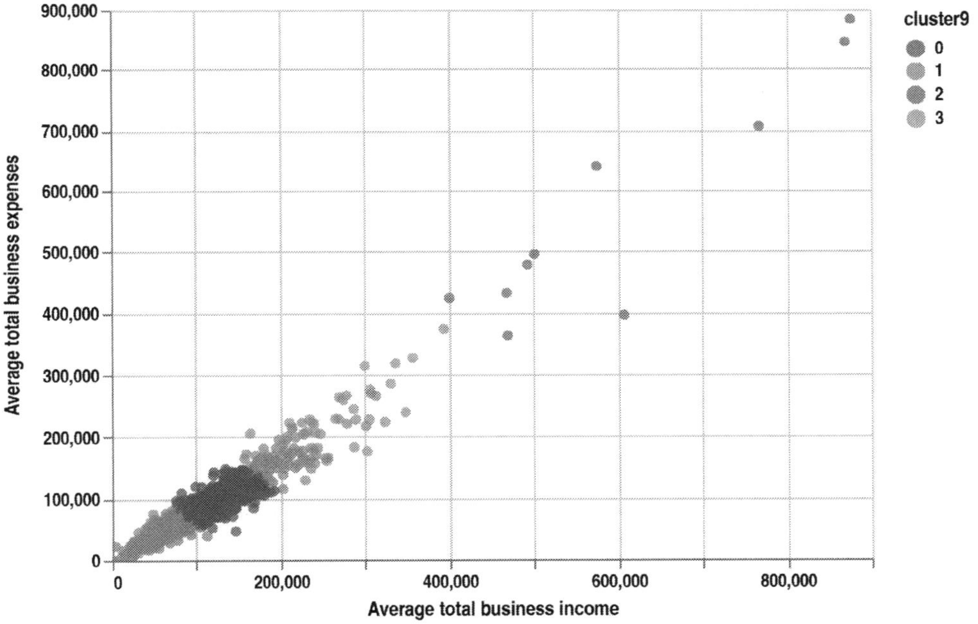

Figure 5.54: Scatter plot of k-means results using the z-score-standardized data

> **NOTE**
>
> To access the source code for this specific section, please refer to https://packt.live/2Q2BSND.
>
> This section does not currently have an online interactive example, but can be run as usual on Google Colab.

The k-means clustering results are very similar between min-max and z-score standardization, which are the outputs for *Steps 10* and *13*. Compared to the results in *Exercise 5.04, Using Different Initialization Parameters to Achieve a Suitable Outcome*, we can see that the boundaries between clusters 1 and 2 are slightly lower after standardization. The reason why these results are very close to each other is due to the fact that the range of values for the two variables (average total business income and average total business expenses) are almost identical: between 0 and 900,000. Therefore, k-means is not putting more weight toward one of these variables.

You've completed the final exercise of this chapter. You have learned how to preprocess data before fitting a k-means model with two very popular methods: min-max scaling and z-score.

ACTIVITY 5.01: PERFORM CUSTOMER SEGMENTATION ANALYSIS IN A BANK USING K-MEANS

You are working for an international bank. The credit department is reviewing its offerings and wants to get a better understanding of its current customers. You have been tasked with performing customer segmentation analysis. You will perform cluster analysis with k-means to identify groups of similar customers.

The following steps will help you complete this activity:

1. Download the dataset and load it into Python.
2. Read the CSV file using the **`read_csv()`** method.

> **NOTE**
>
> This dataset is in the **`.dat`** file format. You can still load the file using **`read_csv()`** but you will need to specify the following parameter: **`header=None, sep= '\s\s+' and prefix='X'`**.

3. You will be using the fourth and tenth columns (**`X3`** and **`X9`**). Extract these.
4. Perform data standardization by instantiating a **`StandardScaler`** object.
5. Analyze and define the optimal number of clusters.
6. Fit a k-means algorithm with the number of clusters you've defined.

7. Create a scatter plot of the clusters.

> **NOTE**
>
> This is the German Credit Dataset from the UCI Machine Learning Repository. It is available from the Packt repository at https://packt.live/31L2c2b.
> Even though all the columns in this dataset are integers, most of them are actually categorical variables. The data in these columns is not continuous. Only two variables are really numeric. Those are the ones you will use for your clustering.

You should get something similar to the following output:

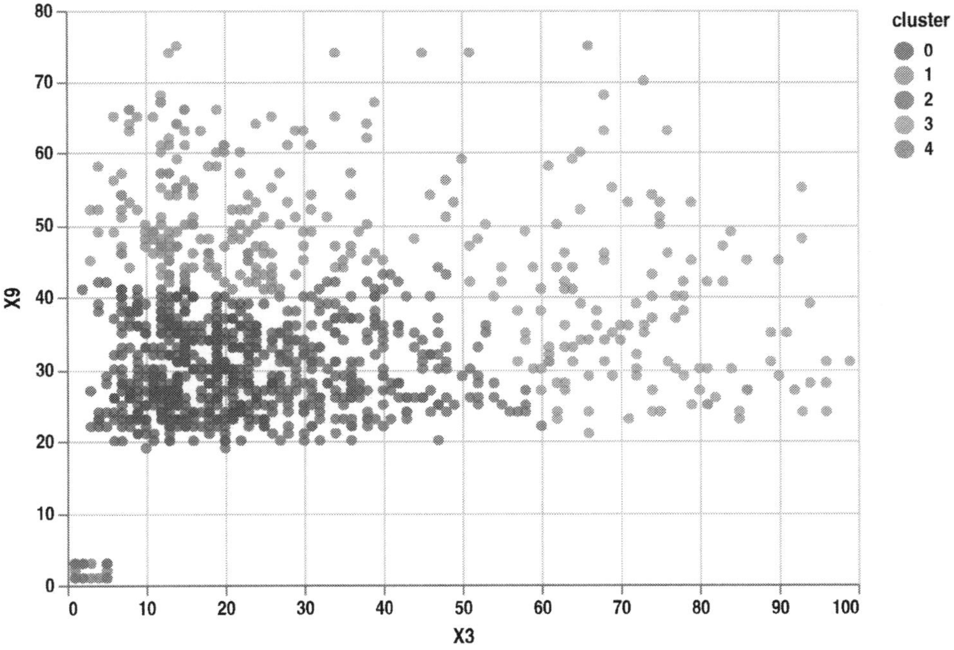

Figure 5.55: Scatter plot of the four clusters found

> **NOTE**
>
> The solution to this activity can be found at the following address: https://packt.live/2GbJloz.

SUMMARY

You are now ready to perform cluster analysis with the k-means algorithm on your own dataset. This type of analysis is very popular in the industry for segmenting customer profiles as well as detecting suspicious transactions or anomalies.

We learned about a lot of different concepts, such as centroids and squared Euclidean distance. We went through the main k-means hyperparameters: **`init`** (initialization method), **`n_init`** (number of initialization runs), **`n_clusters`** (number of clusters), and **`random_state`** (specified seed). We also discussed the importance of choosing the optimal number of clusters, initializing centroids properly, and standardizing data. You have learned how to use the following Python packages: **`pandas`**, **`altair`**, **`sklearn`**, and **`KMeans`**.

In this chapter, we only looked at k-means, but it is not the only clustering algorithm. There are quite a lot of algorithms that use different approaches, such as hierarchical clustering, principal component analysis, and the Gaussian mixture model, to name a few. If you are interested in this field, you now have all the basic knowledge you need to explore these other algorithms on your own.

Next, you will see how we can assess the performance of these models and what tools can be used to make them even better.

6

HOW TO ASSESS PERFORMANCE

OVERVIEW

This chapter will introduce you to model evaluation, where you evaluate or assess the performance of each model that you train before you decide to put it into production. By the end of this chapter, you will be able to create an evaluation dataset. You will be equipped to assess the performance of linear regression models using **mean absolute error** (**MAE**) and **mean squared error** (**MSE**). You will also be able to evaluate the performance of logistic regression models using accuracy, precision, recall, and F1 score.

INTRODUCTION

When you assess the performance of a model, you look at certain measurements or values that tell you how well the model is performing under certain conditions, and that helps you make an informed decision about whether or not to make use of the model that you have trained in the real world. Some of the measurements you will encounter in this chapter are MAE, precision, recall, and R^2 score.

You learned how to train a regression model in *Chapter 2, Regression*, and how to train classification models in *Chapter 3, Binary Classification*. Consider the task of predicting whether or not a customer is likely to purchase a term deposit, which you addressed in *Chapter 3, Binary Classification*. You have learned how to train a model to perform this sort of classification. You are now concerned with how useful this model might be. You might start by training one model, and then evaluating how often the predictions from that model are correct. You might then proceed to train more models and evaluate whether they perform better than previous models you have trained.

You have already seen an example of splitting data using **`train_test_split`** in *Exercise 3.06, A Logistic Regression Model for Predicting the Propensity of Term Deposit Purchases in a Bank*. You will go further into the necessity and application of splitting data in *Chapter 7, The Generalization of Machine Learning Models*, but for now, you should note that it is important to split your data into one set that is used for training a model, and a second set that is used for validating the model. It is this validation step that helps you decide whether or not to put a model into production.

SPLITTING DATA

You will learn more about splitting data in *Chapter 7, The Generalization of Machine Learning Models*, where we will cover the following:

- Simple data splits using **`train_test_split`**
- Multiple data splits using cross-validation

For now, you will learn how to split data using a function from **`sklearn`** called **`train_test_split`**.

It is very important that you do not use all of your data to train a model. You must set aside some data for validation, and this data must not have been used previously for training. When you train a model, it tries to generate an equation that fits your data. The longer you train, the more complex the equation becomes so that it passes through as many of the data points as possible.

When you shuffle the data and set some aside for validation, it ensures that the model learns to not overfit the hypotheses you are trying to generate.

EXERCISE 6.01: IMPORTING AND SPLITTING DATA

In this exercise, you will import data from a repository and split it into a training and an evaluation set to train a model. Splitting your data is required so that you can evaluate the model later. This exercise will get you familiar with the process of splitting data; this is something you will be doing frequently.

> **NOTE**
>
> The Car dataset that you will be using in this chapter can be found in our GitHub repository: https://packt.live/30I594E.
>
> It was taken from the UCI Machine Learning Repository.

This dataset is about cars. A text file is provided with the following information:

- **`buying`** – the cost of purchasing this vehicle
- **`maint`** – the maintenance cost of the vehicle
- **`doors`** – the number of doors the vehicle has
- **`persons`** – the number of persons the vehicle is capable of transporting
- **`lug_boot`** – the cargo capacity of the vehicle
- **`safety`** – the safety rating of the vehicle
- **`car`** – this is the category that the model attempts to predict

The following steps will help you complete the exercise:

1. Open a new Colab notebook.

2. Import the required libraries:

```
import pandas as pd
from sklearn.model_selection import train_test_split
```

   You started by importing a library called **pandas** in the first line. This library is useful for reading files into a data structure that is called a **DataFrame**, which you have used in previous chapters. This structure is like a spreadsheet or a table with rows and columns that we can manipulate. Because you might need to reference the library lots of times, we have created an alias for it, **pd**.

   In the second line, you import a function called **train_test_split** from a module called **model_selection**, which is within **sklearn**. This function is what you will make use of to split the data that you read in using **pandas**.

3. Create a Python list:

```
# data doesn't have headers, so let's create headers
_headers = ['buying', 'maint', 'doors', 'persons', \
            'lug_boot', 'safety', 'car']
```

   The data that you are reading in is stored as a CSV file.

The browser will download the file to your computer. You can open the file using a text editor. If you do, you will see something similar to the following:

car - Notepad

File Edit Format View Help

```
vhigh,vhigh,2,2,small,low,unacc
vhigh,vhigh,2,2,small,med,unacc
vhigh,vhigh,2,2,small,high,unacc
vhigh,vhigh,2,2,med,low,unacc
vhigh,vhigh,2,2,med,med,unacc
vhigh,vhigh,2,2,med,high,unacc
vhigh,vhigh,2,2,big,low,unacc
vhigh,vhigh,2,2,big,med,unacc
vhigh,vhigh,2,2,big,high,unacc
vhigh,vhigh,2,4,small,low,unacc
vhigh,vhigh,2,4,small,med,unacc
vhigh,vhigh,2,4,small,high,unacc
vhigh,vhigh,2,4,med,low,unacc
vhigh,vhigh,2,4,med,med,unacc
vhigh,vhigh,2,4,med,high,unacc
vhigh,vhigh,2,4,big,low,unacc
```

Figure 6.1: The car dataset without headers

> **NOTE**
>
> Alternatively, you can enter the dataset URL in the browser to view the dataset.

CSV files normally have the name of each column written in the first row of the data. For instance, have a look at this dataset's CSV file, which you used in *Chapter 3, Binary Classification*:

```
"age";"job";"marital";"education";"default";"balance";"housing";"loan";"contact";"day";"month";"duration";"campaign";"pdays";"previous";"poutcome";"y"
58;"management";"married";"tertiary";"no";2143;"yes";"no";"unknown";5;"may";261;1;-1;0;"unknown";"no"
44;"technician";"single";"secondary";"no";29;"yes";"no";"unknown";5;"may";151;1;-1;0;"unknown";"no"
33;"entrepreneur";"married";"secondary";"no";2;"yes";"yes";"unknown";5;"may";76;1;-1;0;"unknown";"no"
47;"blue-collar";"married";"unknown";"no";1506;"yes";"no";"unknown";5;"may";92;1;-1;0;"unknown";"no"
33;"unknown";"single";"unknown";"no";1;"no";"no";"unknown";5;"may";198;1;-1;0;"unknown";"no"
35;"management";"married";"tertiary";"no";231;"yes";"no";"unknown";5;"may";139;1;-1;0;"unknown";"no"
28;"management";"single";"tertiary";"no";447;"yes";"yes";"unknown";5;"may";217;1;-1;0;"unknown";"no"
42;"entrepreneur";"divorced";"tertiary";"yes";2;"yes";"no";"unknown";5;"may";380;1;-1;0;"unknown";"no"
58;"retired";"married";"primary";"no";121;"yes";"no";"unknown";5;"may";50;1;-1;0;"unknown";"no"
43;"technician";"single";"secondary";"no";593;"yes";"no";"unknown";5;"may";55;1;-1;0;"unknown";"no"
41;"admin.";"divorced";"secondary";"no";270;"yes";"no";"unknown";5;"may";222;1;-1;0;"unknown";"no"
29;"admin.";"single";"secondary";"no";390;"yes";"no";"unknown";5;"may";137;1;-1;0;"unknown";"no"
53;"technician";"married";"secondary";"no";6;"yes";"no";"unknown";5;"may";517;1;-1;0;"unknown";"no"
58;"technician";"married";"unknown";"no";71;"yes";"no";"unknown";5;"may";71;1;-1;0;"unknown";"no"
57;"services";"married";"secondary";"no";162;"yes";"no";"unknown";5;"may";174;1;-1;0;"unknown";"no"
51;"retired";"married";"primary";"no";229;"yes";"no";"unknown";5;"may";353;1;-1;0;"unknown";"no"
45;"admin.";"single";"unknown";"no";13;"yes";"no";"unknown";5;"may";98;1;-1;0;"unknown";"no"
57;"blue-collar";"married";"primary";"no";52;"yes";"no";"unknown";5;"may";38;1;-1;0;"unknown";"no"
60;"retired";"married";"primary";"no";60;"yes";"no";"unknown";5;"may";219;1;-1;0;"unknown";"no"
33;"services";"married";"secondary";"no";0;"yes";"no";"unknown";5;"may";54;1;-1;0;"unknown";"no"
28;"blue-collar";"married";"secondary";"no";723;"yes";"yes";"unknown";5;"may";262;1;-1;0;"unknown";"no"
56;"management";"married";"tertiary";"no";779;"yes";"no";"unknown";5;"may";164;1;-1;0;"unknown";"no"
32;"blue-collar";"single";"primary";"no";23;"yes";"yes";"unknown";5;"may";160;1;-1;0;"unknown";"no"
25;"services";"married";"secondary";"no";50;"yes";"no";"unknown";5;"may";342;1;-1;0;"unknown";"no"
```

Figure 6.2: CSV file without headers

But, in this case, the column name is missing. That is not a problem, however. The code in this step creates a Python list called **_headers** that contains the name of each column. You will supply this list when you read in the data in the next step.

4. Read the data:

```
df = pd.read_csv('https://raw.githubusercontent.com/'\
                 'PacktWorkshops/The-Data-Science-Workshop/'\
                 'master/Chapter06/Dataset/car.data', \
                 names=_headers, index_col=None)
```

In this step, the code reads in the file using a function called **read_csv**. The first parameter, **'https://raw.githubusercontent.com/PacktWorkshops/The-Data-Science-Workshop/master/Chapter06/Dataset/car.data'**, is mandatory and is the location of the file. In our case, the file is on the internet. It can also be optionally downloaded, and we can then point to the local file's location.

The second parameter (**names=_headers**) asks the function to add the row headers to the data after reading it in. The third parameter (**index_col=None**) asks the function to generate a new index for the table because the data doesn't contain an index. The function will produce a DataFrame, which we assign to a variable called **df**.

5. Print out the top five records:

```
df.head()
```

The code in this step is used to print the top five rows of the DataFrame. The output from that operation is shown in the following screenshot:

	buying	maint	doors	persons	lug_boot	safety	car
0	vhigh	vhigh	2	2	small	low	unacc
1	vhigh	vhigh	2	2	small	med	unacc
2	vhigh	vhigh	2	2	small	high	unacc
3	vhigh	vhigh	2	2	med	low	unacc
4	vhigh	vhigh	2	2	med	med	unacc

Figure 6.3: The top five rows of the DataFrame

6. Create a training and an evaluation DataFrame:

```
training, evaluation = train_test_split(df, test_size=0.3, \
                                        random_state=0)
```

The preceding code will split the DataFrame containing your data into two new DataFrames. The first is called **`training`** and is used for training the model. The second is called **`evaluation`** and will be further split into two in the next step. We mentioned earlier that you must separate your dataset into a training and an evaluation dataset, the former for training your model and the latter for evaluating your model.

At this point, the **`train_test_split`** function takes two parameters. The first parameter is the data we want to split. The second is the ratio we would like to split it by. What we have done is specified that we want our evaluation data to be 30% of our data.

> **NOTE**
>
> The third parameter random_state is set to 0 to ensure reproducibility of results.

7. Create a validation and test dataset:

```
validation, test = train_test_split(evaluation, test_size=0.5, \
                                    random_state=0)
```

This code is similar to the code in *Step 6*. In this step, the code splits our evaluation data into two equal parts because we specified **0.5**, which means **50%**.

> **NOTE**
>
> To access the source code for this specific section, please refer to https://packt.live/3haKvl3.
>
> You can also run this example online at https://packt.live/3g8zl9R.

In previous chapters, we've seen how to split your data into train and test sets, but here, we'll go one step further and split it into three: one to train a model, one to evaluate the model during training, and one to evaluate the model before putting it into production.

Now that you have your data split into different sets, you may proceed to train and evaluate models.

ASSESSING MODEL PERFORMANCE FOR REGRESSION MODELS

When you create a regression model, you create a model that predicts a continuous numerical variable, as you learned in *Chapter 2, Regression*. When you set aside your evaluation dataset, you have something that you can use to compare the quality of your model.

What you need to do to assess your model quality is compare the quality of your prediction to what is called the ground truth, which is the actual observed value that you are trying to predict. Take a look at *Figure 6.4*, in which the first column contains the ground truth (called actuals) and the second column contains the predicted values:

	actuals	predicted
0	4.891	4.132270
1	4.194	4.364320
2	4.984	4.440703
3	3.109	2.954363
4	5.115	4.987951

Figure 6.4: Actual versus predicted values

Line `0` in the output compares the actual value in our evaluation dataset to what our model predicted. The actual value from our evaluation dataset is **`4.891`**. The value that the model predicted is **`4.132270`**.

Line **`1`** compares the actual value of **`4.194`** to what the model predicted, which is **`4.364320`**.

In practice, the evaluation dataset will contain a lot of records, so you will not be making this comparison visually. Instead, you will make use of some equations.

You would carry out this comparison by computing the loss. The loss is the difference between the actuals and the predicted values in the preceding screenshot. In data mining, it is called a **distance measure**. There are various approaches to computing distance measures that give rise to different loss functions. Two of these are:

- Manhattan distance
- Euclidean distance

There are various loss functions for regression, but in this book, we will be looking at two of the commonly used loss functions for regression, which are:

- Mean absolute error (MAE) – this is based on Manhattan distance
- Mean squared error (MSE) – this is based on Euclidean distance

The goal of these functions is to measure the usefulness of your models by giving you a numerical value that shows how much deviation there is between the ground truths and the predicted values from your models.

Your mission is to train new models with consistently lower errors. Before we do that, let's have a quick introduction to some data structures.

DATA STRUCTURES – VECTORS AND MATRICES

In this section, we will look at different data structures, as follows.

SCALARS

A scalar variable is a simple number, such as 23. Whenever you make use of numbers on their own, they are scalars. You assign them to variables, such as in the following expression:

```
temperature = 23
```

If you had to store the temperature for 5 days, you would need to store the values in 5 different values, such as in the following code snippet:

```
temp_1 = 23
temp_2 = 24
temp_3 = 23
temp_4 = 22
temp_5 = 22
```

In data science, you will frequently work with a large number of data points, such as hourly temperature measurements for an entire year. A more efficient way of storing lots of values is called a vector. Let's look at vectors in the next topic.

VECTORS

A vector is a collection of scalars. Consider the five temperatures in the previous code snippet. A vector is a data type that lets you collect all of the previous temperatures in one variable that supports arithmetic operations. Vectors look similar to Python lists and can be created from Python lists. Consider the following code snippet for creating a Python list:

```
temps_list = [23, 24, 23, 22, 22]
```

You can create a vector from the list using the **`.array()`** method from **`numpy`** by first importing **`numpy`** and then using the following snippet:

```
import numpy as np
temps_ndarray = np.array(temps_list)
```

You can proceed to verify the data type using the following code snippet:

```
print(type(temps_ndarray))
```

The code snippet will cause the compiler to print out the following:

```
<class 'numpy.ndarray'>
```

Figure 6.5: The temps_ndarray vector data type

You may inspect the contents of the vector using the following code snippet:

```
print(temps_ndarray)
```

This generates the following output:

```
[23 24 23 22 22]
```

Figure 6.6: The temps_ndarray vector

Note that the output contains single square brackets, `[` and `]`, and the numbers are separated by spaces. This is different from the output from a Python list, which you can obtain using the following code snippet:

```
print(temps_list)
```

The code snippet yields the following output:

```
[23, 24, 23, 22, 22]
```

Figure 6.7: List of elements in temps_list

Note that the output contains single square brackets, `[` and `]`, and the numbers are separated by commas.

Vectors have a shape and a dimension. Both of these can be determined by using the following code snippet:

```
print(temps_ndarray.shape)
```

The output is a Python data structure called a **tuple** and looks like this:

```
(5,)
```

Figure 6.8: Shape of the temps_ndarray vector

Notice that the output consists of brackets, **(** and **)**, with a number and a comma. The single number followed by a comma implies that this object has only one dimension. The value of the number is the number of elements. The output is read as "a vector with five elements." This is very important because it is very different from a matrix, which we will discuss next.

MATRICES

A matrix is also made up of scalars but is different from a scalar in the sense that a matrix has both rows and columns3

There are times when you need to convert between vectors and matrices. Let's revisit **temps_ndarray**. You may recall that it has five elements because the shape was **(5,)**. To convert it into a matrix with five rows and one column, you would use the following snippet:

```
temps_matrix = temps_ndarray.reshape(-1, 1)
```

The code snippet makes use of the **.reshape()** method. The first parameter, **-1**, instructs the interpreter to keep the first dimension constant. The second parameter, **1**, instructs the interpreter to add a new dimension. This new dimension is the column. To see the new shape, use the following snippet:

```
print(temps_matrix.shape)
```

You will get the following output:

```
(5, 1)
```

Figure 6.9: Shape of the matrix

Notice that the tuple now has two numbers, **5** and **1**. The first number, **5**, represents the rows, and the second number, **1**, represents the columns. You can print out the value of the matrix using the following snippet:

```
print(temps_matrix)
```

The output of the code is as follows:

```
[[23]
 [24]
 [23]
 [22]
 [22]]
```

Figure 6.10: Elements of the matrix

Notice that the output is different from that of the vector. First, we have an outer set of square brackets. Then, each row has its element enclosed in square brackets. Each row contains only one number because the matrix has only one column.

You may reshape the matrix to contain **1** row and **5** columns and print out the value using the following code snippet:

```
print(temps_matrix.reshape(1,5))
```

The output will be as follows:

```
[[23 24 23 22 22]]
```

Figure 6.11: Reshaping the matrix

Notice that you now have all the numbers on one row because this matrix has one row and five columns. The outer square brackets represent the matrix, while the inner square brackets represent the row.

Finally, you can convert the matrix back into a vector by dropping the column using the following snippet:

```
vector = temps_matrix.reshape(-1)
```

You can print out the value of the vector to confirm that you get the following:

```
[23 24 23 22 22]
```

Figure 6.12: The value of the vector

Notice that you now have only one set of square brackets. You still have the same number of elements.

Let's now look at an important metric – R^2 score.

R^2 SCORE

The R^2 score (pronounced "r squared") is sometimes called the "score" and measures the coefficient of determination of the model. Think of it as the model's ability to make good and reliable predictions. This measure is accessed using the **`score()`** method of the model and is available for every model.

Your goal is to train successive models with a higher R^2 score. The R^2 score has a range between **0** and **1**. Your goal is to try and get the model to have a score that is close to **1**.

EXERCISE 6.02: COMPUTING THE R^2 SCORE OF A LINEAR REGRESSION MODEL

As mentioned in the preceding sections, R^2 score is an important factor in evaluating the performance of a model. Thus, in this exercise, we will be creating a linear regression model and then calculating the R^2 score for it.

> **NOTE**
>
> The fish toxicity dataset that you will be using in this chapter can be found in our GitHub repository: https://packt.live/2sNChvv.
>
> This dataset was taken from the UCI Machine Learning Repository: https://packt.live/2TSyJTB.

The following attributes are useful for our task:

- CIC0: information indices
- SM1_Dz(Z): 2D matrix-based descriptors
- GATS1i: 2D autocorrelations
- NdsCH: Pimephales promelas

- NdssC: atom-type counts
- MLOGP: molecular properties
- Quantitative response, LC50 [-LOG(mol/L)]: This attribute represents the concentration that causes death in 50% of test fish over a test duration of 96 hours.

The following steps will help you to complete the exercise:

1. Open a new Colab notebook to write and execute your code.
2. Next, import the libraries mentioned in the following code snippet:

```
# import libraries
import pandas as pd
from sklearn.model_selection import train_test_split
from sklearn.linear_model import LinearRegression
```

   In this step, you import **pandas**, which you will use to read your data. You also import **train_test_split()**, which you will use to split your data into training and validation sets, and you import **LinearRegression**, which you will use to train your model.

3. Now, read the data from the dataset:

```
# column headers
_headers = ['CIC0', 'SM1', 'GATS1i', 'NdsCH', 'Ndssc', \
            'MLOGP', 'response']
# read in data
df = pd.read_csv('https://raw.githubusercontent.com/'\
                 'PacktWorkshops/The-Data-Science-Workshop/'\
                 'master/Chapter06/Dataset/'\
                 'qsar_fish_toxicity.csv', \
                 names=_headers, sep=';')
```

In this step, you create a Python list to hold the names of the columns in your data. You do this because the CSV file containing the data does not have a first row that contains the column headers. You proceed to read in the file and store it in a variable called **df** using the **read_csv()** method in pandas. You specify the list containing column headers by passing it into the **names** parameter. This CSV uses semi-colons as column separators, so you specify that using the **sep** parameter. You can use **df.head()** to see what the DataFrame looks like:

	CIC0	SM1	GATS1i	NdsCH	Ndssc	MLOGP	response
0	3.260	0.829	1.676	0	1	1.453	3.770
1	2.189	0.580	0.863	0	0	1.348	3.115
2	2.125	0.638	0.831	0	0	1.348	3.531
3	3.027	0.331	1.472	1	0	1.807	3.510
4	2.094	0.827	0.860	0	0	1.886	5.390

Figure 6.13: The first five rows of the DataFrame

4. Split the data into features and labels and into training and evaluation datasets:

```
# Let's split our data
features = df.drop('response', axis=1).values
labels = df[['response']].values

X_train, X_eval, y_train, y_eval = train_test_split\
                                   (features, labels, \
                                    test_size=0.2, \
                                    random_state=0)
X_val, X_test, y_val, y_test = train_test_split(X_eval, y_eval,\
                                                random_state=0)
```

In this step, you create two **numpy** arrays called **features** and **labels**. You then proceed to split them twice. The first split produces a **training** set and an **evaluation** set. The second split creates a **validation** set and a **test** set.

5. Create a linear regression model:

```
model = LinearRegression()
```

In this step, you create an instance of **LinearRegression** and store it in a variable called **model**. You will make use of this to train on the training dataset.

6. Train the model:

```
model.fit(X_train, y_train)
```

In this step, you train the model using the **fit()** method and the training dataset that you made in *Step 4*. The first parameter is the **features** NumPy array, and the second parameter is **labels**.

You should get an output similar to the following:

```
LinearRegression(copy_X=True, fit_intercept=True, n_jobs=None, normalize=False)
```

Figure 6.14: Training the model

7. Make a prediction, as shown in the following code snippet:

```
y_pred = model.predict(X_val)
```

In this step, you make use of the validation dataset to make a prediction. This is stored in **y_pred**.

8. Compute the R^2 score:

```
r2 = model.score(X_val, y_val)
print('R^2 score: {}'.format(r2))
```

In this step, you compute **r2**, which is the R^2 score of the model. The R^2 score is computed using the **score()** method of the model. The next line causes the interpreter to print out the R^2 score.

The output is similar to the following:

```
R^2 score: 0.5623861754188693
```

Figure 6.15: R2 score

> **NOTE**
>
> The MAE and R^2 score may vary depending on the distribution of the datasets.

9. You see that the R^2 score we achieved is **0.56238**, which is not close to 1. In the next step, we will be making comparisons.

10. Compare the predictions to the actual ground truth:

```
_ys = pd.DataFrame(dict(actuals=y_val.reshape(-1), \
                        predicted=y_pred.reshape(-1)))
_ys.head()
```

In this step, you take a cursory look at the predictions compared to the ground truth. In *Step 8*, you will have noticed that the R^2 score you computed for the model is far from perfect (perfect is a score of 1). In this step, in the first line, you create a DataFrame by making use of the **DataFrame** method in pandas. You provide a dictionary as an argument. The dictionary has two keys: **actuals** and **predicted**. **actuals** contains **y_vals**, which is the actual labels in the validation dataset. **predicted** contains **y_pred**, which contains the predictions. Both **y_vals** and **y_pred** are two-dimensional matrices, so you reshape them to 1D vectors by using **.reshape(-1)**, which drops the second axis.

The second line causes the interpreter to display the top five records.

The output looks similar to the following:

	actuals	predicted
0	3.742	4.155885
1	6.143	6.398238
2	4.674	5.183181
3	4.865	3.771333
4	4.732	4.593059

Figure 6.16: The actual versus predicted values of the model

> **NOTE**
>
> To access the source code for this specific section, please refer to https://packt.live/31aw6QE.
>
> You can also run this example online at https://packt.live/3aASLbE.

In this exercise, we computed the R^2 score, which is an evaluation metric that can be used for comparing models.

In the next topic, we will be looking at the mean absolute error, which is another evaluation metric.

MEAN ABSOLUTE ERROR

The **mean absolute error** (**MAE**) is an evaluation metric for regression models that measures the absolute distance between your predictions and the ground truth. The absolute distance is the distance regardless of the sign, whether positive or negative. For example, if the ground truth is 6 and you predict 5, the distance is 1. However, if you predict 7, the distance becomes -1. The absolute distance, without taking the signs into consideration, is 1 in both cases. This is called the **magnitude**. The MAE is computed by summing all of the magnitudes and dividing by the number of observations.

EXERCISE 6.03: COMPUTING THE MAE OF A MODEL

The goal of this exercise is to find the score and loss of a model using the same dataset as *Exercise 6.02, Computing the R2 Score of a Linear Regression Model*.

In this exercise, we will be calculating the MAE of a model.

The following steps will help you with this exercise:

1. Open a new Colab notebook file.
2. Import the necessary libraries:

```
# Import libraries
import pandas as pd
from sklearn.model_selection import train_test_split
from sklearn.linear_model import LinearRegression
from sklearn.metrics import mean_absolute_error
```

   In this step, you import the function called **`mean_absolute_error`** from **`sklearn.metrics`**.

3. Import the data:

```
# column headers
_headers = ['CIC0', 'SM1', 'GATS1i', 'NdsCH', 'Ndssc', \
            'MLOGP', 'response']
# read in data
df = pd.read_csv('https://raw.githubusercontent.com/'\
                 'PacktWorkshops/The-Data-Science-Workshop/'\
                 'master/Chapter06/Dataset/'\
                 'qsar_fish_toxicity.csv', \
                 names=_headers, sep=';')
```

In the preceding code, you read in your data. This data is hosted online and contains some information about fish toxicity. The data is stored as a CSV but does not contain any headers. Also, the columns in this file are not separated by a comma, but rather by a semi-colon. The Python list called **_headers** contains the names of the column headers.

In the next line, you make use of the function called **read_csv**, which is contained in the **pandas** library, to load the data. The first parameter specifies the file location. The second parameter specifies the Python list that contains the names of the columns in the data. The third parameter specifies the character that is used to separate the columns in the data.

4. Split the data into **features** and **labels** and into training and evaluation sets:

```
# Let's split our data
features = df.drop('response', axis=1).values
labels = df[['response']].values

X_train, X_eval, y_train, y_eval = train_test_split\
                                   (features, labels, \
                                    test_size=0.2, \
                                    random_state=0)
X_val, X_test, y_val, y_test = train_test_split(X_eval, y_eval,\
                                                random_state=0)
```

In this step, you split your data into training, validation, and test datasets. In the first line, you create a **numpy** array in two steps. In the first step, the **drop** method takes a parameter with the name of the column to drop from the DataFrame. In the second step, you use **values** to convert the DataFrame into a two-dimensional **numpy** array that is a tabular structure with rows and columns. This array is stored in a variable called **features**.

In the second line, you convert the column into a **numpy** array that contains the label that you would like to predict. You do this by picking out the column from the DataFrame and then using **values** to convert it into a **numpy** array.

In the third line, you split the **features** and **labels** using **train_test_split** and a ratio of 80:20. The training data is contained in **X_train** for the features and **y_train** for the labels. The evaluation dataset is contained in **X_eval** and **y_eval**.

In the fourth line, you split the evaluation dataset into validation and testing using **train_test_split**. Because you don't specify the **test_size**, a value of **25%** is used. The validation data is stored in **X_val** and **y_val**, while the test data is stored in **X_test** and **y_test**.

5. Create a simple linear regression model and train it:

```
# create a simple Linear Regression model
model = LinearRegression()
# train the model
model.fit(X_train, y_train)
```

In this step, you make use of your training data to train a model. In the first line, you create an instance of **LinearRegression**, which you call **model**. In the second line, you train the model using **X_train** and **y_train**. **X_train** contains the **features**, while **y_train** contains the **labels**.

6. Now predict the values of our validation dataset:

```
# let's use our model to predict on our validation dataset
y_pred = model.predict(X_val)
```

At this point, your model is ready to use. You make use of the **predict** method to predict on your data. In this case, you are passing **X_val** as a parameter to the function. Recall that **X_val** is your validation dataset. The result is assigned to a variable called **y_pred** and will be used in the next step to compute the MAE of the model.

7. Compute the MAE:

```
# Let's compute our MEAN ABSOLUTE ERROR
mae = mean_absolute_error(y_val, y_pred)
print('MAE: {}'.format(mae))
```

In this step, you compute the MAE of the model by using the **mean_absolute_error** function and passing in **y_val** and **y_pred**. **y_val** is the label that was provided with your training data, and **y_pred** is the prediction from the model. The preceding code should give you an MAE value of ~ 0.72434:

```
MAE: 0.7243440846447939
```

Figure 6.17 MAE score

Both **y_val** and **y_pred** are a **numpy** array that contains the same number of elements. The **mean_absolute_error** function subtracts **y_pred** from **y_val**. This results in a new array. The elements in the resulting array have the absolute function applied to them so that all negative signs are dropped. The average of the elements is then computed.

8. Compute the R^2 score of the model:

```
# Let's get the R2 score
r2 = model.score(X_val, y_val)
print('R^2 score: {}'.format(r2))
```

You should get an output similar to the following:

```
R^2 score: 0.5623861754188693
```

Figure 6.18: The R2 score of the model

> **NOTE**
>
> The MAE and R^2 score may vary depending on the distribution of the datasets.

A higher R^2 score means a better model and uses an equation that computes the coefficient of determination.

> **NOTE**
>
> To access the source code for this specific section, please refer to https://packt.live/349mG9P.
>
> You can also run this example online at https://packt.live/3aA1rza.

In this exercise, we have calculated the MAE, which is a significant parameter when it comes to evaluating models.

You will now train a second model and compare its R^2 score and MAE to the first model to evaluate which is a better performing model.

EXERCISE 6.04: COMPUTING THE MEAN ABSOLUTE ERROR OF A SECOND MODEL

In this exercise, we will be engineering new features and finding the score and loss of a new model.

The following steps will help you with this exercise:

1. Open a new Colab notebook file.
2. Import the required libraries:

```
# Import libraries
import pandas as pd
from sklearn.model_selection import train_test_split
from sklearn.linear_model import LinearRegression
from sklearn.metrics import mean_absolute_error
# pipeline
from sklearn.pipeline import Pipeline
# preprocessing
from sklearn.preprocessing import MinMaxScaler
from sklearn.preprocessing import StandardScaler
from sklearn.preprocessing import PolynomialFeatures
```

In the first step, you will import libraries such as **train_test_split**, **LinearRegression**, and **mean_absolute_error**. We make use of a pipeline to quickly transform our features and engineer new features using **MinMaxScaler** and **PolynomialFeatures**. **MinMaxScaler** reduces the variance in your data by adjusting all values to a range between 0 and 1. It does this by subtracting the mean of the data and dividing by the range, which is the minimum value subtracted from the maximum value. **PolynomialFeatures** will engineer new features by raising the values in a column up to a certain power and creating new columns in your DataFrame to accommodate them.

3. Read in the data from the dataset:

```
# column headers
_headers = ['CIC0', 'SM1', 'GATS1i', 'NdsCH', 'Ndssc', \
            'MLOGP', 'response']

# read in data
df = pd.read_csv('https://raw.githubusercontent.com/'\
                 'PacktWorkshops/The-Data-Science-Workshop/'\
                 'master/Chapter06/Dataset/'\
                 'qsar_fish_toxicity.csv', \
                 names=_headers, sep=';')
```

In this step, you will read in your data. While the data is stored in a CSV, it doesn't have a first row that lists the names of the columns. The Python list called **_headers** will hold the column names that you will supply to the **pandas** method called **read_csv**.

In the next line, you call the **read_csv pandas** method and supply the location and name of the file to be read in, along with the header names and the file separator. Columns in the file are separated with a semi-colon.

4. Split the data into training and evaluation sets:

```
# Let's split our data
features = df.drop('response', axis=1).values
labels = df[['response']].values

X_train, X_eval, y_train, y_eval = train_test_split\
                                   (features, labels, \
                                    test_size=0.2, \
                                    random_state=0)
X_val, X_test, y_val, y_test = train_test_split(X_eval, y_eval,\
                                                random_state=0)
```

In this step, you begin by splitting the DataFrame called **df** into two. The first DataFrame is called **features** and contains all of the independent variables that you will use to make your predictions. The second is called **labels** and contains the values that you are trying to predict.

In the third line, you split **features** and **labels** into four sets using **train_test_split**. **X_train** and **y_train** contain 80% of the data and are used for training your model. **X_eval** and **y_eval** contain the remaining 20%.

In the fourth line, you split **X_eval** and **y_eval** into two additional sets. **X_val** and **y_val** contain 75% of the data because you did not specify a ratio or size. **X_test** and **y_test** contain the remaining 25%.

5. Create a pipeline:

```
# create a pipeline and engineer quadratic features
steps = [('scaler', MinMaxScaler()),\
         ('poly', PolynomialFeatures(2)),\
         ('model', LinearRegression())]
```

In this step, you begin by creating a Python list called **steps**. The list contains three tuples, each one representing a transformation of a model. The first tuple represents a scaling operation. The first item in the tuple is the name of the step, which you call **scaler**. This uses **MinMaxScaler** to transform the data. The second, called **poly**, creates additional features by crossing the columns of data up to the degree that you specify. In this case, you specify **2**, so it crosses these columns up to a power of 2. Next comes your **LinearRegression** model.

6. Create a pipeline:

```
# create a simple Linear Regression model with a pipeline
model = Pipeline(steps)
```

In this step, you create an instance of **Pipeline** and store it in a variable called **model**. **Pipeline** performs a series of transformations, which are specified in the steps you defined in the previous step. This operation works because the transformers (**MinMaxScaler** and **PolynomialFeatures**) implement two methods called **fit()** and **fit_transform()**. You may recall from previous examples that models are trained using the **fit()** method that **LinearRegression** implements.

7. Train the model:

```
# train the model
model.fit(X_train, y_train)
```

On the next line, you call the **fit** method and provide **X_train** and **y_train** as parameters. Because the model is a pipeline, three operations will happen. First, **X_train** will be scaled. Next, additional features will be engineered. Finally, training will happen using the **LinearRegression** model. The output from this step is similar to the following:

```
Pipeline(memory=None,
         steps=[('scaler', MinMaxScaler(copy=True, feature_range=(0, 1))),
                ('poly',
                 PolynomialFeatures(degree=2, include_bias=True,
                                    interaction_only=False, order='C')),
                ('model',
                 LinearRegression(copy_X=True, fit_intercept=True, n_jobs=None,
                                  normalize=False))],
         verbose=False)
```

Figure 6.19: Training the model

8. Predict using the validation dataset:

```
# let's use our model to predict on our validation dataset
y_pred = model.predict(X_val)
```

9. Compute the MAE of the model:

```
# Let's compute our MEAN ABSOLUTE ERROR
mae = mean_absolute_error(y_val, y_pred)
print('MAE: {}'.format(mae))
```

In the first line, you make use of **mean_absolute_error** to compute the mean absolute error. You supply **y_val** and **y_pred**, and the result is stored in the **mae** variable. In the following line, you print out **mae**:

```
MAE: 0.660552610083608
```

Figure 6.20: MAE score

The loss that you compute at this step is called a validation loss because you make use of the validation dataset. This is different from a training loss that is computed using the training dataset. This distinction is important to note as you study other documentation or books, which might refer to both.

10. Compute the R^2 score:

```
# Let's get the R2 score
r2 = model.score(X_val, y_val)
print('R^2 score: {}'.format(r2))
```

In the final two lines, you compute the R^2 score and also display it, as shown in the following screenshot:

```
R^2 score: 0.6284921344153387
```

Figure 6.21: R2 score

At this point, you should see a difference between the R^2 score and the MAE of the first model and the second model (in the first model, the **MAE** and R^2 scores were `0.781629` and `0.498688` respectively).

> **NOTE**
>
> To access the source code for this specific section, please refer to https://packt.live/2EjCaNn.
>
> You can also run this example online at https://packt.live/2Yb5vRd.

In this exercise, you engineered new features that give you a model with a hypothesis of a higher polynomial degree. This model should perform better than simpler models up to a certain point. After engineering and training the new model, you computed the R^2 score and MAE, which you can use to compare this model with the model you trained previously. We can conclude that this model is better as it has a higher R^2 score and a lower MAE.

OTHER EVALUATION METRICS

While we made use of **`mean_absolute_error`**, there are other model evaluation functions for regression. Recall that these are all cost (or loss) functions. These include **`max_error`**, **`mean_squared_error`**, **`mean_squared_log_error`**, and **`median_absolute_error`**. If you are working on a project with a data scientist, they will normally be responsible for telling you what evaluation metric to make use of. If not, then you can choose any metric of your liking.

The MAE is computed by subtracting every prediction from the ground truth, finding the absolute value, summing all the absolute values, and dividing by the number of observations. This type of distance measure is called Manhattan distance in data mining.

The **mean squared error** (**MSE**) is computed by taking the squares of the differences between the ground truths and the predictions, summing them, and then dividing by the number of observations. The MSE is large, and sometimes the square root of this is used, which is the **root mean squared error** (**RMSE**).

The **mean squared logarithmic error** (**MSLE**) introduces logarithms into the equation by adding one to both the ground truth and the prediction before taking the logarithms, then squaring the differences, then summing them, and dividing by the number of observations. MSLE has the property of having a lower cost for predictions that are above the ground truth than for those that are below it.

Finally, `median_absolute_error` finds the median value of the absolute errors, which are the differences between the ground truths and the predictions.

Let's now move toward evaluating the performance of classification models.

ASSESSING MODEL PERFORMANCE FOR CLASSIFICATION MODELS

Classification models are used for predicting which class a group of features will fall under. You learned to create binary classification models in *Chapter 3*, *Binary Classification*, and multi-class classification models in *Chapter 4, Multiclass Classification with RandomForest*.

When you consider a classification model, you might start to ask yourself how accurate the model is. But how do you evaluate accuracy?

You need to create a classification model before you can start assessing it.

EXERCISE 6.05: CREATING A CLASSIFICATION MODEL FOR COMPUTING EVALUATION METRICS

In this exercise, you will create a classification model that you will make use of later on for model assessment.

You will make use of the cars dataset from the UCI Machine Learning Repository. You will use this dataset to classify cars as either acceptable or unacceptable based on the following categorical features:

- **buying**: the purchase price of the car
- **maint**: the maintenance cost of the car
- **doors**: the number of doors on the car
- **persons**: the carrying capacity of the vehicle
- **lug_boot**: the size of the luggage boot
- **safety**: the estimated safety of the car

> **NOTE**
>
> You can find the dataset here: https://packt.live/30I594E.

The following steps will help you achieve the task:

1. Open a new Colab notebook.
2. Import the libraries you will need:

```
# import libraries
import pandas as pd
from sklearn.model_selection import train_test_split
from sklearn.linear_model import LogisticRegression
```

In this step, you import **pandas** and alias it as **pd**. **pandas** is needed for reading data into a DataFrame. You also import **train_test_split**, which is needed for splitting your data into training and evaluation datasets. Finally, you also import the **LogisticRegression** class.

3. Import your data:

```
# data doesn't have headers, so let's create headers
_headers = ['buying', 'maint', 'doors', 'persons', \
            'lug_boot', 'safety', 'car']
# read in cars dataset
df = pd.read_csv('https://raw.githubusercontent.com/'\
                 'PacktWorkshops/The-Data-Science-Workshop/'\
                 'master/Chapter06/Dataset/car.data', \
                 names=_headers, index_col=None)
df.head()
```

In this step, you create a Python list called **`_headers`** to hold the names of the columns in the file you will be importing because the file doesn't have a header. You then proceed to read the file into a DataFrame named **`df`** by using **`pd.read_csv`** and specifying the file location as well as the list containing the file headers. Finally, you display the first five rows using **`df.head()`**.

You should get an output similar to the following:

	buying	maint	doors	persons	lug_boot	safety	car
0	vhigh	vhigh	2	2	small	low	unacc
1	vhigh	vhigh	2	2	small	med	unacc
2	vhigh	vhigh	2	2	small	high	unacc
3	vhigh	vhigh	2	2	med	low	unacc
4	vhigh	vhigh	2	2	med	med	unacc

Figure 6.22: Inspecting the DataFrame

4. Encode categorical variables as shown in the following code snippet:

```
# encode categorical variables
_df = pd.get_dummies(df, columns=['buying', 'maint', 'doors',\
                                  'persons', 'lug_boot', \
                                  'safety'])
_df.head()
```

In this step, you convert categorical columns into numeric columns using a technique called one-hot encoding. You saw an example of this in *Step 13* of *Exercise 3.04, Feature Engineering – Creating New Features from Existing Ones*. You need to do this because the inputs to your model must be numeric. You get numeric variables from categorical variables using **get_dummies** from the **pandas** library. You provide your DataFrame as input and specify the columns to be encoded. You assign the result to a new DataFrame called **_df**, and then inspect the result using **head()**.

The output should now resemble the following screenshot:

	car	buying_high	buying_low	buying_med	buying_vhigh	maint_high	maint_low	maint_med	maint_vhigh	doors_2
0	unacc	0	0	0	1	0	0	0	1	1
1	unacc	0	0	0	1	0	0	0	1	1
2	unacc	0	0	0	1	0	0	0	1	1
3	unacc	0	0	0	1	0	0	0	1	1
4	unacc	0	0	0	1	0	0	0	1	1

5 rows × 22 columns

Figure 6.23: Encoding categorical variables

> **NOTE**
>
> The output has been truncated for presentation purposes. Please find the complete output at https://packt.live/3aBNlg7.

5. Split the data into training and validation sets:

```
# split data into training and evaluation datasets
features = _df.drop('car', axis=1).values
labels = _df['car'].values

X_train, X_eval, y_train, y_eval = train_test_split\
                                   (features, labels, \
                                    test_size=0.3, \
                                    random_state=0)
X_val, X_test, y_val, y_test = train_test_split(X_eval, y_eval,\
                                                test_size=0.5, \
                                                random_state=0)
```

In this step, you begin by extracting your feature columns and your labels into two NumPy arrays called **features** and **labels**. You then proceed to extract 70% into **X_train** and **y_train**, with the remaining 30% going into **X_eval** and **y_eval**. You then further split **X_eval** and **y_eval** into two equal parts and assign those to **X_val** and **y_val** for validation, and **X_test** and **y_test** for testing much later.

6. Train a logistic regression model:

```
# train a Logistic Regression model
model = LogisticRegression()
model.fit(X_train, y_train)
```

In this step, you create an instance of **LogisticRegression** and train the model on your training data by passing in **X_train** and **y_train** to the **fit** method.

You should get an output that looks similar to the following:

```
LogisticRegression(C=1.0, class_weight=None, dual=False, fit_intercept=True,
                   intercept_scaling=1, l1_ratio=None, max_iter=100,
                   multi_class='warn', n_jobs=None, penalty='l2',
                   random_state=None, solver='warn', tol=0.0001, verbose=0,
                   warm_start=False)
```

Figure 6.24: Training a logistic regression model

7. Make a prediction:

```
# make predictions for the validation set
y_pred = model.predict(X_val)
```

In this step, you make a prediction on the validation dataset, **X_val**, and store the result in **y_pred**. A look at the first 10 predictions (by executing **y_pred[0:9]**) should provide an output similar to the following:

```
array(['unacc', 'acc', 'unacc', 'unacc', 'acc', 'acc', 'vgood', 'unacc',
       'unacc'], dtype=object)
```

Figure 6.25: Prediction for the validation set

This model works because you are able to use it to make predictions. The predictions classify each car as acceptable (**acc**) or unacceptable (**unacc**) based on the features of the car. At this point, you are ready to apply various assessments to the model.

> **NOTE**
>
> To access the source code for this specific section, please refer to https://packt.live/3aBNlg7.
>
> You can also run this example online at https://packt.live/34eg7CH.

Thus, we have successfully created a classification model to make predictions, and we will assess the performance of the model in future exercises.

In this exercise, we trained this logistic regression model once so that we don't need to do it repeatedly because of the number of steps involved. In the next section, you will be looking at confusion matrices.

THE CONFUSION MATRIX

You encountered the confusion matrix in *Chapter 3, Binary Classification*. You may recall that the confusion matrix compares the number of classes that the model predicted against the actual occurrences of those classes in the validation dataset. The output is a square matrix that has the number of rows and columns equal to the number of classes you are predicting. The columns represent the actual values, while the rows represent the predictions. You get a confusion matrix by using **confusion_matrix** from **sklearn.metrics**.

EXERCISE 6.06: GENERATING A CONFUSION MATRIX FOR THE CLASSIFICATION MODEL

The goal of this exercise is to create a confusion matrix for the classification model you trained in *Exercise 6.05, Creating a Classification Model for Computing Evaluation Metrics*.

> **NOTE**
>
> You should continue this exercise in the same notebook as that used in *Exercise 6.05, Creating a Classification Model for Computing Evaluation Metrics.* If you wish to use a new notebook, make sure you copy and run the entire code from *Exercise 6.05, Creating a Classification Model for Computing Evaluation Metrics*, and then begin with the execution of the code of this exercise.

The following steps will help you achieve the task:

1. Open a new Colab notebook file.
2. Import **confusion_matrix**:

```
from sklearn.metrics import confusion_matrix
```

   In this step, you import **confusion_matrix** from **sklearn.metrics**. This function will let you generate a confusion matrix.

3. Generate a confusion matrix:

```
confusion_matrix(y_val, y_pred)
```

   In this step, you generate a confusion matrix by supplying **y_val**, the actual classes, and **y_pred**, the predicted classes.

   The output should look similar to the following:

```
array([[ 41,   1,   9,   0],
       [  7,   2,   0,   1],
       [  7,   0, 178,   0],
       [  1,   0,   0,  12]])
```

Figure 6.26: Confusion matrix

> **NOTE**
>
> To access the source code for this specific section, please refer to https://packt.live/3hbreQz.
>
> You can also run this example online at https://packt.live/2EebSMD.

We can see that our data has four classes. The first column shows all of the data that should belong to the first class. The first row shows the number of predictions that were correctly placed in the first class. In this example, that number is **41**. The second row shows the number of predictions that were placed in the second class but should have been in the first class. In this example, that number is **7**. In the third row, you see the number of items that were predicted to be in the third class but should have been in the first class. That number is **7**. Finally, in the fourth row, you see the number of items that were wrongly classified into the fourth class when they should have been in the first class. In this case, the number is **1**.

MORE ON THE CONFUSION MATRIX

The confusion matrix helps you analyze the impact of the choices you would have to make if you put the model into production. Let's consider the example of predicting the presence of a disease based on the inputs to the model. This is a binary classification problem, where 1 implies that the disease is present and 0 implies the disease is absent. The confusion matrix for this model would have two columns and two rows.

The first column would show the items that fall into class **0**. The first row would show the items that were correctly classified into class **0** and are called **`true negatives`**. The second row would show the items that were wrongly classified as **1** but should have been **0**. These are **`false positives`**.

The second column would show the items that fall into class **1**. The first row would show the items that were wrongly classified into class 0 when they should have been **1** and are called **`false negatives`**. Finally, the second row shows items that were correctly classified into class 1 and are called **`true positives`**.

False positives are the cases in which the samples were wrongly predicted to be infected when they are actually healthy. The implication of this is that these cases would be treated for a disease that they do not have.

False negatives are the cases that were wrongly predicted to be healthy when they actually have the disease. The implication of this is that these cases would not be treated for a disease that they actually have.

The question you need to ask about this model depends on the nature of the disease and requires domain expertise about the disease. For example, if the disease is contagious, then the untreated cases will be released into the general population and could infect others. What would be the implication of this versus placing cases into quarantine and observing them for symptoms?

On the other hand, if the disease is not contagious, the question becomes that of the implications of treating people for a disease they do not have versus the implications of not treating cases of a disease.

It should be clear that there isn't a definite answer to these questions. The model would need to be tuned to provide performance that is acceptable to the users.

PRECISION

Precision was introduced in *Chapter 3, Binary Classification*; however, we will be looking at it in more detail in this chapter. The precision is the total number of cases that were correctly classified as positive (called **true positive** and abbreviated as **TP**) divided by the total number of cases in that prediction (that is, the total number of entries in the row, both correctly classified (TP) and wrongly classified (FP) from the confusion matrix). Suppose 10 entries were classified as positive. If 7 of the entries were actually positive, then TP would be 7 and FP would be 3. The precision would, therefore, be 0.7. The equation is given as follows:

$$\frac{tp}{tp + fp}$$

Figure 6.27: Equation for precision

In the preceding equation:

- **`tp`** is true positive – the number of predictions that were correctly classified as belonging to that class.
- **`fp`** is false positive – the number of predictions that were wrongly classified as belonging to that class.
- The function in **`sklearn.metrics`** to compute precision is called **`precision_score`**. Go ahead and give it a try.

EXERCISE 6.07: COMPUTING PRECISION FOR THE CLASSIFICATION MODEL

In this exercise, you will be computing the precision for the classification model you trained in *Exercise 6.05, Creating a Classification Model for Computing Evaluation Metrics*.

> **NOTE**
>
> You should continue this exercise in the same notebook as that used in *Exercise 6.05, Creating a Classification Model for Computing Evaluation Metrics.* If you wish to use a new notebook, make sure you copy and run the entire code from *Exercise 6.05, Creating a Classification Model for Computing Evaluation Metrics*, and then begin with the execution of the code of this exercise.

The following steps will help you achieve the task:

1. Import the required libraries:

```
from sklearn.metrics import precision_score
```

   In this step, you import **precision_score** from **sklearn.metrics**.

2. Next, compute the precision score as shown in the following code snippet:

```
precision_score(y_val, y_pred, average='macro')
```

   In this step, you compute the precision score using **precision_score**.

   The output is a floating-point number between 0 and 1. It might look like this:

```
0.8184395261601145
```

Figure 6.28: Precision score

> **NOTE**
>
> The precision score can vary depending on the data.

In this exercise, you see the precision score for the classification model is **`0.9245`**. **92%** could be a good score and is acceptable in some domains, but is a low score in certain domains. So there is scope for improvement.

> **NOTE**
>
> To access the source code for this specific section, please refer to https://packt.live/3kROW6R.
>
> You can also run this example online at https://packt.live/3aCS8ye.

Think of the precision score as asking how often does this model make the correct prediction for a class? The value needs to be much closer to 1 than the score we just achieved.

RECALL

Recall is the total number of predictions that were true divided by the number of predictions for the class, both true and false. Think of it as the true positive divided by the sum of entries in the column. The equation is given as follows:

$$\frac{tp}{tp + fn}$$

Figure 6.29: Equation for recall

The function for this is **`recall_score`**, which is available from **`sklearn.metrics`**.

EXERCISE 6.08: COMPUTING RECALL FOR THE CLASSIFICATION MODEL

The goal of this exercise is to compute the recall for the classification model you trained in *Exercise 6.05, Creating a Classification Model for Computing Evaluation Metrics*.

> **NOTE**
>
> You should continue this exercise in the same notebook as that used in *Exercise 6.05, Creating a Classification Model for Computing Evaluation Metrics.* If you wish to use a new notebook, make sure you copy and run the entire code from *Exercise 6.05, Creating a Classification Model for Computing Evaluation Metrics*, and then begin with the execution of the code of this exercise.

The following steps will help you accomplish the task:

1. Open a new Colab notebook file.
2. Now, import the required libraries:

```
from sklearn.metrics import recall_score
```

   In this step, you import **recall_score** from **sklearn.metrics**. This is the function that you will make use of in the second step.

3. Compute the recall:

```
recall_score(y_val, y_pred, average='macro')
```

   In this step, you compute the recall by using **recall_score**. You need to specify **y_val** and **y_pred** as parameters to the function. The documentation for **recall_score** explains the values that you can supply to **average**. If your model does binary prediction and the labels are **0** and **1**, you can set **average** to **binary**. Other options are **micro**, **macro**, **weighted**, and **samples**. You should read the documentation to see what they do.

You should get an output that looks like the following:

```
0.7222901634666341
```

Figure 6.30: Recall score

> **NOTE**
>
> The recall score can vary, depending on the data.

As you can see, we have calculated the recall score in the exercise, which is **`0.622`**. This means that of the total number of classes that were predicted, **`62%`** of them were correctly predicted. On its own, this value might not mean much until it is compared to the recall score from another model.

> **NOTE**
>
> To access the source code for this specific section, please refer to https://packt.live/31axPp6.
>
> You can also run this example online at https://packt.live/2YdNv8O.

Let's now move toward calculating the F1 score, which also helps greatly in evaluating the model performance, which in turn aids in making better decisions when choosing models.

F1 SCORE

The F1 score is another important parameter that helps us to evaluate the model performance. It considers the contribution of both precision and recall using the following equation:

$$\frac{2 * precision * recall}{precision + recall}$$

Figure 6.31: F1 score

The F1 score ranges from 0 to 1, with 1 being the best possible score. You compute the F1 score using **`f1_score`** from **`sklearn.metrics`**.

EXERCISE 6.09: COMPUTING THE F1 SCORE FOR THE CLASSIFICATION MODEL

In this exercise, you will compute the F1 score for the classification model you trained in *Exercise 6.05, Creating a Classification Model for Computing Evaluation Metrics*.

> **NOTE**
>
> You should continue this exercise in the same notebook as that used in *Exercise 6.05, Creating a Classification Model for Computing Evaluation Metrics*. If you wish to use a new notebook, make sure you copy and run the entire code from *Exercise 6.05, Creating a Classification Model for Computing Evaluation Metrics*, and then begin with the execution of the code of this exercise.

The following steps will help you accomplish the task:

1. Open a new Colab notebook file.
2. Import the necessary modules:

```
from sklearn.metrics import f1_score
```

   In this step, you import the **f1_score** method from **sklearn.metrics**. This score will let you compute evaluation metrics.

3. Compute the F1 score:

```
f1_score(y_val, y_pred, average='macro')
```

   In this step, you compute the F1 score by passing in **y_val** and **y_pred**. You also specify **average='macro'** because this is not binary classification.

   You should get an output similar to the following:

```
0.7385284045669938
```

Figure 6.32: F1 score

> **NOTE**
>
> To access the source code for this specific section, please refer to https://packt.live/3iWCqkq.
>
> You can also run this example online at https://packt.live/2Q84epY.

By the end of this exercise, you will see that the **F1** score we achieved is **0.6746**. There is a lot of room for improvement, and you would engineer new features and train a new model to try and get a better F1 score.

ACCURACY

Accuracy is an evaluation metric that is applied to classification models. It is computed by counting the number of labels that were correctly predicted, meaning that the predicted label is exactly the same as the ground truth. The **accuracy_score()** function exists in **sklearn.metrics** to provide this value.

EXERCISE 6.10: COMPUTING MODEL ACCURACY FOR THE CLASSIFICATION MODEL

The goal of this exercise is to compute the accuracy score of the model trained in *Exercise 6.04, Computing the Mean Absolute Error of a Second Model*.

> **NOTE**
>
> You should continue this exercise in the same notebook as that used in *Exercise 6.05, Creating a Classification Model for Computing Evaluation Metrics*. If you wish to use a new notebook, make sure you copy and run the entire code from *Exercise 6.05, Creating a Classification Model for Computing Evaluation Metrics*, and then begin with the execution of the code of this exercise.

The following steps will help you accomplish the task:

1. Continue from where the code for *Exercise 6.05, Creating a Classification Model for Computing Evaluation Metrics*, ends in your notebook.
2. Import **accuracy_score()**:

```
from sklearn.metrics import accuracy_score
```

In this step, you import **accuracy_score()**, which you will use to compute the model accuracy.

3. Compute the accuracy:

```
_accuracy = accuracy_score(y_val, y_pred)
print(_accuracy)
```

In this step, you compute the model accuracy by passing in **y_val** and **y_pred** as parameters to **accuracy_score()**. The interpreter assigns the result to a variable called **c**. The **print()** method causes the interpreter to render the value of **_accuracy**.

The result is similar to the following:

```
0.8996138996138996
```

Figure 6.33 Accuracy score

> **NOTE**
>
> To access the source code for this specific section, please refer to https://packt.live/2Q6K5Ao.
>
> You can also run this example online at https://packt.live/2Ye55JT.

Thus, we have successfully calculated the accuracy of the model as being **0.876**. The goal of this exercise is to show you how to compute the accuracy of a model and to compare this accuracy value to that of another model that you will train in the future.

LOGARITHMIC LOSS

The logarithmic loss (or log loss) is the loss function for categorical models. It is also called categorical cross-entropy. It seeks to penalize incorrect predictions. The **sklearn** documentation defines it as "the negative log-likelihood of the true values given your model predictions."

EXERCISE 6.11: COMPUTING THE LOG LOSS FOR THE CLASSIFICATION MODEL

The goal of this exercise is to predict the log loss of the model trained in *Exercise 6.05, Creating a Classification Model for Computing Evaluation Metrics*.

> **NOTE**
>
> You should continue this exercise in the same notebook as that used in *Exercise 6.05, Creating a Classification Model for Computing Evaluation Metrics*. If you wish to use a new notebook, make sure you copy and run the entire code from *Exercise 6.05* and then begin with the execution of the code of this exercise.

The following steps will help you accomplish the task:

1. Open your Colab notebook and continue from where *Exercise 6.05, Creating a Classification Model for Computing Evaluation Metrics*, stopped.
2. Import the required libraries:

```
from sklearn.metrics import log_loss
```

   In this step, you import **log_loss()** from **sklearn.metrics**.

3. Compute the log loss:

```
_loss = log_loss(y_val, model.predict_proba(X_val))
print(_loss)
```

In this step, you compute the log loss and store it in a variable called **_loss**. You need to observe something very important: previously, you made use of **y_val**, the ground truths, and **y_pred**, the predictions.

In this step, you do not make use of predictions. Instead, you make use of predicted probabilities. You see that in the code where you specify **model.predict_proba()**. You specify the validation dataset and it returns the predicted probabilities.

The **print()** function causes the interpreter to render the log loss.

This should look like the following:

```
0.22578836752298448
```

Figure 6.34: Log loss output

> **NOTE**
>
> The value of loss can vary for different data.
>
> To access the source code for this specific section, please refer to https://packt.live/2Q5plZR.
>
> You can also run this example online at https://packt.live/34eMIsm.

Thus, we have successfully calculated the `log_loss` for a classification model.

RECEIVER OPERATING CHARACTERISTIC CURVE

Recall the True Positive Rate, which we discussed earlier. It is also called **sensitivity**. Also recall that what we try to do with a logistic regression model is find a threshold value such that above that threshold value, we predict that our input falls into a certain class, and below that threshold, we predict that it doesn't.

The Receiver Operating Characteristic (ROC) curve is a plot that shows how the true positive and false positive rates vary for a model as the threshold is changed.

Let's do an exercise to enhance our understanding of the ROC curve.

EXERCISE 6.12: COMPUTING AND PLOTTING ROC CURVE FOR A BINARY CLASSIFICATION PROBLEM

The goal of this exercise is to plot the ROC curve for a binary classification problem. The data for this problem is used to predict whether or not a mother will require a caesarian section to give birth.

> **NOTE**
>
> The dataset that you will be using in this chapter can be found in our GitHub repository: https://packt.live/36dyEg5.
>
> From the UCI Machine Learning Repository, the abstract for this dataset follows: "This dataset contains information about caesarian section results of 80 pregnant women with the most important characteristics of delivery problems in the medical field." The attributes of interest are age, delivery number, delivery time, blood pressure, and heart status.

The following steps will help you accomplish this task:

1. Open a Colab notebook file.
2. Import the required libraries:

```
# import libraries
import pandas as pd
from sklearn.model_selection import train_test_split
from sklearn.linear_model import LogisticRegression
from sklearn.metrics import roc_curve
from sklearn.metrics import auc
```

   In this step, you import **pandas**, which you will use to read in data. You also import **train_test_split** for creating training and validation datasets, and **LogisticRegression** for creating a model.

3. Read in the data:

```
# data doesn't have headers, so let's create headers
_headers = ['Age', 'Delivery_Nbr', 'Delivery_Time', \
            'Blood_Pressure', 'Heart_Problem', 'Caesarian']
# read in cars dataset
df = pd.read_csv('https://raw.githubusercontent.com/'\
                 'PacktWorkshops/The-Data-Science-Workshop/'\
                 'master/Chapter06/Dataset/caesarian.csv.arff',\
                 names=_headers, index_col=None, skiprows=15)
df.head()
# target column is 'Caesarian'
```

   In this step, you read in your data. The dataset has an interesting format. The bottom part contains the data in CSV format, but the upper part contains some file descriptors. If you download and open the file from https://packt.live/38qJe4A and open the file using Notepad, you will see the following:

```
@relation caesarian



@attribute 'Age' { 22,26,28,27,32,36,33,23,20,29,25,37,24,18,30,40,31,19,21,35,17,38 }
@attribute 'Delivery number' { 1,2,3,4 }
@attribute 'Delivery time' { 0,1,2 }
@attribute 'Blood of Pressure' { 2,1,0 }

@attribute 'Heart Problem' { 1,0 }
@attribute Caesarian { 0,1 }


@data


22,1,0,2,0,0
26,2,0,1,0,1
26,2,1,1,0,0
28,1,0,2,0,0
22,2,0,1,0,1
```

Figure 6.35: Reading the dataset

You will need to do a few things to work with this file. Skip 15 rows and specify the column headers and read the file without an index.

The code shows how you do that by creating a Python list to hold your column headers and then read in the file using **`read_csv()`**. The parameters that you pass in are the file's location, the column headers as a Python list, the name of the index column (in this case, it is None), and the number of rows to skip.

The **head()** method will print out the top five rows and should look similar to the following:

	Age	Delivery_Nbr	Delivery_Time	Blood_Pressure	Heart_Problem	Caesarian
0	22	1	0	2	0	0
1	26	2	0	1	0	1
2	26	2	1	1	0	0
3	28	1	0	2	0	0
4	22	2	0	1	0	1

Figure 6.36: The top five rows of the DataFrame

4. Split the data:

```
# target column is 'Caesarian'
features = df.drop(['Caesarian'], axis=1).values
labels = df[['Caesarian']].values

# split 80% for training and 20% into an evaluation set
X_train, X_eval, y_train, y_eval = train_test_split\
                                   (features, labels, \
                                    test_size=0.2, \
                                    random_state=0)

"""
further split the evaluation set into validation and test sets
of 10% each
"""
X_val, X_test, y_val, y_test = train_test_split(X_eval, y_eval,\
                                                test_size=0.5, \
                                                random_state=0)
```

In this step, you begin by creating two **numpy** arrays, which you call **features** and **labels**. You then split these arrays into a **training** and an **evaluation** dataset. You further split the **evaluation** dataset into **validation** and **test** datasets.

5. Now, train and fit a logistic regression model:

```
model = LogisticRegression()
model.fit(X_train, y_train)
```

In this step, you begin by creating an instance of a logistic regression model. You then proceed to train or fit the model on the training dataset.

The output should be similar to the following:

```
LogisticRegression(C=1.0, class_weight=None, dual=False, fit_intercept=True,
                   intercept_scaling=1, l1_ratio=None, max_iter=100,
                   multi_class='warn', n_jobs=None, penalty='l2',
                   random_state=None, solver='warn', tol=0.0001, verbose=0,
                   warm_start=False)
```

Figure 6.37: Training a logistic regression model

6. Predict the probabilities, as shown in the following code snippet:

```
y_proba = model.predict_proba(X_val)
```

In this step, the model predicts the probabilities for each entry in the validation dataset. It stores the results in **`y_proba`**.

7. Compute the true positive rate, the false positive rate, and the thresholds:

```
_false_positive, _true_positive, _thresholds = roc_curve\
                                               (y_val, \
                                                y_proba[:, 0])
```

In this step, you make a call to **`roc_curve()`** and specify the ground truth and the first column of the predicted probabilities. The result is a tuple of false positive rate, true positive rate, and thresholds.

8. Explore the false positive rates:

```
print(_false_positive)
```

In this step, you instruct the interpreter to print out the false positive rate. The output should be similar to the following:

```
[0.  0.  0.  0.5 0.5 1.  1. ]
```

Figure 6.38: False positive rates

> **NOTE**
>
> The false positive rates can vary, depending on the data.

9. Explore the true positive rates:

```
print(_true_positive)
```

In this step, you instruct the interpreter to print out the true positive rates. This should be similar to the following:

```
[0.         0.16666667 0.33333333 0.33333333 0.83333333 0.83333333
 1.        ]
```

Figure 6.39: True positive rates

10. Explore the thresholds:

```
print(_thresholds)
```

In this step, you instruct the interpreter to display the thresholds. The output should be similar to the following:

```
[1.55519917 0.55519917 0.55005086 0.48008433 0.32085037 0.22083119
 0.19657847]
```

Figure 6.40: Thresholds

11. Now, plot the ROC curve:

```
# Plot the RoC
import matplotlib.pyplot as plt
%matplotlib inline

plt.plot(_false_positive, _true_positive, lw=2, \
         label='Receiver Operating Characteristic')
plt.xlim(0.0, 1.2)
plt.ylim(0.0, 1.2)
plt.xlabel('False Positive Rate')
plt.ylabel('True Positive Rate')
plt.title('Receiver Operating Characteristic')
plt.show()
```

In this step, you import **`matplotlib.pyplot`** as your plotting library. You alias it as **`plt`**. You then proceed to plot a line chart by specifying the false positive rates and true positive rates. The rest of the code decorates the chart with a title and labels for the horizontal and vertical axes.

The output should look similar to the following:

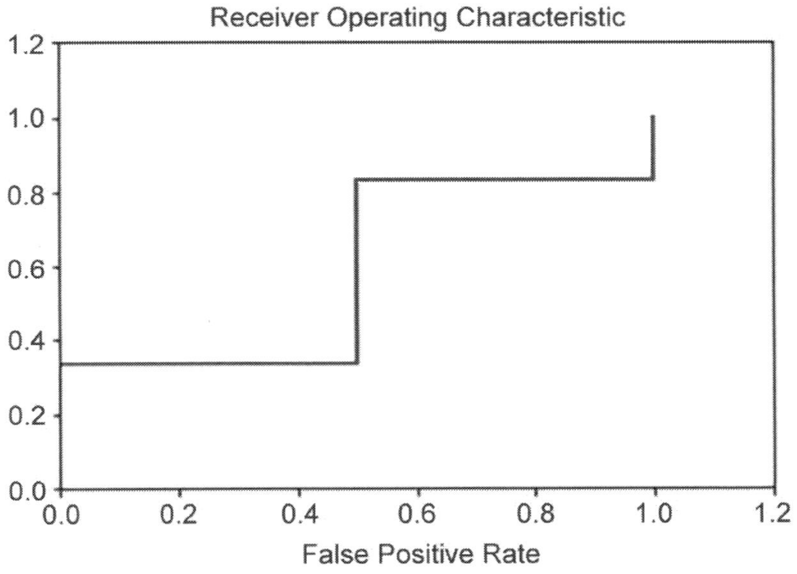

Figure 6.41: ROC curve

> **NOTE**
>
> To access the source code for this specific section, please refer to https://packt.live/322jiLa.
>
> You can also run this example online at https://packt.live/324ii9s.

In this exercise, you learned to plot how the true positive rate and false positive rate of the model vary as you change the prediction threshold. Recall that what the model does is output a value between 0 and 1. This value is called a logit. Your job as a data scientist is to decide on a threshold value, for example, 0.5. If the logit is above that threshold, you predict that the input falls into one class (positive, if it is a positive-or-negative prediction). If the logit is below the threshold, you will predict that the input belongs to the negative class.

For example, if your threshold is 0.5, then a logit of 0.33 is predicted as negative, while a logit of 0.80 is predicted as positive.

However, if your threshold is 0.95, then a logit of 0.33 is predicted as negative, and a logit of 0.80 is still predicted as negative.

Now, recall that what you want your model to do is correctly classify as many data points as possible. Classification is controlled by your chosen threshold value. The logit (predicted probability) from the model will always be the same, but the class assigned to the prediction will depend on the threshold.

As you vary the threshold, the predictions change, and the number of true positives and true negatives changes.

The RoC shows you how the percentage of true positives and true negatives changes as the threshold varies from 0 to 1.

The higher the threshold, the more confident the model needs to be before you classify a prediction as positive. Recall that the logit is the probability that the input belongs to a class and is a confidence score from 0 to 1.

AREA UNDER THE ROC CURVE

The **Area Under the Receiver Operating Characteristic Curve** (**ROC AUC**) is a measure of the likelihood that the model will rank a randomly chosen positive example higher than a randomly chosen negative example. Another way of putting it is to say that the higher this measure is, the better the model is at predicting a negative class as negative, and a positive class as positive. The value ranges from 0 to 1. If the AUC is 0.6, it means that the model has a 60% probability of correctly distinguishing a negative class from a positive class based on the inputs. This measure is used to compare models.

EXERCISE 6.13: COMPUTING THE ROC AUC FOR THE CAESARIAN DATASET

The goal of this exercise is to compute the ROC AUC for the binary classification model that you trained in *Exercise 6.12, Computing and Plotting ROC Curve for a Binary Classification Problem*.

> **NOTE**
>
> You should continue this exercise in the same notebook as that used in *Exercise 6.12, Computing and Plotting ROC Curve for a Binary Classification Problem.* If you wish to use a new notebook, make sure you copy and run the entire code from *Exercise 6.12* and then begin with the execution of the code of this exercise.

The following steps will help you accomplish the task:

1. Open a Colab notebook to the code for *Exercise 6.12, Computing and Plotting ROC Curve for a Binary Classification Problem,* and continue writing your code.
2. Predict the probabilities:

```
y_proba = model.predict_proba(X_val)
```

   In this step, you compute the probabilities of the classes in the validation dataset. You store the result in **y_proba**.

3. Compute the ROC AUC:

```
from sklearn.metrics import roc_auc_score
_auc = roc_auc_score(y_val, y_proba[:, 0])
print(_auc)
```

In this step, you compute the ROC AUC and store the result in **_auc**. You then proceed to print this value out. The result should look similar to the following:

```
0.5833333333333334
```

Figure 6.42: Computing the ROC AUC

> **NOTE**
>
> The AUC can be different, depending on the data.
>
> To access the source code for this specific section, please refer to https://packt.live/32jCrIT.
>
> You can also run this example online at https://packt.live/319zoDy.

In this exercise, you learned to compute the ROC AUC, which is the measure of the likelihood that the model will rank a randomly chosen positive example higher than a randomly chosen negative example. In this example, the AUC is 0.1944, and there is room for improvement with this model.

When you are done selecting a model, you might be interested in saving it for use in the future. The next topic explores saving and loading models.

SAVING AND LOADING MODELS

You will eventually need to transfer some of the models you have trained to a different computer so they can be put into production. There are various utilities for doing this, but the one we will discuss is called **joblib**.

joblib supports saving and loading models, and it saves the models in a format that is supported by other machine learning architectures, such as **ONNX**.

joblib is found in the **sklearn.externals** module.

EXERCISE 6.14: SAVING AND LOADING A MODEL

In this exercise, you will train a simple model and use it for prediction. You will then proceed to save the model and then load it back in. You will use the loaded model for a second prediction, and then compare the predictions from the first model to those from the second model. You will make use of the car dataset for this exercise.

The following steps will guide you toward the goal:

1. Open a Colab notebook.
2. Import the required libraries:

```
import pandas as pd
from sklearn.model_selection import train_test_split
from sklearn.linear_model import LinearRegression
```

3. Read in the data:

```
_headers = ['CIC0', 'SM1', 'GATS1i', 'NdsCH', 'Ndssc', \
            'MLOGP', 'response']

# read in data
df = pd.read_csv('https://raw.githubusercontent.com/'\
                 'PacktWorkshops/The-Data-Science-Workshop/'\
                 'master/Chapter06/Dataset/'\
                 'qsar_fish_toxicity.csv', \
                 names=_headers, sep=';')
```

4. Inspect the data:

```
df.head()
```

The output should be similar to the following:

	CIC0	SM1	GATS1i	NdsCH	Ndssc	MLOGP	response
0	3.260	0.829	1.676	0	1	1.453	3.770
1	2.189	0.580	0.863	0	0	1.348	3.115
2	2.125	0.638	0.831	0	0	1.348	3.531
3	3.027	0.331	1.472	1	0	1.807	3.510
4	2.094	0.827	0.860	0	0	1.886	5.390

Figure 6.43: Inspecting the first five rows of the DataFrame

5. Split the data into **features** and **labels**, and into training and validation sets:

```
features = df.drop('response', axis=1).values
labels = df[['response']].values

X_train, X_eval, y_train, y_eval = train_test_split\
                                   (features, labels, \
                                    test_size=0.2, \
                                    random_state=0)
X_val, X_test, y_val, y_test = train_test_split(X_eval, y_eval,\
                                                random_state=0)
```

6. Create a linear regression model:

```
model = LinearRegression()
print(model)
```

The output will be as follows:

```
LinearRegression(copy_X=True, fit_intercept=True, n_jobs=None, normalize=False)
```

Figure 6.44: Training a linear regression model

7. Fit the training data to the model:

```
model.fit(X_train, y_train)
```

8. Use the model for prediction:

```
y_pred = model.predict(X_val)
```

9. Import **joblib**:

```
from sklearn.externals import joblib
```

10. Save the model:

```
joblib.dump(model, './model.joblib')
```

The output should be similar to the following:

```
['./model.joblib']
```

Figure 6.45: Saving the model

11. Load it as a new model:

```
m2 = joblib.load('./model.joblib')
```

12. Use the new model for predictions:

```
m2_preds = m2.predict(X_val)
```

13. Compare the predictions:

```
ys = pd.DataFrame(dict(predicted=y_pred.reshape(-1), \
                       m2=m2_preds.reshape(-1)))
ys.head()
```

The output should be similar to the following:

	predicted	m2
0	4.155885	4.155885
1	6.398238	6.398238
2	5.183181	5.183181
3	3.771333	3.771333
4	4.593059	4.593059

Figure 6.46: Comparing predictions

> **NOTE**
>
> To access the source code for this specific section, please refer to https://packt.live/322VxTb.
>
> You can also run this example online at https://packt.live/3aAUz4q.

You can see that the predictions from the model before it was saved are exactly the same as the predictions from the model after it was saved and loaded back in. It is safe to conclude that saving and loading models does not affect their quality.

In this exercise, you learned how to save and load models. You also checked and confirmed that the model predictions remain the same even when you save and load them.

ACTIVITY 6.01: TRAIN THREE DIFFERENT MODELS AND USE EVALUATION METRICS TO PICK THE BEST PERFORMING MODEL

You work as a data scientist at a bank. The bank would like to implement a model that predicts the likelihood of a customer purchasing a term deposit. The bank provides you with a dataset, which is the same as the one in *Chapter 3, Binary Classification*. You have previously learned how to train a logistic regression model for binary classification. You have also heard about other non-parametric modeling techniques and would like to try out a decision tree as well as a random forest to see how well they perform against the logistic regression models you have been training.

In this activity, you will train a logistic regression model and compute a classification report. You will then proceed to train a decision tree classifier and compute a classification report. You will compare the models using the classification reports. Finally, you will train a random forest classifier and generate the classification report. You will then compare the logistic regression model with the random forest using the classification reports to determine which model you should put into production.

The steps to accomplish this task are:

1. Open a Colab notebook.
2. Load the necessary libraries.
3. Read in the data.
4. Explore the data.
5. Convert categorical variables using **`pandas.get_dummies()`**.
6. Prepare the **`X`** and **`y`** variables.
7. Split the data into training and evaluation sets.
8. Create an instance of **`LogisticRegression`**.
9. Fit the training data to the **`LogisticRegression`** model.
10. Use the evaluation set to make a prediction.
11. Use the prediction from the **`LogisticRegression`** model to compute the classification report.

12. Create an instance of **DecisionTreeClassifier**:

```
dt_model = DecisionTreeClassifier(max_depth= 6)
```

13. Fit the training data to the **DecisionTreeClassifier** model:

```
dt_model.fit(train_X, train_y)
```

14. Using the **DecisionTreeClassifier** model, make a prediction on the evaluation dataset:

```
dt_preds = dt_model.predict(val_X)
```

15. Use the prediction from the **DecisionTreeClassifier** model to compute the classification report:

```
dt_report = classification_report(val_y, dt_preds)
print(dt_report)
```

> **NOTE**
>
> We will be studying decision trees in detail in *Chapter 7, The Generalization of Machine Learning Models*.

16. Compare the classification report from the linear regression model and the classification report from the decision tree classifier to determine which is the better model.
17. Create an instance of **RandomForestClassifier**.
18. Fit the training data to the **RandomForestClassifier** model.
19. Using the **RandomForestClassifier** model, make a prediction on the evaluation dataset.
20. Using the prediction from the random forest classifier, compute the classification report.
21. Compare the classification report from the linear regression model with the classification report from the random forest classifier to decide which model to keep or improve upon.

22. Compare the R^2 scores of all three models. The output should be similar to the following:

```
Linear Score: 0.9087083198446099, DecisionTree Score: 0.917125283263192, RandomForest Score: 0.9153987266645
```

Figure 6.47: Comparing the R^2 scores

> **NOTE**
>
> The solution to this activity can be found at the following address: https://packt.live/2GbJloz.

SUMMARY

In this chapter we observed that some of the evaluation metrics for classification models require a binary classification model. We saw that when we worked with more than two classes, we were required to use the one-versus-all approach. The one-versus-all approach builds one model for each class and tries to predict the probability that the input belongs to a specific class. We saw that once this was done, we then predicted that the input belongs to the class where the model has the highest prediction probability. We also split our evaluation dataset into two, it's because **`X_test`** and **`y_test`** are used once for a final evaluation of the model's performance. You can make use of them before putting your model into production to see how the model would perform in a production environment.

You have learned how to assess the quality of a regression model by observing how the loss changes. You saw examples using the MAE, and also learned of the existence of MSE. You also learned about how to assess the quality of classification models in the activity. In the next chapter, you will learn how to train multiple models using cross-validation and also implement regularization techniques.

7

THE GENERALIZATION OF MACHINE LEARNING MODELS

OVERVIEW

This chapter will teach you how to make use of the data you have to train better models by either splitting your data if it is sufficient or making use of cross-validation if it is not. By the end of this chapter, you will know how to split your data into training, validation, and test datasets. You will be able to identify the ratio in which data has to be split and also consider certain features while splitting. You will also be able to implement cross-validation to use limited data for testing and use regularization to reduce overfitting in models.

INTRODUCTION

In the previous chapter, you learned about model assessment using various metrics such as R2 score, MAE, and accuracy. These metrics help you decide which models to keep and which ones to discard. In this chapter, you will learn some more techniques for training better models.

Generalization deals with getting your models to perform well enough on data points that they have not encountered in the past (that is, during training). We will address two specific areas:

- How to make use of as much of your data as possible to train a model
- How to reduce overfitting in a model

OVERFITTING

A model is said to overfit the training data when it generates a hypothesis that accounts for every example. What this means is that it correctly predicts the outcome of every example. The problem with this scenario is that the model equation becomes extremely complex, and such models have been observed to be incapable of correctly predicting new observations.

Overfitting occurs when a model has been over-engineered. Two of the ways in which this could occur are:

- The model is trained on too many features.
- The model is trained for too long.

We'll discuss each of these two points in the following sections.

TRAINING ON TOO MANY FEATURES

When a model trains on too many features, the hypothesis becomes extremely complicated. Consider a case in which you have one column of features and you need to generate a hypothesis. This would be a simple linear equation, as shown here:

$$y = w . x_1$$

Figure 7.1: Equation for a hypothesis for a line

Now, consider a case in which you have two columns, and in which you cross the columns by multiplying them. The hypothesis becomes the following:

$$y = w_1.x_1 + w_2.x_2 + w_3.x_1.x_2 + b$$

Figure 7.2: Equation for a hypothesis for a curve

While the first equation yields a line, the second equation yields a curve, because it is now a quadratic equation. But the same two features could become even more complicated depending on how you engineer your features. Consider the following equation:

$$y = w_1.x_1 + w_2.x_2 + w_3.x_1.x_2 + w_4.x_1^2 + w_5.x_2^3 + b$$

Figure 7.3: Cubic equation for a hypothesis

The same set of features has now given rise to a cubic equation. This equation will have the property of having a large number of weights, for example:

- The simple linear equation has one weight and one bias.
- The quadratic equation has three weights and one bias.
- The cubic equation has five weights and one bias.

One solution to overfitting as a result of too many features is to eliminate certain features. The technique for this is called lasso regression.

A second solution to overfitting as a result of too many features is to provide more data to the model. This might not always be a feasible option, but where possible, it is always a good idea to do so.

TRAINING FOR TOO LONG

The model starts training by initializing the vector of weights such that all values are equal to zero. During training, the weights are updated according to the gradient update rule. This systematically adds or subtracts a small value to each weight. As training progresses, the magnitude of the weights increases. If the model trains for too long, these model weights become too large.

The solution to overfitting as a result of large weights is to reduce the magnitude of the weights to as close to zero as possible. The technique for this is called ridge regression.

UNDERFITTING

Consider an alternative situation in which the data has 10 features, but you only make use of 1 feature. Your model hypothesis would still be the following:

$$y = w . x_1$$

Figure 7.4: Equation for a hypothesis for a line

However, that is the equation of a straight line, but your model is probably ignoring a lot of information. The model is over-simplified and is said to underfit the data.

The solution to underfitting is to provide the model with more features, or conversely, less data to train on; but more features is the better approach.

DATA

In the world of machine learning, the data that you have is not used in its entirety to train your model. Instead, you need to separate your data into three sets, as mentioned here:

- A training dataset, which is used to train your model and measure the training loss.
- An evaluation or validation dataset, which you use to measure the validation loss of the model to see whether the validation loss continues to reduce as well as the training loss.
- A test dataset for final testing to see how well the model performs before you put it into production.

THE RATIO FOR DATASET SPLITS

The evaluation dataset is set aside from your entire training data and is never used for training. There are various schools of thought around the particular ratio that is set aside for evaluation, but it generally ranges from a high of 30% to a low of 10%. This evaluation dataset is normally further split into a validation dataset that is used during training and a test dataset that is used at the end for a sanity check. If you are using 10% for evaluation, you might set 5% aside for validation and the remaining 5% for testing. If using 30%, you might set 20% aside for validation and 10% for testing.

To summarize, you might split your data into 70% for training, 20% for validation, and 10% for testing, or you could split your data into 80% for training, 15% for validation, and 5% for test. Or, finally, you could split your data into 90% for training, 5% for validation, and 5% for testing.

The choice of what ratio to use is dependent on the amount of data that you have. If you are working with 100,000 records, for example, then 20% validation would give you 20,000 records. However, if you were working with 100,000,000 records, then 5% would give you 5 million records for validation, which would be more than sufficient.

CREATING DATASET SPLITS

At a very basic level, splitting your data involves random sampling. Let's say you have 10 items in a bowl. To get 30% of the items, you would reach in and take any 3 items at random.

In the same way, because you are writing code, you could do the following:

1. Create a Python list.
2. Place 10 numbers in the list.
3. Generate 3 non-repeating random whole numbers from 0 to 9.
4. Pick items whose indices correspond to the random numbers previously generated.

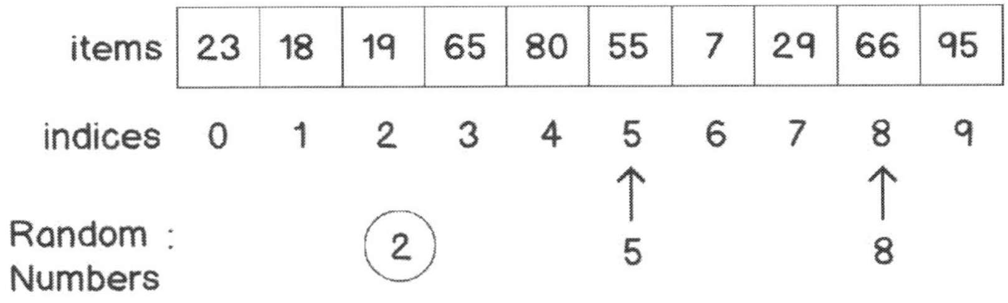

Figure 7.5: Visualization of data splitting

This is something you will only do once for a particular dataset. You might write a function for it. If it is something that you need to do repeatedly and you also need to handle advanced functionality, you might want to write a class for it.

`sklearn` has a class called **`train_test_split`**, which provides the functionality for splitting data. It is available as **`sklearn.model_selection.train_test_split`**. This function will let you split a DataFrame into two parts.

Have a look at the following exercise on importing and splitting data.

EXERCISE 7.01: IMPORTING AND SPLITTING DATA

The goal of this exercise is to import data from a repository and to split it into a training and an evaluation set.

We will be using the Cars dataset from the UCI Machine Learning Repository.

> **NOTE**
>
> You can find the dataset here: https://packt.live/2RE5rWi
>
> The dataset can also be found on our GitHub, here: https://packt.live/36cvyc4

You will be using this dataset throughout the exercises in this chapter.

This dataset is about the cost of owning cars with certain attributes. The abstract from the website states: "*Derived from simple hierarchical decision model, this database may be useful for testing constructive induction and structure discovery methods*." Here are some of the key attributes of this dataset:

```
CAR car acceptability
. PRICE overall price
. . buying buying price
. . maint price of the maintenance
. TECH technical characteristics
. . COMFORT comfort
. . . doors number of doors
. . . persons capacity in terms of persons to carry
. . . lug_boot the size of luggage boot
. . safety estimated safety of the car
```

The following steps will help you complete the exercise:

1. Open a new Colab notebook file.
2. Import the necessary libraries:

```
# import libraries
import pandas as pd
from sklearn.model_selection import train_test_split
```

In this step, you have imported **pandas** and aliased it as **pd**. As you know, **pandas** is required to read in the file. You also import **train_test_split** from **sklearn.model_selection** to split the data into two parts.

3. Before reading the file into your notebook, open and inspect the file (**car.data**) with an editor. You should see an output similar to the following:

car.data

```
vhigh,vhigh,2,2,small,low,unacc
vhigh,vhigh,2,2,small,med,unacc
vhigh,vhigh,2,2,small,high,unacc
vhigh,vhigh,2,2,med,low,unacc
vhigh,vhigh,2,2,med,med,unacc
vhigh,vhigh,2,2,med,high,unacc
vhigh,vhigh,2,2,big,low,unacc
vhigh,vhigh,2,2,big,med,unacc
vhigh,vhigh,2,2,big,high,unacc
vhigh,vhigh,2,4,small,low,unacc
vhigh,vhigh,2,4,small,med,unacc
vhigh,vhigh,2,4,small,high,unacc
vhigh,vhigh,2,4,med,low,unacc
vhigh,vhigh,2,4,med,med,unacc
vhigh,vhigh,2,4,med,high,unacc
vhigh,vhigh,2,4,big,low,unacc
vhigh,vhigh,2,4,big,med,unacc
vhigh,vhigh,2,4,big,high,unacc
vhigh,vhigh,2,more,small,low,unacc
vhigh,vhigh,2,more,small,med,unacc
vhigh,vhigh,2,more,small,high,unacc
vhigh,vhigh,2,more,med,low,unacc
vhigh,vhigh,2,more,med,med,unacc
vhigh,vhigh,2,more,med,high,unacc
vhigh,vhigh,2,more,big,low,unacc
vhigh,vhigh,2,more,big,med,unacc
vhigh,vhigh,2,more,big,high,unacc
vhigh,vhigh,3,2,small,low,unacc
vhigh,vhigh,3,2,small,med,unacc
vhigh,vhigh,3,2,small,high,unacc
```

Figure 7.6: Car data

You will notice from the preceding screenshot that the file doesn't have a first row containing the headers.

4. Create a Python list to hold the headers for the data:

```
# data doesn't have headers, so let's create headers
_headers = ['buying', 'maint', 'doors', 'persons', \
            'lug_boot', 'safety', 'car']
```

5. Now, import the data as shown in the following code snippet:

```
# read in cars dataset
df = pd.read_csv('https://raw.githubusercontent.com/'\
                 'PacktWorkshops/The-Data-Science-Workshop/'\
                 'master/Chapter07/Dataset/car.data', \
                 names=_headers, index_col=None)
```

   You then proceed to import the data into a variable called **df** by using **pd.read_csv**. You specify the location of the data file, as well as the list of column headers. You also specify that the data does not have a column index.

6. Show the top five records:

```
df.info()
```

   In order to get information about the columns in the data as well as the number of records, you make use of the **info()** method. You should get an output similar to the following:

```
<class 'pandas.core.frame.DataFrame'>
RangeIndex: 1728 entries, 0 to 1727
Data columns (total 7 columns):
buying      1728 non-null object
maint       1728 non-null object
doors       1728 non-null object
persons     1728 non-null object
lug_boot    1728 non-null object
safety      1728 non-null object
car         1728 non-null object
dtypes: object(7)
memory usage: 94.6+ KB
```

   Figure 7.7: The top five records of the DataFrame

   The **RangeIndex** value shows the number of records, which is **1728**.

7. Now, you need to split the data contained in **df** into a training dataset and an evaluation dataset:

```
#split the data into 80% for training and 20% for evaluation
training_df, eval_df = train_test_split(df, train_size=0.8, \
                                        random_state=0)
```

In this step, you make use of **train_test_split** to create two new DataFrames called **training_df** and **eval_df**.

You specify a value of **0.8** for **train_size** so that **80%** of the data is assigned to **training_df**.

random_state ensures that your experiments are reproducible. Without **random_state**, the data is split differently every time using a different random number. With **random_state**, the data is split the same way every time. We will be studying **random_state** in depth in the next chapter.

8. Check the information of **training_df**:

```
training_df.info()
```

In this step, you make use of **.info()** to get the details of **training_df**. This will print out the column names as well as the number of records.

You should get an output similar to the following:

```
<class 'pandas.core.frame.DataFrame'>
Int64Index: 1382 entries, 1713 to 1240
Data columns (total 7 columns):
buying      1382 non-null object
maint       1382 non-null object
doors       1382 non-null object
persons     1382 non-null object
lug_boot    1382 non-null object
safety      1382 non-null object
car         1382 non-null object
dtypes: object(7)
memory usage: 86.4+ KB
```

Figure 7.8: Information on training_df

You should observe that the column names match those in **df**, but you should have **80%** of the records that you did in **df**, which is **1382** out of **1728**.

9. Check the information on **eval_df**:

```
eval_df.info()
```

In this step, you print out the information about **eval_df**. This will give you the column names and the number of records. The output should be similar to the following:

```
<class 'pandas.core.frame.DataFrame'>
Int64Index: 346 entries, 1194 to 1086
Data columns (total 7 columns):
buying      346 non-null object
maint       346 non-null object
doors       346 non-null object
persons     346 non-null object
lug_boot    346 non-null object
safety      346 non-null object
car         346 non-null object
dtypes: object(7)
memory usage: 21.6+ KB
```

Figure 7.9: Information on eval_df

> **NOTE**
>
> To access the source code for this specific section, please refer to https://packt.live/3294avL.
>
> You can also run this example online at https://packt.live/2E8FHhT.

Now you know how to split your data. Whenever you split your data, the records are going to be exactly the same. You could repeat the exercise a number of times and notice the range of entries in the index for **eval_df**.

The implication of this is that you cannot repeat your experiments. If you run the same code, you will get different results every time. Also, if you share your code with your colleagues, they will get different results. This is because the compiler makes use of random numbers.

These random numbers are not actually random but make use of something called a pseudo-random number generator. The generator has a pre-determined set of random numbers that it uses, and as a result, you can specify a random state that will cause it to use a particular set of random numbers.

RANDOM STATE

The key to reproducing the same results is called random state. You simply specify a number, and whenever that number is used, the same results will be produced. This works because computers don't have an actual random number generator. Instead, they have a pseudo-random number generator. This means that you can generate the same sequence of random numbers if you set a random state.

Consider the following figure as an example. The columns are your random states. If you pick 0 as the random state, the following numbers will be generated: 41, 52, 38, 56...

However, if you pick 1 as the random state, a different set of numbers will be generated, and so on.

0	1	2	3	4	5	6	7	8	9	10
41	12	77	91	5	85	48	61	83	41	32
52	41	84	37	43	99	34	19	67	94	18
38	76	84	73	88	36	90	12	39	86	94
56	7	36	88	32	35	90	30	19	14	2
69	26	15	74	60	43	85	49	82	7	41
28	28	7	0	75	72	29	40	82	9	87
25	35	19	36	35	88	9	55	33	80	41
37	83	2	29	6	20	31	75	98	96	16
72	50	52	7	50	67	9	1	45	12	0
95	20	21	80	35	2	48	68	39	62	95
1	86	5	54	74	4	44	85	86	73	64
86	16	70	23	20	45	1	95	83	98	49
96	49	26	57	88	35	59	26	40	19	97
20	3	41	21	81	99	19	93	14	62	7
97	96	87	92	82	71	6	54	69	86	16
3	42	41	70	5	59	28	90	41	74	73
51	9	3	23	14	7	95	10	75	9	12
19	42	33	71	51	11	51	50	87	28	45
85	72	57	36	91	9	86	19	54	23	32
40	45	54	17	39	49	58	18	3	54	53
80	62	48	7	86	4	58	69	72	10	22
28	21	44	97	28	14	82	37	77	12	10
24	35	81	63	64	20	78	98	2	69	8
56	49	30	0	91	12	93	8	75	69	55
36	22	25	95	67	66	27	53	11	51	36
33	58	4	91	78	25	27	20	61	15	80
45	94	22	14	67	25	55	9	92	74	52
72	0	4	53	27	40	42	37	95	76	60
70	44	99	89	81	50	65	39	14	0	52
76	99	54	95	22	37	40	84	43	14	58

Figure 7.10: Numbers generated using random state

In the previous exercise, you set the random state to 0 so that the experiment was repeatable.

EXERCISE 7.02: SETTING A RANDOM STATE WHEN SPLITTING DATA

The goal of this exercise is to have a reproducible way of splitting the data that you imported in *Exercise 7.01, Importing and Splitting Data*.

> **NOTE**
>
> We going to refactor the code from the previous exercise. Hence, if you are using a new Colab notebook then make sure you copy the code from the previous exercise. Alternatively, you can make a copy of the notebook used in *Exercise 7.01* and use the revised the code as suggested in the following steps.

The following steps will help you complete the exercise:

1. Continue from the previous *Exercise 7.01* notebook.
2. Set the random state as **1** and split the data:

```
"""
split the data into 80% for training and 20% for evaluation
using a random state
"""
training_df, eval_df = train_test_split(df, train_size=0.8, \
                                        random_state=1)
```

   In this step, you specify a **random_state** value of 1 to the **train_test_split** function.

3. Now, view the top five records in **training_df**:

```
#view the head of training_eval
training_df.head()
```

   In this step, you print out the first five records in **training_df**.

The output should be similar to the following:

	buying	maint	doors	persons	lug_boot	safety	car
1579	low	med	4	4	med	med	good
634	high	high	5more	4	med	med	acc
299	vhigh	med	5more	2	small	high	unacc
1085	med	med	2	2	med	high	unacc
1659	low	low	3	4	med	low	unacc

Figure 7.11: The top five rows for the training evaluation set

4. View the top five records in **eval_df**:

```
#view the top of eval_df
eval_df.head()
```

In this step, you print out the first five records in **eval_df**.

The output should be similar to the following:

	buying	maint	doors	persons	lug_boot	safety	car
1233	med	low	3	more	small	low	unacc
592	high	high	3	more	big	med	acc
625	high	high	5more	2	med	med	unacc
1546	low	med	3	2	big	med	unacc
730	high	med	5more	2	small	med	unacc

Figure 7.12: The top five rows of eval_df

> **NOTE**
>
> To access the source code for this specific section, please refer to https://packt.live/2Q6Jb7e.
>
> You can also run this example online at https://packt.live/2EjFvMp.

The goal of this exercise is to get reproducible splits. If you run the code, you will get the same records in both **`training_df`** and **`eval_df`**. You may proceed to run that code a few times on every system and verify that you get the same records in both datasets.

Whenever you change **`random_state`**, you will get a different set of training and validation data.

But how do you find the best dataset split to train your model? When you don't have a lot of data, the recommended approach is to make use of all of your data.

But how do you retain validation data if you make use of all of your data?

The answer is to split the data into a number of parts. This approach is called cross-validation, which we will be looking at in the next section.

CROSS-VALIDATION

Consider an example where you split your data into five parts of 20% each. You would then make use of four parts for training and one part for evaluation. Because you have five parts, you can make use of the data five times, each time using one part for validation and the remaining data for training.

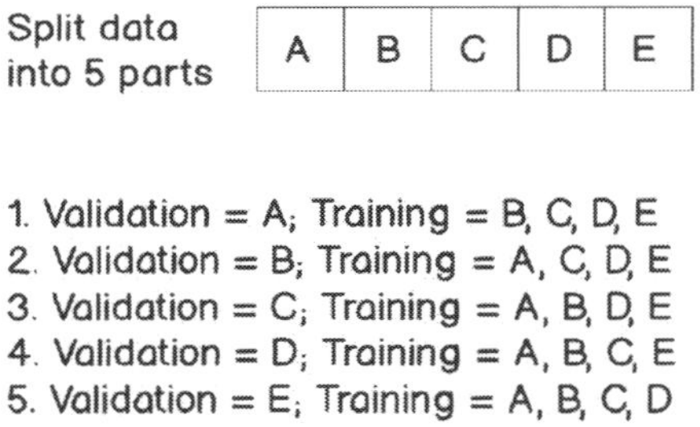

Figure 7.13: Cross-validation

Cross-validation is an approach to splitting your data where you make multiple splits and then make use of some of them for training and the rest for validation. You then make use of all of the combinations of data to train multiple models.

This approach is called n-fold cross-validation or k-fold cross-validation.

> **NOTE**
>
> For more information on k-fold cross-validation, refer to https://packt.live/36eXyfi.

KFOLD

The **KFold** class in **sklearn.model_selection** returns a generator that provides a tuple with two indices, one for training and another for testing or validation. A generator function lets you declare a function that behaves like an iterator, thus letting you use it in a loop.

EXERCISE 7.03: CREATING A FIVE-FOLD CROSS-VALIDATION DATASET

The goal of this exercise is to create a five-fold cross-validation dataset from the data that you imported in *Exercise 7.01*, *Importing and Splitting Data*.

> **NOTE**
>
> If you are using a new Colab notebook then make sure you copy the code from *Exercise 7.01*, *Importing and Splitting Data*. Alternatively, you can make a copy of the notebook used in *Exercise 7.01* and then use the code as suggested in the following steps.

The following steps will help you complete the exercise:

1. Continue from the notebook file of *Exercise 7.01*.
2. Import all the necessary libraries:

```
from sklearn.model_selection import KFold
```

   In this step, you import **KFold** from **sklearn.model_selection**.

3. Now create an instance of the class:

```
_kf = KFold(n_splits=5)
```

   In this step, you create an instance of **KFold** and assign it to a variable called **_kf**. You specify a value of **5** for the **n_splits** parameter so that it splits the dataset into five parts.

4. Now split the data as shown in the following code snippet:

```
indices = _kf.split(df)
```

   In this step, you call the **split** method, which is **.split()** on **_kf**. The result is stored in a variable called **indices**.

5. Find out what data type **indices** has:

```
print(type(indices))
```

In this step, you inspect the call to split the output returns.

The output should be a **generator**, as seen in the following output:

```
<class 'generator'>
```

Figure 7.14: Data type for indices

6. Get the first set of indices:

```
#first set
train_indices, val_indices = next(indices)
```

In this step, you make use of the **next()** Python function on the generator function. Using **next()** is the way that you get a generator to return results to you. You asked for five splits, so you can call **next()** five times on this particular generator. Calling **next()** a sixth time will cause the Python runtime to raise an exception.

The call to **next()** yields a tuple. In this case, it is a pair of indices. The first one contains your training indices and the second one contains your validation indices. You assign these to **train_indices** and **val_indices**.

7. Create a training dataset as shown in the following code snippet:

```
train_df = df.drop(val_indices)
train_df.info()
```

In this step, you create a new DataFrame called **train_df** by dropping the validation indices from **df**, the DataFrame that contains all of the data. This is a subtractive operation similar to what is done in set theory. The **df** set is a union of **train** and **val**. Once you know what **val** is, you can work backward to determine **train** by subtracting **val** from **df**. If you consider **df** to be a set called **A**, **val** to be a set called **B**, and train to be a set called **C**, then the following holds true:

$$A = B \cup C$$

Figure 7.15: Dataframe A

Similarly, set **C** can be the difference between set **A** and set **B**, as depicted in the following:

$$C = A - B$$

Figure 7.16: Dataframe C

The way to accomplish this with a pandas DataFrame is to drop the rows with the indices of the elements of **B** from **A**, which is what you see in the preceding code snippet.

You can see the result of this by calling the **info()** method on the new DataFrame.

The result of that call should be similar to the following screenshot:

```
<class 'pandas.core.frame.DataFrame'>
Int64Index: 1382 entries, 346 to 1727
Data columns (total 7 columns):
buying      1382 non-null object
maint       1382 non-null object
doors       1382 non-null object
persons     1382 non-null object
lug_boot    1382 non-null object
safety      1382 non-null object
car         1382 non-null object
dtypes: object(7)
memory usage: 86.4+ KB
```

Figure 7.17: Information on the new dataframe

8. Create a validation dataset:

```
val_df = df.drop(train_indices)
val_df.info()
```

In this step, you create the **val_df** validation dataset by dropping the training indices from the **df** DataFrame. Again, you can see the details of this new DataFrame by calling the **info()** method.

The output should be similar to the following:

```
<class 'pandas.core.frame.DataFrame'>
Int64Index: 346 entries, 0 to 345
Data columns (total 7 columns):
buying      346 non-null object
maint       346 non-null object
doors       346 non-null object
persons     346 non-null object
lug_boot    346 non-null object
safety      346 non-null object
car         346 non-null object
dtypes: object(7)
memory usage: 21.6+ KB
```

Figure 7.18: Information for the validation dataset

> **NOTE**
>
> To access the source code for this specific section, please refer to https://packt.live/3kRRaDf.
>
> You can also run this example online at https://packt.live/3kTNPnf.

You could program all of the preceding in a loop so that you do not need to manually make a call to **next()** five times. This is what we will be doing in the next exercise.

EXERCISE 7.04: CREATING A FIVE-FOLD CROSS-VALIDATION DATASET USING A LOOP FOR CALLS

The goal of this exercise is to create a five-fold cross-validation dataset from the data that you imported in *Exercise 7.01, Importing and Splitting Data*. You will make use of a loop for calls to the generator function.

> **NOTE**
>
> If you are using a new Colab notebook then make sure you copy the code from *Exercise 7.01, Importing and Splitting Data*. Alternatively, you can make a copy of the notebook used in *Exercise 7.01* and then use the code as suggested in the following steps. The link to notebook for this exercise can be found here: https://packt.live/3g83AmU

The following steps will help you complete this exercise:

1. Open a new Colab notebook and repeat the steps you used to import data in *Exercise 7.01*, *Importing and Splitting Data*.
2. Define the number of splits you would like:

```
from sklearn.model_selection import KFold
#define number of splits
n_splits = 5
```

   In this step, you set the number of splits to **5**. You store this in a variable called **n_splits**.

3. Create an instance of **Kfold**:

```
#create an instance of KFold
_kf = KFold(n_splits=n_splits)
```

   In this step, you create an instance of **Kfold**. You assign this instance to a variable called **_kf**.

4. Generate the split indices:

```
#create splits as _indices
_indices = _kf.split(df)
```

   In this step, you call the **split()** method on **_kf**, which is the instance of **KFold** that you defined earlier. You provide **df** as a parameter so that the splits are performed on the data contained in the DataFrame called **df**. The resulting generator is stored as **_indices**.

5. Create two Python lists:

```
_t, _v = [], []
```

   In this step, you create two Python lists. The first is called **_t** and holds the training DataFrames, and the second is called **_v** and holds the validation DataFrames.

6. Iterate over the generator and create DataFrames called **train_idx**, **val_idx**, **_train_df** and **_val_df**:

```
#iterate over _indices
for i in range(n_splits):
    train_idx, val_idx = next(_indices)
    _train_df = df.drop(val_idx)
```

```
        _t.append(_train_df)
        _val_df = df.drop(train_idx)
        _v.append(_val_df)
```

In this step, you create a loop using **range** to determine the number of iterations. You specify the number of iterations by providing **n_splits** as a parameter to **range()**. On every iteration, you execute **next()** on the **_indices** generator and store the results in **train_idx** and **val_idx**. You then proceed to create **_train_df** by dropping the validation indices, **val_idx**, from **df**. You also create **_val_df** by dropping the training indices from **df**.

7. Iterate over the training list:

```
for d in _t:
    print(d.info())
```

In this step, you verify that the compiler created the DataFrames. You do this by iterating over the list and using the **.info()** method to print out the details of each element. The output is similar to the following screenshot, which is incomplete due to the size of the output. Each element in the list is a DataFrame with 1,382 entries:

```
<class 'pandas.core.frame.DataFrame'>
Int64Index: 1382 entries, 346 to 1727
Data columns (total 7 columns):
 #   Column    Non-Null Count  Dtype 
---  ------    --------------  ----- 
 0   buying    1382 non-null   object
 1   maint     1382 non-null   object
 2   doors     1382 non-null   object
 3   persons   1382 non-null   object
 4   lug_boot  1382 non-null   object
 5   safety    1382 non-null   object
 6   car       1382 non-null   object
dtypes: object(7)
memory usage: 86.4+ KB
None
<class 'pandas.core.frame.DataFrame'>
Int64Index: 1382 entries, 0 to 1727
Data columns (total 7 columns):
 #   Column    Non-Null Count  Dtype 
---  ------    --------------  ----- 
 0   buying    1382 non-null   object
 1   maint     1382 non-null   object
 2   doors     1382 non-null   object
 3   persons   1382 non-null   object
 4   lug_boot  1382 non-null   object
 5   safety    1382 non-null   object
 6   car       1382 non-null   object
dtypes: object(7)
memory usage: 86.4+ KB
None
<class 'pandas.core.frame.DataFrame'>
Int64Index: 1382 entries, 0 to 1727
```

Figure 7.19: Iterating over the training list

> **NOTE**
>
> The preceding output is a truncated version of the actual output.

8. Iterate over the validation list:

```
for d in _v:
    print(d.info())
```

In this step, you iterate over the validation list and make use of **`.info()`** to print out the details of each element. The output is similar to the following screenshot, which is incomplete due to the size. Each element is a DataFrame with 346 entries:

```
<class 'pandas.core.frame.DataFrame'>
Int64Index: 346 entries, 0 to 345
Data columns (total 7 columns):
 #   Column    Non-Null Count  Dtype 
---  ------    --------------  ----- 
 0   buying    346 non-null    object
 1   maint     346 non-null    object
 2   doors     346 non-null    object
 3   persons   346 non-null    object
 4   lug_boot  346 non-null    object
 5   safety    346 non-null    object
 6   car       346 non-null    object
dtypes: object(7)
memory usage: 21.6+ KB
None
<class 'pandas.core.frame.DataFrame'>
Int64Index: 346 entries, 346 to 691
Data columns (total 7 columns):
 #   Column    Non-Null Count  Dtype 
---  ------    --------------  ----- 
 0   buying    346 non-null    object
 1   maint     346 non-null    object
 2   doors     346 non-null    object
 3   persons   346 non-null    object
 4   lug_boot  346 non-null    object
 5   safety    346 non-null    object
 6   car       346 non-null    object
dtypes: object(7)
memory usage: 21.6+ KB
None
<class 'pandas.core.frame.DataFrame'>
```

Figure 7.20: Iterating over the validation list

> **NOTE**
>
> The preceding output is a truncated version of the actual output.
>
> To access the source code for this specific section, please refer to https://packt.live/3g83AmU.
>
> You can also run this example online at https://packt.live/3iXwEPR.

In this exercise, you have learned how to use a loop for k-fold cross-validation to extract training and validation datasets. You can make use of these datasets to train and evaluate multiple models.

The essence of creating cross-validation datasets is that you can train and evaluate multiple models. What if you didn't have to train those models in a loop?

The good news is that you can avoid training multiple models in a loop because if you did that, you would need arrays to track lots of metrics.

CROSS_VAL_SCORE

The **`cross_val_score()`** function is available in **`sklearn.model_selection`**. Up until this point, you have learned how to create cross-validation datasets in a loop. If you made use of that approach, you would need to keep track of all of the models that you are training and evaluating inside of that loop.

`cross_val_score` takes care of the following:

- Creating cross-validation datasets
- Training models by fitting them to the training data
- Evaluating the models on the validation data
- Returning a list of the R2 score of each model that is trained

For all of the preceding actions to happen, you will need to provide the following inputs:

- An instance of an estimator (for example, **`LinearRegression`**)
- The original dataset
- The number of splits to create (which is also the number of models that will be trained and evaluated)

EXERCISE 7.05: GETTING THE SCORES FROM FIVE-FOLD CROSS-VALIDATION

The goal of this exercise is to create a five-fold cross-validation dataset from the data that you imported in *Exercise 7.01*, *Importing and Splitting Data*. You will then use **cross_val_score** to get the scores of models trained on those datasets.

> **NOTE**
>
> If you are using a new Colab notebook then make sure you copy the code from *Exercise 7.01*, *Importing and Splitting Data*. Alternatively, you can make a copy of the notebook used in *Exercise 7.01* and then use the revised code as suggested in the following steps. The link to notebook for this exercise can be found here: https://packt.live/2DWTkAY.

The following steps will help you complete the exercise:

1. Open a new Colab notebook and repeat *steps 1-6* that you took to import data in *Exercise 7.01*, *Importing and Splitting Data*.

2. Encode the categorical variables in the dataset:

```
# encode categorical variables
_df = pd.get_dummies(df, columns=['buying', 'maint', 'doors', \
                                  'persons', 'lug_boot', \
                                  'safety'])
_df.head()
```

   In this step, you make use of **pd.get_dummies()** to convert categorical variables into an encoding. You store the result in a new DataFrame variable called **_df**. You then proceed to take a look at the first five records.

The result should look similar to the following:

	car	buying_high	buying_low	buying_med	buying_vhigh	maint_high	maint_low
0	unacc	0	0	0	1	0	0
1	unacc	0	0	0	1	0	0
2	unacc	0	0	0	1	0	0
3	unacc	0	0	0	1	0	0
4	unacc	0	0	0	1	0	0

5 rows × 22 columns

Figure 7.21: Encoding categorical variables

3. Split the data into features and labels:

```
# separate features and labels DataFrames
features = _df.drop(['car'], axis=1).values
labels = _df[['car']].values
```

In this step, you create a **features** DataFrame by dropping **car** from **_df**. You also create **labels** by selecting only **car** in a new DataFrame. Here, a feature and a label are similar in the Cars dataset.

4. Create an instance of the **LogisticRegression** class to be used later:

```
from sklearn.linear_model import LogisticRegression
# create an instance of LogisticRegression
_lr = LogisticRegression()
```

In this step, you import **LogisticRegression** from **sklearn.linear_model**. We use **LogisticRegression** because it lets us create a classification model, as you learned in *Chapter 3, Binary Classification*. You then proceed to create an instance and store it as **_lr**.

5. Import the **cross_val_score** function:

```
from sklearn.model_selection import cross_val_score
```

In this step now, you import **cross_val_score**, which you will make use of to compute the scores of the models.

6. Compute the cross-validation scores:

```
_scores = cross_val_score(_lr, features, labels, cv=5)
```

In this step, you the compute cross-validation scores and store the result in a Python list, which you call **_scores**. You do this using **cross_cal_score**. The function requires the following four parameters: the model to make use of (in our case, it's called **_lr**); the features of the dataset; the labels of the dataset; and the number of cross-validation splits to create (five, in our case).

7. Now, display the scores as shown in the following code snippet:

```
print(_scores)
```

In this step, you display the scores using **print()**.

The output should look similar to the following:

```
[0.69942197 0.83236994 0.72254335 0.80346821 0.73546512]
```

Figure 7.22: Printing the cross-validation scores

> **NOTE**
>
> You may get slightly different outputs but the best score should belong to second split.
>
> To access the source code for this specific section, please refer to https://packt.live/2DWTkAY.
>
> You can also run this example online at https://packt.live/34d5aS8.

In the preceding output, you see that the Python list stored in **variable _scores** contains five results. Each result is the R2 score of a **LogisticRegression** model. As mentioned before the exercise, the data will be split into five sets, and each combination of the five sets will be used to train and evaluate a model, after which the R2 score is computed.

You should observe from the preceding example that the same model trained on five different datasets yields different scores. This implies the importance of your data as well as how it is split.

By completing this exercise, we see that the best score is **0.832**, which belongs to the second split. This is our conclusion here.

You have seen that cross-validation yields different models.

But how do you get the best model to work with? There are some models or estimators with in-built cross-validation. Let's explain those.

UNDERSTANDING ESTIMATORS THAT IMPLEMENT CV

The goal of using cross-validation is to find the best performing model using the data that you have. The process for this is:

1. Split the data using something like **`Kfold()`**.
2. Iterate over the number of splits and create an estimator.
3. Train and evaluate each estimator.
4. Pick the estimator with the best metrics to use. You have already seen various approaches to doing that.

Cross-validation is a popular technique, so estimators exist for cross-validation. For example, **`LogisticRegressionCV`** exists as a class that implements cross-validation inside **`LogisticRegression`**. When you make use of **`LogisticRegressionCV`**, it returns an instance of **`LogisticRegression`**. The instance it returns is the best performing instance.

When you create an instance of **`LogisticRegressionCV`**, you will need to specify the number of **`cv`** parts that you want. For example, if you set **`cv`** to **3**, **`LogisticRegressionCV`** will train three instances of **`LogisticRegression`** and then evaluate them and return the best performing instance.

You do not have to make use of **`LogisticRegressionCV`**. You can continue to make use of **`LogisticRegression`** with **`Kfold`** and iterations. **`LogisticRegressionCV`** simply exists as a convenience.

In a similar manner, **`LinearRegressionCV`** exists as a convenient way of implementing cross-validation using **`LinearRegression`**.

So, just to be clear, you do not have to use convenience methods such as **`LogisticRegressionCV`**. Also, they are not a replacement for their primary implementations, such as **`LogisticRegression`**. Instead, you make use of the convenience methods when you need to implement cross-validation but would like to cut out the four preceding steps.

LOGISTICREGRESSIONCV

LogisticRegressionCV is a class that implements cross-validation inside it. This class will train multiple **LogisticRegression** models and return the best one.

EXERCISE 7.06: TRAINING A LOGISTIC REGRESSION MODEL USING CROSS-VALIDATION

The goal of this exercise is to train a logistic regression model using cross-validation and get the optimal R2 result. We will be making use of the Cars dataset that you worked with previously.

The following steps will help you complete the exercise:

1. Open a new Colab notebook.
2. Import the necessary libraries:

```
# import libraries
import pandas as pd
from sklearn.model_selection import train_test_split
```

   In this step, you import **pandas** and alias it as **pd**. You will make use of pandas to read in the file you will be working with.

3. Create headers for the data:

```
# data doesn't have headers, so let's create headers
_headers = ['buying', 'maint', 'doors', 'persons', \
            'lug_boot', 'safety', 'car']
```

   In this step, you start by creating a Python list to hold the **headers** column for the file you will be working with. You store this list as **_headers**.

4. Read the data:

```
# read in cars dataset
df = pd.read_csv('https://raw.githubusercontent.com/'\
                 'PacktWorkshops/The-Data-Science-Workshop/'\
                 'master/Chapter07/Dataset/car.data', \
                 names=_headers, index_col=None)
```

   You then proceed to read in the file and store it as **df**. This is a DataFrame.

5. Print out the top five records:

```
df.info()
```

Finally, you look at the summary of the DataFrame using **.info()**.

The output looks similar to the following:

```
<class 'pandas.core.frame.DataFrame'>
RangeIndex: 1728 entries, 0 to 1727
Data columns (total 7 columns):
buying      1728 non-null object
maint       1728 non-null object
doors       1728 non-null object
persons     1728 non-null object
lug_boot    1728 non-null object
safety      1728 non-null object
car         1728 non-null object
dtypes: object(7)
memory usage: 94.6+ KB
```

Figure 7.23: The top five records of the dataframe

6. Encode the categorical variables as shown in the following code snippet:

```
# encode categorical variables
_df = pd.get_dummies(df, columns=['buying', 'maint', 'doors', \
                                  'persons', 'lug_boot', \
                                  'safety'])
_df.head()
```

In this step, you convert categorical variables into encodings using the **get_dummies()** method from pandas. You supply the original DataFrame as a parameter and also specify the columns you would like to encode.

Finally, you take a peek at the top five rows. The output looks similar to the following:

	car	buying_high	buying_low	buying_med	buying_vhigh	maint_high	maint_low	maint_med
0	unacc	0	0	0	1	0	0	0
1	unacc	0	0	0	1	0	0	0
2	unacc	0	0	0	1	0	0	0
3	unacc	0	0	0	1	0	0	0
4	unacc	0	0	0	1	0	0	0

5 rows × 22 columns

Figure 7.24: Encoding categorical variables

7. Split the DataFrame into features and labels:

```
# separate features and labels DataFrames
features = _df.drop(['car'], axis=1).values
labels = _df[['car']].values
```

In this step, you create two NumPy arrays. The first, called **features**, contains the independent variables. The second, called **labels**, contains the values that the model learns to predict. These are also called **targets**.

8. Import logistic regression with cross-validation:

```
from sklearn.linear_model import LogisticRegressionCV
```

In this step, you import the **LogisticRegressionCV** class.

9. Instantiate **LogisticRegressionCV** as shown in the following code snippet:

```
model = LogisticRegressionCV(max_iter=2000, multi_class='auto',\
                             cv=5)
```

In this step, you create an instance of **LogisticRegressionCV**. You specify the following parameters:

max_iter : You set this to **2000** so that the trainer continues training for **2000** iterations to find better weights.

multi_class: You set this to **auto** so that the model automatically detects that your data has more than two classes.

cv: You set this to **5**, which is the number of cross-validation sets you would like to train on.

10. Now fit the model:

```
model.fit(features, labels.ravel())
```

In this step, you train the model. You pass in **features** and **labels**. Because **labels** is a 2D array, you make use of **ravel()** to convert it into a 1D array or vector.

The interpreter produces an output similar to the following:

```
LogisticRegressionCV(Cs=10, class_weight=None, cv=5, dual=False,
                     fit_intercept=True, intercept_scaling=1.0, l1_ratios
=None,
                     max_iter=2000, multi_class='auto', n_jobs=None,
                     penalty='l2', random_state=None, refit=True, scoring
=None,
                     solver='lbfgs', tol=0.0001, verbose=0)
```

Figure 7.25: Fitting the model

In the preceding output, you see that the model fits the training data. The output shows you the parameters that were used in training, so you are not taken by surprise. Notice, for example, that **max_iter** is **2000**, which is the value that you set. Other parameters you didn't set make use of default values, which you can find out more about from the documentation.

11. Evaluate the training R2:

```
print(model.score(features, labels.ravel()))
```

In this step, we make use of the training dataset to compute the R2 score. While we didn't set aside a specific validation dataset, it is important to note that the model only saw 80% of our training data, so it still has new data to work with for this evaluation.

The output looks similar to the following:

```
0.9456018518518519
```

Figure 7.26: Computing the R2 score

> **NOTE**
>
> To access the source code for this specific section, please refer to https://packt.live/34eD1du.
>
> You can also run this example online at https://packt.live/2Yey40k.

In the preceding output, you see that the final model has an **R2** score of **0.95**, which is a good score.

At this point, you should see a much better **R2** score than you have previously encountered.

What if you were working with other types of models that don't have cross-validation built into them? Can you make use of cross-validation to train models and find the best one? Let's find out.

HYPERPARAMETER TUNING WITH GRIDSEARCHCV

GridSearchCV will take a model and parameters and train one model for each permutation of the parameters. At the end of the training, it will provide access to the parameters and the model scores. This is called hyperparameter tuning and you will be looking at this in much more depth in *Chapter 8, Hyperparameter Tuning*.

The usual practice is to make use of a small training set to find the optimal parameters using hyperparameter tuning and then to train a final model with all of the data.

Before the next exercise, let's take a brief look at decision trees, which are a type of model or estimator.

DECISION TREES

A decision tree works by generating a separating hyperplane or a threshold for the features in data. It does this by considering every feature and finding the correlation between the spread of the values in that feature and the label that you are trying to predict.

Consider the following data about balloons. The label you need to predict is called **inflated**. This dataset is used for predicting whether the balloon is inflated or deflated given the features. The features are:

- **color**
- **size**
- **act**
- **age**

The following table displays the distribution of features:

	color	size	act	age	inflated
0	YELLOW	SMALL	STRETCH	ADULT	T
1	YELLOW	SMALL	STRETCH	ADULT	T
2	YELLOW	SMALL	STRETCH	CHILD	F
3	YELLOW	SMALL	DIP	ADULT	F
4	YELLOW	SMALL	DIP	CHILD	F
5	YELLOW	LARGE	STRETCH	ADULT	T
6	YELLOW	LARGE	STRETCH	ADULT	T
7	YELLOW	LARGE	STRETCH	CHILD	F
8	YELLOW	LARGE	DIP	ADULT	F
9	YELLOW	LARGE	DIP	CHILD	F
10	PURPLE	SMALL	STRETCH	ADULT	T
11	PURPLE	SMALL	STRETCH	ADULT	T
12	PURPLE	SMALL	STRETCH	CHILD	F
13	PURPLE	SMALL	DIP	ADULT	F
14	PURPLE	SMALL	DIP	CHILD	F
15	PURPLE	LARGE	STRETCH	ADULT	T
16	PURPLE	LARGE	STRETCH	ADULT	T
17	PURPLE	LARGE	STRETCH	CHILD	F
18	PURPLE	LARGE	DIP	ADULT	F
19	PURPLE	LARGE	DIP	CHILD	F

Figure 7.27: Tabular data for balloon features

Now consider the following charts, which are visualized depending on the spread of the features against the label:

- If you consider the `Color` feature, the values are **`PURPLE`** and **`YELLOW`**, but the number of observations is the same, so you can't infer whether the balloon is inflated or not based on the color, as you can see in the following figure:

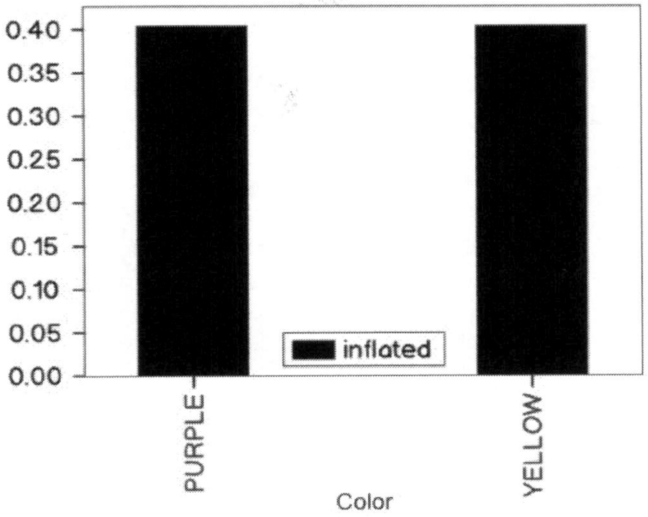

Figure 7.28: Barplot for the color feature

- The **`Size`** feature has two values: **`LARGE`** and **`SMALL`**. These are equally spread, so we can't infer whether the balloon is inflated or not based on the color, as you can see in the following figure:

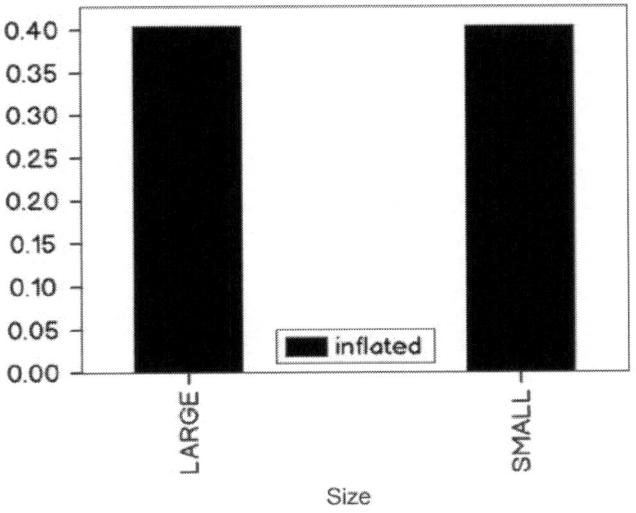

Figure 7.29: Barplot for the size feature

- The **Act** feature has two values: **DIP** and **STRETCH**. You can see from the chart that the majority of the **STRETCH** values are inflated. If you had to make a guess, you could easily say that if **Act** is **STRETCH**, then the balloon is inflated. Consider the following figure:

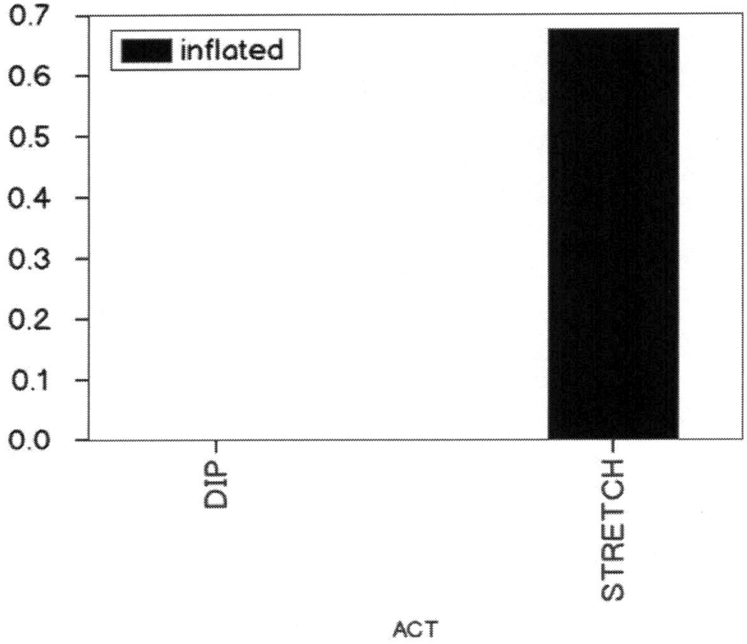

Figure 7.30: Barplot for the act feature

- Finally, the **`Age`** feature also has two values: **`ADULT`** and **`CHILD`**. It's also visible from the chart that the **`ADULT`** value constitutes the majority of inflated balloons:

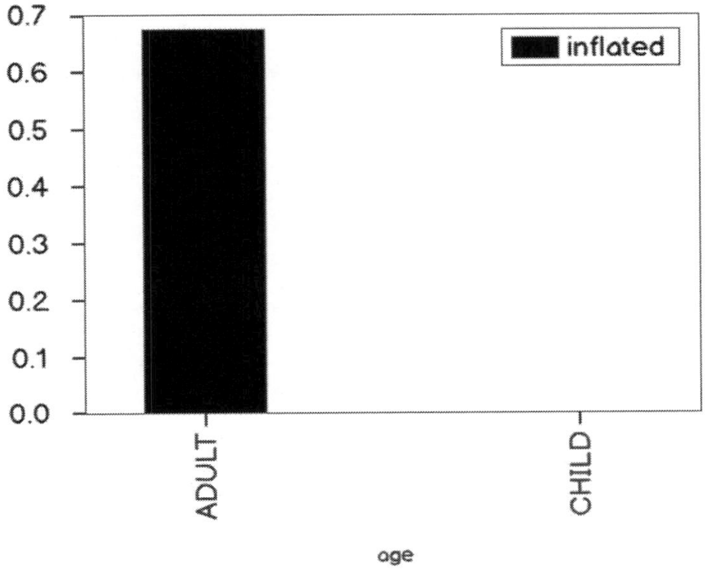

Figure 7.31: Barplot for the age feature

The two features that are useful to the decision tree are **`Act`** and **`Age`**. The tree could start by considering whether **`Act`** is **`STRETCH`**. If it is, the prediction will be true. This tree would look like the following figure:

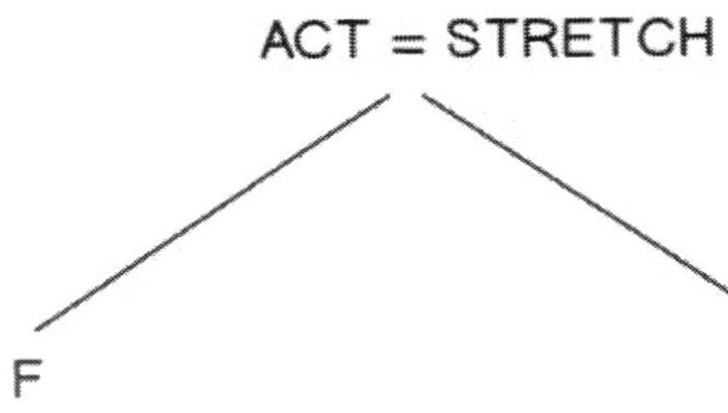

Figure 7.32: Decision tree with depth=1

The left side evaluates to the condition being false, and the right side evaluates to the condition being true. This tree has a depth of 1. F means that the prediction is false, and T means that the prediction is true.

To get better results, the decision tree could introduce a second level. The second level would utilize the **Age** feature and evaluate whether the value is **ADULT**. It would look like the following figure:

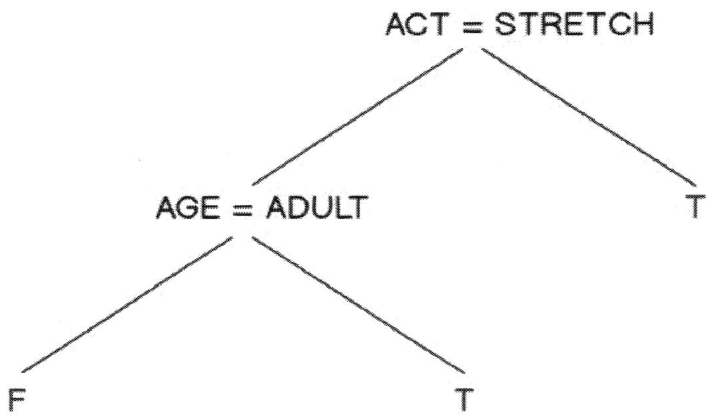

Figure 7.33: Decision tree with depth=2

This tree has a depth of 2. At the first level, it predicts true if **Act** is **STRETCH**. If **Act** is not **STRETCH**, it checks whether **Age** is **ADULT**. If it is, it predicts true, otherwise, it predicts false.

The decision tree can have as many levels as you like but starts to overfit at a certain point. As with everything in data science, the optimal depth depends on the data and is a hyperparameter, meaning you need to try different values to find the optimal one.

In the following exercise, we will be making use of grid search with cross-validation to find the best parameters for a decision tree estimator.

EXERCISE 7.07: USING GRID SEARCH WITH CROSS-VALIDATION TO FIND THE BEST PARAMETERS FOR A MODEL

The goal of this exercise is to make use of grid search to find the best parameters for a **DecisionTree** classifier. We will be making use of the Cars dataset that you worked with previously.

The following steps will help you complete the exercise:

1. Open a Colab notebook file.
2. Import **pandas**:

```
import pandas as pd
```

   In this step, you import **pandas**. You alias it as **pd**. **Pandas** is used to read in the data you will work with subsequently.

3. Create **headers**:

```
_headers = ['buying', 'maint', 'doors', 'persons', \
            'lug_boot', 'safety', 'car']
```

4. Read in the **headers**:

```
# read in cars dataset
df = pd.read_csv('https://raw.githubusercontent.com/'\
                 'PacktWorkshops/The-Data-Science-Workshop/'\
                 'master/Chapter07/Dataset/car.data', \
                 names=_headers, index_col=None)
```

5. Inspect the top five records:

```
df.info()
```

The output looks similar to the following:

```
<class 'pandas.core.frame.DataFrame'>
RangeIndex: 1728 entries, 0 to 1727
Data columns (total 7 columns):
buying      1728 non-null object
maint       1728 non-null object
doors       1728 non-null object
persons     1728 non-null object
lug_boot    1728 non-null object
safety      1728 non-null object
car         1728 non-null object
dtypes: object(7)
memory usage: 94.6+ KB
```

Figure 7.34: The top five records of the dataframe

6. Encode the categorical variables:

```
_df = pd.get_dummies(df, columns=['buying', 'maint', 'doors',\
                                  'persons', 'lug_boot', \
                                  'safety'])
_df.head()
```

In this step, you utilize **.get_dummies()** to convert the categorical variables into encodings. The **.head()** method instructs the Python interpreter to output the top five columns.

The output is similar to the following:

	car	buying_high	buying_low	buying_med	buying_vhigh	maint_high	maint_low	maint_med
0	unacc	0	0	0	1	0	0	0
1	unacc	0	0	0	1	0	0	0
2	unacc	0	0	0	1	0	0	0
3	unacc	0	0	0	1	0	0	0
4	unacc	0	0	0	1	0	0	0

5 rows × 22 columns

Figure 7.35: Encoding categorical variables

7. Separate **features** and **labels**:

```
features = _df.drop(['car'], axis=1).values
labels = _df[['car']].values
```

In this step, you create two **numpy** arrays, **features** and **labels**, the first containing independent variables or predictors, and the second containing dependent variables or targets.

8. Import more libraries – **numpy**, **DecisionTreeClassifier**, and **GridSearchCV**:

```
import numpy as np
from sklearn.tree import DecisionTreeClassifier
from sklearn.model_selection import GridSearchCV
```

In this step, you import **numpy**. NumPy is a numerical computation library. You alias it as **np**. You also import **DecisionTreeClassifier**, which you use to create decision trees. Finally, you import **GridSearchCV**, which will use cross-validation to train multiple models.

9. Instantiate the decision tree:

```
clf = DecisionTreeClassifier()
```

In this step, you create an instance of **DecisionTreeClassifier** as **clf**. This instance will be used repeatedly by the grid search.

10. Create parameters – **max_depth**:

```
params = {'max_depth': np.arange(1, 8)}
```

In this step, you create a dictionary of parameters. There are two parts to this dictionary:

The key of the dictionary is a parameter that is passed into the model. In this case, **max_depth** is a parameter that **DecisionTreeClassifier** takes.

The value is a Python list that grid search iterates over and passes to the model. In this case, we create an array that starts at 1 and ends at 7, inclusive.

11. Instantiate the grid search as shown in the following code snippet:

```
clf_cv = GridSearchCV(clf, param_grid=params, cv=5)
```

In this step, you create an instance of **GridSearchCV**. The first parameter is the model to train. The second parameter is the parameters to search over. The third parameter is the number of cross-validation splits to create.

12. Now train the models:

```
clf_cv.fit(features, labels)
```

In this step, you train the models using the features and labels. Depending on the type of model, this could take a while. Because we are using a decision tree, it trains quickly.

The output is similar to the following:

```
GridSearchCV(cv=5, error_score='raise-deprecating',
             estimator=DecisionTreeClassifier(class_weight=None,
                                              criterion='gini', max_depth
=None,
                                              max_features=None,
                                              max_leaf_nodes=None,
                                              min_impurity_decrease=0.0,
                                              min_impurity_split=None,
                                              min_samples_leaf=1,
                                              min_samples_split=2,
                                              min_weight_fraction_leaf=0.
0,
                                              presort=False, random_state
=None,
                                              splitter='best'),
             iid='warn', n_jobs=None,
             param_grid={'max_depth': array([1, 2, 3, 4, 5, 6, 7])},
             pre_dispatch='2*n_jobs', refit=True, return_train_score=Fals
e,
             scoring=None, verbose=0)
```

Figure 7.36: Training the model

You can learn a lot by reading the output, such as the number of cross-validation datasets created (called **cv** and equal to **5**), the estimator used (**DecisionTreeClassifier**), and the parameter search space (called **param_grid**).

13. Print the best parameter:

```
print("Tuned Decision Tree Parameters: {}"\
      .format(clf_cv.best_params_))
```

In this step, you print out what the best parameter is. In this case, what we were looking for was the best **max_depth**. The output looks like the following:

```
Tuned Decision Tree Parameters: {'max_depth': 2}
```

Figure 7.37: Printing the best parameter

In the preceding output, you see that the best performing model is one with a **max_depth** of **2**.

Accessing **best_params_** lets you train another model with the best-known parameters using a larger training dataset.

14. Print the best **R2**:

```
print("Best score is {}".format(clf_cv.best_score_))
```

In this step, you print out the **R2** score of the best performing model.

The output is similar to the following:

```
Best score is 0.7777777777777778
```

In the preceding output, you see that the best performing model has an **R2** score of **0.778**.

15. Access the best model:

```
model = clf_cv.best_estimator_
model
```

In this step, you access the best model (or estimator) using **`best_estimator_`**. This will let you analyze the model, or optionally use it to make predictions and find other metrics. Instructing the Python interpreter to print the best estimator will yield an output similar to the following:

```
DecisionTreeClassifier(class_weight=None, criterion='gini', max_depth=2,
                       max_features=None, max_leaf_nodes=None,
                       min_impurity_decrease=0.0, min_impurity_split=Non
e,
                       min_samples_leaf=1, min_samples_split=2,
                       min_weight_fraction_leaf=0.0, presort=False,
                       random_state=None, splitter='best')
```

Figure 7.38: Accessing the model

In the preceding output, you see that the best model is **`DecisionTreeClassifier`** with a **`max_depth`** of **2**.

> **NOTE**
>
> To access the source code for this specific section, please refer to https://packt.live/2E6TdCD.
>
> You can also run this example online at https://packt.live/3aCg30V.

Grid search is one of the first techniques that is taught for hyperparameter tuning. However, as the search space increases in size, it quickly becomes expensive. The search space increases as you increase the parameter options because every possible combination of parameter options is considered.

Consider the case in which the model (or estimator) takes more than one parameter. The search space becomes a multiple of the number of parameters. For example, if we want to train a random forest classifier, we will need to specify the number of trees in the forest, as well as the max depth. If we specified a max depth of 1, 2, and 3, and a forest with 1,000, 2,000, and 3,000 trees, we would need to train 9 different estimators. If we added any more parameters (or hyperparameters), our search space would increase geometrically.

HYPERPARAMETER TUNING WITH RANDOMIZEDSEARCHCV

Grid search goes over the entire search space and trains a model or estimator for every combination of parameters. Randomized search goes over only some of the combinations. This is a more optimal use of resources and still provides the benefits of hyperparameter tuning and cross-validation. You will be looking at this in depth in *Chapter 8, Hyperparameter Tuning*.

Have a look at the following exercise.

EXERCISE 7.08: USING RANDOMIZED SEARCH FOR HYPERPARAMETER TUNING

The goal of this exercise is to perform hyperparameter tuning using randomized search and cross-validation.

The following steps will help you complete this exercise:

1. Open a new Colab notebook file.
2. Import **pandas**:

```
import pandas as pd
```

   In this step, you import **pandas**. You will make use of it in the next step.

3. Create **headers**:

```
_headers = ['buying', 'maint', 'doors', 'persons', \
            'lug_boot', 'safety', 'car']
```

4. Read in the data:

```
# read in cars dataset
df = pd.read_csv('https://raw.githubusercontent.com/'\
                 'PacktWorkshops/The-Data-Science-Workshop/'\
                 'master/Chapter07/Dataset/car.data', \
                 names=_headers, index_col=None)
```

5. Check the first five rows:

```
df.info()
```

   You need to provide a Python list of column headers because the data does not contain column headers. You also inspect the DataFrame that you created.

The output is similar to the following:

```
<class 'pandas.core.frame.DataFrame'>
RangeIndex: 1728 entries, 0 to 1727
Data columns (total 7 columns):
buying      1728 non-null object
maint       1728 non-null object
doors       1728 non-null object
persons     1728 non-null object
lug_boot    1728 non-null object
safety      1728 non-null object
car         1728 non-null object
dtypes: object(7)
memory usage: 94.6+ KB
```

Figure 7.39: The top five rows of the DataFrame

6. Encode categorical variables as shown in the following code snippet:

```
_df = pd.get_dummies(df, columns=['buying', 'maint', 'doors',\
                                  'persons', 'lug_boot', \
                                  'safety'])
_df.head()
```

In this step, you find a numerical representation of text data using one-hot encoding. The operation results in a new DataFrame. You will see that the resulting data structure looks similar to the following:

	car	buying_high	buying_low	buying_med	buying_vhigh	maint_high	maint_low	maint_med
0	unacc	0	0	0	1	0	0	0
1	unacc	0	0	0	1	0	0	0
2	unacc	0	0	0	1	0	0	0
3	unacc	0	0	0	1	0	0	0
4	unacc	0	0	0	1	0	0	0

5 rows × 22 columns

Figure 7.40: Encoding categorical variables

7. Separate the data into independent and dependent variables, which are the **features** and **labels**:

```
features = _df.drop(['car'], axis=1).values
labels = _df[['car']].values
```

   In this step, you separate the DataFrame into two **numpy** arrays called **features** and **labels**. **Features** contains the independent variables, while **labels** contains the target or dependent variables.

8. Import additional libraries – **numpy**, **RandomForestClassifier**, and **RandomizedSearchCV**:

```
import numpy as np
from sklearn.ensemble import RandomForestClassifier
from sklearn.model_selection import RandomizedSearchCV
```

   In this step, you import **numpy** for numerical computations, **RandomForestClassifier** to create an ensemble of estimators, and **RandomizedSearchCV** to perform a randomized search with cross-validation.

9. Create an instance of **RandomForestClassifier**:

```
clf = RandomForestClassifier()
```

   In this step, you instantiate **RandomForestClassifier**. A random forest classifier is a voting classifier. It makes use of multiple decision trees, which are trained on different subsets of the data. The results from the trees contribute to the output of the random forest by using a voting mechanism.

10. Specify the parameters:

```
params = {'n_estimators':[500, 1000, 2000], \
          'max_depth': np.arange(1, 8)}
```

   RandomForestClassifier accepts many parameters, but we specify two: the number of trees in the forest, called **n_estimators**, and the depth of the nodes in each tree, called **max_depth**.

11. Instantiate a randomized search:

```
clf_cv = RandomizedSearchCV(clf, param_distributions=params, \
                            cv=5)
```

In this step, you specify three parameters when you instantiate the **clf** class, the estimator, or model to use, which is a random forest classifier, **param_distributions**, the parameter search space, and **cv**, the number of cross-validation datasets to create.

12. Perform the search:

```
clf_cv.fit(features, labels.ravel())
```

In this step, you perform the search by calling **fit()**. This operation trains different models using the cross-validation datasets and various combinations of the hyperparameters. The output from this operation is similar to the following:

```
RandomizedSearchCV(cv=5, error_score='raise-deprecating',
                   estimator=RandomForestClassifier(bootstrap=True,
                                                    class_weight=None,
                                                    criterion='gini',
                                                    max_depth=None,
                                                    max_features='auto',
                                                    max_leaf_nodes=None,
                                                    min_impurity_decrease
=0.0,
                                                    min_impurity_split=No
ne,
                                                    min_samples_leaf=1,
                                                    min_samples_split=2,
                                                    min_weight_fraction_l
eaf=0.0,
                                                    n_estimators='warn',
                                                    n_jobs=None,
                                                    oob_score=False,
                                                    random_state=None,
                                                    verbose=0,
                                                    warm_start=False),
                   iid='warn', n_iter=10, n_jobs=None,
                   param_distributions={'max_depth': array([1, 2, 3, 4,
5, 6, 7]),
                                        'n_estimators': [500, 1000, 200
0]},
                   pre_dispatch='2*n_jobs', random_state=None, refit=Tru
e,
                   return_train_score=False, scoring=None, verbose=0)
```

Figure 7.41: Output of the search operation

In the preceding output, you see that the randomized search will be carried out using cross-validation with five splits (**cv=5**). The estimator to be used is **RandomForestClassifier**.

13. Print the best parameter combination:

```
print("Tuned Random Forest Parameters: {}"\
      .format(clf_cv.best_params_))
```

In this step, you print out the best hyperparameters.

The output is similar to the following:

```
Tuned Random Forest Parameters: {'n_estimators': 500, 'max_depth': 5}
```

Figure 7.42: Printing the best parameter combination

In the preceding output, you see that the best estimator is a Random Forest classifier with 1,000 trees (**n_estimators=1000**) and **max_depth=5**. You can print the best score by executing **print("Best score is {}".format(clf_cv.best_score_))**. For this exercise, this value is ~ **0.76**.

14. Inspect the best model:

```
model = clf_cv.best_estimator_
model
```

In this step, you find the best performing estimator (or model) and print out its details. The output is similar to the following:

```
RandomForestClassifier(bootstrap=True, class_weight=None, criterion='gin
i',
                       max_depth=5, max_features='auto', max_leaf_nodes=N
one,
                       min_impurity_decrease=0.0, min_impurity_split=Non
e,
                       min_samples_leaf=1, min_samples_split=2,
                       min_weight_fraction_leaf=0.0, n_estimators=1000,
                       n_jobs=None, oob_score=False, random_state=None,
                       verbose=0, warm_start=False)
```

Figure 7.43: Inspecting the model

In the preceding output, you see that the best estimator is **RandomForestClassifier** with **n_estimators=1000** and **max_depth=5**.

NOTE

To access the source code for this specific section, please refer to https://packt.live/3aDFijn.

You can also run this example online at https://packt.live/3kWMQ5r.

In this exercise, you learned to make use of cross-validation and random search to find the best model using a combination of hyperparameters. This process is called hyperparameter tuning, in which you find the best combination of hyperparameters to use to train the model that you will put into production.

MODEL REGULARIZATION WITH LASSO REGRESSION

As mentioned at the beginning of this chapter models can overfit training data. One reason for this is having too many features with large coefficients (also called weights). The key to solving this type of overfitting problem is reducing the magnitude of the coefficients.

You may recall that weights are optimized during model training. One method for optimizing weights is called gradient descent. The gradient update rule makes use of a differentiable loss function. Examples of differentiable loss functions are:

- Mean Absolute Error (MAE)
- Mean Squared Error (MSE)

For lasso regression, a penalty is introduced in the loss function. The technicalities of this implementation are hidden by the class. The penalty is also called a regularization parameter.

Consider the following exercise in which you over-engineer a model to introduce overfitting, and then use lasso regression to get better results.

EXERCISE 7.09: FIXING MODEL OVERFITTING USING LASSO REGRESSION

The goal of this exercise is to teach you how to identify when your model starts overfitting, and to use lasso regression to fix overfitting in your model.

> **NOTE**
>
> The data you will be making use of is the Combined Cycle Power Plant Data Set from the UCI Machine Learning Repository. It contains 9568 data points collected from a Combined Cycle Power Plant. Features include temperature, pressure, humidity, and exhaust vacuum. These are used to predict the net hourly electrical energy output of the plant. See the following link: https://packt.live/2v9ohwK.

The attribute information states "Features consist of hourly average ambient variables:

- Temperature (T) in the range 1.81°C and 37.11°C,
- Ambient Pressure (AP) in the range 992.89-1033.30 millibar,
- Relative Humidity (RH) in the range 25.56% to 100.16%
- Exhaust Vacuum (V) in the range 25.36-81.56 cm Hg
- Net hourly electrical energy output (EP) 420.26-495.76 MW

The averages are taken from various sensors located around the plant that record the ambient variables every second. The variables are given without normalization."

The following steps will help you complete the exercise:

1. Open a Colab notebook.
2. Import the required libraries:

```
import pandas as pd
from sklearn.model_selection import train_test_split
from sklearn.linear_model import LinearRegression, Lasso
from sklearn.metrics import mean_squared_error
from sklearn.pipeline import Pipeline
from sklearn.preprocessing import MinMaxScaler, \
PolynomialFeatures
```

3. Read in the data:

```
_df = pd.read_csv('https://raw.githubusercontent.com/'\
                  'PacktWorkshops/The-Data-Science-Workshop/'\
                  'master/Chapter07/Dataset/ccpp.csv')
```

4. Inspect the DataFrame:

```
_df.info()
```

The **.info()** method prints out a summary of the DataFrame, including the names of the columns and the number of records. The output might be similar to the following:

```
<class 'pandas.core.frame.DataFrame'>
RangeIndex: 9568 entries, 0 to 9567
Data columns (total 5 columns):
AT     9568 non-null float64
V      9568 non-null float64
AP     9568 non-null float64
RH     9568 non-null float64
PE     9568 non-null float64
dtypes: float64(5)
memory usage: 373.9 KB
```

Figure 7.44: Inspecting the dataframe

You can see from the preceding figure that the DataFrame has 5 columns and 9,568 records. You can see that all columns contain numeric data and that the columns have the following names: **AT**, **V**, **AP**, **RH**, and **PE**.

5. Extract features into a column called **X**:

```
X = _df.drop(['PE'], axis=1).values
```

6. Extract labels into a column called **y**:

```
y = _df['PE'].values
```

7. Split the data into training and evaluation sets:

```
train_X, eval_X, train_y, eval_y = train_test_split\
                                   (X, y, train_size=0.8, \
                                    random_state=0)
```

8. Create an instance of a **LinearRegression** model:

```
lr_model_1 = LinearRegression()
```

9. Fit the model on the training data:

```
lr_model_1.fit(train_X, train_y)
```

The output from this step should look similar to the following:

```
LinearRegression(copy_X=True, fit_intercept=True, n_jobs=None, normalize=False)
```

Figure 7.45: Fitting the model on training data

10. Use the model to make predictions on the evaluation dataset:

```
lr_model_1_preds = lr_model_1.predict(eval_X)
```

11. Print out the **R2** score of the model:

```
print('lr_model_1 R2 Score: {}'\
      .format(lr_model_1.score(eval_X, eval_y)))
```

The output of this step should look similar to the following:

```
lr_model_1 R2 Score: 0.9325315554761302
```

Figure 7.46: Printing the R2 score

You will notice that the **R2** score for this model is **0.926**. You will make use of this figure to compare with the next model you train. Recall that this is an evaluation metric.

12. Print out the Mean Squared Error (MSE) of this model:

```
print('lr_model_1 MSE: {}'\
      .format(mean_squared_error(eval_y, lr_model_1_preds)))
```

The output of this step should look similar to the following:

```
lr_model_1 MSE: 19.733699303497648
```

Figure 7.47: Printing the MSE

You will notice that the MSE is **21.675**. This is an evaluation metric that you will use to compare this model to subsequent models.

The first model was trained on four features. You will now train a new model on four cubed features.

13. Create a list of tuples to serve as a pipeline:

```
steps = [('scaler', MinMaxScaler()),\
         ('poly', PolynomialFeatures(degree=3)),\
         ('lr', LinearRegression())]
```

In this step, you create a list with three tuples. The first tuple represents a scaling operation that makes use of **MinMaxScaler**. The second tuple represents a feature engineering step and makes use of **PolynomialFeatures**. The third tuple represents a **LinearRegression** model.

The first element of the tuple represents the name of the step, while the second element represents the class that performs a transformation or an estimator.

14. Create an instance of a pipeline:

```
lr_model_2 = Pipeline(steps)
```

15. Train the instance of the pipeline:

```
lr_model_2.fit(train_X, train_y)
```

The pipeline implements a **`.fit()`** method, which is also implemented in all instances of transformers and estimators. The **`.fit()`** method causes **`.fit_transform()`** to be called on transformers, and causes **`.fit()`** to be called on estimators. The output of this step is similar to the following:

```
Pipeline(memory=None,
         steps=[('scaler', MinMaxScaler(copy=True, feature_range=(0, 1))),
                ('poly',
                 PolynomialFeatures(degree=3, include_bias=True,
                                    interaction_only=False, order='C')),
                ('lr',
                 LinearRegression(copy_X=True, fit_intercept=True, n_jobs=None,
                                  normalize=False))],
         verbose=False)
```

Figure 7.48: Training the instance of the pipeline

You can see from the output that a pipeline was trained. You can see that the steps are made up of **`MinMaxScaler`** and **`PolynomialFeatures`**, and that the final step is made up of **`LinearRegression`**.

16. Print out the **R2** score of the model:

```
print('lr_model_2 R2 Score: {}'\
      .format(lr_model_2.score(eval_X, eval_y)))
```

The output is similar to the following:

```
lr_model_2 R2 Score: 0.9443678654045208
```

Figure 7.49: The R2 score of the model

You can see from the preceding that the **R2** score is **`0.944`**, which is better than the **R2** score of the first model, which was **`0.932`**. You can start to observe that the metrics suggest that this model is better than the first one.

17. Use the model to predict on the evaluation data:

```
lr_model_2_preds = lr_model_2.predict(eval_X)
```

18. Print the MSE of the second model:

```
print('lr_model_2 MSE: {}'\
      .format(mean_squared_error(eval_y, lr_model_2_preds)))
```

The output is similar to the following:

```
lr_model_2 MSE: 16.271722632207666
```

Figure 7.50: The MSE of the second model

You can see from the output that the MSE of the second model is **`16.27`**. This is less than the MSE of the first model, which is **`19.73`**. You can safely conclude that the second model is better than the first.

19. Inspect the model coefficients (also called weights):

```
print(lr_model_2[-1].coef_)
```

In this step, you will note that **`lr_model_2`** is a pipeline. The final object in this pipeline is the model, so you make use of list addressing to access this by setting the index of the list element to **`-1`**.

Once you have the model, which is the final element in the pipeline, you make use of **`.coef_`** to get the model coefficients. The output is similar to the following:

```
[ 7.72661789e-14 -1.77278028e+02 -4.60337188e+01 -1.60520675e+02
 -1.23076123e+02  6.23358210e+00  8.19655844e+00  1.45478576e+02
  1.88658651e+02  2.43740192e+01  1.80553150e+02 -1.08058561e+02
  1.09713294e+02  1.79121906e+02  1.06460596e+02  2.67290613e+01
  7.79833654e+01  3.69241324e+01 -1.13863997e+02 -1.42673215e+02
 -9.69606773e+01  1.90706809e+02 -5.56429546e+01 -1.32595225e+02
 -9.41682917e+01  9.40112729e+01 -1.18732510e+02 -7.64871610e+01
 -4.18714081e+01  6.36772260e+01  4.42340977e+01 -3.81114691e+01
 -4.71547759e+01 -9.16797074e+01 -2.52346805e+01]
```

Figure 7.51: Print the model coefficients

You will note from the preceding output that the majority of the values are in the tens, some values are in the hundreds, and one value has a really small magnitude.

20. Check for the number of coefficients in this model:

```
print(len(lr_model_2[-1].coef_))
```

The output for this step is similar to the following:

```
35
```

You can see from the preceding screenshot that the second model has **35** coefficients.

21. Create a **steps** list with **PolynomialFeatures** of degree **10**:

```
steps = [('scaler', MinMaxScaler()),\
         ('poly', PolynomialFeatures(degree=10)),\
         ('lr', LinearRegression())]
```

22. Create a third model from the preceding steps:

```
lr_model_3 = Pipeline(steps)
```

23. Fit the third model on the training data:

```
lr_model_3.fit(train_X, train_y)
```

The output from this step is similar to the following:

```
Pipeline(memory=None,
         steps=[('scaler', MinMaxScaler(copy=True, feature_range=(0, 1))),
                ('poly',
                 PolynomialFeatures(degree=10, include_bias=True,
                                    interaction_only=False, order='C')),
                ('lr',
                 LinearRegression(copy_X=True, fit_intercept=True, n_jobs=None,
                                  normalize=False))],
         verbose=False)
```

Figure 7.52: Fitting the third model on the data

You can see from the output that the pipeline makes use of **PolynomialFeatures** of degree **10**. You are doing this in the hope of getting a better model.

24. Print out the **R2** score of this model:

```
print('lr_model_3 R2 Score: {}'\
      .format(lr_model_3.score(eval_X, eval_y)))
```

The output of this model is similar to the following:

```
lr_model_3 R2 Score: 0.5683459493202576
```

Figure 7.53: R2 score of the model

You can see from the preceding figure that the R2 score is now **0.56**. The previous model had an **R2** score of **0.944**. This model has an R2 score that is considerably worse than the one of the previous model, **lr_model_2**. This happens when your model is overfitting.

25. Use **lr_model_3** to predict on evaluation data:

```
lr_model_3_preds = lr_model_3.predict(eval_X)
```

26. Print out the MSE for **lr_model_3**:

```
print('lr_model_3 MSE: {}'\
      .format(mean_squared_error(eval_y, lr_model_3_preds)))
```

The output for this step might be similar to the following:

```
lr_model_3 MSE: 126.25355896914343
```

Figure 7.54: The MSE of the model

You can see from the preceding figure that the MSE is also considerably worse. The MSE is **126.25**, as compared to **16.27** for the previous model.

27. Print out the number of coefficients (also called weights) in this model:

```
print(len(lr_model_3[-1].coef_))
```

The output might resemble the following:

```
1001
```

Figure 7.55: Printing the number of coefficients

You can see that the model has 1,001 coefficients.

28. Inspect the first 35 coefficients to get a sense of the individual magnitudes:

```
print(lr_model_3[-1].coef_[:35])
```

The output might be similar to the following:

```
[ 3.92417572e+05 -6.90884957e+07 -4.12728037e+07  2.27928559e+07
 -4.76788092e+07  2.96663457e+08  2.73267484e+08  1.07844757e+08
  3.73718995e+08  8.79698968e+07 -2.35367959e+07  2.46251982e+08
 -2.61104947e+08  1.86087661e+07  1.41131196e+08 -6.53886924e+08
 -8.90633353e+08 -1.06074814e+09 -1.29264510e+09 -4.28435046e+08
  5.31626843e+07 -1.30408977e+09  4.41024830e+08 -8.86228713e+08
 -8.78160515e+08 -1.97377311e+06 -5.39375259e+08 -3.68352714e+08
  9.82113559e+08 -2.76718687e+08 -6.28824872e+08  8.14257203e+08
  5.43205856e+08 -2.03045074e+08 -2.42929048e+08]
```

Figure 7.56: Inspecting the first 35 coefficients

You can see from the output that the coefficients have significantly larger magnitudes than the coefficients from **`lr_model_2`**.

In the next steps, you will train a lasso regression model on the same set of features to reduce overfitting.

29. Create a list of steps for the pipeline you will create later on:

```
steps = [('scaler', MinMaxScaler()),\
         ('poly', PolynomialFeatures(degree=10)),\
         ('lr', Lasso(alpha=0.01))]
```

You create a list of steps for the pipeline you will create. Note that the third step in this list is an instance of lasso. The parameter called **`alpha`** in the call to **`Lasso()`** is the regularization parameter. You can play around with any values from 0 to 1 to see how it affects the performance of the model that you train.

30. Create an instance of a pipeline:

```
lasso_model = Pipeline(steps)
```

31. Fit the pipeline on the training data:

```
lasso_model.fit(train_X, train_y)
```

The output from this operation might be similar to the following:

```
Pipeline(memory=None,
         steps=[('scaler', MinMaxScaler(copy=True, feature_range=(0, 1))),
                ('poly',
                 PolynomialFeatures(degree=10, include_bias=True,
                                    interaction_only=False, order='C')),
                ('lr',
                 Lasso(alpha=0.01, copy_X=True, fit_intercept=True,
                       max_iter=1000, normalize=False, positive=False,
                       precompute=False, random_state=None, selection='cyclic',
                       tol=0.0001, warm_start=False))],
         verbose=False)
```

Figure 7.57: Fitting the pipeline on the training data

You can see from the output that the pipeline trained a lasso model in the final step. The regularization parameter was **`0.01`** and the model trained for a maximum of 1,000 iterations.

32. Print the **`R2`** score of **`lasso_model`**:

```
print('lasso_model R2 Score: {}'\
      .format(lasso_model.score(eval_X, eval_y)))
```

The output of this step might be similar to the following:

```
lasso_model R2 Score: 0.9418109161488483
```

Figure 7.58: R2 score

You can see that the **`R2`** score has climbed back up to **`0.94`**, which is considerably better than the score of **`0.56`** that **`lr_model_3`** had. This is already looking like a better model.

33. Use **`lasso_model`** to predict on the evaluation data:

```
lasso_preds = lasso_model.predict(eval_X)
```

34. Print the MSE of **`lasso_model`**:

```
print('lasso_model MSE: {}'\
      .format(mean_squared_error(eval_y, lasso_preds)))
```

The output might be similar to the following:

```
lasso_model MSE: 17.019599185488644
```

Figure 7.59: MSE of lasso model

You can see from the output that the MSE is **17.01**, which is way lower than the MSE value of **126.25** that **lr_model_3** had. You can safely conclude that this is a much better model.

35. Print out the number of coefficients in **lasso_model**:

```
print(len(lasso_model[-1].coef_))
```

The output might be similar to the following:

```
1001
```

You can see that this model has 1,001 coefficients, which is the same number of coefficients that **lr_model_3** had.

36. Print out the values of the first 35 coefficients:

```
print(lasso_model[-1].coef_[:35])
```

The output might be similar to the following:

```
[ 0.          -69.23283545 -12.97913161   5.59999369  -0.
  0.           -0.           0.          -0.71670158  -0.53479946
  0.           -1.25577296   0.          -0.          -0.
  0.            0.           0.          -0.           0.
  0.           -0.           0.          -0.          -9.10662876
 -0.            0.          -0.           0.          -0.
 -3.04193695  -0.          -0.          -0.          -0.        ]
```

Figure 7.60: Printing the values of 35 coefficients

You can see from the preceding output that some of the coefficients are set to **0**. This has the effect of ignoring the corresponding column of data in the input. You can also see that the remaining coefficients have magnitudes of less than 100. This goes to show that the model is no longer overfitting.

> **NOTE**
>
> To access the source code for this specific section, please refer to https://packt.live/319S6en.
>
> You can also run this example online at https://packt.live/319AAXD.

This exercise taught you how to fix overfitting by using **LassoRegression** to train a new model.

In the next section, you will learn about using ridge regression to solve overfitting in a model.

RIDGE REGRESSION

You just learned about lasso regression, which introduces a penalty and tries to eliminate certain features from the data. Ridge regression takes an alternative approach by introducing a penalty that penalizes large weights. As a result, the optimization process tries to reduce the magnitude of the coefficients without completely eliminating them.

EXERCISE 7.10: FIXING MODEL OVERFITTING USING RIDGE REGRESSION

The goal of this exercise is to teach you how to identify when your model starts overfitting, and to use ridge regression to fix overfitting in your model.

> **NOTE**
>
> You will be using the same dataset as in *Exercise 7.09*, *Fixing Model Overfitting Using Lasso Regression.*

The following steps will help you complete the exercise:

1. Open a Colab notebook.
2. Import the required libraries:

```
import pandas as pd
from sklearn.model_selection import train_test_split
from sklearn.linear_model import LinearRegression, Ridge
from sklearn.metrics import mean_squared_error
from sklearn.pipeline import Pipeline
from sklearn.preprocessing import MinMaxScaler, \
PolynomialFeatures
```

3. Read in the data:

```
_df = pd.read_csv('https://raw.githubusercontent.com/'\
                  'PacktWorkshops/The-Data-Science-Workshop/'\
                  'master/Chapter07/Dataset/ccpp.csv')
```

4. Inspect the DataFrame:

```
_df.info()
```

The **.info()** method prints out a summary of the DataFrame, including the names of the columns and the number of records. The output might be similar to the following:

```
<class 'pandas.core.frame.DataFrame'>
RangeIndex: 9568 entries, 0 to 9567
Data columns (total 5 columns):
 #   Column  Non-Null Count  Dtype
---  ------  --------------  -----
 0   AT      9568 non-null   float64
 1   V       9568 non-null   float64
 2   AP      9568 non-null   float64
 3   RH      9568 non-null   float64
 4   PE      9568 non-null   float64
dtypes: float64(5)
memory usage: 373.9 KB
```

Figure 7.61: Inspecting the dataframe

You can see from the preceding figure that the DataFrame has 5 columns and 9,568 records. You can see that all columns contain numeric data and that the columns have the names: **AT**, **V**, **AP**, **RH**, and **PE**.

5. Extract features into a column called **X**:

```
X = _df.drop(['PE'], axis=1).values
```

6. Extract labels into a column called **y**:

```
y = _df['PE'].values
```

7. Split the data into training and evaluation sets:

```
train_X, eval_X, train_y, eval_y = train_test_split\
                                    (X, y, train_size=0.8, \
                                     random_state=0)
```

8. Create an instance of a **LinearRegression** model:

```
lr_model_1 = LinearRegression()
```

9. Fit the model on the training data:

```
lr_model_1.fit(train_X, train_y)
```

The output from this step should look similar to the following:

```
LinearRegression(copy_X=True, fit_intercept=True, n_jobs=None, normalize=False)
```

Figure 7.62: Fitting the model on data

10. Use the model to make predictions on the evaluation dataset:

```
lr_model_1_preds = lr_model_1.predict(eval_X)
```

11. Print out the **R2** score of the model:

```
print('lr_model_1 R2 Score: {}'\
      .format(lr_model_1.score(eval_X, eval_y)))
```

The output of this step should look similar to the following:

```
lr_model_1 R2 Score: 0.9325315554761303
```

Figure 7.63: R2 score

You will notice that the R2 score for this model is `0.933`. You will make use of this figure to compare it with the next model you train. Recall that this is an evaluation metric.

12. Print out the MSE of this model:

```
print('lr_model_1 MSE: {}'\
      .format(mean_squared_error(eval_y, lr_model_1_preds)))
```

The output of this step should look similar to the following:

```
lr_model_1 MSE: 19.733699303497637
```

Figure 7.64: The MSE of the model

You will notice that the MSE is `19.734`. This is an evaluation metric that you will use to compare this model to subsequent models.

The first model was trained on four features. You will now train a new model on four cubed features.

13. Create a list of tuples to serve as a pipeline:

```
steps = [('scaler', MinMaxScaler()),\
         ('poly', PolynomialFeatures(degree=3)),\
         ('lr', LinearRegression())]
```

In this step, you create a list with three tuples. The first tuple represents a scaling operation that makes use of **MinMaxScaler**. The second tuple represents a feature engineering step and makes use of **PolynomialFeatures**. The third tuple represents a **LinearRegression** model.

The first element of the tuple represents the name of the step, while the second element represents the class that performs a transformation or an estimation.

14. Create an instance of a pipeline:

```
lr_model_2 = Pipeline(steps)
```

15. Train the instance of the pipeline:

```
lr_model_2.fit(train_X, train_y)
```

The pipeline implements a **.fit()** method, which is also implemented in all instances of transformers and estimators. The **.fit()** method causes **.fit_transform()** to be called on transformers, and causes **.fit()** to be called on estimators. The output of this step is similar to the following:

```
Pipeline(memory=None,
         steps=[('scaler', MinMaxScaler(copy=True, feature_range=(0, 1))),
                ('poly',
                 PolynomialFeatures(degree=3, include_bias=True,
                                    interaction_only=False, order='C')),
                ('lr',
                 LinearRegression(copy_X=True, fit_intercept=True, n_jobs=None,
                                  normalize=False))],
         verbose=False)
```

Figure 7.65: Training the instance of a pipeline

You can see from the output that a pipeline was trained. You can see that the steps are made up of **MinMaxScaler** and **PolynomialFeatures**, and that the final step is made up of **LinearRegression**.

16. Print out the **R2** score of the model:

```
print('lr_model_2 R2 Score: {}'\
      .format(lr_model_2.score(eval_X, eval_y)))
```

The output is similar to the following:

```
lr_model_2 R2 Score: 0.9443678654045208
```

Figure 7.66: R2 score

You can see from the preceding that the R2 score is **0.944**, which is better than the R2 score of the first model, which was **0.933**. You can start to observe that the metrics suggest that this model is better than the first one.

17. Use the model to predict on the evaluation data:

```
lr_model_2_preds = lr_model_2.predict(eval_X)
```

18. Print the MSE of the second model:

```
print('lr_model_2 MSE: {}'\
      .format(mean_squared_error(eval_y, lr_model_2_preds)))
```

The output is similar to the following:

```
lr_model_2 MSE: 16.27172263220766
```

Figure 7.67: The MSE of the model

You can see from the output that the MSE of the second model is **16.272**. This is less than the MSE of the first model, which is **19.734**. You can safely conclude that the second model is better than the first.

19. Inspect the model coefficients (also called weights):

```
print(lr_model_2[-1].coef_)
```

In this step, you will note that **lr_model_2** is a pipeline. The final object in this pipeline is the model, so you make use of list addressing to access this by setting the index of the list element to **-1**.

Once you have the model, which is the final element in the pipeline, you make use of **.coef_** to get the model coefficients. The output is similar to the following:

```
[ 7.72661789e-14 -1.77278028e+02 -4.60337188e+01 -1.60520675e+02
 -1.23076123e+02  6.23358210e+00  8.19655844e+00  1.45478576e+02
  1.88658651e+02  2.43740192e+01  1.80553150e+02 -1.08058561e+02
  1.09713294e+02  1.79121906e+02  1.06460596e+02  2.67290613e+01
  7.79833654e+01  3.69241324e+01 -1.13863997e+02 -1.42673215e+02
 -9.69606773e+01  1.90706809e+02 -5.56429546e+01 -1.32595225e+02
 -9.41682917e+01  9.40112729e+01 -1.18732510e+02 -7.64871610e+01
 -4.18714081e+01  6.36772260e+01  4.42340977e+01 -3.81114691e+01
 -4.71547759e+01 -9.16797074e+01 -2.52346805e+01]
```

Figure 7.68: Printing model coefficients

You will note from the preceding output that the majority of the values are in the tens, some values are in the hundreds, and one value has a really small magnitude.

20. Check the number of coefficients in this model:

```
print(len(lr_model_2[-1].coef_))
```

The output of this step is similar to the following:

```
35
```

Figure 7.69: Checking the number of coefficients

You will see from the preceding that the second model has 35 coefficients.

21. Create a **steps** list with **PolynomialFeatures** of degree **10**:

```
steps = [('scaler', MinMaxScaler()),\
         ('poly', PolynomialFeatures(degree=10)),\
         ('lr', LinearRegression())]
```

22. Create a third model from the preceding steps:

```
lr_model_3 = Pipeline(steps)
```

23. Fit the third model on the training data:

```
lr_model_3.fit(train_X, train_y)
```

The output from this step is similar to the following:

```
Pipeline(memory=None,
         steps=[('scaler', MinMaxScaler(copy=True, feature_range=(0, 1))),
                ('poly',
                 PolynomialFeatures(degree=10, include_bias=True,
                                    interaction_only=False, order='C')),
                ('lr',
                 LinearRegression(copy_X=True, fit_intercept=True, n_jobs=None,
                                  normalize=False))],
         verbose=False)
```

Figure 7.70: Fitting lr_model_3 on the training data

You can see from the output that the pipeline makes use of **PolynomialFeatures** of degree **10**. You are doing this in the hope of getting a better model.

24. Print out the **R2** score of this model:

```
print('lr_model_3 R2 Score: {}'\
      .format(lr_model_3.score(eval_X, eval_y)))
```

The output of this model is similar to the following:

```
lr_model_3 R2 Score: 0.5683441691963667
```

Figure 7.71: R2 score

You can see from the preceding figure that the **R2** score is now **0.568** The previous model had an **R2** score of **0.944**. This model has an **R2** score that is worse than the one of the previous model, **lr_model_2**. This happens when your model is overfitting.

25. Use **lr_model_3** to predict on evaluation data:

```
lr_model_3_preds = lr_model_3.predict(eval_X)
```

26. Print out the MSE for **lr_model_3**:

```
print('lr_model_3 MSE: {}'\
      .format(mean_squared_error(eval_y, lr_model_3_preds)))
```

The output of this step might be similar to the following:

```
lr_model_3 MSE: 126.25407963372724
```

Figure 7.72: The MSE of lr_model_3

You can see from the preceding figure that the MSE is also worse. The MSE is **126.254**, as compared to **16.271** for the previous model.

27. Print out the number of coefficients (also called weights) in this model:

```
print(len(lr_model_3[-1].coef_))
```

The output might resemble the following:

```
1001
```

You can see that the model has **1,001** coefficients.

28. Inspect the first **35** coefficients to get a sense of the individual magnitudes:

```
print(lr_model_3[-1].coef_[:35])
```

The output might be similar to the following:

```
[ 3.92493073e+05 -6.90880756e+07 -4.12730736e+07  2.27928296e+07
 -4.76786535e+07  2.96660772e+08  2.73269211e+08  1.07842470e+08
  3.73716530e+08  8.79698224e+07 -2.35343276e+07  2.46253110e+08
 -2.61104544e+08  1.86081203e+07  1.41130624e+08 -6.53879247e+08
 -8.90635637e+08 -1.06073301e+09 -1.29263356e+09 -4.28438465e+08
  5.31481876e+07 -1.30409467e+09  4.41030510e+08 -8.86215800e+08
 -8.78154429e+08 -1.97221576e+06 -5.39374275e+08 -3.68353450e+08
  9.82103996e+08 -2.76727773e+08 -6.28826853e+08  8.14255868e+08
  5.43206968e+08 -2.03042423e+08 -2.42927974e+08]
```

Figure 7.73: Inspecting 35 coefficients

You can see from the output that the coefficients have significantly larger magnitudes than the coefficients from **lr_model_2**.

In the next steps, you will train a ridge regression model on the same set of features to reduce overfitting.

29. Create a list of steps for the pipeline you will create later on:

```
steps = [('scaler', MinMaxScaler()),\
         ('poly', PolynomialFeatures(degree=10)),\
         ('lr', Ridge(alpha=0.9))]
```

You create a list of steps for the pipeline you will create. Note that the third step in this list is an instance of **Ridge**. The parameter called **alpha** in the call to **Ridge()** is the regularization parameter. You can play around with any values from 0 to 1 to see how it affects the performance of the model that you train.

30. Create an instance of a pipeline:

```
ridge_model = Pipeline(steps)
```

31. Fit the pipeline on the training data:

```
ridge_model.fit(train_X, train_y)
```

The output of this operation might be similar to the following:

```
Pipeline(memory=None,
         steps=[('scaler', MinMaxScaler(copy=True, feature_range=(0, 1))),
                ('poly',
                 PolynomialFeatures(degree=10, include_bias=True,
                                    interaction_only=False, order='C')),
                ('lr',
                 Ridge(alpha=0.9, copy_X=True, fit_intercept=True,
                       max_iter=None, normalize=False, random_state=None,
                       solver='auto', tol=0.001))],
         verbose=False)
```

Figure 7.74: Fitting the pipeline on training data

You can see from the output that the pipeline trained a ridge model in the final step. The regularization parameter was **0**.

32. Print the R2 score of **ridge_model**:

```
print('ridge_model R2 Score: {}'\
      .format(ridge_model.score(eval_X, eval_y)))
```

The output of this step might be similar to the following:

```
ridge_model R2 Score: 0.9451949082623442
```

Figure 7.75: R2 score

You can see that the R2 score has climbed back up to **0.945**, which is way better than the score of **0.568** that **lr_model_3** had. This is already looking like a better model.

33. Use **ridge_model** to predict on the evaluation data:

```
ridge_model_preds = ridge_model.predict(eval_X)
```

34. Print the MSE of **ridge_model**:

```
print('ridge_model MSE: {}'\
      .format(mean_squared_error(eval_y, ridge_model_preds)))
```

The output might be similar to the following:

```
ridge_model MSE: 16.029822656855167
```

Figure 7.76: The MSE of ridge_model

You can see from the output that the MSE is **16.030**, which is lower than the MSE value of **126.254** that **lr_model_3** had. You can safely conclude that this is a much better model.

35. Print out the number of coefficients in **ridge_model**:

```
print(len(ridge_model[-1].coef_))
```

The output might be similar to the following:

```
1001
```

Figure 7.77: The number of coefficients in the ridge model

You can see that this model has **1001** coefficients, which is the same number of coefficients that **lr_model_3** had.

36. Print out the values of the first 35 coefficients:

```
print(ridge_model[-1].coef_[:35])
```

The output might be similar to the following:

```
[  0.         -39.79803902  -7.77413135   6.07694837   3.10326786
 -18.17945028  -9.45440071  -7.4037462  -16.97192766  -9.10799691
   6.96959155  -1.55574911   4.49242992   0.31127893   5.27565009
  -4.07568831  -0.95958324   2.38995687  -6.1583696   -2.05510604
   2.3741985   -1.30281151  -1.7837005   -4.53024264  -8.30749466
  -3.42801698   0.65288784  -2.74767783   5.47711767   4.68241474
  -2.1214614   -0.47331885   0.43221968  -0.28909998   4.64549348]
```

Figure 7.78: The values of the first 35 coefficients

You can see from the preceding output that the coefficient values no longer have large magnitudes. A lot of the coefficients have a magnitude that is less than 10, with none we can see exceeding 100. This goes to show that the model is no longer overfitting.

> **NOTE**
>
> To access the source code for this specific section, please refer to https://packt.live/3248PPx.
>
> You can also run this example online at https://packt.live/2E4LWDu.

This exercise taught you how to fix overfitting by using `RidgeRegression` to train a new model.

ACTIVITY 7.01: FIND AN OPTIMAL MODEL FOR PREDICTING THE CRITICAL TEMPERATURES OF SUPERCONDUCTORS

You work as a data scientist for a cable manufacturer. Management has decided to start shipping low-resistance cables to clients around the world. To ensure that the right cables are shipped to the right countries, they would like to predict the critical temperatures of various cables based on certain observed readings.

In this activity, you will train a linear regression model and compute the R2 score and the MSE. You will proceed to engineer new features using polynomial features of degree 3. You will compare the R2 score and MSE of this new model to those of the first model to determine overfitting. You will then use regularization to train a model that generalizes to previously unseen data.

> **NOTE**
>
> You will find the dataset required for the activity here: https://packt.live/2tJFVqu.
>
> The original dataset can be found here: https://packt.live/3ay3aoe.
>
> Citation:
>
> Hamidieh, Kam, A data-driven statistical model for predicting the critical temperature of a superconductor, Computational Materials Science, Volume 154, November 2018, pages 346-354.

The steps to accomplish this task are:

1. Open a Colab notebook.
2. Load the necessary libraries.
3. Read in the data from the **superconduct** folder.
4. Prepare the **X** and **y** variables.
5. Split the data into training and evaluation sets.
6. Create a baseline linear regression model.
7. Print out the R2 score and MSE of the model.
8. Create a pipeline to engineer polynomial features and train a linear regression model.
9. Print out the R2 score and MSE.
10. Determine that this new model is overfitting.
11. Create a pipeline to engineer polynomial features and train a ridge or lasso model.
12. Print out the R2 score and MSE.

    The output will be as follows:

```
Lasso Model R2 Score: 0.8325230040978594
```

Figure 7.79: The R2 score and MSE of the ridge model

13. Determine that this model is no longer overfitting. This is the model to put into production.

    The coefficients for the ridge model are as shown in the following figure:

```
[ 0.00000000e+00  8.74340500e-02 -7.95095837e+00 -1.30139088e-01
 -0.00000000e+00  0.00000000e+00  0.00000000e+00  3.38565726e+01
  0.00000000e+00 -0.00000000e+00 -4.13763260e+00 -2.65279487e-02
 -0.00000000e+00 -0.00000000e+00 -0.00000000e+00 -0.00000000e+00
 -0.00000000e+00  1.22329305e+01  0.00000000e+00 -0.00000000e+00
 -0.00000000e+00 -1.12633645e+01  0.00000000e+00  0.00000000e+00
  0.00000000e+00  0.00000000e+00 -0.00000000e+00  0.00000000e+00
  0.00000000e+00 -9.08364155e+00]
```

Figure 7.80: The coefficients for the ridge model

> **NOTE**
>
> The solution to this activity can be found at the following address: https://packt.live/2GbJloz.

SUMMARY

In this chapter, we studied the importance of withholding some of the available data to evaluate models. We also learned how to make use of all of the available data with a technique called cross-validation to find the best performing model from a set of models you are training. We also made use of evaluation metrics to determine when a model starts to overfit and made use of ridge and lasso regression to fix a model that is overfitting.

In the next chapter, we will go into hyperparameter tuning in depth. You will learn about various techniques for finding the best hyperparameters to train your models.

8

HYPERPARAMETER TUNING

OVERVIEW

In this chapter, each hyperparameter tuning strategy will be first broken down into its key steps before any high-level scikit-learn implementations are demonstrated. This is to ensure that you fully understand the concept behind each of the strategies before jumping to the more automated methods.

By the end of this chapter, you will be able to find further predictive performance improvements via the systematic evaluation of estimators with different hyperparameters. You will successfully deploy manual, grid, and random search strategies to find the optimal hyperparameters. You will be able to parameterize **k-nearest neighbors** (**k-NN**), **support vector machines** (**SVMs**), ridge regression, and random forest classifiers to optimize model performance.

INTRODUCTION

In previous chapters, we discussed several methods to arrive at a model that performs well. These include transforming the data via preprocessing, feature engineering and scaling, or simply choosing an appropriate estimator (algorithm) type from the large set of possible estimators made available to the users of scikit-learn.

Depending on which estimator you eventually select, there may be settings that can be adjusted to improve overall predictive performance. These settings are known as hyperparameters, and deriving the best hyperparameters is known as tuning or optimizing. Properly tuning your hyperparameters can result in performance improvements well into the double-digit percentages, so it is well worth doing in any modeling exercise.

This chapter will discuss the concept of hyperparameter tuning and will present some simple strategies that you can use to help find the best hyperparameters for your estimators.

In previous chapters, we have seen some exercises that use a range of estimators, but we haven't conducted any hyperparameter tuning. After reading this chapter, we recommend you revisit these exercises, apply the techniques taught, and see if you can improve the results.

WHAT ARE HYPERPARAMETERS?

Hyperparameters can be thought of as a set of dials and switches for each estimator that change how the estimator works to explain relationships in the data.

Have a look at *Figure 8.1*:

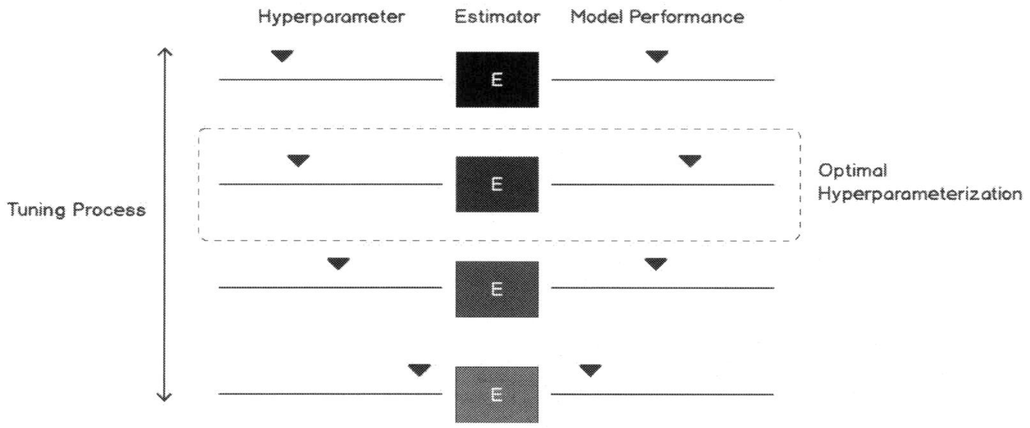

Figure 8.1: How hyperparameters work

If you read from left to right in the preceding figure, you can see that during the tuning process we change the value of the hyperparameter, which results in a change to the estimator. This in turn causes a change in model performance. Our objective is to find hyperparameterization that leads to the best model performance. This will be the *optimal* hyperparameterization.

Estimators can have hyperparameters of varying quantities and types, which means that sometimes you can be faced with a very large number of possible hyperparameterizations to choose for an estimator.

For instance, scikit-learn's implementation of the SVM classifier (`sklearn.svm.SVC`), which you will be introduced to later in the chapter, is an estimator that has multiple possible hyperparameterizations. We will test out only a small subset of these, namely using a linear kernel or a polynomial kernel of degree 2, 3, or 4.

Some of these hyperparameters are continuous in nature, while others are discrete, and the presence of continuous hyperparameters means that the number of possible hyperparameterizations is theoretically infinite. Of course, when it comes to producing a model with good predictive performance, some hyperparameterizations are much better than others, and it is your job as a data scientist to find them.

In the next section, we will be looking at setting these hyperparameters in more detail. But first, some clarification of terms.

Difference between Hyperparameters and Statistical Model Parameters

In your reading on data science, particularly in the area of statistics, you will come across terms such as "model parameters," "parameter estimation," and "(non)-parametric models." These terms relate to the parameters that feature in the mathematical formulation of models. The simplest example is that of the single variable linear model with no intercept term that takes the following form:

$$\mathrm{y} = \beta \mathrm{X}$$

Figure 8.2: Equation for a single variable linear model

Here, β is the statistical model parameter, and if this formulation is chosen, it is the data scientist's job to use data to estimate what value it takes. This could be achieved using **Ordinary Least Squares** (**OLS**) regression modeling, or it could be achieved through a method called median regression.

Hyperparameters are different in that they are external to the mathematical form. An example of a hyperparameter in this case is the way in which β will be estimated (OLS, or median regression). In some cases, hyperparameters can change the algorithm completely (that is, generating a completely different mathematical form). You will see examples of this occurring throughout this chapter.

In the next section, you will be looking at how to set a hyperparameter.

SETTING HYPERPARAMETERS

In *Chapter 7, The Generalization of Machine Learning Models*, you were introduced to the k-NN model for classification and you saw how varying k, the number of nearest neighbors, resulted in changes in model performance with respect to the prediction of class labels. Here, k is a hyperparameter, and the act of manually trying different values of k is a simple form of hyperparameter tuning.

Each time you initialize a scikit-learn estimator, it will take on a hyperparameterization as determined by the values you set for its arguments. If you specify no values, then the estimator will take on a default hyperparameterization. If you would like to see how the hyperparameters have been set for your estimator, and what hyperparameters you can adjust, simply print the output of the **estimator.get_params()** method.

For instance, say we initialize a k-NN estimator without specifying any arguments (empty brackets). To see the default hyperparameterization, we can run:

```
from sklearn import neighbors
# initialize with default hyperparameters
knn = neighbors.KNeighborsClassifier()
# examine the defaults
print(knn.get_params())
```

You should get the following output:

```
{'algorithm': 'auto', 'leaf_size': 30, 'metric': 'minkowski',
 'metric_params': None, 'n_jobs': None, 'n_neighbors': 5,
 'p': 2, 'weights': 'uniform'}
```

A dictionary of all the hyperparameters is now printed to the screen, revealing their default settings. Notice **k**, our number of nearest neighbors, is set to **5**.

To get more information as to what these parameters mean, how they can be changed, and what their likely effect may be, you can run the following command and view the help file for the estimator in question.

For our k-NN estimator:

```
?knn
```

The output will be as follows:

```
Type:           KNeighborsClassifier
String form:
KNeighborsClassifier(algorithm='auto', leaf_size=30, metric='minkowski',
                     metric_params=None, n_jobs=None, n_neighbors=5, p=2,
                     weights='uniform')
File:           /usr/local/lib/python3.6/dist-packages/sklearn/neighbors/classification.py
Docstring:
Classifier implementing the k-nearest neighbors vote.

Read more in the :ref:`User Guide <classification>`.

Parameters
----------
n_neighbors : int, optional (default = 5)
    Number of neighbors to use by default for :meth:`kneighbors` queries.

weights : str or callable, optional (default = 'uniform')
    weight function used in prediction.  Possible values:

    - 'uniform' : uniform weights.  All points in each neighborhood
      are weighted equally.
    - 'distance' : weight points by the inverse of their distance.
      in this case, closer neighbors of a query point will have a
      greater influence than neighbors which are further away.
    - [callable] : a user-defined function which accepts an
      array of distances, and returns an array of the same shape
      containing the weights.
```

Figure 8.3: Help file for the k-NN estimator

If you look closely at the help file, you will see the default hyperparameterization for the estimator under the **`String form`** heading, along with an explanation of what each hyperparameter means under the **`Parameters`** heading.

Coming back to our example, if we want to change the hyperparameterization from **`k = 5`** to **`k = 15`**, just re-initialize the estimator and set the **`n_neighbors`** argument to **`15`**, which will override the default:

```
"""
initialize with k = 15 and all other hyperparameters as default
"""
knn = neighbors.KNeighborsClassifier(n_neighbors=15)

# examine
print(knn.get_params())
```

You should get the following output:

```
{'algorithm': 'auto', 'leaf_size': 30, 'metric': 'minkowski',
 'metric_params': None, 'n_jobs': None, 'n_neighbors': 15,
 'p': 2, 'weights': 'uniform'}
```

You may have noticed that k is not the only hyperparameter available for k-NN classifiers. Setting multiple hyperparameters is as easy as specifying the relevant arguments. For example, let's increase the number of neighbors from **5** to **15** and force the algorithm to take the distance of points in the neighborhood, rather than a simple majority vote, into account when training. For more information, see the description for the **weights** argument in the help file (**?knn**):

```
"""
initialize with k = 15, weights = distance and all other
hyperparameters as default
"""
knn = neighbors.KNeighborsClassifier(n_neighbors=15, \
                                     weights='distance')

# examine
print(knn.get_params())
```

The output will be as follows:

```
{'algorithm': 'auto', 'leaf_size': 30, 'metric': 'minkowski',
 'metric_params': None, 'n_jobs': None, 'n_neighbors': 15,
 'p': 2, 'weights': 'distance'}
```

In the output, you can see **n_neighbors** (**k**) is now set to **15**, and **weights** is now set to **distance**, rather than **uniform**.

> **NOTE**
>
> The code for this section can be found at https://packt.live/2tN5CH1.

A NOTE ON DEFAULTS

Generally, efforts have been made by the developers of machine learning libraries to set sensible default hyperparameters for estimators. That said, for certain datasets, significant performance improvements may be achieved through tuning.

FINDING THE BEST HYPERPARAMETERIZATION

The best hyperparameterization depends on your overall objective in building a machine learning model in the first place. In most cases, this is to find the model that has the highest predictive performance on unseen data, as measured by its ability to correctly label data points (classification) or predict a number (regression).

The prediction of unseen data can be simulated using hold-out test sets or cross-validation, the former being the method used in this chapter. Performance is evaluated differently in each case, for instance, **Mean Squared Error** (**MSE**) for regression and accuracy for classification. We seek to reduce the MSE or increase the accuracy of our predictions.

Let's implement manual hyperparameterization in the following exercise.

EXERCISE 8.01: MANUAL HYPERPARAMETER TUNING FOR A K-NN CLASSIFIER

In this exercise, we will manually tune a k-NN classifier, which was covered in *Chapter 7, The Generalization of Machine Learning Models*, our goal being to predict incidences of malignant or benign breast cancer based on cell measurements sourced from the affected breast sample.

> **NOTE**
>
> The dataset to be used in this exercise can be found on our GitHub repository at https://packt.live/36dsxIF.

These are the important attributes of the dataset:

- ID number
- Diagnosis (M = malignant, B = benign)
- 3-32)

10 real-valued features are computed for each cell nucleus as follows:

- Radius (mean of distances from the center to points on the perimeter)
- Texture (standard deviation of grayscale values)
- Perimeter
- Area

- Smoothness (local variation in radius lengths)
- Compactness (perimeter^2 / area - 1.0)
- Concavity (severity of concave portions of the contour)
- Concave points (number of concave portions of the contour)
- Symmetry
- Fractal dimension (refers to the complexity of the tissue architecture; "coastline approximation" - 1)

> **NOTE**
>
> Details on the attributes of the dataset can be found at https://packt.live/30HzGQ6.

The following steps will help you complete this exercise:

1. Create a new notebook in Google Colab.
2. Next, import **neighbors**, **datasets**, and **model_selection** from scikit-learn:

```
from sklearn import neighbors, datasets, model_selection
```

3. Load the data. We will call this object **cancer**, and isolate the target **y**, and the features, **X**:

```
# dataset
cancer = datasets.load_breast_cancer()

# target
y = cancer.target

# features
X = cancer.data
```

4. Initialize a k-NN classifier with its default hyperparameterization:

```
# no arguments specified
knn = neighbors.KNeighborsClassifier()
```

5. Feed this classifier into a 10-fold cross-validation (**cv**), calculating the precision score for each fold. Assume that maximizing precision (the proportion of true positives in all positive classifications) is the primary objective of this exercise:

```
# 10 folds, scored on precision
cv = model_selection.cross_val_score(knn, X, y, cv=10,\
                                     scoring='precision')
```

6. Printing **cv** shows the precision score calculated for each fold:

```
# precision scores
print(cv)
```

You will see the following output:

```
[0.91666667 0.85       0.91666667 0.94736842 0.94594595
 0.94444444 0.97222222 0.92105263 0.96969697 0.97142857]
```

7. Calculate and print the mean precision score for all folds. This will give us an idea of the overall performance of the model, as shown in the following code snippet:

```
# average over all folds
print(round(cv.mean(), 2))
```

You should get the following output:

```
0.94
```

You should see the mean score is close to 94%. Can this be improved upon?

8. Run everything again, this time setting hyperparameter **k** to **15**. You can see that the result is actually marginally worse (1% lower):

```
# k = 15
knn = neighbors.KNeighborsClassifier(n_neighbors=15)

cv = model_selection.cross_val_score(knn, X, y, cv=10, \
                                     scoring='precision')

print(round(cv.mean(), 2))
```

The output will be as follows:

```
0.93
```

9. Try again with **k** = **7**, **3**, and **1**. In this case, it seems reasonable that the default value of 5 is the best option. To avoid repetition, you may like to define and call a Python function as follows:

```
def evaluate_knn(k):
    knn = neighbors.KNeighborsClassifier(n_neighbors=k)
    cv = model_selection.cross_val_score(knn, X, y, cv=10, \
                                         scoring='precision')
    print(round(cv.mean(), 2))
evaluate_knn(k=7)

evaluate_knn(k=3)

evaluate_knn(k=1)
```

The output will be as follows:

```
0.93
0.93
0.92
```

Nothing beats 94%.

10. Let's alter a second hyperparameter. Setting **k = 5**, what happens if we change the k-NN weighing system to depend on **distance** rather than having **uniform** weights? Run all code again, this time with the following hyperparameterization:

```
# k =5, weights evaluated using distance
knn = neighbors.KNeighborsClassifier(n_neighbors=5, \
                                     weights='distance')

cv = model_selection.cross_val_score(knn, X, y, cv=10, \
                                     scoring='precision')
print(round(cv.mean(), 2))
```

Did performance improve?

You should see no further improvement on the default hyperparameterization because the output is:

```
0.93
```

We therefore conclude that the default hyperparameterization is the optimal one in this case.

> **NOTE**
>
> To access the source code for this specific section, please refer to https://packt.live/322lWk4.
>
> You can also run this example online at https://packt.live/3gbOyfU.

ADVANTAGES AND DISADVANTAGES OF A MANUAL SEARCH

Of all the strategies for hyperparameter tuning, the manual process gives you the most control. As you go through the process, you can get a feel for how your estimators might perform under different hyperparameterizations, and this means you can adjust them in line with your expectations without having to try a large number of possibilities unnecessarily. However, this strategy is feasible only when there is a small number of possibilities you would like to try. When the number of possibilities exceeds about five, this strategy becomes too labor-intensive to be practical.

In the following sections, we will introduce two strategies to better deal with this situation.

TUNING USING GRID SEARCH

In the context of machine learning, grid search refers to a strategy of systematically testing out every hyperparameterization from a pre-defined set of possibilities for your chosen estimator. You decide the criteria used to evaluate performance, and once the search is complete, you may manually examine the results and choose the best hyperparameterization, or let your computer automatically choose it for you.

The overall objective is to try and find an optimal hyperparameterization that leads to improved performance when predicting unseen data.

Before we get to the implementations of grid search in scikit-learn, let's first demonstrate the strategy using simple Python `for` loops.

SIMPLE DEMONSTRATION OF THE GRID SEARCH STRATEGY

In the following demonstration of the grid search strategy, we will use the breast cancer prediction dataset we saw in *Exercise 8.01*, *Manual Hyperparameter Tuning for a k-NN Classifier*, where we manually tuned the hyperparameters of the k-NN classifier to optimize for the precision of cancer predictions.

This time, instead of manually fitting models with different values of **`k`** we just define the **`k`** values we would like to try, that is, **`k = 1, 3, 5, 7`** in a Python dictionary. This dictionary will be the grid we will search through to find the optimal hyperparameterization.

> **NOTE**
>
> The code for this section can be found at https://packt.live/2U1Y0Li.

The code will be as follows:

```
from sklearn import neighbors, datasets, model_selection

# load data
cancer = datasets.load_breast_cancer()

# target
y = cancer.target

# features
X = cancer.data

# hyperparameter grid
grid = {'k': [1, 3, 5, 7]}
```

In the code snippet, we have used a dictionary **`{}`** and set the **`k`** values in a Python dictionary.

In the next part of the code snippet, to conduct the search, we iterate through the grid, fitting a model for each value of **`k`**, each time evaluating the model through 10-fold cross-validation.

At the end of each iteration, we extract, format, and report back the mean precision score after cross-validation via the **`print`** method:

```
# for every value of k in the grid
for k in grid['k']:
    # initialize the knn estimator
    knn = neighbors.KNeighborsClassifier(n_neighbors=k)
    # conduct a 10-fold cross-validation
    cv = model_selection.cross_val_score(knn, X, y, cv=10, \
                                         scoring='precision')
    # calculate the average precision value over all folds
    cv_mean = round(cv.mean(), 3)
    # report the result
    print('With k = {}, mean precision = {}'.format(k, cv_mean))
```

The output will be as follows:

```
With k = 1, mean precision = 0.919
With k = 3, mean precision = 0.928
With k = 5, mean precision = 0.936
With k = 7, mean precision = 0.931
```

Figure 8.4: Average precisions for all folds

We can see from the output that **`k = 5`** is the best hyperparameterization found, with a mean precision score of roughly 94%. Increasing **`k`** to **`7`** didn't significantly improve performance. It is important to note that the only parameter we are changing here is k and that each time the k-NN estimator is initialized, it is done with the remaining hyperparameters set to their default values.

To make this point clear, we can run the same loop, this time just printing the hyperparameterization that will be tried:

```
# for every value of k in the grid
for k in grid['k']:
    # initialize the knn estimator
    knn = neighbors.KNeighborsClassifier(n_neighbors=k)
    # print the hyperparameterization
    print(knn.get_params())
```

The output will be as follows:

```
{'algorithm': 'auto', 'leaf_size': 30, 'metric': 'minkowski',
 'metric_params': None, 'n_jobs': None, 'n_neighbors': 1,
 'p': 2, 'weights': 'uniform'}
{'algorithm': 'auto', 'leaf_size': 30, 'metric': 'minkowski',
 'metric_params': None, 'n_jobs': None, 'n_neighbors': 3,
 'p': 2, 'weights': 'uniform'}
{'algorithm': 'auto', 'leaf_size': 30, 'metric': 'minkowski',
 'metric_params': None, 'n_jobs': None, 'n_neighbors': 5,
 'p': 2, 'weights': 'uniform'}
{'algorithm': 'auto', 'leaf_size': 30, 'metric': 'minkowski',
 'metric_params': None, 'n_jobs': None, 'n_neighbors': 7,
 'p': 2, 'weights': 'uniform'}
```

You can see from the output that the only parameter we are changing is k; everything else remains the same in each iteration.

Simple, single-loop structures are fine for a grid search of a single hyperparameter, but what if we would like to try a second one? Remember that for k-NN we also have weights that can take values **`uniform`** or **`distance`**, the choice of which influences how k-NN learns how to classify points.

To proceed, all we need to do is create a dictionary containing both the values of k and the weight functions we would like to try as separate key/value pairs:

```
# hyperparameter grid
grid = {'k': [1, 3, 5, 7],\
        'weight_function': ['uniform', 'distance']}

# for every value of k in the grid
for k in grid['k']:
    # and every possible weight_function in the grid
    for weight_function in grid['weight_function']:
        # initialize the knn estimator
        knn = neighbors.KNeighborsClassifier\
              (n_neighbors=k, \
               weights=weight_function)

        # conduct a 10-fold cross-validation
```

```
        cv = model_selection.cross_val_score(knn, X, y, cv=10, \
                                            scoring='precision')

        # calculate the average precision value over all folds
        cv_mean = round(cv.mean(), 3)

        # report the result
        print('With k = {} and weight function = {}, '\
              'mean precision = {}'\
              .format(k, weight_function, cv_mean))
```

The output will be as follows:

```
With k = 1 and weight function = uniform, mean precision = 0.919
With k = 1 and weight function = distance, mean precision = 0.919
With k = 3 and weight function = uniform, mean precision = 0.928
With k = 3 and weight function = distance, mean precision = 0.929
With k = 5 and weight function = uniform, mean precision = 0.936
With k = 5 and weight function = distance, mean precision = 0.93
With k = 7 and weight function = uniform, mean precision = 0.931
With k = 7 and weight function = distance, mean precision = 0.926
```

Figure 8.5: Average precision values for all folds for different values of k

You can see that when **`k = 5`**, the weight function is not based on distance and all the other hyperparameters are kept as their default values, and the mean precision comes out highest. As we discussed earlier, if you would like to see the full set of hyperparameterizations evaluated for k-NN, just add **`print(knn.get_params())`** inside the **`for`** loop after the estimator is initialized:

```
# for every value of k in the grid
for k in grid['k']:
    # and every possible weight_function in the grid
    for weight_function in grid['weight_function']:

        # initialize the knn estimator
        knn = neighbors.KNeighborsClassifier\
              (n_neighbors=k, \
               weights=weight_function)

        # print the hyperparameterizations
        print(knn.get_params())
```

The output will be as follows:

```
{'algorithm': 'auto', 'leaf_size': 30, 'metric': 'minkowski',
 'metric_params': None, 'n_jobs': None, 'n_neighbors': 1,
 'p': 2, 'weights': 'uniform'}
{'algorithm': 'auto', 'leaf_size': 30, 'metric': 'minkowski',
 'metric_params': None, 'n_jobs': None, 'n_neighbors': 1,
 'p': 2, 'weights': 'distance'}
{'algorithm': 'auto', 'leaf_size': 30, 'metric': 'minkowski',
 'metric_params': None, 'n_jobs': None, 'n_neighbors': 3,
 'p': 2, 'weights': 'uniform'}
{'algorithm': 'auto', 'leaf_size': 30, 'metric': 'minkowski',
 'metric_params': None, 'n_jobs': None, 'n_neighbors': 3,
 'p': 2, 'weights': 'distance'}
{'algorithm': 'auto', 'leaf_size': 30, 'metric': 'minkowski',
 'metric_params': None, 'n_jobs': None, 'n_neighbors': 5,
 'p': 2, 'weights': 'uniform'}
{'algorithm': 'auto', 'leaf_size': 30, 'metric': 'minkowski',
 'metric_params': None, 'n_jobs': None, 'n_neighbors': 5,
 'p': 2, 'weights': 'distance'}
{'algorithm': 'auto', 'leaf_size': 30, 'metric': 'minkowski',
 'metric_params': None, 'n_jobs': None, 'n_neighbors': 7,
 'p': 2, 'weights': 'uniform'}
{'algorithm': 'auto', 'leaf_size': 30, 'metric': 'minkowski',
 'metric_params': None, 'n_jobs': None, 'n_neighbors': 7,
 'p': 2, 'weights': 'distance'}
```

This implementation, while great for demonstrating how the grid search process works, may not practical when trying to evaluate estimators that have **3**, **4**, or even **10** different types of hyperparameters, each with a multitude of possible settings.

To carry on in this way will mean writing and keeping track of multiple **for** loops, which can be tedious. Thankfully, **scikit-learn**'s **model_selection** module gives us a method called **GridSearchCV** that is much more user-friendly. We will be looking at this in the topic ahead.

GRIDSEARCHCV

GridsearchCV is a method of tuning wherein the model can be built by evaluating the combination of parameters mentioned in a grid. In the following figure, we will see how **GridSearchCV** is different from manual search and look at grid search in a muchdetailed way in a table format.

TUNING USING GRIDSEARCHCV

We can conduct a grid search much more easily in practice by leveraging **model_selection.GridSearchCV**.

For the sake of comparison, we will use the same breast cancer dataset and k-NN classifier as before:

```
from sklearn import model_selection, datasets, neighbors

# load the data
cancer = datasets.load_breast_cancer()

# target
y = cancer.target

# features
X = cancer.data
```

The next thing we need to do after loading the data is to initialize the class of the estimator we would like to evaluate under different hyperparameterizations:

```
# initialize the estimator
knn = neighbors.KNeighborsClassifier()
```

We then define the grid:

```
# grid contains k and the weight function
grid = {'n_neighbors': [1, 3, 5, 7],\
        'weights': ['uniform', 'distance']}
```

To set up the search, we pass the freshly initialized estimator and our grid of hyperparameters to **model_selection.GridSearchCV()**. We must also specify a scoring metric, which is the method that will be used to evaluate the performance of the various hyperparameterizations tried during the search.

The last thing to do is set the number splits to be used using cross-validation via the **cv** argument. We will set this to **10**, thereby conducting 10-fold cross-validation:

```
"""
 set up the grid search with scoring on precision and
number of folds = 10
"""
gscv = model_selection.GridSearchCV(estimator=knn, \
                                    param_grid=grid, \
                                    scoring='precision', cv=10)
```

The last step is to feed data to this object via its **fit()** method. Once this has been done, the grid search process will be kick-started:

```
# start the search
gscv.fit(X, y)
```

By default, information relating to the search will be printed to the screen, allowing you to see the exact estimator parameterizations that will be evaluated for the k-NN estimator:

```
GridSearchCV(cv=10, error_score=nan,
             estimator=KNeighborsClassifier(algorithm='auto', leaf_size=30,
                                            metric='minkowski',
                                            metric_params=None, n_jobs=None,
                                            n_neighbors=5, p=2,
                                            weights='uniform'),
             iid='deprecated', n_jobs=None,
             param_grid={'n_neighbors': [1, 3, 5, 7],
                         'weights': ['uniform', 'distance']},
             pre_dispatch='2*n_jobs', refit=True, return_train_score=False,
             scoring='precision', verbose=0)
```

Figure 8.6: Estimator parameterizations for the k-NN estimator

Once the search is complete, we can examine the results by accessing and printing the **cv_results_** attribute. **cv_results_** is a dictionary containing helpful information regarding model performance under each hyperparameterization, such as the mean test-set value of your scoring metric (**mean_test_score**, the lower the better), the complete list of hyperparameterizations tried (**params**), and the model ranks as they relate to the **mean_test_score** (**rank_test_score**).

The best model found will have rank = 1, the second-best model will have rank = 2, and so on, as you can see in *Figure 8.8*. The model fitting times are reported through **mean_fit_time**.

Although not usually a consideration for smaller datasets, this value can be important because in some cases you may find that a marginal increase in model performance through a certain hyperparameterization is associated with a significant increase in model fit time, which, depending on the computing resources you have available, may render that hyperparameterization infeasible because it will take too long to fit:

```
# view the results
print(gscv.cv_results_)
```

The output will be as follows:

```
{'mean_fit_time': array([0.00055282, 0.00043252, 0.00045586, 0.00044289, 0.00042443,
       0.00044796, 0.00044997, 0.0004324 ]), 'std_fit_time': array([2.26088859e-04, 3.34712853e-06, 4.32680787e-05,
6.06286024e-05,
       1.17754644e-05, 4.16436731e-05, 3.92637181e-05, 1.40615227e-05]), 'mean_score_time': array([0.00221133, 0.0010
2084, 0.00203059, 0.00103009, 0.00206087,
       0.00111656, 0.0021332 , 0.00115821]), 'std_score_time': array([3.21795421e-04, 2.84032587e-05, 7.50346451e-05,
3.56917072e-05,
       6.77137685e-05, 9.23788651e-05, 6.50428475e-05, 9.99759607e-05]), 'param_n_neighbors': masked_array(data=[1,
1, 3, 3, 5, 5, 7, 7],
             mask=[False, False, False, False, False, False, False, False],
       fill_value='?',
            dtype=object), 'param_weights': masked_array(data=['uniform', 'distance', 'uniform', 'distance',
                   'uniform', 'distance', 'uniform', 'distance'],
             mask=[False, False, False, False, False, False, False, False],
       fill_value='?',
            dtype=object), 'params': [{'n_neighbors': 1, 'weights': 'uniform'}, {'n_neighbors': 1, 'weights': 'distan
ce'}, {'n_neighbors': 3, 'weights': 'uniform'}, {'n_neighbors': 3, 'weights': 'distance'}, {'n_neighbors': 5, 'weight
s': 'uniform'}, {'n_neighbors': 5, 'weights': 'distance'}, {'n_neighbors': 7, 'weights': 'uniform'}, {'n_neighbors':
7, 'weights': 'distance'}], 'split0_test_score': array([0.92105263, 0.92105263, 0.8974359 , 0.8974359 , 0.91891892,
```

Figure 8.7: GridsearchCV results

The model ranks can be seen in the following image:

```
ce'}, {'n_neighbors': 3, 'weights': 'uniform'}, {'n_neighbors': 3, 'weights': 'distance'}, {'n_neighbors': 5, 'weight
s': 'uniform'}, {'n_neighbors': 5, 'weights': 'distance'}, {'n_neighbors': 7, 'weights': 'uniform'}, {'n_neighbors':
7, 'weights': 'distance'}], 'split0_test_score': array([0.92105263, 0.92105263, 0.8974359 , 0.8974359 , 0.91891892,
       0.91891892, 0.92105263, 0.92105263]), 'split1_test_score': array([0.86486486, 0.86486486, 0.83333333, 0.833333
33, 0.85365854,
       0.85365854, 0.83333333, 0.83333333]), 'split2_test_score': array([0.92105263, 0.92105263, 0.91666667, 0.918918
92, 0.91666667,
       0.91891892, 0.91891892, 0.91891892]), 'split3_test_score': array([0.92105263, 0.92105263, 0.94594595, 0.945945
95, 0.94736842,
       0.94736842, 0.94736842, 0.94736842]), 'split4_test_score': array([0.8974359 , 0.8974359 , 0.94594595, 0.945945
95, 0.94594595,
       0.94594595, 0.92105263, 0.92105263]), 'split5_test_score': array([0.91666667, 0.91666667, 0.94594595, 0.945945
95, 0.94444444,
       0.94444444, 0.94444444, 0.94444444]), 'split6_test_score': array([0.92105263, 0.92105263, 0.94736842, 0.947368
42, 0.97222222,
       0.94594595, 0.97222222, 0.94594595]), 'split7_test_score': array([0.94444444, 0.94444444, 0.94444444, 0.944444
44, 0.91891892,
       0.91891892, 0.94285714, 0.94285714]), 'split8_test_score': array([0.93939394, 0.93939394, 0.96875   , 0.969696
97, 0.96875   ,
       0.94117647, 0.96875   , 0.94117647]), 'split9_test_score': array([0.94444444, 0.94444444, 0.94285714, 0.942857
14, 0.97142857,
       0.97142857, 0.94444444, 0.94444444]), 'mean_test_score': array([0.91892952, 0.91892952, 0.92852418, 0.928843
, 0.93556744,
       0.93044707, 0.93114526, 0.92579928]), 'std_test_score': array([0.02271376, 0.02271376, 0.03697908, 0.03701478,
0.03431266,
       0.0302332 , 0.03733588, 0.0330005 ]), 'rank_test_score': array([7, 7, 5, 4, 1, 3, 2, 6], dtype=int32)}
```

Figure 8.8: Model ranks

> **NOTE**
>
> For the purpose of presentation, the output has been truncated. You can see the complete output here: https://packt.live/2uD12uP.

In the output, it is worth noting that this dictionary can be easily transformed into a pandas DataFrame, which makes information much clearer to read and allows us to selectively display the metrics we are interested in.

For example, say we are only interested in each hyperparameterization (**params**) and mean cross-validated test score (**mean_test_score**) for the top five high - performing models:

```
import pandas as pd

# convert the results dictionary to a dataframe
results = pd.DataFrame(gscv.cv_results_)

"""
select just the hyperparameterizations tried,
the mean test scores, order by score and show the top 5 models
"""
print(results.loc[:,['params','mean_test_score']]\
      .sort_values('mean_test_score', ascending=False).head(5))
```

Running this code produces the following output:

```
                                          params  mean_test_score
4   {'n_neighbors': 5, 'weights': 'uniform'}          0.935567
6   {'n_neighbors': 7, 'weights': 'uniform'}          0.931145
5  {'n_neighbors': 5, 'weights': 'distance'}          0.930447
3  {'n_neighbors': 3, 'weights': 'distance'}          0.928843
2   {'n_neighbors': 3, 'weights': 'uniform'}          0.928524
```

Figure 8.9: mean_test_score for top 5 models

We can also use pandas to produce visualizations of the result as follows:

```
# visualise the result
results.loc[:,['params','mean_test_score']]\
      .plot.barh(x = 'params')
```

The output will be as follows:

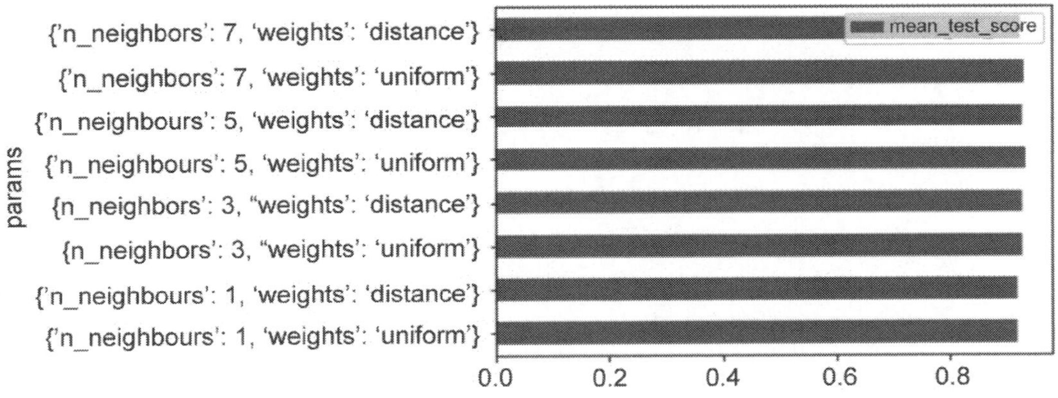

Figure 8.10: Using pandas to visualize the output

When you look at the preceding figure, you see that the best hyperparameterization found is where **`n_neighbors = 5`** and **`weights = 'uniform'`**, because this results in the highest mean test score (precision).

> **NOTE**
>
> The code for this section can be found at https://packt.live/2uD12uP.

SUPPORT VECTOR MACHINE (SVM) CLASSIFIERS

The **SVM** classifier is basically a supervised machine learning model. It is a commonly used class of estimator that can be used for both binary and multi-class classification. It is known to perform well in cases where the data is limited, hence it is a reliable model. It is relatively fast to train compared to highly iterative or ensemble methods such as artificial neural networks or random forests, which makes it a good option if there is a limit on your computer's processing power.

It makes its predictions by leveraging a special mathematical formulation known as a kernel function. This function can take several forms with some functions, such as the polynomial kernel function with a degree (squared, cubed, and so on), that have their own adjustable parameters.

SVMs have been shown to perform well in the context of image classification, which you will see in the following exercise.

> **NOTE**
>
> For more information on support vector machines, see https://packt.live/37iDytw and also refer to https://packt.live/38xaPkC.

EXERCISE 8.02: GRID SEARCH HYPERPARAMETER TUNING FOR AN SVM

In this exercise, we will employ a class of estimator called an SVM classifier and tune its hyperparameters using a grid search strategy.

The supervised learning objective we will focus on here is the classification of handwritten digits (0-9) based solely on images. The dataset we will use contains 1,797 labeled images of handwritten digits.

> **NOTE**
>
> The dataset to be used in this exercise can be found on our GitHub repository at https://packt.live/2vdbHg9.
>
> Details on the attributes of the dataset can be found on the original dataset's URL: https://packt.live/36cX35b.

1. Create a new notebook in Google Colab.
2. Import **datasets**, **svm**, and **model_selection** from scikit-learn:

```
from sklearn import datasets, svm, model_selection
```

3. Load the data. We will call this object images, and then we'll isolate the target **y** and the features **X**. In the training step, the SVM classifier will learn how **y** relates to **X** and will therefore be able to predict new **y** values when given new **X** values:

```
# load data
digits = datasets.load_digits()

# target
```

```
y = digits.target

# features
X = digits.data
```

4. Initialize the estimator as a multi-class SVM classifier and set the **gamma** argument to **scale**:

```
# support vector machine classifier
clr = svm.SVC(gamma='scale')
```

> **NOTE**
>
> For more information on the gamma argument, go to https://packt.live/2Ga2l79.

5. Define our grid to cover four distinct hyperparameterizations of the classifier with a linear kernel and with a polynomial kernel of degrees **2**, **3**, and **4**. We want to see which of the four hyperparameterizations leads to more accurate predictions:

```
# hyperparameter grid. contains linear and polynomial kernels
grid = [{'kernel': ['linear']},\
        {'kernel': ['poly'], 'degree': [2, 3, 4]}]
```

6. Set up grid search k-fold cross-validation with **10** folds and a scoring measure of accuracy. Make sure it has our **grid** and **estimator** objects as inputs:

```
"""
setting up the grid search to score on accuracy and
evaluate over 10 folds
"""
cv_spec = model_selection.GridSearchCV\
          (estimator=clr, param_grid=grid, \
           scoring='accuracy', cv=10)
```

7. Start the search by providing data to the **.fit()** method. Details of the process, including the hyperparameterizations tried and the scoring method selected, will be printed to the screen:

```
# start the grid search
cv_spec.fit(X, y)
```

You should see the following output:

```
GridSearchCV(cv=10, error_score=nan,
             estimator=SVC(C=1.0, break_ties=False, cache_size=200,
                           class_weight=None, coef0=0.0,
                           decision_function_shape='ovr', degree=3,
                           gamma='scale', kernel='rbf', max_iter=-1,
                           probability=False, random_state=None, shrinking=True,
                           tol=0.001, verbose=False),
             iid='deprecated', n_jobs=None,
             param_grid=[{'kernel': ['linear']},
                         {'degree': [2, 3, 4], 'kernel': ['poly']}],
             pre_dispatch='2*n_jobs', refit=True, return_train_score=False,
             scoring='accuracy', verbose=0)
```

Figure 8.11: Grid Search using the .fit() method

8. To examine all of the results, simply print **cv_spec.cv_results_** to the screen. You will see that the results are structured as a dictionary, allowing you to access the information you require using the keys:

```
# what is the available information
print(cv_spec.cv_results_.keys())
```

You will see the following information:

```
dict_keys(['mean_fit_time', 'std_fit_time', 'mean_score_time', 'std_score_time', 'param_kernel', 'param_de
gree', 'params', 'split0_test_score', 'split1_test_score', 'split2_test_score', 'split3_test_score', 'spli
t4_test_score', 'split5_test_score', 'split6_test_score', 'split7_test_score', 'split8_test_score', 'split
9_test_score', 'mean_test_score', 'std_test_score', 'rank_test_score'])
```

Figure 8.12: Results as a dictionary

9. For this exercise, we are primarily concerned with the test-set performance of each distinct hyperparameterization. You can see the first hyperparameterization through **cv_spec.cv_results_['mean_test_score']**, and the second through **cv_spec.cv_results_['params']**.

Let's convert the results dictionary to a **pandas** DataFrame and find the best hyperparameterization:

```
import pandas as pd

# convert the dictionary of results to a pandas dataframe
results = pd.DataFrame(cv_spec.cv_results_)
# show hyperparameterizations
print(results.loc[:,['params','mean_test_score']]\
      .sort_values('mean_test_score', ascending=False))
```

You will see the following results:

	params	mean_test_score
2	{'degree': 3, 'kernel': 'poly'}	0.977734
3	{'degree': 4, 'kernel': 'poly'}	0.973284
1	{'degree': 2, 'kernel': 'poly'}	0.970500
0	{'kernel': 'linear'}	0.960487

Figure 8.13: Parameterization results

> **NOTE**
>
> You may get slightly different results. However, the values you obtain should largely agree with those in the preceding output.

10. It is best practice to visualize any results you produce. **pandas** makes this easy. Run the following code to produce a visualization:

```
# visualize the result
(results.loc[:,['params','mean_test_score']]\
        .sort_values('mean_test_score', ascending=True)\
        .plot.barh(x='params', xlim=(0.8)))
```

The output will be as follows:

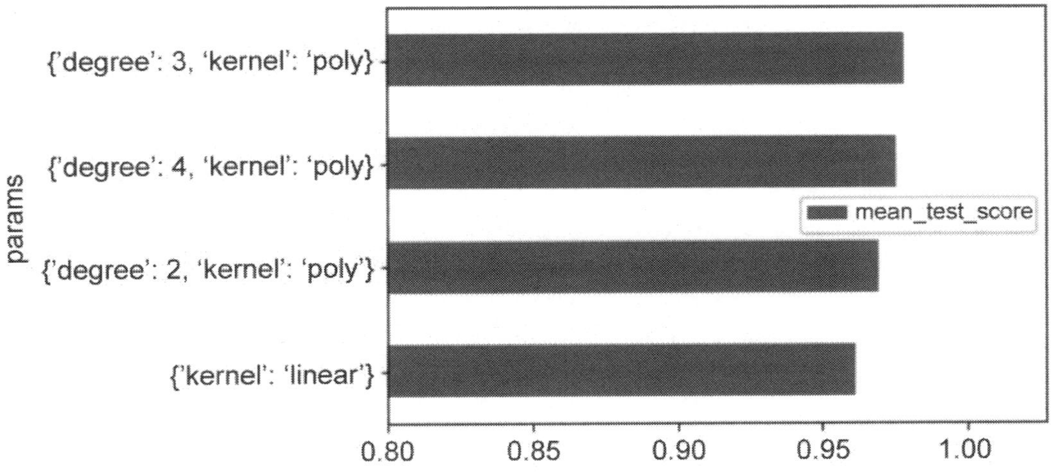

Figure 8.14: Using pandas to visualize the results

> **NOTE**
>
> To access the source code for this specific section, please refer to https://packt.live/36At2MO.
>
> You can also run this example online at https://packt.live/2YdQsGq.

We can see that an SVM classifier with a third-degree polynomial kernel function has the highest accuracy of all the hyperparameterizations evaluated in our search. Feel free to add more hyperparameterizations to the grid and see if you can improve on the score.

ADVANTAGES AND DISADVANTAGES OF GRID SEARCH

The primary advantage of the grid search compared to a manual search is that it is an automated process that one can simply set and forget. Additionally, you have the power to dictate the exact hyperparameterizations evaluated, which can be a good thing when you have prior knowledge of what kind of hyperparameterizations might work well in your context. It is also easy to understand exactly what will happen during the search thanks to the explicit definitions of the grid.

The major drawback of the grid search strategy is that it is computationally very expensive; that is, when the number of hyperparameterizations to try increases substantially, processing times can be very slow. Also, when you define your grid, you may inadvertently omit an hyperparameterization that would in fact be optimal. If it is not specified in your grid, it will never be tried

To overcome these drawbacks, we will be looking at random search in the next section.

RANDOM SEARCH

Instead of searching through every hyperparameterizations in a pre-defined set, as is the case with a grid search, in a random search we sample from a distribution of possibilities by assuming each hyperparameter to be a random variable. Before we go through the process in depth, it will be helpful to briefly review what random variables are and what we mean by a distribution.

RANDOM VARIABLES AND THEIR DISTRIBUTIONS

A random variable is non-constant (its value can change) and its variability can be described in terms of distribution. There are many different types of distributions, but each falls into one of two broad categories: discrete and continuous. We use discrete distributions to describe random variables whose values can take only whole numbers, such as counts.

An example is the count of visitors to a theme park in a day, or the number of attempted shots it takes a golfer to get a hole-in-one.

We use continuous distributions to describe random variables whose values lie along a continuum made up of infinitely small increments. Examples include human height or weight, or outside air temperature. Distributions often have parameters that control their shape.

Discrete distributions can be described mathematically using what's called a probability mass function, which defines the exact probability of the random variable taking a certain value. Common notation for the left-hand side of this function is **`P(X=x)`**, which in plain English means that the probability that the random variable **`X`** equals a certain value **`x`** is **`P`**. Remember that probabilities range between **`0`** (impossible) and **`1`** (certain).

By definition, the summation of each **`P(X=x)`** for all possible **`x`**'s will be equal to 1, or if expressed another way, the probability that **`X`** will take any value is 1. A simple example of this kind of distribution is the discrete uniform distribution, where the random variable **`X`** will take only one of a finite range of values and the probability of it taking any particular value is the same for all values, hence the term uniform.

For example, if there are 10 possible values the probability that **`X`** is any particular value is exactly 1/10. If there were 6 possible values, as in the case of a standard 6-sided die, the probability would be 1/6, and so on. The probability mass function for the discrete uniform distribution is:

$$P(X = x) = \frac{1}{n}$$

Figure 8.15: Probability mass function for the discrete uniform distribution

The following code will allow us to see the form of this distribution with 10 possible values of X.

First, we create a list of all the possible values **X** can take:

```
# list of all xs
X = list(range(1, 11))

print(X)
```

The output will be as follows:

```
[1, 2, 3, 4, 5, 6, 7, 8, 9, 10]
```

We then calculate the probability that **X** will take up any value of **x (P(X=x))**:

```
# pmf, 1/n * n = 1
p_X_x = [1/len(X)] * len(X)

# sums to 1
print(p_X_x)
```

As discussed, the summation of probabilities will equal 1, and this is the case with any distribution. We now have everything we need to visualize the distribution:

```
import matplotlib.pyplot as plt

plt.bar(X, p_X_x)
plt.xlabel('X')
plt.ylabel('P(X=x)')
```

The output will be as follows:

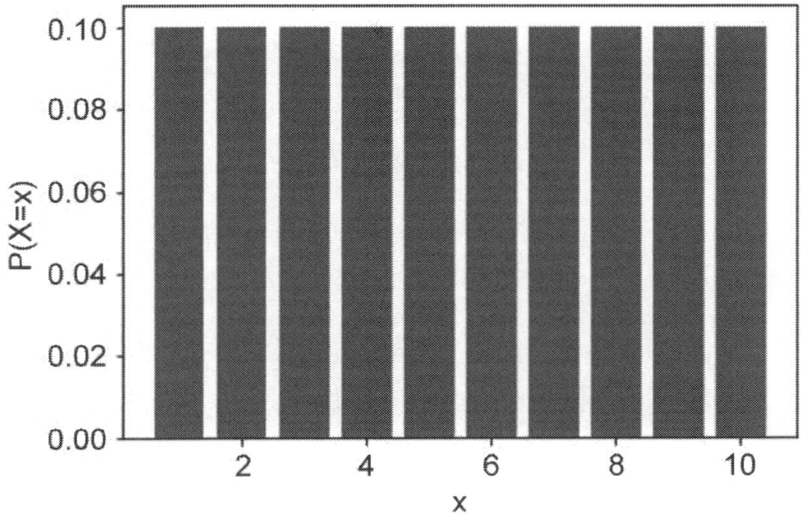

Figure 8.16: Visualizing the bar chart

In the visual output, we see that the probability of **X** being a specific whole number between 1 and 10 is equal to 1/10.

> **NOTE**
>
> Other discrete distributions you commonly see include the binomial, negative binomial, geometric, and Poisson distributions, all of which we encourage you to investigate. Type these terms into a search engine to find out more.

Distributions of continuous random variables are a bit more challenging in that we cannot calculate an exact `P(X=x)` directly because **X** lies on a continuum. We can, however, use integration to approximate probabilities between a range of values, but this is beyond the scope of this book. The relationship between **X** and probability is described using a probability density function, `P(X)`. Perhaps the most well-known continuous distribution is the normal distribution, which visually takes the form of a bell.

The normal distribution has two parameters that describe its shape, mean (μ) and variance (σ^2). The probability density function for the normal distribution is:

$$P(X) = \frac{1}{\sqrt{2\pi\sigma^2}} e^{-\frac{(x-\mu)^2}{2\sigma^2}}$$

Figure 8.17: Probability density function for the normal distribution

The following code shows two normal distributions with the same mean (μ = **0**) but different variance parameters (σ**2** = **1** and σ**2** = **2.25**). Let's first generate 100 evenly spaced values from **-10** to **10** using NumPy's **.linspace** method:

```
import numpy as np

# range of xs
x = np.linspace(-10, 10, 100)
```

We then generate the approximate **X** probabilities for both normal distributions.

Using **scipy.stats** is a good way to work with distributions, and its **pdf** method allows us to easily visualize the shape of probability density functions:

```
import scipy.stats as stats

# first normal distribution with mean = 0, variance = 1
p_X_1 = stats.norm.pdf(x=x, loc=0.0, scale=1.0**2)

# second normal distribution with mean = 0, variance = 2.25
p_X_2 = stats.norm.pdf(x=x, loc=0.0, scale=1.5**2)
```

> **NOTE**
>
> In this case, **loc** corresponds to μ, while **scale** corresponds to the standard deviation, which is the square root of σ**2**, hence why we square the inputs.

We then visualize the result. Notice that $\sigma\mathbf{2}$ controls how fat the distribution is and therefore how variable the random variable is:

```
plt.plot(x,p_X_1, color='blue')
plt.plot(x, p_X_2, color='orange')
plt.xlabel('X')
plt.ylabel('P(X)')
```

The output will be as follows:

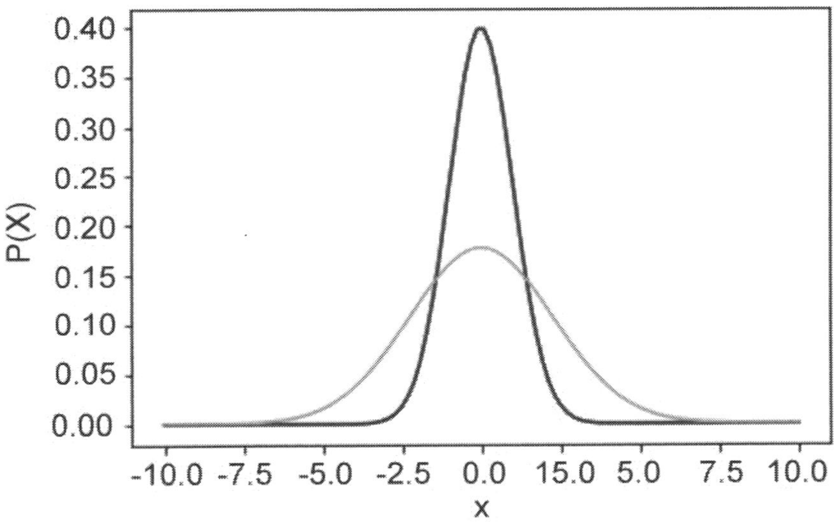

Figure 8.18: Visualizing the normal distribution

Other discrete distributions you commonly see include the gamma, exponential, and beta distributions, which we encourage you to investigate.

> **NOTE**
>
> The code for this section can be found at https://packt.live/38Mfyzm.

SIMPLE DEMONSTRATION OF THE RANDOM SEARCH PROCESS

Again, before we get to the scikit-learn implementation of random search parameter tuning, we will step through the process using simple Python tools. Up until this point, we have only been using classification problems to demonstrate tuning concepts, but now we will look at a regression problem. Can we find a model that's able to predict the progression of diabetes in patients based on characteristics such as BMI and age?

> **NOTE**
>
> The original dataset can be found at https://packt.live/2O4XN6v.
>
> The code for this section can be found at https://packt.live/3aOudvK.

We first load the data:

```
from sklearn import datasets, linear_model, model_selection

# load the data
diabetes = datasets.load_diabetes()

# target
y = diabetes.target

# features
X = diabetes.data
```

To get a feel for the data, we can examine the disease progression for the first patient:

```
# the first patient has index 0
print(y[0])
```

The output will be as follows:

```
151.0
```

Let's now examine their characteristics:

```
# let's look at the first patients data
print(dict(zip(diabetes.feature_names, X[0])))
```

We should see the following:

```
{'age': 0.0380759064334241, 'sex': 0.0506801187398187, 'bmi': 0.0616962065186885, 'bp': 0.021872354994955
8, 's1': -0.0442234984244464, 's2': -0.0348207628376986, 's3': -0.0434008456520269, 's4': -0.0025922619981
8282, 's5': 0.0199084208763183, 's6': -0.0176461251598052}
```

Figure 8.19: Dictionary for patient characteristics

For this scenario, we will try a technique called ridge regression, which will fit a linear model to the data. Ridge regression is a special method that allows us to directly employ regularization to help mitigate the problem of overfitting. Ridge regression has one key hyperparameter, α, which controls the level of regularization in the model fit. If α is set to 1, no regularization will be employed, which is actually a special case in which a ridge regression model fit will be exactly equal to the fit of an OLS' linear regression model. Increase the value of α and you increase the degree of regularization.

> **NOTE**
>
> We covered ridge regression in *Chapter 7*, *The Generalization of Machine Learning Models*.
>
> For more information on ridge regression and regularization, see https://packt.live/2NR3GUq.

In the context of random search parameter tuning, we assume α is a random variable and it is up to us to specify a likely distribution.

For this example, we will assume alpha follows a gamma distribution. This distribution takes two parameters, k and θ, which control the shape and scale of the distribution respectively.

For ridge regression, we believe the optimal α to be somewhere near 1, becoming less likely as you move away from 1. A parameterization of the gamma distribution that reflects this idea is where k and θ are both equal to 1. To visualize the form of this distribution, we can run the following:

```
import numpy as np
from scipy import stats
import matplotlib.pyplot as plt

# values of alpha
```

```
x = np.linspace(1, 20, 100)

# probabilities
p_X = stats.gamma.pdf(x=x, a=1, loc=1, scale=2)

plt.plot(x,p_X)
plt.xlabel('alpha')
plt.ylabel('P(alpha)')
```

The output will be as follows:

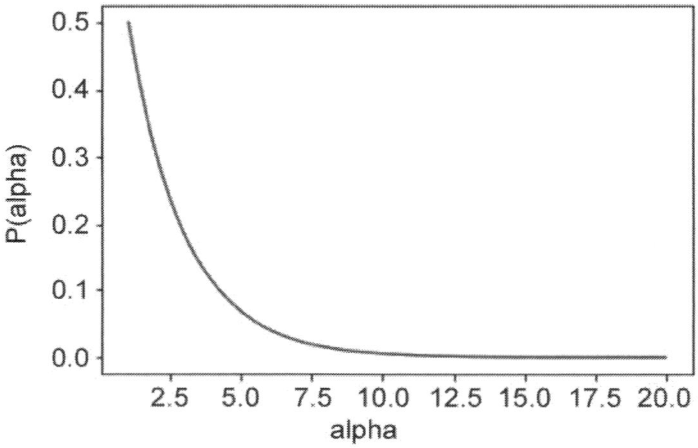

Figure 8.20: Visualization of probabilities

In the graph, you can see how probability decays sharply for smaller values of α, then decays more slowly for larger values.

The next step in the random search process is to sample n values from the chosen distribution. In this example, we will draw 100 α values. Remember that the probability of drawing out a particular value of α is related to its probability as defined by this distribution:

```
# n sample values
n_iter = 100
```

```
# sample from the gamma distribution
samples = stats.gamma.rvs(a=1, loc=1, scale=2, \
                          size=n_iter, random_state=100)
```

> **NOTE**
>
> We set a random state to ensure reproducible results.

Plotting a histogram of the sample, as shown in the following figure, reveals a shape that approximately conforms to the distribution that we have sampled from. Note that as your sample sizes increases, the more the histogram conforms to the distribution:

```
# visualize the sample distribution
plt.hist(samples)
plt.xlabel('alpha')
plt.ylabel('sample count')
```

The output will be as follows:

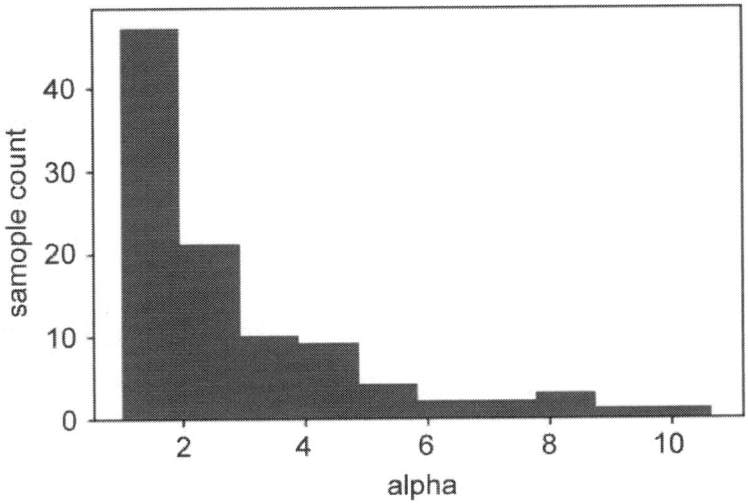

Figure 8.21: Visualization of the sample distribution

A model will then be fitted for each value of α sampled and assessed for performance. As we have seen with the other approaches to hyperparameter tuning in this chapter, performance will be assessed using k-fold cross-validation (with **k =10**) but because we are dealing with a regression problem, the performance metric will be the test-set negative MSE.

Using this metric means larger values are better. We will store the results in a dictionary with each α value as the key and the corresponding cross-validated negative MSE as the value:

```
# we will store the results inside a dictionary
result = {}

# for each sample
for sample in samples:
    """
    initialize a ridge regression estimator with alpha set
    to the sample value
    """
    reg = linear_model.Ridge(alpha=sample)
    """
    conduct a 10-fold cross validation scoring on
    negative mean squared error
    """
    cv = model_selection.cross_val_score\
         (reg, X, y, cv=10, \
          scoring='neg_mean_squared_error')
    # retain the result in the dictionary
    result[sample] = [cv.mean()]
```

Instead of examining the raw dictionary of results, we will convert it to a pandas DataFrame, transpose it, and give the columns names. Sorting by descending negative mean squared error reveals that the optimal level of regularization for this problem is actually when α is approximately 1, meaning that we did not find evidence to suggest regularization is necessary for this problem and that the OLS linear model will suffice:

```
import pandas as pd
"""
convert the result dictionary to a pandas dataframe,
transpose and reset the index
"""
```

```
df_result = pd.DataFrame(result).T.reset_index()

# give the columns sensible names
df_result.columns = ['alpha', 'mean_neg_mean_squared_error']

print(df_result.sort_values('mean_neg_mean_squared_error', \
                            ascending=False).head())
```

The output will be as follows:

```
       alpha  mean_neg_mean_squared_error
4   1.009460                 -3368.572167
26  1.011409                 -3369.403727
29  1.030745                 -3377.629026
43  1.041302                 -3382.102466
34  1.074316                 -3396.012056
```

Figure 8.22: Output for the random search process

> **NOTE**
>
> The results will be different, depending on the data used.

It is always beneficial to visualize results where possible. Plotting α by negative mean squared error as a scatter plot makes it clear that venturing away from $\alpha = 1$ does not result in improvements in predictive performance:

```
plt.scatter(df_result.alpha, \
            df_result.mean_neg_mean_squared_error)
plt.xlabel('alpha')
plt.ylabel('-MSE')
```

The output will be as follows:

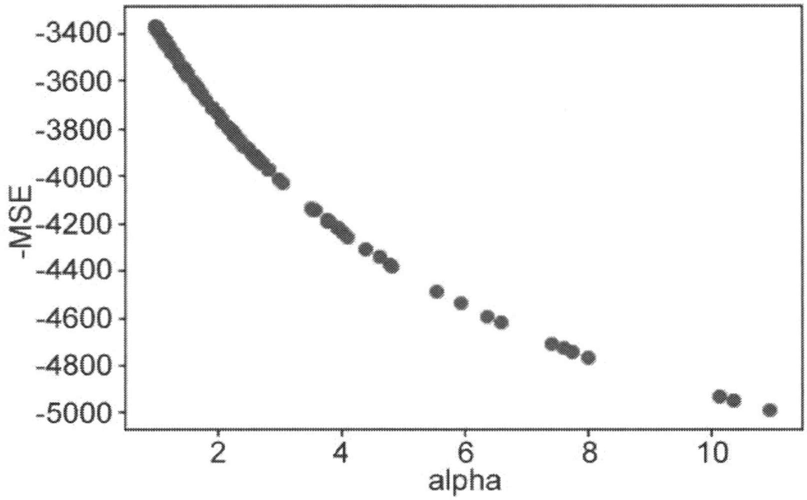

Figure 8.23: Plotting the scatter plot

The fact that we found the optimal α to be 1 (its default value) is a special case in hyperparameter tuning in that the optimal hyperparameterization is the default one.

TUNING USING RANDOMIZEDSEARCHCV

In practice, we can use the **RandomizedSearchCV** method inside scikit-learn's **model_selection** module to conduct the search. All you need to do is pass in your estimator, the hyperparameters you wish to tune along with their distributions, the number of samples you would like to sample from each distribution, and the metric by which you would like to assess model performance. These correspond to the **param_distributions**, **n_iter**, and **scoring** arguments respectively. For the sake of demonstration, let's conduct the search we completed earlier using **RandomizedSearchCV**. First, we load the data and initialize our ridge regression estimator:

```
from sklearn import datasets, model_selection, linear_model

# load the data
diabetes = datasets.load_diabetes()

# target
y = diabetes.target
```

```
# features
X = diabetes.data

# initialise the ridge regression
reg = linear_model.Ridge()
```

We then specify that the hyperparameter we would like to tune is **alpha** and that we would like α to be distributed **gamma**, with **k = 1** and θ **= 1**:

```
from scipy import stats

# alpha ~ gamma(1,1)
param_dist = {'alpha': stats.gamma(a=1, loc=1, scale=2)}
```

Next, we set up and run the random search process, which will sample 100 values from our **gamma(1,1)** distribution, fit the ridge regression, and evaluate its performance using cross-validation scored on the negative mean squared error metric:

```
"""
set up the random search to sample 100 values and
score on negative mean squared error
"""
rscv = model_selection.RandomizedSearchCV\
       (estimator=reg, param_distributions=param_dist, \
        n_iter=100, scoring='neg_mean_squared_error')

# start the search
rscv.fit(X,y)
```

After completing the search, we can extract the results and generate a pandas DataFrame, as we have done previously. Sorting by **rank_test_score** and viewing the first five rows aligns with our conclusion that alpha should be set to 1 and regularization does not seem to be required for this problem:

```
import pandas as pd

# convert the results dictionary to a pandas data frame
results = pd.DataFrame(rscv.cv_results_)

# show the top 5 hyperparamaterizations
print(results.loc[:,['params','rank_test_score']]\
      .sort_values('rank_test_score').head(5))
```

The output will be as follows:

```
                                  params  rank_test_score
47   {'alpha': 1.082807253775902}                      1
72  {'alpha': 1.0996845885124735}                      2
18  {'alpha': 1.1006233499723193}                      3
52  {'alpha': 1.1012596885127424}                      4
59  {'alpha': 1.1267717423087455}                      5
```

Figure 8.24: Output for tuning using RandomizedSearchCV

> **NOTE**
>
> The preceding results may vary, depending on the data.

EXERCISE 8.03: RANDOM SEARCH HYPERPARAMETER TUNING FOR A RANDOM FOREST CLASSIFIER

In this exercise, we will revisit the handwritten digit classification problem, this time using a random forest classifier with hyperparameters tuned using a random search strategy. The random forest is a popular method used for both single-class and multi-class classification problems. It learns by growing **`n`** simple tree models that each progressively split the dataset into areas that best separate the points of different classes.

The final model produced can be thought of as the average of each of the n tree models. In this way, the random forest is an **`ensemble`** method. The parameters we will tune in this exercise are **`criterion`** and **`max_features`**.

`criterion` refers to the way in which each split is evaluated from a class purity perspective (the purer the splits, the better) and **`max_features`** is the maximum number of features the random forest can use when finding the best splits.

The following steps will help you complete the exercise.

1. Create a new notebook in Google Colab.
2. Import the data and isolate the features **X** and the target **y**:

```
from sklearn import datasets

# import data
digits = datasets.load_digits()

# target
y = digits.target

# features
X = digits.data
```

3. Initialize the random forest classifier estimator. We will set the **n_estimators** hyperparameter to **100**, which means the predictions of the final model will essentially be an average of **100** simple tree models. Note the use of a random state to ensure the reproducibility of results:

```
from sklearn import ensemble

# an ensemble of 100 estimators
rfc = ensemble.RandomForestClassifier(n_estimators=100, \
                                      random_state=100)
```

4. One of the parameters we will be tuning is **max_features**. Let's find out the maximum value this could take:

```
# how many features do we have in our dataset?
n_features = X.shape[1]

print(n_features)
```

You should see that we have 64 features:

```
64
```

Now that we know the maximum value of **max_features** we are free to define our hyperparameter inputs to the randomized search process. At this point, we have no reason to believe any particular value of **max_features** is more optimal.

5. Set a discrete uniform distribution covering the range **`1`** to **`64`**. Remember the probability mass function, **`P(X=x) = 1/n`**, for this distribution, so **`P(X=x) = 1/64`** in our case. Because **`criterion`** has only two discrete options, this will also be sampled as a discrete uniform distribution with **`P(X=x) = ½`**:

```
from scipy import stats

"""
we would like to smaple from criterion and
max_features as discrete uniform distributions
"""
param_dist = {'criterion': ['gini', 'entropy'],\
              'max_features': stats.randint(low=1, \
                                            high=n_features)}
```

6. We now have everything we need to set up the randomized search process. As before, we will use accuracy as the metric of model evaluation. Note the use of a random state:

```
from sklearn import model_selection
"""
setting up the random search sampling 50 times and
conducting 5-fold cross-validation
"""
rscv = model_selection.RandomizedSearchCV\
       (estimator=rfc, param_distributions=param_dist, \
        n_iter=50, cv=5, scoring='accuracy' , random_state=100)
```

7. Let's kick off the process with the. **`fit`** method. Please note that both fitting random forests and cross-validation are computationally expensive processes due to their internal processes of iteration. Generating a result may take some time:

```
# start the process
rscv.fit(X,y)
```

You should see the following:

```
RandomizedSearchCV(cv=5, error_score='raise-deprecating',
                   estimator=RandomForestClassifier(bootstrap=True,
                                                    class_weight=None,
                                                    criterion='gini',
                                                    max_depth=None,
                                                    max_features='auto',
                                                    max_leaf_nodes=None,
                                                    min_impurity_decrease=0.0,
                                                    min_impurity_split=None,
                                                    min_samples_leaf=1,
                                                    min_samples_split=2,
                                                    min_weight_fraction_leaf=0.0,
                                                    n_estimators=100,
                                                    n_jobs=None,
                                                    oob_score=False,
                                                    random_state=100, verbose=0,
                                                    warm_start=False),
                   iid='warn', n_iter=50, n_jobs=None,
                   param_distributions={'criterion': ['gini', 'entropy'],
                                        'max_features': <scipy.stats._distn_infrastructure.rv_frozen
object at 0x7f1f8d772e10>},
                   pre_dispatch='2*n_jobs', random_state=100, refit=True,
                   return_train_score=False, scoring='accuracy', verbose=0)
```

Figure 8.25: RandomizedSearchCV results

8. Next, you need to examine the results. Create a **pandas** DataFrame from the **results** attribute, order by the **rank_test_score**, and look at the top five model hyperparameterizations. Note that because the random search draws samples of hyperparameterizations at random, it is possible to have duplication. We remove the duplicate entries from the DataFrame:

```
import pandas as pd

# convert the dictionary of results to a pandas dataframe
results = pd.DataFrame(rscv.cv_results_)

# removing duplication
distinct_results = results.loc[:,['params',\
                                  'mean_test_score']]

# convert the params dictionaries to string data types
distinct_results.loc[:,'params'] = distinct_results.loc\
                                   [:,'params'].astype('str')
```

```
# remove duplicates
distinct_results.drop_duplicates(inplace=True)

# look at the top 5 best hyperparamaterizations
distinct_results.sort_values('mean_test_score', \
                             ascending=False).head(5)
```

You should get the following output:

```
                                           params  mean_test_score
3     {'criterion': 'gini', 'max_features': 11}          0.940470
48     {'criterion': 'gini', 'max_features': 4}          0.939913
19     {'criterion': 'gini', 'max_features': 5}          0.937700
14     {'criterion': 'gini', 'max_features': 3}          0.937694
21  {'criterion': 'entropy', 'max_features': 8}          0.936582
```

Figure 8.26: Top five hyperparameterizations

> **NOTE**
>
> You may get slightly different results. However, the values you obtain should largely agree with those in the preceding output.

9. The last step is to visualize the result. Including every parameterization will result in a cluttered plot, so we will filter on parameterizations that resulted in a mean test score > 0.93:

```
# top performing models
distinct_results[distinct_results.mean_test_score > 0.93]\
                 .sort_values('mean_test_score')\
                 .plot.barh(x='params', xlim=(0.9))
```

The output will be as follows:

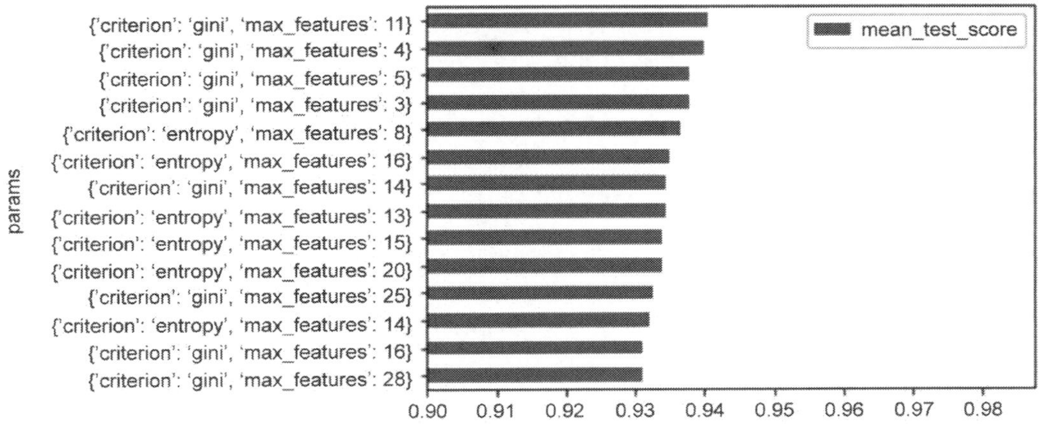

Figure 8.27: Visualizing the test scores of the top-performing models

> **NOTE**
>
> To access the source code for this specific section, please refer to https://packt.live/2uDVct8.
>
> You can also run this example online at https://packt.live/3gbQMvw.

We have found the best hyperparameterization to be a random forest classifier using the **`gini`** criterion with the maximum features set to 4.

ADVANTAGES AND DISADVANTAGES OF A RANDOM SEARCH

Because a random search takes a finite sample from a range of possible hyperparameterizations (**`n_iter`** in **`model_selection.RandomizedSearchCV`**), it is feasible to expand the range of your hyperparameter search beyond what would be practical with a grid search. This is because a grid search has to try everything in the range, and setting a large range of values may be too slow to process. Searching this wider range gives you the chance of discovering a truly optimal solution.

Compared to the manual and grid search strategies, you do sacrifice a level of control to obtain this benefit. The other consideration is that setting up random search is a bit more involved than other options in that you have to specify distributions. There is always a chance of getting this wrong. That said, if you are unsure about what distributions to use, stick with discrete or continuous uniform for the respective variable types as this will assign an equal probability of selection to all options.

ACTIVITY 8.01: IS THE MUSHROOM POISONOUS?

Imagine you are a data scientist working for the biology department at your local university. Your colleague who is a mycologist (a biologist who specializes in fungi) has requested that you help her develop a machine learning model capable of discerning whether a particular mushroom species is poisonous or not given attributes relating to its appearance.

The objective of this activity is to employ the grid and randomized search strategies to find an optimal model for this purpose.

> **NOTE**
>
> The dataset to be used in this exercise can be found on our GitHub repository at https://packt.live/38zdhaB.
>
> Details on the attributes of the dataset can be found on the original dataset site: https://packt.live/36j0jfA.

1. Load the data into Python using the **pandas.read_csv()** method, calling the object **mushrooms**.

   Hint: The dataset is in CSV format and has no header. Set **header=None** in **pandas.read_csv()**.

2. Separate the target, **y** and features, **X** from the dataset.

   Hint: The target can be found in the first column (**mushrooms.iloc[:,0]**) and the features in the remaining columns (**mushrooms.iloc[:,1:]**).

3. Recode the target, **y**, so that poisonous mushrooms are represented as **1** and edible mushrooms as **0**.

4. Transform the columns of the feature set **X** into a **numpy** array with a binary representation. This is known as one-hot encoding.

   Hint: Use **preprocessing.OneHotEncoder()** to transform **X**.

5. Conduct both a grid and random search to find an optimal hyperparameterization for a random forest classifier. Use accuracy as your method of model evaluation. Make sure that when you initialize the classifier and when you conduct your random search, **random_state = 100**.

   For the grid search, use the following:

```
{'criterion': ['gini', 'entropy'],\
 'max_features': [2, 4, 6, 8, 10, 12, 14]}
```

   For the randomized search, use the following:

```
{'criterion': ['gini', 'entropy'],\
 'max_features': stats.randint(low=1, high=max_features)}
```

6. Plot the mean test score versus hyperparameterization for the top 10 models found using random search.

   You should see a plot similar to the following:

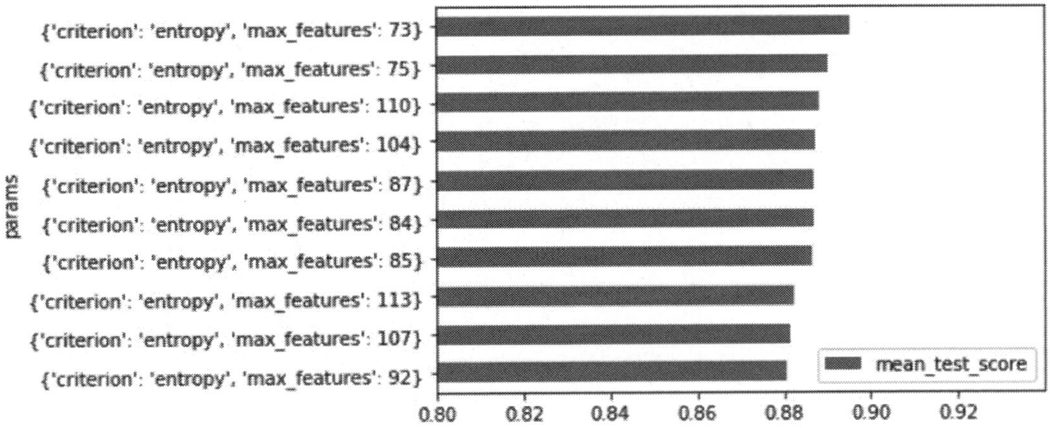

Figure 8.28: Mean test score plot

> **NOTE**
>
> The solution to the activity can be found here: https://packt.live/2GbJloz.

SUMMARY

In this chapter, we have covered three strategies for hyperparameter tuning based on searching for estimator hyperparameterizations that improve performance.

The manual search is the most hands-on of the three but gives you a unique feel for the process. It is suitable for situations where the estimator in question is simple (a low number of hyperparameters).

The grid search is an automated method that is the most systematic of the three but can be very computationally intensive to run when the range of possible hyperparameterizations increases.

The random search, while the most complicated to set up, is based on sampling from distributions of hyperparameters, which allows you to expand the search range, thereby giving you the chance to discover a good solution that you may miss with the grid or manual search options.

In the next chapter, we will be looking at how to visualize results, summarize models, and articulate feature importance and weights.

9

INTERPRETING A MACHINE LEARNING MODEL

OVERVIEW

This chapter will show you how to interpret a machine learning model's results and get deeper insights into the patterns it found. By the end of the chapter, you will be able to analyze weights from linear models and variable importance for **`RandomForest`**. You will be able to implement variable importance via permutation to analyze feature importance. You will use a partial dependence plot to analyze single variables and make use of the lime package for local interpretation.

INTRODUCTION

In the previous chapter, you saw how to find the optimal hyperparameters of some of the most popular machine learning algorithms in order to get better predictive performance (that is, more accurate predictions).

Machine learning algorithms are always referred to as black box where we can only see the inputs and outputs and the implementation inside the algorithm is quite opaque, so people don't know what is happening inside.

With each day that passes, we can sense the elevated need for more transparency in machine learning models. In the last few years, we have seen some cases where algorithms have been accused of discriminating against groups of people. For instance, a few years ago, a not-for-profit news organization called ProPublica highlighted bias in the COMPAS algorithm, built by the Northpointe company. The objective of the algorithm is to assess the likelihood of re-offending for a criminal. It was shown that the algorithm was predicting a higher level of risk for specific groups of people based on their demographics rather than other features. This example highlighted the importance of interpreting the results of your model and its logic properly and clearly.

Luckily, some machine learning algorithms provide methods to understand the parameters they learned for a given task and dataset. There are also some functions that are model-agnostic and can help us to better understand the predictions made. So, there are different techniques that are either model-specific or model-agnostic for interpreting a model.

These techniques can also differ in their scope. In the literature, we either have a global or local interpretation. A global interpretation means we are looking at the variables for all observations from a dataset and we want to understand which features have the biggest overall influence on the target variable. For instance, if you are predicting customer churn for a telco company, you may find the most important features for your model are customer usage and the average monthly amount paid. Local interpretation, on the other hand, focuses only on a single observation and analyzes the impact of the different variables. We will look at a single specific case and see what led the model to make its final prediction. For example, you will look at a specific customer who is predicted to churn and will discover that they usually buy the new iPhone model every year, in September.

In this chapter, we will go through some techniques on how to interpret your models or their results.

LINEAR MODEL COEFFICIENTS

In *Chapter 2, Regression*, and *Chapter 3, Binary Classification*, you saw that linear regression models learn function parameters in the form of the following:

$$\hat{y} = f\,(X) = \mathrm{w}_0 + \mathrm{w}_1 * x_1 + \mathrm{w}_2 * x_2 + \ldots + \mathrm{w}_\mathrm{n} * x_n$$

Figure 9.1: Function parameters for linear regression models

The objective is to find the best parameters (w_1, w_2 ..., w_n) that will get the predictions, $\hat{y}$, very close to the actual target values, **y**. So, once you have trained your model and are getting good predictive performance without much overfitting, you can use these parameters (or coefficients) to understand which variables largely impacted the predictions. If a coefficient is close to 0, this means the related feature didn't impact much the outcome. On the other hand, if it is quite high (positively or negatively), it means its feature is influencing the prediction outcome vastly.

Let's take the example of the following function: $\mathbf{100 + 0.2 * x_1 + 200 * x_2 - 180 * x_3}$. The coefficient of x_1 is only **0.2**. It is quite low compared to the other ones. It doesn't have much impact on the final outcome. The coefficient of x_2 is positive, so it will positively impact the prediction. It is the opposite of the x_3 coefficient because the x_3 coefficient is negative.

But to be able to compare apples versus apples, you need to rescale the features so that they have the same scale so you can compare their coefficients. If not, then maybe x_1 ranges from 1 million to 5 million, while x_2 and x_3 are between **1** and **88**. In this case, even though the x_1 coefficient is small, a small change in the x_1 value has a drastic impact on the prediction. On the other hand, if all 3 coefficients are between -1 and 1, then we can say the key drivers in predicting the target variable are the features x_2 and x_3.

In **sklearn**, it is extremely easy to get the coefficient of a linear model; you just need to call the **coef_** attribute. Let's implement this on a real example with the Diabetes dataset from **sklearn**:

```
from sklearn.datasets import load_diabetes
from sklearn.linear_model import LinearRegression
data = load_diabetes()

# fit a linear regression model to the data
lr_model = LinearRegression()
lr_model.fit(data.data, data.target)
lr_model.coef_
```

The output will be as follows:

```
array([ -10.01219782, -239.81908937,  519.83978679,  324.39042769,
       -792.18416163,  476.74583782,  101.04457032,  177.06417623,
        751.27932109,   67.62538639])
```

Figure 9.2: Coefficients of the linear regression parameters

Let's create a DataFrame with these values and column names:

```
import pandas as pd
coeff_df = pd.DataFrame()
coeff_df['feature'] = data.feature_names
coeff_df['coefficient'] = lr_model.coef_
coeff_df.head()
```

The output will be as follows:

	feature	coefficient
0	age	-10.012198
1	sex	-239.819089
2	bmi	519.839787
3	bp	324.390428
4	s1	-792.184162

Figure 9.3: Coefficients of the linear regression model

A large positive or a large negative number for a feature coefficient means it has a strong influence on the outcome. On the other hand, if the coefficient is close to 0, this means the variable does not have much impact on the prediction.

From this table, we can see that column **`s1`** has a very low coefficient (a large negative number) so it negatively influences the final prediction. If **`s1`** increases by a unit of 1, the prediction value will decrease by **`-792.184162`**. On the other hand, **`bmi`** has a large positive number (**`519.839787`**) on the prediction, so the risk of diabetes is highly linked to this feature: an increase in body mass index (BMI) means a significant increase in the risk of diabetes.

EXERCISE 9.01: EXTRACTING THE LINEAR REGRESSION COEFFICIENT

In this exercise, we will train a linear regression model to predict the customer drop-out ratio and extract its coefficients.

> **NOTE**
>
> The dataset we will be using is shared by Carl Rasmussen from the University of Toronto: https://packt.live/37hInDr.
>
> This dataset was synthetically generated from a simulation for predicting the fraction of bank customers who leave a bank because of long queues.
>
> The CSV version of this dataset can be found here: https://packt.live/3kZrggU.
>
> A data dictionary presenting the variables in this dataset can be found here:
>
> https://packt.live/3aBGhQD.

The following steps will help you complete the exercise:

1. Open a new Colab notebook.
2. Import the following packages: **pandas**, **train_test_split** from **sklearn.model_selection**, **StandardScaler** from **sklearn.preprocessing**, **LinearRegression** from **sklearn.linear_model**, **mean_squared_error** from **sklearn.metrics**, and **altair**:

```
import pandas as pd
from sklearn.model_selection import train_test_split
from sklearn.preprocessing import StandardScaler
from sklearn.linear_model import LinearRegression
from sklearn.metrics import mean_squared_error
import altair as alt
```

3. Create a variable called **file_url** that contains the URL to the dataset:

```
file_url = 'https://raw.githubusercontent.com/'\
           'PacktWorkshops/The-Data-Science-Workshop/'\
           'master/Chapter09/Dataset/phpYYZ4Qc.csv'
```

4. Load the dataset into a DataFrame called **df** using **.read_csv()**:

```
df = pd.read_csv(file_url)
```

5. Print the first five rows of the DataFrame:

```
df.head()
```

You should get the following output:

	a1cx	a1cy	a1sx	a1sy	a1rho	a1pop	a2cx
0	0.413010	0.607442	0.332608	0.406812	-0.151224	1.525222	-0.144368
1	-0.602384	0.350618	0.429196	0.414476	-0.124489	4.597991	0.579458
2	-0.322881	-0.538491	1.602260	0.039605	0.196023	1.909005	-0.675672
3	-0.233570	-0.936451	1.710192	2.179527	0.438461	4.742055	-0.163625
4	0.403126	0.313367	0.822382	1.393975	0.253435	9.398630	0.312528

Figure 9.4: First five rows of the loaded DataFrame

> **NOTE**
>
> The output has been truncated for presentation purposes. Please refer https://packt.live/3kZrggU for complete output.

6. Extract the **rej** column using **.pop()** and save it into a variable called **y**:

```
y = df.pop('rej')
```

7. Print the summary of the DataFrame using **.describe()**.

```
df.describe()
```

You should get the following output:

	a1cx	a1cy	a1sx	a1sy	a1rho
count	8192.000000	8192.000000	8192.000000	8192.000000	8192.000000
mean	-0.003230	-0.000939	1.011966	1.004934	-0.001786
std	0.579124	0.577033	1.027579	1.001369	0.288346
min	-0.999409	-0.999864	0.000191	0.000055	-0.499944
25%	-0.499372	-0.500793	0.293154	0.283420	-0.253597
50%	-0.013944	0.001390	0.692698	0.690240	-0.001311
75%	0.506926	0.494132	1.394602	1.398254	0.246830
max	0.999881	0.999828	10.303770	8.856675	0.499937

Figure 9.5: Statistical measures of the DataFrame

> **NOTE**
>
> The preceding figure is a truncated version of the output.

From this output, we can see the data is not standardized. The variables have different scales.

8. Split the DataFrame into training and testing sets using **train_test_split()** with **test_size=0.3** and **random_state = 1**:

```
X_train, X_test, y_train, y_test = train_test_split\
                                   (df, y, test_size=0.3, \
                                    random_state=1)
```

9. Instantiate **StandardScaler**:

```
scaler = StandardScaler()
```

10. Train **StandardScaler** on the training set and standardize it using **.fit_transform()**:

```
X_train = scaler.fit_transform(X_train)
```

11. Standardize the testing set using **`.transform()`**:

```
X_test = scaler.transform(X_test)
```

12. Instantiate **`LinearRegression`** and save it to a variable called **`lr_model`**:

```
lr_model = LinearRegression()
```

13. Train the model on the training set using **`.fit()`**:

```
lr_model.fit(X_train, y_train)
```

You should get the following output:

```
LinearRegression(copy_X=True, fit_intercept=True, n_jobs=None, normalize=False)
```

Figure 9.6: Logs of LinearRegression

14. Predict the outcomes of the training and testing sets using **`.predict()`**:

```
preds_train = lr_model.predict(X_train)
preds_test = lr_model.predict(X_test)
```

15. Calculate the mean squared error on the training set and print its value:

```
train_mse = mean_squared_error(y_train, preds_train)
train_mse
```

You should get the following output:

```
0.007062801218218886
```

Figure 9.7: MSE score of the training set

We achieved quite a low MSE score on the training set.

16. Calculate the mean squared error on the testing set and print its value:

```
test_mse = mean_squared_error(y_test, preds_test)
test_mse
```

You should get the following output:

```
0.006571073840504757
```

Figure 9.8: MSE score of the testing set

We also have a low MSE score on the testing set that is very similar to the training one. So, our model is not overfitting.

> **NOTE**
>
> You may get slightly different outputs than those present here. However, the values you would obtain should largely agree with those obtained in this exercise.

17. Print the coefficients of the linear regression model using **.coef_**:

```
lr_model.coef_
```

You should get the following output:

```
array([-4.94784409e-04, -9.33729668e-04, -2.81877324e-03, -3.29306515e-03,
        5.93297658e-05,  4.02235021e-02,  1.98044098e-03, -3.39452179e-04,
       -5.44949336e-03, -4.82500415e-03,  8.22897305e-05,  6.24226133e-02,
       -2.66390121e-04,  5.69511279e-04, -2.30657474e-03, -2.51428876e-03,
       -1.31637908e-03,  3.96978126e-02, -1.05127088e-02,  3.02116023e-04,
       -3.89728413e-04,  3.57359816e-03, -1.43282556e-02, -1.13460794e-03,
       -1.02515456e-03,  5.50201521e-03, -4.02044201e-03, -1.15164578e-03,
        2.15908520e-04,  5.59779791e-03, -2.42464365e-03, -1.75240320e-02])
```

Figure 9.9: Coefficients of the linear regression model

18. Create an empty DataFrame called **coef_df**:

```
coef_df = pd.DataFrame()
```

19. Create a new column called **feature** for this DataFrame with the name of the columns of **df** using **.columns**:

```
coef_df['feature'] = df.columns
```

20. Create a new column called **coefficient** for this DataFrame with the coefficients of the linear regression model using **.coef_**:

```
coef_df['coefficient'] = lr_model.coef_
```

21. Print the first five rows of **coef_df**:

```
coef_df.head()
```

You should get the following output:

	feature	coefficient
0	a1cx	-0.000495
1	a1cy	-0.000934
2	a1sx	-0.002819
3	a1sy	-0.003293
4	a1rho	0.000059

Figure 9.10: The first five rows of coef_df

From this output, we can see the variables **a1sx** and **a1sy** have the lowest value (the biggest negative value) so they are contributing more to the prediction than the three other variables shown here.

22. Plot a bar chart with Altair using **coef_df** and **coefficient** as the **x** axis and **feature** as the **y** axis:

```
alt.Chart(coef_df).mark_bar().encode(x='coefficient',\
                                     y="feature")
```

You should get the following output:

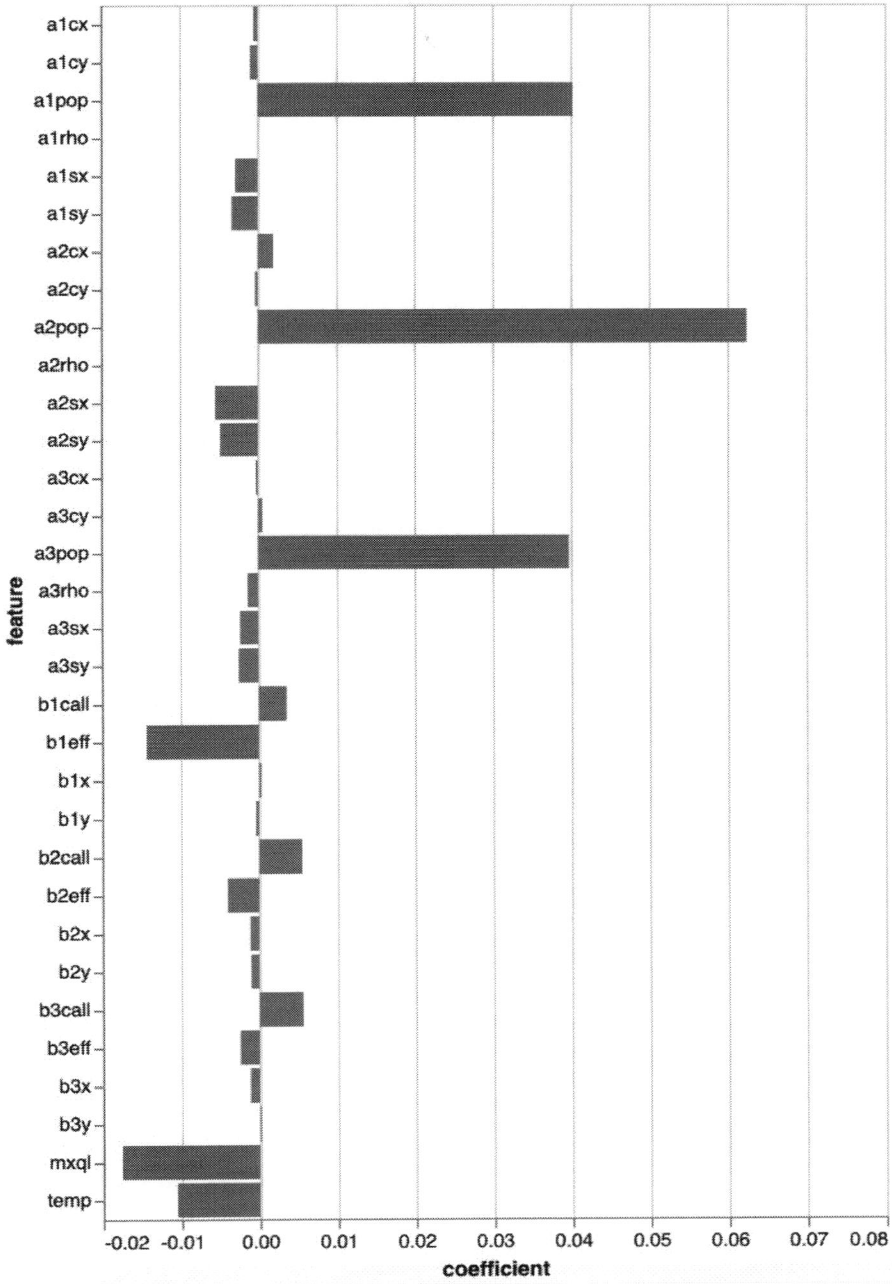

Figure 9.11: Graph showing the coefficients of the linear regression model

From this output, we can see the variables that impacted the prediction the most were:

- **a2pop**, which corresponds to the population of area 2
- **a1pop**, which corresponds to the population of area 1
- **a3pop**, which corresponds to the population of area 3
- **mxql**, which is the maximum length of the queues
- **b1eff**, which is the level of efficiency of bank 1
- **temp**, which is the temperature

The first three variables impacted the outcome positively (increasing the target variable value). This means as the population grows in any of the three areas, the chance of customer churn increases. On the other hand, the last three features negatively impacted the target variable (decreasing the target variable value): if the maximum length, bank-1 efficiency level, or temperature increases, the risk of customers leaving decreases.

> **NOTE**
>
> To access the source code for this specific section, please refer to https://packt.live/3kZrggU.
>
> This section does not currently have an online interactive example, but can be run as usual on Google Colab.

In this exercise, you learned how to extract the coefficients learned by a linear regression model and identified which variables make the biggest contribution to the prediction.

RANDOMFOREST VARIABLE IMPORTANCE

Chapter 4, Multiclass Classification with RandomForest, introduced you to a very powerful tree-based algorithm: **RandomForest**. It is one of the most popular algorithms in the industry, not only because it achieves very good results in terms of prediction but also for the fact that it provides several tools for interpreting it, such as variable importance.

Remember from *Chapter 4, Multiclass Classification with RandomForest*, that **RandomForest** builds multiple independent trees and then averages their results to make a final prediction. We also learned that it creates nodes in each tree to find the best split that will clearly separate the observations into two groups. **RandomForest** uses different measures to find the best split. In **sklearn**, you can either use the Gini or Entropy measure for the classification task and MSE or MAE for regression. Without going into the details of each of them, these measures calculate the level of impurity of a given split. This level of impurity looks at how different the observations are from each other within a node. For instance, if a group has all the same values within a feature, it will have a high level of purity. On the other hand, if the group has a lot of different values, it will have a high level of impurity.

Each sub-tree built will decrease this impurity score. So, we can use this impurity score to assess the importance of each variable for the final prediction. This technique is not specific to **RandomForest** only; it can be applied to any tree-based algorithm, such as decision tree or gradient-boosted tree.

After training **RandomForest**, you can assess its variable importance (or feature importance) with the **feature_importances_** attribute.

Let's see how to extract this information from the Breast Cancer dataset from **sklearn**:

```
from sklearn.datasets import load_breast_cancer
from sklearn.ensemble import RandomForestClassifier
data = load_breast_cancer()
X, y = data.data, data.target
rf_model = RandomForestClassifier(random_state=168)
rf_model.fit(X, y)
rf_model.feature_importances_
```

The output will be as shown in the following figure:

```
array([0.03854056, 0.02053266, 0.04877917, 0.06475535, 0.00611284,
       0.00627651, 0.06487147, 0.10810024, 0.0037876 , 0.00390689,
       0.01179614, 0.00535536, 0.0040302 , 0.03232201, 0.00470869,
       0.00466341, 0.00708819, 0.00341199, 0.00282266, 0.00505392,
       0.11991176, 0.01938264, 0.10187395, 0.10452031, 0.01187623,
       0.01984074, 0.03877298, 0.12437077, 0.0055569 , 0.00697787])
```

Figure 9.12: Feature importance of a Random Forest model

> **NOTE**
>
> Due to randomization, you may get a slightly different result.

It might be a little difficult to evaluate which importance value corresponds to which variable from this output. Let's create a DataFrame that will contain these values with the name of the columns:

```
import pandas as pd
varimp_df = pd.DataFrame()
varimp_df['feature'] = data.feature_names
varimp_df['importance'] = rf_model.feature_importances_
varimp_df.head()
```

The output will be as follows:

	feature	importance
0	mean radius	0.073053
1	mean texture	0.041600
2	mean perimeter	0.075311
3	mean area	0.059660
4	mean smoothness	0.002494

Figure 9.13: RandomForest variable importance for the first five features of the Breast Cancer dataset

From this output, we can see that **`mean radius`** and **`mean perimeter`** have the highest scores, which means they are the most important in predicting the target variable. The **`mean smoothness`** column has a very low value, so it seems it doesn't influence the model much to predict the output.

> **NOTE**
>
> The range of values of variable importance is different for datasets; it is not a standardized measure.

Let's plot these variable importance values onto a graph using **altair**:

```
import altair as alt
alt.Chart(varimp_df).mark_bar().encode(x='importance',\
                                        y="feature")
```

The output will be as follows:

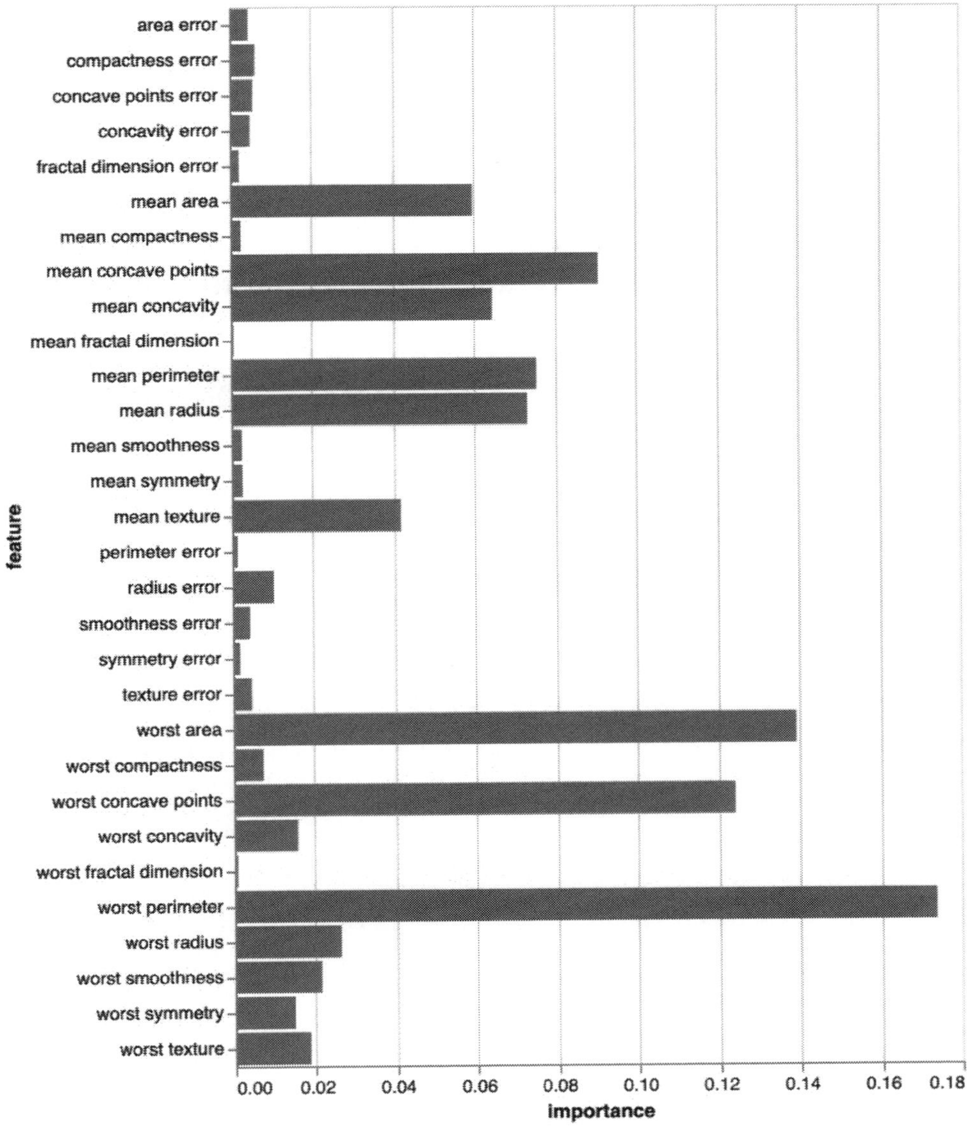

Figure 9.14: Graph showing RandomForest variable importance

From this graph, we can see the most important features for this Random Forest model are **worst perimeter**, **worst area**, and **worst concave points**. So now we know these features are the most important ones in predicting whether a tumor is benign or malignant for this Random Forest model.

EXERCISE 9.02: EXTRACTING RANDOMFOREST FEATURE IMPORTANCE

In this exercise, we will extract the feature importance of a Random Forest classifier model trained to predict the customer drop-out ratio.

We will be using the same dataset as in the previous exercise.

The following steps will help you complete the exercise:

1. Open a new Colab notebook.
2. Import the following packages: **pandas**, **train_test_split** from **sklearn.model_selection**, and **RandomForestRegressor** from **sklearn.ensemble**:

```
import pandas as pd
from sklearn.model_selection import train_test_split
from sklearn.ensemble import RandomForestRegressor
from sklearn.metrics import mean_squared_error
import altair as alt
```

3. Create a variable called **file_url** that contains the URL to the dataset:

```
file_url = 'https://raw.githubusercontent.com/'\
           'PacktWorkshops/The-Data-Science-Workshop/'\
           'master/Chapter09/Dataset/phpYYZ4Qc.csv'
```

4. Load the dataset into a DataFrame called **df** using **.read_csv()**:

```
df = pd.read_csv(file_url)
```

5. Extract the **rej** column using **.pop()** and save it into a variable called **y**:

```
y = df.pop('rej')
```

6. Split the DataFrame into training and testing sets using **train_test_split()** with **test_size=0.3** and **random_state = 1**:

```
X_train, X_test, y_train, y_test = train_test_split\
                                    (df, y, test_size=0.3, \
                                     random_state=1)
```

7. Instantiate **RandomForestRegressor** with **random_state=1**, **n_estimators=50**, **max_depth=6**, and **min_samples_leaf=60**:

```
rf_model = RandomForestRegressor(random_state=1, \
                                 n_estimators=50, max_depth=6,\
                                 min_samples_leaf=60)
```

8. Train the model on the training set using **.fit()**:

```
rf_model.fit(X_train, y_train)
```

You should get the following output:

```
RandomForestRegressor(bootstrap=True, criterion='mse', max_depth=6,
                      max_features='auto', max_leaf_nodes=None,
                      min_impurity_decrease=0.0, min_impurity_split=None,
                      min_samples_leaf=60, min_samples_split=2,
                      min_weight_fraction_leaf=0.0, n_estimators=50,
                      n_jobs=None, oob_score=False, random_state=1, verbose=0,
                      warm_start=False)
```

Figure 9.15: Logs of the Random Forest model

9. Predict the outcomes of the training and testing sets using **.predict()**:

```
preds_train = rf_model.predict(X_train)
preds_test = rf_model.predict(X_test)
```

10. Calculate the mean squared error on the training set and print its value:

```
train_mse = mean_squared_error(y_train, preds_train)
train_mse
```

You should get the following output:

```
0.007315982781336234
```

Figure 9.16: MSE score of the training set

We achieved quite a low MSE score on the training set.

11. Calculate the MSE on the testing set and print its value:

```
test_mse = mean_squared_error(y_test, preds_test)
test_mse
```

You should get the following output:

```
0.007489642004973965
```

Figure 9.17: MSE score of the testing set

We also have a low MSE score on the testing set that is very similar to the training one. So, our model is not overfitting.

12. Print the variable importance using **`.feature_importances_`**:

```
rf_model.feature_importances_
```

You should get the following output:

```
array([0.00000000e+00, 7.56405224e-04, 8.89442010e-05, 9.46275333e-04,
       4.08153931e-05, 1.97210546e-01, 5.03587073e-04, 2.31999967e-04,
       6.15222081e-03, 3.52461267e-03, 0.00000000e+00, 5.69504288e-01,
       1.13616416e-04, 4.90638284e-04, 1.87909452e-04, 3.20591202e-04,
       2.12958787e-04, 1.90764978e-01, 5.75581836e-03, 4.67864791e-04,
       0.00000000e+00, 0.00000000e+00, 1.75187909e-02, 3.51906210e-04,
       4.85916389e-04, 2.89740583e-05, 1.27170564e-03, 1.12059338e-03,
       1.97954549e-04, 3.01220348e-04, 0.00000000e+00, 1.44886927e-03])
```

Figure 9.18: MSE score of the testing set

13. Create an empty DataFrame called **`varimp_df`**:

```
varimp_df = pd.DataFrame()
```

14. Create a new column called **feature** for this DataFrame with the name of the columns of **df**, using **.columns**:

```
varimp_df['feature'] = df.columns
varimp_df['importance'] = rf_model.feature_importances_
```

15. Print the first five rows of **varimp_df**:

```
varimp_df.head()
```

You should get the following output:

	feature	importance
0	a1cx	0.000000
1	a1cy	0.000756
2	a1sx	0.000089
3	a1sy	0.000946
4	a1rho	0.000041

Figure 9.19: Variable importance of the first five variables

From this output, we can see the variables **a1cy** and **a1sy** have the highest value, so they are more important for predicting the target variable than the three other variables shown here.

16. Plot a bar chart with Altair using **coef_df** and **importance** as the **x** axis and **feature** as the **y** axis:

```
alt.Chart(varimp_df).mark_bar().encode(x='importance',\
                                       y="feature")
```

You should get the following output:

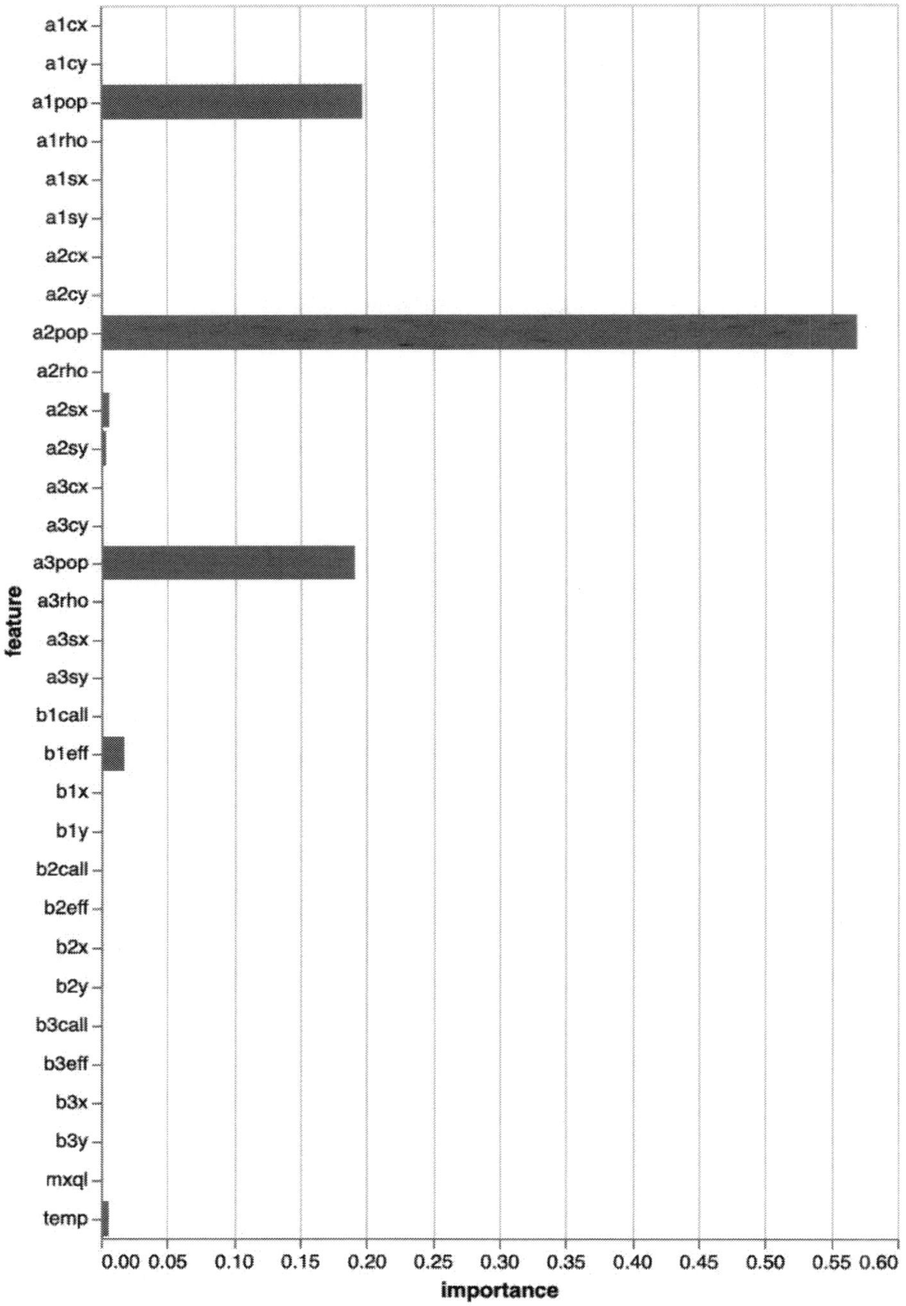

Figure 9.20: Graph showing the variable importance of the first five variables

From this output, we can see the variables that impact the prediction the most for this Random Forest model are **a2pop**, **a1pop**, **a3pop**, **b1eff**, and **temp**, by decreasing order of importance.

> **NOTE**
>
> To access the source code for this specific section, please refer to https://packt.live/327Pi0i.
>
> This section does not currently have an online interactive example, but can be run as usual on Google Colab.

In this exercise, you learned how to extract the feature importance learned by a Random Forest model and identified which variables are the most important for its predictions.

VARIABLE IMPORTANCE VIA PERMUTATION

In the previous section, we saw how to extract feature importance for RandomForest. There is actually another technique that shares the same name, but its underlying logic is different and can be applied to any algorithm, not only tree-based ones.

This technique can be referred to as variable importance via permutation. Let's say we trained a model to predict a target variable with five classes and achieved an accuracy of 0.95. One way to assess the importance of one of the features is to remove and train a model and see the new accuracy score. If the accuracy score dropped significantly, then we could infer that this variable has a significant impact on the prediction. On the other hand, if the score slightly decreased or stayed the same, we could say this variable is not very important and doesn't influence the final prediction much. So, we can use this difference between the model's performance to assess the importance of a variable.

The drawback of this method is that you need to retrain a new model for each variable. If it took you a few hours to train the original model and you have 100 different features, it would take quite a while to compute the importance of each variable. It would be great if we didn't have to retrain different models. So, another solution would be to generate noise or new values for a given column and predict the final outcomes from this modified data and compare the accuracy score. For example, if you have a column with values between 0 and 100, you can take the original data and randomly generate new values for this column (keeping all other variables the same) and predict the class for them.

This option also has a catch. The randomly generated values can be very different from the original data. Going back to the same example we saw before, if the original range of values for a column is between 0 and 100 and we generate values that can be negative or take a very high value, it is not very representative of the real distribution of the original data. So, we will need to understand the distribution of each variable before generating new values.

Rather than generating random values, we can simply swap (or permute) values of a column between different rows and use these modified cases for predictions. Then, we can calculate the related accuracy score and compare it with the original one to assess the importance of this variable. For example, we have the following rows in the original dataset:

X1		X2	X3	target
1		0.213	-23	0
42		0.783	-13	0
12		0.0013	-321	1

Figure 9.21: Example of the dataset

We can swap the values for the X1 column and get a new dataset:

X1	X2	X3	Target
42	0.213	-23	0
12	0.783	-13	1
1	0.0013	-321	1

Figure 9.22: Example of a swapped column from the dataset

The **mlxtend** package provides a function to perform variable permutation and calculate variable importance values: **feature_importance_permutation**. Let's see how to use it with the Breast Cancer dataset from **sklearn**.

First, let's load the data and train a Random Forest model:

```
from sklearn.datasets import load_breast_cancer
from sklearn.ensemble import RandomForestClassifier

data = load_breast_cancer()
X, y = data.data, data.target
rf_model = RandomForestClassifier(random_state=168)
rf_model.fit(X, y)
```

Then, we will call the **feature_importance_permutation** function from **mlxtend.evaluate**. This function takes the following parameters:

- **predict_method**: A function that will be called for model prediction. Here, we will provide the **predict** method from our trained **rf_model** model.
- **X**: The features from the dataset. It needs to be in NumPy array form.
- **y**: The target variable from the dataset. It needs to be in **Numpy** array form.
- **metric**: The metric used for comparing the performance of the model. For the classification task, we will use accuracy.
- **num_round**: The number of rounds **mlxtend** will perform permutation on the data and assess the performance change.
- **seed**: The seed set for getting reproducible results.

Consider the following code snippet:

```
from mlxtend.evaluate import feature_importance_permutation

imp_vals, _ = feature_importance_permutation\
              (predict_method=rf_model.predict, X=X, y=y, \
               metric='r2', num_rounds=1, seed=2)
imp_vals
```

The output should be as follows:

```
array([0.        , 0.        , 0.        , 0.        , 0.        , 0.        ,
       0.        , 0.        , 0.        , 0.        , 0.0075181, 0.        ,
       0.        , 0.0075181, 0.        , 0.        , 0.        , 0.        ,
       0.        , 0.        , 0.        , 0.0075181, 0.0075181, 0.        ,
       0.        , 0.        , 0.0075181, 0.        , 0.        , 0.        ])
```

Figure 9.23: Variable importance by permutation

Let's create a DataFrame containing these values and the names of the features and plot them on a graph with **altair**:

```
import pandas as pd
varimp_df = pd.DataFrame()
varimp_df['feature'] = data.feature_names
varimp_df['importance'] = imp_vals
varimp_df.head()
import altair as alt
```

```
alt.Chart(varimp_df).mark_bar().encode(x='importance',\
                                       y="feature")
```

The output should be as follows:

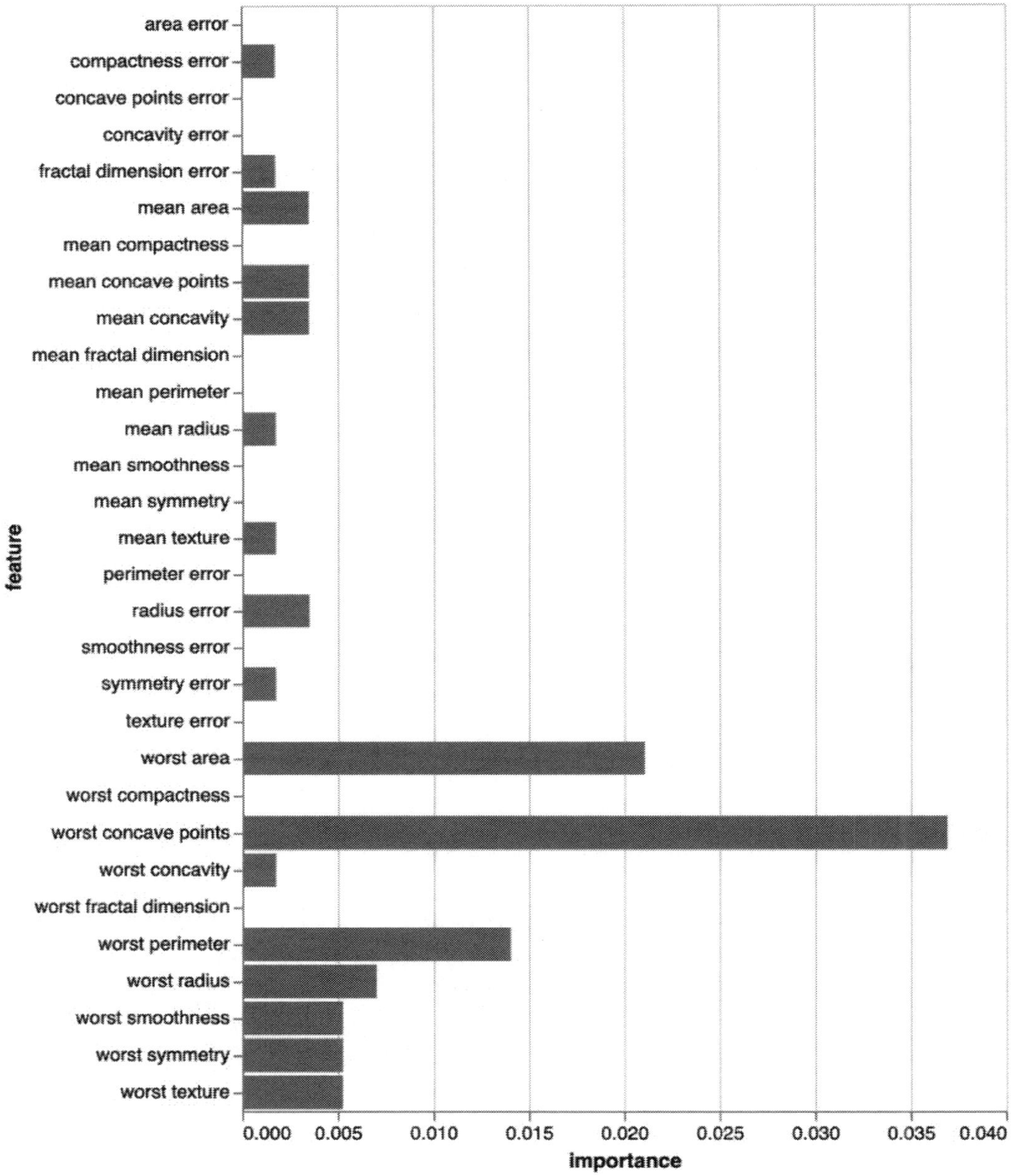

Figure 9.24: Graph showing variable importance by permutation

These results are different from the ones we got from **RandomForest** in the previous section. Here, worst concave points is the most important, followed by worst area, and worst perimeter has a higher value than mean radius. So, we got the same list of the most important variables but in a different order. This confirms these three features are indeed the most important in predicting whether a tumor is malignant or not. The variable importance from **RandomForest** and the permutation have different logic, therefore, you might get different outputs when you run the code given in the preceding section.

EXERCISE 9.03: EXTRACTING FEATURE IMPORTANCE VIA PERMUTATION

In this exercise, we will compute and extract feature importance by permutating a Random Forest classifier model trained to predict the customer drop-out ratio.

We will using the same dataset as in the previous exercise.

The following steps will help you complete the exercise:

1. Open a new Colab notebook.
2. Import the following packages: **pandas**, **train_test_split** from **sklearn.model_selection**, **RandomForestRegressor** from **sklearn.ensemble**, **feature_importance_permutation** from **mlxtend.evaluate**, and **altair**:

```
import pandas as pd
from sklearn.model_selection import train_test_split
from sklearn.ensemble import RandomForestRegressor
from mlxtend.evaluate import feature_importance_permutation
import altair as alt
```

3. Create a variable called **file_url** that contains the URL of the dataset:

```
file_url = 'https://raw.githubusercontent.com/'\
           'PacktWorkshops/The-Data-Science-Workshop/'\
           'master/Chapter09/Dataset/phpYYZ4Qc.csv'
```

4. Load the dataset into a DataFrame called **df** using **.read_csv()**:

```
df = pd.read_csv(file_url)
```

5. Extract the **rej** column using **.pop()** and save it into a variable called **y**:

```
y = df.pop('rej')
```

6. Split the DataFrame into training and testing sets using **train_test_split()** with **test_size=0.3** and **random_state = 1**:

```
X_train, X_test, y_train, y_test = train_test_split\
                                   (df, y, test_size=0.3, \
                                    random_state=1)
```

7. Instantiate **RandomForestRegressor** with **random_state=1**, **n_estimators=50**, **max_depth=6**, and **min_samples_leaf=60**:

```
rf_model = RandomForestRegressor(random_state=1, \
                                 n_estimators=50, max_depth=6, \
                                 min_samples_leaf=60)
```

8. Train the model on the training set using **.fit()**:

```
rf_model.fit(X_train, y_train)
```

You should get the following output:

```
RandomForestRegressor(bootstrap=True, criterion='mse', max_depth=6,
                      max_features='auto', max_leaf_nodes=None,
                      min_impurity_decrease=0.0, min_impurity_split=None,
                      min_samples_leaf=60, min_samples_split=2,
                      min_weight_fraction_leaf=0.0, n_estimators=50,
                      n_jobs=None, oob_score=False, random_state=1, verbose=0,
                      warm_start=False)
```

Figure 9.25: Logs of RandomForest

9. Extract the feature importance via permutation using **feature_importance_permutation** from **mlxtend** with the Random Forest model, the testing set, **r2** as the metric used, **num_rounds=1**, and **seed=2**. Save the results into a variable called **imp_vals** and print its values:

```
imp_vals, _ = feature_importance_permutation\
              (predict_method=rf_model.predict, \
               X=X_test.values, y=y_test.values, \
               metric='r2', num_rounds=1, seed=2)
imp_vals
```

You should get the following output:

```
array([ 0.00000000e+00, -3.34728428e-05, -2.83476215e-05,  1.03738033e-04,
        4.61246775e-06,  1.96879681e-01,  8.71635991e-05, -7.16980150e-05,
        3.28788126e-04,  1.05860288e-03,  0.00000000e+00,  5.56589408e-01,
       -4.31208212e-05,  1.13215046e-04,  2.22409533e-05,  5.96895938e-05,
        5.35704113e-05,  1.76990072e-01,  2.81084956e-03,  6.79193119e-05,
        0.00000000e+00,  0.00000000e+00,  1.16553234e-02,  2.77582324e-05,
        1.40812233e-04,  1.96362926e-06,  3.66606090e-04, -1.82522826e-04,
        1.14460108e-05,  3.72080724e-05,  0.00000000e+00,  5.54878998e-04])
```

Figure 9.26: Variable importance by permutation

It is quite hard to interpret the raw results. Let's plot the variable importance by permutating the model on a graph.

10. Create a DataFrame called **varimp_df** with two columns: **feature** containing the name of the columns of **df**, using **.columns** and **'importance'** containing the values of **imp_vals**:

```
varimp_df = pd.DataFrame({'feature': df.columns, \
                          'importance': imp_vals})
```

11. Plot a bar chart with Altair using **coef_df** and **importance** as the **x** axis and **feature** as the **y** axis:

```
alt.Chart(varimp_df).mark_bar().encode(x='importance',\
                                       y="feature")
```

You should get the following output:

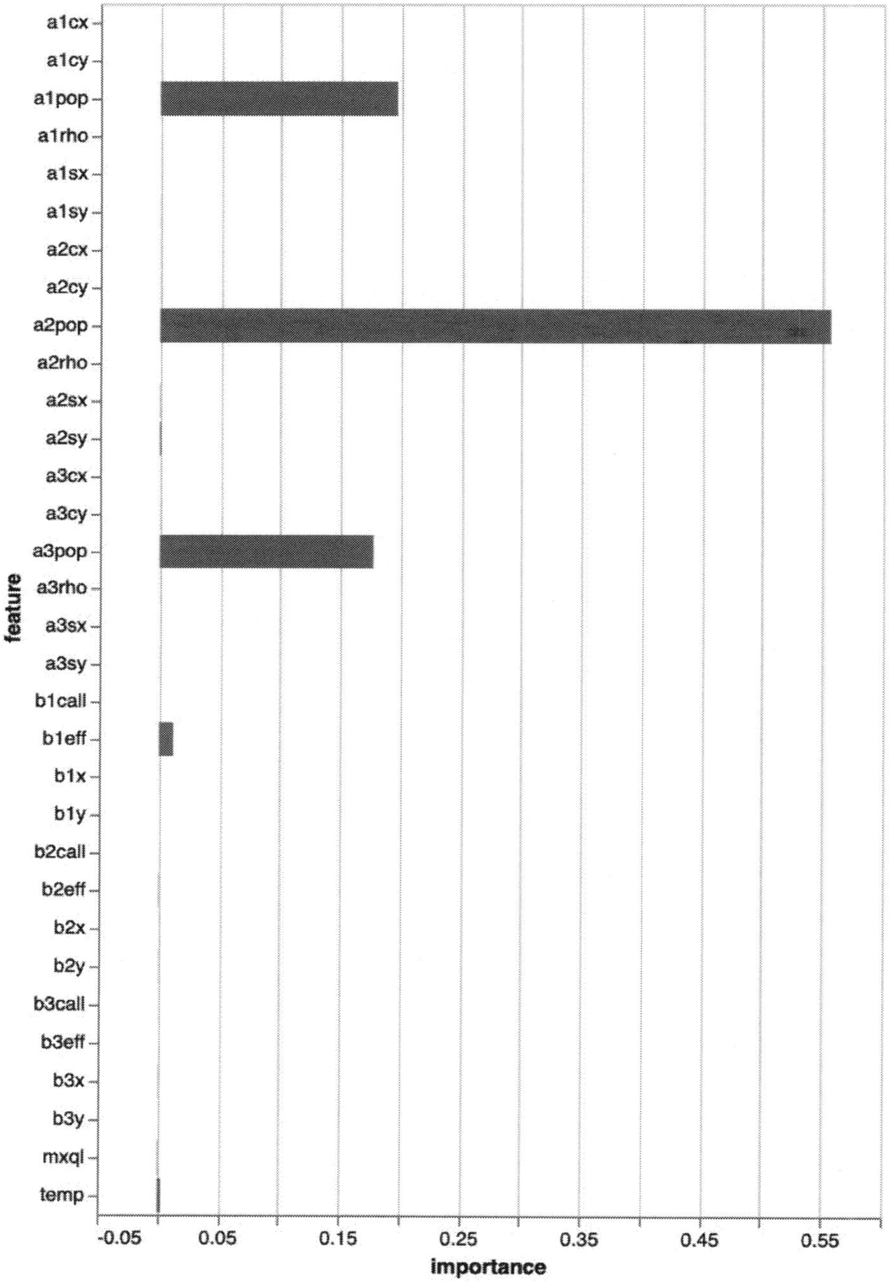

Figure 9.27: Graph showing the variable importance by permutation

From this output, we can see the variables that impact the prediction the most for this Random Forest model are: **a2pop**, **a1pop**, **a3pop**, **b1eff**, and **temp**, in decreasing order of importance. This is very similar to the results of *Exercise 9.02, Extracting RandomForest Feature Importance*.

> **NOTE**
>
> To access the source code for this specific section, please refer to https://packt.live/2YdstY9.
>
> This section does not currently have an online interactive example, but can be run as usual on Google Colab.

You successfully extracted the feature importance by permutating this model and identified which variables are the most important for its predictions.

PARTIAL DEPENDENCE PLOTS

Another tool that is model-agnostic is a partial dependence plot. It is a visual tool for analyzing the effect of a feature on the target variable. To achieve this, we can plot the values of the feature we are interested in analyzing on the **x**-axis and the target variable on the **y**-axis and then show all the observations from the dataset on this graph. Let's try it on the Breast Cancer dataset from **sklearn**:

```
from sklearn.datasets import load_breast_cancer
import pandas as pd

data = load_breast_cancer()
df = pd.DataFrame(data.data, columns=data.feature_names)
df['target'] = data.target
```

Now that we have loaded the data and converted it to a DataFrame, let's have a look at the worst concave points column:

```
import altair as alt

alt.Chart(df).mark_circle(size=60)\
            .encode(x='worst concave points', y='target')
```

The resulting plot is as follows:

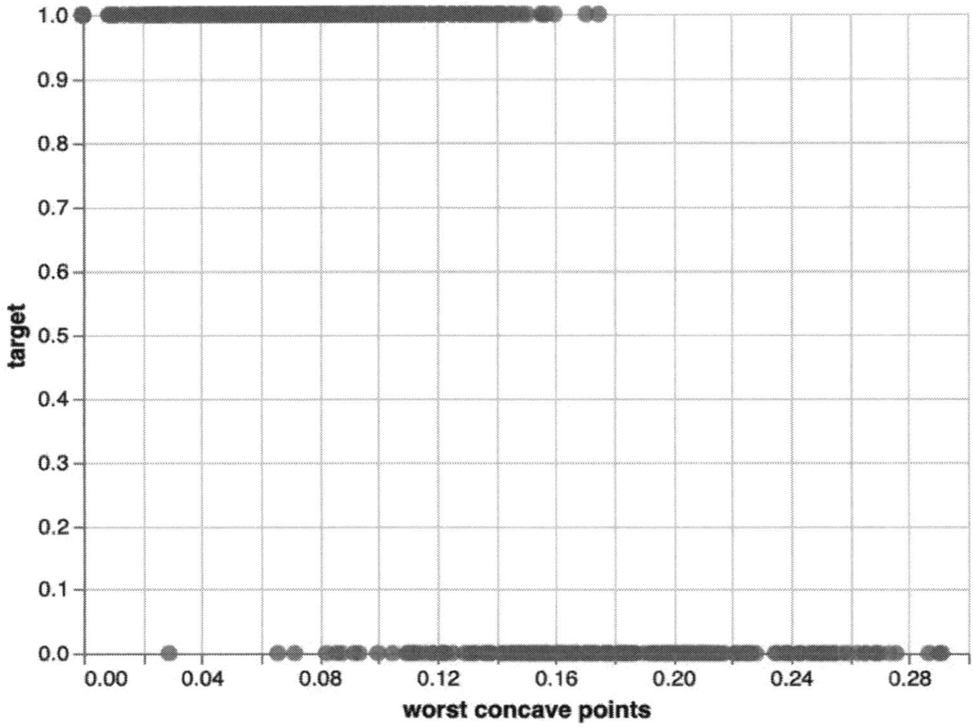

Figure 9.28: Scatter plot of the worst concave points and target variables

> **NOTE**
>
> The preceding code and figure are just examples. We encourage you to analyze different features by changing the values assigned to **`x`** and **`y`** in the preceding code. For example, you can possibly analyze worst concavity versus worst perimeter by setting **`x='worst concavity'`** and **`y='worst perimeter'`** in the preceding code.

From this plot, we can see:

- Most cases with 1 for the target variable have values under 0.16 for the worst concave points column.
- Cases with a 0 value for the target have values of over 0.08 for worst concave points.

With this plot, we are not too sure about which outcome (0 or 1) we will get for the values between 0.08 and 0.16 for worst concave points. There are multiple possible reasons why the outcome of the observations within this range of values is uncertain, such as the fact that there are not many records that fall into this case, or other variables might influence the outcome for these cases. This is where a partial dependence plot can help.

The logic is very similar to variable importance via permutation but rather than randomly replacing the values in a column, we will test every possible value within that column for all observations and see what predictions it leads to. If we take the example from figure 9.21, from the three observations we had originally, this method will create six new observations by keeping columns **X2** and **X3** as they were and replacing the values of **X1**:

	X1	X2	X3	target
Original records	1	0.213	-23	0
	42	0.783	-13	0
	12	0.0013	-321	1
Generated records	42	0.213	-23	0
	12	0.213	-23	1
	1	0.783	-13	1
	12	0.783	-13	0
	1	0.0013	-321	1
	42	0.0013	-321	1

Figure 9.29: Example of records generated from a partial dependence plot

With this new data, we can see, for instance, whether the value 12 really has a strong influence on predicting 1 for the target variable. The original records, with the values 42 and 1 for the **X1** column, lead to outcome 0 and only value 12 generated a prediction of 1. But if we take the same observations for **X1**, equal to 42 and 1, and replace that value with 12, we can see whether the new predictions will lead to 1 for the target variable. This is exactly the logic behind a partial dependence plot, and it will assess all the permutations possible for a column and plot the average of the predictions.

sklearn provides a function called **plot_partial_dependence()** to display the partial dependence plot for a given feature. Let's see how to use it on the Breast Cancer dataset. First, we need to get the index of the column we are interested in. We will use the **.get_loc()** method from **pandas** to get the index for the **worst concave points** column:

```
import altair as alt
from sklearn.inspection import plot_partial_dependence
feature_index = df.columns.get_loc("worst concave points")
```

Now we can call the **plot_partial_dependence()** function. We need to provide the following parameters: the trained model, the training set, and the indices of the features to be analyzed:

```
plot_partial_dependence(rf_model, df, \
                        features=[feature_index])
```

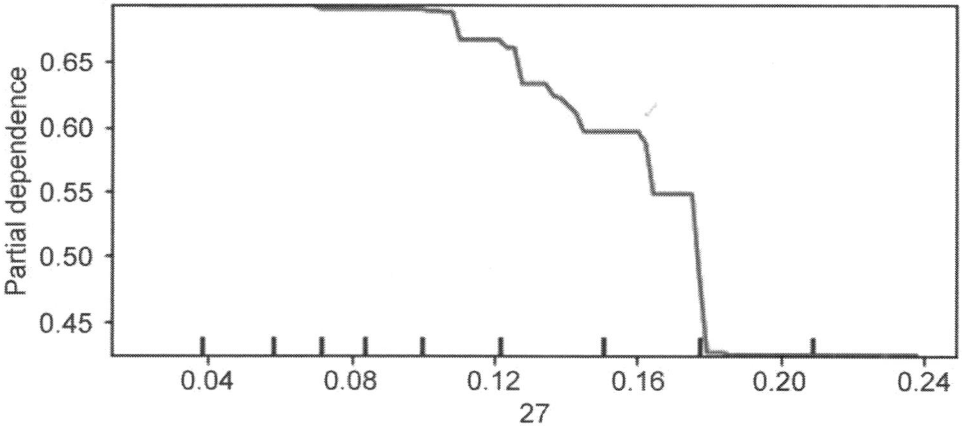

Figure 9.30: Partial dependence plot for the worst concave points column

This partial dependence plot shows us that, on average, all the observations with a value under 0.17 for the worst concave points column will most likely lead to a prediction of 1 for the target (probability over 0.5) and all the records over 0.17 will have a prediction of 0 (probability under 0.5).

EXERCISE 9.04: PLOTTING PARTIAL DEPENDENCE

In this exercise, we will plot partial dependence plots for two variables, **a1pop** and **temp**, from a Random Forest classifier model trained to predict the customer drop-out ratio.

We will using the same dataset as in the previous exercise.

1. Open a new Colab notebook.
2. Import the following packages: **pandas**, **train_test_split** from **sklearn.model_selection**, **RandomForestRegressor** from **sklearn.ensemble**, **plot_partial_dependence** from **sklearn.inspection**, and **altair**:

```
import pandas as pd
from sklearn.model_selection import train_test_split
from sklearn.ensemble import RandomForestRegressor
from sklearn.inspection import plot_partial_dependence
import altair as alt
```

3. Create a variable called **file_url** that contains the URL for the dataset:

```
file_url = 'https://raw.githubusercontent.com/'\
           'PacktWorkshops/The-Data-Science-Workshop/'\
           'master/Chapter09/Dataset/phpYYZ4Qc.csv'
```

4. Load the dataset into a DataFrame called **df** using **.read_csv()**:

```
df = pd.read_csv(file_url)
```

5. Extract the **rej** column using **.pop()** and save it into a variable called **y**:

```
y = df.pop('rej')
```

6. Split the DataFrame into training and testing sets using **train_test_split()** with **test_size=0.3** and **random_state = 1**:

```
X_train, X_test, y_train, y_test = train_test_split\
                                   (df, y, test_size=0.3, \
                                    random_state=1)
```

7. Instantiate **RandomForestRegressor** with **random_state=1**, **n_estimators=50**, **max_depth=6**, and **min_samples_leaf=60**:

```
rf_model = RandomForestRegressor(random_state=1, \
                                 n_estimators=50, max_depth=6,\
                                 min_samples_leaf=60)
```

8. Train the model on the training set using **.fit()**:

```
rf_model.fit(X_train, y_train)
```

You should get the following output:

```
RandomForestRegressor(bootstrap=True, criterion='mse', max_depth=6,
                      max_features='auto', max_leaf_nodes=None,
                      min_impurity_decrease=0.0, min_impurity_split=None,
                      min_samples_leaf=60, min_samples_split=2,
                      min_weight_fraction_leaf=0.0, n_estimators=50,
                      n_jobs=None, oob_score=False, random_state=1, verbose=0,
                      warm_start=False)
```

Figure 9.31: Logs of RandomForest

9. Plot the partial dependence plot using **plot_partial_dependence()** from **sklearn** with the Random Forest model, the testing set, and the index of the **a1pop** column:

```
plot_partial_dependence(rf_model, X_test, \
                        features=[df.columns.get_loc('a1pop')])
```

You should get the following output:

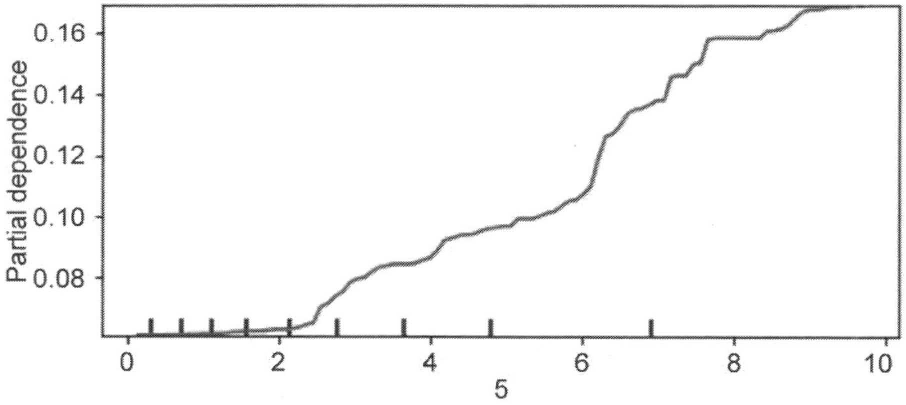

Figure 9.32: Partial dependence plot for a1pop

This partial dependence plot shows that, on average, the **a1pop** variable doesn't affect the target variable much when its value is below 2, but from there the target increases linearly by 0.04 for each unit increase of **a1pop**. This means if the population size of area 1 is below the value of 2, the risk of churn is almost null. But over this limit, every increment of population size for area 1 increases the chance of churn by **4%**.

10. Plot the partial dependence plot using **plot_partial_dependence()** from **sklearn** with the Random Forest model, the testing set, and the index of the **temp** column:

```
plot_partial_dependence(rf_model, X_test, \
                        features=[df.columns.get_loc('temp')])
```

You should get the following output:

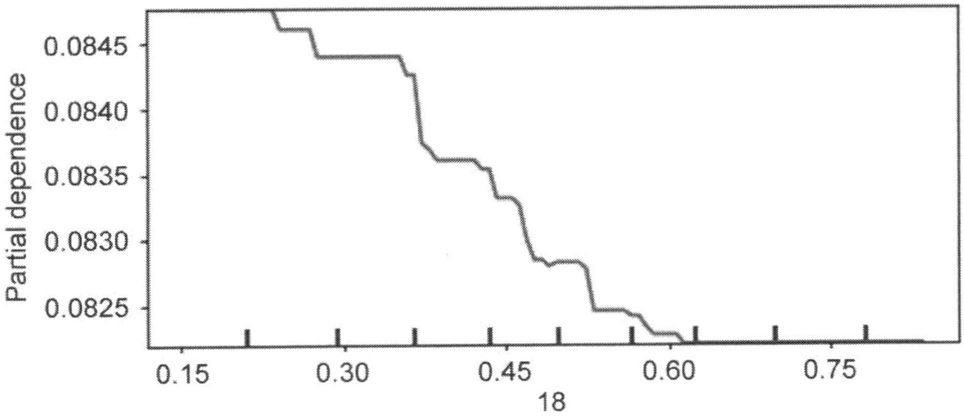

Figure 9.33: Partial dependence plot for temp

This partial dependence plot shows that, on average, the **temp** variable has a negative linear impact on the target variable: when **temp** increases by 1, the target variable will decrease by 0.12. This means if the temperature increases by a degree, the chance of leaving the queue decreases by 12%.

> **NOTE**
>
> To access the source code for this specific section, please refer to https://packt.live/2DWnSmn.
>
> You can also run this example online at https://packt.live/2DWnUL1.

You learned how to plot and analyze a partial dependence plot for the **a1pop** and **temp** features. In this exercise, we saw that **a1pop** has a positive linear impact on the target, while **temp** has a negative linear influence.

LOCAL INTERPRETATION WITH LIME

After training our model, we usually use it for predicting outcomes on unseen data. The global interpretations we saw earlier, such as model coefficient, variable importance, and the partial dependence plot, gave us a lot of information on the features at an overall level. Sometimes we want to understand what has influenced the model for a specific case to predict a specific outcome. For instance, if your model is to assess the risk of offering credit to a new client, you may want to understand why it rejected the case for a specific lead. This is what local interpretation is for: analyzing a single observation and understanding the rationale behind the model's decision. In this section, we will introduce you to a technique called **Locally Interpretable Model-Agnostic Explanations** (**LIME**).

If we are using a linear model, it is extremely easy to understand the contribution of each variable to the predicted outcome. We just need to look at the coefficients of the model. For instance, the model will learn the following function: $y = 100 + 0.2 * x_1 + 200 * x_2 - 180 * x_3$. So, if we received an observation of x_1=0, x_2=2 and x_3=1, we would know the contribution of:

- x_1 was 0.2 * 0 = 0
- x_2 was 200 * 2 = +400
- x_3 was -180 * 1 = -180

So, the final prediction (100 +0 + 400 -180 = 320) was mainly driven by x_2.

But for a nonlinear model, it is quite hard to get such a clear view. LIME is one way to get more visibility in such cases. The underlying logic of LIME is to approximate the original nonlinear model with a linear one. Then, it uses the coefficients of that linear model in order to explain the contribution of each variable, as we just saw in the preceding example. But rather than trying to approximate the entire model for the whole dataset, LIME tries to approximate it locally around the observation you are interested in. LIME uses the trained model to predict new data points near your observation and then fit a linear regression on that predicted data.

Let's see how we can use it on the Breast Cancer dataset. First, we will load the data and train a Random Forest model:

```
from sklearn.datasets import load_breast_cancer
from sklearn.model_selection import train_test_split
from sklearn.ensemble import RandomForestClassifier
data = load_breast_cancer()
X, y = data.data, data.target
```

```
X_train, X_test, y_train, y_test = train_test_split\
                                   (X, y, test_size=0.3, \
                                    random_state=1)
rf_model = RandomForestClassifier(random_state=168)
rf_model.fit(X_train, y_train)
```

The **`lime`** package is not directly accessible on Google Colab, so we need to manually install it with the following command:

```
!pip install lime
```

The output will be as follows:

```
Collecting lime
  Downloading https://files.pythonhosted.org/packages/b5/e0/60070b461a589b2fee0dbc45df9987f150fca83667c2f8a064cef7dbac6b/lime-0.1.1.37.tar.gz (275kB)
     |████████████████████████████████| 276kB 3.5MB/s
Requirement already satisfied: numpy in /usr/local/lib/python3.6/dist-packages (from lime) (1.17.5)
Requirement already satisfied: scipy in /usr/local/lib/python3.6/dist-packages (from lime) (1.4.1)
Collecting progressbar
  Downloading https://files.pythonhosted.org/packages/a3/a6/b8e451f6cff1c99b4747a2f7235aa904d2d49e8e1464e0b798272aa84358/progressbar-2.5.tar.gz
Requirement already satisfied: scikit-learn>=0.18 in /usr/local/lib/python3.6/dist-packages (from lime) (0.22.1)
Requirement already satisfied: matplotlib in /usr/local/lib/python3.6/dist-packages (from lime) (3.1.2)
Requirement already satisfied: scikit-image>=0.12 in /usr/local/lib/python3.6/dist-packages (from lime) (0.16.2)
Requirement already satisfied: joblib>=0.11 in /usr/local/lib/python3.6/dist-packages (from scikit-learn>=0.18->lime) (0.14.1)
Requirement already satisfied: python-dateutil>=2.1 in /usr/local/lib/python3.6/dist-packages (from matplotlib->lime) (2.6.1)
Requirement already satisfied: pyparsing!=2.0.4,!=2.1.2,!=2.1.6,>=2.0.1 in /usr/local/lib/python3.6/dist-packages (from matplotlib->lime) (2.4.6)
Requirement already satisfied: kiwisolver>=1.0.1 in /usr/local/lib/python3.6/dist-packages (from matplotlib->lime) (1.1.0)
Requirement already satisfied: cycler>=0.10 in /usr/local/lib/python3.6/dist-packages (from matplotlib->lime) (0.10.0)
Requirement already satisfied: networkx>=2.0 in /usr/local/lib/python3.6/dist-packages (from scikit-image>=0.12->lime) (2.4)
Requirement already satisfied: pillow>=4.3.0 in /usr/local/lib/python3.6/dist-packages (from scikit-image>=0.12->lime) (6.2.2)
Requirement already satisfied: PyWavelets>=0.4.0 in /usr/local/lib/python3.6/dist-packages (from scikit-image>=0.12->lime) (1.1.1)
Requirement already satisfied: imageio>=2.3.0 in /usr/local/lib/python3.6/dist-packages (from scikit-image>=0.12->lime) (2.4.1)
Requirement already satisfied: six>=1.5 in /usr/local/lib/python3.6/dist-packages (from python-dateutil>=2.1->matplotlib->lime) (1.12.0)
Requirement already satisfied: setuptools in /usr/local/lib/python3.6/dist-packages (from kiwisolver>=1.0.1->matplotlib->lime) (42.0.2)
Requirement already satisfied: decorator>=4.3.0 in /usr/local/lib/python3.6/dist-packages (from networkx>=2.0->scikit-image>=0.12->lime) (4.4.1)
Building wheels for collected packages: lime, progressbar
  Building wheel for lime (setup.py) ... done
  Created wheel for lime: filename=lime-0.1.1.37-cp36-none-any.whl size=284277 sha256=4a26b91294e4a192b234e31171003837d9050835dc017b325ae4b0de3bdcbdc
  Stored in directory: /root/.cache/pip/wheels/c1/38/e7/50d75d4fb75afa604570dc42f20c5c5f5ab26d3fbe8d6ef27b
  Building wheel for progressbar (setup.py) ... done
  Created wheel for progressbar: filename=progressbar-2.5-cp36-none-any.whl size=12073 sha256=fba4ccb035d6a61d4a19c2081852a8016d508cf296af67060a32b13
  Stored in directory: /root/.cache/pip/wheels/c0/e9/6b/ea01090205e285175842339aa3b491adeb4015206cda272ff0
Successfully built lime progressbar
Installing collected packages: progressbar, lime
Successfully installed lime-0.1.1.37 progressbar-2.5
```

Figure 9.34: Installation logs for the lime package

Once installed, we will instantiate the **`LimeTabularExplainer`** class by providing the training data, the names of the features, the names of the classes to be predicted, and the task type (in this example, it is **`classification`**):

```
from lime.lime_tabular import LimeTabularExplainer

lime_explainer = LimeTabularExplainer\
                 (X_train, feature_names=data.feature_names,\
                 class_names=data.target_names,\
                 mode='classification')
```

Then, we will call the **`.explain_instance()`** method with the observations we are interested in (here, it will be the second observation from the testing set) and the function that will predict the outcome probabilities (here, it is **`.predict_proba()`**). Finally, we will call the **`.show_in_notebook()`** method to display the results from **`lime`**:

```
exp = lime_explainer.explain_instance\
      (X_test[1], rf_model.predict_proba, num_features=10)
exp.show_in_notebook()
```

The output will be as follows:

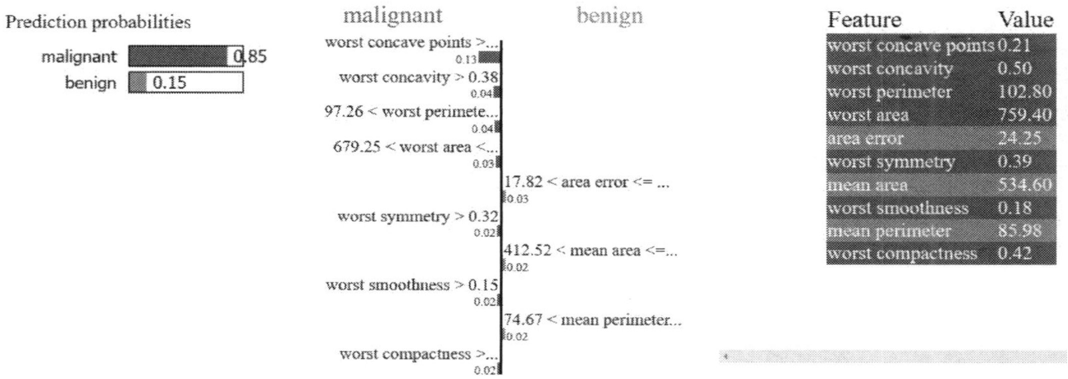

Figure 9.35: Output of LIME

> **NOTE**
>
> Your output may differ slightly. This is due to the random sampling process of LIME.

There is a lot of information in the preceding output. Let's go through it a bit at a time. The left-hand side shows the prediction probabilities for the two classes of the target variable. For this observation, the model thinks there is a 0.85 probability that the predicted value will be malignant:

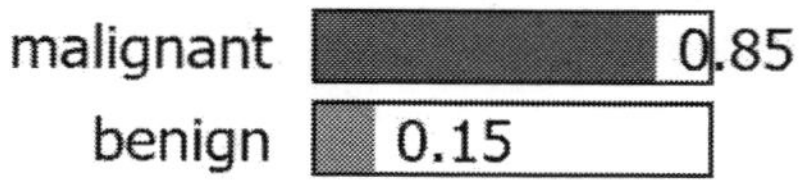

Figure 9.36: Prediction probabilities from LIME

The right-hand side shows the value of each feature for this observation. Each feature is color-coded to highlight its contribution toward the possible classes of the target variable. The list sorts the features by decreasing importance. In this example, the mean perimeter, mean area, and area error contributed to the model to increase the probability toward class 1. All the other features influenced the model to predict outcome 0:

Feature	Value
worst concave points	0.21
worst symmetry	0.39
worst compactness	0.42
mean perimeter	85.98
worst texture	27.95
worst area	759.40
worst perimeter	102.80
area error	24.25
worst concavity	0.50
mean concavity	0.12

Figure 9.37: Value of the feature for the observation of interest

Finally, the central part shows how each variable contributed to the final prediction. In this example, the **`worst concave points`** and **`worst compactness`** variables led to an increase of, respectively, 0.10 and 0.05 probability in predicting outcome 0. On the other hand, **`mean perimeter`** and **`mean area`** both contributed to an increase of 0.03 probability of predicting class 1:

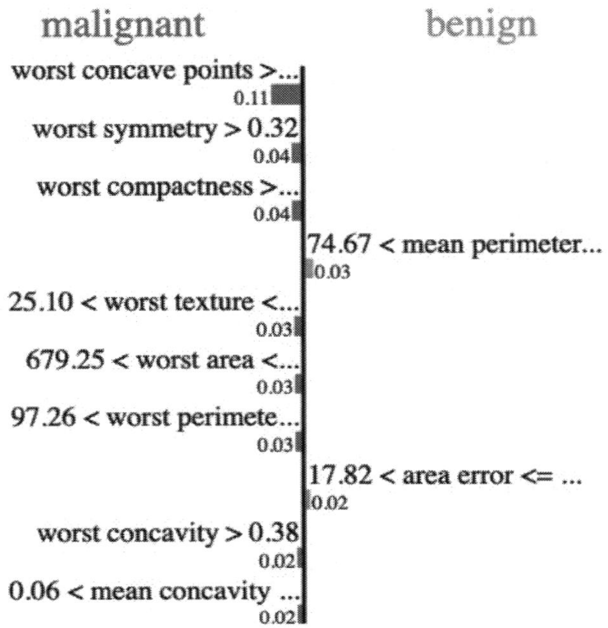

Figure 9.38: Contribution of each feature to the final prediction

It's as simple as that. With LIME, we can easily see how each variable impacted the probabilities of predicting the different outcomes of the model. As you saw, the LIME package not only computes the local approximation but also provides a visual representation of its results. It is much easier to interpret than looking at raw outputs. It is also very useful for presenting your findings and illustrating how different features influenced the prediction of a single observation.

EXERCISE 9.05: LOCAL INTERPRETATION WITH LIME

In this exercise, we will analyze some predictions from a Random Forest classifier model trained to predict the customer drop-out ratio using LIME.

We will be using the same dataset as in the previous exercise.

1. Open a new Colab notebook.
2. Import the following packages: **`pandas`**, **`train_test_split`** from **`sklearn.model_selection`**, and **`RandomForestRegressor`** from **`sklearn.ensemble`**:

```
import pandas as pd
from sklearn.model_selection import train_test_split
from sklearn.ensemble import RandomForestRegressor
```

3. Create a variable called **file_url** that contains the URL of the dataset:

```
file_url = 'https://raw.githubusercontent.com/'\
           'PacktWorkshops/The-Data-Science-Workshop/'\
           'master/Chapter09/Dataset/phpYYZ4Qc.csv'
```

4. Load the dataset into a DataFrame called **df** using **.read_csv()**:

```
df = pd.read_csv(file_url)
```

5. Extract the **rej** column using **.pop()** and save it into a variable called **y**:

```
y = df.pop('rej')
```

6. Split the DataFrame into training and testing sets using **train_test_split()** with **test_size=0.3** and **random_state = 1**:

```
X_train, X_test, y_train, y_test = train_test_split\
                                   (df, y, test_size=0.3, \
                                    random_state=1)
```

7. Instantiate **RandomForestRegressor** with **random_state=1**, **n_estimators=50**, **max_depth=6**, and **min_samples_leaf=60**:

```
rf_model = RandomForestRegressor(random_state=1, \
                                 n_estimators=50, max_depth=6,\
                                 min_samples_leaf=60)
```

8. Train the model on the training set using **.fit()**:

```
rf_model.fit(X_train, y_train)
```

You should get the following output:

```
RandomForestRegressor(bootstrap=True, criterion='mse', max_depth=6,
                      max_features='auto', max_leaf_nodes=None,
                      min_impurity_decrease=0.0, min_impurity_split=None,
                      min_samples_leaf=60, min_samples_split=2,
                      min_weight_fraction_leaf=0.0, n_estimators=50,
                      n_jobs=None, oob_score=False, random_state=1, verbose=0,
                      warm_start=False)
```

Figure 9.39: Logs of RandomForest

9. Install the lime package using the **!pip** install command:

```
!pip install lime
```

10. Import **LimeTabularExplainer** from **lime.lime_tabular**:

```
from lime.lime_tabular import LimeTabularExplainer
```

11. Instantiate **LimeTabularExplainer** with the training set and **mode='regression'**:

```
lime_explainer = LimeTabularExplainer\
                    (X_train.values, \
                     feature_names=X_train.columns, \
                     mode='regression')
```

12. Display the LIME analysis on the first row of the testing set using **.explain_instance()** and **.show_in_notebook()**:

```
exp = lime_explainer.explain_instance\
      (X_test.values[0], rf_model.predict)
exp.show_in_notebook()
```

You should get the following output:

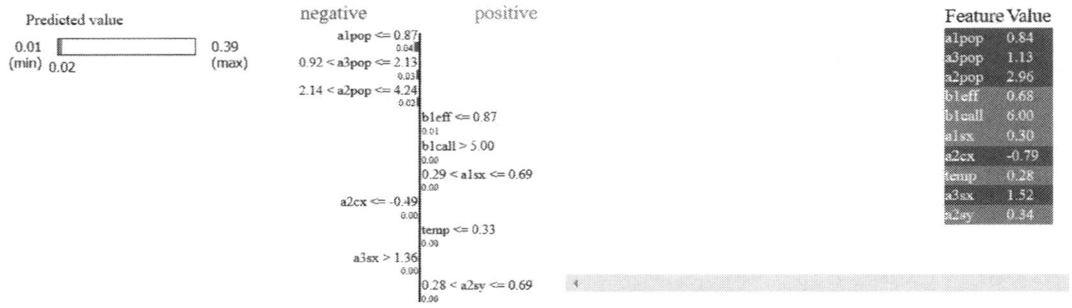

Figure 9.40: LIME output for the first observation of the testing set

This output shows that the predicted value for this observation is a 0.02 chance of customer drop-out and it has been mainly influenced by the **a1pop**, **a3pop**, **a2pop**, and **b2eff** features. For instance, the fact that **a1pop** was under 0.87 has decreased the value of the target variable by 0.01.

13. Display the LIME analysis on the third row of the testing set using **.explain_instance()** and **.show_in_notebook()**:

```
exp = lime_explainer.explain_instance\
        (X_test.values[2], rf_model.predict)
exp.show_in_notebook()
```

You should get the following output:

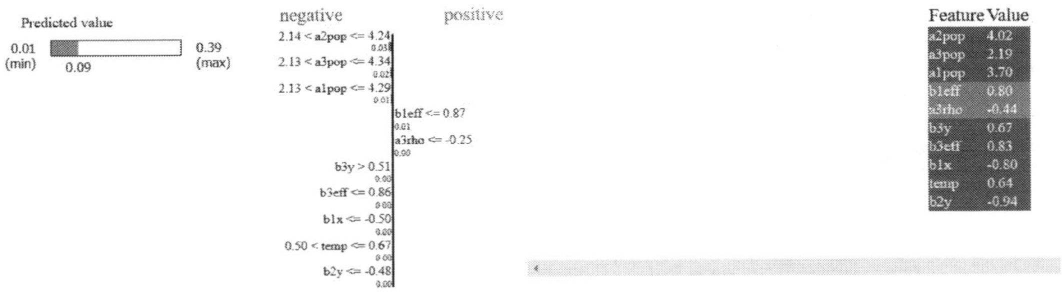

Figure 9.41: LIME output for the third observation of the testing set

This output shows that the predicted value for this observation is a 0.09 chance of customer drop-out and it has been mainly influenced by the **a2pop**, **a3pop**, **a1pop**, and **b1eff** features. For instance, the fact that **b1eff** was under 0.87 has increased the value of the target variable by 0.01. The **b1eff** feature represents the level of efficiency of bank 1, so the results from LIME are telling us that the chance of customers leaving increases if this level of efficiency goes lower than 0.87.

> **NOTE**
>
> To access the source code for this specific section, please refer to https://packt.live/2Q5i3Fp.
>
> You can also run this example online at https://packt.live/327Nl3Z.

You have completed the last exercise of this chapter. You saw how to use LIME to interpret the prediction of single observations. We learned that the **a1pop**, **a2pop**, and **a3pop** features have a strong negative impact on the first and third observations of the training set.

ACTIVITY 9.01: TRAIN AND ANALYZE A NETWORK INTRUSION DETECTION MODEL

You are working for a cybersecurity company and you have been tasked with building a model that can recognize network intrusion then analyze its feature importance, plot partial dependence, and perform local interpretation on a single observation using LIME.

The dataset provided contains data from 7 weeks of network traffic.

> **NOTE**
>
> The dataset used in this activity is from KDD Cup 1999:
>
> https://packt.live/2tFKUIV.
>
> The CSV version of this dataset can be found here:
>
> https://packt.live/2RyVsBm.

The following steps will help you to complete this activity:

1. Download and load the dataset using **`.read_csv()`** from **`pandas`**.
2. Extract the response variable using **`.pop()`** from **`pandas`**.
3. Split the dataset into training and test sets using **`train_test_split()`** from **`sklearn.model_selection`**.
4. Create a function that will instantiate and fit **`RandomForestClassifier`** using **`.fit()`** from **`sklearn.ensemble`**.
5. Create a function that will predict the outcome for the training and testing sets using **`.predict()`**.
6. Create a function that will print the accuracy score for the training and testing sets using **`accuracy_score()`** from **`sklearn.metrics`**.
7. Compute the feature importance via permutation with **`feature_importance_permutation()`** and display it on a bar chart using **`altair`**.
8. Plot the partial dependence plot using **`plot_partial_dependence`** on the **`src_bytes`** variable.
9. Install **`lime`** using **`!pip install`**.
10. Perform a LIME analysis on row **`99893`** with **`explain_instance()`**.

The output should be as follows:

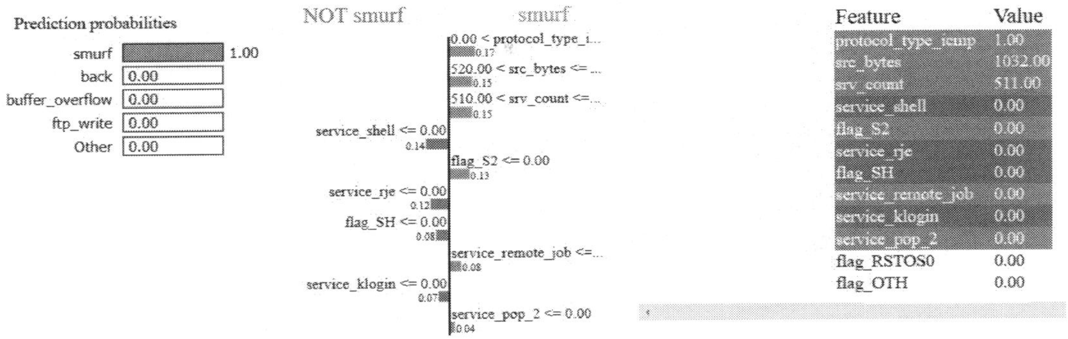

Figure 9.42: Output for LIME analysis

You have successfully trained a Random Forest model to predict the type of network connection. You have also analyzed which features are the most important for this Random Forest model and learned that it mainly relies on the **`src_bytes`** feature. We also analyzed the partial dependence plot for this feature in order to understand its impact on the **`normal`** class. Finally, we used LIME to analyze a single observation and found out which variables led to the predicted outcome.

SUMMARY

In this chapter, we learned a few techniques for interpreting machine learning models. We saw that there are techniques that are specific to the model used: coefficients for linear models and variable importance for tree-based models. There are also some methods that are model-agnostic, such as variable importance via permutation.

All these techniques are global interpreters, which look at the entire dataset and analyze the overall contribution of each variable to predictions. We can use this information not only to identify which variables have the most impact on predictions but also to shortlist them. Rather than keeping all features available from a dataset, we can just keep the ones that have a stronger influence. This can significantly reduce the computation time for training a model or calculating predictions.

We also went through a local interpreter scenario with LIME, which analyzes a single observation. It helped us to better understand the decisions made by the model in predicting the final outcome for a given case. This is a very powerful tool to assess whether a model is biased toward a specific variable that could contain sensitive information such as personal details or demographic data. We can also use it to compare two different observations and understand the rationale for getting different outcomes from the model.

In the next chapter, we will be focusing on analyzing a dataset and will learn exploratory data analysis and data visualization techniques to get a good understanding of the information it contains.

10

ANALYZING A DATASET

OVERVIEW

By the end of this chapter, you will be able to explain the key steps involved in performing exploratory data analysis; identify the types of data contained in the dataset; summarize the dataset and at a detailed level for each variable; visualize the data distribution in each column; find relationships between variables and analyze missing values and outliers for each variable

This chapter will introduce you to the art of performing exploratory data analysis and visualizing the data in order to identify quality issues, potential data transformations, and interesting patterns.

INTRODUCTION

The previous chapter was all about improving our machine learning model, and interpreting its results and parameters to provide meaningful insights to the business. This chapter opens the third part of this book: *enhancing your dataset*. In the next three chapters, we are taking a step back and will be focusing on the key input of any machine learning model: the dataset. We will learn how to explore a new dataset, prepare it for the modeling stage, and create new variables (also called **feature engineering**). These are very exciting and important topics to learn about, so let's jump in.

When we mention data science, most people think about building fancy machine learning algorithms for predicting future outcomes. They usually do not think about all the other critical tasks involved in a data science project. In reality, the modeling step covers only a small part of such a project. You may have already heard about the *rule of thumb* stating that data scientists spend only 20% of their time fitting a model and the other 80% on understanding and preparing the data. This is actually quite close to reality.

A very popular methodology that's used in the industry for running data science projects is **CRISP-DM**.

> **NOTE**
>
> We will not go into too much detail about this methodology as it is out of the scope of this book. But if you are interested in learning more about it, you can find the description of CRISP-DM here: https://packt.live/2QMRepG.

This methodology breaks down a data science project into six different stages:

1. Business understanding
2. Data understanding
3. Data preparation
4. Modeling
5. Evaluation
6. Deployment

As you can see, modeling represents only one phase out of the six and it happens quite close toward the end of the project. In this chapter, we will mainly focus on the second step of CRISP-DM: the data understanding stage.

You may wonder why it is so important to understand the data and why we shouldn't spend more time on modeling. Some researchers have actually shown that training very simple models on high-quality data outperformed extremely complex models with bad data.

If your data is not right, even the most advanced model will not be able to find the relevant patterns and predict the right outcome. This is *garbage in, garbage out*, which means that the wrong input will lead to the wrong output. Therefore, we need to have a good grasp of the limitations and issues of our dataset and fix them before fitting it into a model.

The second reason why it is so important to understand the input data is because it will also help us to define the right approach and shortlist the relevant algorithms accordingly. For instance, if you see that a specific class is less represented compared to other ones in your dataset, you may want to use specific algorithms that can handle imbalanced data or use some resampling techniques beforehand to make the classes more evenly distributed.

In this chapter, you will learn about some of the key concepts and techniques for getting a deep and good understanding of your data.

EXPLORING YOUR DATA

If you are running your project by following the CRISP-DM methodology, the first step will be to discuss the project with the stakeholders and clearly define their requirements and expectations. Only once this is clear can you start having a look at the data and see whether you will be able to achieve these objectives.

After receiving a dataset, you may want to make sure that the dataset contains the information you need for your project. For instance, if you are working on a supervised project, you will check whether this dataset contains the target variable you need and whether there are any missing or incorrect values for this field. You may also check how many observations (rows) and variables (columns) there are. These are the kind of questions you will have initially with a new dataset. This section will introduce you to some techniques you can use to get the answers to these questions.

For the rest of this section, we will be working with a dataset containing transactions from an online retail store.

> **NOTE**
>
> This dataset is in our GitHub repository: https://packt.live/36s4XIN.
>
> It was sourced from https://packt.live/2Qu5XqC, courtesy of Daqing Chen, Sai Liang Sain, and Kun Guo, Data mining for the online retail industry, UCI Machine Learning Repository.

Our dataset is an Excel spreadsheet. Luckily, the **pandas** package provides a method we can use to load this type of file: **read_excel()**.

Let's read the data using the **.read_excel()** method and store it in a **pandas** DataFrame, as shown in the following code snippet:

```
import pandas as pd
file_url = 'https://github.com/PacktWorkshops/'\
           'The-Data-Science-Workshop/blob/'\
           'master/Chapter10/dataset/'\
           'Online%20Retail.xlsx?raw=true'
df = pd.read_excel(file_url)
```

After loading the data into a DataFrame, we want to know the size of this dataset, that is, its number of rows and columns. To get this information, we just need to call the **.shape** attribute from **pandas**:

```
df.shape
```

You should get the following output:

```
(541909, 8)
```

This attribute returns a tuple containing the number of rows as the first element and the number of columns as the second element. The loaded dataset contains **541909** rows and **8** different columns.

Since this attribute returns a tuple, we can access each of its elements independently by providing the relevant index. Let's extract the number of rows (index **0**):

```
df.shape[0]
```

You should get the following output:

```
541909
```

Similarly, we can get the number of columns with the second index:

```
df.shape[1]
```

You should get the following output:

```
8
```

Usually, the first row of a dataset is the header. It contains the name of each column. By default, the **read_excel()** method assumes that the first row of the file is the header. If the **header** is stored in a different row, you can specify a different index for the header with the parameter header from **read_excel()**, such as **pd.read_excel(header=1)** for specifying the header column is the second row.

Once loaded into a **pandas** DataFrame, you can print out its content by calling it directly:

```
df
```

You should get the following output:

	InvoiceNo	StockCode	Description	Quantity	InvoiceDate	UnitPrice	CustomerID	Country
0	536365	85123A	WHITE HANGING HEART T-LIGHT HOLDER	6	2010-12-01 08:26:00	2.55	17850.0	United Kingdom
1	536365	71053	WHITE METAL LANTERN	6	2010-12-01 08:26:00	3.39	17850.0	United Kingdom
2	536365	84406B	CREAM CUPID HEARTS COAT HANGER	8	2010-12-01 08:26:00	2.75	17850.0	United Kingdom
3	536365	84029G	KNITTED UNION FLAG HOT WATER BOTTLE	6	2010-12-01 08:26:00	3.39	17850.0	United Kingdom
4	536365	84029E	RED WOOLLY HOTTIE WHITE HEART.	6	2010-12-01 08:26:00	3.39	17850.0	United Kingdom
5	536365	22752	SET 7 BABUSHKA NESTING BOXES	2	2010-12-01 08:26:00	7.65	17850.0	United Kingdom
6	536365	21730	GLASS STAR FROSTED T-LIGHT HOLDER	6	2010-12-01 08:26:00	4.25	17850.0	United Kingdom
7	536366	22633	HAND WARMER UNION JACK	6	2010-12-01 08:28:00	1.85	17850.0	United Kingdom

Figure 10.1: First few rows of the loaded online retail DataFrame

To access the names of the columns for this DataFrame, we can call the **.columns** attribute:

```
df.columns
```

You should get the following output:

```
Index(['InvoiceNo', 'StockCode', 'Description', 'Quantity', 'InvoiceDate',
       'UnitPrice', 'CustomerID', 'Country'],
      dtype='object')
```

Figure 10.2: List of the column names for the online retail DataFrame

The columns from this dataset are **InvoiceNo**, **StockCode**, **Description**, **Quantity**, **InvoiceDate**, **UnitPrice**, **CustomerID**, and **Country**. We can infer that a row from this dataset represents the sale of an article for a given quantity and price for a specific customer at a particular date.

Looking at these names, we can potentially guess what types of information are contained in these columns, however, to be sure, we can use the **dtypes** attribute, as shown in the following code snippet:

```
df.dtypes
```

You should get the following output:

```
InvoiceNo              object
StockCode              object
Description            object
Quantity                int64
InvoiceDate    datetime64[ns]
UnitPrice             float64
CustomerID            float64
Country                object
dtype: object
```

Figure 10.3: Description of the data type for each column of the DataFrame

From this output, we can see that the **InvoiceDate** column is a date type (**datetime64[ns]**), **Quantity** is an integer (**int64**), and that **UnitPrice** and **CustomerID** are decimal numbers (**float64**). The remaining columns are text (**object**).

The **pandas** package provides a single method that can display all the information we have seen so far, that is, the **info()** method:

```
df.info()
```

You should get the following output:

```
<class 'pandas.core.frame.DataFrame'>
RangeIndex: 541909 entries, 0 to 541908
Data columns (total 8 columns):
InvoiceNo       541909 non-null object
StockCode       541909 non-null object
Description     540455 non-null object
Quantity        541909 non-null int64
InvoiceDate     541909 non-null datetime64[ns]
UnitPrice       541909 non-null float64
CustomerID      406829 non-null float64
Country         541909 non-null object
dtypes: datetime64[ns](1), float64(2), int64(1), object(4)
memory usage: 33.1+ MB
```

Figure 10.4: Output of the info() method

In just a few lines of code, we learned some high-level information about this dataset, such as its size, the column names, and their types.

In the next section, we will analyze the content of a dataset.

ANALYZING YOUR DATASET

Previously, we learned about the overall structure of a dataset and the kind of information it contains. Now, it is time to really dig into it and look at the values of each column.

First, we need to import the **pandas** package:

```
import pandas as pd
```

Then, we'll load the data into a **pandas** DataFrame:

```
file_url = 'https://github.com/PacktWorkshops/'\
           'The-Data-Science-Workshop/blob/'\
           'master/Chapter10/dataset/'\
           'Online%20Retail.xlsx?raw=true'
df = pd.read_excel(file_url)
```

The **pandas** package provides several methods so that you can display a snapshot of your dataset. The most popular ones are **head()**, **tail()**, and **sample()**.

The **head()** method will show the top rows of your dataset. By default, **pandas** will display the first five rows:

```
df.head()
```

You should get the following output:

	InvoiceNo	StockCode	Description	Quantity	InvoiceDate	UnitPrice	CustomerID	Country
0	536365	85123A	WHITE HANGING HEART T-LIGHT HOLDER	6	2010-12-01 08:26:00	2.55	17850.0	United Kingdom
1	536365	71053	WHITE METAL LANTERN	6	2010-12-01 08:26:00	3.39	17850.0	United Kingdom
2	536365	84406B	CREAM CUPID HEARTS COAT HANGER	8	2010-12-01 08:26:00	2.75	17850.0	United Kingdom
3	536365	84029G	KNITTED UNION FLAG HOT WATER BOTTLE	6	2010-12-01 08:26:00	3.39	17850.0	United Kingdom
4	536365	84029E	RED WOOLLY HOTTIE WHITE HEART.	6	2010-12-01 08:26:00	3.39	17850.0	United Kingdom

Figure 10.5: Displaying the first five rows using the head() method

The output of the **head()** method shows that the **InvoiceNo**, **StockCode**, and **CustomerID** columns are unique identifier fields for each purchasing invoice, item sold, and customer. The **Description** field is text describing the item sold. **Quantity** and **UnitPrice** are the number of items sold and their unit price, respectively. **Country** is a text field that can be used for specifying where the customer or the item is located or from which country version of the online store the order has been made. In a real project, you may reach out to the team who provided this dataset and confirm what the meaning of the **Country** column is, or any other column details that you may need, for that matter.

With **pandas**, you can specify the number of top rows to be displayed with the **head()** method by providing an integer as its parameter. Let's try this by displaying the first **10** rows:

```
df.head(10)
```

You should get the following output:

	InvoiceNo	StockCode	Description	Quantity	InvoiceDate	UnitPrice	CustomerID	Country
0	536365	85123A	WHITE HANGING HEART T-LIGHT HOLDER	6	2010-12-01 08:26:00	2.55	17850.0	United Kingdom
1	536365	71053	WHITE METAL LANTERN	6	2010-12-01 08:26:00	3.39	17850.0	United Kingdom
2	536365	84406B	CREAM CUPID HEARTS COAT HANGER	8	2010-12-01 08:26:00	2.75	17850.0	United Kingdom
3	536365	84029G	KNITTED UNION FLAG HOT WATER BOTTLE	6	2010-12-01 08:26:00	3.39	17850.0	United Kingdom
4	536365	84029E	RED WOOLLY HOTTIE WHITE HEART.	6	2010-12-01 08:26:00	3.39	17850.0	United Kingdom
5	536365	22752	SET 7 BABUSHKA NESTING BOXES	2	2010-12-01 08:26:00	7.65	17850.0	United Kingdom
6	536365	21730	GLASS STAR FROSTED T-LIGHT HOLDER	6	2010-12-01 08:26:00	4.25	17850.0	United Kingdom
7	536366	22633	HAND WARMER UNION JACK	6	2010-12-01 08:28:00	1.85	17850.0	United Kingdom
8	536366	22632	HAND WARMER RED POLKA DOT	6	2010-12-01 08:28:00	1.85	17850.0	United Kingdom
9	536367	84879	ASSORTED COLOUR BIRD ORNAMENT	32	2010-12-01 08:34:00	1.69	13047.0	United Kingdom

Figure 10.6: Displaying the first 10 rows using the head() method

Looking at this output, we can assume that the data is sorted by the **InvoiceDate** column and grouped by **CustomerID** and **InvoiceNo**. We can only see one value in the **Country** column: **United Kingdom**. Let's check whether this is really the case by looking at the last rows of the dataset. This can be achieved by calling the **tail()** method. Like **head()**, this method, by default, will display only five rows, but you can specify the number of rows you want as a parameter. Here, we will display the last eight rows:

```
df.tail(8)
```

You should get the following output:

	InvoiceNo	StockCode	Description	Quantity	InvoiceDate	UnitPrice	CustomerID	Country
541901	581587	22367	CHILDRENS APRON SPACEBOY DESIGN	8	2011-12-09 12:50:00	1.95	12680.0	France
541902	581587	22629	SPACEBOY LUNCH BOX	12	2011-12-09 12:50:00	1.95	12680.0	France
541903	581587	23256	CHILDRENS CUTLERY SPACEBOY	4	2011-12-09 12:50:00	4.15	12680.0	France
541904	581587	22613	PACK OF 20 SPACEBOY NAPKINS	12	2011-12-09 12:50:00	0.85	12680.0	France
541905	581587	22899	CHILDREN'S APRON DOLLY GIRL	6	2011-12-09 12:50:00	2.10	12680.0	France
541906	581587	23254	CHILDRENS CUTLERY DOLLY GIRL	4	2011-12-09 12:50:00	4.15	12680.0	France
541907	581587	23255	CHILDRENS CUTLERY CIRCUS PARADE	4	2011-12-09 12:50:00	4.15	12680.0	France
541908	581587	22138	BAKING SET 9 PIECE RETROSPOT	3	2011-12-09 12:50:00	4.95	12680.0	France

Figure 10.7: Displaying the last eight rows using the tail() method

It seems that we were right in assuming that the data is sorted in ascending order by the **InvoiceDate** column. We can also confirm that there is actually more than one value in the **Country** column.

We can also use the **sample()** method to randomly pick a given number of rows from the dataset with the **n** parameter. You can also specify a **seed** (which we covered in *Chapter 5, Performing Your First Cluster Analysis*) in order to get reproducible results if you run the same code again with the **random_state** parameter:

```
df.sample(n=5, random_state=1)
```

You should get the following output:

	InvoiceNo	StockCode	Description	Quantity	InvoiceDate	UnitPrice	CustomerID	Country
94801	C544414	22960	JAM MAKING SET WITH JARS	-2	2011-02-18 14:54:00	3.75	13408.0	United Kingdom
210111	555276	48111	DOORMAT 3 SMILEY CATS	1	2011-06-01 17:28:00	15.79	NaN	United Kingdom
455946	575656	22952	60 CAKE CASES VINTAGE CHRISTMAS	48	2011-11-10 14:29:00	0.55	13319.0	United Kingdom
403542	571636	20674	GREEN POLKADOT BOWL	16	2011-10-18 11:41:00	1.25	13509.0	United Kingdom
471951	576657	22556	PLASTERS IN TIN CIRCUS PARADE	12	2011-11-16 11:03:00	1.65	12720.0	Germany

Figure 10.8: Displaying five random sampled rows using the sample() method

In this output, we can see an additional value in the **Country** column: **Germany**. We can also notice a few interesting points:

- **InvoiceNo** can also contain alphabetical letters (row **94,801** starts with a **C**, which may have a special meaning).
- **Quantity** can have negative values: **-2** (row **94801**).
- **CustomerID** contains missing values: **NaN** (row **210111**).

EXERCISE 10.01: EXPLORING THE AMES HOUSING DATASET WITH DESCRIPTIVE STATISTICS

In this exercise, we will explore the **Ames Housing dataset** in order to get a good understanding of it by analyzing its structure and looking at some of its rows.

The dataset we will be using in this exercise is the Ames Housing dataset, which can be found on our GitHub repository: https://packt.live/35kRKAo.

> **NOTE**
>
> This dataset was compiled by Dean De Cock.
>
> This dataset contains a list of residential house sales in the city of Ames, Iowa, between 2016 and 2010.
>
> More information about each variable can be found at https://packt.live/2sT88L4.

The following steps will help you to complete this exercise:

1. Open a new Colab notebook.
2. Import the **pandas** package:

```
import pandas as pd
```

3. Assign the link to the AMES dataset to a variable called **file_url**:

```
file_url = 'https://raw.githubusercontent.com/'\
           'PacktWorkshops/The-Data-Science-Workshop/'\
           'master/Chapter10/dataset/ames_iowa_housing.csv'
```

4. Use the **.read_csv()** method from the **pandas** package and load the dataset into a new variable called **df**:

```
df = pd.read_csv(file_url)
```

5. Print the number of rows and columns of the DataFrame using the **shape** attribute from the **pandas** package:

```
df.shape
```

You should get the following output:

```
(1460, 81)
```

We can see that this dataset contains **1460** rows and **81** different columns.

6. Print the names of the variables contained in this DataFrame using the **columns** attribute from the **pandas** package:

```
df.columns
```

You should get the following output:

```
Index(['Id', 'MSSubClass', 'MSZoning', 'LotFrontage', 'LotArea', 'Street',
       'Alley', 'LotShape', 'LandContour', 'Utilities', 'LotConfig',
       'LandSlope', 'Neighborhood', 'Condition1', 'Condition2', 'BldgType',
       'HouseStyle', 'OverallQual', 'OverallCond', 'YearBuilt', 'YearRemodAdd',
       'RoofStyle', 'RoofMatl', 'Exterior1st', 'Exterior2nd', 'MasVnrType',
       'MasVnrArea', 'ExterQual', 'ExterCond', 'Foundation', 'BsmtQual',
       'BsmtCond', 'BsmtExposure', 'BsmtFinType1', 'BsmtFinSF1',
       'BsmtFinType2', 'BsmtFinSF2', 'BsmtUnfSF', 'TotalBsmtSF', 'Heating',
       'HeatingQC', 'CentralAir', 'Electrical', '1stFlrSF', '2ndFlrSF',
       'LowQualFinSF', 'GrLivArea', 'BsmtFullBath', 'BsmtHalfBath', 'FullBath',
       'HalfBath', 'BedroomAbvGr', 'KitchenAbvGr', 'KitchenQual',
       'TotRmsAbvGrd', 'Functional', 'Fireplaces', 'FireplaceQu', 'GarageType',
       'GarageYrBlt', 'GarageFinish', 'GarageCars', 'GarageArea', 'GarageQual',
       'GarageCond', 'PavedDrive', 'WoodDeckSF', 'OpenPorchSF',
       'EnclosedPorch', '3SsnPorch', 'ScreenPorch', 'PoolArea', 'PoolQC',
       'Fence', 'MiscFeature', 'MiscVal', 'MoSold', 'YrSold', 'SaleType',
       'SaleCondition', 'SalePrice'],
      dtype='object')
```

Figure 10.9: List of columns in the housing dataset

We can infer the type of information contained in some of the variables by looking at their names, such as **LotArea** (property size), **YearBuilt** (year of construction), and **SalePrice** (property sale price).

7. Print out the type of each variable contained in this DataFrame using the **dtypes** attribute from the **pandas** package:

```
df.dtypes
```

You should get the following output:

```
Id                 int64
MSSubClass         int64
MSZoning          object
LotFrontage      float64
LotArea            int64
                   ...
MoSold             int64
YrSold             int64
SaleType          object
SaleCondition     object
SalePrice          int64
Length: 81, dtype: object
```

Figure 10.10: List of columns and their type from the housing dataset

We can see that the variables are either numerical or text types. There is no date column in this dataset.

8. Display the top rows of the DataFrame using the **head()** method from **pandas**:

```
df.head()
```

You should get the following output:

	Id	MSSubClass	MSZoning	LotFrontage	LotArea	Street	Alley	LotShape	LandContour	Utilities	LotConfig
0	1	60	RL	65.0	8450	Pave	NaN	Reg	Lvl	AllPub	Inside
1	2	20	RL	80.0	9600	Pave	NaN	Reg	Lvl	AllPub	FR2
2	3	60	RL	68.0	11250	Pave	NaN	IR1	Lvl	AllPub	Inside
3	4	70	RL	60.0	9550	Pave	NaN	IR1	Lvl	AllPub	Corner
4	5	60	RL	84.0	14260	Pave	NaN	IR1	Lvl	AllPub	FR2

5 rows × 81 columns

Figure 10.11: First five rows of the housing dataset

9. Display the last five rows of the DataFrame using the **tail()** method from **pandas**:

```
df.tail()
```

You should get the following output:

	Id	MSSubClass	MSZoning	LotFrontage	LotArea	Street	Alley	LotShape	LandContour	Utilities	LotConfig
1455	1456	60	RL	62.0	7917	Pave	NaN	Reg	Lvl	AllPub	Inside
1456	1457	20	RL	85.0	13175	Pave	NaN	Reg	Lvl	AllPub	Inside
1457	1458	70	RL	66.0	9042	Pave	NaN	Reg	Lvl	AllPub	Inside
1458	1459	20	RL	68.0	9717	Pave	NaN	Reg	Lvl	AllPub	Inside
1459	1460	20	RL	75.0	9937	Pave	NaN	Reg	Lvl	AllPub	Inside

5 rows × 81 columns

Figure 10.12: Last five rows of the housing dataset

It seems that the **Alley** column has a lot of missing values, which are represented by the **NaN** value (which stands for **Not a Number**). The **Street** and **Utilities** columns seem to have only one value.

10. Now, display **5** random sampled rows of the DataFrame using the **sample()** method from **pandas** and pass it a **'random_state'** of **8**:

```
df.sample(n=5, random_state=8)
```

You should get the following output:

	Id	MSSubClass	MSZoning	LotFrontage	LotArea	Street	Alley	LotShape	LandContour	Utilities	LotConfig
1260	1261	60	RL	NaN	24682	Pave	NaN	IR3	Lvl	AllPub	CulDSac
274	275	20	RL	76.0	8314	Pave	NaN	Reg	Lvl	AllPub	Corner
51	52	50	RM	52.0	6240	Pave	NaN	Reg	Lvl	AllPub	Inside
117	118	20	RL	74.0	8536	Pave	NaN	Reg	Lvl	AllPub	Corner
789	790	60	RL	NaN	12205	Pave	NaN	IR1	Low	AllPub	Inside

5 rows × 81 columns

Figure 10.13: Five randomly sampled rows of the housing dataset

With these random samples, we can see that the **LotFrontage** column also has some missing values. We can also see that this dataset contains both numerical and text data (object types). We will analyze them more in detail in *Exercise 10.02, Analyzing the Categorical Variables from the Ames Housing Dataset*, and *Exercise 10.03, Analyzing Numerical Variables from the Ames Housing Dataset*.

> **NOTE**
>
> To access the source code for this specific section, please refer to https://packt.live/2E8HMdH.
>
> You can also run this example online at https://packt.live/3g62zLT.

We learned quite a lot about this dataset in just a few lines of code, such as the number of rows and columns, the data type of each variable, and their information. We also identified some issues with missing values.

ANALYZING THE CONTENT OF A CATEGORICAL VARIABLE

Now that we've got a good feel for the kind of information contained in the **online retail dataset**, we want to dig a little deeper into each of its columns:

```
import pandas as pd
file_url = 'https://github.com/PacktWorkshops/'\
           'The-Data-Science-Workshop/blob'\
           '/master/Chapter10/dataset/'\
           'Online%20Retail.xlsx?raw=true'
df = pd.read_excel(file_url)
```

For instance, we would like to know how many different values are contained in each of the variables by calling the **nunique()** method. This is particularly useful for a categorical variable with a limited number of values, such as **Country**:

```
df['Country'].nunique()
```

You should get the following output:

```
38
```

We can see that there are 38 different countries in this dataset. It would be great if we could get a list of all the values in this column. Thankfully, the **pandas** package provides a method to get these results: **unique()**:

```
df['Country'].unique()
```

You should get the following output:

```
array(['United Kingdom', 'France', 'Australia', 'Netherlands', 'Germany',
       'Norway', 'EIRE', 'Switzerland', 'Spain', 'Poland', 'Portugal',
       'Italy', 'Belgium', 'Lithuania', 'Japan', 'Iceland',
       'Channel Islands', 'Denmark', 'Cyprus', 'Sweden', 'Austria',
       'Israel', 'Finland', 'Bahrain', 'Greece', 'Hong Kong', 'Singapore',
       'Lebanon', 'United Arab Emirates', 'Saudi Arabia',
       'Czech Republic', 'Canada', 'Unspecified', 'Brazil', 'USA',
       'European Community', 'Malta', 'RSA'], dtype=object)
```

Figure 10.14: List of unique values for the 'Country' column

We can see that there are multiple countries from different continents, but most of them come from Europe. We can also see that there is a value called **Unspecified** and another one for **European Community**, which may be for all the countries of the eurozone that are not listed separately.

Another very useful method from **pandas** is **value_counts()**. This method lists all the values from a given column but also their occurrence. By providing the **dropna=False** and **normalise=True** parameters, this method will include the missing value in the listing and calculate the number of occurrences as a ratio, respectively:

```
df['Country'].value_counts(dropna=False, normalize=True)
```

You should get the following output:

```
United Kingdom      0.914320
Germany             0.017521
France              0.015790
EIRE                0.015124
Spain               0.004674
Netherlands         0.004375
Belgium             0.003818
Switzerland         0.003694
Portugal            0.002803
Australia           0.002323
Norway              0.002004
Italy               0.001482
Channel Islands     0.001399
Finland             0.001283
Cyprus              0.001148
Sweden              0.000853
Unspecified         0.000823
Austria             0.000740
Denmark             0.000718
```

Figure 10.15: A truncated list of unique values and their occurrence percentage for the 'Country' column

From this output, we can see that the **`United Kingdom`** value is totally dominating this column as it represents over 91% of the rows and that other values such as **`Austria`** and **`Denmark`** are quite rare as they represent less than 1% of this dataset.

EXERCISE 10.02: ANALYZING THE CATEGORICAL VARIABLES FROM THE AMES HOUSING DATASET

In this exercise, we will continue our dataset exploration by analyzing the categorical variables of this dataset. To do so, we will implement our own **`describe`** functions.

The dataset we will be using in this exercise is the Ames Housing dataset, which can be found on our GitHub repository: https://packt.live/35kRKAo. Let's get started:

1. Open a new Colab notebook.
2. Import the **`pandas`** package:

```
import pandas as pd
```

3. Assign the following link to the AMES dataset to a variable called **file_url**:

```
file_url = 'https://raw.githubusercontent.com/'\
           'PacktWorkshops/The-Data-Science-Workshop/'\
           'master/Chapter10/dataset/ames_iowa_housing.csv'
```

4. Use the **.read_csv()** method from the **pandas** package and load the dataset into a new variable called **df**:

```
df = pd.read_csv(file_url)
```

5. Create a new DataFrame called **obj_df** with only the columns that are of numerical types using the **select_dtypes** method from **pandas** package. Then, pass in the **object** value to the **include** parameter:

```
obj_df = df.select_dtypes(include='object')
```

6. Using the **columns** attribute from **pandas**, extract the list of columns of this DataFrame, **obj_df**, assign it to a new variable called **obj_cols**, and print its content:

```
obj_cols = obj_df.columns
obj_cols
```

You should get the following output:

```
Index(['MSZoning', 'Street', 'Alley', 'LotShape', 'LandContour', 'Utilities',
       'LotConfig', 'LandSlope', 'Neighborhood', 'Condition1', 'Condition2',
       'BldgType', 'HouseStyle', 'RoofStyle', 'RoofMatl', 'Exterior1st',
       'Exterior2nd', 'MasVnrType', 'ExterQual', 'ExterCond', 'Foundation',
       'BsmtQual', 'BsmtCond', 'BsmtExposure', 'BsmtFinType1', 'BsmtFinType2',
       'Heating', 'HeatingQC', 'CentralAir', 'Electrical', 'KitchenQual',
       'Functional', 'FireplaceQu', 'GarageType', 'GarageFinish', 'GarageQual',
       'GarageCond', 'PavedDrive', 'PoolQC', 'Fence', 'MiscFeature',
       'SaleType', 'SaleCondition'],
      dtype='object')
```

Figure 10.16: List of categorical variables

7. Create a function called **describe_object** that takes a **pandas** DataFrame and a column name as input parameters. Then, inside the function, print out the name of the given column, its number of unique values using the **nunique()** method, and the list of values and their occurrence using the **value_counts()** method, as shown in the following code snippet:

```
def describe_object(df, col_name):
    print(f"\nCOLUMN: {col_name}")
    print(f"{df[col_name].nunique()} different values")
    print(f"List of values:")
    print(df[col_name].value_counts\
                   (dropna=False, normalize=True))
```

8. Test this function by providing the **df** DataFrame and the **'MSZoning'** column:

```
describe_object(df, 'MSZoning')
```

You should get the following output:

```
COLUMN: MSZoning
5 different values
List of values:
RL          0.788356
RM          0.149315
FV          0.044521
RH          0.010959
C (all)     0.006849
Name: MSZoning, dtype: float64
```

Figure 10.17: Display of the created function for the MSZoning column

For the **MSZoning** column, the **RL** value represents almost **79%** of the values, while **C (all)** is only present in less than **1%** of the rows.

9. Create a **for** loop that will call the created function for every element from the **obj_cols** list:

```
for col_name in obj_cols:
    describe_object(df, col_name)
```

You should get the following output:

```
COLUMN: MSZoning
5 different values
List of values:
RL          0.788356
RM          0.149315
FV          0.044521
RH          0.010959
C (all)     0.006849
Name: MSZoning, dtype: float64

COLUMN: Street
2 different values
List of values:
Pave    0.99589
Grvl    0.00411
Name: Street, dtype: float64

COLUMN: Alley
2 different values
List of values:
NaN     0.937671
```

Figure 10.18: Display of the created function for the first columns contained in obj_cols

The output of the previous step is truncated in *Figure 10.18*. We can confirm that the **`Street`** column is almost constant as 99.6% of the rows contain the same value: **`Pave`**. For the column, that is, **`Alley`**, almost 94% of the rows have missing values.

> **NOTE**
>
> To access the source code for this specific section, please refer to https://packt.live/3kWoRn2.
>
> You can also run this example online at https://packt.live/3gbPnp0.

We just analyzed all the categorical variables from this dataset. We saw how to look at the distribution of all the values contained in any feature. We also found that some of them are dominated by a single value and others have mainly missing values in them.

SUMMARIZING NUMERICAL VARIABLES

Now, let's have a look at a numerical column and get a good understanding of its content. We will use some statistical measures that summarize a variable. All of these measures are referred to as descriptive statistics. In this chapter, we will introduce you to the most popular ones.

With the **`pandas`** package, a lot of these measures have been implemented as methods. For instance, if we want to know what the highest value contained in the **`'Quantity'`** column is, we can use the **`.max()`** method:

```
df['Quantity'].max()
```

You should get the following output:

```
80995
```

We can see that the maximum quantity of an item sold in this dataset is **`80995`**, which seems extremely high for a retail business. In a real project, this kind of unexpected value will have to be discussed and confirmed with the data owner or key stakeholders to see whether this is a genuine or an incorrect value. Now, let's have a look at the lowest value for **`'Quantity'`** using the **`.min()`** method:

```
df['Quantity'].min()
```

You should get the following output:

```
-80995
```

The lowest value in this variable is extremely low. We can think that having negative values is possible for returned items, but here, the minimum (**`-80995`**) is very low. This, again, will be something to be confirmed with the relevant people in your organization.

Now, we are going to have a look at the central tendency of this column. **Central tendency** is a statistical term referring to the central point where the data will cluster around. The most famous central tendency measure is the average (or mean). The average is calculated by summing all the values of a column and dividing them by the number of values.

If we plot the **Quantity** column on a graph with its average, it would look as follows:

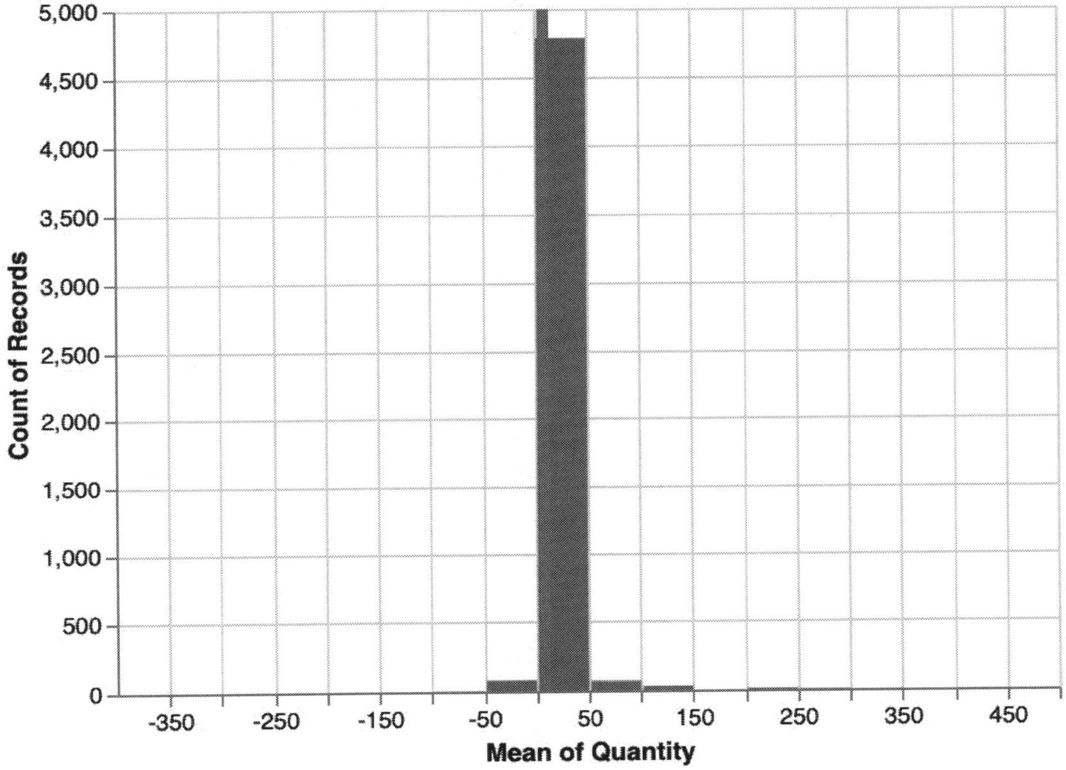

Figure 10.19: Average value for the 'Quantity' column

We can see the average for the **Quantity** column is very close to 0 and most of the data is between **-50** and **+50**.

We can get the average value of a feature by using the **mean()** method from **pandas**:

```
df['Quantity'].mean()
```

You should get the following output:

```
9.55224954743324
```

In this dataset, the average quantity of items sold is around **9.55**. The average measure is very sensitive to outliers and, as we saw previously, the minimum and maximum values of the **Quantity** column are quite extreme (**-80995 to +80995**).

We can use the median instead as another measure of central tendency. The median is calculated by splitting the column into two groups of equal lengths and getting the value of the middle point by separating these two groups, as shown in the following example:

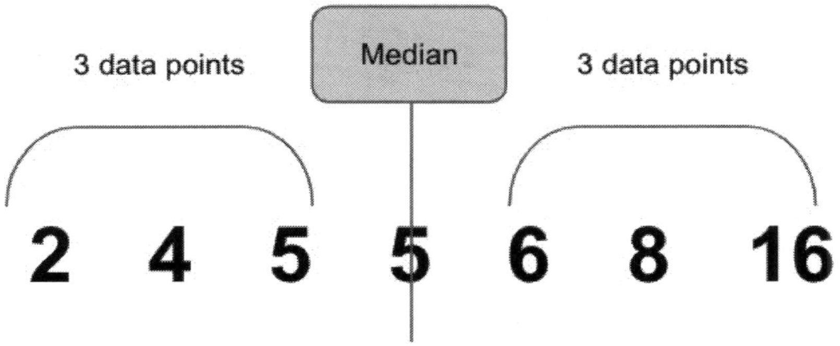

Figure 10.20: Sample median example

In **pandas**, you can call the **median()** method to get this value:

```
df['Quantity'].median()
```

You should get the following output:

```
3.0
```

The median value for this column is 3, which is quite different from the mean (**9.55**) we found earlier. This tells us that there are some outliers in this dataset and we will have to decide on how to handle them after we've done more investigation (this will be covered in *Chapter 11*, *Data Preparation*).

We can also evaluate the spread of this column (how much the data points vary from the central point). A common measure of spread is the standard deviation. The smaller this measure is, the closer the data is to its mean. On the other hand, if the standard deviation is high, this means there are some observations that are far from the average. We will use the **std()** method from **pandas** to calculate this measure:

```
df['Quantity'].std()
```

You should get the following output:

```
218.08115784986612
```

As expected, the standard deviation for this column is quite high, so the data is quite spread from the average, which is **9.55** in this example.

In the **pandas** package, there is a method that can display most of these descriptive statistics with one single line of code: **describe()**:

```
df.describe()
```

You should get the following output:

	Quantity	UnitPrice	CustomerID
count	541909.000000	541909.000000	406829.000000
mean	9.552250	4.611114	15287.690570
std	218.081158	96.759853	1713.600303
min	-80995.000000	-11062.060000	12346.000000
25%	1.000000	1.250000	13953.000000
50%	3.000000	2.080000	15152.000000
75%	10.000000	4.130000	16791.000000
max	80995.000000	38970.000000	18287.000000

Figure 10.21: Output of the describe() method

We got the exact same values for the **Quantity** column as we saw previously. This method has calculated the descriptive statistics for the three numerical columns (**Quantity**, **UnitPrice**, and **CustomerID**).

Even though the **CustomerID** column contains only numerical data, we know these values are used to identify each customer and have no mathematical meaning. For instance, it will not make sense to add customer ID **12680 to 17850** in the table or calculate the mean of these identifiers. This column is not actually numerical but categorical.

The **describe()** method doesn't know this information and just noticed there are numbers, so it assumed this is a numerical variable. This is the perfect example of why you should understand your dataset perfectly and identify the issues to be fixed before feeding the data to an algorithm. In this case, we will have to change the type of this column to categorical. In *Chapter 11*, *Data Preparation*, we will see how we can handle this kind of issue, but for now, we will look at some graphical tools and techniques that will help us have an even better understanding of the data.

EXERCISE 10.03: ANALYZING NUMERICAL VARIABLES FROM THE AMES HOUSING DATASET

In this exercise, we will continue our dataset exploration by analyzing the numerical variables of this dataset. To do so, we will implement our own **describe** functions.

The dataset we will be using in this exercise is the Ames Housing dataset, which can be found on our GitHub repository: https://packt.live/35kRKAo. Let's get started:

1. Open a new Colab notebook.
2. Import the **pandas** package:

```
import pandas as pd
```

3. Assign the link to the AMES dataset to a variable called **file_url**:

```
file_url = 'https://raw.githubusercontent.com/'\
           'PacktWorkshops/The-Data-Science-Workshop/'\
           'master/Chapter10/dataset/ames_iowa_housing.csv'
```

4. Use the **.read_csv()** method from the **pandas** package and load the dataset into a new variable called **df**:

```
df = pd.read_csv(file_url)
```

5. Create a new DataFrame called **num_df** with only the columns that are numerical using the **select_dtypes** method from the **pandas** package and pass in the **'number'** value to the **include** parameter:

```
num_df = df.select_dtypes(include='number')
```

6. Using the **columns** attribute from **pandas**, extract the list of columns of this DataFrame, **num_df**, assign it to a new variable called **num_cols**, and print its content:

```
num_cols = num_df.columns
num_cols
```

You should get the following output:

```
Index(['Id', 'MSSubClass', 'LotFrontage', 'LotArea', 'OverallQual',
       'OverallCond', 'YearBuilt', 'YearRemodAdd', 'MasVnrArea', 'BsmtFinSF1',
       'BsmtFinSF2', 'BsmtUnfSF', 'TotalBsmtSF', '1stFlrSF', '2ndFlrSF',
       'LowQualFinSF', 'GrLivArea', 'BsmtFullBath', 'BsmtHalfBath', 'FullBath',
       'HalfBath', 'BedroomAbvGr', 'KitchenAbvGr', 'TotRmsAbvGrd',
       'Fireplaces', 'GarageYrBlt', 'GarageCars', 'GarageArea', 'WoodDeckSF',
       'OpenPorchSF', 'EnclosedPorch', '3SsnPorch', 'ScreenPorch', 'PoolArea',
       'MiscVal', 'MoSold', 'YrSold', 'SalePrice'],
      dtype='object')
```

Figure 10.22: List of numerical columns

7. Create a function called **describe_numeric** that takes a **pandas** DataFrame and a column name as input parameters. Then, inside the function, print out the name of the given column, its minimum value using **min()**, its maximum value using **max()**, its average value using **mean()**, its standard deviation using **std()**, and its **median** using **median()**:

```
def describe_numeric(df, col_name):
    print(f"\nCOLUMN: {col_name}")
    print(f"Minimum: {df[col_name].min()}")
    print(f"Maximum: {df[col_name].max()}")
    print(f"Average: {df[col_name].mean()}")
    print(f"Standard Deviation: {df[col_name].std()}")
    print(f"Median: {df[col_name].median()}")
```

8. Now, test this function by providing the **df** DataFrame and the **SalePrice** column:

```
describe_numeric(df, 'SalePrice')
```

You should get the following output:

```
COLUMN: SalePrice
Minimum: 34900
Maximum: 755000
Average: 180921.19589041095
Standard Deviation: 79442.50288288663
Median: 163000.0
```

Figure 10.23: The display of the created function for the 'SalePrice' column

The sale price ranges from **34,900** to **755,000** with an average of **180,921**. The median is slightly lower than the average, which tells us there are some outliers with high sales prices.

9. Create a **for** loop that will call the created function for every element from the **num_cols** list:

```
for col_name in num_cols:
    describe_numeric(df, col_name)
```

You should get the following output:

```
COLUMN: Id
Minimum: 1
Maximum: 1460
Average: 730.5
Standard Deviation: 421.6100093688479
Median: 730.5

COLUMN: MSSubClass
Minimum: 20
Maximum: 190
Average: 56.897260273972606
Standard Deviation: 42.30057099381035
Median: 50.0

COLUMN: LotFrontage
Minimum: 21.0
Maximum: 313.0
Average: 70.04995836802665
Standard Deviation: 24.284751774483183
Median: 69.0

COLUMN: LotArea
Minimum: 1300
Maximum: 215245
```

Figure 10.24: Display of the created function for the first few columns contained in 'num_cols'

Figure 10.25 displays the truncated output. The **`Id`** column ranges from **`1`** to **`1460`**, which is the exact value as the number of rows in this dataset. This means this column is definitely a unique identifier of the property that was sold. It appears the values from the **`MSSubClass`** are all rounded. This may indicate that the information contained in this column has either been clustered into groups of 10 or categorical variable.

> **NOTE**
>
> To access the source code for this specific section, please refer to https://packt.live/2Q2TJEc.
>
> You can also run this example online at https://packt.live/2Yez18U.

We saw how to explore a newly received dataset with just a few lines of code. This helped us to understand its structure, the type of information contained in each variable, and also helped us identify some potential data quality issues, such as missing values or incorrect values.

VISUALIZING YOUR DATA

In the previous section, we saw how to explore a new dataset and calculate some simple descriptive statistics. These measures helped summarize the dataset into interpretable metrics, such as the average or maximum values. Now it is time to dive even deeper and get a more granular view of each column using data visualization.

In a data science project, data visualization can be used either for data analysis or communicating gained insights. Presenting results in a visual way that stakeholders can easily understand and interpret them in is definitely a must-have skill for any good data scientist.

However, in this chapter, we will be focusing on using data visualization for analyzing data. Most people tend to interpret information more easily on a graph than reading written information. For example, when looking at the following descriptive statistics and the scatter plot for the same variable, which one do you think is easier to interpret? Let's take a look:

```
count     5000.000000
mean         3.895058
std         14.928765
min          0.000000
25%          1.250000
50%          2.080000
75%          4.130000
max        557.720000
Name: UnitPrice, dtype: float64
```

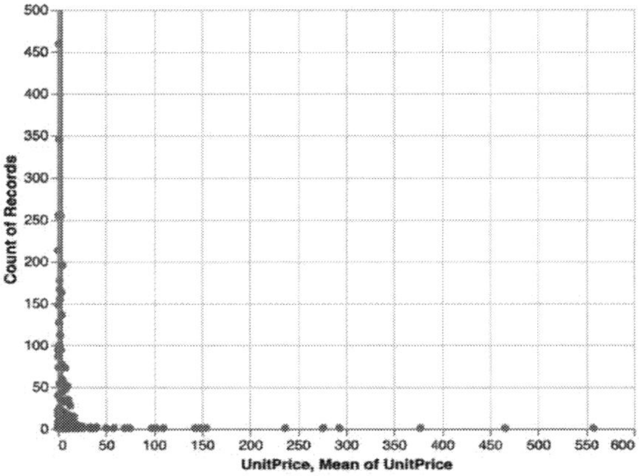

Figure 10.25: Sample visual data analysis

Even though the information shown with the descriptive statistics are more detailed, by looking at the graph, you have already seen that the data is stretched and mainly concentrated around the value 0. It probably took you less than 1 or 2 seconds to come up with this conclusion, that is, there is a cluster of points near the 0 value and that it gets reduced while moving away from it. Coming to this conclusion would have taken you more time if you were interpreting the descriptive statistics. This is the reason why data visualization is a very powerful tool for effectively analyzing data.

USING THE ALTAIR API

We will be using a package called **`altair`** (if you recall, we already briefly used it in *Chapter 5, Performing Your First Cluster Analysis*). There are quite a lot of Python packages for data visualization on the market, such as **`matplotlib`**, **`seaborn`**, or **`Bokeh`**, and compared to them, **`altair`** is relatively new, but its community of users is growing fast thanks to its simple API syntax.

Let's see how we can display a bar chart step by step on the online retail dataset.

First, import the **pandas** and **altair** packages:

```
import pandas as pd
import altair as alt
```

Then, load the data into a **pandas** DataFrame:

```
file_url = 'https://github.com/PacktWorkshops/'\
           'The-Data-Science-Workshop/blob/'\
           'master/Chapter10/dataset/'\
           'Online%20Retail.xlsx?raw=true'
df = pd.read_excel(file_url)
```

We will randomly sample 5,000 rows of this DataFrame using the **sample()** method (**altair** requires additional steps in order to display a larger dataset):

```
sample_df = df.sample(n=5000, random_state=8)
```

Now instantiate a **Chart** object from **altair** with the **pandas** DataFrame as its input parameter:

```
base = alt.Chart(sample_df)
```

Next, we call the **mark_circle()** method to specify the type of graph we want to plot: a scatter plot:

```
chart = base.mark_circle()
```

Finally, we specify the names of the columns that will be displayed on the *x* and *y* axes using the **encode()** method:

```
chart.encode(x='Quantity', y='UnitPrice')
```

We just plotted a scatter plot in seven lines of code:

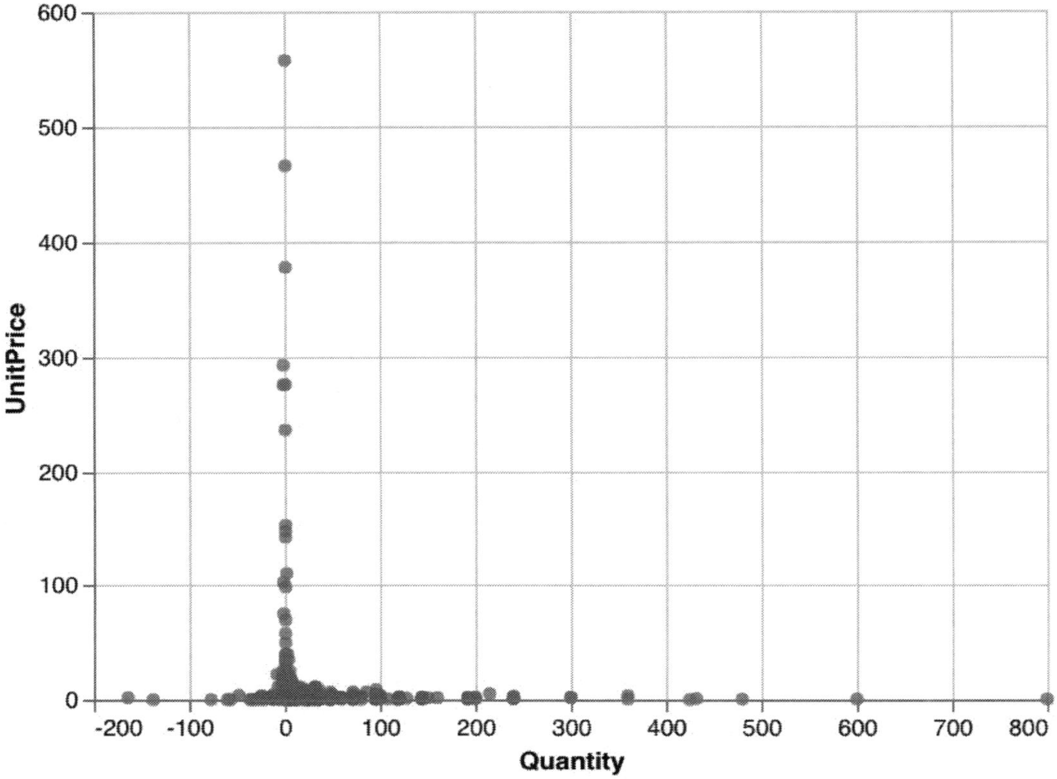

Figure 10.26: Output of the scatter plot

Altair provides the option for combining its methods all together into one single line of code, like this:

```
alt.Chart(sample_df).mark_circle()\
    .encode(x='Quantity', y='UnitPrice')
```

You should get the following output:

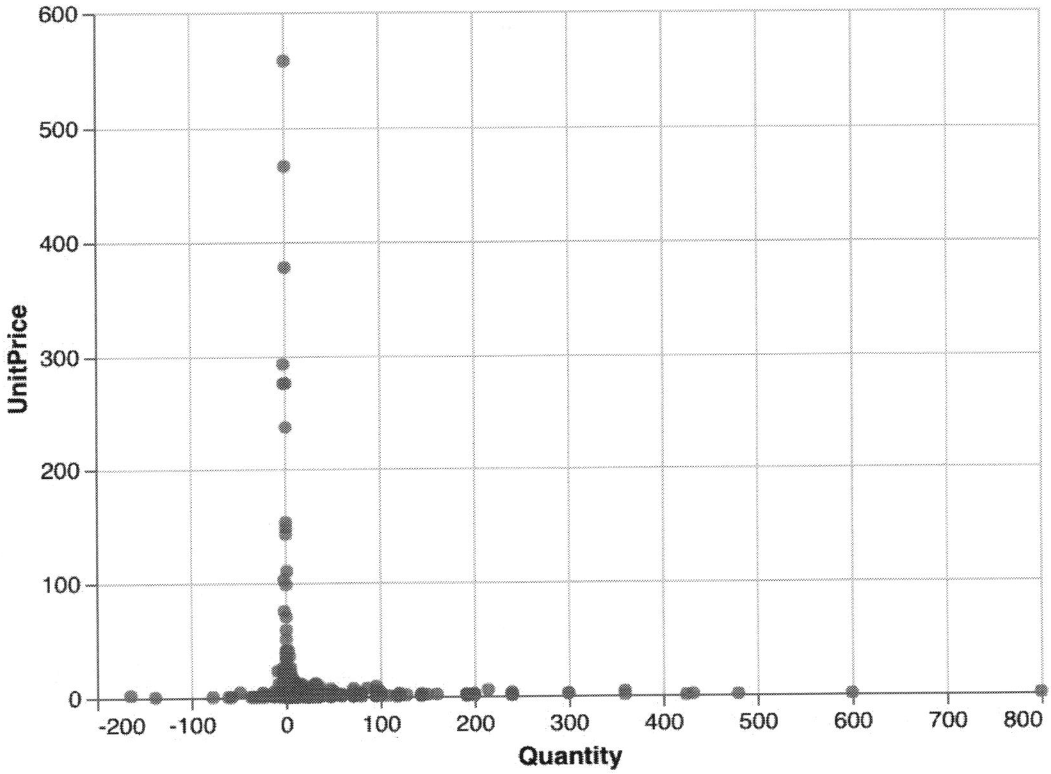

Figure 10.27: Output of the scatter plot with combined altair methods

We can see that we got the exact same output as before. This graph shows us that there are a lot of outliers (extreme values) for both variables: most of the values of **UnitPrice** are below 100, but there are some over 300, and **Quantity** ranges from -200 to 800, while most of the observations are between -50 to 150. We can also notice a pattern where items with a high unit price have lower quantity (items over 50 in terms of unit price have a quantity close to 0) and the opposite is also true (items with a quantity over 100 have a unit price close to 0).

Now, let's say we want to visualize the same plot while adding the **Country** column's information. One easy way to do this is to use the **color** parameter from the **encode()** method. This will color all the data points according to their value in the **Country** column:

```
alt.Chart(sample_df).mark_circle()\
    .encode(x='Quantity', y='UnitPrice', color='Country')
```

You should get the following output:

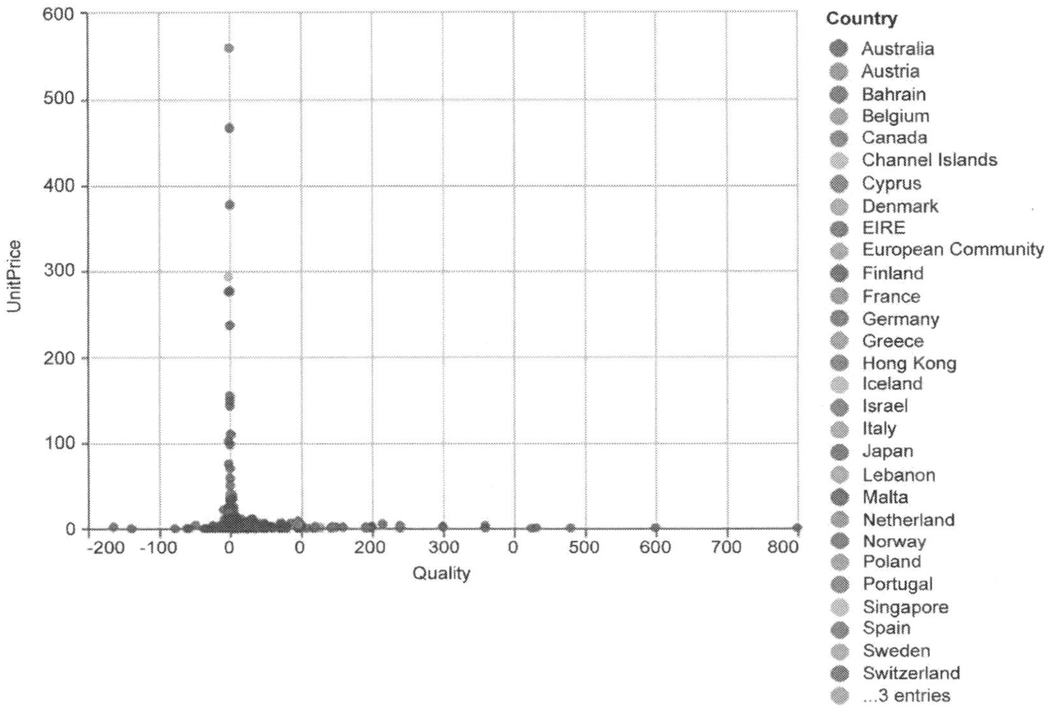

Figure 10.28: Scatter plot with colors based on the 'Country' column

We added the information from the **Country** column into the graph, but as we can see, there are too many values and it is hard to differentiate between countries: there are a lot of blue points, but it is hard to tell which countries they are representing.

With **altair**, we can easily add some interactions on the graph in order to display more information for each observation; we just need to use the **tooltip** parameter from the **encode()** method and specify the list of columns to be displayed and then call the **interactive()** method to make the whole thing interactive (as seen previously in *Chapter 5, Performing Your First Cluster Analysis*):

```
alt.Chart(sample_df).mark_circle()\
   .encode(x='Quantity', y='UnitPrice', color='Country', \
           tooltip=['InvoiceNo','StockCode','Description',\
                    'InvoiceDate','CustomerID']).interactive()
```

You should get the following output:

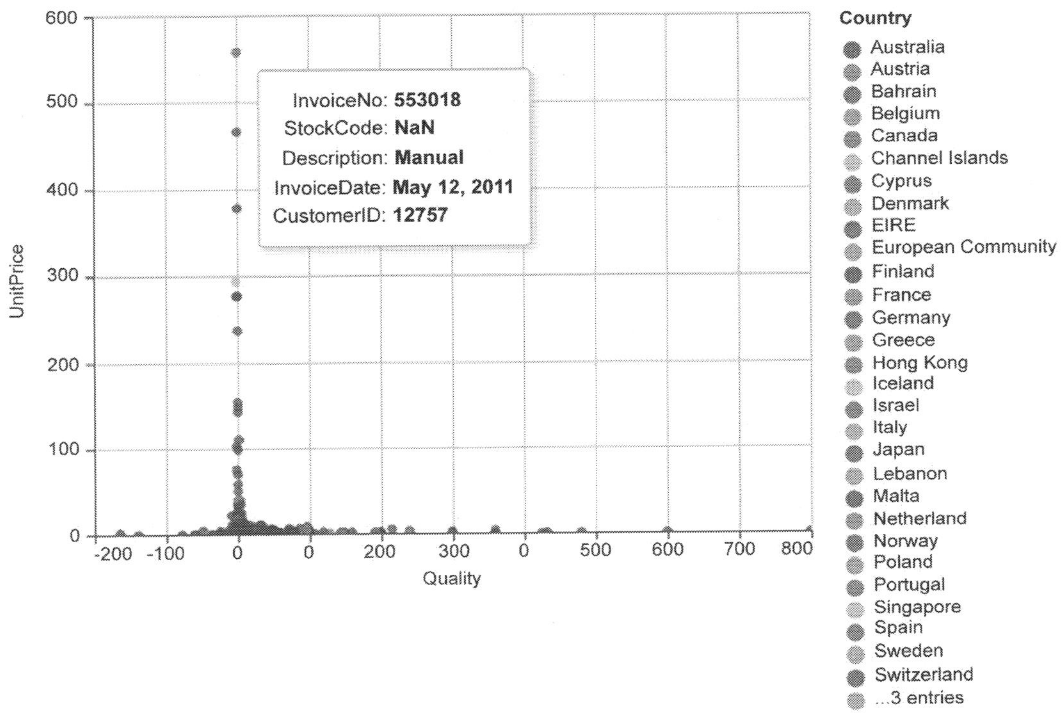

Figure 10.29: Interactive scatter plot with tooltip

Now, if we hover on the observation with the highest **`UnitPrice`** value (the one near 600), we can see the information displayed by the tooltip: this observation doesn't have any value for **`StockCode`** and its **`Description`** is **`Manual`**. So, it seems that this is not a normal transaction to happen on the website. It may be a special order that has been manually entered into the system. This is something you will have to discuss with your stakeholder and confirm.

HISTOGRAM FOR NUMERICAL VARIABLES

Now that we are familiar with the **altair** API, let's have a look at some specific type of charts that will help us analyze and understand each variable. First, let's focus on numerical variables such as **UnitPrice** or **Quantity** in the online retail dataset.

For this type of variable, a histogram is usually used to show the distribution of a given variable. The x axis of a histogram will show the possible values in this column and the y axis will plot the number of observations that fall under each value. Since the number of possible values can be very high for a numerical variable (potentially an infinite number of potential values), it is better to group these values by chunks (also called bins). For instance, we can group prices into bins of 10 steps (that is, groups of 10 items each) such as 0 to 10, 11 to 20, 21 to 30, and so on.

Let's look at this by using a real example. We will plot a histogram for **'UnitPrice'** using the **mark_bar()** and **encode()** methods with the following parameters:

- **alt.X("UnitPrice:Q", bin=True)**: This is another **altair** API syntax that allows you to tune some of the parameters for the x axis. Here, we are telling altair to use the **'UnitPrice'** column as the axis. **':Q'** specifies that this column is quantitative data (that is, numerical) and **bin=True** forces the grouping of the possible values into bins.
- **y='count()'**: This is used for calculating the number of observations and plotting them on the y axis, like so:

```
alt.Chart(sample_df).mark_bar()\
    .encode(alt.X("UnitPrice:Q", bin=True), \
            y='count()')
```

You should get the following output:

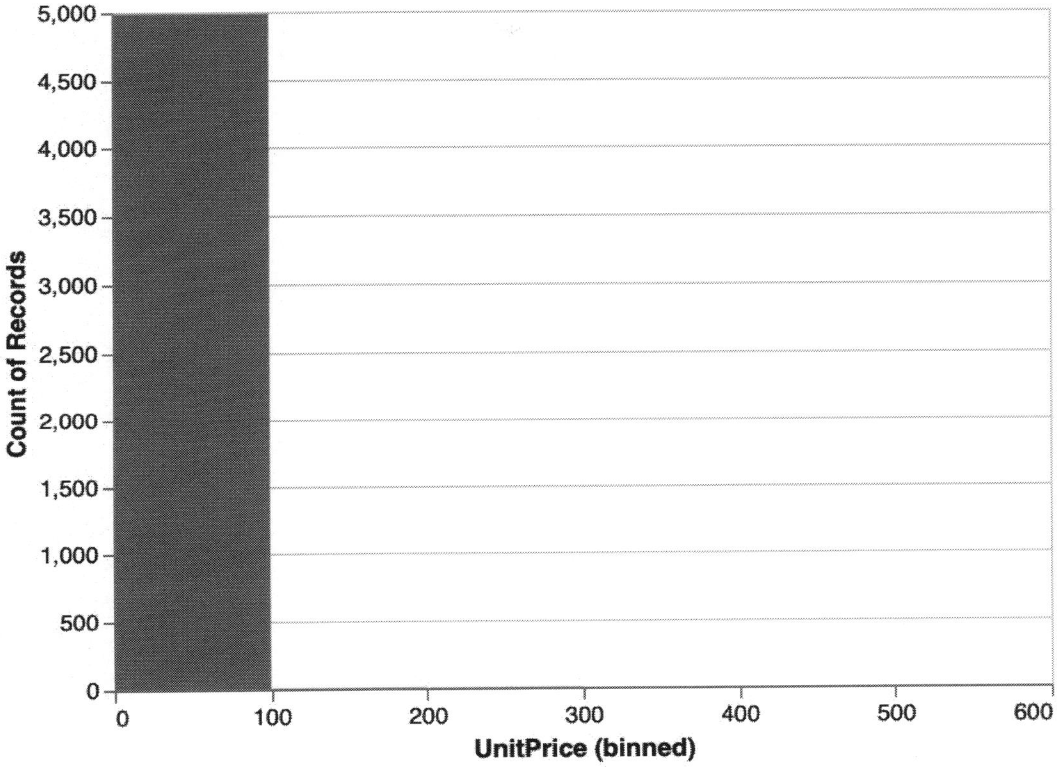

Figure 10.30: Histogram for UnitPrice with the default bin step size

By default, **`altair`** grouped the observations by bins of 100 steps: 0 to 100, then 100 to 200, and so on. The step size that was chosen is not optimal as almost all the observations fell under the first bin (0 to 100) and we can't see any other bin. With **`altair`**, we can specify the values of the parameter bin and we will try this with 5, that is, **`alt.Bin(step=5)`**:

```
alt.Chart(sample_df).mark_bar()\
    .encode(alt.X("UnitPrice:Q", bin=alt.Bin(step=5)), \
            y='count()')
```

You should get the following output:

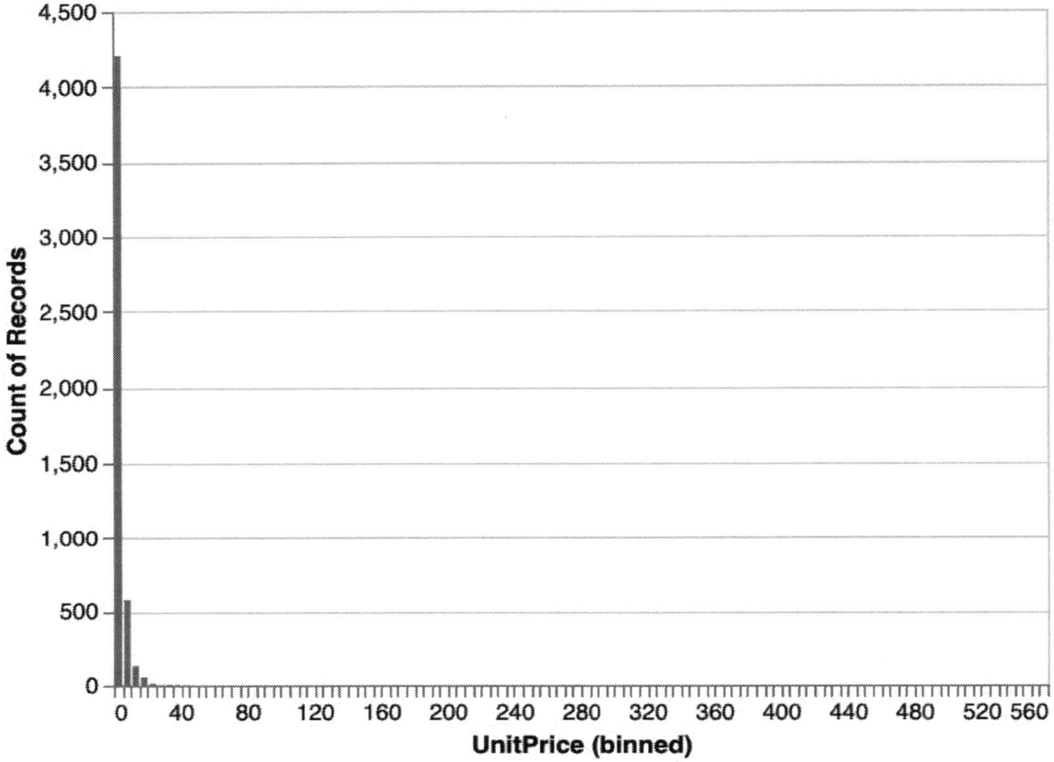

Figure 10.31: Histogram for UnitPrice with a bin step size of 5

This is much better. With this step size, we can see that most of the observations have a unit price under 5 (almost 4,200 observations). We can also see that a bit more than 500 data points have a unit price under 10. The count of records keeps decreasing as the unit price increases.

Let's plot the histogram for the **`Quantity`** column with a bin step size of 10:

```
alt.Chart(sample_df).mark_bar()\
    .encode(alt.X("Quantity:Q", bin=alt.Bin(step=10)), \
            y='count()')
```

You should get the following output:

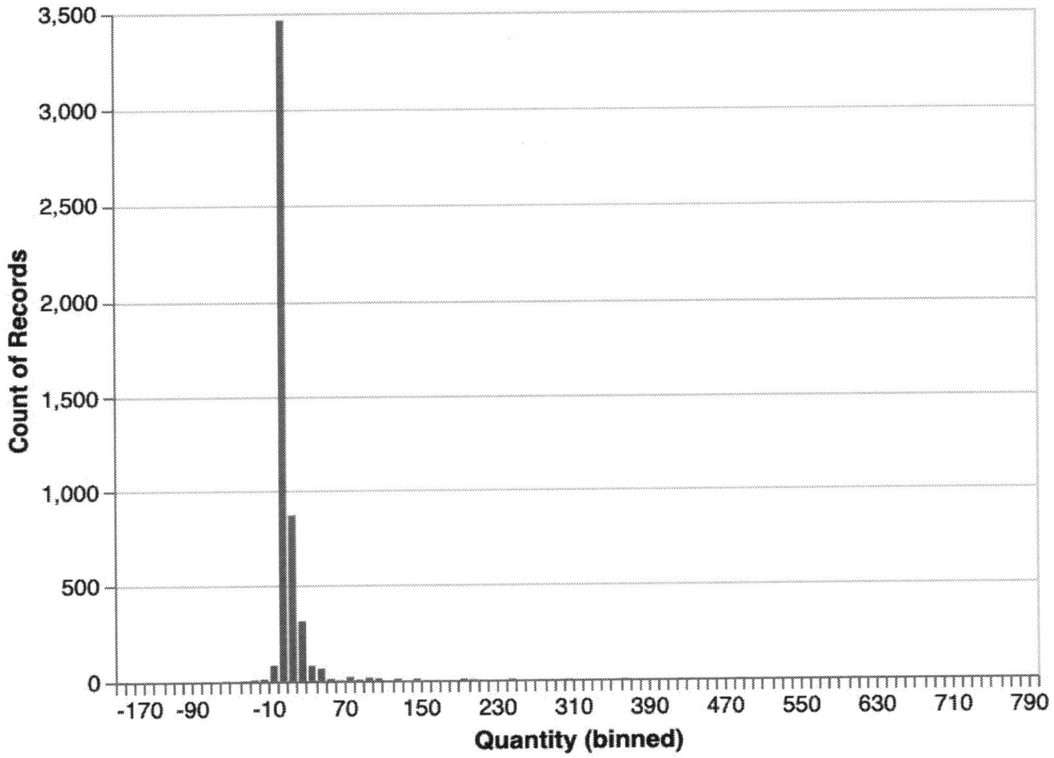

Figure 10.32: Histogram for Quantity with a bin step size of 10

In this histogram, most of the records have a positive quantity between 0 and 30 (first three highest bins). There is also a bin with around 50 observations that have a negative quantity from -10 to 0. As we mentioned earlier, these may be returned items from customers.

BAR CHART FOR CATEGORICAL VARIABLES

Now, we are going to have a look at categorical variables. For such variables, there is no need to group the values into bins as, by definition, they have a limited number of potential values. We can still plot the distribution of such columns using a simple bar chart. In **`altair`**, this is very simple – it is similar to plotting a histogram but without the **`bin`** parameter. Let's try this on the **`Country`** column and look at the number of records for each of its values:

```
alt.Chart(sample_df).mark_bar()\
    .encode(x='Country',y='count()')
```

You should get the following output:

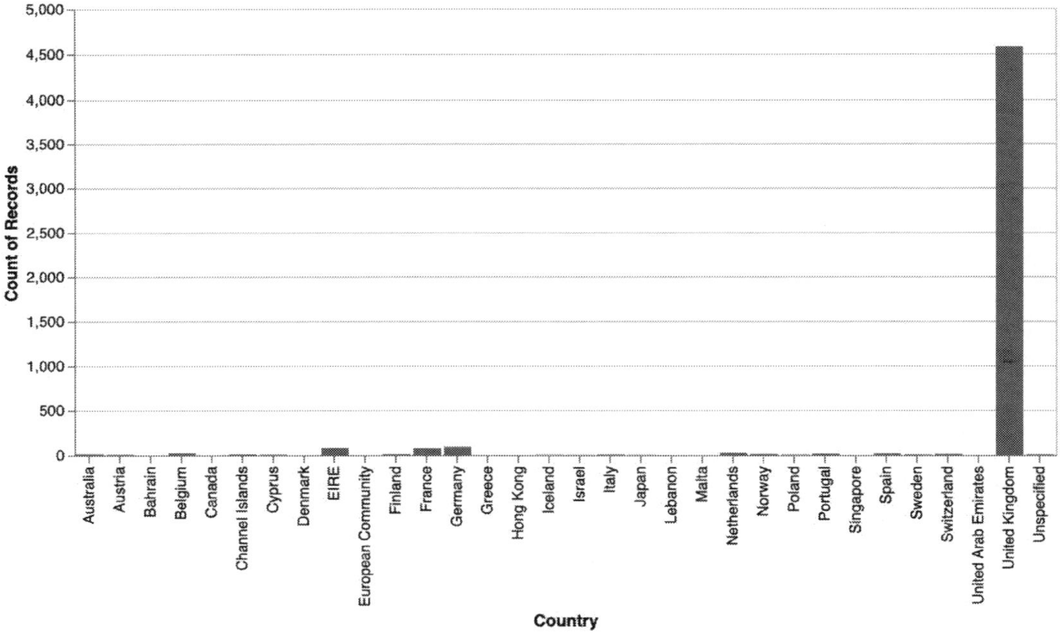

Figure 10.33: Bar chart of the Country column's occurrence

We can confirm that **`United Kingdom`** is the most represented country in this dataset (and by far), followed by **`Germany`**, **`France`**, and **`EIRE`**. We clearly have imbalanced data that may affect the performance of a predictive model. In *Chapter 13, Imbalanced Datasets*, we will look at how we can handle this situation.

Now, let's analyze the datetime column, that is, **`InvoiceDate`**. The **`altair`** package provides some functionality that we can use to group datetime information by period, such as day, day of week, month, and so on. For instance, if we want to have a monthly view of the distribution of a variable, we can use the **`yearmonth`** function to group datetimes. We also need to specify that the type of this variable is ordinal (there is an order between the values) by adding **`:O`** to the column name:

```
alt.Chart(sample_df).mark_bar()\
    .encode(alt.X('yearmonth(InvoiceDate):O'),\
            y='count()')
```

You should get the following output:

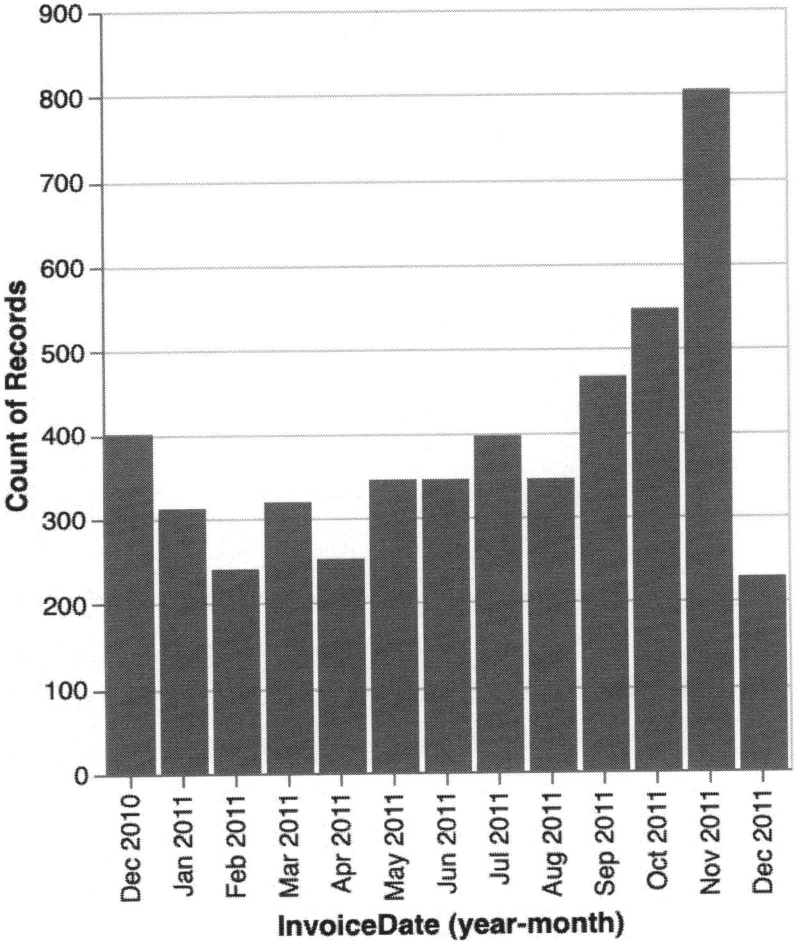

Figure 10.34: Distribution of InvoiceDate by month

This graph tells us that there was a huge spike of items sold in November 2011. It peaked to 800 items sold in this month, while the average is around 300. Was there a promotion or an advertising campaign run at that time that can explain this increase? These are the questions you may want to ask your stakeholders so that they can confirm this sudden increase of sales.

BOXPLOTS

Now, we will have a look at another specific type of chart called a **boxplot**. This kind of graph is used to display the distribution of a variable based on its quartiles. Quartiles are the values that split a dataset into quarters. Each quarter contains exactly 25% of the observations. For example, in the following sample data, the quartiles will be as follows:

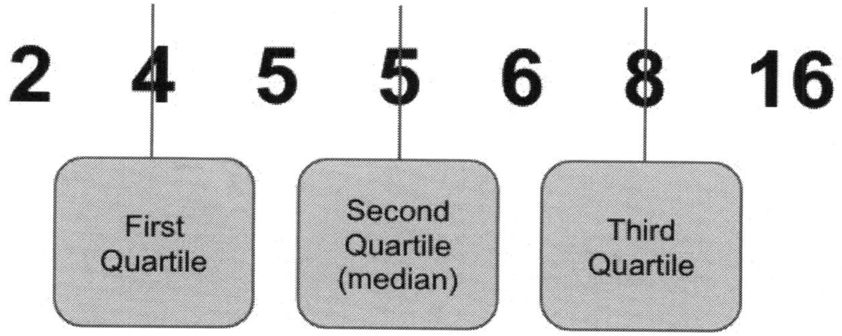

Figure 10.35: Example of quartiles for the given data

So, the first quartile (usually referred to as Q1) is 4; the second one (Q2), which is also the median, is 5; and the third quartile (Q3) is 8.

A boxplot will show these quartiles but also additional information, such as the following:

- The **interquartile range (or IQR)**, which corresponds to Q3 - Q1
- The *lowest* value, which corresponds to Q1 - (1.5 * IQR)
- The *highest* value, which corresponds to Q3 + (1.5 * IQR)
- Outliers, that is, any point outside of the lowest and highest points:

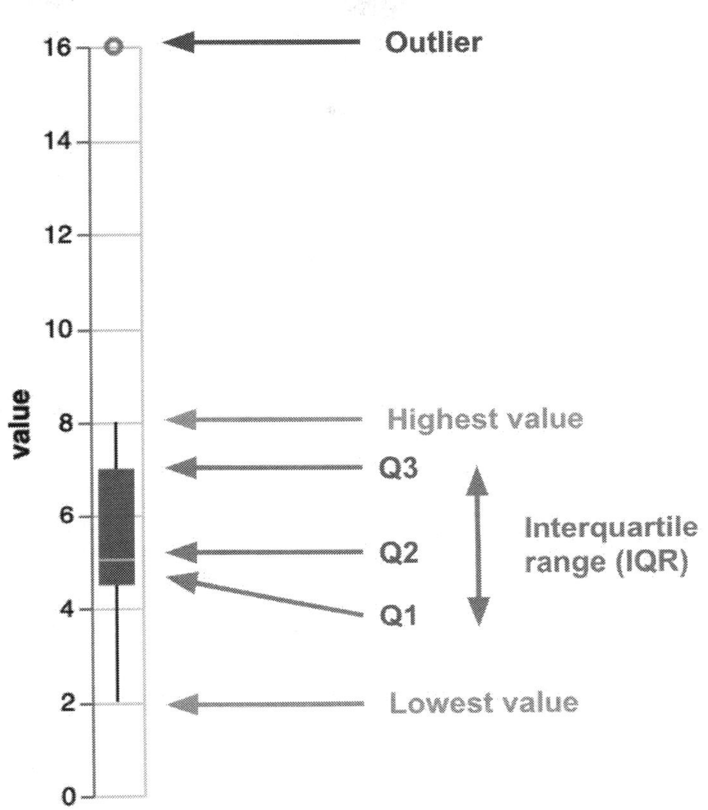

Figure 10.36: Example of a boxplot

With a boxplot, it is quite easy to see the central point (median), where 50% of the data falls under (IQR), and the outliers.

Another benefit of using a boxplot is to plot the distribution of categorical variables against a numerical variable and compare them. Let's try it with the **`Country`** and **`Quantity`** columns using the **`mark_boxplot()`** method:

```
alt.Chart(sample_df).mark_boxplot()\
    .encode(x='Country:O', y='Quantity:Q')
```

You should receive the following output:

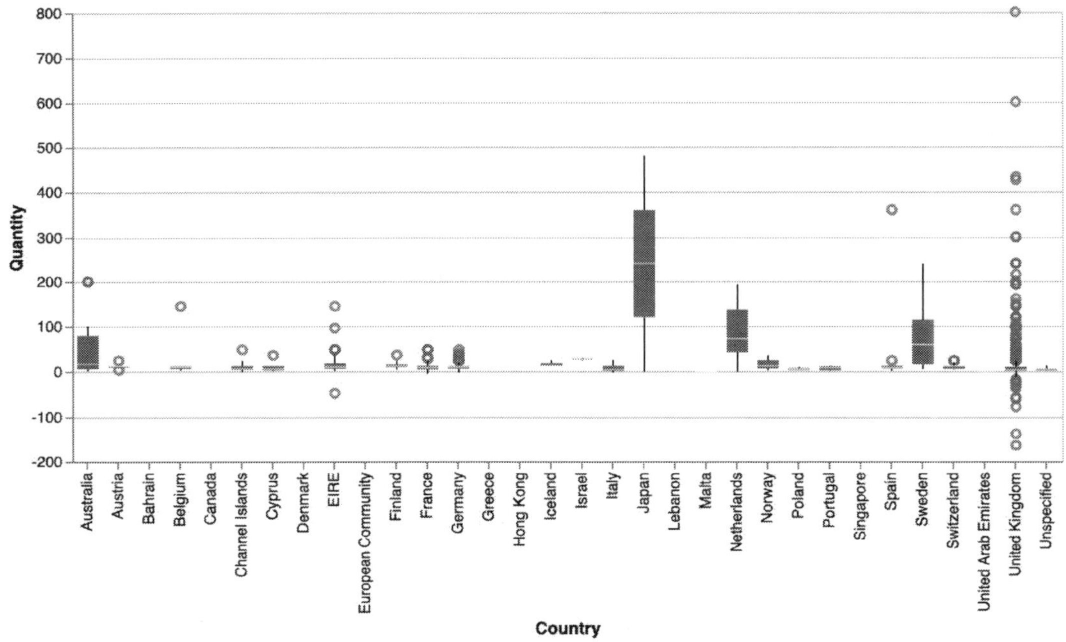

Figure 10.37: Boxplot of the 'Country' and 'Quantity' columns

This chart shows us how the **`Quantity`** variable is distributed across the different countries for this dataset. We can see that **`United Kingdom`** has a lot of outliers, especially in the negative values. **`Eire`** is another country that has negative outliers. Most of the countries have very low value quantities except for **`Japan`**, **`Netherlands`**, and **`Sweden`**, who sold more items.

In this section, we saw how to use the **`altair`** package to generate graphs that helped us get additional insights about the dataset and identify some potential issues.

EXERCISE 10.04: VISUALIZING THE AMES HOUSING DATASET WITH ALTAIR

In this exercise, we will learn how to get a better understanding of a dataset and the relationship between variables using data visualization features such as histograms, scatter plots, or boxplots.

> **NOTE**
>
> You will be using the same Ames housing dataset that was used in the previous exercises.

1. Open a new Colab notebook.
2. Import the **pandas** and **altair** packages:

```
import pandas as pd
import altair as alt
```

3. Assign the link to the AMES dataset to a variable called **file_url**:

```
file_url = 'https://raw.githubusercontent.com/'\
           'PacktWorkshops/The-Data-Science-Workshop/'\
           'master/Chapter10/dataset/ames_iowa_housing.csv'
```

4. Using the **read_csv** method from the pandas package, load the dataset into a new variable called **'df'**:

```
df = pd.read_csv(file_url)
```

Plot the histogram for the **SalePrice** variable using the **mark_bar()** and **encode()** methods from the **altair** package. Use the **alt.X** and **alt.Bin** APIs to specify the number of bin steps, that is, **50000**:

```
alt.Chart(df).mark_bar()\
   .encode(alt.X("SalePrice:Q", bin=alt.Bin(step=50000)),\
           y='count()')
```

You should get the following output:

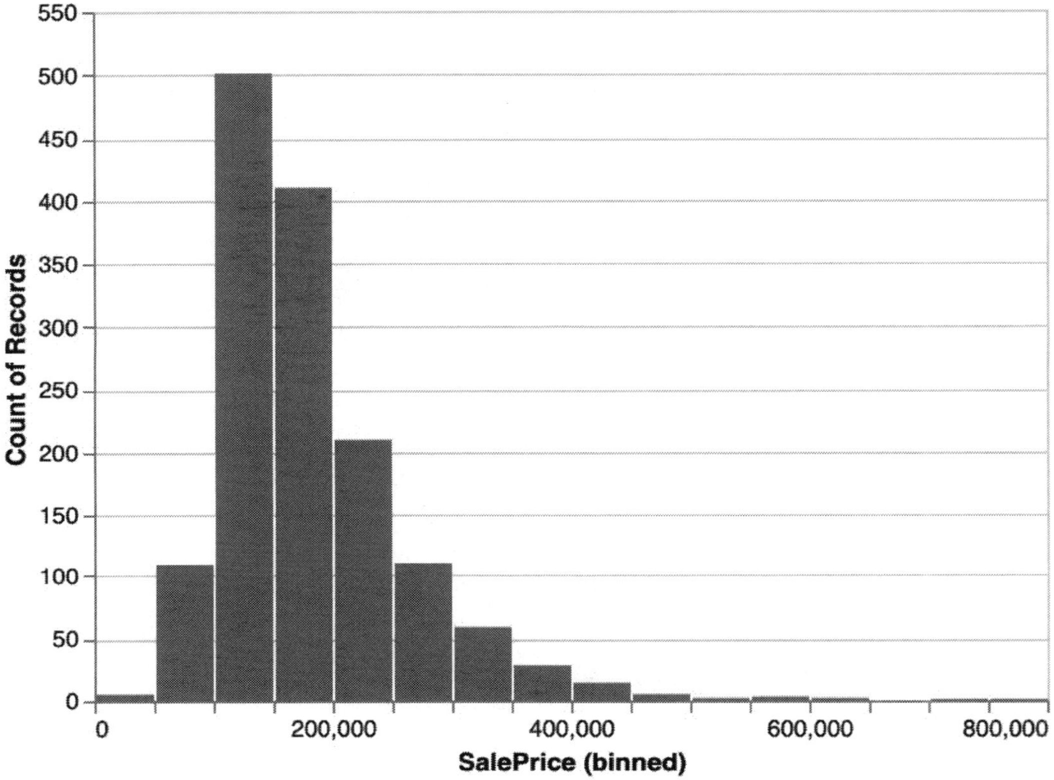

Figure 10.38: Histogram of SalePrice

This chart shows that most of the properties have a sale price centered around **`100,000 – 150,000`**. There are also a few outliers with a high sale price over **`500,000`**.

5. Now, let's plot the histogram for **`LotArea`** but this time with a bin step size of **`10000`**:

```
alt.Chart(df).mark_bar()\
    .encode(alt.X("LotArea:Q", bin=alt.Bin(step=10000)),\
            y='count()')
```

You should get the following output:

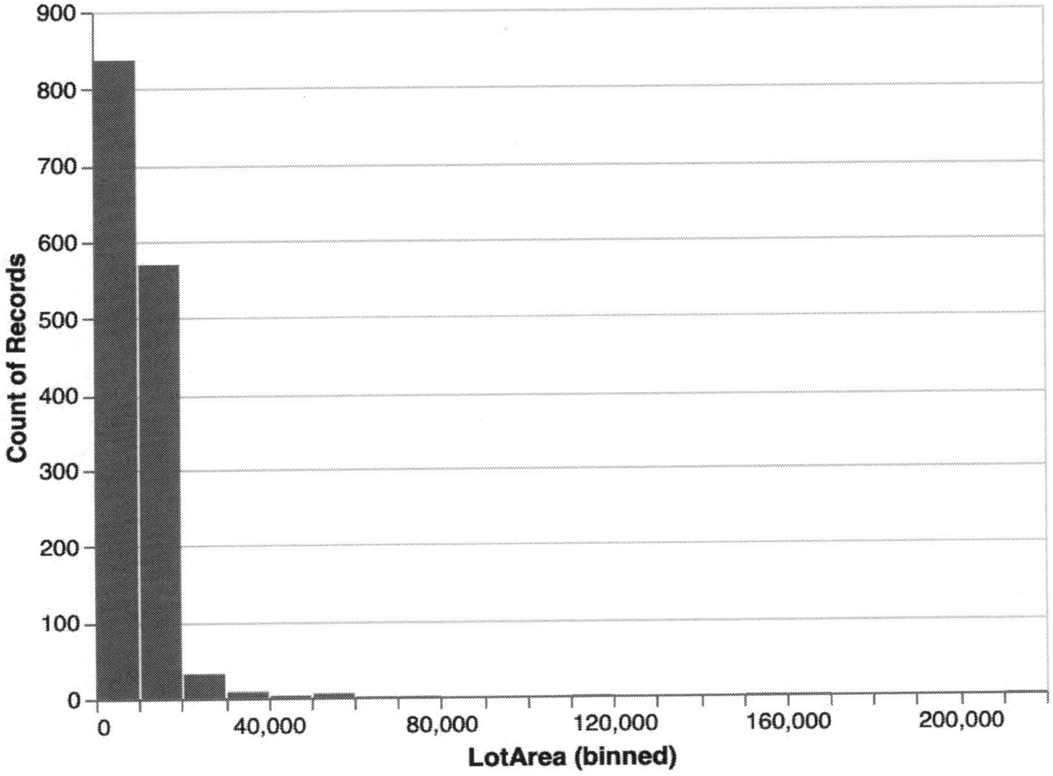

Figure 10.39: Histogram of LotArea

`LotArea` has a totally different distribution compared to **`SalePrice`**. Most of the observations are between **`0`** and **`20,000`**. The rest of the observations represent a small portion of the dataset. We can also notice some extreme outliers over **`150,000`**.

6. Now, plot a scatter plot with **`LotArea`** as the *x* axis and **`SalePrice`** as the *y* axis to understand the interactions between these two variables:

```
alt.Chart(df).mark_circle()\
    .encode(x='LotArea:Q', y='SalePrice:Q')
```

You should get the following output:

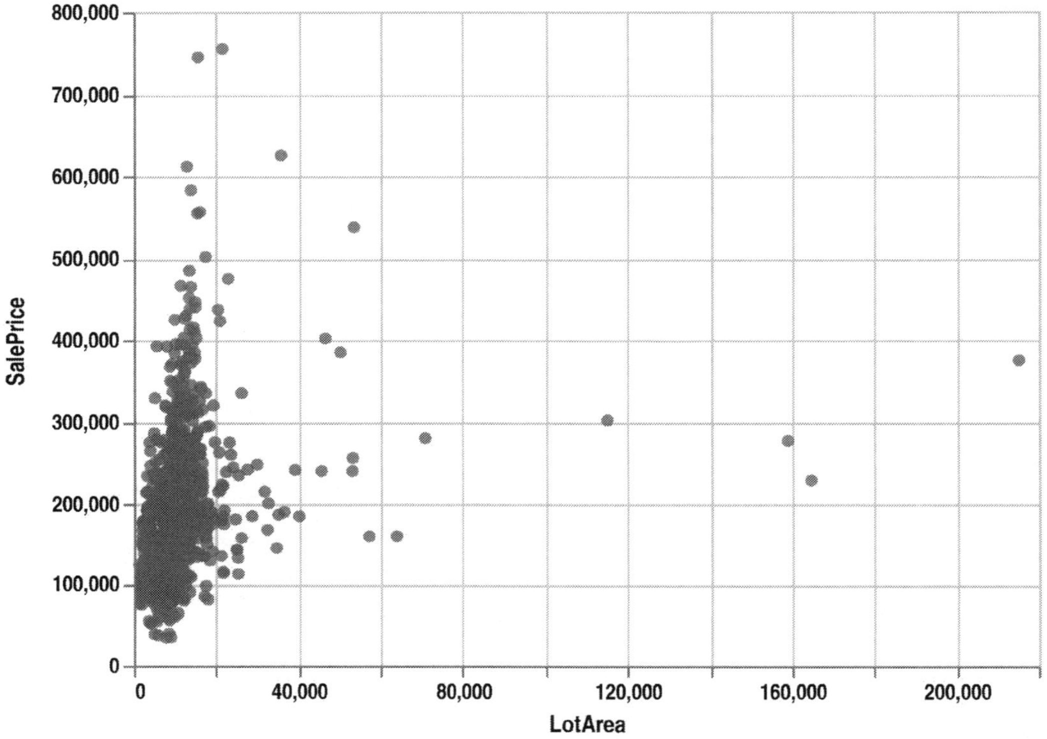

Figure 10.40: Scatter plot of SalePrice and LotArea

There is clearly a correlation between the size of the property and the sale price. If we look only at the properties with **LotArea** under 50,000, we can see a linear relationship: if we draw a straight line from the (**0,0**) coordinates to the (**20000,800000**) coordinates, we can say that **SalePrice** increases by 40,000 for each additional increase of 1,000 for **LotArea**. The formula of this straight line (or regression line) will be **SalePrice = 40000 * LotArea / 1000**. We can also see that, for some properties, although their size is quite high, their price didn't follow this pattern. For instance, the property with a size of 160,000 has been sold for less than 300,000.

7. Now, let's plot the histogram for **OverallCond**, but this time with the default bin step size, that is, (**bin=True**):

```
alt.Chart(df).mark_bar()\
    .encode(alt.X("OverallCond", bin=True), \
            y='count()')
```

You should get the following output:

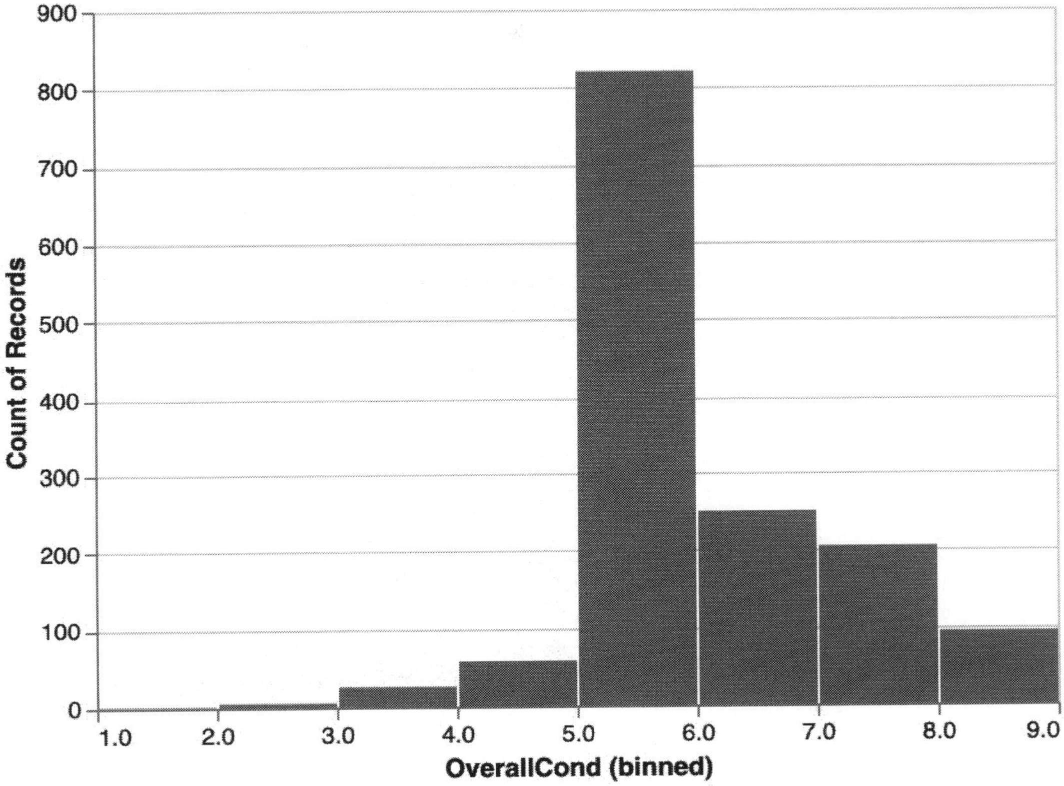

Figure 10.41: Histogram of OverallCond

We can see that the values contained in this column are discrete: they can only take a finite number of values (any integer between **1** and **9**). This variable is not numerical, but ordinal: the order matters, but you can't perform some mathematical operations on it such as adding value **2** to value **8**. This column is an arbitrary mapping to assess the overall quality of the property. In the next chapter, we will look at how we can change the type of such a column.

8. Build a boxplot with **OverallCond:O** (**':O'** is for specifying that this column is ordinal) on the *x* axis and **SalePrice** on the *y* axis using the **mark_boxplot()** method, as shown in the following code snippet:

```
alt.Chart(df).mark_boxplot()\
    .encode(x='OverallCond:O', y='SalePrice:Q')
```

You should get the following output:

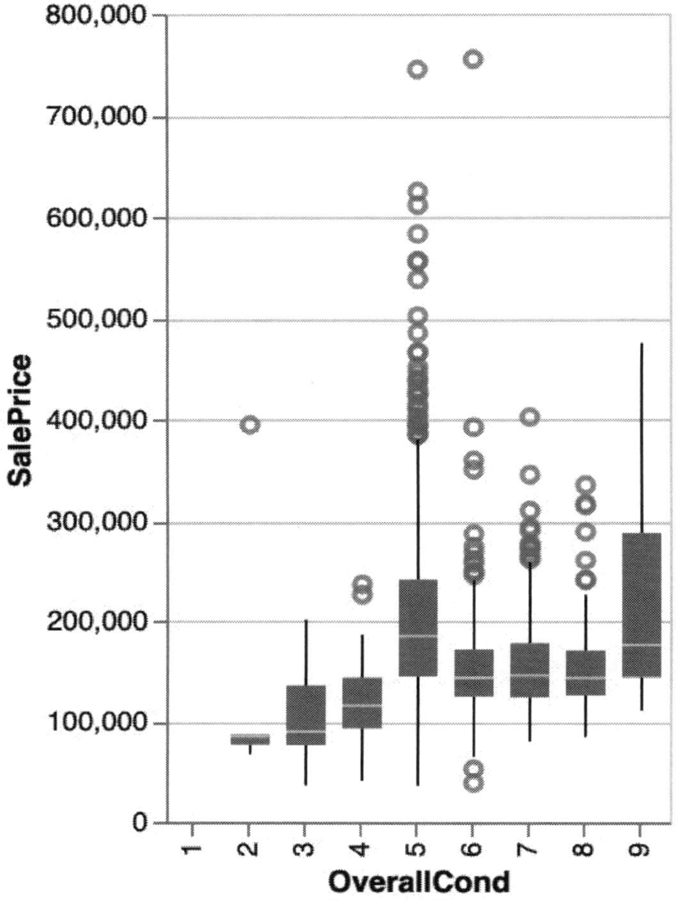

Figure 10.42: Boxplot of OverallCond

It seems that the **OverallCond** variable is in ascending order: the sales price is higher if the condition value is high. However, we will notice that **SalePrice** is quite high for the value 5, which seems to represent a medium condition. There may be other factors impacting the sales price for this category, such as higher competition between buyers for such types of properties.

9. Now, let's plot a bar chart for **YrSold** as its *x* axis and **count()** as its *y* axis. Don't forget to specify that **YrSold** is an ordinal variable and not numerical using **':O'**:

```
alt.Chart(df).mark_bar()\
    .encode(alt.X('YrSold:O'), y='count()')
```

You should get the following output:

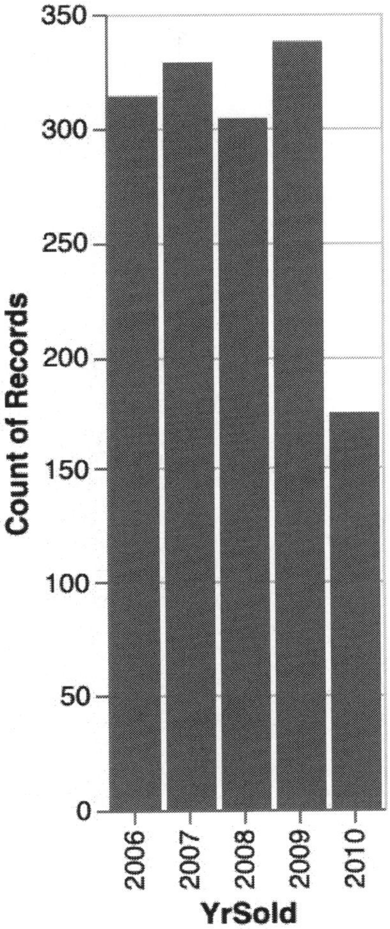

Figure 10.43: Bar chart of YrSold

We can see that, roughly, the same number of properties are sold every year, except for 2010. From 2006 to 2009, there was, on average, 310 properties sold per year, while there were only 170 in 2010.

10. Plot a boxplot similar to the one shown in *Step 8* but for **`YrSold`** as its *x* axis:

```
alt.Chart(df).mark_boxplot()\
    .encode(x='YrSold:O', y='SalePrice:Q')
```

You should get the following output:

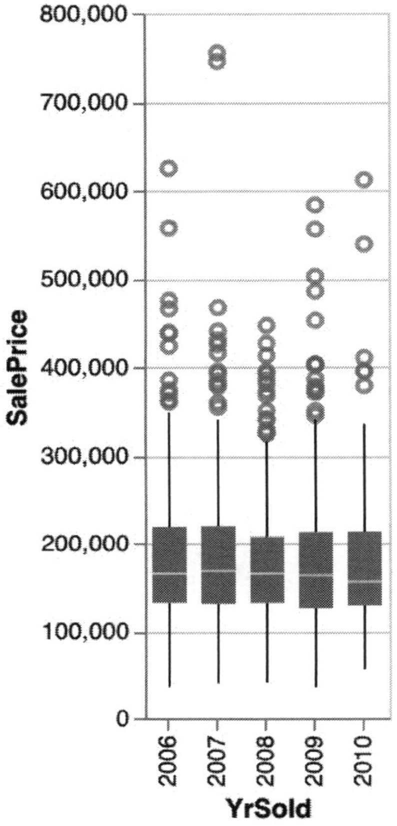

Figure 10.44: Boxplot of YrSold and SalePrice

Overall, the median sale price is quite stable across the years, with a slight decrease in 2010.

11. Let's analyze the relationship between **SalePrice** and **Neighborhood** by plotting a bar chart, similar to the one shown in *Step 9*:

```
alt.Chart(df).mark_bar()\
    .encode(x='Neighborhood',y='count()')
```

You should get the following output:

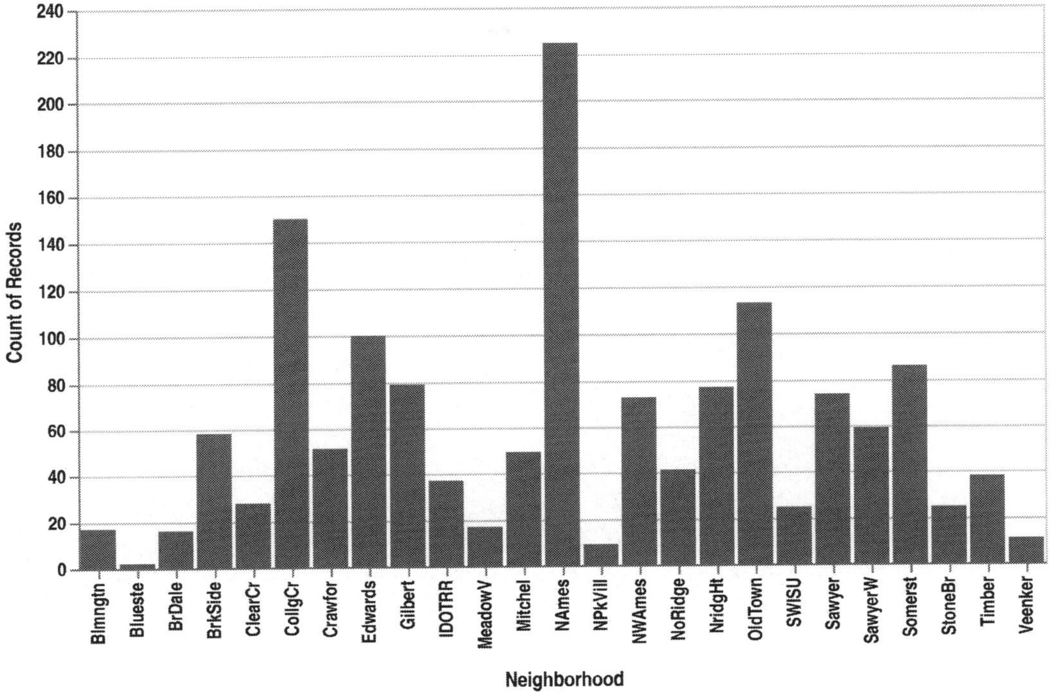

Figure 10.45: Bar chart of Neighborhood

The number of sold properties differs, depending on their location. The **'NAmes'** neighborhood has the higher number of properties sold: over 220. On the other hand, neighborhoods such as **'Blueste'** or **'NPkVill'** only had a few properties sold.

12. Let's analyze the relationship between **SalePrice** and **Neighborhood** by plotting a boxplot chart similar to the one in *Step 10*:

```
alt.Chart(df).mark_boxplot()\
    .encode(x='Neighborhood:O', y='SalePrice:Q')
```

You should get the following output:

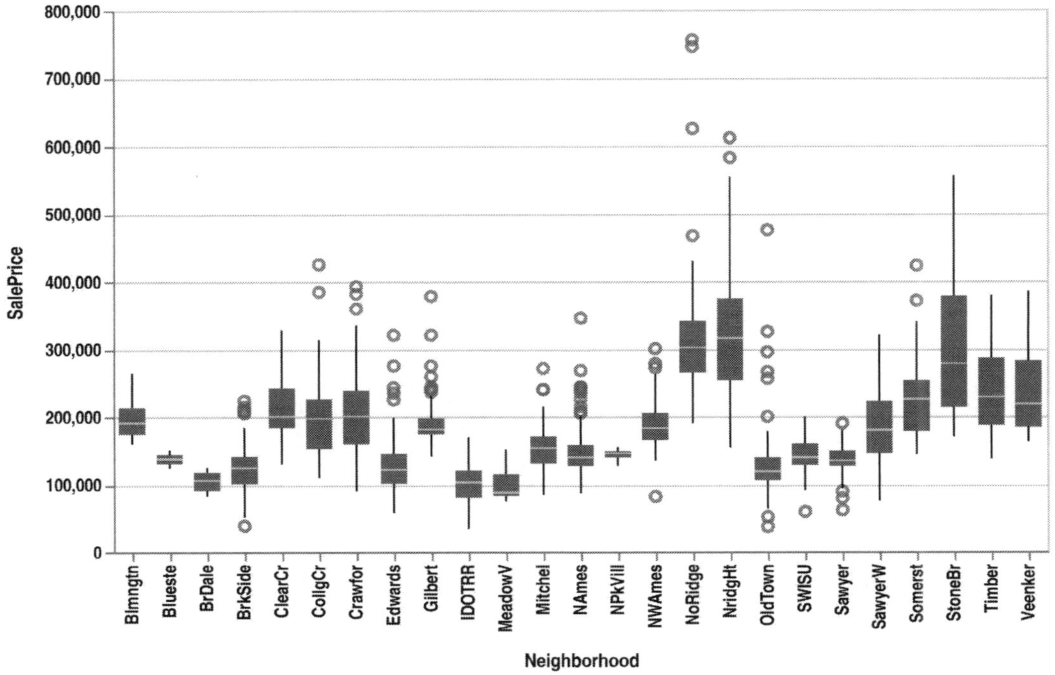

Figure 10.46: Boxplot of Neighborhood and SalePrice

The location of the properties that were sold has a significant impact on the sale price. The **`noRidge`**, **`NridgHt`**, and **`StoneBr`** neighborhoods have a higher price overall. It is also worth noting that there are some extreme outliers for **`NoRidge`** where some properties have been sold with a price that's much higher than other properties in this neighborhood.

> **NOTE**
>
> To access the source code for this specific section, please refer to https://packt.live/2CDWfO4.
>
> This section does not currently have an online interactive example, but can be run as usual on Google Colab.

With this analysis, we've completed this exercise. We saw that, by using data visualization, we can get some valuable insights about the dataset. For instance, using a scatter plot, we identified a linear relationship between **SalePrice** and **LotArea**, where the price tends to increase as the size of the property gets bigger. Histograms helped us to understand the distribution of the numerical variables and bar charts gave us a similar view for categorical variables. For example, we saw that there are more sold properties in some neighborhoods compared to others. Finally, we were able to analyze and compare the impact of different values of a variable on **SalePrice** through the use of a boxplot. We saw that the better condition a property is in, the higher the sale price will be. Data visualization is a very important tool for data scientists so that they can explore and analyze datasets.

ACTIVITY 10.01: ANALYZING CHURN DATA USING VISUAL DATA ANALYSIS TECHNIQUES

You are working for a major telecommunications company. The marketing department has noticed a recent spike of customer churn (*customers that stopped using or canceled their service from the company*).

You have been asked to analyze the customer profiles and predict future customer churn. Before building the predictive model, your first task is to analyze the data the marketing department has shared with you and assess its overall quality.

> **NOTE**
>
> The dataset to be used in this activity can be found on our GitHub repository: https://packt.live/2s1yquq.
>
> The dataset we are going to be using was has originally shared by Eduardo Arino De La Rubia on Data.World: https://packt.live/2s1ynie.

The following steps will help you complete this activity:

1. Download and load the dataset into Python using **.read_csv()**.
2. Explore the structure and content of the dataset by using **.shape**, **.dtypes**, **.head()**, **.tail()**, or **.sample()**.
3. Calculate and interpret descriptive statistics with **.describe()**.
4. Analyze each variable using data visualization with bar charts, histograms, or boxplots.

5. Identify areas that need clarification from the marketing department and potential data quality issues.

Expected Output

Here is the expected bar chart output:

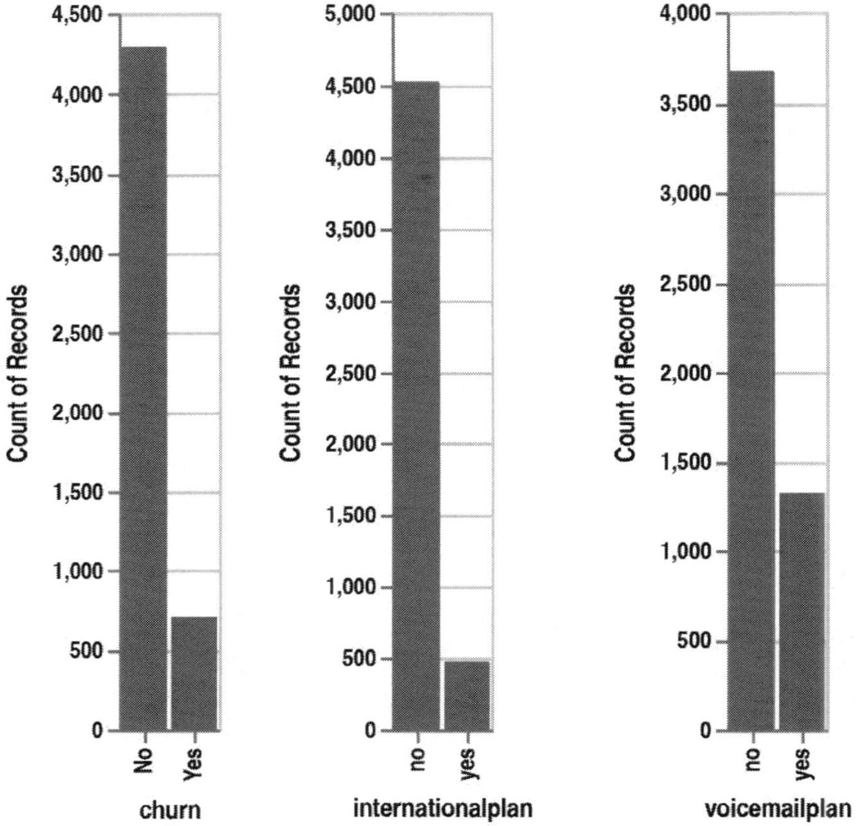

Figure 10.47: Expected bar chart output

Here is the expected histogram output:

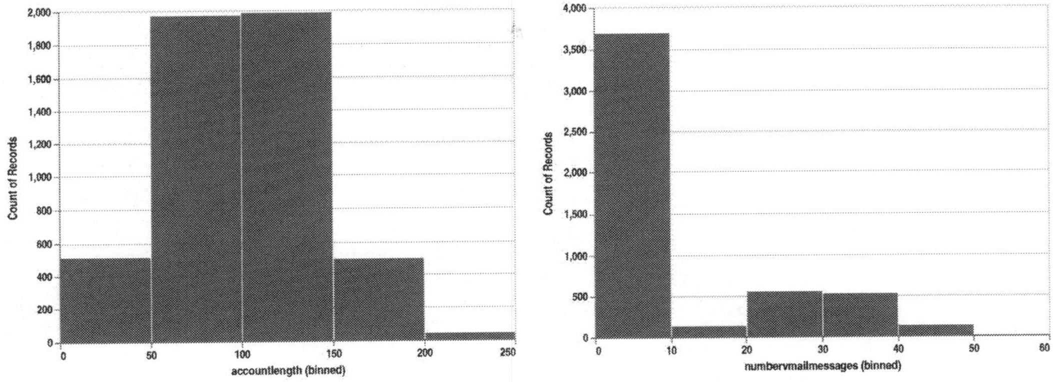

Figure 10.48: Expected histogram output

Here is the expected boxplot output:

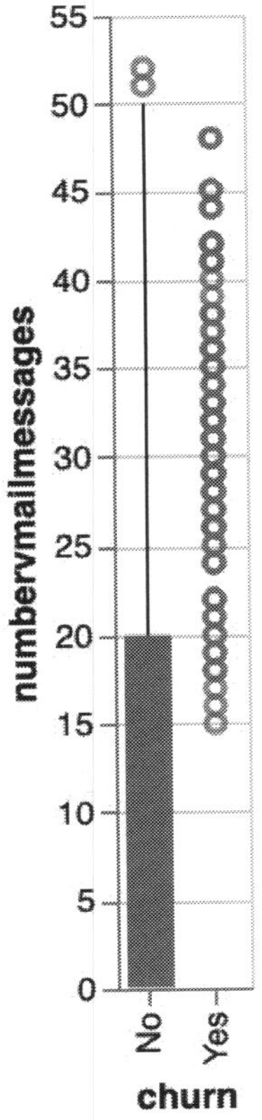

Figure 10.49: Expected boxplot output

> **NOTE**
>
> The solution to this activity can be found here: https://packt.live/2GbJloz.

You just completed the activity for this chapter. You have analyzed the dataset related to customer churn. You learned a lot about this dataset using descriptive statistics and data visualization. In a few lines of codes, you understood the structure of the DataFrame (number of rows and columns) and the type of information contained in each variable. By plotting the distribution of some columns, we learned there are specific charges for day, evening, or international calls. We also saw that the churn variable is imbalanced: there are roughly only 10% of customers who churn. Finally, we saw that one of the variables, **`numbervmailmessages`**, has a very different distribution for customers who churned or not. This may be a strong predictor for customer churn.

SUMMARY

You just learned a lot regarding how to analyze a dataset. This a very critical step in any data science project. Getting a deep understanding of the dataset will help you to better assess the feasibility of achieving the requirements from the business.

Getting the right data in the right format at the right level of quality is key for getting good predictive performance for any machine learning algorithm. This is why it is so important to take the time analyzing the data before proceeding to the next stage. This task is referred to as the data understanding phase in the CRISP-DM methodology and can also be called **Exploratory Data Analysis** (**EDA**).

You learned how to use descriptive statistics to summarize key attributes of the dataset such as the average value of a numerical column, its spread with standard deviation or its range (minimum and maximum values), the unique values of a categorical variable, and its most frequent values. You also saw how to use data visualization to get valuable insights for each variable. Now, you know how to use scatter plots, bar charts, histograms, and boxplots to understand the distribution of a column.

While analyzing the data, we came across additional questions that, in a normal project, need to be addressed with the business. We also spotted some potential data quality issues, such as missing values, outliers, or incorrect values that need to be fixed. This is the topic we will cover in the next chapter: preparing the data. Stay tuned.

11

DATA PREPARATION

OVERVIEW

By the end of this chapter you will be able to filter DataFrames with specific conditions; remove duplicate or irrelevant records or columns; convert variables into different data types; replace values in a column and handle missing values and outlier observations.

This chapter will introduce you to the main techniques you can use to handle data issues in order to achieve high quality for your dataset prior to modeling it.

INTRODUCTION

In the previous chapter, you saw how critical it was to get a very good understanding of your data and learned about different techniques and tools to achieve this goal. While performing **Exploratory Data Analysis** (**EDA**) on a given **dataset**, you may find some potential issues that need to be addressed before the modeling stage. This is exactly the topic that will be covered in this chapter. You will learn how you can handle some of the most frequent data quality issues and prepare the dataset properly.

This chapter will introduce you to the issues that you will encounter frequently during your data scientist career (such as **duplicated rows**, incorrect data types, incorrect values, and missing values) and you will learn about the techniques you can use to easily fix them. But be careful – some issues that you come across don't necessarily need to be fixed. Some of the suspicious or unexpected values you find may be genuine from a business point of view. This includes values that crop up very rarely but are totally genuine. Therefore, it is extremely important to get confirmation either from your stakeholder or the data engineering team before you alter the dataset. It is your responsibility to make sure you are making the right decisions for the business while preparing the dataset.

For instance, in *Chapter 10, Analyzing a Dataset*, you looked at the *Online Retail dataset*, which had some negative values in the **`Quantity`** column. Here, we expected only positive values. But before fixing this issue straight away (by either dropping the records or transforming them into positive values), it is preferable to get in touch with your stakeholders first and get confirmation that these values are not significant for the business. They may tell you that these values are extremely important as they represent returned items and cost the company a lot of money, so they want to analyze these cases in order to reduce these numbers. If you had moved to the data cleaning stage straight away, you would have missed this critical piece of information and potentially came up with incorrect results.

HANDLING ROW DUPLICATION

Most of the time, the datasets you will receive or have access to will not have been 100% cleaned. They usually have some issues that need to be fixed. One of these issues could be duplicated rows. Row duplication means that several observations contain the exact same information in the dataset. With the **`pandas`** package, it is extremely easy to find these cases.

Let's use the example that we saw in *Chapter 10, Analyzing a Dataset*.

Start by **importing** the dataset into a DataFrame:

```
import pandas as pd
file_url = 'https://github.com/PacktWorkshops/'\
           'The-Data-Science-Workshop/blob/'\
           'master/Chapter10/dataset/'\
           'Online%20Retail.xlsx?raw=true'
df = pd.read_excel(file_url)
```

The **duplicated()** method from **pandas** checks whether any of the rows are duplicates and returns a **boolean** value for each row, **True** if the row is a duplicate and **False** if not:

```
df.duplicated()
```

You should get the following output:

```
0         False
1         False
2         False
3         False
4         False
          ...
541904    False
541905    False
541906    False
541907    False
541908    False
Length: 541909, dtype: bool
```

Figure 11.1: Output of the duplicated() method

> **NOTE**
>
> The outputs in this chapter have been truncated to effectively use the page area.

In Python, the **True** and **False** binary values correspond to the numerical values 1 and 0, respectively. To find out how many rows have been identified as duplicates, you can use the **sum()** method on the output of **duplicated()**. This will add all the 1s (that is, **True** values) and gives us the count of duplicates:

```
df.duplicated().sum()
```

You should get the following output:

```
5268
```

Since the output of the **duplicated()** method is a **pandas** series of binary values for each row, you can also use it to subset the rows of a DataFrame. The **pandas** package provides different APIs for subsetting a DataFrame, as follows:

- df[<rows> or <columns>]
- df.loc[<rows>, <columns>]
- df.iloc[<rows>, <columns>]

The first API subsets the DataFrame by **row** or **column**. To filter specific columns, you can provide a list that contains their names. For instance, if you want to keep only the variables, that is, **InvoiceNo**, **StockCode**, **InvoiceDate**, and **CustomerID**, you need to use the following code:

```
df[['InvoiceNo', 'StockCode', 'InvoiceDate', 'CustomerID']]
```

You should get the following output:

	InvoiceNo	StockCode	InvoiceDate	CustomerID
0	536365	85123A	2010-12-01 08:26:00	17850.0
1	536365	71053	2010-12-01 08:26:00	17850.0
2	536365	84406B	2010-12-01 08:26:00	17850.0
3	536365	84029G	2010-12-01 08:26:00	17850.0
4	536365	84029E	2010-12-01 08:26:00	17850.0
...	...	...	...	...
541904	581587	22613	2011-12-09 12:50:00	12680.0
541905	581587	22899	2011-12-09 12:50:00	12680.0
541906	581587	23254	2011-12-09 12:50:00	12680.0
541907	581587	23255	2011-12-09 12:50:00	12680.0
541908	581587	22138	2011-12-09 12:50:00	12680.0

541909 rows × 4 columns

Figure 11.2: Subsetting columns

If you only want to filter the rows that are considered duplicates, you can use the same API call with the output of the **`duplicated()`** method. It will only keep the rows with **True** as a value:

```
df[df.duplicated()]
```

You should get the following output:

	InvoiceNo	StockCode	Description	Quantity	InvoiceDate	UnitPrice	CustomerID	Country
517	536409	21866	UNION JACK FLAG LUGGAGE TAG	1	2010-12-01 11:45:00	1.25	17908.0	United Kingdom
527	536409	22866	HAND WARMER SCOTTY DOG DESIGN	1	2010-12-01 11:45:00	2.10	17908.0	United Kingdom
537	536409	22900	SET 2 TEA TOWELS I LOVE LONDON	1	2010-12-01 11:45:00	2.95	17908.0	United Kingdom
539	536409	22111	SCOTTIE DOG HOT WATER BOTTLE	1	2010-12-01 11:45:00	4.95	17908.0	United Kingdom
555	536412	22327	ROUND SNACK BOXES SET OF 4 SKULLS	1	2010-12-01 11:49:00	2.95	17920.0	United Kingdom
...	...	...	...	...	...	...	...	...
541675	581538	22068	BLACK PIRATE TREASURE CHEST	1	2011-12-09 11:34:00	0.39	14446.0	United Kingdom
541689	581538	23318	BOX OF 6 MINI VINTAGE CRACKERS	1	2011-12-09 11:34:00	2.49	14446.0	United Kingdom
541692	581538	22992	REVOLVER WOODEN RULER	1	2011-12-09 11:34:00	1.95	14446.0	United Kingdom
541699	581538	22694	WICKER STAR	1	2011-12-09 11:34:00	2.10	14446.0	United Kingdom
541701	581538	23343	JUMBO BAG VINTAGE CHRISTMAS	1	2011-12-09 11:34:00	2.08	14446.0	United Kingdom

5268 rows × 8 columns

Figure 11.3: Subsetting the duplicated rows

If you want to subset the rows and columns at the same time, you must use one of the other two available APIs: **.loc** or **.iloc**. These APIs do the exact same thing but **.loc** uses labels or names while **.iloc** only takes indices as input. You will use the **.loc** API to subset the duplicated rows and keep only the selected four columns, as shown in the previous example:

```
df.loc[df.duplicated(), ['InvoiceNo', 'StockCode', \
                         'InvoiceDate', 'CustomerID']]
```

You should get the following output:

	InvoiceNo	StockCode	InvoiceDate	CustomerID
517	536409	21866	2010-12-01 11:45:00	17908.0
527	536409	22866	2010-12-01 11:45:00	17908.0
537	536409	22900	2010-12-01 11:45:00	17908.0
539	536409	22111	2010-12-01 11:45:00	17908.0
555	536412	22327	2010-12-01 11:49:00	17920.0
...	...	...	...	...
541675	581538	22068	2011-12-09 11:34:00	14446.0
541689	581538	23318	2011-12-09 11:34:00	14446.0
541692	581538	22992	2011-12-09 11:34:00	14446.0
541699	581538	22694	2011-12-09 11:34:00	14446.0
541701	581538	23343	2011-12-09 11:34:00	14446.0

5268 rows × 4 columns

Figure 11.4: Subsetting the duplicated rows and selected columns using .loc

This preceding output shows that the first few duplicates are row numbers **517**, **527**, **537**, and so on. By default, **pandas** doesn't mark the first occurrence of duplicates as duplicates: all the same, duplicates will have a value of **True** except for the first occurrence. You can change this behavior by specifying the **keep** parameter. If you want to keep the last duplicate, you need to specify **keep='last'**:

```
df.loc[df.duplicated(keep='last'), ['InvoiceNo', 'StockCode', \
                                    'InvoiceDate', 'CustomerID']]
```

You should get the following output:

	InvoiceNo	StockCode	InvoiceDate	CustomerID
485	536409	22111	2010-12-01 11:45:00	17908.0
489	536409	22866	2010-12-01 11:45:00	17908.0
494	536409	21866	2010-12-01 11:45:00	17908.0
521	536409	22900	2010-12-01 11:45:00	17908.0
548	536412	22327	2010-12-01 11:49:00	17920.0
...	...	...	...	...
541640	581538	22992	2011-12-09 11:34:00	14446.0
541644	581538	22694	2011-12-09 11:34:00	14446.0
541646	581538	23275	2011-12-09 11:34:00	14446.0
541656	581538	23318	2011-12-09 11:34:00	14446.0
541666	581538	23343	2011-12-09 11:34:00	14446.0

5268 rows × 4 columns

Figure 11.5: Subsetting the last duplicated rows

As you can see from the previous outputs, row **`485`** has the same value as row **`539`**. As expected, row **`539`** is not marked as a duplicate anymore. If you want to mark all the duplicate records as duplicates, you will have to use **`keep=False`**:

```
df.loc[df.duplicated(keep=False), ['InvoiceNo', 'StockCode',\
                                   'InvoiceDate', 'CustomerID']]
```

You should get the following output:

	InvoiceNo	StockCode	InvoiceDate	CustomerID
485	536409	22111	2010-12-01 11:45:00	17908.0
489	536409	22866	2010-12-01 11:45:00	17908.0
494	536409	21866	2010-12-01 11:45:00	17908.0
517	536409	21866	2010-12-01 11:45:00	17908.0
521	536409	22900	2010-12-01 11:45:00	17908.0
...	...	...	...	...
541675	581538	22068	2011-12-09 11:34:00	14446.0
541689	581538	23318	2011-12-09 11:34:00	14446.0
541692	581538	22992	2011-12-09 11:34:00	14446.0
541699	581538	22694	2011-12-09 11:34:00	14446.0
541701	581538	23343	2011-12-09 11:34:00	14446.0

10147 rows × 4 columns

Figure 11.6: Subsetting all the duplicated rows

This time, rows **485** and **539** have been listed as duplicates. Now that you know how to identify duplicate observations, you can decide whether you wish to remove them from the dataset. As we mentioned previously, you must be careful when changing the data. You may want to confirm with the business that they are comfortable with you doing so. You will have to explain the reason why you want to remove these rows. In the Online Retail dataset, if you take rows **485** and **539** as an example, these two observations are identical. From a business perspective, this means that a specific customer (**CustomerID 17908**) has bought the same item (**StockCode 22111**) at the exact same date and time (**InvoiceDate 2010-12-01 11:45:00**) on the same invoice (**InvoiceNo 536409**). This is highly suspicious. When you're talking with the business, they may tell you that new software was released at that time and there was a bug that was splitting all the purchased items into single-line items.

In this case, you know that you shouldn't remove these rows. On the other hand, they may tell you that duplication shouldn't happen and that it may be due to human error as the data was entered or during the data extraction step. Let's assume this is the case; now, it is safe for you to remove these rows.

To do so, you can use the **drop_duplicates()** method from **pandas**. It has the same **keep** parameter as **duplicated()**, which specifies which duplicated record you want to keep or if you want to remove all of them. In this case, we want to keep at least one duplicate row. Here, we want to keep the first occurrence:

```
df.drop_duplicates(keep='first')
```

You should get the following output:

	InvoiceNo	StockCode	Description	Quantity	InvoiceDate	UnitPrice	CustomerID	Country
0	536365	85123A	WHITE HANGING HEART T-LIGHT HOLDER	6	2010-12-01 08:26:00	2.55	17850.0	United Kingdom
1	536365	71053	WHITE METAL LANTERN	6	2010-12-01 08:26:00	3.39	17850.0	United Kingdom
2	536365	84406B	CREAM CUPID HEARTS COAT HANGER	8	2010-12-01 08:26:00	2.75	17850.0	United Kingdom
3	536365	84029G	KNITTED UNION FLAG HOT WATER BOTTLE	6	2010-12-01 08:26:00	3.39	17850.0	United Kingdom
4	536365	84029E	RED WOOLLY HOTTIE WHITE HEART.	6	2010-12-01 08:26:00	3.39	17850.0	United Kingdom
5	536365	22752	SET 7 BABUSHKA NESTING BOXES	2	2010-12-01 08:26:00	7.65	17850.0	United Kingdom

Figure 11.7: Dropping duplicate rows with keep='first'

The output of this method is a new DataFrame that contains unique records where only the first occurrence of duplicates has been kept. If you want to replace the existing DataFrame rather than getting a new DataFrame, you need to use the **inplace=True** parameter.

The **drop_duplicates()** and **duplicated()** methods also have another very useful parameter: **subset**. This parameter allows you to specify the list of columns to consider while looking for duplicates. By default, all the columns of a DataFrame are used to find duplicate rows. Let's see how many duplicate rows there are while only looking at the **InvoiceNo**, **StockCode**, **invoiceDate**, and **CustomerID** columns:

```
df.duplicated(subset=['InvoiceNo', 'StockCode', 'InvoiceDate',\
                      'CustomerID'], keep='first').sum()
```

You should get the following output:

```
10677
```

By looking only at these four columns instead of all of them, we can see that the number of duplicate rows has increased from **5268** to **10677**. This means that there are rows that have the exact same values as these four columns but have different values in other columns, which means they may be different records. In this case, it is better to use all the columns to identify duplicate records.

EXERCISE 11.01: HANDLING DUPLICATES IN A BREAST CANCER DATASET

In this exercise, you will learn how to identify duplicate records and how to handle such issues so that the dataset only contains **unique** records. Let's get started:

> **NOTE**
>
> The dataset that we're using in this exercise is the Breast Cancer Detection dataset, which has been shared by Dr. William H. Wolberg from the University of Wisconsin Hospitals and is hosted by the UCI Machine Learning Repository. The attribute information for this dataset can be found here: https://packt.live/39LaIDx.
>
> This dataset can also be found in this book's GitHub repository: https://packt.live/2QqbHBC.

1. Open a new **Colab** notebook.
2. Import the **pandas** package:

```
import pandas as pd
```

3. Assign the link to the **Breast Cancer** dataset to a variable called **file_url**:

```
file_url = 'https://raw.githubusercontent.com/'\
           'PacktWorkshops/The-Data-Science-Workshop/'\
           'master/Chapter11/dataset/'\
           'breast-cancer-wisconsin.data'
```

4. Using the **read_csv()** method from the **pandas** package, load the dataset into a new variable called **df** with the **header=None** parameter. We're doing this because this file doesn't contain column names:

```
df = pd.read_csv(file_url, header=None)
```

5. Create a variable called **col_names** that contains the names of the columns: **Sample code number, Clump Thickness, Uniformity of Cell Size, Uniformity of Cell Shape, Marginal Adhesion, Single Epithelial Cell Size, Bare Nuclei, Bland Chromatin, Normal Nucleoli, Mitoses**, and **Class**:

> **NOTE**
>
> Information about the names that have been specified in this file can be found here: https://packt.live/39J7hgT.

```
col_names = ['Sample code number','Clump Thickness',\
             'Uniformity of Cell Size',\
             'Uniformity of Cell Shape',\
             'Marginal Adhesion','Single Epithelial Cell Size',\
             'Bare Nuclei','Bland Chromatin',\
             'Normal Nucleoli','Mitoses','Class']
```

6. Assign the column names of the DataFrame using the **columns** attribute:

```
df.columns = col_names
```

7. Display the shape of the DataFrame using the **.shape** attribute:

```
df.shape
```

You should get the following output:

```
(699, 11)
```

This DataFrame contains **699** rows and **11** columns.

8. Display the first five rows of the DataFrame using the **head()** method:

```
df.head()
```

You should get the following output:

	Sample code number	Clump Thickness	Uniformity of Cell Size	Uniformity of Cell Shape	Marginal Adhesion
0	1000025	5	1	1	1
1	1002945	5	4	4	5
2	1015425	3	1	1	1
3	1016277	6	8	8	1
4	1017023	4	1	1	3

Figure 11.8: The first five rows of the Breast Cancer dataset

All the variables are numerical. The Sample code number column is an identifier for the measurement samples.

9. Find the number of duplicate rows using the **duplicated()** and **sum()** methods:

```
df.duplicated().sum()
```

You should get the following output:

```
8
```

Looking at the 11 columns in this dataset, we can see that there are **8** duplicate rows.

10. Display the duplicate rows using the **loc()** and **duplicated()** methods:

```
df.loc[df.duplicated()]
```

You should get the following output:

	Sample code number	Clump Thickness	Uniformity of Cell Size	Uniformity of Cell Shape	Marginal Adhesion
208	1218860	1	1	1	1
253	1100524	6	10	10	2
254	1116116	9	10	10	1
258	1198641	3	1	1	1
272	320675	3	3	5	2
338	704097	1	1	1	1
561	1321942	5	1	1	1
684	466906	1	1	1	1

Figure 11.9: Duplicate records

The following rows are duplicates: **208**, **253**, **254**, **258**, **272**, **338**, **561**, and **684**.

11. Display the duplicate rows just like we did in *Step 9*, but with the **keep='last'** parameter instead:

```
df.loc[df.duplicated(keep='last')]
```

You should get the following output:

	Sample code number	Clump Thickness	Uniformity of Cell Size	Uniformity of Cell Shape	Marginal Adhesion
42	1100524	6	10	10	2
62	1116116	9	10	10	1
168	1198641	3	1	1	1
207	1218860	1	1	1	1
267	320675	3	3	5	2
314	704097	1	1	1	1
560	1321942	5	1	1	1
683	466906	1	1	1	1

Figure 11.10: Duplicate records with keep='last'

By using the **keep='last'** parameter, the following rows are considered duplicates: **42**, **62**, **168**, **207**, **267**, **314**, **560**, and **683**. By comparing this output to the one from the previous step, we can see that rows 253 and 42 are identical.

12. Remove the duplicate rows using the **drop_duplicates()** method along with the **keep='first'** parameter and save this into a new DataFrame called **df_unique**:

```
df_unique = df.drop_duplicates(keep='first')
```

13. Display the shape of **df_unique** with the **.shape** attribute:

```
df_unique.shape
```

You should get the following output:

```
(691, 11)
```

Now that we have removed the eight duplicate records, only **691** rows remain. Now, the dataset only contains unique observations.

> **NOTE**
>
> To access the source code for this specific section, please refer to https://packt.live/2EiArYI.
>
> You can also run this example online at https://packt.live/349tLat.

In this exercise, you learned how to identify and remove duplicate records from a real-world dataset.

CONVERTING DATA TYPES

Another problem you may face in a project is incorrect data types being inferred for some columns. As we saw in *Chapter 10*, *Analyzing a Dataset*, the **pandas** package provides us with a very easy way to display the data type of each column using the **.dtypes** attribute. You may be wondering, when did **pandas** identify the type of each column? The types are detected when you load the dataset into a **pandas** DataFrame using methods such as **read_csv()**, **read_excel()**, and so on.

When you've done this, **pandas** will try its best to automatically find the best type according to the values contained in each column. Let's see how this works on the **Online Retail** dataset.

First, you must import **pandas**:

```
import pandas as pd
```

Then, you need to assign the URL to the dataset to a new variable:

```
file_url = 'https://github.com/PacktWorkshops/'\
           'The-Data-Science-Workshop/blob/'\
           'master/Chapter10/dataset/'\
           'Online%20Retail.xlsx?raw=true'
```

Let's load the dataset into a **pandas** DataFrame using **read_excel()**:

```
df = pd.read_excel(file_url)
```

Finally, let's print the data type of each column:

```
df.dtypes
```

You should get the following output:

```
InvoiceNo              object
StockCode              object
Description            object
Quantity                int64
InvoiceDate    datetime64[ns]
UnitPrice             float64
CustomerID            float64
Country                object
dtype: object
```

Figure 11.11: The data type of each column of the Online Retail dataset

The preceding output shows the data types that have been assigned to each column. **Quantity**, **UnitPrice**, and **CustomerID** have been identified as numerical variables (**int64**, **float64**), **InvoiceDate** is a **datetime** variable, and all the other columns are considered text (**object**). This is not too bad. **pandas** did a great job of recognizing non-text columns.

But what if you want to change the types of some columns? You have two ways to achieve this.

The first way is to reload the dataset, but this time, you will need to specify the data types of the columns of interest using the **dtype** parameter. This parameter takes a dictionary with the column names as keys and the correct data types as values, such as {'col1': np.float64, 'col2': np.int32}, as input. Let's try this on **CustomerID**. We know this isn't a numerical variable as it contains a unique **identifier** (code). Here, we are going to change its type to **object**:

```
df = pd.read_excel(file_url, dtype={'CustomerID': 'category'})
df.dtypes
```

You should get the following output:

```
InvoiceNo              object
StockCode              object
Description            object
Quantity                int64
InvoiceDate    datetime64[ns]
UnitPrice             float64
CustomerID           category
Country                object
dtype: object
```

Figure 11.12: The data types of each column after converting CustomerID

As you can see, the data type for **CustomerID** has effectively changed to a **category** type.

Now, let's look at the second way of converting a single column into a different type. In **pandas**, you can use the **astype()** method and specify the new data type that it will be converted into as its **parameter**. It will return a new column (a new **pandas** series, to be more precise), so you need to reassign it to the same column of the DataFrame. For instance, if you want to change the **InvoiceNo** column into a categorical variable, you would do the following:

```
df['InvoiceNo'] = df['InvoiceNo'].astype('category')
df.dtypes
```

You should get the following output:

```
InvoiceNo              category
StockCode                object
Description              object
Quantity                  int64
InvoiceDate      datetime64[ns]
UnitPrice               float64
CustomerID             category
Country                  object
dtype: object
```

Figure 11.13: The data types of each column after converting InvoiceNo

As you can see, the data type for **`InvoiceNo`** has changed to a categorical variable. The difference between **`object`** and **`category`** is that the latter has a finite number of possible values (also called discrete variables). Once these have been changed into categorical variables, **`pandas`** will automatically list all the values. They can be accessed using the **`.cat.categories`** attribute:

```
df['InvoiceNo'].cat.categories
```

You should get the following output:

```
Index([   536365,    536366,    536367,    536368,    536369,    536370,
          536371,    536372,    536373,    536374,
       ...
       'C581464', 'C581465', 'C581466', 'C581468', 'C581470', 'C581484',
       'C581490', 'C581499', 'C581568', 'C581569'],
      dtype='object', length=25900)
```

Figure 11.14: List of categories (possible values) for the InvoiceNo categorical variable

`pandas` has identified that there are 25,900 different values in this column and has listed all of them. Depending on the data type that's assigned to a variable, **`pandas`** provides different attributes and methods that are very handy for data transformation or feature engineering (this will be covered in *Chapter 12, Feature Engineering*).

As a final note, you may be wondering when you would use the first way of changing the types of certain columns (while loading the dataset). To find out the current type of each variable, you must load the data first, so why will you need to reload the data again with new data types? It will be easier to change the type with the **astype()** method after the first load. There are a few reasons why you would use it. One reason could be that you have already explored the dataset on a different tool, such as Excel, and already know what the correct data types are.

The second reason could be that your dataset is big, and you cannot load it in its entirety. As you may have noticed, by default, **pandas** use 64-bit encoding for numerical variables. This requires a lot of memory and may be overkill.

For example, the **Quantity** column has an int64 data type, which means that the range of possible values is -9,223,372,036,854,775,808 to 9,223,372,036,854,775,807. However, in *Chapter 10, Analyzing a Dataset* while analyzing the distribution of this column, you learned that the range of values for this column is only from -80,995 to 80,995. You don't need to use so much space. By reducing the data type of this variable to int32 (which ranges from -2,147,483,648 to 2,147,483,647), you may be able to reload the entire dataset.

EXERCISE 11.02: CONVERTING DATA TYPES FOR THE AMES HOUSING DATASET

In this exercise, you will prepare a dataset by converting its variables into the correct data types.

You will use the Ames Housing dataset to do this, which we also used in *Chapter 10, Analyzing a Dataset*. For more information about this dataset, refer to the following note. Let's get started:

> **NOTE**
>
> The dataset that's being used in this exercise is the Ames Housing dataset, which has been compiled by Dean De Cock: https://packt.live/2QTbTbq.
>
> For your convenience, this dataset has been uploaded to this book's GitHub repository: https://packt.live/2ZUk4bz.

1. Open a new Colab notebook.
2. Import the **pandas** package:

```
import pandas as pd
```

3. Assign the link to the Ames dataset to a variable called **file_url**:

```
file_url = 'https://raw.githubusercontent.com/'\
           'PacktWorkshops/The-Data-Science-Workshop/'\
           'master/Chapter10/dataset/ames_iowa_housing.csv'
```

4. Using the **read_csv** method from the **pandas** package, load the dataset into a new variable called **df**:

```
df = pd.read_csv(file_url)
```

5. Print the data type of each column using the **dtypes** attribute:

```
df.dtypes
```

You should get the following output:

```
Id               int64
MSSubClass       int64
MSZoning        object
LotFrontage    float64
LotArea          int64
Street          object
Alley           object
LotShape        object
LandContour     object
Utilities       object
```

Figure 11.15: List of columns and their assigned data types

> **NOTE**
>
> The preceding output has been truncated.

From *Chapter 10, Analyzing a Dataset* you know that the **Id**, **MSSubClass**, **OverallQual**, and **OverallCond** columns have been incorrectly classified as numerical variables. They have a finite number of unique values and you can't perform any mathematical operations on them. For example, it doesn't make sense to add, remove, multiply, or divide two different values from the **Id** column. Therefore, you need to convert them into categorical variables.

6. Using the **astype()** method, convert the **'Id'** column into a categorical variable, as shown in the following code snippet:

```
df['Id'] = df['Id'].astype('category')
```

7. Convert the **'MSSubClass'**, **'OverallQual'**, and **'OverallCond'** columns into categorical variables, like we did in the previous step:

```
df['MSSubClass'] = df['MSSubClass'].astype('category')
df['OverallQual'] = df['OverallQual'].astype('category')
df['OverallCond'] = df['OverallCond'].astype('category')
```

8. Create a for loop that will iterate through the four categorical columns **('Id', 'MSSubClass', 'OverallQual',** and **'OverallCond')** and print their names and categories using the **.cat.categories** attribute:

```
for col_name in ['Id', 'MSSubClass', 'OverallQual', \
                 'OverallCond']:
    print(col_name)
    print(df[col_name].cat.categories)
```

You should get the following output:

```
Id
Int64Index([   1,    2,    3,    4,    5,    6,    7,    8,    9,   10,
            ...
            1451, 1452, 1453, 1454, 1455, 1456, 1457, 1458, 1459, 1460],
           dtype='int64', length=1460)
MSSubClass
Int64Index([20, 30, 40, 45, 50, 60, 70, 75, 80, 85, 90, 120, 160, 180, 190], dtype='int64')
OverallQual
Int64Index([1, 2, 3, 4, 5, 6, 7, 8, 9, 10], dtype='int64')
OverallCond
Int64Index([1, 2, 3, 4, 5, 6, 7, 8, 9], dtype='int64')
```

Figure 11.16: List of categories for the four newly converted variables

Now, these four columns have been converted into categorical variables. From the output of *Step 5*, we can see that there are a lot of variables of the **object** type. Let's have a look at them and see if they need to be converted as well.

9. Create a new DataFrame called **obj_df** that will only contain variables of the **object** type using the **select_dtypes** method along with the **include='object'** parameter:

```
obj_df = df.select_dtypes(include='object')
```

10. Create a new variable called **obj_cols** that contains a list of column names from the **obj_df** DataFrame using the **.columns** attribute and display its content:

```
obj_cols = obj_df.columns
obj_cols
```

You should get the following output:

```
Index(['MSZoning', 'Street', 'Alley', 'LotShape', 'LandContour', 'Utilities',
       'LotConfig', 'LandSlope', 'Neighborhood', 'Condition1', 'Condition2',
       'BldgType', 'HouseStyle', 'RoofStyle', 'RoofMatl', 'Exterior1st',
       'Exterior2nd', 'MasVnrType', 'ExterQual', 'ExterCond', 'Foundation',
       'BsmtQual', 'BsmtCond', 'BsmtExposure', 'BsmtFinType1', 'BsmtFinType2',
       'Heating', 'HeatingQC', 'CentralAir', 'Electrical', 'KitchenQual',
       'Functional', 'FireplaceQu', 'GarageType', 'GarageFinish', 'GarageQual',
       'GarageCond', 'PavedDrive', 'PoolQC', 'Fence', 'MiscFeature',
       'SaleType', 'SaleCondition'],
      dtype='object')
```

Figure 11.17: List of variables of the 'object' type

11. Like we did in *Step 8*, create a **for** loop that will iterate through the column names contained in **obj_cols** and print their names and unique values using the **unique()** method:

```
for col_name in obj_cols:
    print(col_name)
    print(df[col_name].unique())
```

You should get the following output:

```
MSZoning
['RL' 'RM' 'C (all)' 'FV' 'RH']
Street
['Pave' 'Grvl']
Alley
[nan 'Grvl' 'Pave']
LotShape
['Reg' 'IR1' 'IR2' 'IR3']
LandContour
['Lvl' 'Bnk' 'Low' 'HLS']
Utilities
['AllPub' 'NoSeWa']
LotConfig
['Inside' 'FR2' 'Corner' 'CulDSac' 'FR3']
LandSlope
['Gtl' 'Mod' 'Sev']
Neighborhood
['CollgCr' 'Veenker' 'Crawfor' 'NoRidge' 'Mitchel' 'Somerst' 'NWAmes'
 'OldTown' 'BrkSide' 'Sawyer' 'NridgHt' 'NAmes' 'SawyerW' 'IDOTRR'
```

Figure 11.18: List of unique values for each variable of the 'object' type

As you can see, all these columns have a finite number of unique values that are composed of text, which shows us that they are categorical variables.

12. Now, create a **`for`** loop that will iterate through the column names contained in **`obj_cols`** and convert each of them into a categorical variable using the **`astype()`** method:

```
for col_name in obj_cols:
    df[col_name] = df[col_name].astype('category')
```

13. Print the data type of each column using the **`dtypes`** attribute:

```
df.dtypes
```

You should get the following output:

```
Id                  category
MSSubClass          category
MSZoning            category
LotFrontage          float64
LotArea                int64
Street              category
Alley               category
LotShape            category
LandContour         category
Utilities           category
LotConfig           category
LandSlope           category
Neighborhood        category
```

Figure 11.19: List of variables and their new data types

> **NOTE**
>
> The preceding output has been truncated.
>
> To access the source code for this specific section, please refer to https://packt.live/2FvR8R6.
>
> You can also run this example online at https://packt.live/3aAmKka.

You have successfully converted the columns that have incorrect data types (numerical or object) into categorical variables. Your dataset is now one step closer to being prepared for modeling.

In the next section, we will look at handling incorrect values.

HANDLING INCORRECT VALUES

Another issue you may face with a new dataset is incorrect values for some of the observations in the dataset. Sometimes, this is due to a syntax error; for instance, the name of a country may be written all in lower case, all in upper case, as a title (where only the first letter is capitalized), or may even be abbreviated. France may take different values, such as 'France', 'FRANCE', 'france', 'FR', and so on. If you define 'France' as the standard format, then all the other variants are considered incorrect values in the dataset and need to be fixed.

If this kind of issue is not handled before the modeling phase, it can lead to incorrect results. The model will think these different variants are completely different values and may pay less attention to these values since they have separated frequencies. For instance, let's say that 'France' represents 2% of the value, 'FRANCE' 2% and 'FR' 1%. You know that these values correspond to the same country and should represent 5% of the values, but the model will consider them as different countries.

Let's learn how to detect such issues in real life by using the **Online Retail** dataset.

First, you need to load the data into a **pandas** DataFrame:

```
import pandas as pd
file_url = 'https://github.com/PacktWorkshops/'\
           'The-Data-Science-Workshop/blob/'\
           'master/Chapter10/dataset/'\
           'Online%20Retail.xlsx?raw=true'
df = pd.read_excel(file_url)
```

In this dataset, there are two variables that seem to be related to each other: **StockCode** and **Description**. The first one contains the identifier code of the items sold and the other one contains their descriptions. However, if you look at some of the examples, such as **StockCode 23131**, the **Description** column has different values:

```
df.loc[df['StockCode'] == 23131, 'Description'].unique()
```

You should get the following output

```
array(['MISTLETOE HEART WREATH CREAM', 'MISELTOE HEART WREATH WHITE',
       'MISELTOE HEART WREATH CREAM', '?', 'had been put aside', nan],
      dtype=object)
```

Figure 11.20: List of unique values for the Description column and StockCode 23131

There are multiple issues in the preceding output. One issue is that the word **Mistletoe** has been misspelled so that it reads **Miseltoe**. The other errors are unexpected values and missing values, which will be covered in the next section. It seems that the **Description** column has been used to record comments such as **had been put aside**.

Let's focus on the misspelling issue. What we need to do here is modify the incorrect spelling and replace it with the correct value. First, let's create a new column called **StockCodeDescription**, which is an exact copy of the **Description** column:

```
df['StockCodeDescription'] = df['Description']
```

You will use this new column to fix the misspelling issue. To do this, use the subsetting technique you learned about earlier in this chapter. You need to use **.loc** and filter the rows and columns you want, that is, all rows with **StockCode == 21131** and **Description == MISELTOE HEART WREATH CREAM** and the **Description** column:

```
df.loc[(df['StockCode'] == 23131) \
       & (df['StockCodeDescription'] \
           == 'MISELTOE HEART WREATH CREAM'), \
       'StockCodeDescription'] = 'MISTLETOE HEART WREATH CREAM'
```

If you reprint the value for this issue, you will see that the misspelling value has been fixed and is not present anymore:

```
df.loc[df['StockCode'] == 23131, 'StockCodeDescription'].unique()
```

You should get the following output:

```
array(['MISTLETOE HEART WREATH CREAM', 'MISELTOE HEART WREATH WHITE', '?',
       'had been put aside', nan], dtype=object)
```

Figure 11.21: List of unique values for the Description column and StockCode 23131 after fixing the first misspelling issue

As you can see, there are still five different values for this product, but for one of them, that is, **MISTLETOE**, has been spelled incorrectly: **MISELTOE**.

This time, rather than looking at an exact match (a word must be the same as another one), we will look at performing a partial match (part of a word will be present in another word). In our case, instead of looking at the spelling of **MISELTOE**, we will only look at **MISEL**. The **pandas** package provides a method called **.str.contains()** that we can use to look for observations that partially match with a given expression.

Let's use this to see if we have the same misspelling issue (**MISEL**) in the entire dataset. You will need to add one additional parameter since this method doesn't handle missing values. You will also have to subset the rows that don't have missing values for the **Description** column. This can be done by providing the **na=False** parameter to the **.str.contains()** method:

```
df.loc[df['StockCodeDescription']\
  .str.contains('MISEL', na=False),]
```

You should get the following output:

	InvoiceNo	StockCode	Description
186760	552882	23131	MISELTOE HEART WREATH WHITE
186761	552882	23130	MISELTOE HEART WREATH
195286	553711	23130	MISELTOE HEART WREATH
195288	553711	23131	MISELTOE HEART WREATH WHITE
372887	569252	23130	MISELTOE HEART WREATH
373325	569324	23131	MISELTOE HEART WREATH WHITE
373327	569324	23130	MISELTOE HEART WREATH
377632	569558	23131	MISELTOE HEART WREATH WHITE
377635	569558	23130	MISELTOE HEART WREATH

Figure 11.22: Displaying all the rows containing the misspelling 'MISELTOE'

This misspelling issue (**MISELTOE**) is not only related to **StockCode 23131**, but also to other items. You will need to fix all of these using the **str.replace()** method. This method takes the string of characters to be replaced and the replacement string as parameters:

```
df['StockCodeDescription'] = df['StockCodeDescription']\
                             .str.replace\
                             ('MISELTOE', 'MISTLETOE')
```

Now, if you print all the rows that contain the misspelling of **MISEL**, you will see that no such rows exist anymore:

```
df.loc[df['StockCodeDescription']\
  .str.contains('MISEL', na=False),]
```

You should get the following output

InvoiceNo	StockCode	Description	Quantity	InvoiceDate	UnitPrice	CustomerID	Country	StockCodeDescription

Figure 11.23: Displaying all the rows containing the misspelling MISELTOE after cleaning up

You just saw how easy it is to clean observations that have incorrect values using the **`.str.contains`** and **`.str.replace()`** methods that are provided by the **`pandas`** package. These methods can only be used for variables containing strings, but the same logic can be applied to numerical variables and can also be used to handle extreme values or outliers. You can use the ==, >, <, >=, or <= operator to subset the rows you want and then replace the observations with the correct values.

EXERCISE 11.03: FIXING INCORRECT VALUES IN THE STATE COLUMN

In this exercise, you will clean the **`State`** variable in a modified version of a dataset by listing all the finance officers in the USA. We are doing this because the dataset contains some incorrect values. Let's get started:

> **NOTE**
>
> The original dataset was shared by Forest Gregg and Derek Eder and can be found at https://packt.live/2rTJVns.
>
> The modified dataset that we're using here is available in this book's GitHub repository: https://packt.live/2MZJsrk.

1. Open a new Colab notebook.
2. Import the **`pandas`** package:

```
import pandas as pd
```

3. Assign the link to the dataset to a variable called **`file_url`**:

```
file_url = 'https://raw.githubusercontent.com/'\
           'PacktWorkshops/The-Data-Science-Workshop/'\
           'master/Chapter11/dataset/officers.csv'
```

4. Using the **`read_csv()`** method from the **`pandas`** package, load the dataset into a new variable called **`df`**:

```
df = pd.read_csv(file_url)
```

5. Print the first five rows of the DataFrame using the **`.head()`** method:

```
df.head()
```

You should get the following output:

	ID	City	State	Zip	Title	RedactionRequested
0	804	Glenview	IL	60025	Treasurer	False
1	9177	Harrisburg	IL	62946	Treasurer	False
2	53011	Chicago	IL	60606	Treasurer	False
3	9176	Harrisburg	IL	62946	Chairman	False
4	33020	Mechanicsburg	IL	62545	Chairman	False

Figure 11.24: The first five rows of the finance officers dataset

6. Print out all the unique values of the **`State`** variable:

```
df['State'].unique()
```

You should get the following output:

```
array(['IL', 'PA', 'DC', 'Il', nan, 'WI', 'CA', 'MO', 'NC', 'IA', 'MA',
       'IN', 'MI', 'TN', 'NY', 'ng', 'TX', 'CO', 'NV', 'il', 'WA', '8I',
       'In', 'iL', 'OH', 'SC', 'VA', 'NM', 'FL', 'LA', 'GA', 'II', 'NJ',
       'MD', 'I', 'AR', 'KS', 'DE', '60', 'SD', 'MN', 'VT', 'OK', 'KY',
       'CT', 'NH', 'AZ', 'OR', 'PR', 'RI'], dtype=object)
```

Figure 11.25: List of unique values in the State column

All the states have been encoded into a two-capitalized character format. As you can see, there are some incorrect values with non-capitalized characters, such as **`il`** and **`iL`** (they look like spelling errors for Illinois), and unexpected values such as **`8I`**, **`I`**, and **`60`**. In the next few steps, you are going to fix these issues.

7. Print out the rows that have the **il** value in the **State** column using the **pandas .str.contains()** method and the subsetting API, that is, DataFrame [condition]. You will also have to set the **na** parameter to **False** in **str.contains()** in order to exclude observations with missing values:

```
df[df['State'].str.contains('il', na=False)]
```

You should get the following output:

	ID	City	State	Zip	Title	RedactionRequested
4245	47448	Chicago	il	60619	Treasurer	False
4651	47447	Chicago	il	60623-1614	Chairman	False
4652	54025	Chicago	il	60623-1614	Chairman	False
18939	39418	Kingston	il	60145	Chairman	False
29699	27124	Hampshire	il	60140	Chairman	False
43761	29179	McHenry	il	60050	Admin Asst	False

Figure 11.26: Observations with a value of il

As you can see, all the cities with the **il** value are from the state of Illinois. So, the correct **State** value should be **IL**. You may be thinking that the following values are also referring to Illinois: **Il**, **iL**, and **Il**. We'll have a look at them next.

8. Now, create a **for** loop that will iterate through the following values in the **State** column: **Il**, **iL**, **Il**. Then, print out the values of the City and State variables using the **pandas** method for subsetting, that is, **.loc()**: DataFrame.loc[row_condition, column condition]. Do this for each observation:

```
for state in ['Il', 'iL', 'Il']:
    print(df.loc[df['State'] == state, ['City', 'State']])
```

You should get the following output:

```
             City State
43         Ottawa    Il
44         Ottawa    Il
493     Galesburg    Il
613       Chicago    Il
614       Chicago    Il
...           ...   ...
54915     Chicago    Il
54916     Chicago    Il
54918     Chicago    Il
54919     Chicago    Il
54921     Chicago    Il

[665 rows x 2 columns]
          City State
7052  Wheaton    iL
             City State
43         Ottawa    Il
44         Ottawa    Il
493     Galesburg    Il
613       Chicago    Il
614       Chicago    Il
...           ...   ...
54915     Chicago    Il
54916     Chicago    Il
54918     Chicago    Il
54919     Chicago    Il
54921     Chicago    Il

[665 rows x 2 columns]
```

Figure 11.27: Observations with the il value

> **NOTE**
>
> The preceding output has been truncated.

As you can see, all these cities belong to the state of Illinois. Let's replace them with the correct values.

9. Create a condition mask (**il_mask**) to subset all the rows that contain the four incorrect values (**il**, **Il**, **iL**, and **Il**) by using the **isin()** method and a list of these values as a parameter. Then, save the result into a variable called **il_mask**:

```
il_mask = df['State'].isin(['il', 'Il', 'iL', 'Il'])
```

10. Print the number of rows that match the condition we set in **il_mask** using the **.sum()** method. This will sum all the rows that have a value of **True** (they match the condition):

```
il_mask.sum()
```

You should get the following output:

```
672
```

11. Using the **pandas .loc()** method, subset the rows with the **il_mask** condition mask and replace the value of the **State** column with **IL**:

```
df.loc[il_mask, 'State'] = 'IL'
```

12. Print out all the unique values of the **State** variable once more:

```
df['State'].unique()
```

You should get the following output:

```
array(['IL', 'PA', 'DC', nan, 'WI', 'CA', 'MO', 'NC', 'IA', 'MA', 'IN',
       'MI', 'TN', 'NY', 'ng', 'TX', 'CO', 'NV', 'WA', '8I', 'In', 'OH',
       'SC', 'VA', 'NM', 'FL', 'LA', 'GA', 'II', 'NJ', 'MD', 'I', 'AR',
       'KS', 'DE', '60', 'SD', 'MN', 'VT', 'OK', 'KY', 'CT', 'NH', 'AZ',
       'OR', 'PR', 'RI'], dtype=object)
```

Figure 11.28: List of unique values for the 'State' column

As you can see, the four incorrect values are not present anymore. Let's have a look at the other remaining incorrect values: **II**, **I**, **8I**, and **60**. We will look at dealing **II** in the next step.

Print out the rows that have a value of **II** into the **State** column using the **pandas** subsetting API, that is, DataFrame.loc[row_condition, column_condition]:

```
df.loc[df['State'] == 'II',]
```

You should get the following output:

	ID	City	State	Zip	Title	RedactionRequested
14340	28039	Bloomington	II	61704	Co-Chairman	False
14341	31994	Bloomington	II	61704	Chairman	False

Figure 11.29: Subsetting the rows with a value of IL in the State column

There are only two cases where the **II** value has been used for the **State** column and both have **Bloomington** as the city, which is in Illinois. Here, the correct **State** value should be **IL**.

13. Now, create a **for** loop that iterates through the three incorrect values (**I**, **8I**, and **60**) and print out the subsetted rows using the same logic that we used in *Step 12*. Only display the **City** and **State** columns:

```
for val in ['I', '8I', '60']:
    print(df.loc[df['State'] == val, ['City', 'State']])
```

You should get the following output:

```
              City State
17596  Bloomington     I
             City State
5513  Springfield    8I
          City State
28060  Chicago    60
```

Figure 11.30: Observations with incorrect values (I, 8I, and 60)

All the observations that have incorrect values are cities in Illinois. Let's fix them now.

14. Create a **for** loop that iterates through the four incorrect values (**II**, **I**, **8I**, and **60**) and reuse the subsetting logic from *Step 12* to replace the value in **State** with **IL**:

```
for val in ['II', 'I', '8I', '60']:
    df.loc[df['State'] == val, 'State'] = 'IL'
```

15. Print out all the unique values of the **State** variable:

```
df['State'].unique()
```

You should get the following output:

```
array(['IL', 'PA', 'DC', nan, 'WI', 'CA', 'MO', 'NC', 'IA', 'MA', 'IN',
       'MI', 'TN', 'NY', 'ng', 'TX', 'CO', 'NV', 'WA', 'OH', 'SC', 'VA',
       'NM', 'FL', 'LA', 'GA', 'NJ', 'MD', 'AR', 'KS', 'DE', 'SD', 'MN',
       'VT', 'OK', 'KY', 'CT', 'NH', 'AZ', 'OR', 'PR', 'RI'], dtype=object)
```

Figure 11.31: List of unique values for the State column

You fixed the issues for the state of Illinois. However, there are two more incorrect values in this column: **In** and **ng**.

16. Repeat *Step 13*, but iterate through the **In** and **ng** values instead:

```
for val in ['In', 'ng']:
    print(df.loc[df['State'] == val, ['City', 'State']])
```

You should get the following output:

```
            City State
5733   Sherville    In
              City State
2428   none given    ng
2961   none given    ng
```

Figure 11.32: Observations with incorrect values (In, ng)

The rows that have the **ng** value in **State** are missing values. We will cover this topic in the next section. The observation that has **In** as its **State** is a city in Indiana, so the correct value should be **IN**. Let's fix this.

17. Subset the rows containing the **In** value in **State** using the **.loc()** and **.str.contains()** methods and replace the state value with **IN**. Don't forget to specify the **na=False** parameter as **.str.contains()**:

```
df.loc[df['State']\
  .str.contains('In', na=False), 'State'] = 'IN'
```

Print out all the unique values of the **State** variable:

```
df['State'].unique()
```

You should get the following output:

```
array(['IL', 'PA', 'DC', nan, 'WI', 'CA', 'MO', 'NC', 'IA', 'MA', 'IN',
       'MI', 'TN', 'NY', 'ng', 'TX', 'CO', 'NV', 'WA', 'OH', 'SC', 'VA',
       'NM', 'FL', 'LA', 'GA', 'NJ', 'MD', 'AR', 'KS', 'DE', 'SD', 'MN',
       'VT', 'OK', 'KY', 'CT', 'NH', 'AZ', 'OR', 'PR', 'RI'], dtype=object)
```

Figure 11.33: List of unique values for the State column

> **NOTE**
>
> To access the source code for this specific section, please refer to https://packt.live/319pfGX.
>
> You can also run this example online at https://packt.live/2E8ICHn.

You just fixed all the incorrect values for the **State** variable using the methods provided by the **pandas** package. In the next section, we are going to look at handling missing values.

HANDLING MISSING VALUES

So far, you have looked at a variety of issues when it comes to datasets. Now it is time to discuss another issue that occurs quite frequently: missing values. As you may have guessed, this type of issue means that certain values are missing for certain variables.

The **pandas** package provides a method that we can use to identify missing values in a DataFrame: **.isna()**. Let's see it in action on the **Online Retail** dataset. First, you need to import **pandas** and load the data into a DataFrame:

```
import pandas as pd
file_url = 'https://github.com/PacktWorkshops/'\
           'The-Data-Science-Workshop/blob/'\
           'master/Chapter10/dataset/'\
           'Online%20Retail.xlsx?raw=true'
df = pd.read_excel(file_url)
```

The **.isna()** method returns a **pandas** series with a binary value for each cell of a DataFrame and states whether it is missing a value (**True**) or not (**False**):

```
df.isna()
```

You should get the following output:

	InvoiceNo	StockCode	Description	Quantity	InvoiceDate
0	False	False	False	False	False
1	False	False	False	False	False
2	False	False	False	False	False
3	False	False	False	False	False
4	False	False	False	False	False

Figure 11.34: Output of the .isna() method

As we saw previously, we can give the output of a binary variable to the **.sum()** method, which will add all the **True** values together (cells that have missing values) and provide a summary for each column:

```
df.isna().sum()
```

You should get the following output:

```
InvoiceNo           0
StockCode           0
Description      1454
Quantity            0
InvoiceDate         0
UnitPrice           0
CustomerID     135080
Country             0
dtype: int64
```

Figure 11.35: Summary of missing values for each variable

As you can see, there are **1454** missing values in the **Description** column and **135080** in the **CustomerID** column. Let's have a look at the missing value observations for **Description**. You can use the output of the **.isna()** method to subset the rows with missing values:

```
df[df['Description'].isna()]
```

You should get the following output:

	InvoiceNo	StockCode	Description	Quantity	InvoiceDate	UnitPrice	CustomerID	Country
622	536414	22139	NaN	56	2010-12-01 11:52:00	0.0	NaN	United Kingdom
1970	536545	21134	NaN	1	2010-12-01 14:32:00	0.0	NaN	United Kingdom
1971	536546	22145	NaN	1	2010-12-01 14:33:00	0.0	NaN	United Kingdom
1972	536547	37509	NaN	1	2010-12-01 14:33:00	0.0	NaN	United Kingdom
1987	536549	85226A	NaN	1	2010-12-01 14:34:00	0.0	NaN	United Kingdom
1988	536550	85044	NaN	1	2010-12-01 14:34:00	0.0	NaN	United Kingdom

Figure 11.36: Subsetting the rows with missing values for Description

From the preceding output, you can see that all the rows with missing values have **0.0** as the unit price and are missing the **CustomerID** column. In a real project, you will have to discuss these cases with the business and check whether these transactions are genuine or not. If the business confirms that these observations are irrelevant, then you will need to remove them from the dataset.

The **pandas** package provides a method that we can use to easily remove missing values: **.dropna()**. This method returns a new DataFrame without all the rows that have missing values. By default, it will look at all the columns. You can specify a list of columns for it to look for with the **subset** parameter:

```
df.dropna(subset=['Description'])
```

This method returns a new DataFrame with no missing values for the specified columns. If you want to replace the original dataset directly, you can use the **inplace=True** parameter:

```
df.dropna(subset=['Description'], inplace=True)
```

Now, look at the summary of the missing values for each variable:

```
df.isna().sum()
```

You should get the following output:

```
InvoiceNo            0
StockCode            0
Description          0
Quantity             0
InvoiceDate          0
UnitPrice            0
CustomerID      133626
Country              0
dtype: int64
```

Figure 11.37: Summary of missing values for each variable

As you can see, there are no more missing values in the **Description** column. Let's have a look at the **CustomerID** column:

```
df[df['CustomerID'].isna()]
```

You should get the following output:

	InvoiceNo	StockCode	Description	Quantity	InvoiceDate	UnitPrice	CustomerID	Country
1443	536544	21773	DECORATIVE ROSE BATHROOM BOTTLE	1	2010-12-01 14:32:00	2.51	NaN	United Kingdom
1444	536544	21774	DECORATIVE CATS BATHROOM BOTTLE	2	2010-12-01 14:32:00	2.51	NaN	United Kingdom
1445	536544	21786	POLKADOT RAIN HAT	4	2010-12-01 14:32:00	0.85	NaN	United Kingdom
1446	536544	21787	RAIN PONCHO RETROSPOT	2	2010-12-01 14:32:00	1.66	NaN	United Kingdom
1447	536544	21790	VINTAGE SNAP CARDS	9	2010-12-01 14:32:00	1.66	NaN	United Kingdom
...	...	...	...	...	...	...	...	...
541536	581498	85099B	JUMBO BAG RED RETROSPOT	5	2011-12-09 10:26:00	4.13	NaN	United Kingdom
541537	581498	85099C	JUMBO BAG BAROQUE BLACK WHITE	4	2011-12-09 10:26:00	4.13	NaN	United Kingdom
541538	581498	85150	LADIES & GENTLEMEN METAL SIGN	1	2011-12-09 10:26:00	4.96	NaN	United Kingdom
541539	581498	85174	S/4 CACTI CANDLES	1	2011-12-09 10:26:00	10.79	NaN	United Kingdom
541540	581498	DOT	DOTCOM POSTAGE	1	2011-12-09 10:26:00	1714.17	NaN	United Kingdom

133626 rows × 8 columns

Figure 11.38: Rows with missing values in CustomerID

This time, all the transactions look normal, except they are missing values for the **CustomerID** column; all the other variables have been filled in with values that seem genuine. There is no other way to infer the missing values for the **CustomerID** column. These rows represent almost 25% of the dataset, so we can't remove them.

However, most algorithms require a value for each observation, so you need to provide one for these cases. We will use the **.fillna()** method from **pandas** to do this. Provide the value to be imputed as **Missing** and use **inplace=True** as a parameter:

```
df['CustomerID'].fillna('Missing', inplace=True)
df[1443:1448]
```

You should get the following output:

	InvoiceNo	StockCode	Description	Quantity	InvoiceDate	UnitPrice	CustomerID
1444	536544	21774	DECORATIVE CATS BATHROOM BOTTLE	2	2010-12-01 14:32:00	2.51	Missing
1445	536544	21786	POLKADOT RAIN HAT	4	2010-12-01 14:32:00	0.85	Missing
1446	536544	21787	RAIN PONCHO RETROSPOT	2	2010-12-01 14:32:00	1.66	Missing
1447	536544	21790	VINTAGE SNAP CARDS	9	2010-12-01 14:32:00	1.66	Missing
1448	536544	21791	VINTAGE HEADS AND TAILS CARD GAME	2	2010-12-01 14:32:00	2.51	Missing

Figure 11.39: Examples of rows where missing values for CustomerID have been replaced with Missing

Let's see if we have any missing values in the dataset:

```
df.isna().sum()
```

You should get the following output:

```
InvoiceNo      0
StockCode      0
Description    0
Quantity       0
InvoiceDate    0
UnitPrice      0
CustomerID     0
Country        0
dtype: int64
```

Figure 11.40: Summary of missing values for each variable

You have successfully fixed all the missing values in this dataset. These methods also work when we want to handle missing numerical variables. We will look at this in the following exercise. All you need to do is provide a numerical value when you want to impute a value with **.fillna()**.

EXERCISE 11.04: FIXING MISSING VALUES FOR THE HORSE COLIC DATASET

In this exercise, you will be cleaning out all the missing values for all the numerical variables in the **Horse Colic** dataset.

Colic is a painful condition that horses can suffer from, and this dataset contains various pieces of information related to specific cases of this condition. You can use the link provided in the Note section if you want to find out more about the dataset's attributes. Let's get started:

> **NOTE**
>
> This dataset is from the UCI Machine Learning Repository. The attributes information can be found at https://packt.live/2MZwSrW.
>
> For your convenience, the dataset file that we'll be using in this exercise has been uploaded to this book's GitHub repository: https://packt.live/35qESZq.

1. Open a new Colab notebook.

2. Import the **pandas** package:

```
import pandas as pd
```

3. Assign the link to the dataset to a variable called **file_url**:

```
file_url = 'http://raw.githubusercontent.com/'\
           'PacktWorkshops/The-Data-Science-Workshop/'\
           'master/Chapter11/dataset/horse-colic.data'
```

4. Using the **.read_csv()** method from the **pandas** package, load the dataset into a new variable called **df** and specify the **header=None**, **sep='\s+'**, and **prefix='X'** parameters:

```
df = pd.read_csv(file_url, header=None, \
                 sep='\s+', prefix='X')
```

5. Print the first five rows of the DataFrame using the **.head()** method:

```
df.head()
```

You should get the following output:

	X0	X1	X2	X3	X4	X5	X6	X7	X8	X9	X10	X11	X12	X13	X14
0	2	1	530101	38.50	66	28	3	3	?	2	5	4	4	?	?
1	1	1	534817	39.2	88	20	?	?	4	1	3	4	2	?	?
2	2	1	530334	38.30	40	24	1	1	3	1	3	3	1	?	?
3	1	9	5290409	39.10	164	84	4	1	6	2	2	4	4	1	2
4	2	1	530255	37.30	104	35	?	?	6	2	?	?	?	?	?

Figure 11.41: The first five rows of the Horse Colic dataset

As you can see, the authors have used the **?** character for missing values, but the **pandas** package thinks that this is a normal value. You need to transform them into missing values.

6. Reload the dataset into a **pandas** DataFrame using the **.read_csv()** method, but this time, add the **na_values='?'** parameter in order to specify that this value needs to be treated as a missing value:

```
df = pd.read_csv(file_url, header=None, sep='\s+', \
                 prefix='X', na_values='?')
```

7. Print the first five rows of the DataFrame using the **.head()** method:

```
df.head()
```

You should get the following output:

	X0	X1	X2	X3	X4	X5	X6	X7	X8	X9	X10	X11	X12	X13	X14
0	2.0	1	530101	38.5	66.0	28.0	3.0	3.0	NaN	2.0	5.0	4.0	4.0	NaN	NaN
1	1.0	1	534817	39.2	88.0	20.0	NaN	NaN	4.0	1.0	3.0	4.0	2.0	NaN	NaN
2	2.0	1	530334	38.3	40.0	24.0	1.0	1.0	3.0	1.0	3.0	3.0	1.0	NaN	NaN
3	1.0	9	5290409	39.1	164.0	84.0	4.0	1.0	6.0	2.0	2.0	4.0	4.0	1.0	2.0
4	2.0	1	530255	37.3	104.0	35.0	NaN	NaN	6.0	2.0	NaN	NaN	NaN	NaN	NaN

Figure 11.42: The first five rows of the Horse Colic dataset

Now, you can see that **pandas** have converted all the **?** values into missing values.

8. Print the data type of each column using the **dtypes** attribute:

```
df.dtypes
```

You should get the following output:

```
X0     float64
X1       int64
X2       int64
X3     float64
X4     float64
X5     float64
X6     float64
X7     float64
X8     float64
X9     float64
X10    float64
X11    float64
X12    float64
X13    float64
```

Figure 11.43: Data type of each column

9. Print the number of missing values for each column by combining the **.isna()** and **.sum()** methods:

```
df.isna().sum()
```

You should get the following output:

```
X0      1
X1      0
X2      0
X3     60
X4     24
X5     58
X6     56
X7     69
X8     47
X9     32
X10    55
```

Figure 11.44: Number of missing values for each column

10. Create a condition mask called **x0_mask** so that you can find the missing values in the **X0** column using the **.isna()** method:

```
x0_mask = df['X0'].isna()
```

11. Display the number of missing values for this column by using the **.sum()** method on **x0_mask**:

```
x0_mask.sum()
```

You should get the following output:

```
1
```

Here, you got the exact same number of missing values for **X0** that you did in *Step 9*.

12. Extract the mean of **X0** using the **.median()** method and store it in a new variable called **x0_median**. Print its value:

```
x0_median = df['X0'].median()
print(x0_median)
```

You should get the following output:

```
1.0
```

The median value for this column is **1**. You will replace all the missing values with this value in the **X0** column.

13. Replace all the missing values in the **X0** variable with their median using the **.fillna()** method, along with the **inplace=True** parameter:

```
df['X0'].fillna(x0_median, inplace=True)
```

14. Print the number of missing values for **X0** by combining the **.isna()** and **.sum()** methods:

```
df['X0'].isna().sum()
```

You should get the following output:

```
0
```

There are no more missing values in the variables.

15. Create a **for** loop that will iterate through all the columns of the DataFrame. In the for loop, calculate the median for each and save them into a variable called **col_median**. Then, impute missing values with this median value using the **.fillna()** method, along with the **inplace=True** parameter, and print the name of the column and its median value:

```
for col_name in df.columns:
    col_median = df[col_name].median()
    df[col_name].fillna(col_median, inplace=True)
    print(col_name)
    print(col_median)
```

You should get the following output:

```
X0
1.0
X1
1.0
X2
530305.5
X3
38.2
X4
64.0
X5
24.5
```

Figure 11.45: Median values for each column

16. Print the number of missing values for each column by combining the **.isna()** and **.sum()** methods:

```
df.isna().sum()
```

You should get the following output:

```
X0     0
X1     0
X2     0
X3     0
X4     0
X5     0
X6     0
X7     0
X8     0
X9     0
X10    0
```

Figure 11.46: Number of missing values for each column

> **NOTE**
>
> To access the source code for this specific section, please refer to https://packt.live/34c1zUd.
>
> You can also run this example online at https://packt.live/324mHt0.

You have successfully fixed the missing values for all the numerical variables using the methods provided by the **pandas** package: **.isna()** and **.fillna()**.

ACTIVITY 11.01: PREPARING THE SPEED DATING DATASET

As an entrepreneur, you are planning to launch a new dating app into the market. The key feature that will differentiate your app from other competitors will be your high performing user-matching algorithm. Before building this model, you have partnered with a speed dating company to collect data from real events. You just received the dataset from your partner company but realized it is not as clean as you expected; there are missing and incorrect values. Your task is to fix the main data quality issues in this dataset.

The following steps will help you complete this activity:

1. Download and load the dataset into Python using **.read_csv()**.
2. Print out the dimensions of the DataFrame using **.shape**.

3. Check for duplicate rows by using `.duplicated()` and `.sum()` on all the columns.
4. Check for duplicate rows by using `.duplicated()` and `.sum()` for the identifier columns (`iid`, `id`, `partner`, and `pid`).
5. Check for unexpected values for the following numerical variables: `'imprace'`, `'imprelig'`, `'sports'`, `'tvsports'`, `'exercise'`, `'dining'`, `'museums'`, `'art'`, `'hiking'`, `'gaming'`, `'clubbing'`, `'reading'`, `'tv'`, `'theater'`, `'movies'`, `'concerts'`, `'music'`, `'shopping'`, and `'yoga'`.
6. Replace the identified incorrect values.
7. Check the data type of the different columns using `.dtypes`.
8. Change the data types to categorical for the columns that don't contain numerical values using `.astype()`.
9. Check for any missing values using `.isna()` and `.sum()` for each numerical variable.
10. Replace the missing values for each numerical variable with their corresponding mean or median values using `.fillna()`, `.mean()`, and `.median()`.

> **NOTE**
>
> The dataset for this activity can be found in this book's GitHub repository: https://packt.live/36u0jtR.
>
> The original dataset has been shared by Ray Fisman and Sheena Iyengar from Columbia Business School: https://packt.live/2Fp5rUg.
>
> The authors have provided a very useful document that describes the dataset and its features: https://packt.live/2Qrp7gD.

You should get the following output. The figure represents the number of rows with unexpected values for **`imprace`** and a list of unexpected values:

```
imprace
8
[0.]
```

Figure 11.47: Number of rows with unexpected values for 'imprace' and a list of unexpected values

The following figure illustrates the number of rows with unexpected values and a list of unexpected values for each column:

```
imprace
8
[0.]
museums
18
[0.]
art
18
[0.]
```

Figure 11.48: Number of rows with unexpected values and a list of unexpected values for each column

The following figure illustrates a list of unique values for gaming:

```
gaming
[ 1.   5.   4.   6.   2.   3.   7.   8.  10.  nan   9.   0.]
```

Figure 11.49: List of unique values for gaming

The following figure displays the data types of each column:

```
iid           int64
id          float64
gender        int64
idg           int64
condtn        int64
wave          int64
round         int64
```

Figure 11.50: Data types of each column

The following figure displays the updated data types of each column:

```
iid         category
id          category
gender      category
idg         category
condtn      category
wave        category
round          int64
position    category
```

Figure 11.51: Data types of each column

The following figure displays the number of missing values for numerical variables:

```
round          0
order          0
int_corr     158
age           95
mn_sat      5245
income      4099
expnum      6578
dtype: int64
```

Figure 11.52: Number of missing values for numerical variables

The following figure displays the list of unique values for **int_corr**:

```
array([ 0.14,  0.54,  0.16,  0.61,  0.21,  0.25,  0.34,  0.5 ,  0.28,
       -0.36,  0.29,  0.18,  0.1 , -0.21,  0.32,  0.73,  0.6 ,  0.07,
        0.11,  0.39, -0.24, -0.14,  0.09, -0.04, -0.3 , -0.26, -0.15,
       -0.47, -0.18,  0.05,  0.37,  0.35,  0.15, -0.19, -0.43,  0.  ,
       -0.17,  0.08, -0.16,  0.06, -0.05, -0.13, -0.06,  0.33, -0.51,
        0.12,  0.19,  0.47,  0.03,  0.46,  0.43,  0.52, -0.46, -0.27,
        0.59,  0.31, -0.34, -0.03, -0.11,  0.42, -0.4 , -0.23,  0.17,
        0.68, -0.01, -0.35,  0.3 ,  0.65,  0.24,  0.41,  0.49,  0.01,
        0.22, -0.08,  0.27,  0.44,  0.62, -0.2 , -0.02, -0.33, -0.52,
       -0.1 ,  0.58, -0.57, -0.31, -0.07, -0.32,  0.04, -0.12,  0.48,
```

Figure 11.53: List of unique values for 'int_corr'

The following figure displays the list of unique values for numerical variables:

```
age
[21. 24. 25. 23. 22. 26. 27. 30. 28. nan 29. 34. 35. 32. 39. 20. 19. 18.
 37. 33. 36. 31. 42. 38. 55.]
mn_sat
[  nan 1070. 1258. 1400. 1290. 1460. 1430. 1215. 1330. 1450. 1155. 1140.
 1360. 1402. 1250. 1210. 1220. 1410. 1260. 1380. 1030. 1309. 1308. 1050.
 1100. 1310. 1490. 1188. 1097. 1212. 1340. 1034. 1185. 1242. 1160. 1099.
 1214. 1270. 1110. 1178. 1060. 1157. 1180. 1014. 1341.  990. 1320. 1159.
 1370. 1105. 1365. 1011. 1130. 1206. 1331. 1191.  914. 1200. 1080. 1090.
 1092. 1470. 1149. 1134. 1230. 1267. 1280. 1227. 1239.]
income
```

Figure 11.54: List of unique values for numerical variables

The following figure displays the number of missing values for numerical variables:

```
age
0
mn_sat
0
income
0
expnum
0
```

Figure 11.55: Number of missing values for numerical variables

> **NOTE**
>
> The solution to this activity can be found at the following address: https://packt.live/2GbJloz.

SUMMARY

In this chapter, you learned how important it is to prepare any given dataset and fix the main quality issues it has. This is critical because the cleaner a dataset is, the easier it will be for any machine learning model to easily learn about the relevant patterns. On top of this, most algorithms can't handle issues such as missing values, so they must be handled prior to the modeling phase. In this chapter, you covered the most frequent issues that are faced in data science projects: duplicate rows, incorrect data types, unexpected values, and missing values.

The goal of this chapter was to introduce you to the concepts that will help you to spot some of these issues and easily fix them so that you have the basic toolkit to be able to handle other cases. As a final note, throughout this chapter, we emphasized how important it is to discuss the issues you find with the business or the data engineering team you are working with. For instance, if you've detected unexpected values in a dataset, you may want to confirm that they don't have any special meaning from a business point of view before removing or replacing them.

You also need to be very careful when fixing issues: you don't want to alter the dataset too much so that it creates additional unexpected patterns. This is exactly why it is recommended that you replace any of the missing values of numerical variables with their **mean** or **median**. Otherwise, you will change its distribution drastically. For example, if the values of a variable are between 0 and 10, replacing all the missing values with -999 will drastically change their mean and **standard deviation**.

In the next chapter, we will discuss the interesting topic of feature engineering.

12

FEATURE ENGINEERING

OVERVIEW

By the end of this chapter, you will be able to merge multiple datasets together; bin categorical and numerical variables; perform aggregation on data; and manipulate dates using **`pandas`**.

This chapter will introduce you to some of the key techniques for creating new variables on an existing dataset.

INTRODUCTION

In the previous chapters, we learned how to analyze and prepare a dataset in order to increase its level of quality. In this chapter, we will introduce you to another interesting topic: creating new features, also known as feature engineering. You already saw some of these concepts in *Chapter 3*, *Binary Classification*, but we will dive a bit deeper into it in this chapter.

The objective of feature engineering is to provide more information for the analysis you are performing on or the machine learning algorithms you will train on. Adding more information will help you to achieve better and more accurate results.

New features can come from internal data sources such as another table from databases or from different systems. For instance, you may want to link data from the CRM tool used in your company to the data from a marketing tool. The added features can also come from external sources such as open-source data or shared data from partners or providers. For example, you may want to link the volume of sales with a weather API or with governmental census data. But it can also come from the original dataset by creating new variables from existing ones.

Let's pause for a second and understand why feature engineering is so important for training machine learning algorithms. We are all aware that these algorithms have achieved incredible results in recent years in finding extremely complex patterns from data. But their main limitations lie in the fact that they can only analyze and find meaningful patterns within the data provided as input. If the data is incorrect, incomplete, or missing important features, the algorithms will not be able to perform correctly.

On the other hand, we humans tend to understand the broader context and see the bigger picture quite easily. For instance, if you were tasked with analyzing customer churn, even before looking at the existing data, you would already expect it to have some features describing customer attributes such as demographics, services or products subscribed to, and subscription date. And once we receive the data, we can highlight the features that we think are important and missing from the dataset. This is the reason why data scientists, with their expertise and experience, need to think about the additional information that will help algorithms to understand and detect more meaningful patterns from this enriched data. Without further ado, let's jump in.

MERGING DATASETS

Most organizations store their data in data stores such as databases, data warehouses, or data lakes. The flow of information can come from different systems or tools. Most of the time, the data is stored in a relational database composed of multiple tables rather than a single one with well-defined relationships between them.

For instance, an online store could have multiple tables for recording all the purchases made on its platform. One table might contain information relating to existing customers, another one might list all existing and past products in the catalog, and a third one might contain all of the transactions that occurred, and so on.

If you were working on a project recommending products to customers for an e-commerce platform such as Amazon, you may have been given only the data from the transactions table. In that case, you would like to get some attributes for each product and customer and would have to ask to extract these additional tables you need and then merge the three tables together before building your recommendation system.

Let's see how we can merge multiple data sources with a real example: the Online Retail dataset we used in the previous chapter. We will add new information regarding whether the transactions happened on public holidays in the UK or not. This additional data may help the model to understand whether there are some correlations between sales and some public holidays such as Christmas or the Queen's birthday, which is a holiday in countries such as Australia.

> **NOTE**
>
> The list of public holidays in the UK will be extracted from this site: https://packt.live/2twsFVR.

First, we need to import the Online Retail dataset into a **pandas** DataFrame:

```
import pandas as pd
file_url = 'https://github.com/PacktWorkshops/'\
           'The-Data-Science-Workshop/blob/'\
           'master/Chapter12/Dataset/'\
           'Online%20Retail.xlsx?raw=true'
df = pd.read_excel(file_url)
df.head()
```

You should get the following output.

	InvoiceNo	StockCode	Description	Quantity	InvoiceDate	UnitPrice	CustomerID	Country
0	536365	85123A	WHITE HANGING HEART T-LIGHT HOLDER	6	2010-12-01 08:26:00	2.55	17850.0	United Kingdom
1	536365	71053	WHITE METAL LANTERN	6	2010-12-01 08:26:00	3.39	17850.0	United Kingdom
2	536365	84406B	CREAM CUPID HEARTS COAT HANGER	8	2010-12-01 08:26:00	2.75	17850.0	United Kingdom
3	536365	84029G	KNITTED UNION FLAG HOT WATER BOTTLE	6	2010-12-01 08:26:00	3.39	17850.0	United Kingdom
4	536365	84029E	RED WOOLLY HOTTIE WHITE HEART.	6	2010-12-01 08:26:00	3.39	17850.0	United Kingdom

Figure 12.1: First five rows of the Online Retail dataset

Next, we are going to load all the public holidays in the UK into another **pandas** DataFrame. From *Chapter 10, Analyzing a Dataset* we know the records of this dataset are only for the years 2010 and 2011. So we are going to extract public holidays for those two years, but we need to do so in two different steps as the API provided by **date.nager** is split into single years only.

Let's focus on 2010 first:

```
uk_holidays_2010 = pd.read_csv\
                   ('https://date.nager.at/PublicHoliday/'\
                    'Country/GB/2010/CSV')
```

We can print its shape to see how many rows and columns it has:

```
uk_holidays_2010.shape
```

You should get the following output.

```
(13, 8)
```

We can see there were **13** public holidays in that year and there are **8** different columns.

Let's print the first five rows of this DataFrame:

```
uk_holidays_2010.head()
```

You should get the following output:

	Date	LocalName	Name	CountryCode	Fixed	Global	LaunchYear	Type
0	2010-01-01	New Year's Day	New Year's Day	GB	False	True	NaN	Public
1	2010-01-04	New Year's Day	New Year's Day	GB	False	False	NaN	Public
2	2010-03-17	Saint Patrick's Day	Saint Patrick's Day	GB	True	False	NaN	Public
3	2010-04-02	Good Friday	Good Friday	GB	False	True	NaN	Public
4	2010-04-05	Easter Monday	Easter Monday	GB	False	False	NaN	Public

Figure 12.2: First five rows of the UK 2010 public holidays DataFrame

Now that we have the list of public holidays for 2010, let's extract the ones for 2011:

```
uk_holidays_2011 = pd.read_csv\
                   ('https://date.nager.at/PublicHoliday/'\
                    'Country/GB/2011/CSV')
uk_holidays_2011.shape
```

You should get the following output.

```
(15, 8)
```

There were **15** public holidays in 2011. Now we need to combine the records of these two DataFrames. We will use the **.append()** method from **pandas** and assign the results into a new DataFrame:

```
uk_holidays = uk_holidays_2010.append(uk_holidays_2011)
```

Let's check we have the right number of rows after appending the two DataFrames:

```
uk_holidays.shape
```

You should get the following output:

```
(28, 8)
```

We got **28** records, which corresponds with the total number of public holidays in 2010 and 2011.

In order to merge two DataFrames together, we need to have at least one common column between them, meaning the two DataFrames should have at least one column that contains the same type of information. In our example, we are going to merge this DataFrame using the **Date** column with the Online Retail DataFrame on the **InvoiceDate** column. We can see that the data format of these two columns is different: one is a date (**yyyy-mm-dd**) and the other is a datetime (**yyyy-mm-dd hh:mm:ss**).

So, we need to transform the **InvoiceDate** column into date format (**yyyy-mm-dd**). One way to do it (we will see another one later in this chapter) is to transform this column into text and then extract the first 10 characters for each cell using the **.str.slice()** method.

For example, the date 2010-12-01 08:26:00 will first be converted into a string and then we will keep only the first 10 characters, which will be 2010-12-01. We are going to save these results into a new column called **InvoiceDay**:

```
df['InvoiceDay'] = df['InvoiceDate'].astype(str)\
                                    .str.slice(stop=10)
df.head()
```

The output is as follows:

	InvoiceNo	StockCode	Description	Quantity	InvoiceDate	UnitPrice	CustomerID	Country	InvoiceDay
0	536365	85123A	WHITE HANGING HEART T-LIGHT HOLDER	6	2010-12-01 08:26:00	2.55	17850.0	United Kingdom	2010-12-01
1	536365	71053	WHITE METAL LANTERN	6	2010-12-01 08:26:00	3.39	17850.0	United Kingdom	2010-12-01
2	536365	84406B	CREAM CUPID HEARTS COAT HANGER	8	2010-12-01 08:26:00	2.75	17850.0	United Kingdom	2010-12-01
3	536365	84029G	KNITTED UNION FLAG HOT WATER BOTTLE	6	2010-12-01 08:26:00	3.39	17850.0	United Kingdom	2010-12-01
4	536365	84029E	RED WOOLLY HOTTIE WHITE HEART.	6	2010-12-01 08:26:00	3.39	17850.0	United Kingdom	2010-12-01

Figure 12.3: First five rows after creating InvoiceDay

Now **InvoiceDay** from the online retail DataFrame and **Date** from the UK public holidays DataFrame have similar information, so we can merge these two DataFrames together using **.merge()** from **pandas**.

There are multiple ways to join two tables together:

- The left join
- The right join
- The inner join
- The outer join

THE LEFT JOIN

The left join will keep all the rows from the first DataFrame, which is the *Online Retail* dataset (the left-hand side) and join it to the matching rows from the second DataFrame, which is the *UK Public Holidays* dataset (the right-hand side), as shown in *Figure 12.04*:

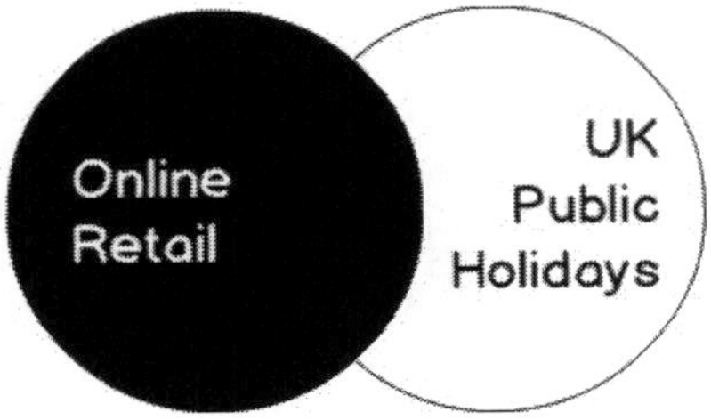

Figure 12.4: Venn diagram for left join

To perform a left join, we need to specify to the .merge() method the following parameters:

- **how = 'left'** for a left join
- **left_on = InvoiceDay** to specify the column used for merging from the left-hand side (here, the **Invoiceday** column from the Online Retail DataFrame)
- **right_on = Date** to specify the column used for merging from the right-hand side (here, the **Date** column from the UK Public Holidays DataFrame)

These parameters are clubbed together as shown in the following code snippet:

```
df_left = pd.merge(df, uk_holidays, left_on='InvoiceDay', \
                   right_on='Date', how='left')
df_left.shape
```

You should get the following output:

```
(541909, 17)
```

We got the exact same number of rows as the original Online Retail DataFrame, which is expected for a left join. Let's have a look at the first five rows:

```
df_left.head()
```

You should get the following output:

	InvoiceNo	StockCode	Description	Quantity	InvoiceDate	UnitPrice	CustomerID	Country	InvoiceDay	Date	LocalName	Name	CountryCode	Fixed
0	536365	85123A	WHITE HANGING HEART T-LIGHT HOLDER	6	2010-12-01 08:26:00	2.55	17850.0	United Kingdom	2010-12-01	NaN	NaN	NaN	NaN	NaN
1	536365	71053	WHITE METAL LANTERN	6	2010-12-01 08:26:00	3.39	17850.0	United Kingdom	2010-12-01	NaN	NaN	NaN	NaN	NaN
2	536365	84406B	CREAM CUPID HEARTS COAT HANGER	8	2010-12-01 08:26:00	2.75	17850.0	United Kingdom	2010-12-01	NaN	NaN	NaN	NaN	NaN
3	536365	84029G	KNITTED UNION FLAG HOT WATER BOTTLE	6	2010-12-01 08:26:00	3.39	17850.0	United Kingdom	2010-12-01	NaN	NaN	NaN	NaN	NaN
4	536365	84029E	RED WOOLLY HOTTIE WHITE HEART.	6	2010-12-01 08:26:00	3.39	17850.0	United Kingdom	2010-12-01	NaN	NaN	NaN	NaN	NaN

Figure 12.5: First five rows of the left-merged DataFrame

We can see that the eight columns from the public holidays DataFrame have been merged to the original one. If no row has been matched from the second DataFrame (in this case, the public holidays one), **`pandas`** will fill all the cells with missing values (**`NaT`** or **`NaN`**), as shown in *Figure 12.05*.

THE RIGHT JOIN

The right join is similar to the left join except it will keep all the rows from the second DataFrame (the right-hand side) and tries to match it with the first one (the left-hand side), as shown in *Figure 12.06*:

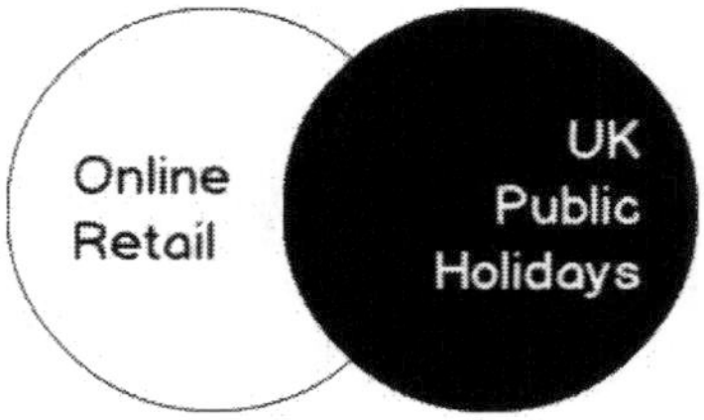

Figure 12.6: Venn diagram for right join

We just need to specify the parameters:

- **`how= 'right'`** to the **`.merge()`** method to perform this type of join.
- We will use the exact same columns used for merging as the previous example, which is **`InvoiceDay`** for the Online Retail DataFrame and **`Date`** for the UK Public Holidays one.

These parameters are clubbed together as shown in the following code snippet:

```
df_right = df.merge(uk_holidays, left_on='InvoiceDay', \
                    right_on='Date', how='right')
df_right.shape
```

You should get the following output:

```
(9602, 17)
```

We can see there are fewer rows as a result of the right join, but it doesn't get the same number as for the Public Holidays DataFrame. This is because there are multiple rows from the Online Retail DataFrame that match one single date in the public holidays one.

For instance, looking at the first rows of the merged DataFrame, we can see there were multiple purchases on January 4, 2011, so all of them have been matched with the corresponding public holiday. Have a look at the following code snippet:

```
df_right.head()
```

You should get the following output:

	InvoiceNo	StockCode	Description	Quantity	InvoiceDate	UnitPrice	CustomerID	Country	InvoiceDay	Date	LocalName	Name	CountryCode	Fixed
0	539993	22386	JUMBO BAG PINK POLKADOT	10.0	2011-01-04 10:00:00	1.95	13313.0	United Kingdom	2011-01-04	2011-01-04	New Year's Day	New Year's Day	GB	False
1	539993	21499	BLUE POLKADOT WRAP	25.0	2011-01-04 10:00:00	0.42	13313.0	United Kingdom	2011-01-04	2011-01-04	New Year's Day	New Year's Day	GB	False
2	539993	21498	RED RETROSPOT WRAP	25.0	2011-01-04 10:00:00	0.42	13313.0	United Kingdom	2011-01-04	2011-01-04	New Year's Day	New Year's Day	GB	False
3	539993	22379	RECYCLING BAG RETROSPOT	5.0	2011-01-04 10:00:00	2.10	13313.0	United Kingdom	2011-01-04	2011-01-04	New Year's Day	New Year's Day	GB	False
4	539993	20718	RED RETROSPOT SHOPPER BAG	10.0	2011-01-04 10:00:00	1.25	13313.0	United Kingdom	2011-01-04	2011-01-04	New Year's Day	New Year's Day	GB	False

Figure 12.7: First five rows of the right-merged DataFrame

There are two other types of merging: inner and outer.

An inner join will only keep the rows that match between the two tables:

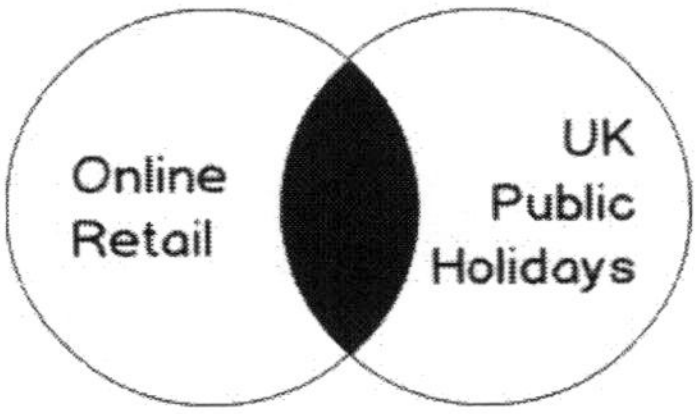

Figure 12.8: Venn diagram for inner join

You just need to specify the **`how = 'inner'`** parameter in the **`.merge()`** method.

These parameters are clubbed together as shown in the following code snippet:

```
df_inner = df.merge(uk_holidays, left_on='InvoiceDay', \
                    right_on='Date', how='inner')
df_inner.shape
```

You should get the following output:

```
(9579, 17)
```

We can see there are only 9,579 observations that happened during a public holiday in the UK.

The outer join will keep all rows from both tables (matched and unmatched), as shown in *Figure 12.09*:

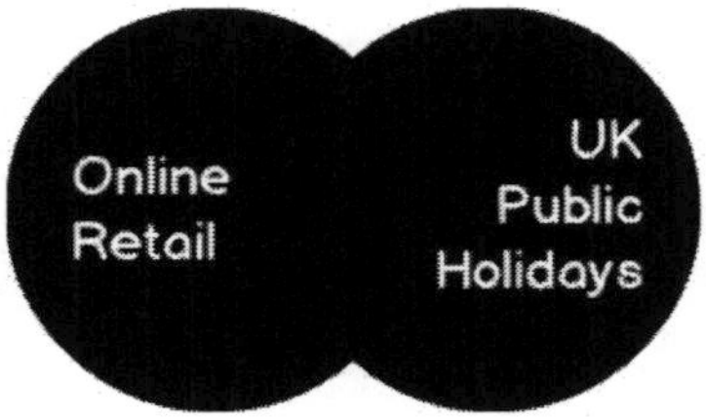

Figure 12.9: Venn diagram for outer join

As you may have guessed, you just need to specify the **`how == 'outer'`** parameter in the **`.merge()`** method:

```
df_outer = df.merge(uk_holidays, left_on='InvoiceDay', \
                    right_on='Date', how='outer')
df_outer.shape
```

You should get the following output:

```
(541932, 17)
```

Before merging two tables, it is extremely important for you to know what your focus is. If your objective is to expand the number of features from an original dataset by adding the columns from another one, then you will probably use a left or right join. But be aware you may end up with more observations due to potentially multiple matches between the two tables. On the other hand, if you are interested in knowing which observations matched or didn't match between the two tables, you will either use an inner or outer join.

EXERCISE 12.01: MERGING THE ATO DATASET WITH THE POSTCODE DATA

In this exercise, we will merge the ATO dataset (28 columns) with the Postcode dataset (150 columns) to get a richer dataset with an increased number of columns.

> **NOTE**
>
> The Australian Taxation Office (ATO) dataset can be found in the Packt GitHub repository: https://packt.live/39B146q.
>
> The Postcode dataset can be found here: https://packt.live/2sHAPLc.
>
> The sources of the dataset are as follows:
>
> The **Australian Taxation Office** (**ATO**): https://packt.live/361i1p3.
>
> The Postcode dataset: https://packt.live/2umIn6u.

The following steps will help you complete the exercise:

1. Open up a new Colab notebook.
2. Now, begin with the **import** of the **pandas** package:

```
import pandas as pd
```

3. Assign the link to the ATO dataset to a variable called **file_url**:

```
file_url = 'https://raw.githubusercontent.com/'\
           'PacktWorkshops/The-Data-Science-Workshop/'\
           'master/Chapter12/Dataset/taxstats2015.csv'
```

4. Using the **.read_csv()** method from the **pandas** package, load the dataset into a new DataFrame called **df**:

```
df = pd.read_csv(file_url)
```

5. Display the dimensions of this DataFrame using the **.shape** attribute:

```
df.shape
```

You should get the following output:

```
(2473, 28)
```

The ATO dataset contains **2471** rows and **28** columns.

6. Display the first five rows of the ATO DataFrame using the **.head()** method:

```
df.head()
```

You should get the following output:

	Postcode	Count taxable income or loss	Average taxable income or loss	Median taxable income or loss	Count salary and wages	Average salary and wages	Median salary and wages	Count net rent	Average net rent	Median net rent	Count total income or loss	Average total income or loss	Median total income or loss	Count total deductions	Average total deductions	Median total deductions	Count total business income	Average total business income	Median total business income	Count total business expenses
0	2000	36185	47723	18213	31293	38710	17992	3614	558	207	36185	50148	18596	36185	2071	0	1928	210901	19684	1331
1	2006	83	80905	58150	74	82733	67658	21	1042	-807	83	84710	64709	83	3804	641	4	69983	42054	4
2	2007	4769	46549	31474	4153	47386	34366	548	-1242	-794	4769	48309	32568	4769	1740	300	384	575099	19960	334
3	2008	5607	108816	41151	5008	53418	42892	612	1818	-1728	5607	112819	42741	5607	3917	430	548	53329	19722	481
4	2009	9726	82938	50604	8167	74068	55243	1714	-2412	-1520	9726	86503	53311	9726	3433	570	736	237539	26044	666

Figure 12.10: First five rows of the ATO dataset

Both DataFrames have a column called **Postcode** containing postcodes, so we will use it to merge them together.

> **NOTE**
>
> Postcode is the name used in Australia for zip code. It is an identifier for postal areas.

We are interested in learning more about each of these postcodes. Let's make sure they are all unique in this dataset.

7. Display the number of unique values for the **Postcode** variable using the **.nunique()** method:

```
df['Postcode'].nunique()
```

You should get the following output:

```
2473
```

There are **2473** unique values in this column and the DataFrame has **2473** rows, so we are sure the **Postcode** variable contains only unique values.

8. Now, assign the link to the second Postcode dataset to a variable called **postcode_df**:

```
postcode_url = 'https://github.com/PacktWorkshops/'\
               'The-Data-Science-Workshop/blob/'\
               'master/Chapter12/Dataset/'\
               'taxstats2016individual06taxablestatusstate'\
               'territorypostcodetaxableincome%20(2).xlsx?'\
               'raw=true'
```

9. Load the second Postcode dataset into a new DataFrame called **postcode_df** using the **.read_excel()** method.

   We will only load the *Individuals Table 6B* sheet as this is where the data is located so we need to provide this name to the **sheet_name** parameter. Also, the header row (containing the name of the variables) in this spreadsheet is located on the third row so we need to specify it to the header parameter.

> **NOTE**
>
> Don't forget the **index** starts with 0 in Python.

   Have a look at the following code snippet:

```
postcode_df = pd.read_excel(postcode_url, \
                            sheet_name='Individuals Table 6B', \
                            header=2)
```

10. Print the dimensions of **postcode_df** using the **.shape** attribute:

```
postcode_df.shape
```

   You should get the following output:

```
(2567, 150)
```

   This DataFrame contains **2567** rows for **150** columns. By merging it with the ATO dataset, we will get additional information for each postcode.

11. Print the first five rows of **postcode_df** using the **.head()** method:

```
postcode_df.head()
```

You should get the following output:

	State/ Territory1	Postcode	Number of individuals\nno.	Taxable income or loss3 \nno.	Taxable income or loss3 \n$	Tax on taxable income \nno.	Tax on taxable income \n$	Medicare levy \nno.	Medicare levy \n$	Medicare levy surcharge \nno.	Medicare levy surcharge \n$	Total Medicare levy liability \nno.	Total Medicare levy liability \n$	Net tax \nno.	Net tax \n$	HELP assessment debt \nno.	HELP assessment debt \n$
0	ACT	2600	5581	5557	569612119	4905	163820305	4384	10548612	119	148593	4386	10685434	4656	169683313	383	1899448
1	ACT	2601	2658	2637	183288078	1941	46542933	1660	3203840	88	106660	1662	3308839	1827	48971292	285	1350343
2	ACT	2602	19457	19367	1379212924	16595	326786223	14594	24937105	565	689813	14603	25618479	15652	339564080	1582	6765600
3	ACT	2603	6478	6439	796053195	5701	249451322	5176	15002971	131	177083	5177	15176478	5473	263200195	549	2550578
4	ACT	2604	7387	7341	637350002	6534	165676071	5787	11512325	248	340226	5795	11837486	6262	173062197	882	4221697

5 rows × 150 columns

Figure 12.11: First five rows of the Postcode dataset

We can see that the second column contains the postcode value, and this is the one we will use to merge on with the ATO dataset. Let's check if they are unique.

12. Print the number of unique values in this column using the **.nunique()** method as shown in the following code snippet:

```
postcode_df['Postcode'].nunique()
```

You should get the following output:

```
2567
```

There are **2567** unique values, and this corresponds exactly to the number of rows of this DataFrame, so we're absolutely sure this column contains unique values. This also means that after merging the two tables, there will be only one-to-one matches. We won't have a case where we get multiple rows from one of the datasets matching with only one row of the other one. For instance, postcode **2029** from the ATO DataFrame will have exactly one match in the second Postcode DataFrame.

13. Perform a left join on the two DataFrames using the **.merge()** method and save the results into a new DataFrame called **merged_df**. Specify the **how='left'** and **on='Postcode'** parameters:

```
merged_df = pd.merge(df, postcode_df, \
                     how='left', on='Postcode')
```

14. Print the dimensions of the new merged DataFrame using the **.shape** attribute:

```
merged_df.shape
```

You should get the following output:

```
(2473, 177)
```

We got exactly **2473** rows after merging, which is what we expect as we used a left join and there was a one-to-one match on the **Postcode** column from both original DataFrames. Also, we now have **177** columns, which is the objective of this exercise. But before concluding it, we want to see whether there are any postcodes that didn't match between the two datasets. To do so, we will be looking at one column from the right-hand side DataFrame (the Postcode dataset) and see if there are any missing values.

15. Print the total number of missing values from the **'State/Territory1'** column by combining the **.isna()** and **.sum()** methods:

```
merged_df['State/ Territory1'].isna().sum()
```

You should get the following output:

```
4
```

There are four postcodes from the ATO dataset that didn't match the Postcode code.

Let's see which ones they are.

16. Print the missing postcodes using the **.iloc()** method, as shown in the following code snippet:

```
merged_df.loc[merged_df['State/ Territory1'].isna(), \
              'Postcode']
```

You should get the following output:

```
631     3010
1494    4462
2072    6068
2332    6758
Name: Postcode, dtype: object
```

Figure 12.12: List of unmatched postcodes

The missing postcodes from the Postcode dataset are **3010**, **4462**, **6068**, and **6758**. In a real project, you would have to get in touch with your stakeholders or the data team to see if you are able to get this data.

We have successfully merged the two datasets of interest and have expanded the number of features from **28** to **177**. We now have a much richer dataset and will be able to perform a more detailed analysis of it.

> **NOTE**
>
> To access the source code for this specific section, please refer to https://packt.live/324bV67.
>
> You can also run this example online at https://packt.live/2CDYv80.

In the next topic, you will be introduced to the binning variables.

BINNING VARIABLES

As mentioned earlier, feature engineering is not only about getting information not present in a dataset. Quite often, you will have to create new features from existing ones. One example of this is consolidating values from an existing column to a new list of values.

For instance, you may have a very high number of unique values for some of the categorical columns in your dataset, let's say over 1,000 values for each variable. This is actually quite a lot of information that will require extra computation power for an algorithm to process and learn the patterns from. This can have a significant impact on the project cost if you are using cloud computing services or on the delivery time of the project.

One possible solution is to not use these columns and drop them, but in that case, you may lose some very important and critical information for the business. Another solution is to create a more consolidated version of these columns by reducing the number of unique values to a smaller number, let's say 100. This would drastically speed up the training process for the algorithm without losing too much information. This kind of transformation is called binning and, traditionally, it refers to numerical variables, but the same logic can be applied to categorical variables as well.

Let's see how we can achieve this on the Online Retail dataset. First, we need to load the data:

```
import pandas as pd
file_url = 'https://github.com/PacktWorkshops/'\
           'The-Data-Science-Workshop/blob/'\
           'master/Chapter12/Dataset/'\
           'Online%20Retail.xlsx?raw=true'
df = pd.read_excel(file_url)
```

In *Chapter 10, Analyzing a Dataset* we learned that the **Country** column contains **38** different unique values:

```
df['Country'].unique()
```

You should get the following output:

```
array(['United Kingdom', 'France', 'Australia', 'Netherlands', 'Germany',
       'Norway', 'EIRE', 'Switzerland', 'Spain', 'Poland', 'Portugal',
       'Italy', 'Belgium', 'Lithuania', 'Japan', 'Iceland',
       'Channel Islands', 'Denmark', 'Cyprus', 'Sweden', 'Austria',
       'Israel', 'Finland', 'Bahrain', 'Greece', 'Hong Kong', 'Singapore',
       'Lebanon', 'United Arab Emirates', 'Saudi Arabia',
       'Czech Republic', 'Canada', 'Unspecified', 'Brazil', 'USA',
       'European Community', 'Malta', 'RSA'], dtype=object)
```

Figure 12.13: List of unique values for the Country column

We are going to group some of the countries together into regions such as Asia, the Middle East, and America. We will leave the European countries as is.

First, let's create a new column called **Country_bin** by copying the **Country** column:

```
df['Country_bin'] = df['Country']
```

Then, we are going to create a list called **asian_countries** containing the name of Asian countries from the list of unique values for the **Country** column:

```
asian_countries = ['Japan', 'Hong Kong', 'Singapore']
```

And finally, using the **.loc()** and **.isin()** methods from **pandas**, we are going to change the value of **Country_bin** to **Asia** for all of the countries that are present in the **asian_countries** list:

```
df.loc[df['Country'].isin(asian_countries), \
       'Country_bin'] = 'Asia'
```

Now, if we print the list of unique values for this new column, we will see the three Asian countries (**`Japan`**, **`Hong Kong`**, and **`Singapore`**) have been replaced by the value **`Asia`**:

```
df['Country_bin'].unique()
```

You should get the following output:

```
array(['United Kingdom', 'France', 'Australia', 'Netherlands', 'Germany',
       'Norway', 'EIRE', 'Switzerland', 'Spain', 'Poland', 'Portugal',
       'Italy', 'Belgium', 'Lithuania', 'Asia', 'Iceland',
       'Channel Islands', 'Denmark', 'Cyprus', 'Sweden', 'Austria',
       'Israel', 'Finland', 'Bahrain', 'Greece', 'Lebanon',
       'United Arab Emirates', 'Saudi Arabia', 'Czech Republic', 'Canada',
       'Unspecified', 'Brazil', 'USA', 'European Community', 'Malta',
       'RSA'], dtype=object)
```

Figure 12.14: List of unique values for the Country_bin column after binning Asian countries

Let's perform the same process for Middle Eastern countries:

```
m_east_countries = ['Israel', 'Bahrain', 'Lebanon', \
                    'United Arab Emirates', 'Saudi Arabia']
df.loc[df['Country'].isin(m_east_countries), \
       'Country_bin'] = 'Middle East'
df['Country_bin'].unique()
```

You should get the following output:

```
array(['United Kingdom', 'France', 'Australia', 'Netherlands', 'Germany',
       'Norway', 'EIRE', 'Switzerland', 'Spain', 'Poland', 'Portugal',
       'Italy', 'Belgium', 'Lithuania', 'Asia', 'Iceland',
       'Channel Islands', 'Denmark', 'Cyprus', 'Sweden', 'Austria',
       'Middle East', 'Finland', 'Greece', 'Czech Republic', 'Canada',
       'Unspecified', 'Brazil', 'USA', 'European Community', 'Malta',
       'RSA'], dtype=object)
```

Figure 12.15: List of unique values for the Country_bin column after binning Middle Eastern countries

Finally, let's group all countries from North and South America together:

```
american_countries = ['Canada', 'Brazil', 'USA']
df.loc[df['Country'].isin(american_countries), \
       'Country_bin'] = 'America'
df['Country_bin'].unique()
```

You should get the following output:

```
array(['United Kingdom', 'France', 'Australia', 'Netherlands', 'Germany',
       'Norway', 'EIRE', 'Switzerland', 'Spain', 'Poland', 'Portugal',
       'Italy', 'Belgium', 'Lithuania', 'Asia', 'Iceland',
       'Channel Islands', 'Denmark', 'Cyprus', 'Sweden', 'Austria',
       'Middle East', 'Finland', 'Greece', 'Czech Republic', 'America',
       'Unspecified', 'European Community', 'Malta', 'RSA'], dtype=object)
```

Figure 12.16: List of unique values for the Country_bin column after binning countries from North and South America

```
df['Country_bin'].nunique()
```

You should get the following output:

```
30
```

`30` is the number of unique values for the **`Country_bin`** column. So we reduced the number of unique values in this column from **`38`** to **`30`**:

We just saw how to group categorical values together, but the same process can be applied to numerical values as well. For instance, it is quite common to group people's ages into bins such as 20s (20 to 29 years old), 30s (30 to 39), and so on.

Have a look at *Exercise 12.02, Binning the YearBuilt variable from the AMES Housing dataset*.

EXERCISE 12.02: BINNING THE YEARBUILT VARIABLE FROM THE AMES HOUSING DATASET

In this exercise, we will create a new feature by binning an existing numerical column in order to reduce the number of unique values from **`112`** to **`15`**.

> **NOTE**
>
> The dataset we will be using in this exercise is the Ames Housing dataset and it can be found in our GitHub repository: https://packt.live/35r2ahN.
>
> This dataset was compiled by Dean De Cock: https://packt.live/2uojqHR.
>
> This dataset contains the list of residential home sales in the city of Ames, Iowa between 2010 and 2016.
>
> More information about each variable can be found here: https://packt.live/2sT88L4.

1. Open up a new Colab notebook.

2. Import the **pandas** and **altair** packages:

```
import pandas as pd
import altair as alt
```

3. Assign the link to the dataset to a variable called **file_url**:

```
file_url = 'https://raw.githubusercontent.com/'\
           'PacktWorkshops/The-Data-Science-Workshop/'\
           'master/Chapter12/Dataset/ames_iowa_housing.csv'
```

4. Using the **.read_csv()** method from the **pandas** package, load the dataset into a new DataFrame called **df**:

```
df = pd.read_csv(file_url)
```

5. Display the first five rows using the **.head()** method:

```
df.head()
```

You should get the following output:

	Id	MSSubClass	MSZoning	LotFrontage	LotArea	Street	Alley	LotShape	LandContour	Utilities	LotConfig	LandSlope	Neighborhood	Condition1	Condition2	BldgType	HouseStyle
0	1	60	RL	65.0	8450	Pave	NaN	Reg	Lvl	AllPub	Inside	Gtl	CollgCr	Norm	Norm	1Fam	2Story
1	2	20	RL	80.0	9600	Pave	NaN	Reg	Lvl	AllPub	FR2	Gtl	Veenker	Feedr	Norm	1Fam	1Story
2	3	60	RL	68.0	11250	Pave	NaN	IR1	Lvl	AllPub	Inside	Gtl	CollgCr	Norm	Norm	1Fam	2Story
3	4	70	RL	60.0	9550	Pave	NaN	IR1	Lvl	AllPub	Corner	Gtl	Crawfor	Norm	Norm	1Fam	2Story
4	5	60	RL	84.0	14260	Pave	NaN	IR1	Lvl	AllPub	FR2	Gtl	NoRidge	Norm	Norm	1Fam	2Story

5 rows × 81 columns

Figure 12.17: First five rows of the AMES housing DataFrame

6. Display the number of unique values on the column using **.nunique()**:

```
df['YearBuilt'].nunique()
```

You should get the following output:

```
112
```

There are **112** different or unique values in the **YearBuilt** column:

7. Print a scatter plot using **altair** to visualize the number of records built per year. Specify **YearBuilt:O** as the x-axis and **count()** as the y-axis in the **.encode()** method:

```
alt.Chart(df).mark_circle().encode(alt.X('YearBuilt:O'),\
                                   y='count()')
```

You should get the following output:

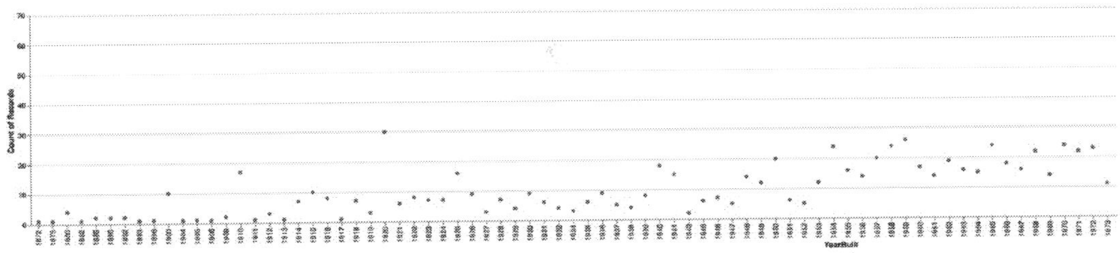

Figure 12.18: First five rows of the AMES housing DataFrame

> **NOTE**
>
> The output is not shown on GitHub due to its limitations. If you run this on your Colab file, the graph will be displayed.

There weren't many properties sold in some of the years. So, you can group them by decades (groups of 10 years).

8. Create a list called **`year_built`** containing all the unique values in the **`YearBuilt`** column:

```
year_built = df['YearBuilt'].unique()
```

9. Create another list that will compute the decade for each year in **`year_built`**. Use list comprehension to loop through each year and apply the following formula: **`year - (year % 10)`**.

   For example, this formula applied to the year 2015 will give 2015 - (2015 % 10), which is 2015 – 5 equals 2010.

> **NOTE**
>
> % corresponds to the modulo operator and will return the last digit of each year.

Have a look at the following code snippet:

```
decade_list = [year - (year % 10) for year in year_built]
```

10. Create a sorted list of unique values from **decade_list** and save the result into a new variable called **decade_built**. To do so, transform **decade_list** into a set (this will exclude all duplicates) and then use the **sorted()** function as shown in the following code snippet:

```
decade_built = sorted(set(decade_list))
```

11. Print the values of **decade_built**:

```
decade_built
```

You should get the following output:

```
[1870,
 1880,
 1890,
 1900,
 1910,
 1920,
 1930,
 1940,
 1950,
 1960,
 1970,
 1980,
 1990,
 2000,
 2010]
```

Figure 12.19: List of decades

Now we have the list of decades we are going to bin the **YearBuilt** column with.

12. Create a new column on the **df** DataFrame called **DecadeBuilt** that will bin each value from **YearBuilt** into a decade. You will use the **.cut()** method from **pandas** and specify the **bins=decade_built** parameter:

```
df['DecadeBuilt'] = pd.cut(df['YearBuilt'], \
                           bins=decade_built)
```

13. Print the first five rows of the DataFrame but only for the **'YearBuilt'** and **'DecadeBuilt'** columns:

```
df[['YearBuilt', 'DecadeBuilt']].head()
```

You should get the following output:

	YearBuilt	DecadeBuilt
0	2003	(2000, 2010]
1	1976	(1970, 1980]
2	2001	(2000, 2010]
3	1915	(1910, 1920]
4	2000	(1990, 2000]

Figure 12.20: First five rows after binning

We can see each year has been properly assigned to the relevant decade.

> **NOTE**
>
> To access the source code for this specific section, please refer to https://packt.live/3kXnC7c.
>
> This section does not currently have an online interactive example, but can be run as usual on Google Colab.

We have successfully created a new feature from the **YearBuilt** column by binning its values into groups of decades. We have reduced the number of unique values from **112** to **15**.

MANIPULATING DATES

In most datasets you will be working on, there will be one or more columns containing date information. Usually, you will not feed that type of information directly as input to a machine learning algorithm. The reason is you don't want it to learn extremely specific patterns, such as customer A bought product X on August 3, 2012, at 08:11 a.m. The model would be overfitting in that case and wouldn't be able to generalize to future data.

What you really want is the model to learn patterns, such as customers with young kids tending to buy unicorn toys in December, for instance. Rather than providing the raw dates, you want to extract some cyclical characteristics such as the month of the year, the day of the week, and so on. We will see in this section how easy it is to get this kind of information using the **pandas** package.

> **NOTE**
>
> There is an exception to this rule of thumb. If you are performing a time-series analysis, this kind of algorithm requires a date column as an input feature, but this is out of the scope of this book.

In *Chapter 10, Analyzing a Dataset* you were introduced to the concept of data types in **pandas**. At that time, we mainly focused on numerical variables and categorical ones but there is another important one: **datetime**. Let's have a look again at the type of each column from the Online Retail dataset:

```
import pandas as pd
file_url = 'https://github.com/PacktWorkshops/'\
           'The-Data-Science-Workshop/blob/'\
           'master/Chapter12/Dataset/'\
           'Online%20Retail.xlsx?raw=true'
df = pd.read_excel(file_url)
df.dtypes
```

You should get the following output:

```
InvoiceNo               object
StockCode               object
Description             object
Quantity                 int64
InvoiceDate     datetime64[ns]
UnitPrice              float64
CustomerID             float64
Country                 object
dtype: object
```

Figure 12.21: Data types for the variables in the Online Retail dataset

We can see that **pandas** automatically detected that **InvoiceDate** is of type **datetime**. But for some other datasets, it may not recognize dates properly. In this case, you will have to manually convert them using the **.to_datetime()** method:

```
df['InvoiceDate'] = pd.to_datetime(df['InvoiceDate'])
```

Once the column is converted to **datetime**, pandas provides a lot of attributes and methods for extracting time-related information. For instance, if you want to get the year of a date, you use the **.dt.year** attribute:

```
df['InvoiceDate'].dt.year
```

You should get the following output:

```
0         2010
1         2010
2         2010
3         2010
4         2010
          ...
541904    2011
541905    2011
541906    2011
541907    2011
541908    2011
Name: InvoiceDate, Length: 541909, dtype: int64
```

Figure 12.22: Extracted year for each row for the InvoiceDate column

As you may have guessed, there are attributes for extracting the month and day of a date: **.dt.month** and **.dt.day** respectively. You can get the day of the week from a date using the **.dt.dayofweek** attribute:

```
df['InvoiceDate'].dt.dayofweek
```

You should get the following output.

```
0         2
1         2
2         2
3         2
4         2
         ..
541904    4
541905    4
541906    4
541907    4
541908    4
Name: InvoiceDate, Length: 541909, dtype: int64
```

Figure 12.23: Extracted day of the week for each row for the InvoiceDate column

> **NOTE**
>
> You can find the whole list of available attributes here: https://packt.live/2ZUe02R.

With datetime columns, you can also perform some mathematical operations. We can, for instance, add **3** days to each date by using pandas time-series offset object, **pd.tseries.offsets.Day(3)**:

```
df['InvoiceDate'] + pd.tseries.offsets.Day(3)
```

You should get the following output:

```
0        2010-12-04 08:26:00
1        2010-12-04 08:26:00
2        2010-12-04 08:26:00
3        2010-12-04 08:26:00
4        2010-12-04 08:26:00
                 ...
541904   2011-12-12 12:50:00
541905   2011-12-12 12:50:00
541906   2011-12-12 12:50:00
541907   2011-12-12 12:50:00
541908   2011-12-12 12:50:00
Name: InvoiceDate, Length: 541909, dtype: datetime64[ns]
```

Figure 12.24: InvoiceDate column offset by three days

You can also offset days by business days using **pd.tseries.offsets.BusinessDay()**. For instance, if we want to get the previous business days, we do:

```
df['InvoiceDate'] + pd.tseries.offsets.BusinessDay(-1)
```

You should get the following output:

```
0        2010-11-30 08:26:00
1        2010-11-30 08:26:00
2        2010-11-30 08:26:00
3        2010-11-30 08:26:00
4        2010-11-30 08:26:00
                 ...
541904   2011-12-08 12:50:00
541905   2011-12-08 12:50:00
541906   2011-12-08 12:50:00
541907   2011-12-08 12:50:00
541908   2011-12-08 12:50:00
Name: InvoiceDate, Length: 541909, dtype: datetime64[ns]
```

Figure 12.25: InvoiceDate column offset by -1 business day

Another interesting date manipulation operation is to apply a specific time-frequency using **pd.Timedelta()**. For instance, if you want to get the first day of the month from a date, you do:

```
df['InvoiceDate'] + pd.Timedelta(1, unit='MS')
```

You should get the following output:

```
0        2010-12-01 08:26:00.001
1        2010-12-01 08:26:00.001
2        2010-12-01 08:26:00.001
3        2010-12-01 08:26:00.001
4        2010-12-01 08:26:00.001
                 ...
541904   2011-12-09 12:50:00.001
541905   2011-12-09 12:50:00.001
541906   2011-12-09 12:50:00.001
541907   2011-12-09 12:50:00.001
541908   2011-12-09 12:50:00.001
Name: InvoiceDate, Length: 541909, dtype: datetime64[ns]
```

Figure 12.26: InvoiceDate column transformed to the start of the month

As you have seen in this section, the **pandas** package provides a lot of different APIs for manipulating dates. You have learned how to use a few of the most popular ones. You can now explore the other ones on your own.

EXERCISE 12.03: DATE MANIPULATION ON FINANCIAL SERVICES CONSUMER COMPLAINTS

In this exercise, we will learn how to extract time-related information from two existing date columns using **pandas** in order to create six new columns:

> **NOTE**
>
> The dataset we will be using in this exercise is the Financial Services Customer Complaints dataset and it can be found on our GitHub repository: https://packt.live/2ZYm9Dp.
>
> The original dataset can be found here: https://packt.live/35mFhMw.

1. Open up a new Colab notebook.
2. Import the **pandas** package:

```
import pandas as pd
```

3. Assign the link to the dataset to a variable called **file_url**:

```
file_url = 'https://raw.githubusercontent.com/'\
           'PacktWorkshops/The-Data-Science-Workshop/'\
           'master/Chapter12/Dataset/Consumer_Complaints.csv'
```

4. Use the **.read_csv()** method from the **pandas** package and load the dataset into a new DataFrame called **df**:

```
df = pd.read_csv(file_url)
```

5. Display the first five rows using the **.head()** method:

```
df.head()
```

You should get the following output:

	Complaint ID	Product	Sub-product	Issue	Sub-issue	State	ZIP code	Submitted via	Date received	Date sent to company	Company	Company response	Timely response?	Consumer disputed?
0	1114245	Debt collection	Medical	Disclosure verification of debt	Not given enough info to verify debt	FL	32219.0	Web	11/13/2014	11/13/2014	Choice Recovery, Inc.	Closed with explanation	Yes	NaN
1	1114488	Debt collection	Medical	Disclosure verification of debt	Right to dispute notice not received	TX	75006.0	Web	11/13/2014	11/13/2014	Expert Global Solutions, Inc.	In progress	Yes	NaN
2	1114255	Bank account or service	Checking account	Deposits and withdrawals	NaN	NY	11102.0	Web	11/13/2014	11/13/2014	FNIS (Fidelity National Information Services, ...	In progress	Yes	NaN
3	1115106	Debt collection	Other (phone, health club, etc.)	Communication tactics	Frequent or repeated calls	GA	31721.0	Web	11/13/2014	11/13/2014	Expert Global Solutions, Inc.	In progress	Yes	NaN
4	1115890	Credit reporting	NaN	Incorrect information on credit report	Information is not mine	FL	33461.0	Web	11/12/2014	11/13/2014	TransUnion	In progress	Yes	NaN

Figure 12.27: First five rows of the Customer Complaint DataFrame

6. Print out the data types for each column using the **`.dtypes`** attribute:

```
df.dtypes
```

You should get the following output:

```
Complaint ID               int64
Product                   object
Sub-product               object
Issue                     object
Sub-issue                 object
State                     object
ZIP code                 float64
Submitted via             object
Date received             object
Date sent to company      object
Company                   object
Company response          object
Timely response?          object
Consumer disputed?        object
dtype: object
```

Figure 12.28: Data types for the Customer Complaint DataFrame

The **`Date received`** and **`Date sent to company`** columns haven't been recognized as datetime, so we need to manually convert them.

7. Convert the **`Date received`** and **`Date sent to company`** columns to datetime using the **`pd.to_datetime()`** method:

```
df['Date received'] = pd.to_datetime(df['Date received'])
df['Date sent to company'] = pd.to_datetime\
                             (df['Date sent to company'])
```

8. Print out the data types for each column using the **.dtypes** attribute:

```
df.dtypes
```

You should get the following output:

```
Complaint ID                     int64
Product                         object
Sub-product                     object
Issue                           object
Sub-issue                       object
State                           object
ZIP code                       float64
Submitted via                   object
Date received           datetime64[ns]
Date sent to company    datetime64[ns]
Company                         object
Company response                object
Timely response?                object
Consumer disputed?              object
dtype: object
```

Figure 12.29: Data types for the Customer Complaint DataFrame after conversion

Now these two columns have the right data types. Now let's create some new features from these two dates.

9. Create a new column called **YearReceived**, which will contain the year of each date from the **Date Received** column using the **.dt.year** attribute:

```
df['YearReceived'] = df['Date received'].dt.year
```

10. Create a new column called **MonthReceived**, which will contain the month of each date using the **.dt.month** attribute:

```
df['MonthReceived'] = df['Date received'].dt.month
```

11. Create a new column called **DayReceived**, which will contain the day of the month for each date using the **.dt.day** attribute:

```
df['DomReceived'] = df['Date received'].dt.day
```

12. Create a new column called **DowReceived**, which will contain the day of the week for each date using the **.dt.dayofweek** attribute:

```
df['DowReceived'] = df['Date received'].dt.dayofweek
```

13. Display the first five rows using the **.head()** method:

```
df.head()
```

You should get the following output:

	Complaint ID	Product	Sub-product	Issue	Sub-issue	State	ZIP code	Submitted via	Date received	Date sent to company	Company	Company response	Timely response?	Consumer disputed?	YearReceived	MonthReceived	DomReceived
0	1114245	Debt collection	Medical	Disclosure verification of debt	Not given enough info to verify debt	FL	32219.0	Web	2014-11-13	2014-11-13	Choice Recovery, Inc.	Closed with explanation	Yes	NaN	2014	11	13
1	1114488	Debt collection	Medical	Disclosure verification of debt	Right to dispute notice not received	TX	75006.0	Web	2014-11-13	2014-11-13	Expert Global Solutions, Inc.	In progress	Yes	NaN	2014	11	13
2	1114255	Bank account or service	Checking account	Deposits and withdrawals	NaN	NY	11102.0	Web	2014-11-13	2014-11-13	FNIS (Fidelity National Information Services, ...	In progress	Yes	NaN	2014	11	13
3	1115106	Debt collection	Other (phone, health club, etc.)	Communication tactics	Frequent or repeated calls	GA	31721.0	Web	2014-11-13	2014-11-13	Expert Global Solutions, Inc.	In progress	Yes	NaN	2014	11	13
4	1115890	Credit reporting	NaN	Incorrect information on credit report	Information is not mine	FL	33461.0	Web	2014-11-12	2014-11-13	TransUnion	In progress	Yes	NaN	2014	11	12

Figure 12.30: First five rows of the Customer Complaint DataFrame after creating four new features

We can see we have successfully created four new features: **YearReceived**, **MonthReceived**, **DayReceived**, and **DowReceived**. Now let's create another that will indicate whether the date was during a weekend or not.

14. Create a new column called **IsWeekendReceived**, which will contain binary values indicating whether the **DowReceived** column is over or equal to **5** (**0** corresponds to Monday, **5** and **6** correspond to Saturday and Sunday respectively):

```
df['IsWeekendReceived'] = df['DowReceived'] >= 5
```

15. Display the first **5** rows using the **.head()** method:

```
df.head()
```

You should get the following output:

Issue	Sub-issue	State	ZIP code	Submitted via	Date received	Date sent to company	Company	Company response	Timely response?	Consumer disputed?	YearReceived	MonthReceived	DomReceived	DowReceived	IsWeekendReceived
Disclosure verification of debt	Not given enough info to verify debt	FL	32219.0	Web	2014-11-13	2014-11-13	Choice Recovery, Inc.	Closed with explanation	Yes	NaN	2014	11	13	3	False
Disclosure verification of debt	Right to dispute notice not received	TX	75006.0	Web	2014-11-13	2014-11-13	Expert Global Solutions, Inc.	In progress	Yes	NaN	2014	11	13	3	False
Deposits and withdrawals	NaN	NY	11102.0	Web	2014-11-13	2014-11-13	FNIS (Fidelity National Information Services, ...	In progress	Yes	NaN	2014	11	13	3	False
Communication tactics	Frequent or repeated calls	GA	31721.0	Web	2014-11-13	2014-11-13	Expert Global Solutions, Inc.	In progress	Yes	NaN	2014	11	13	3	False
Incorrect information on credit report	Information is not mine	FL	33461.0	Web	2014-11-12	2014-11-13	TransUnion	In progress	Yes	NaN	2014	11	12	2	False

Figure 12.31: First five rows of the Customer Complaint DataFrame after creating the weekend feature

We have created a new feature stating whether each complaint was received during a weekend or not. Now we will feature engineer a new column with the numbers of days between **`Date sent to company`** and **`Date received`**.

16. Create a new column called **`RoutingDays`**, which will contain the difference between **`Date sent to company`** and **`Date received`**:

```
df['RoutingDays'] = df['Date sent to company'] \
                    - df['Date received']
```

17. Print out the data type of the new **`'RoutingDays'`** column using the **`.dtype`** attribute:

```
df['RoutingDays'].dtype
```

You should get the following output:

```
dtype('<m8[ns]')
```

Figure 12.32: Data type of the RoutingDays column

The result of subtracting two datetime columns is a new datetime column (**`dtype('<M8[ns]')`**, which is a specific datetime type for the **`numpy`** package). We need to convert this data type into an **`int`** to get the number of days between these two days.

18. Transform the **RoutingDays** column using the **.dt.days** attribute:

```
df['RoutingDays'] = df['RoutingDays'].dt.days
```

19. Display the first five rows using the **.head()** method:

```
df.head()
```

You should get the following output:

Submitted via	Date received	Date sent to company	Company	Company response	Timely response?	Consumer disputed?	YearReceived	MonthReceived	DayReceived	DowReceived	IsWeekendReceived	RoutingDays
Web	2014-11-13	2014-11-13	Choice Recovery, Inc.	Closed with explanation	Yes	NaN	2014	11	13	3	False	0
Web	2014-11-13	2014-11-13	Expert Global Solutions, Inc.	In progress	Yes	NaN	2014	11	13	3	False	0
Web	2014-11-13	2014-11-13	FNIS (Fidelity National Information Services, ...	In progress	Yes	NaN	2014	11	13	3	False	0
Web	2014-11-13	2014-11-13	Expert Global Solutions, Inc.	In progress	Yes	NaN	2014	11	13	3	False	0
Web	2014-11-12	2014-11-13	TransUnion	In progress	Yes	NaN	2014	11	12	2	False	1

Figure 12.33: First five rows of the Customer Complaint DataFrame after creating RoutingDays

In this exercise, you put into practice different techniques to feature engineer new variables from datetime columns on a real-world dataset. From the two **Date sent to company** and **Date received** columns, you successfully created six new features that will provide additional valuable information.

> **NOTE**
>
> To access the source code for this specific section, please refer to https://packt.live/3kWvhmf.
>
> You can also run this example online at https://packt.live/316YT8z.

For instance, we were able to find patterns such as the number of complaints tends to be higher in November or on a Friday. We also found that routing the complaints takes more time when they are received during the weekend, which may be due to the limited number of staff at that time of the week.

PERFORMING DATA AGGREGATION

Alright. We are getting close to the end of this chapter. But before we wrap it up, there is one more technique to explore for creating new features: data aggregation. The idea behind it is to summarize a numerical column for specific groups from another column. We already saw an example of how to aggregate two numerical variables from the ATO dataset (Average net tax and Average total deductions) for each cluster found by k-means using the **`.pivot_table()`** method in *Chapter 5, Performing Your First Cluster Analysis*. But at that time, we aggregated the data not to create new features but to understand the difference between these clusters.

You may wonder to yourself in which cases you would want to perform feature engineering using data aggregation. If you already have a numerical column that contains a value for each record, why would you need to summarize it and add this information back to the DataFrame? It feels like we are just adding the same information but with fewer details. But there are actually multiple good reasons for using this technique.

One potential reason might be that you want to normalize another numerical column using this aggregation. For instance, if you are working on a dataset for a retailer that contains all the sales for each store around the world, the volume of sales may differ drastically for a country compared to another one as they don't have the same population. In this case, rather than using the raw sales figures for each store, you would calculate a ratio (or a percentage) of the sales of a store divided by the total volume of sales in its country. With this new ratio feature, some of the stores that looked as though they were underperforming because their raw volume of sales was not as high as for other countries may actually be performing much better than the average in its country.

In **`pandas`**, it is quite easy to perform data aggregation. We just need to combine the following methods successively: **`.groupby()`** and **`.agg()`**.

We will need to specify the list of columns that will be grouped together to the **`.groupby()`** method. If you are familiar with pivot tables in Excel, this corresponds to the **`Rows`** field.

The **`.agg()`** method expects a dictionary with the name of a column as a key and the aggregation function as a value such as **`{'column_name': 'aggregation_function'}`**. In an Excel pivot table, the aggregated column is referred to as **`values`**.

Let's see how to do it on the Online Retail dataset. First, we need to import the data:

```
import pandas as pd
file_url = 'https://github.com/PacktWorkshops/'\
           'The-Data-Science-Workshop/blob/'\
           'master/Chapter12/Dataset/'\
           'Online%20Retail.xlsx?raw=true'
df = pd.read_excel(file_url)
```

Let's calculate the total quantity of items sold for each country. We will specify the **Country** column as the grouping column:

```
df.groupby('Country').agg({'Quantity': 'sum'})
```

You should get the following output:

	Quantity
Country	
Australia	83653
Austria	4827
Bahrain	260
Belgium	23152
Brazil	356
Canada	2763
Channel Islands	9479

Figure 12.34: Sum of Quantity per Country (truncated)

This result gives the total volume of items sold for each country. We can see that Australia has almost sold four times more items than Belgium. This level of information may be too high-level and we may want a bit more granular detail. Let's perform the same aggregation but this time we will group on two columns: **Country** and **StockCode**. We just need to provide the names of these columns as a list to the **.groupby()** method:

```
df.groupby(['Country', 'StockCode']).agg({'Quantity': 'sum'})
```

You should get the following output:

		Quantity
Country	StockCode	
Australia	15036	600
	20665	6
	20675	216
	20676	216
	20677	216
...	...	...
Unspecified	85049A	1
	85179A	1
	85179C	1
	85180A	2
	85180B	1

19839 rows × 1 columns

Figure 12.35: Sum of Quantity per Country and StockCode

We can see how many items have been sold for each country. We can note that Australia has sold the same quantity of products **`20675`**, **`20676`**, and **`20677`** (**`216`** each). This may indicate that these products are always sold together.

We can add one more layer of information and get the number of items sold for each country, the product, and the date. To do so, we first need to create a new feature that will extract the date component of **`InvoiceDate`** (we just learned how to do this in the previous section):

```
df['Invoice_Date'] = df['InvoiceDate'].dt.date
```

Then, we can add this new column in the **`.groupby()`** method:

```
df.groupby(['Country', 'StockCode', \
            'Invoice_Date']).agg({'Quantity': 'sum'})
```

You should get the following output:

			Quantity
Country	**StockCode**	**Invoice_Date**	
Australia	**15036**	**2011-05-17**	600
	20665	**2011-03-24**	6
	20675	**2011-01-06**	72
		2011-03-03	144
	20676	**2011-01-06**	72
...	**...**	**...**	...
Unspecified	**85049A**	**2011-07-28**	1
	85179A	**2011-07-28**	1
	85179C	**2011-07-28**	1
	85180A	**2011-07-28**	2
	85180B	**2011-07-28**	1

310015 rows × 1 columns

Figure 12.36: Sum of Quantity per Country, StockCode, and Invoice_Date

We have generated a new DataFrame with the total quantity of items sold per country, item ID, and date. We can see the item with **StockCode 15036** was quite popular on **2011-05-17** in **Australia** – there were **600** sold items. On the other hand, only **6** items of **Stockcode 20665** were sold on **2011-03-24** in **Australia**.

We can now merge this additional information back into the original DataFrame. But before that, there is an additional data transformation step required: reset the column index. The **pandas** package creates a multi-level index after data aggregation by default. You can think of it as though the column names were stored in multiple rows instead of one only. To change it back to a single level, you need to call the **.reset_index()** method:

```
df_agg = df.groupby(['Country', 'StockCode', 'Invoice_Date'])\
        .agg({'Quantity': 'sum'}).reset_index()
df_agg.head()
```

You should get the following output:

	Country	StockCode	Invoice_Date	Quantity
0	Australia	15036	2011-05-17	600
1	Australia	20665	2011-03-24	6
2	Australia	20675	2011-01-06	72
3	Australia	20675	2011-03-03	144
4	Australia	20676	2011-01-06	72

Figure 12.37: DataFrame containing data aggregation information

Now we can merge this new DataFrame into the original one using the **`.merge()`** method we saw earlier in this chapter:

```
df_merged = pd.merge(df, df_agg, how='left', \
                     on = ['Country', 'StockCode', \
                           'Invoice_Date'])
df_merged
```

You should get the following output:

InvoiceNo	StockCode	Description	Quantity_x	InvoiceDate	UnitPrice	CustomerID	Country	Invoice_Date	Quantity_y
536365	85123A	WHITE HANGING HEART T-LIGHT HOLDER	6	2010-12-01 08:26:00	2.55	17850.0	United Kingdom	2010-12-01	454
536365	71053	WHITE METAL LANTERN	6	2010-12-01 08:26:00	3.39	17850.0	United Kingdom	2010-12-01	33
536365	84406B	CREAM CUPID HEARTS COAT HANGER	8	2010-12-01 08:26:00	2.75	17850.0	United Kingdom	2010-12-01	40
536365	84029G	KNITTED UNION FLAG HOT WATER BOTTLE	6	2010-12-01 08:26:00	3.39	17850.0	United Kingdom	2010-12-01	59

Figure 12.38: Merged DataFrame (truncated)

We can see there are two columns called **`Quantity_x`** and **`Quantity_y`** instead of **`Quantity`**.

The reason is that, after merging, there were two different columns with the exact same name (**Quantity**), so by default, pandas added a suffix to differentiate them.

We can fix this situation either by replacing the name of one of those two columns before merging or we can replace both of them after merging. To replace column names, we can use the **.rename()** method from **pandas** by providing a dictionary with the old name as the key and the new name as the value, such as **{'old_name': 'new_name'}**.

Let's replace the column names after merging with **Quantity** and **DailyQuantity**:

```
df_merged.rename(columns={"Quantity_x": "Quantity", \
                          "Quantity_y": "DailyQuantity"}, \
                 inplace=True)
df_merged
```

You should get the following output:

InvoiceNo	StockCode	Description	Quantity	InvoiceDate	UnitPrice	CustomerID	Country	Invoice_Date	DailyQuantity
536365	85123A	WHITE HANGING HEART T-LIGHT HOLDER	6	2010-12-01 08:26:00	2.55	17850.0	United Kingdom	2010-12-01	454
536365	71053	WHITE METAL LANTERN	6	2010-12-01 08:26:00	3.39	17850.0	United Kingdom	2010-12-01	33
536365	84406B	CREAM CUPID HEARTS COAT HANGER	8	2010-12-01 08:26:00	2.75	17850.0	United Kingdom	2010-12-01	40
		KNITTED							

Figure 12.39: Renamed DataFrame (truncated)

Now we can create a new feature that will calculate the ratio between the items sold with the daily total quantity of sold items in the corresponding country:

```
df_merged['QuantityRatio'] = df_merged['Quantity'] \
                             / df_merged['DailyQuantity']
df_merged
```

You should get the following output:

	InvoiceNo	StockCode	Description	Quantity	InvoiceDate	UnitPrice	CustomerID	Country	Invoice_Date	DailyQuantity	QuantityRatio
0	536365	85123A	WHITE HANGING HEART T-LIGHT HOLDER	6	2010-12-01 08:26:00	2.55	17850.0	United Kingdom	2010-12-01	454	0.013216
1	536365	71053	WHITE METAL LANTERN	6	2010-12-01 08:26:00	3.39	17850.0	United Kingdom	2010-12-01	33	0.181818
2	536365	84406B	CREAM CUPID HEARTS COAT HANGER	8	2010-12-01 08:26:00	2.75	17850.0	United Kingdom	2010-12-01	40	0.200000
3	536365	84029G	KNITTED UNION FLAG HOT WATER BOTTLE	6	2010-12-01 08:26:00	3.39	17850.0	United Kingdom	2010-12-01	59	0.101695
4	536365	84029E	RED WOOLLY HOTTIE WHITE HEART.	6	2010-12-01 08:26:00	3.39	17850.0	United Kingdom	2010-12-01	551	0.010889
...	...	...	...	...	...	...	...	...	...	...	...
541904	581587	22613	PACK OF 20 SPACEBOY NAPKINS	12	2011-12-09 12:50:00	0.85	12680.0	France	2011-12-09	12	1.000000
541905	581587	22899	CHILDREN'S APRON DOLLY GIRL	6	2011-12-09 12:50:00	2.10	12680.0	France	2011-12-09	6	1.000000
541906	581587	23254	CHILDRENS CUTLERY DOLLY GIRL	4	2011-12-09 12:50:00	4.15	12680.0	France	2011-12-09	4	1.000000
541907	581587	23255	CHILDRENS CUTLERY CIRCUS PARADE	4	2011-12-09 12:50:00	4.15	12680.0	France	2011-12-09	4	1.000000
541908	581587	22138	BAKING SET 9 PIECE RETROSPOT	3	2011-12-09 12:50:00	4.95	12680.0	France	2011-12-09	3	1.000000

541909 rows × 11 columns

Figure 12.40: Final DataFrame with new QuantityRatio feature

In this section, we learned how performing data aggregation can help us to create new features by calculating the ratio or percentage for each grouping of interest. Looking at the first and second rows, we can see there were **6** items sold for **`StockCode`** transactions **`84123A`** and **`71053`**. But if we look at the newly created **`DailyQuantity`** column, we can see that **`StockCode 84123A`** is more popular: on that day (**`2010-12-01`**), the store sold **`454`** units of it but only **`33`** of **`StockCode 71053`**. **`QuantityRatio`** is showing us the third transaction sold **`8`** items of **`StockCode 84406B`** and this single transaction accounted for 20% of the sales of that item on that day. By performing data aggregation, we have gained additional information for each record and have put the original information from the dataset into perspective.

EXERCISE 12.04: FEATURE ENGINEERING USING DATA AGGREGATION ON THE AMES HOUSING DATASET

In this exercise, we will create new features using data aggregation. First, we'll calculate the maximum **`SalePrice`** and **`LotArea`** for each neighborhood and by **`YrSold`**. Then, we will add this information back to the dataset, and finally, we will calculate the ratio of each property sold with these two maximum values:

> **NOTE**
>
> The dataset we will be using in this exercise is the Ames Housing dataset and it can be found in our GitHub repository: https://packt.live/35r2ahN.

1. Open up a new Colab notebook.
2. Import the **pandas** and **altair** packages:

```
import pandas as pd
```

3. Assign the link to the dataset to a variable called **file_url**:

```
file_url = 'https://raw.githubusercontent.com/'\
           'PacktWorkshops/The-Data-Science-Workshop/'\
           'master/Chapter12/Dataset/ames_iowa_housing.csv'
```

4. Using the **.read_csv()** method from the **pandas** package, load the dataset into a new DataFrame called **df**:

```
df = pd.read_csv(file_url)
```

5. Perform data aggregation to find the maximum **SalePrice** for each **Neighborhood** and the **YrSold** using the **.groupby.agg()** method and save the results in a new DataFrame called **df_agg**:

```
df_agg = df.groupby(['Neighborhood', 'YrSold'])\
           .agg({'SalePrice': 'max'}).reset_index()
```

6. Rename the **df_agg** columns to **Neighborhood**, **YrSold**, and **SalePriceMax**:

```
df_agg.columns = ['Neighborhood', 'YrSold', 'SalePriceMax']
```

7. Print out the first five rows of **df_agg**:

```
df_agg.head()
```

You should get the following output:

	Neighborhood	YrSold	SalePriceMax
0	Blmngtn	2006	264561
1	Blmngtn	2007	194201
2	Blmngtn	2008	191000
3	Blmngtn	2009	192500
4	Blmngtn	2010	192000

Figure 12.41: First five rows of the aggregated DataFrame

8. Merge the original DataFrame, **df**, to **df_agg** using a left join (**how='left'**) on the **Neighborhood** and **YrSold** columns using the **merge()** method and save the results into a new DataFrame called **df_new**:

```
df_new = pd.merge(df, df_agg, how='left', \
                  on=['Neighborhood', 'YrSold'])
```

9. Print out the first five rows of **df_new**:

```
df_new.head()
```

You should get the following output:

Feature	MiscVal	MoSold	YrSold	SaleType	SaleCondition	SalePrice	SalePriceMax
NaN	0	2	2008	WD	Normal	208500	287000
NaN	0	5	2007	WD	Normal	181500	294000
NaN	0	9	2008	WD	Normal	223500	287000
NaN	0	2	2006	WD	Abnorml	140000	250000
NaN	0	12	2008	WD	Normal	250000	350000

Figure 12.42: First five rows of df_new

Note that we are displaying the last eight columns of the output.

10. Create a new column called **SalePriceRatio** by dividing **SalePrice** by **SalePriceMax**:

```
df_new['SalePriceRatio'] = df_new['SalePrice'] \
                           / df_new['SalePriceMax']
```

11. Print out the first five rows of **df_new**:

```
df_new.head()
```

You should get the following output:

SaleType	SaleCondition	SalePrice	SalePriceMax	SalePriceRatio
WD	Normal	208500	287000	0.726481
WD	Normal	181500	294000	0.617347
WD	Normal	223500	287000	0.778746
WD	Abnorml	140000	250000	0.560000
WD	Normal	250000	350000	0.714286

Figure 12.43: First five rows of df_new after feature engineering

Note that we are displaying the last eight columns of the output.

12. Perform data aggregation to find the maximum **LotArea** for each **Neighborhood** and **YrSold** using the **.groupby.agg()** method and save the results in a new DataFrame called **df_agg2**:

```
df_agg2 = df.groupby(['Neighborhood', 'YrSold'])\
          .agg({'LotArea': 'max'}).reset_index()
```

13. Rename the column of **df_agg2** to **Neighborhood**, **YrSold**, and **LotAreaMax** and print out the first five columns:

```
df_agg2.columns = ['Neighborhood', 'YrSold', 'LotAreaMax']
df_agg2.head()
```

You should get the following output:

	Neighborhood	YrSold	LotAreaMax
0	Blmngtn	2006	4045
1	Blmngtn	2007	3922
2	Blmngtn	2008	3182
3	Blmngtn	2009	3684
4	Blmngtn	2010	3182

Figure 12.44: First five rows of the aggregated DataFrame

14. Merge the original DataFrame, **df**, to **df_agg2** using a left join (**how='left'**) on the **Neighborhood** and **YrSold** columns using the **merge()** method and save the results into a new DataFrame called **df_final**:

```
df_final = pd.merge(df_new, df_agg2, how='left', \
                    on=['Neighborhood', 'YrSold'])
```

15. Create a new column called **LotAreaRatio** by dividing **LotArea** by **LotAreaMax**:

```
df_final['LotAreaRatio'] = df_final['LotArea'] \
                           / df_final['LotAreaMax']
```

16. Print out the first five rows of **df_final** for the following columns: **Id**, **Neighborhood**, **YrSold**, **SalePrice**, **SalePriceMax**, **SalePriceRatio**, **LotArea**, **LotAreaMax**, **LotAreaRatio**:

```
df_final[['Id', 'Neighborhood', 'YrSold', 'SalePrice', \
          'SalePriceMax', 'SalePriceRatio', 'LotArea', \
          'LotAreaMax', 'LotAreaRatio']].head()
```

You should get the following output:

	Id	Neighborhood	YrSold	SalePrice	SalePriceMax	SalePriceRatio	LotArea	LotAreaMax	LotAreaRatio
0	1	CollgCr	2008	208500	287000	0.726481	8450	13125	0.643810
1	2	Veenker	2007	181500	294000	0.617347	9600	17542	0.547258
2	3	CollgCr	2008	223500	287000	0.778746	11250	13125	0.857143
3	4	Crawfor	2006	140000	250000	0.560000	9550	16560	0.576691
4	5	NoRidge	2008	250000	350000	0.714286	14260	14303	0.996994

Figure 12.45: First five rows of the final DataFrame

> **NOTE**
>
> To access the source code for this specific section, please refer to https://packt.live/2Q8a5eU.
>
> You can also run this example online at https://packt.live/2Q8dhXI.

This is it. We just created two new features that give the ratio of **SalePrice** and **LotArea** for a property compared to the highest one that was sold in the same year and the same neighborhood. We can now easily and fairly compare the properties. For instance, from the output of the last step, we can note that the fifth property size (**Id** 5 and **LotArea** 14260) was almost as close (**LotAreaRatio** 0.996994) as the biggest property sold (**LotArea** 14303) in the same area and the same year. But its sale price (**SalePrice** 250000) was significantly lower (**SalePriceRatio** is 0.714286) than the highest one (**SalePrice** 350000). This indicates that other features of the property had an impact on the sale price.

ACTIVITY 12.01: FEATURE ENGINEERING ON A FINANCIAL DATASET

You are working for a major bank in the Czech Republic and you have been tasked to analyze the transactions of existing customers. The data team has extracted all the tables from their database they think will be useful for you to analyze the dataset. You will need to consolidate the data from those tables into a single DataFrame and create new features in order to get an enriched dataset from which you will be able to perform an in-depth analysis of customers' banking transactions.

You will be using only the following four tables:

- **account**: The characteristics of a customer's bank account for a given branch
- **client**: Personal information related to the bank's customers
- **disp**: A table that links an account to a customer
- **trans**: A list of all historical transactions by account

> **NOTE**
>
> If you want to know more about these tables, you can look at the data dictionary for this dataset: https://packt.live/2QSev9F.

The following steps will help you complete this activity:

1. Download and load the different tables from this dataset into Python.
2. Analyze each table with the **.shape** and **.head()** methods.
3. Find the common/similar column(s) between tables that will be used for merging based on the analysis from *Step 2*.

4. There should be four common tables. Merge the four tables together using **`pd.merge()`**.
5. Rename the column names after merging with **`.rename()`**.
6. Check there is no duplication after merging with **`.duplicated()`** and **`.sum()`**.
7. Transform the data type for date columns using **`.to_datetime()`**.
8. Create two separate features from **`birth_number`** to get the date of birth and sex for each customer.

> **NOTE**
>
> This is the rule used for coding the data related to birthday and sex in this column: the number is in the YYMMDD format for men, the number is in the YYMM+50DD format for women, where YYMMDD is the date of birth.

9. Fix data quality issues with **`.isna()`**.
10. Create a new feature that will calculate customers' ages when they opened an account using date operations:

> **NOTE**
>
> The dataset was originally shared by Berka, Petr for the Discovery Challenge PKDD'99: https://packt.live/2ZVaG7J.
>
> The datasets you will be using in this activity can be found on our GitHub repository:
>
> https://packt.live/2QpUOXC.
>
> https://packt.live/36sN2BR.
>
> https://packt.live/2MZLzLB.
>
> https://packt.live/2rW9hkE.
>
> The CSV version can be found here: https://packt.live/2N150nn.

Expected output:

frequency	account_creation	disp_id	client_id	client_type	birth_number	is_female	age_at_creation
POPLATEK MESICNE	1993-01-01	2873	2873	OWNER	1975-03-24	True	18.0
POPLATEK MESICNE	1993-01-01	692	692	OWNER	NaT	False	NaN
POPLATEK MESICNE	1993-01-01	844	844	OWNER	NaT	False	NaN
POPLATEK MESICNE	1993-01-01	4601	4601	OWNER	NaT	False	NaN
POPLATEK MESICNE	1993-01-02	2397	2397	OWNER	NaT	False	NaN

Figure 12.46: Expected output with the merged rows

> **NOTE**
>
> The solution to this activity can be found at the following address: https://packt.live/2GbJloz.

SUMMARY

We first learned how to analyze a dataset and get a very good understanding of its data using data summarization and data visualization. This is very useful for finding out what the limitations of a dataset are and identifying data quality issues. We saw how to handle and fix some of the most frequent issues (duplicate rows, type conversion, value replacement, and missing values) using `pandas`' APIs.

Finally, we went through several feature engineering techniques. It was not possible to cover all the existing techniques for creating features. The objective of this chapter was to introduce you to critical steps that can significantly improve the quality of your analysis and the performance of your model. But remember to regularly get in touch with either the business or the data engineering team to get confirmation before transforming data too drastically. Preparing a dataset does not always mean having the cleanest dataset possible but rather getting the one that is closest to the true information the business is interested in. Otherwise, you may find incorrect or meaningless patterns. As we say, *with great power comes great responsibility*.

The next chapter opens a new part of this book that presents data science use cases end to end. *Chapter 13*, *Imbalanced Datasets*, will walk you through an example of an imbalanced dataset and how to deal with such a situation.

13

IMBALANCED DATASETS

OVERVIEW

By the end of this chapter, you will be able to identify use cases where datasets are likely to be imbalanced; formulate strategies for dealing with imbalanced datasets; build classification models, such as logistic regression models, after balancing datasets; and analyze classification metrics to validate whether adopted strategies are yielding the desired results.

In this chapter, you will be dealing with imbalanced datasets, which are very prevalent in real-life scenarios. You will be using techniques such as **`SMOTE`**, **`MSMOTE`**, and random undersampling to address imbalanced datasets.

INTRODUCTION

In the previous chapter, *Chapter 12, Feature Engineering*, where we dealt with data points related to dates, we were addressing scenarios pertaining to features. In this chapter, we will deal with scenarios where the proportions of examples in the overall dataset pose challenges.

Let's revisit the dataset we dealt with in *Chapter 3, Binary Classification*, in which the examples pertaining to 'No' for term deposits far outnumbered the ones with 'Yes' with a ratio of 88% to 12%. We also determined that one reason for suboptimal results with a logistic regression model on that dataset was the skewed proportion of examples. Datasets like the one we analyzed in *Chapter 3, Binary Classification*, which are called imbalanced datasets, are very common in real-world use cases.

Some of the use cases where we encounter imbalanced datasets include the following:

- Fraud detection for credit cards or insurance claims
- Medical diagnoses where we must detect the presence of rare diseases
- Intrusion detection in networks

In all of these use cases, we can see that what we really want to detect will be minority cases. For instance, in domains such as the medical diagnosis of rare diseases, examples where rare diseases exist could even be less than 1% of the total examples. One inherent characteristic of use cases with imbalanced datasets is that the quality of the classifier is not apparent if the right metric is not used. This makes the problem of imbalanced datasets really challenging.

In this chapter, we will discuss strategies for identifying imbalanced datasets and ways to mitigate the effects of imbalanced datasets.

UNDERSTANDING THE BUSINESS CONTEXT

The business head of the bank for which you are working as a data scientist recently raised the alarm about the results of the term deposit propensity model that you built in *Chapter 3, Binary Classification*. It has been observed that a large proportion of customers who were identified as potential cases for targeted marketing for term deposits have turned down the offer. This has made a big dent in the sales team's metrics on upselling and cross-selling. The business team urgently requires your help in fixing the issue to meet the required sales targets for the quarter. Don't worry, though – this is the problem that we will be solving later in this chapter.

First, we begin with an analysis of the issue.

EXERCISE 13.01: BENCHMARKING THE LOGISTIC REGRESSION MODEL ON THE DATASET

In this exercise, we will be analyzing the problem of predicting whether a customer will buy a term deposit. For this, you will be fitting a logistic regression model, as you did in *Chapter 3, Binary Classification*, and you will look closely at the metrics:

> **NOTE**
>
> The dataset you will be using in this exercise can be found on our GitHub repository: https://packt.live/2twFgIM.

1. Open a new notebook in Google Colab.
2. Next, import **pandas** and load the data from the GitHub repository:

```
import pandas as pd
filename = 'https://raw.githubusercontent.com/PacktWorkshops'\
           '/The-Data-Science-Workshop/master/'\
           'Chapter13/Dataset/bank-full.csv'
```

3. Now, load the data using **pandas**

```
#Loading the data using pandas
bankData = pd.read_csv(filename,sep=";")
bankData.head()
```

Your output would be as follows:

	age	job	marital	education	default	balance	housing	loan	contact	day	month	duration	campaign	pdays	previous	poutcome	y
0	58	management	married	tertiary	no	2143	yes	no	unknown	5	may	261	1	-1	0	unknown	no
1	44	technician	single	secondary	no	29	yes	no	unknown	5	may	151	1	-1	0	unknown	no
2	33	entrepreneur	married	secondary	no	2	yes	yes	unknown	5	may	76	1	-1	0	unknown	no
3	47	blue-collar	married	unknown	no	1506	yes	no	unknown	5	may	92	1	-1	0	unknown	no
4	33	unknown	single	unknown	no	1	no	no	unknown	5	may	198	1	-1	0	unknown	no

Figure 13.1: The first 5 rows of bankData

Now, to break the dataset down further, let's perform some feature-engineering steps.

4. Normalize the numerical features (age, balance, and duration) through scaling, which was covered in *Chapter 3, Binary Classification*. Enter the following code:

```
from sklearn.preprocessing import RobustScaler
rob_scaler = RobustScaler()
```

In the preceding code snippet, we used a scaling function called **RobustScaler()** to scale the numerical data. **RobustScaler()** is a scaling function similar to **MinMaxScaler** in *Chapter 3*, *Binary Classification*.

5. After scaling the numerical data, we convert each of the columns to a scaled version, as in the following code snippet:

```
# Converting each of the columns to scaled version
bankData['ageScaled'] = rob_scaler.fit_transform\
                        (bankData['age'].values.reshape(-1,1))
bankData['balScaled'] = rob_scaler.fit_transform\
                        (bankData['balance']\
                         .values.reshape(-1,1))
bankData['durScaled'] = rob_scaler.fit_transform\
                        (bankData['duration']\
                         .values.reshape(-1,1))
```

6. Now, drop the original features after we introduce the scaled features using the **.drop()** function:

```
# Dropping the original columns
bankData.drop(['age','balance','duration'], \
              axis=1, inplace=True)
```

7. Display the first five columns using the **.head()** function:

```
bankData.head()
```

The output is as follows:

	job	marital	education	default	housing	loan	contact	day	month	campaign	pdays	previous	poutcome	y	ageScaled	balScaled	durScaled
0	management	married	tertiary	no	yes	no	unknown	5	may	1	-1	0	unknown	no	1.266667	1.250000	0.375000
1	technician	single	secondary	no	yes	no	unknown	5	may	1	-1	0	unknown	no	0.333333	-0.308997	-0.134259
2	entrepreneur	married	secondary	no	yes	yes	unknown	5	may	1	-1	0	unknown	no	-0.400000	-0.328909	-0.481481
3	blue-collar	married	unknown	no	yes	no	unknown	5	may	1	-1	0	unknown	no	0.533333	0.780236	-0.407407
4	unknown	single	unknown	no	no	no	unknown	5	may	1	-1	0	unknown	no	-0.400000	-0.329646	0.083333

Figure 13.2: bankData with scaled features

The categorical features in the dataset must be converted into numerical values by transforming them into dummy values, which was covered in *Chapter 3*, *Binary Classification*.

8. Convert all the categorical variables to dummy variables using the **`.get_dummies()`** function:

```
bankCat = pd.get_dummies(bankData[['job','marital','education',\
                                    'default','housing','loan',\
                                    'contact','month',\
                                    'poutcome']])
```

9. Separate the numerical data and observe the shape:

```
bankNum = bankData[['ageScaled','balScaled','day',\
                    'durScaled','campaign','pdays','previous']]
bankNum.shape
```

The output would be as follows:

```
(45211, 7)
```

After the categorical values are transformed, they must be combined with the scaled numerical values of the data frame to get the feature-engineered dataset.

10. Create the independent variables, **X**, and dependent variables, **Y**, from the combined dataset for modeling, as in the following code snippet:

```
# Merging with the original data frame
# Preparing the X variables
X = pd.concat([bankCat, bankNum], axis=1)
print(X.shape)
# Preparing the Y variable
Y = bankData['y']
print(Y.shape)
X.head()
```

The output is as follows:

```
(45211, 51)
(45211,)
```

	job_admin.	job_blue-collar	job_entrepreneur	job_housemaid	job_management	job_retired	job_self-employed	job_services	job_student	job_technician
0	0	0	0	0	1	0	0	0	0	0
1	0	0	0	0	0	0	0	0	0	1
2	0	0	1	0	0	0	0	0	0	0
3	0	1	0	0	0	0	0	0	0	0
4	0	0	0	0	0	0	0	0	0	0

Figure 13.3: The independent variables and the combined data (truncated)

We are now ready for the modeling task. Let's first import the necessary packages.

11. Now, **`import`** the necessary functions of **`train_test_split()`** and **`LogisticRegression`** from **`sklearn`**:

```
from sklearn.model_selection import train_test_split
from sklearn.linear_model import LogisticRegression
```

12. Split the data into train and test sets at a **70:30** ratio using the **`test_size = 0.3`** variable in the splitting function. We also set **`random_state`** for the reproducibility of the code:

```
X_train, X_test, y_train, y_test = train_test_split\
                                   (X, Y, test_size=0.3, \
                                    random_state=123)
```

13. Now, fit the model using **`.fit`** on the training data:

```
# Defining the LogisticRegression function
bankModel = LogisticRegression()
bankModel.fit(X_train, y_train)
```

Your output should be as follows:

```
/usr/local/lib/python3.6/dist-packages/sklearn/linear_model/_logistic.py:940: ConvergenceWarning: lbfgs failed to converge (status=1):
STOP: TOTAL NO. of ITERATIONS REACHED LIMIT.

Increase the number of iterations (max_iter) or scale the data as shown in:
    https://scikit-learn.org/stable/modules/preprocessing.html
Please also refer to the documentation for alternative solver options:
    https://scikit-learn.org/stable/modules/linear_model.html#logistic-regression
  extra_warning_msg=_LOGISTIC_SOLVER_CONVERGENCE_MSG)
LogisticRegression(C=1.0, class_weight=None, dual=False, fit_intercept=True,
                   intercept_scaling=1, l1_ratio=None, max_iter=100,
                   multi_class='auto', n_jobs=None, penalty='l2',
                   random_state=None, solver='lbfgs', tol=0.0001, verbose=0,
                   warm_start=False)
```

Figure 13.4: Fitting the model

Now that the model is fit, let's now predict the test set and generate the metrics.

14. Next, find the prediction on the test set and print the accuracy scores:

```
pred = bankModel.predict(X_test)
print('Accuracy of Logistic regression model prediction on '\
      'test set: {:.2f}'\
      .format(bankModel.score(X_test, y_test)))
```

You should get the following output:

```
Accuracy of Logistic regression model prediction on test set: 0.90
```

15. Now, use both the **`confusion_matrix()`** and **`classification_report()`** functions to generate the metrics for further analysis, which we will cover in the *Analysis of the Result* section:

```
# Confusion Matrix for the model
from sklearn.metrics import confusion_matrix
confusionMatrix = confusion_matrix(y_test, pred)
print(confusionMatrix)

from sklearn.metrics import classification_report
print(classification_report(y_test, pred))
```

You should get the following output:

```
[[11696   302]
 [ 1073   493]]
              precision    recall  f1-score   support

          no       0.92      0.97      0.94     11998
         yes       0.62      0.31      0.42      1566

    accuracy                           0.90     13564
   macro avg       0.77      0.64      0.68     13564
weighted avg       0.88      0.90      0.88     13564
```

Figure 13.5: Metrics showing the accuracy result along with the confusion matrix

> **NOTE**
>
> You will get metrics similar to the following. However, the values will vary due to the variability in the modeling process.

In this exercise, we have found a report that may have caused the issue with the number of customers expected to purchase the term deposit plan. From the metrics, we can see that the number of values for **No** is relatively higher than that for **Yes**.

> **NOTE**
>
> To access the source code for this specific section, please refer to https://packt.live/3hapnvB.
>
> You can also run this example online at https://packt.live/3hh6Xta.

To understand more about the reasons behind the skewed results, we will analyze these metrics in detail in the following section.

ANALYSIS OF THE RESULT

To analyze the results obtained in the previous section, let's expand the confusion matrix in the form:

Actual	Predicted	
	Propensity: 'No'	Propensity: 'Yes'
Propensity: 'No'	True positive (TP) = 11707	False negative (FN) = 291
Propensity: 'Yes'	False positive (FP) = 1060	True negative (TN) = 506

Figure 13.6: Confusion matrix of the resulting metrics obtained

We enter the values **11707**, **291**, **1060**, and **506** from the output we got from the previous exercise. We then place these values as shown in the diagram. We will represent the propensity to take a term deposit (**No**) as the positive class and the other as the negative class. So, from the confusion matrix, we can calculate the accuracy measures, which were covered in *Chapter 3*, *Binary Classification*. The accuracy of the model is given by:

$$Accuracy\ of\ a\ model = \frac{(\mathrm{TP} + \mathrm{TN})}{(\mathrm{TP} + \mathrm{FP} + \mathrm{FN} + \mathrm{TN})}$$

Figure 13.7: Accuracy of a model

In our case, it will be (11707 + 506) / (11707 + 1060 + 291 + 506), or 90%.

From the accuracy perspective, the model would seem like it is doing a reasonable job. However, the reality might be quite different. To find out what's really the case, let's look at the precision and recall values, which are available from the classification report we obtained. The formulae for precision for any class was covered in *Chapter 3, Binary Classification*

The precision value of any class is given by:

$$Precision\ value = \frac{Correct\ prediction\ of\ the\ class}{Total\ predictions\ for\ that\ class}$$

Figure 13.8: Precision of a model

In our case, for the positive class, the precision is *TP/(TP + FP)*, which is 11707/ (11707 + 1060), which comes to approximately 92%.

In the case of the negative class, the precision could be written as *TN / (TN + FN)*, which is 506 / (506 + 291), which comes to approximately 63%.

Similarly, the recall value for any class can be represented as follows:

$$Recall\ value = \frac{Correct\ prediction\ of\ the\ class}{Total\ examples\ of\ the\ class}$$

Figure 13.9: Recalling a model

The recall value for the positive class, *TP / (TP + FN)* = 11707 / (11707 + 291), comes to approximately 98%.

The recall value for the negative class, *TN / (TN + FP)* = 506 / (506 + 1060), comes to approximately 32%.

Recall indicates the ability of the classifier to correctly identify the respective classes. From the metrics, we see that the model that we built does a good job of identifying the positive classes, but does a very poor job of correctly identifying the negative class.

Why do you think that the classifier is biased toward one class? The answer to this can be unearthed by looking at the class balance in the training set.

The following code will generate the percentages of the classes in the training data:

```
print('Percentage of negative class :',\
      (y_train[y_train=='yes'].value_counts()\
       /len(y_train) ) * 100)
print('Percentage of positive class :',\
      (y_train[y_train=='no'].value_counts()\
       /len(y_train) ) * 100)
```

You should get the following output:

```
Percentage of negative class: yes    11.764148
Name: y, dtype: float64
Percentage of positive class: no    88.235852
Name: y, dtype: float64
```

From this, we can see that the majority of the training set (88%) is made up of the positive class. This imbalance is one of the major reasons behind the poor metrics that we have had with the logistic regression classifier we have selected.

Now, let's look at the challenges of imbalanced datasets.

CHALLENGES OF IMBALANCED DATASETS

As seen from the classifier example, one of the biggest challenges with imbalanced datasets is the bias toward the majority class, which ended up being 88% in the previous example. This will result in suboptimal results. However, what makes such cases even more challenging is the deceptive nature of results if the right metric is not used.

Let's take, for example, a dataset where the negative class is around 99% and the positive class is 1% (as in a use case where a rare disease has to be detected, for instance).

Have a look at the following code snippet:

```
Data set Size: 10,000 examples
Negative class : 9910
Positive Class : 90
```

Suppose we had a poor classifier that was capable of only predicting the negative class; we would get the following confusion matrix:

Actual	Predicted	
	Propensity : 'Yes'	Propensity : 'No'
Probability of disease : 'Yes'	True positive (TP)= 0	False negative (FN) = 90
Probability of disease : 'No'	False positive (FP) = 0	True negative (TN) = 9900

Figure 13.10: Confusion matrix of the poor classifier

From the confusion matrix, let's calculate the accuracy measures. Have a look at the following code snippet:

```
# Classifier biased to only negative class
Accuracy = (TP + TN ) / ( TP + FP + FN + TN)
 = (0 + 9900) / ( 0 + 0 + 90 + 9900) = 9900/10000
 = 99%
```

With such a classifier, if we were to use a metric such as accuracy, we still would get a result of around 99%, which, in normal circumstances, would look outstanding. However, in this case, the classifier is doing a bad job. Think of the real-life impact of using such a classifier and a metric such as accuracy. The impact on patients who have rare diseases and who get wrongly classified as not having the disease could be fatal.

Therefore, it is important to identify cases with imbalanced datasets and equally important to pick the right metric for analyzing such datasets. The right metric in this example would have been to look at the recall values for both the classes:

```
Recall Positive class  = TP / ( TP + FN ) = 0 / ( 0 + 90)
 = 0
Recall Negative Class = TN / ( TN + FP) = 9900 / ( 9900 + 0)
= 100%
```

From the recall values, we could have identified the bias of the classifier toward the majority class, prompting us to look at strategies for mitigating such biases, which is the next topic we will focus on.

STRATEGIES FOR DEALING WITH IMBALANCED DATASETS

Now that we have identified the challenges of imbalanced datasets, let's look at strategies for combatting imbalanced datasets:

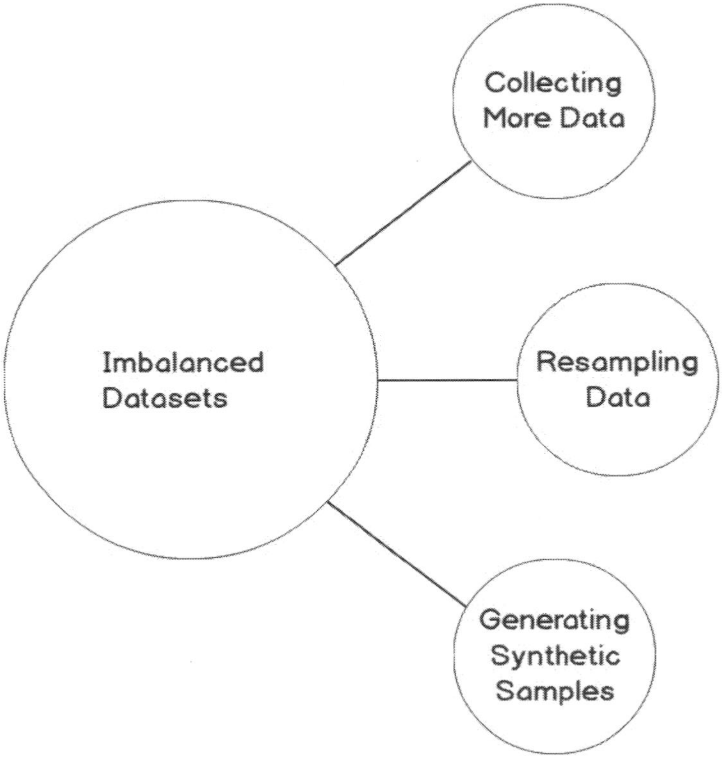

Figure 13.11: Strategies for dealing with imbalanced datasets

COLLECTING MORE DATA

Having encountered an imbalanced dataset, one of the first questions you need to ask is whether it is possible to get more data. This might appear naïve, but collecting more data, especially from the minority class, and then balancing the dataset should be the first strategy for addressing the class imbalance.

RESAMPLING DATA

In many circumstances, collecting more data, especially from minority classes, can be challenging as data points for the minority class will be very minimal. In such circumstances, we need to adopt different strategies to work with our constraints and still strive to balance our dataset. One effective strategy is to resample our dataset to make the dataset more balanced. Resampling would mean taking samples from the available dataset to create a new dataset, thereby making the new dataset balanced.

Let's look at the idea in detail:

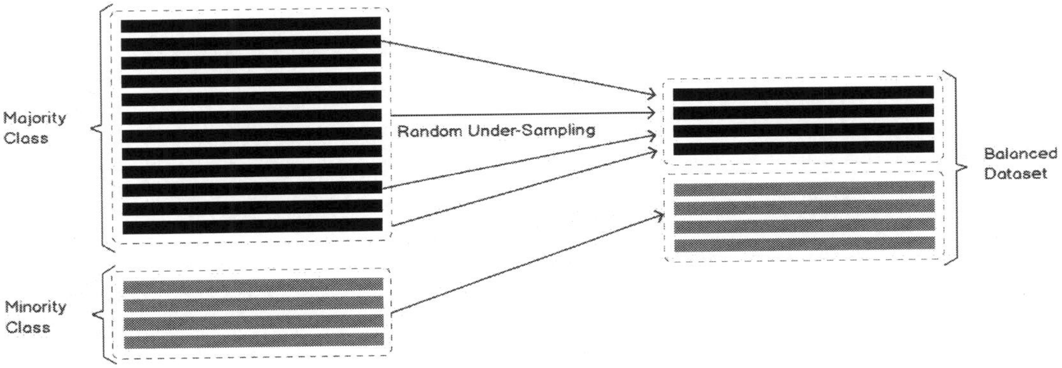

Figure 13.12: Random undersampling of the majority class

As seen in *Figure 13.8*, the idea behind resampling is to randomly pick samples from the majority class to make the final dataset more balanced. In the diagram, we can see that the minority class has the same number of examples as the original dataset and that the majority class is under-sampled to make the final dataset more balanced. Resampling examples of this type is called random undersampling as we are undersampling the majority class. We will perform random undersampling in the following exercise.

EXERCISE 13.02: IMPLEMENTING RANDOM UNDERSAMPLING AND CLASSIFICATION ON OUR BANKING DATASET TO FIND THE OPTIMAL RESULT

In this exercise, you will undersample the majority class (propensity **'No'**) and then make the dataset balanced. On the new balanced dataset, you will fit a logistic regression model and then analyze the results:

> **NOTE**
>
> The dataset you will be using in this exercise can be found on our GitHub repository: https://packt.live/2twFgIM.

1. Open a new Colab notebook for this exercise.
2. Perform the initial 12 steps of *Exercise 13.01*, *Benchmarking the Logistic Regression Model on the Dataset*, such that the dataset is split into training and testing sets.
3. Now, join the **X** and **y** variables for the training set before resampling:

```
"""
Let us first join the train_x and train_y for ease of operation
"""
trainData = pd.concat([X_train,y_train],axis=1)
```

   In this step, we concatenated the **X_train** and **y_train** datasets to one single dataset. This is done to make the resampling process in the subsequent steps easier. To concatenate the two datasets, we use the **.concat()** function from **pandas**. In the code, we use **axis = 1** to indicate that the concatenation is done horizontally, which is along the columns.

4. Now, display the new data with the **.head()** function:

```
trainData.head()
```

   You should get the following output

	job_admin.	job_blue-collar	job_entrepreneur	job_housemaid	job_management	job_retired	job_self-employed	job_services	job_student	job_technician	job_unemployed
19100	1	0	0	0	0	0	0	0	0	0	0
37958	1	0	0	0	0	0	0	0	0	0	0
12451	0	1	0	0	0	0	0	0	0	0	0
18263	0	0	0	0	1	0	0	0	0	0	0
5128	0	0	0	0	0	0	0	1	0	0	0

Figure 13.13: Displaying the first five rows of the dataset using .head()

The preceding output shows some of the columns of the dataset.

Now, let's move onto separating the minority and majority classes into separate datasets.

What we will do next is separate the minority class and the majority class. This is required because we have to sample separately from the majority class to make a balanced dataset. To separate the minority class, we have to identify the indexes of the dataset where the dataset has 'yes.' The indexes are identified using **`.index()`** function.

Once those indexes are identified, they are separated from the main dataset using the **`.loc()`** function and stored in a new variable for the minority class. The shape of the minority dataset is also printed. A similar process is followed for the majority class and, after these two steps, we have two datasets: one for the minority class and one for the majority class.

5. Next, find the indexes of the sample dataset where the propensity is **`yes`**:

```
ind = trainData[trainData['y']=='yes'].index
print(len(ind))
```

You should get the following output:

```
3723
```

6. Separate by the minority class as in the following code snippet:

```
minData = trainData.loc[ind]
print(minData.shape)
```

You should get the following output:

```
(3723, 52)
```

7. Now, find the indexes of the majority class:

```
ind1 = trainData[trainData['y']=='no'].index
print(len(ind1))
```

You should get the following output:

```
27924
```

8. Separate by the majority class as in the following code snippet:

```
majData = trainData.loc[ind1]
print(majData.shape)
majData.head()
```

You should get the following output:

```
(27924, 52)
```

	job_admin.	job_blue-collar	job_entrepreneur	job_housemaid	job_management	job_retired	job_self-employed	job_services	job_student	job_technician
19100	1	0	0	0	0	0	0	0	0	0
37958	1	0	0	0	0	0	0	0	0	0
12451	0	1	0	0	0	0	0	0	0	0
18263	0	0	0	0	1	0	0	0	0	0
5128	0	0	0	0	0	0	0	1	0	0

Figure 13.14: Output after separating the majority classes

Once the majority class is separated, we can proceed with sampling from the majority class. Once the sampling is done, the shape of the majority class dataset and its head are printed.

Take a random sample equal to the length of the minority class to make the dataset balanced.

9. Extract the samples using the **.sample()** function:

```
majSample = majData.sample(n=len(ind),random_state = 123)
```

The number of examples that are sampled is equal to the number of examples in the minority class. This is implemented with the parameters **(n=len(ind))**.

10. Now that sampling is done, the shape of the majority class dataset and its head is printed:

```
print(majSample.shape)
majSample.head()
```

You should get the following output:

```
(3723, 52)
```

	job_admin.	job_blue-collar	job_entrepreneur	job_housemaid	job_management	job_retired	job_self-employed	job_services	job_student	job_technician	job_unemployed
17387	0	0	0	0	1	0	0	0	0	0	0
34679	0	1	0	0	0	0	0	0	0	0	0
26572	1	0	0	0	0	0	0	0	0	0	0
3280	0	0	0	0	0	1	0	0	0	0	0
4434	0	0	0	0	1	0	0	0	0	0	0

Figure 13.15: Output showing the shape of the majority class dataset

Now, we move onto preparing the new training data

11. After preparing the individual dataset, we can now concatenate them together using the **pd.concat()** function:

```
"""
Concatenating both data sets and then shuffling the data set
"""
balData = pd.concat([minData,majSample],axis = 0)
```

> **NOTE**
>
> In this case, we are concatenating in the vertical direction and, therefore, **axis = 0** is used.

12. Now, shuffle the dataset so that both the minority and majority classes are evenly distributed using the **shuffle()** function:

```
# Shuffling the data set
from sklearn.utils import shuffle
balData = shuffle(balData)
balData.head()
```

You should get the following output:

	job_admin.	job_blue-collar	job_entrepreneur	job_housemaid	job_management	job_retired	job_self-employed	job_services	job_student	job_technician	job_unemployed
44281	0	0	0	0	0	1	0	0	0	0	0
7655	0	0	0	0	1	0	0	0	0	0	0
43702	0	0	0	0	0	0	0	0	0	1	0
22481	0	0	1	0	0	0	0	0	0	0	0
45175	0	0	1	0	0	0	0	0	0	0	0

Figure 13.16: Output after shuffling the dataset

13. Now, separate the shuffled dataset into the independent variables, **X_trainNew**, and dependent variables, **y_trainNew**. The separation is to be done using the index features **0** to **51** for the dependent variables using the **.iloc()** function in **pandas**. The dependent variables are separated by sub-setting with the column name **'y'**:

```
# Making the new X_train and y_train
X_trainNew = balData.iloc[:,0:51]
print(X_trainNew.head())
```

```
y_trainNew = balData['y']
print(y_trainNew.head())
```

You should get the following output:

```
      job_admin.  job_blue-collar  job_entrepreneur  ...  campaign  pdays  previous
40574          0                1                 0  ...         2     -1         0
7560           1                0                 0  ...         2     -1         0
1372           0                0                 0  ...         1     -1         0
14867          0                0                 0  ...         1     -1         0
11057          0                0                 0  ...         2     -1         0

[5 rows x 51 columns]
40574    yes
7560      no
1372     yes
14867     no
11057     no
Name: y, dtype: object
```

Figure 13.17: Shuffling the dataset into independent variables

Now, fit the model on the new data and generate the confusion matrix and classification report for our analysis.

14. First, define the **LogisticRegression** function with the following code snippet:

```
from sklearn.linear_model import LogisticRegression

bankModel1 = LogisticRegression()
bankModel1.fit(X_trainNew, y_trainNew)
```

You should get the following output:

```
/usr/local/lib/python3.6/dist-packages/sklearn/linear_model/_logistic.py:940: ConvergenceWarning: lbfgs failed to converge (status=1):
STOP: TOTAL NO. of ITERATIONS REACHED LIMIT.

Increase the number of iterations (max_iter) or scale the data as shown in:
    https://scikit-learn.org/stable/modules/preprocessing.html
Please also refer to the documentation for alternative solver options:
    https://scikit-learn.org/stable/modules/linear_model.html#logistic-regression
  extra_warning_msg=_LOGISTIC_SOLVER_CONVERGENCE_MSG)
LogisticRegression(C=1.0, class_weight=None, dual=False, fit_intercept=True,
                   intercept_scaling=1, l1_ratio=None, max_iter=100,
                   multi_class='auto', n_jobs=None, penalty='l2',
                   random_state=None, solver='lbfgs', tol=0.0001, verbose=0,
                   warm_start=False)
```

Figure 13.18: Fitting the model

15. Next, perform the prediction on the test with the following code snippet:

```
pred = bankModel1.predict(X_test)
print('Accuracy of Logistic regression model prediction on '\
      'test set for balanced data set: {:.2f}'\
      .format(bankModel1.score(X_test, y_test)))
```

You should get the following output:

```
Accuracy of Logistic regression model prediction on test set for
balanced data set:0.83
```

`{:.2f}'.format` is used to print the string values along with the accuracy score, which is output from **`bankModel1.score(X_test, y_test)`**. In this, **`2f`** means a numerical score with two decimals.

16. Now, generate the confusion matrix for the model and print the results:

```
from sklearn.metrics import confusion_matrix
confusionMatrix = confusion_matrix(y_test, pred)
print(confusionMatrix)

from sklearn.metrics import classification_report
print(classification_report(y_test, pred))
```

You should get the following output:

```
[[10203 1795]
 [ 289  1277]]
              precision    recall  f1-score   support

          no       0.97      0.85      0.91     11998
         yes       0.42      0.82      0.55      1566

    accuracy                           0.85     13564
   macro avg       0.69      0.83      0.73     13564
weighted avg       0.91      0.85      0.87     13564
```

Figure 13.19: Confusion matrix for the model obtained

> **NOTE**
>
> The values can vary in the output as the modeling process is subject to variation.
>
> To access the source code for this specific section, please refer to https://packt.live/348njjY.
>
> You can also run this example online at https://packt.live/318R81I.

ANALYSIS

Let's analyze the results and compare them with those of the benchmark logistic regression model that we built at the beginning of this chapter. In the benchmark model, we had the problem of the model being biased toward the majority class with a very low recall value for the `yes` cases.

Now, by balancing the dataset, we have seen that the recall for the minority class has improved tremendously, from a low of `0.32` to around `0.82`. This means that by balancing the dataset, the classifier has improved its ability to identify negative cases.

However, we can see that our overall accuracy has taken a hit. From a high of around 90%, it has come down to around 85%. One major area where accuracy has taken a hit is the number of false positives, which are those `No` cases that were wrongly predicted as `Yes`.

Analyzing the result from a business perspective, this is a much better scenario than the one we got in the benchmark model. In the benchmark model, out of the total 1,566 `Yes` cases, only 506 were correctly identified. However, after balancing, we were able to identify 1,277 out of 1,566 customers from the dataset who were likely to buy term deposits, which can potentially result in a better conversion rate. However, the flip side of this is that the sales team will also have to spend a lot of time on customers who are unlikely to buy term deposits. From the confusion matrix, we can see that false negatives have gone up to 1,795 from the earlier 291 we got in the benchmark model. Ideally, we would want quadrants 2 and 3 to come down in favor of the other two quadrants.

GENERATING SYNTHETIC SAMPLES

In the previous section, we looked at the undersampling method, where we downsized the majority class to make the dataset balanced. However, when undersampling, we reduced the size of the dataset. In many circumstances, downsizing the dataset can have adverse effects on the predictive power of the classifier. An effective way to counter the downsizing of the dataset is to oversample the minority class. Oversampling is done by generating new synthetic data points similar to those of the minority class, thereby balancing the dataset.

Two very popular methods for generating such synthetic points are:

- **Synthetic Minority Oversampling Technique** (**SMOTE**)
- **Modified SMOTE** (**MSMOTE**)

The way the **`SMOTE`** algorithm generates synthetic data is by looking at the neighborhood of minority classes and generating new data points within the neighborhood:

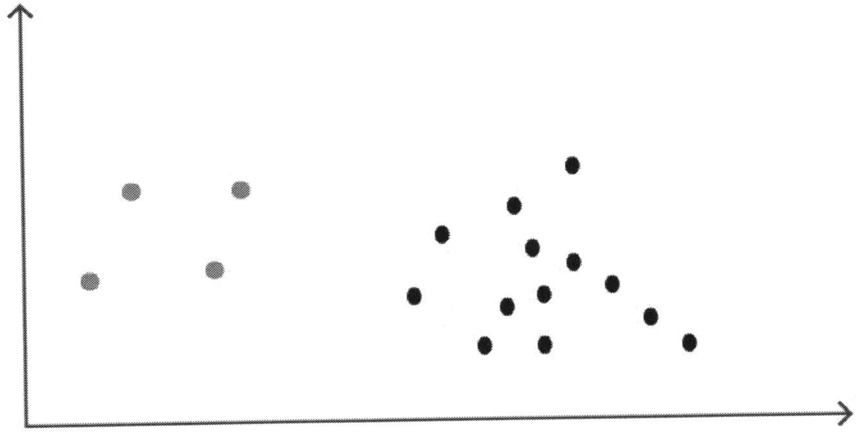

Figure 13.20: Dataset with two classes

Let's explain the concept of generating synthetic datasets with a pictorial representation. Let's assume that *Figure 13.15* represents a dataset with two classes: the grey circles represent the minority class, and the black circles represent the majority class.

In creating synthetic points, an imaginary line connecting all the minority samples in the neighborhood is created and new data points are generated on this line, as shown in *Figure 13.16*, thereby balancing the dataset:

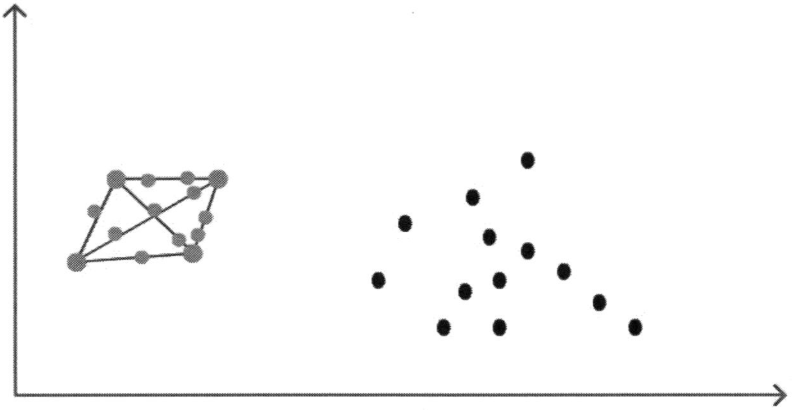

Figure 13.21: Connecting samples in a neighborhood

However, **MSMOTE** is an advancement over the **SMOTE** algorithm and has a different approach to generating synthetic points. **MSMOTE** classifies the minority class into three distinct groups: **security samples**, **border samples**, and **latent noise samples**. Different strategies are adopted to generate neighborhood points based on the group each minority class falls into.

We will see the implementation of both **SMOTE** and **MSMOTE** in the following section.

IMPLEMENTATION OF SMOTE AND MSMOTE

SMOTE and **MSMOTE** can be implemented from a package called **smote-variants** in Python. The library can be installed through **pip install** in the Colab notebook as shown here:

```
!pip install smote-variants
```

> **NOTE**
>
> More details on the package and its different variations can be obtained at https://packt.live/2QsNhat.

Let's now implement both these methods and analyze the results.

EXERCISE 13.03: IMPLEMENTING SMOTE ON OUR BANKING DATASET TO FIND THE OPTIMAL RESULT

In this exercise, we will generate synthetic samples of the minority class using **SMOTE** and then make the dataset balanced. Then, on the new balanced dataset, we will fit a logistic regression model and analyze the results:

1. Implement all the steps of *Exercise 13.01*, *Benchmarking the Logistic Regression Model on the Dataset*, until the splitting of the train and test sets (*Step 12*).
2. Now, print the count of both the classes before we oversample:

```
# Shape before oversampling
print("Before OverSampling count of yes: {}"\
      .format(sum(y_train=='yes')))
print("Before OverSampling count of no: {} \n"\
      .format(sum(y_train=='no')))
```

   You should get the following output:

```
Before OverSampling count of yes: 3694
Before OverSampling count of no: 27953
```

> **NOTE**
>
> The counts mentioned in this output can vary because of a variability in the sampling process.

   Next, we will be oversampling the training set using **SMOTE**.

3. Begin by importing **sv** and **numpy**:

```
!pip install smote-variants
import smote_variants as sv
import numpy as np
```

   The library files that are required for oversampling the training set include the **smote_variants** library, which we installed earlier. This is imported as **sv**. The other library that is required is **numpy**, as the training set will have to be given a **numpy** array for the **smote_variants** library.

4. Now, instantiate the **SMOTE** library to a variable called **oversampler** using the **sv.SMOTE()** function:

```
# Instantiating the SMOTE class
oversampler= sv.SMOTE()
```

   This is a common way of instantiating any of the variants of **SMOTE** from the **smote_variants** library.

5. Now, sample the process using the **.sample()** function of **oversampler**:

```
# Creating new training set
X_train_os, y_train_os = oversampler.sample\
                          (np.array(X_train), np.array(y_train))
```

> **NOTE**
>
> Both the **X** and **y** variables are converted to **numpy** arrays before applying the **.sample()** function.

6. Now, print the shapes of the new **X** and **y** variables and the **counts** of the classes. You will note that the size of the overall dataset has increased from the earlier count of around 31,647 (3694 + 27953) to 55,906. The increase in size can be attributed to the fact that the minority class has been oversampled from 3,694 to 27,953:

```
# Shape after oversampling
print('After OverSampling, the shape of train_X: {}'\
      .format(X_train_os.shape))
print('After OverSampling, the shape of train_y: {} \n'\
      .format(y_train_os.shape))

print("After OverSampling, counts of label 'Yes': {}"\
      .format(sum(y_train_os=='yes')))
print("After OverSampling, counts of label 'no': {}"\
      .format(sum(y_train_os=='no')))
```

You should get the following output:

```
After OverSampling, the shape of train_X: (55906, 51)
After OverSampling, the shape of train_y: (55906,)

After OverSampling, counts of label 'Yes': 27953
After OverSampling, counts of label 'no': 27953
```

> **NOTE**
>
> The counts mentioned in this output can vary because of variability in the sampling process.

Now that we have generated synthetic points using **SMOTE** and balanced the dataset, let's fit a logistic regression model on the new sample and analyze the results using a confusion matrix and a classification report.

7. Define the **LogisticRegression** function:

```
# Training the model with Logistic regression model
from sklearn.linear_model import LogisticRegression

bankModel2 = LogisticRegression()
bankModel2.fit(X_train_os, y_train_os)
```

8. Now, predict using **.predict** on the test set, as mentioned in the following code snippet:

```
pred = bankModel2.predict(X_test)
```

9. Next, **print** the accuracy values:

```
print('Accuracy of Logistic regression model prediction on '\
      'test set for Smote balanced data set: {:.2f}'\
      .format(bankModel2.score(X_test, y_test)))
```

Your output should be as follows:

```
Accuracy of Logistic regression model prediction on test set for
Smote balanced data set: 0.83
```

10. Then, generate **ConfusionMatrix** for the model:

```
from sklearn.metrics import confusion_matrix
confusionMatrix = confusion_matrix(y_test, pred)
print(confusionMatrix)
```

The matrix is as follows:

```
[[10042  1956]
 [  306  1260]]
```

11. Generate **Classification_report** for the model:

```
from sklearn.metrics import classification_report
print(classification_report(y_test, pred))
```

You should get the following output:

```
              precision    recall  f1-score   support

          no       0.97      0.85      0.91     11998
         yes       0.42      0.80      0.55      1566

    accuracy                           0.85     13564
   macro avg       0.69      0.83      0.73     13564
weighted avg       0.91      0.85      0.87     13564
```

Figure 13.22: Classification report for the model

From the generated metrics, we can see that the results are very similar to the undersampling results, with the exception that the recall value of the **'Yes'** cases has reduced from **0.82** to around **0.80**. The results that are generated vary from one use case to the next. **SMOTE** and its variants have been proven to have robust results in balancing data and are therefore the most popular methods used when encountering use cases with highly imbalanced data.

> **NOTE**
>
> The values can vary in the output as the modeling process is subject to variation.
>
> To access the source code for this specific section, please refer to https://packt.live/2Ycxu34.
>
> You can also run this example online at https://packt.live/2FDvTgo.

In the next exercise, we will be implementing **MSMOTE**.

EXERCISE 13.04: IMPLEMENTING MSMOTE ON OUR BANKING DATASET TO FIND THE OPTIMAL RESULT

In this exercise, we will generate synthetic samples of the minority class using **MSMOTE** and then make the dataset balanced. Then, on the new balanced dataset, we will fit a logistic regression model and analyze the results. This exercise will be very similar to the previous one.

1. Implement all the steps of *Exercise 13.01*, *Benchmarking the Logistic Regression Model on the Dataset*, until the splitting of the train and test sets (*Step 12*).

2. Now, print the count of both the classes before we oversample:

```
# Shape before oversampling
print("Before OverSampling count of yes: {}"\
      .format(sum(y_train=='yes')))
print("Before OverSampling count of no: {} \n"\
      .format(sum(y_train=='no')))
```

   You should get the following output:

```
Before OverSampling count of yes: 3723
Before OverSampling count of no: 27924
```

> **NOTE**
>
> The counts mentioned in this output can vary because of variability in the sampling process.

   Next, we will be oversampling the training set using **MSMOTE**.

3. Begin by importing the **sv** and **numpy**:

```
!pip install smote-variants
import smote_variants as sv
import numpy as np
```

   The library files that are required for oversampling the training set include the **smote_variants** library, which we installed earlier. This is imported as **sv**. The other library that is required is **numpy**, as the training set will have to be given a **numpy** array for the **smote_variants** library.

4. Now, instantiate the **MSMOTE** library to a variable called **oversampler** using the **sv.MSMOTE()** function:

```
# Instantiating the MSMOTE class
oversampler= sv.MSMOTE()
```

5. Now, sample the process using the **.sample()** function of **oversampler**:

```
# Creating new training set
X_train_os, y_train_os = oversampler.sample\
                         (np.array(X_train), np.array(y_train))
```

> **NOTE**
>
> Both the **X** and **y** variables are converted to **numpy** arrays before applying the **.sample()** function.

Now, print the shapes of the new **X** and **y** variables and also the **counts** of the classes:

```
# Shape after oversampling

print('After OverSampling, the shape of train_X: {}'\
      .format(X_train_os.shape))
print('After OverSampling, the shape of train_y: {} \n'\
      .format(y_train_os.shape))

print("After OverSampling, counts of label 'Yes': {}"\
      .format(sum(y_train_os=='yes')))
print("After OverSampling, counts of label 'no': {}"\
      .format(sum(y_train_os=='no')))
```

You should get the following output:

```
After OverSampling, the shape of train_X: (55848, 51)
After OverSampling, the shape of train_y: (55848,)

After OverSampling, counts of label 'Yes': 27924
After OverSampling, counts of label 'no': 27924
```

Now that we have generated synthetic points using **MSMOTE** and balanced the dataset, let's fit a logistic regression model on the new sample and analyze the results using a confusion matrix and a classification report.

6. Define the **LogisticRegression** function:

```
# Training the model with Logistic regression model
from sklearn.linear_model import LogisticRegression

# Defining the LogisticRegression function
bankModel3 = LogisticRegression()
bankModel3.fit(X_train_os, y_train_os)
```

7. Now, predict using **.predict** on the test set as in the following code snippet:

```
pred = bankModel3.predict(X_test)
```

8. Next, **print** the accuracy values:

```
print('Accuracy of Logistic regression model prediction on '\
      'test set for MSMOTE balanced data set: {:.2f}'\
      .format(bankModel3.score(X_test, y_test)))
```

You should get the following output:

```
Accuracy of Logistic regression model prediction on test set for
MSMOTE balanced data set: 0.84
```

9. Generate the **ConfusionMatrix** for the model:

```
from sklearn.metrics import confusion_matrix
confusionMatrix = confusion_matrix(y_test, pred)
print(confusionMatrix)
```

The matrix should be as follows:

```
[[10167  1831]
 [  314  1252]]
```

10. Generate the **Classification_report** for the model:

```
from sklearn.metrics import classification_report
print(classification_report(y_test, pred))
```

You should get the following output:

```
[[10288  1710]
 [  331  1235]]
              precision    recall  f1-score   support

          no       0.97      0.86      0.91     11998
         yes       0.42      0.79      0.55      1566

    accuracy                           0.85     13564
   macro avg       0.69      0.82      0.73     13564
weighted avg       0.91      0.85      0.87     13564
```

Figure 13.23: Classification report for the model

> **NOTE**
>
> The values can vary in the output as the modeling process is subject to variation.
>
> To access the source code for this specific section, please refer to https://packt.live/34bCWHd.
>
> You can also run this example online at https://packt.live/2Edccvh.

From the implementation of **MSMOTE**, it is seen that the metrics have degraded compared to the **SMOTE** implementation from *Exercise 13.03, Implementing SMOTE on Our Banking Dataset to Find the Optimal Result*. We can then conclude that **MSMOTE** might not be the best method for this use case.

APPLYING BALANCING TECHNIQUES ON A TELECOM DATASET

Now that we have seen different balancing techniques, let's apply these techniques to a new dataset that is related to the churn of telecom customers. This dataset is available at the following link: https://packt.live/37IvqSX.

This dataset has various variables related to the usage level of a mobile connection, such as total call minutes, call charges, calls made during certain periods of the day, details of international calls, and details of calls to customer services.

The problem statement is to predict whether a customer will churn. This dataset is a highly imbalanced one, with the cases where customers churn being the minority. You will be using this dataset in the following activity.

ACTIVITY 13.01: FINDING THE BEST BALANCING TECHNIQUE BY FITTING A CLASSIFIER ON THE TELECOM CHURN DATASET

You are working as a data scientist for a telecom company. You have encountered a dataset that is highly imbalanced, and you want to correct the class imbalance before fitting the classifier to analyze the churn. You know different methods for correcting the imbalance in datasets and you want to compare them to find the best method before fitting the model.

In this activity, you need to implement all of the three methods that you have come across so far and compare the results.

> **NOTE**
>
> You will be using the telecom churn dataset that you used in *Chapter 10, Analyzing a Dataset*.

Use the **`MinMaxscaler`** function to scale the dataset instead of the robust scaler function you have been using so far. Compare the methods based on the results you get by fitting a logistic regression model on the dataset.

The steps are as follows:

1. Implement all the initial steps, which include installing smote-variants and loading the data using pandas.
2. Normalize the numerical raw data using the **`MinMaxScaler()`** function we learned about in *Chapter 3, Binary Classification*.
3. Create dummy data for the categorical variables using the **`pd.get_dummies()`** function.
4. Separate the numerical data from the original data frame.
5. Concatenate numerical data and dummy categorical data using the **`pd.concat()`** function.

6. Split the earlier dataset into train and test sets using the **train_test_split()** function.

   Since the dataset is imbalanced, you need to perform the various techniques mentioned in the following steps.

7. For the undersampling method, find the index of the minority class using the **.index()** function and separate the minority class. After that, sample the majority class and make the majority dataset equal to the minority class using the **.sample()** function. Concatenate both the minority and under-sampled majority class to form a new dataset. Shuffle the dataset and separate the **X** and **Y** variables.

8. Fit a logistic regression model on the under-sampled dataset and name it **churnModel1**.

9. For the **SMOTE** method, create the oversampler using the **sv.SMOTE()** function and create the new **X** and **Y** training sets.

10. Fit a logistic regression model using **SMOTE** and name it **churnModel2**.

11. Import the **smote-variant** library and instantiate the **MSMOTE** algorithm using the **sv.MSMOTE()** function.

12. Create the oversampled data using the oversampler. Please note that the **X** and **y** variables have to be converted to a **numpy** array before oversampling

13. Fit the logistic regression model using the **MSMOTE** dataset and name the model **churnModel3**.

14. Generate the three separate predictions for each model.

15. Generate separate accuracy metrics, classification reports, and confusion matrices for each of the predictions.

16. Analyze the results and select the best method.

Expected Output:

The final metrics that you can expect will be similar to what you see here.

Undersampling Output

```
[[1027  256]
 [  59  158]]
              precision    recall  f1-score   support

          No       0.95      0.80      0.87      1283
         Yes       0.38      0.73      0.50       217

    accuracy                           0.79      1500
   macro avg       0.66      0.76      0.68      1500
weighted avg       0.86      0.79      0.81      1500
```

Figure 13.24: Undersampling output report

SMOTE Output

```
[[1002  281]
 [  52  165]]
              precision    recall  f1-score   support

          No       0.95      0.78      0.86      1283
         Yes       0.37      0.76      0.50       217

    accuracy                           0.78      1500
   macro avg       0.66      0.77      0.68      1500
weighted avg       0.87      0.78      0.81      1500
```

Figure 13.25: SMOTE output report

MSMOTE Output

```
[[1036  247]
 [  55  162]]
              precision    recall  f1-score   support

          No       0.95      0.81      0.87      1283
         Yes       0.40      0.75      0.52       217

    accuracy                           0.80      1500
   macro avg       0.67      0.78      0.70      1500
weighted avg       0.87      0.80      0.82      1500
```

Figure 13.26: MSMOTE output report

> **NOTE**
>
> You will have different output as the modeling is stochastic in nature.
>
> The solution to the activity can be found here: https://packt.live/2GbJloz.

SUMMARY

In this chapter, we learned about imbalanced datasets and strategies for addressing imbalanced datasets. We introduced the use cases where imbalanced datasets would be encountered. We looked at the challenges posed by imbalanced datasets and we were introduced to the metrics that should be used in the case of an imbalanced dataset. We formulated strategies for dealing with imbalanced datasets and implemented different strategies, such as random undersampling and oversampling, for balancing datasets. We then fit different models after balancing the datasets and analyzed the results.

Balancing datasets is a very effective way to improve the performance of your classifiers. However, it should be noted that there could be a degradation of overall accuracy measures for the majority class due to balancing. What strategies to adopt in what situations should be arrived at based on the problem statement and also after rigorous experiments for those problem statements.

Having learned about methods for dealing with imbalanced datasets, we will now be introduced to another important technique that is prevalent in many modern datasets called dimensionality reduction. Different techniques for dimensionality reduction will be addressed in *Chapter 14*, *Dimensionality Reduction*.

14

DIMENSIONALITY REDUCTION

OVERVIEW

This chapter introduces dimensionality reduction in data science. You will be using the Internet Advertisements dataset to analyze and evaluate different techniques in dimensionality reduction. By the end of this chapter, you will be able to analyze datasets with high dimensions and deal with the challenges posed by these datasets. As well as applying different dimensionality reduction techniques to large datasets, you will fit models based on those datasets and analyze their results. By the end of this chapter, you will be able to deal with huge datasets in the real world.

INTRODUCTION

In the previous chapter on balancing datasets, we dealt with the Bank Marketing dataset, which had 18 variables. We were able to load that dataset very easily, fit a model, and get results. But have you considered the scenario when the number of variables you have to deal with is large, say around 18 million instead of the 18 you dealt with in the last chapter? How do you load such large datasets and analyze them? How do you deal with the computing resources required for modeling with such large datasets?

This is the reality in some modern-day datasets in domains such as:

- Healthcare, where genetics datasets can have millions of features
- High-resolution imaging datasets
- Web data related to advertisements, ranking, and crawling

When dealing with such huge datasets, many challenges can arise:

- Storage and computation challenges: Large datasets with high dimensions require a lot of storage and expensive computational resources for analysis.
- Exploration challenges: When trying to explore data and derive insights, high-dimensional data can be really cumbersome.
- Algorithm challenges: Many algorithms do not scale well in high-dimensional settings.

So, what is the solution when we have to deal with high-dimensional data? This is where dimensionality reduction techniques come to the fore, which we will explore in this chapter.

Dimensionality reduction aims to reduce the dimensions of datasets to get over the challenges posed by high-dimensional data. In this chapter, we will examine some of the popular dimensionality reduction techniques:

- Backward feature elimination or recursive feature elimination
- Forward feature selection
- **Principal Component Analysis** (**PCA**)
- **Independent Component Analysis** (**ICA**)
- Factor analysis

Let's first examine our business context and then apply these techniques to the problem statement.

BUSINESS CONTEXT

The marketing head of your company comes to you with a problem she has been grappling with. Many customers have been complaining about the browsing experience of your company's website because of the number of advertisements that pop up during browsing. Your company wants to build an engine on your web server that identifies potential advertisements and then eliminates them even before they pop up.

To help you to achieve this, you have been given a dataset that contains a set of possible advertisements on a variety of web pages. The features of the dataset represent the geometry of the images in the possible adverts, as well as phrases occurring in the URL, image URLs, anchor text, and words occurring near the anchor text. This dataset has also been labeled, with each possible ad given a label that says whether it is actually an advertisement or not. Using this dataset, you have to build a model that predicts whether something is an advertisement or not. You may think that this is a relatively simple problem that could be solved with any binary classification algorithm. However, there is a challenge in the dataset. The dataset has a large number of features. You have set out to solve this high-dimensional dataset challenge.

This dataset is uploaded in the GitHub repository for working through all the subsequent exercises. The attributes of the dataset are available in the following link: https://packt.live/36rqiCg.

EXERCISE 14.01: LOADING AND CLEANING THE DATASET

In this exercise, we will download the dataset, load it in our Colab notebook, and do some basic explorations, such as printing the dimensions of the dataset using the **`.shape()`** and **`.describe()`** functions, and also cleaning the dataset.

> **NOTE**
>
> The **`internet_ads`** dataset has been uploaded to our GitHub repository and can be accessed at https://packt.live/2sPaVF6.

The following steps will help you complete this exercise:

1. Open a new Colab notebook file.

2. Now, **import pandas** into your Colab notebook:

```
import pandas as pd
```

3. Next, set the path of the drive where the **ad.Data** file is uploaded, as shown in the following code snippet:

```
# Defining file name of the GitHub repository
filename = 'https://raw.githubusercontent.com'\
           '/PacktWorkshops/The-Data-Science-Workshop'\
           '/master/Chapter14/Dataset/ad.data'
```

4. Read the file using the **pd.read_csv()** function from the pandas data frame:

```
adData = pd.read_csv(filename,sep=",",header = None,\
                     error_bad_lines=False)
adData.head()
```

The **pd.read_csv()** function's arguments are the filename as a string and the limit separator of a CSV file, which is **","**. Please note that as there are no headers for the dataset. We specifically mention this using the **header = None** command. The last argument, **error_bad_lines=False**, is to skip any errors in the format of the file and then load data.

After reading the file, the data frame is printed using the **.head()** function.

You should get the following output:

	0	1	2	3	4	5	6	7	8	9	10	11	12	13	14	15	16	17	18	19	20	21	22	23	24	25	26	27	28	29	30	31	32	33	34	35	36	37	38	39	...	1519	1520
0	125	125	1.0	1	0	0	0	0	0	0	0	0	0	0	0	0	0	0	0	0	0	0	0	0	0	0	0	0	0	0	0	0	0	0	0	0	0	0	0	0	...	0	0
1	57	468	8.2105	1	0	0	0	0	0	0	0	0	0	0	0	0	0	0	0	0	0	0	0	0	0	0	0	0	0	0	0	0	0	0	0	0	0	0	0	0	...	0	0
2	33	230	6.9696	1	0	0	0	0	0	0	0	0	0	0	0	0	0	0	0	0	0	0	0	0	0	0	0	0	0	0	0	0	0	0	0	0	0	0	0	0	...	0	0
3	60	468	7.8	1	0	0	0	0	0	0	0	0	0	0	0	0	0	0	0	0	0	0	0	0	0	0	0	0	0	0	0	0	0	0	0	0	0	0	0	0	...	0	0
4	60	468	7.8	1	0	0	0	0	0	0	0	0	0	0	0	0	0	0	0	0	0	0	0	0	0	0	0	0	0	0	0	0	0	0	0	0	0	0	0	0	...	0	0

5 rows × 1559 columns

Figure 14.1: Loading data into the Colab notebook

5. Now, print the shape of the dataset, as shown in the following code snippet:

```
# Printing the shape of the data
print(adData.shape)
```

You should get the following output:

```
(3279, 1559)
```

From the shape, we can see that we have a large number of features, **1559**.

6. Find the summary of the numerical features of the raw data using the **.describe()** function in pandas, as shown in the following code snippet:

```
# Summarizing the statistics of the numerical raw data
adData.describe()
```

You should get the following output:

	4	5	6	7	8	9	10	11	12	13	14	15	16
count	3279.000000	3279.000000	3279.000000	3279.000000	3279.000000	3279.000000	3279.000000	3279.000000	3279.000000	3279.000000	3279.000000	3279.000000	3279.000000
mean	0.004270	0.011589	0.004575	0.003355	0.003965	0.011589	0.003355	0.004880	0.009149	0.004575	0.004880	0.003965	0.005489
std	0.065212	0.107042	0.067491	0.057831	0.062850	0.107042	0.057831	0.069694	0.095227	0.067491	0.069694	0.062850	0.073899
min	0.000000	0.000000	0.000000	0.000000	0.000000	0.000000	0.000000	0.000000	0.000000	0.000000	0.000000	0.000000	0.000000
25%	0.000000	0.000000	0.000000	0.000000	0.000000	0.000000	0.000000	0.000000	0.000000	0.000000	0.000000	0.000000	0.000000
50%	0.000000	0.000000	0.000000	0.000000	0.000000	0.000000	0.000000	0.000000	0.000000	0.000000	0.000000	0.000000	0.000000
75%	0.000000	0.000000	0.000000	0.000000	0.000000	0.000000	0.000000	0.000000	0.000000	0.000000	0.000000	0.000000	0.000000
max	1.000000	1.000000	1.000000	1.000000	1.000000	1.000000	1.000000	1.000000	1.000000	1.000000	1.000000	1.000000	1.000000

Figure 14.2: Loading data into the Colab notebook

As we saw from the shape of the data, the dataset has **3279** examples with **1559** variables. The variable set has both categorical and numerical variables. The summary statistics are only derived for numerical data.

7. Separate the dependent and independent variables from our dataset, as shown in the following code snippet:

```
# Separate the dependent and independent variables
# Preparing the X variables
X = adData.loc[:,0:1557]
print(X.shape)
# Preparing the Y variable
Y = adData[1558]
print(Y.shape)
```

You should get the following output:

```
(3279, 1558)
(3279, )
```

As seen earlier, there are **1559** features in the dataset. The first **1558** features are independent variables. They are separated from the initial **adData** data frame using the **.loc()** function and give the indexes of the corresponding features (**0** to **1557**). The independent variables are loaded into a new variable called **X**. The dependent variable, which is the label of the dataset, is loaded in variable **Y**. The shapes of the dependent and independent variables are also printed.

8. Print the first **15** examples of the independent variables:

```
# Printing the head of the independent variables
X.head(15)
```

You can print as many rows of the data by defining the number within the **head()** function. Here, we have printed out the first **15** rows of the data.

The output is as follows:

	0	1	2	3	4	5	6	7	8	9	10	11	12	13	14	15	16	17	18	19	20	21	22	23	24	25	26	27	28	29	30	31	32	33	34	35	36	37	38	39	...	1518	1519
0	125	125	1.0	1	0	0	0	0	0	0	0	0	0	0	0	0	0	0	0	0	0	0	0	0	0	0	0	0	0	0	0	0	0	0	0	0	0	0	0	0	...	0	0
1	57	468	8.2105	1	0	0	0	0	0	0	0	0	0	0	0	0	0	0	0	0	0	0	0	0	0	0	0	0	0	0	0	0	0	0	0	0	0	0	0	0	...	0	0
2	33	230	6.9696	1	0	0	0	0	0	0	0	0	0	0	0	0	0	0	0	0	0	0	0	0	0	0	0	0	0	0	0	0	0	0	0	0	0	0	0	0	...	0	0
3	60	468	7.8	1	0	0	0	0	0	0	0	0	0	0	0	0	0	0	0	0	0	0	0	0	0	0	0	0	0	0	0	0	0	0	0	0	0	0	0	0	...	0	0
4	60	468	7.8	1	0	0	0	0	0	0	0	0	0	0	0	0	0	0	0	0	0	0	0	0	0	0	0	0	0	0	0	0	0	0	0	0	0	0	0	0	...	0	0
5	60	468	7.8	1	0	0	0	0	0	0	0	0	0	0	0	0	0	0	0	0	0	0	0	0	0	0	0	0	0	0	0	0	0	0	0	0	0	0	0	0	...	0	0
6	59	460	7.7966	1	0	0	0	0	0	0	0	0	0	0	0	0	0	0	0	0	0	0	0	0	0	0	0	0	0	0	0	0	0	0	0	0	0	0	0	0	...	0	0
7	60	234	3.9	1	0	0	0	0	0	0	0	0	0	0	0	0	0	0	0	0	0	0	0	0	0	0	0	0	0	0	0	0	0	0	0	0	0	0	0	0	...	0	0
8	60	468	7.8	1	0	0	0	0	0	0	0	0	0	0	0	0	0	0	0	0	0	0	0	0	0	0	0	0	0	0	0	0	0	0	0	0	0	0	0	0	...	0	0
9	60	468	7.8	1	0	0	0	0	0	0	0	0	0	0	0	0	0	0	0	0	0	0	0	0	0	0	0	0	0	0	0	0	0	0	0	0	0	0	0	0	...	0	0
10	?	?	?		0	0	0	0	0	0	0	0	0	0	0	0	0	0	0	0	0	0	0	0	0	0	0	0	0	0	0	0	0	0	0	0	0	0	0	0	...	0	0
11	90	52	0.5777	1	0	0	0	0	0	0	0	0	0	0	0	0	0	0	0	0	0	0	0	0	0	0	0	0	0	0	0	0	0	0	0	0	0	0	0	0	...	0	0
12	90	60	0.6666	1	0	0	0	0	0	0	0	0	0	0	0	0	0	0	0	0	0	0	0	0	0	0	0	0	0	0	0	0	0	0	0	0	0	0	0	0	...	0	0

Figure 14.3: First 15 examples of independent variables

From the output, we can see that there are many missing values in the dataset, which are represented by **?**. For further analysis, we have to remove these special characters and then replace those cells with assumed values. One popular method of replacing special characters is to impute the mean of the respective feature. Let's adopt this strategy. However, before doing that, let's look at the data types for this dataset to adopt a suitable replacement strategy.

9. Print the data types of the dataset:

```
# Printing the data types
print(X.dtypes)
```

We should get the following output:

```
0       object
1       object
2       object
3       object
4        int64
         ...
1553     int64
1554     int64
1555     int64
1556     int64
1557     int64
Length: 1558, dtype: object
```

Figure 14.4: The data types in our dataset

From the output, we can see that the first four columns are of the object type, which refers to string data, and the others are integer data. When replacing the special characters in the data, we need to be cognizant of the data types.

10. Replace special characters with **NaN** values for the first four columns.

    Replace the special characters in the first four columns, which are of the object type, with **NaN** values. **NaN** is an abbreviation for "not a number." Replacing special characters with **NaN** values makes it easy to further impute data.

    This is achieved through the following code snippet:

```
"""
Replacing special characters in first 3 columns
which are of type object
"""
for i in range(0,3):
    X[i] = X[i].str.replace("?", 'nan')\
              .values.astype(float)
print(X.head(15))
```

To replace the first three columns, we loop through the columns using the **for()** loop and also using the **range()** function. Since the first three columns are of the **object** or **string** type, we use the **.str.replace()** function, which stands for "string replace". After replacing the special characters, **?**, of the data with **nan**, we convert the data type to **float** with the **.values.astype(float)** function, which is required for further processing. By printing the first 15 examples, we can see that all special characters have been replaced with **nan** or **NaN** values

You should get the following output:

	0	1	2	3	4	5	...	1552	1553	1554	1555	1556	1557
0	125.0	125.0	1.0000	1	0	0	...	0	0	0	0	0	0
1	57.0	468.0	8.2105	1	0	0	...	0	0	0	0	0	0
2	33.0	230.0	6.9696	1	0	0	...	0	0	0	0	0	0
3	60.0	468.0	7.8000	1	0	0	...	0	0	0	0	0	0
4	60.0	468.0	7.8000	1	0	0	...	0	0	0	0	0	0
5	60.0	468.0	7.8000	1	0	0	...	0	0	0	0	0	0
6	59.0	460.0	7.7966	1	0	0	...	0	0	0	0	0	0
7	60.0	234.0	3.9000	1	0	0	...	0	0	0	0	0	0
8	60.0	468.0	7.8000	1	0	0	...	0	0	0	0	0	0
9	60.0	468.0	7.8000	1	0	0	...	0	0	0	0	0	0
10	NaN	NaN	NaN	1	0	0	...	0	0	0	0	0	0
11	90.0	52.0	0.5777	1	0	0	...	0	0	0	0	0	0
12	90.0	60.0	0.6666	1	0	0	...	0	0	0	0	0	0
13	90.0	60.0	0.6666	1	0	0	...	0	0	0	0	0	0
14	33.0	230.0	6.9696	1	0	0	...	0	0	0	0	0	0

Figure 14.5: After replacing special characters with NaN

11. Now, replace special characters for the integer features.

As in *Step 9*, let's also replace the special characters from the features of the **int64** data type with the following code snippet:

```
"""
Replacing special characters in the remaining
columns which are of type integer
"""
for i in range(3,1557):
    X[i] = X[i].replace("?", 'NaN').values.astype(float)
```

> **NOTE**
>
> For the integer features, we do not have **.str** before the **.replace()** function, as these features are integer values and not string values.

12. Now, impute the mean of each column for the **NaN** values.

    Now that we have replaced special characters in the data with **NaN** values, we can use the **fillna()** function in pandas to replace the **NaN** values with the mean of the column. This is executed using the following code snippet:

```
import numpy as np

# Impute the 'NaN'  with mean of the values
for i in range(0,1557):
    X[i] = X[i].fillna(X[i].mean())
print(X.head(15))
```

    In the preceding code snippet, the **.mean()** function calculates the mean of each column and then replaces the **nan** values with the mean of the column.

    You should get the following output:

```
             0           1         2    3    4  ...  1553  1554  1555  1556  1557
0   125.000000  125.000000  1.000000  1.0  0.0  ...   0.0   0.0   0.0   0.0     0
1    57.000000  468.000000  8.210500  1.0  0.0  ...   0.0   0.0   0.0   0.0     0
2    33.000000  230.000000  6.969600  1.0  0.0  ...   0.0   0.0   0.0   0.0     0
3    60.000000  468.000000  7.800000  1.0  0.0  ...   0.0   0.0   0.0   0.0     0
4    60.000000  468.000000  7.800000  1.0  0.0  ...   0.0   0.0   0.0   0.0     0
5    60.000000  468.000000  7.800000  1.0  0.0  ...   0.0   0.0   0.0   0.0     0
6    59.000000  460.000000  7.796600  1.0  0.0  ...   0.0   0.0   0.0   0.0     0
7    60.000000  234.000000  3.900000  1.0  0.0  ...   0.0   0.0   0.0   0.0     0
8    60.000000  468.000000  7.800000  1.0  0.0  ...   0.0   0.0   0.0   0.0     0
9    60.000000  468.000000  7.800000  1.0  0.0  ...   0.0   0.0   0.0   0.0     0
10   64.021886  155.344828  3.911953  1.0  0.0  ...   0.0   0.0   0.0   0.0     0
11   90.000000   52.000000  0.577700  1.0  0.0  ...   0.0   0.0   0.0   0.0     0
12   90.000000   60.000000  0.666600  1.0  0.0  ...   0.0   0.0   0.0   0.0     0
13   90.000000   60.000000  0.666600  1.0  0.0  ...   0.0   0.0   0.0   0.0     0
14   33.000000  230.000000  6.969600  1.0  0.0  ...   0.0   0.0   0.0   0.0     0

[15 rows x 1558 columns]
```

Figure 14.6: Mean of the NaN columns

13. Scale the dataset using the **minmaxScaler()** function.

    As in *Chapter 3, Binary Classification*, scaling data is useful in the modeling step. Let's scale the dataset using the **minmaxScaler()** function as learned in *Chapter 3, Binary Classification*.

    This is shown in the following code snippet:

```
# Scaling the data sets
# Import library function
```

```
from sklearn import preprocessing

# Creating the scaling function
minmaxScaler = preprocessing.MinMaxScaler()

# Transforming with the scaler function
X_tran = pd.DataFrame(minmaxScaler.fit_transform(X))

# Printing the output
X_tran.head()
```

You should get the following output. Here, we have displayed the first 24 columns:

	0	1	2	3	4	5	6	7	8	9	10	11	12	13	14	15	16	17	18	19	20	21	22	23	24
0	0.194053	0.194053	0.016642	1.0	0.0	0.0	0.0	0.0	0.0	0.0	0.0	0.0	0.0	0.0	0.0	0.0	0.0	0.0	0.0	0.0	0.0	0.0	0.0	0.0	0.0
1	0.087637	0.730829	0.136820	1.0	0.0	0.0	0.0	0.0	0.0	0.0	0.0	0.0	0.0	0.0	0.0	0.0	0.0	0.0	0.0	0.0	0.0	0.0	0.0	0.0	0.0
2	0.050078	0.358372	0.116138	1.0	0.0	0.0	0.0	0.0	0.0	0.0	0.0	0.0	0.0	0.0	0.0	0.0	0.0	0.0	0.0	0.0	0.0	0.0	0.0	0.0	0.0
3	0.092332	0.730829	0.129978	1.0	0.0	0.0	0.0	0.0	0.0	0.0	0.0	0.0	0.0	0.0	0.0	0.0	0.0	0.0	0.0	0.0	0.0	0.0	0.0	0.0	0.0
4	0.092332	0.730829	0.129978	1.0	0.0	0.0	0.0	0.0	0.0	0.0	0.0	0.0	0.0	0.0	0.0	0.0	0.0	0.0	0.0	0.0	0.0	0.0	0.0	0.0	0.0

5 rows × 1558 columns

Figure 14.7: Scaling the dataset using the MinMaxScaler() function

> **NOTE**
>
> To access the source code for this specific section, please refer to https://packt.live/2Yi7Nym.
>
> You can also run this example online at https://packt.live/2Q6l9ZZ.

You have come to the end of the first exercise. In this exercise, we loaded the dataset, extracted summary statistics, cleaned the data, and also scaled the data. You can see that in the final output, all the raw values have been transformed into scaled values.

In the next section, let's try to augment this dataset with many more features so that this becomes a massive dataset and then fit a simple logistic regression model on this dataset as a benchmark model.

Let's first see how data can be augmented with an example.

CREATING A HIGH-DIMENSIONAL DATASET

In the earlier section, we worked with a dataset that has around **1,558** features. In order to demonstrate the challenges with high-dimensional datasets, let's create an extremely high dimensional dataset from the internet dataset that we already have.

This we will achieve by replicating the existing number of features multiple times so that the dataset becomes really large. To replicate the dataset, we will use a function called **np.tile()**, which copies a data frame multiple times across the axes we want. We will also calculate the time it takes for any activity using the **time()** function.

Let's look at both these functions in action with a toy example.

You begin by importing the necessary library functions:

```
import pandas as pd
import numpy as np
```

Then, to create a dummy data frame, we will use a small dataset with two rows and three columns for this example. We use the **pd.np.array()** function to create a data frame:

```
# Creating a simple data frame
df = pd.np.array([[1, 2, 3], [4, 5, 6]])
print(df.shape)
df
```

You should get the following output:

```
(2,3)
array([[1, 2, 3],
       [4, 5, 6]])
```

Figure 14.8: Array for the sample dummy data frame

Next, you replicate the dummy data frame and this replication of the columns is done using the **pd.np.tile()** function in the following code snippet:

```
# Replicating the data frame and noting the time
import time
# Starting a timing function
t0=time.time()
Newdf = pd.DataFrame(pd.np.tile(df, (1, 5)))
print(Newdf.shape)
```

```
print(Newdf)
# Finding the end time
print("Total time:", round(time.time()-t0, 3), "s")
```

You should get the following output:

```
(2, 15)
   0  1  2  3  4  5  6  7  8  9  10  11  12  13  14
0  1  2  3  1  2  3  1  2  3  1   2   3   1   2   3
1  4  5  6  4  5  6  4  5  6  4   5   6   4   5   6
Total time: 0.033 s
```

Figure 14.9: Replication of the data frame

As we can see in the snippet, the **pd.np.tile()** function accepts two sets of arguments. The first one is the data frame, **df**, that we want to replicate. The next argument, **(1,5)**, defines which axes we want to replicate. In this example, we define that the rows will remain as is because of the **1** argument, and the columns will be replicated **5** times with the **5** argument. We can see from the **shape()** function that the original data frame, which was of shape **(2,3)**, has been transformed into a data frame with a shape of **(2,15)**.

Calculating the total time is done using the **time** library. To start the timing, we invoke the **time.time()** function. In the example, we store the initial time in a variable called **t0** and then subtract this from the end time to find the total time it takes for the process. Thus we have augmented and added more data frames to our exiting internet ads dataset.

ACTIVITY 14.01: FITTING A LOGISTIC REGRESSION MODEL ON A HIGHDIMENSIONAL DATASET

You want to test the performance of your models when the dataset is large. To do this, you are artificially augmenting the internet ads dataset so that the dataset is 300 times bigger in dimension than the original dataset. You will be fitting a logistic regression model on this new dataset and then observe the results.

Hint: In this activity, we will use a notebook similar to *Exercise 14.01, Loading and Cleaning the Dataset*, and we will also be fitting a logistic regression model as done in *Chapter 3, Binary Classification*.

> **NOTE**
>
> We will be using the same ads dataset for this activity.
>
> The **`internet_ads`** dataset has been uploaded to our GitHub repository and can be accessed at https://packt.live/2sPaVF6.

The steps to complete this activity are as follows:

1. Open a new Colab notebook.
2. Implement all steps from *Exercise 14.01, Loading and Cleaning the Dataset*, until the normalization of data. Derive the transformed independent **`X_tran`** variable.
3. Create a high-dimensional dataset by replicating the columns 300 times using the **`pd.np.tile()`** function. Print the shape of the new dataset and observe the number of features in the new dataset.
4. Split the dataset into train and test sets.
5. Fit a logistic regression model on the new dataset and note the time it takes to fit the model. Note the color change for the indicator for RAM on your Colab notebook.

   Expected Output:

   You should get output similar to the following after fitting the logistic regression model on the new dataset:

```
Total training time: 23.86 s
```

Figure 14.10: Google Colab RAM utilization

6. Predict on the test set and print the classification report and confusion matrix.

   You should get the following output:

```
[[112  14]
 [ 18 840]]
              precision    recall  f1-score   support

         ad.       0.86      0.89      0.88       126
      nonad.       0.98      0.98      0.98       858

    accuracy                           0.97       984
   macro avg       0.92      0.93      0.93       984
weighted avg       0.97      0.97      0.97       984
```

Figure 14.11: Confusion matrix and the classification report results

> **NOTE**
>
> The solution to the activity can be found here: https://packt.live/2GbJloz.

In this activity, you will have created a high-dimensional dataset by replicating the columns of the existing database and identified that the resource utilization is quite high with this high dimensional dataset. The resource utilization indicator changed its color to orange because of the large dimensions. The longer time, **23.86** seconds, taken for modeling was also noticed on this dataset. You will have also predicted on the test set to get an accuracy level of around **97%** using the logistic regression model.

First, you need to know why the color of RAM utilization on Colab changed to orange. Because of the huge dataset we created by replication, Colab had to use access RAM, due to which the color changed to orange.

But, out of curiosity, what do you think the impact will be on the RAM utilization if you increased the replication from 300 to 500? Let's have a look at the following example.

> **NOTE**
>
> You don't need to perform this on your Colab notebook.

We begin by defining the path of the dataset for the GitHub repository to our "ads" dataset:

```
# Defining the file name from GitHub
filename = 'https://raw.githubusercontent.com'\
           '/PacktWorkshops/The-Data-Science-Workshop'\
           '/master/Chapter14/Dataset/ad.data'
```

Next, we simply load the data using pandas:

```
# import pandas as pd
# Loading the data using pandas
adData = pd.read_csv(filename,sep=",",header = None,\
                     error_bad_lines=False)
```

Create a high-dimensional dataset with a scaling factor of **500**:

```
# Creating a high dimension dataset
X_hd = pd.DataFrame(pd.np.tile(adData, (1, 500)))
```

You will see the following output:

Figure 14.12: Colab crashing

From the output, you can see that the session crashes because all the RAM provided by Colab has been used. The session will restart, and you will lose all your variables. Hence, it is always good to be mindful of the resources you are provided with, along with the dataset. As a data scientist, if you feel that a dataset is huge with many features but the resources to process that dataset are limited, you need to get in touch with the organization and get the required resources or build an appropriate strategy to address these high-dimensional datasets.

STRATEGIES FOR ADDRESSING HIGH-DIMENSIONAL DATASETS

In *Activity 14.01, Fitting a Logistic Regression Model on a High-Dimensional Dataset*, we witnessed the challenges of high-dimensional datasets. We saw how the resources were challenged when the replication factor was 300. You also saw that the notebook crashes when the replication factor is increased to 500. When the replication factor was 500, the number of features was around 750,000. In our case, our resources would fail to scale up even before we hit the 1 million mark on the number of features. Some modern-day datasets sometimes have hundreds of millions, or in many cases billions, of features. Imagine the kind of resources and time it would take to get any actionable insights from the dataset.

Luckily, we have many robust methods for addressing high-dimensional datasets. Many of these techniques are very effective and have helped to address the challenges raised by huge datasets.

Let's look at some of the techniques for dealing with high-dimensional datasets. In *Figure 14.14*, you can see the strategies we will be coming across in this chapter to deal with such datasets:

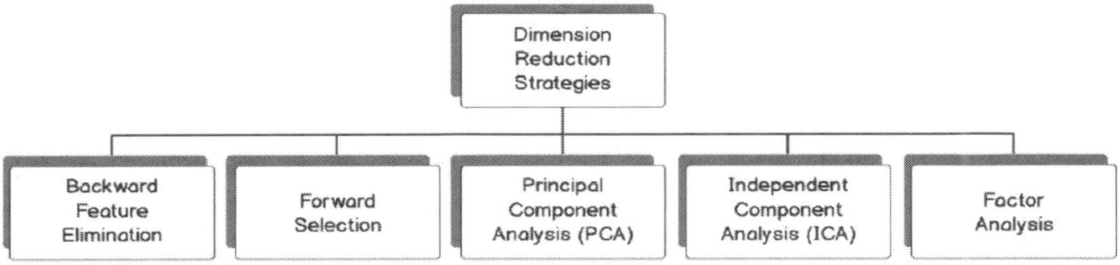

Figure 14.13: Strategies to address high dimensional datasets

BACKWARD FEATURE ELIMINATION (RECURSIVE FEATURE ELIMINATION)

The mechanism behind the backward feature elimination algorithm is the recursive elimination of features and building a model on those features that remain after all the elimination.

Let's look under the hood of this algorithm step by step:

1. Initially, at a given iteration, the selected classification algorithm is first trained on all the `n` features available. For example, let's take the case of the original dataset we had, which had **`1,558`** features. The algorithm starts off with all the **`1,558`** features in the first iteration.
2. In the next step, we remove one feature at a time and train a model with the remaining **`n-1`** features. This process is repeated `n` times. For example, we first remove feature 1 and then fit a model using all the remaining 1,557 variables. In the next iteration, we use feature **`1`** and instead, we eliminate feature **`2`** and then fit the model. This process is repeated `n` times (**`1,558`**) times.
3. For each of the models fitted, the performance of the model (using measures such as accuracy) is calculated.
4. The feature whose replacement has resulted in the smallest change in performance is removed permanently and *Step 2* is repeated with **`n-1`** features.
5. The process is then repeated with **`n-2`** features and so on.

6. The algorithm keeps on eliminating features until the threshold number of features we require is reached.

Let's take a look at the backward feature elimination algorithm in action for the augmented ads dataset in the next exercise.

EXERCISE 14.02: DIMENSIONALITY REDUCTION USING BACKWARD FEATURE ELIMINATION

In this exercise, we will fit a logistic regression model after eliminating features using the backward elimination technique to find the accuracy of the model. We will be using the same ads dataset as before, and we will be enhancing it with additional features for this exercise.

The following steps will help you complete this exercise:

1. Open a new Colab notebook file.
2. Implement all the initial steps similar to *Exercise 14.01*, *Loading and Cleaning the Dataset*, until scaling the dataset using the **`minmaxscaler()`** function:

```
filename = 'https://raw.githubusercontent.com'\
           '/PacktWorkshops/The-Data-Science-Workshop'\
           '/master/Chapter14/Dataset/ad.data'

import pandas as pd
adData = pd.read_csv(filename,sep=",",header = None,\
                     error_bad_lines=False)

X = adData.loc[:,0:1557]
Y = adData[1558]

import numpy as np
for i in range(0,3):
    X[i] = X[i].str.replace("?", 'NaN').values.astype(float)
for i in range(3,1557):
    X[i] = X[i].replace("?", 'NaN').values.astype(float)
for i in range(0,1557):
    X[i] = X[i].fillna(X[i].mean())

from sklearn import preprocessing
minmaxScaler = preprocessing.MinMaxScaler()
X_tran = pd.DataFrame(minmaxScaler.fit_transform(X))
```

3. Next, create a high-dimensional dataset. We'll augment the dataset artificially by a factor of **2**. The process of backward feature elimination is a very compute-intensive process, and using higher dimensions will involve a longer processing time. This is why the augmenting factor has been kept at **2**. This is implemented using the following code snippet:

```
# Creating a high dimension data set
X_hd = pd.DataFrame(pd.np.tile(X_tran, (1, 2)))
print(X_hd.shape)
```

   You should get the following output:

```
(3279, 3116)
```

4. Define the backward elimination model. Backward elimination works by providing two arguments to the **RFE()** function, which is the model we want to try (logistic regression in our case) and the number of features we want the dataset to be reduced to. This is implemented as follows:

```
from sklearn.linear_model import LogisticRegression
from sklearn.feature_selection import RFE

# Defining the Classification function
backModel = LogisticRegression()

"""
Reducing dimensionality to 250 features for the
backward elimination model
"""
rfe = RFE(backModel, 250)
```

   In this implementation, the number of features that we have given, **250**, is identified through trial and error. The process is to first assume an arbitrary number of features and then, based on the final metrics, arrive at the most optimum number of features for the model. In this implementation, our first assumption of **250** implies that we want the backward elimination model to start eliminating features until we get the best **250** features.

5. Fit the backward elimination method to identify the best **250** features.

   We are now ready to fit the backward elimination method on the higher-dimensional dataset. We will also note the time it takes for backward elimination to work. This is implemented using the following code snippet:

```
# Fitting the rfe for selecting the top 250 features

import time
t0 = time.time()
rfe = rfe.fit(X_hd, Y)
t1 = time.time()
print("Backward Elimination time:", \
      round(t1-t0, 3), "s")
```

   Fitting the backward elimination method is done using the **.fit()** function. We give the independent and dependent training sets.

> **NOTE**
>
> The backward elimination method is a compute-intensive process, and therefore this process will take a lot of time to execute. The larger the number of features, the longer it will take.

   The time for backward elimination is at the end of the notifications:

```
/usr/local/lib/python3.6/dist-packages/sklearn/linear_model/logistic.py:432:
  FutureWarning)
Backward Elimination time: 230.357 s
/usr/local/lib/python3.6/dist-packages/sklearn/linear_model/logistic.py:432:
  FutureWarning)
/usr/local/lib/python3.6/dist-packages/sklearn/linear_model/logistic.py:432:
  FutureWarning)
/usr/local/lib/python3.6/dist-packages/sklearn/linear_model/logistic.py:432:
  FutureWarning)
/usr/local/lib/python3.6/dist-packages/sklearn/linear_model/logistic.py:432:
  FutureWarning)
/usr/local/lib/python3.6/dist-packages/sklearn/linear_model/logistic.py:432:
  FutureWarning)
/usr/local/lib/python3.6/dist-packages/sklearn/linear_model/logistic.py:432:
  FutureWarning)
/usr/local/lib/python3.6/dist-packages/sklearn/linear_model/logistic.py:432:
```

Figure 14.14: The time taken for the backward elimination process

You can see that the backward elimination process to find the best **250** features has taken **230.35** seconds to implement.

6. Display the features identified using the backward elimination method. We can display the **250** features that were identified using the backward elimination process using the **get_support()** function. This is implemented as follows:

```
# Getting the indexes of the features used
rfe.get_support(indices = True)
```

You should get the following output:

```
array([   0,    1,   64,   75,   95,  104,  106,  120,  139,  145,  167,
        172,  175,  180,  183,  243,  246,  251,  265,  269,  276,  278,
        307,  317,  346,  351,  357,  359,  370,  372,  379,  381,  398,
        417,  418,  426,  441,  450,  455,  456,  457,  478,  499,  506,
        508,  511,  540,  545,  549,  562,  638,  648,  653,  658,  663,
        679,  680,  686,  723,  730,  766,  803,  807,  818,  819,  849,
        860,  888,  903,  948,  950,  968,  983, 1009, 1011, 1018, 1021,
       1022, 1035, 1043, 1058, 1060, 1081, 1086, 1087, 1114, 1116, 1167,
       1179, 1180, 1228, 1229, 1243, 1264, 1267, 1271, 1278, 1286, 1314,
       1326, 1327, 1341, 1351, 1362, 1364, 1367, 1371, 1380, 1388, 1399,
       1403, 1413, 1416, 1423, 1445, 1455, 1458, 1462, 1465, 1483, 1484,
       1507, 1510, 1527, 1531, 1537, 1539, 1552, 1555, 1558, 1559, 1561,
       1622, 1649, 1652, 1653, 1678, 1691, 1725, 1733, 1741, 1764, 1804,
       1809, 1822, 1823, 1827, 1836, 1865, 1875, 1894, 1904, 1909, 1915,
       1928, 1930, 1939, 1944, 1956, 1975, 1976, 1984, 2013, 2014, 2015,
       2036, 2057, 2064, 2066, 2103, 2107, 2114, 2120, 2211, 2221, 2237,
       2244, 2281, 2308, 2324, 2361, 2365, 2376, 2377, 2407, 2418, 2446,
       2461, 2463, 2472, 2493, 2508, 2526, 2541, 2556, 2567, 2576, 2579,
       2580, 2593, 2601, 2618, 2636, 2639, 2644, 2645, 2658, 2667, 2672,
       2674, 2725, 2737, 2738, 2786, 2787, 2801, 2805, 2820, 2829, 2834,
       2872, 2884, 2885, 2899, 2909, 2922, 2925, 2929, 2938, 2940, 2946,
       2957, 2971, 2974, 2992, 2999, 3003, 3013, 3016, 3020, 3023, 3041,
       3042, 3051, 3085, 3089, 3090, 3091, 3095, 3097])
```

Figure 14.15: The identified features being displayed

These are the best **250** features that were finally selected using the backward elimination process from the entire dataset.

7. Now, split the dataset into training and testing sets for modeling:

```
from sklearn.model_selection import train_test_split
# Splitting the data into train and test sets
X_train, X_test, y_train, y_test = train_test_split\
                                   (X_hd, Y, test_size=0.3,\
                                    random_state=123)
```

```
print('Training set shape',X_train.shape)
print('Test set shape',X_test.shape)
```

You should get the following output:

```
Training set shape (2295, 3116)
Test set shape (984, 3116)
```

From the output, you see the shapes of both the training set and testing sets.

8. Transform the train and test sets. In *step 5*, we identified the top **250** features through backward elimination. Now we need to reduce the train and test sets to those top **250** features. This is done using the **.transform()** function. This is implemented using the following code snippet:

```
# Transforming both train and test sets
X_train_tran = rfe.transform(X_train)
X_test_tran = rfe.transform(X_test)
print("Training set shape",X_train_tran.shape)
print("Test set shape",X_test_tran.shape)
```

You should get the following output:

```
Training set shape (2295, 250)
Test set shape (984, 250)
```

We can see that both the training set and test sets have been reduced to the **250** best features.

9. Fit a logistic regression model on the training set and note the time:

```
# Fitting the logistic regression model
import time
# Defining the LogisticRegression function
RfeModel = LogisticRegression()
# Starting a timing function
t0=time.time()
# Fitting the model
RfeModel.fit(X_train_tran, y_train)
# Finding the end time
print("Total training time:", \
      round(time.time()-t0, 3), "s")
```

You should get the following output:

```
Total training time: 0.016 s
```

As expected, the total time it takes to fit a model on a reduced set of features is much lower than the time it took for the larger dataset in *Activity 14.01, Fitting a Logistic Regression Model on a HighDimensional Dataset*, which was **23.86** seconds. This is a great improvement.

10. Now, predict on the test set and print the accuracy metrics, as shown in the following code snippet:

```
# Predicting on the test set and getting the accuracy
pred = RfeModel.predict(X_test_tran)

print('Accuracy of Logistic regression model after '\
      'backward elimination: {:.2f}'\
      .format(RfeModel.score(X_test_tran, y_test)))
```

You should get the following output:

```
Accuracy of Logistic regression model after backward elimination: 0.98
```

Figure 14.16: The achieved accuracy of the logistic regression model

You can see that the accuracy measure for this model has improved compared to the one we got for the model with higher dimensionality, which was **0.97** in *Activity 14.01, Fitting a Logistic Regression Model on a HighDimensional Dataset*. This increase could be attributed to the identification of non-correlated features from the complete feature set, which could have boosted the performance of the model.

11. Print the confusion matrix:

```
from sklearn.metrics import confusion_matrix
confusionMatrix = confusion_matrix(y_test, pred)
print(confusionMatrix)
```

You should get the following output:

```
[[108  18]
 [  1 857]]
```

Figure 14.17: Confusion matrix

12. Printing the classification report:

```
from sklearn.metrics import classification_report
# Getting the Classification_report
print(classification_report(y_test, pred))
```

You should get the following output:

```
              precision    recall  f1-score   support

         ad.       0.99      0.86      0.92       126
      nonad.       0.98      1.00      0.99       858

    accuracy                           0.98       984
   macro avg       0.99      0.93      0.95       984
weighted avg       0.98      0.98      0.98       984
```

Figure 14.18: Classification matrix

> **NOTE**
>
> To access the source code for this specific section, please refer to https://packt.live/31ca5k6.
>
> You can also run this example online at https://packt.live/329yJkF.

As we can see from the backward elimination process, we were able to get an improved accuracy of **98%** with **250** features, compared to the model in *Activity 14.01, Fitting a Logistic Regression Model on a HighDimensional Dataset,* where an artificially enhanced dataset was used and got an accuracy of **97%**.

However, it should be noted that dimensionality reduction techniques should not be viewed as a method to improve the performance of any model. Dimensionality reduction techniques have to be viewed from the perspective of enabling us to fit a model on datasets with large numbers of features. When dimensions increase, fitting the model becomes intractable. This can be observed if the scaling factor used in *Activity 14.01, Fitting a Logistic Regression Model on a HighDimensional Dataset,* was to be increased from **300** to **500**. In such cases, fitting a model wouldn't happen with the current set of resources.

Dimensionality reduction aids in such scenarios by reducing the number of features, thereby enabling the fitting of a model on reduced dimensions without a large degradation of performance, and can sometimes lead to an improvement in results. However, it should also be noted that methods such as backward elimination are compute-intensive processes. You would have observed this phenomenon as to the time it takes in identifying the top 250 features when the scaling factor was just 2. With much higher scaling factors, it will take far more time and resources to identify the top 250 features.

Having seen the backward elimination method, let's now look at the next technique, which is forward feature selection.

FORWARD FEATURE SELECTION

Forward feature selection works in the reverse order as backward elimination. In this process, we start off with an initial feature, and features are added one by one until no improvement in performance is achieved. The detailed process is as follows:

1. Start model building with one feature.
2. Iterate the model building process *n* times, each time selecting one feature at a time. The feature that gives the highest improvement in performance is selected.
3. Once the first feature is selected, it is the time to select the second feature. The process for selecting the second feature proceeds exactly the same as *step 2*. The remaining *n-1* features are iterated along with the first feature and the performance on the model is observed. The feature that produces the biggest improvement in model performance is selected as the second feature.
4. The iteration of features will continue until a threshold number of features we have determined is extracted.
5. The set of final features selected will be the ones that give the maximum model performance.

Let's now implement this algorithm in the next exercise.

EXERCISE 14.03: DIMENSIONALITY REDUCTION USING FORWARD FEATURE SELECTION

In this exercise, we will fit a logistic regression model by selecting the optimum features through forward feature selection and observing the performance of the model. We will be using the same ads dataset as before, and we will be enhancing it with additional features for this exercise.

The following steps will help you complete this exercise:

1. Open a new Colab notebook.
2. Implement all the initial steps similar to *Exercise 14.01*, *Loading and Cleaning the Dataset*, up until scaling the dataset using **`MinMaxScaler()`**:

```
filename = 'https://raw.githubusercontent.com'\
           '/PacktWorkshops/The-Data-Science-Workshop'\
           '/master/Chapter14/Dataset/ad.data'

import pandas as pd
adData = pd.read_csv(filename,sep=",",header = None,\
                     error_bad_lines=False)

X = adData.loc[:,0:1557]
Y = adData[1558]

import numpy as np
for i in range(0,3):
    X[i] = X[i].str.replace("?", 'NaN')\
              .values.astype(float)
for i in range(3,1557):
    X[i] = X[i].replace("?", 'NaN').values.astype(float)
for i in range(0,1557):
    X[i] = X[i].fillna(X[i].mean())

from sklearn import preprocessing
minmaxScaler = preprocessing.MinMaxScaler()
X_tran = pd.DataFrame(minmaxScaler.fit_transform(X))
```

3. Create a high-dimensional dataset. Now, augment the dataset artificially to a factor of **50**. Augmenting the dataset to higher factors will result in the notebook crashing because of lack of memory. This is implemented using the following code snippet:

```
# Creating a high dimension dataset
X_hd = pd.DataFrame(pd.np.tile(X_tran, (1, 50)))
print(X_hd.shape)
```

You should get the following output:

```
(3279, 77900)
```

4. Split the high dimensional dataset into training and testing sets:

```
from sklearn.model_selection import train_test_split
# Splitting the data into train and test sets
X_train, X_test, y_train, y_test = train_test_split\
                                   (X_hd, Y, test_size=0.3, \
                                    random_state=123)
```

5. Now we define the threshold features. Once the train and test sets are created, the next step is to import the feature selection function, **SelectKBest**. The argument we give to this function is the number of features we want. The features are selected through experimentation and, as a first step, we assume a threshold value. In this example, we assume a threshold value of **250**. This is implemented using the following code snippet:

```
from sklearn.feature_selection import SelectKBest
# feature extraction
feats = SelectKBest(k=250)
```

6. Iterate and get the best set of threshold features. Based on the threshold set of features we defined, we have to fit the training set and get the best set of threshold features. Fitting on the training set is done using the **.fit()** function. We also note the time it takes to find the best set of features. This is executed using the following code snippet:

```
# Fitting the features for training set
import time

t0 = time.time()
fit = feats.fit(X_train, y_train)
```

```
t1 = time.time()
print("Forward selection fitting time:", \
      round(t1-t0, 3), "s")
```

You should get something similar to the following output:

```
Forward selection fitting time: 2.682 s
```

We can see that the forward selection method has taken around **2.68** seconds, which is much lower than the backward selection method.

7. Create new training and test sets. Once we have identified the best set of features, we have to modify our training and test sets so that they have only those selected features. This is accomplished using the **.transform()** function:

```
# Creating new training set and test sets
features_train = fit.transform(X_train)
features_test = fit.transform(X_test)
```

8. Let's verify the shapes of the train and test sets before transformation and after transformation:

```
"""
Printing the shape of training and test sets
before transformation
"""
print('Train shape before transformation',\
      X_train.shape)
print('Test shape before transformation',\
      X_test.shape)

"""
Printing the shape of training and test sets
after transformation
"""
print('Train shape after transformation',\
      features_train.shape)
print('Test shape after transformation',\
      features_test.shape)
```

You should get the following output:

```
Train shape before transformation (2295, 77900)
Test shape before transformation (984, 77900)
Train shape after transformation (2295, 250)
Test shape after transformation (984, 250)
```

Figure 14.19: Shape of the training and testing datasets

You can see that both the training and test sets are reduced to **`250`** features each.

9. Let's now fit a logistic regression model on the transformed dataset and note the time it takes to fit the model:

```
# Fitting a Logistic Regression Model
from sklearn.linear_model import LogisticRegression

import time
t0 = time.time()
forwardModel = LogisticRegression()
forwardModel.fit(features_train, y_train)
t1 = time.time()
```

10. Print the total time:

```
print("Total training time:", round(t1-t0, 3), "s")
```

You should get the following output:

```
Total training time: 0.035 s
```

You can see that the training time is much less than the model that was fit in *Activity 14.01, Fitting a Logistic Regression Model on a HighDimensional Dataset*, which was **`23.86`** seconds. This shorter time is attributed to the number of features in the forward selection model.

11. Now, perform predictions on the test set and print the accuracy metrics:

```
# Predicting with the forward model

pred = forwardModel.predict(features_test)

print('Accuracy of Logistic regression'\
      ' model prediction on test set: {:.2f}'
      .format(forwardModel.score(features_test, y_test)))
```

You should get the following output:

```
Accuracy of Logistic regression model prediction on test set: 0.94
```

12. Print the confusion matrix:

```
from sklearn.metrics import confusion_matrix
confusionMatrix = confusion_matrix(y_test, pred)
print(confusionMatrix)
```

You should get something similar to the following output:

```
[[ 77  49]
 [ 13 845]]
```

Figure 14.20: Resulting confusion matrix

13. Print the classification report:

```
from sklearn.metrics import classification_report
# Getting the Classification_report
print(classification_report(y_test, pred))
```

You should get something similar to the following output:

```
              precision    recall  f1-score   support

         ad.       0.86      0.61      0.71       126
      nonad.       0.95      0.98      0.96       858

    accuracy                           0.94       984
   macro avg       0.90      0.80      0.84       984
weighted avg       0.93      0.94      0.93       984
```

Figure 14.21: Resulting classification report

NOTE

To access the source code for this specific section, please refer to https://packt.live/2YhQE7X.

This section does not currently have an online interactive example, but can be run as usual on Google Colab.

As we can see from the forward selection process, we were able to get an accuracy score of **94%** with **250** features. This score is lower than the one that was achieved with the backward elimination method (**98%**) and also the benchmark model (**97%**) built in *Activity 14.01*, *Fitting a Logistic Regression Model on a HighDimensional Dataset*. However, the time taken to find the best features (2.68 seconds) was substantially less than the backward elimination method (230.35 seconds).

In the next section, we will be looking at Principal Component Analysis (PCA).

PRINCIPAL COMPONENT ANALYSIS (PCA)

PCA is a very effective dimensionality reduction technique that achieves dimensionality reduction without compromising on the information content of the data. The basic idea behind PCA is to first identify correlations among different variables within the dataset. Once correlations are identified, the algorithm decides to eliminate the variables in such a way that the variability of the data is maintained. In other words, PCA aims to find uncorrelated sources of data.

Implementing PCA on raw variables results in transforming them into a completely new set of variables called principal components. Each of these components represents variability in data along an axes that are orthogonal to each other. This means that the first axis is fit in the direction where the maximum variability of data is present. After this, the second axis is selected in such a way that the axis is orthogonal (perpendicular) to the first selected axis and also covers the next highest variability.

Let's look at the idea of PCA with an example.

We will create a sample dataset with 2 variables and 100 random data points in each variable. Random data points are created using the **rand()** function. This is implemented in the following code:

```
import numpy as np
# Setting the seed for reproducibility
seed = np.random.RandomState(123)
# Generating an array of random numbers
X = seed.rand(100,2)
# Printing the shape of the dataset
X.shape
```

The resulting output is: **(100, 2)**.

> **NOTE**
>
> A random state is defined using the **RandomState(123)** function. This is defined to ensure that anyone who reproduces this example gets the same output.

Let's visualize this data using **matplotlib**:

```
import matplotlib.pyplot as plt
%matplotlib inline

plt.scatter(X[:, 0], X[:, 1])
plt.axis('equal')
```

You should get the following output:

```
(-0.04635361265714105,
 1.0325632864350174,
 -0.003996887112708292,
 1.0429468329457663)
```

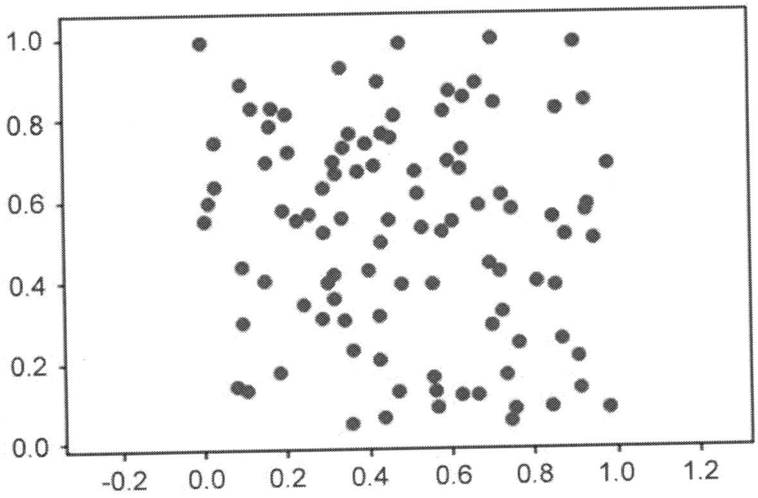

Figure 14.22: Visualization of the data

In the graph, we can see that the data is evenly spread out.

Let's now find the principal components for this dataset. We will reduce this two-dimensional dataset into a one-dimensional dataset. In other words, we will reduce the original dataset into one of its principal components.

This is implemented in code as follows:

```
from sklearn.decomposition import PCA

# Defining one component
pca = PCA(n_components=1)

# Fitting the PCA function
pca.fit(X)

# Getting the new dataset
X_pca = pca.transform(X)

# Printing the shapes
print("Original data set:    ", X.shape)
print("Data set after transformation:", X_pca.shape)
```

You should get the following output:

```
original shape: (100, 2)
transformed shape: (100, 1)
```

As we can see in the code, we first define the number of components using the **`'n_components' = 1`** argument. After this, the PCA algorithm is fit on the input dataset. After fitting on the input data, the initial dataset is transformed into a new dataset with only one variable, which is its principal component.

The algorithm transforms the original dataset into its first principal component by using an axis where the data has the largest variability.

To visualize this concept, let's reverse the transformation of the **`X_pca`** dataset to its original form and then visualize this data along with the original data. To reverse the transformation, we use the **`.inverse_transform()`** function:

```
# Reversing the transformation and plotting
X_reverse = pca.inverse_transform(X_pca)

# Plotting the original data
plt.scatter(X[:, 0], X[:, 1], alpha=0.1)

# Plotting the reversed data
plt.scatter(X_reverse[:, 0], X_reverse[:, 1], alpha=0.9)

plt.axis('equal');
```

You should get the following output:

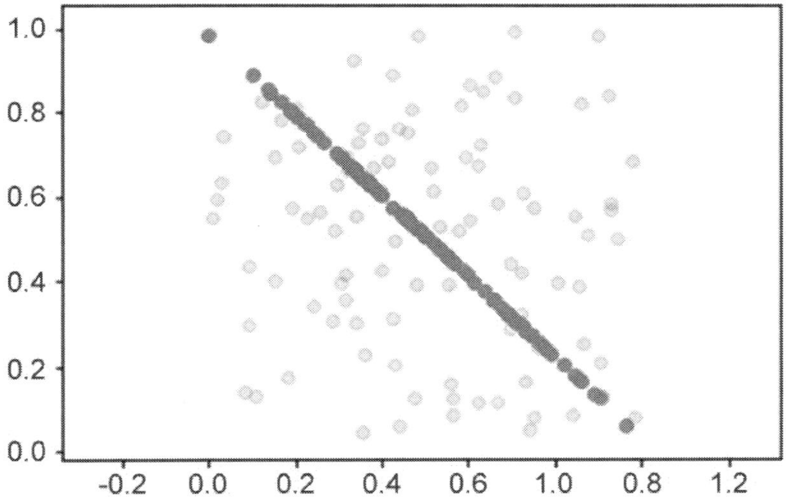

Figure 14.23: Plot with reverse transformation

As we can see in the plot, the data points in orange represent an axis with the highest variability. All the data points were projected to that axis to generate the first principal component.

The data points that are generated when transforming into various principal components will be very different from the original data points before transformation. Each principal component will be in an axis that is orthogonal (perpendicular) to the other principal component. If a second principal component was generated for the preceding example, the second principal component would be along an axis indicated by the blue arrow in the graph. The way we pick the number of principal components for model building is by selecting the number of components that explains a certain threshold of variability.

For example, if there were originally 1,000 features and we reduced it to 100 principal components, and then we find that out of the 100 principal components the first 75 components explain 90% of the variability of data, we would pick those 75 components to build the model. This process is called picking principal components with the percentage of variance explained.

Let's now see how to use PCA as a tool for dimensionality reduction in our use case.

EXERCISE 14.04: DIMENSIONALITY REDUCTION USING PCA

In this exercise, we will fit a logistic regression model by selecting the principal components that explain the maximum variability of the data. We will also observe the performance of the feature selection and model building process. We will be using the same ads dataset as before, and we will be enhancing it with additional features for this exercise.

The following steps will help you complete this exercise:

1. Open a new Colab notebook file.
2. Implement the initial steps from *Exercise 14.01, Loading and Cleaning the Dataset*, up until scaling the dataset using the **minmaxscaler()** function:

```
filename = 'https://raw.githubusercontent.com'\
           '/PacktWorkshops/The-Data-Science-Workshop'\
           '/master/Chapter14/Dataset/ad.data'

import pandas as pd
adData = pd.read_csv(filename,sep=",",header = None,\
                     error_bad_lines=False)
```

```
X = adData.loc[:,0:1557]
Y = adData[1558]

import numpy as np
for i in range(0,3):
    X[i] = X[i].str.replace("?", 'NaN').values.astype(float)
for i in range(3,1557):
    X[i] = X[i].replace("?", 'NaN').values.astype(float)
for i in range(0,1557):
    X[i] = X[i].fillna(X[i].mean())

from sklearn import preprocessing
minmaxScaler = preprocessing.MinMaxScaler()
X_tran = pd.DataFrame(minmaxScaler.fit_transform(X))
```

3. Create a high-dimensional dataset. Let's now augment the dataset artificially to a factor of 50. Augmenting the dataset to higher factors will result in the notebook crashing because of a lack of memory. This is implemented using the following code snippet:

```
# Creating a high dimension data set
X_hd = pd.DataFrame(pd.np.tile(X_tran, (1, 50)))

print(X_hd.shape)
```

You should get the following output

```
(3279, 77900)
```

4. Let's split the high-dimensional dataset to training and test sets:

```
from sklearn.model_selection import train_test_split
# Splitting the data into train and test sets
X_train, X_test, y_train, y_test = train_test_split\
                                   (X_hd, Y, test_size=0.3, \
                                    random_state=123)
```

5. Let's now fit the PCA function on the training set. This is done using the **.fit()** function, as shown in the following snippet. We will also note the time it takes to fit the PCA model on the dataset:

```
from sklearn.decomposition import PCA
import time
t0 = time.time()
pca = PCA().fit(X_train)
t1 = time.time()
print("PCA fitting time:", round(t1-t0, 3), "s")
```

You should get the following output:

```
PCS fitting time: 179.545 s
```

We can see that the time taken to fit the PCA function on the dataset is less than the backward elimination model (230.35 seconds) and higher than the forward selection method (2.682 seconds).

6. We will now determine the number of principal components by plotting the cumulative variance explained by all the principal components. The variance explained is determined by the **pca.explained_variance_ratio_** method. This is plotted in **matplotlib** using the following code snippet:

```
%matplotlib inline
import numpy as np
import matplotlib.pyplot as plt

plt.plot(np.cumsum(pca.explained_variance_ratio_))
plt.xlabel('Number of Principal Components')
plt.ylabel('Cumulative explained variance');
```

In the code, the **np.cumsum()** function is used to get the cumulative variance of each principal component.

You will get the following plot as output:

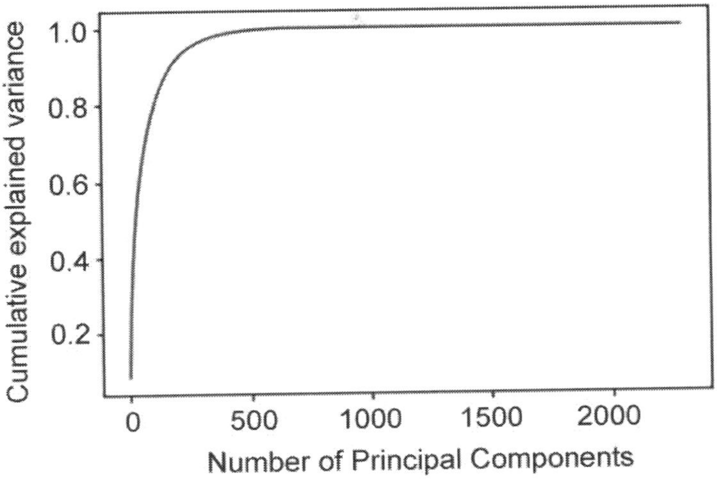

Figure 14.24: The variance graph

From the plot, we can see that the first **250** principal components explain more than **90%** of the variance. Based on this graph, we can decide how many principal components we want to have depending on the variability it explains. Let's select **250** components for fitting our model.

7. Now that we have identified that **250** components explain a lot of the variability, let's refit the training set for **250** components. This is described in the following code snippet:

```
# Defining PCA with 250 components
pca = PCA(n_components=250)

# Fitting PCA on the training set
pca.fit(X_train)
```

8. We now transform the training and test sets with the 200 principal components:

```
# Transforming training set and test set

X_pca = pca.transform(X_train)
X_test_pca = pca.transform(X_test)
```

9. Let's verify the shapes of the train and test sets before transformation and after transformation:

```
"""
Printing the shape of train and test sets before
and after transformation
"""
print("original shape of Training set:    ", \
      X_train.shape)
print("original shape of Test set:    ", \
      X_test.shape)
print("Transformed shape of training set:", \
      X_pca.shape)
print("Transformed shape of test set:", \
      X_test_pca.shape)
```

You should get the following output:

```
original shape of Training set:    (2295, 77900)
original shape of Test set:    (984, 77900)
Transformed shape of training set: (2295, 250)
Transformed shape of test set: (984, 250)
```

Figure 14.25: Transformed and the original training and testing sets

You can see that both the training and test sets are reduced to **250** features each.

10. Let's now fit the logistic regression model on the transformed dataset and note the time it takes to fit the model:

```
# Fitting a Logistic Regression Model
from sklearn.linear_model import LogisticRegression
import time
```

```
pcaModel = LogisticRegression()
t0 = time.time()
pcaModel.fit(X_pca, y_train)
t1 = time.time()
```

11. Print the total time:

```
print("Total training time:", round(t1-t0, 3), "s")
```

You should get the following output:

```
Total training time: 0.293 s
```

You can see that the training time is much lower than the model that was fit in *Activity 14.01, Fitting a Logistic Regression Model on a HighDimensional Dataset*, which was 23.86 seconds. The shorter time is attributed to the smaller number of features, **250**, selected in PCA.

12. Now, predict on the test set and print the accuracy metrics:

```
# Predicting with the pca model
pred = pcaModel.predict(X_test_pca)

print('Accuracy of Logistic regression model '\
      'prediction on test set: {:.2f}'\
      .format(pcaModel.score(X_test_pca, y_test)))
```

You should get the following output:

```
Accuracy of Logistic regression model prediction on test set: 0.98
```

Figure 14.26: Accuracy of the logistic regression model

You can see that the accuracy level is better than the benchmark model with all the features (**97%**) and the forward selection model (**94%**).

13. Print the confusion matrix:

```
from sklearn.metrics import confusion_matrix
confusionMatrix = confusion_matrix(y_test, pred)
print(confusionMatrix)
```

You should get the following output:

```
[[114  12]
 [  9 849]]
```

Figure 14.27: Resulting confusion matrix

14. Print the classification report:

```
from sklearn.metrics import classification_report
# Getting the Classification_report
print(classification_report(y_test, pred))
```

You should get the following output:

```
              precision    recall  f1-score   support

         ad.       0.93      0.90      0.92       126
      nonad.       0.99      0.99      0.99       858

    accuracy                           0.98       984
   macro avg       0.96      0.95      0.95       984
weighted avg       0.98      0.98      0.98       984
```

Figure 14.28: Resulting classification matrix

> **NOTE**
>
> To access the source code for this specific section, please refer to https://packt.live/3iXNVbq.
>
> This section does not currently have an online interactive example, but can be run as usual on Google Colab.

As is evident from the results, we get a score of 98%, which is better than the benchmark model. One reason that could be attributed to the higher performance could be the creation of uncorrelated principal components using the PCA method, which has boosted the performance.

In the next section, we will be looking at Independent Component Analysis (ICA).

INDEPENDENT COMPONENT ANALYSIS (ICA)

ICA is a technique of dimensionality reduction that conceptually follows a similar path as PCA. Both ICA and PCA try to derive new sources of data by linearly combining the original data.

However, the difference between them lies in the method they use to find new sources of data. While PCA attempts to find uncorrelated sources of data, ICA attempts to find independent sources of data.

ICA has a very similar implementation for dimensionality reduction as PCA.

Let's look at the implementation of ICA for our use case.

EXERCISE 14.05: DIMENSIONALITY REDUCTION USING INDEPENDENT COMPONENT ANALYSIS

In this exercise, we will fit a logistic regression model using the ICA technique and observe the performance of the model. We will be using the same ads dataset as before, and we will be enhancing it with additional features for this exercise.

The following steps will help you complete this exercise:

1. Open a new Colab notebook file.
2. Implement all the steps from *Exercise 14.01, Loading and Cleaning the Dataset*, up until scaling the dataset using **MinMaxScaler()**:

```
filename = 'https://raw.githubusercontent.com'\
           '/PacktWorkshops/The-Data-Science-Workshop'\
           '/master/Chapter14/Dataset/ad.data'

import pandas as pd
adData = pd.read_csv(filename,sep=",",header = None,\
                     error_bad_lines=False)

X = adData.loc[:,0:1557]
Y = adData[1558]
```

```
import numpy as np
for i in range(0,3):
    X[i] = X[i].str.replace("?", 'NaN')\
                .values.astype(float)
for i in range(3,1557):
    X[i] = X[i].replace("?", 'NaN')\
                .values.astype(float)
for i in range(0,1557):
    X[i] = X[i].fillna(X[i].mean())

from sklearn import preprocessing
minmaxScaler = preprocessing.MinMaxScaler()
X_tran = pd.DataFrame(minmaxScaler.fit_transform(X))
```

3. Let's now augment the dataset artificially to a factor of **50**. Augmenting the dataset to factors that are higher than **50** will result in the notebook crashing because of a lack of memory. This is implemented using the following code snippet:

```
# Creating a high dimension data set
X_hd = pd.DataFrame(pd.np.tile(X_tran, (1, 50)))
print(X_hd.shape)
```

You should get the following output:

```
(3279, 77900)
```

4. Let's split the high-dimensional dataset into training and testing sets:

```
from sklearn.model_selection import train_test_split
# Splitting the data into train and test sets
X_train, X_test, y_train, y_test = train_test_split\
                                   (X_hd, Y, test_size=0.3,\
                                    random_state=123)
```

5. Let's load the ICA function, **FastICA**, and then define the number of components we require. We will use the same number of components that we used for PCA:

```
# Defining the ICA with number of components
from sklearn.decomposition import FastICA
ICA = FastICA(n_components=250, random_state=123)
```

6. Once the ICA method is defined, we will fit the method on the training set and also transform the training set to get a new training set with the required number of components. We will also note the time taken for fitting and transforming:

```
"""
Fitting the ICA method and transforming the
training set import time
"""
t0 = time.time()
X_ica=ICA.fit_transform(X_train)
t1 = time.time()
print("ICA fitting time:", round(t1-t0, 3), "s")
```

In the code, the **.fit()** function is used to fit on the training set and the **transform()** method is used to get a new training set with the required number of features.

You should get the following output:

```
ICA fitting time: 203.02 s
```

We can see that implementing ICA has taken much more time than PCA (179.54 seconds).

7. We now transform the test set with the **250** components:

```
# Transforming the test set
X_test_ica=ICA.transform(X_test)
```

8. Let's verify the shapes of the train and test sets before transformation and after transformation:

```
"""
Printing the shape of train and test sets
before and after transformation
"""
print("original shape of Training set:   ", \
      X_train.shape)
print("original shape of Test set:   ", \
      X_test.shape)
print("Transformed shape of training set:", \
      X_ica.shape)
```

```
print("Transformed shape of test set:", \
      X_test_ica.shape)
```

You should get the following output:

```
original shape of Training set:    (2295, 77900)
original shape of Test set:    (984, 77900)
Transformed shape of training set: (2295, 250)
Transformed shape of test set: (984, 250)
```

Figure 14.29: Shape of the original and transformed datasets

You can see that both the training and test sets are reduced to **250** features each.

9. Let's now fit the logistic regression model on the transformed dataset and note the time it takes:

```
# Fitting a Logistic Regression Model

from sklearn.linear_model import LogisticRegression
import time
icaModel = LogisticRegression()
t0 = time.time()
icaModel.fit(X_ica, y_train)
t1 = time.time()
```

10. Print the total time:

```
print("Total training time:", round(t1-t0, 3), "s")
```

You should get the following output:

```
Total training time: 0.054 s
```

11. Let's now predict on the test set and print the accuracy metrics:

```
# Predicting with the ica model
pred = icaModel.predict(X_test_ica)

print('Accuracy of Logistic regression model '\
      'prediction on test set: {:.2f}'\
      .format(icaModel.score(X_test_ica, y_test)))
```

You should get the following output:

```
Accuracy of Logistic regression model prediction on test set: 0.87
```

We can see that the ICA model has worse results than other models.

12. Print the confusion matrix:

```
from sklearn.metrics import confusion_matrix
confusionMatrix = confusion_matrix(y_test, pred)
print(confusionMatrix)
```

You should get the following output:

```
[[  0 126]
 [  0 858]]
```

Figure 14.30: Resulting confusion matrix

We can see that the ICA model has done a poor job in classifying the ads. All the examples have been wrongly classified as non-ads. We can conclude that ICA is not suitable for this dataset.

13. Print the classification report:

```
from sklearn.metrics import classification_report
# Getting the Classification_report
print(classification_report(y_test, pred))
```

You should get the following output:

```
              precision    recall  f1-score   support

         ad.       0.00      0.00      0.00       126
      nonad.       0.87      1.00      0.93       858

    accuracy                           0.87       984
   macro avg       0.44      0.50      0.47       984
weighted avg       0.76      0.87      0.81       984
```

Figure 14.31: Resulting classification report

> **NOTE**
>
> To access the source code for this specific section, please refer to https://packt.live/325H88Q.
>
> This section does not currently have an online interactive example, but can be run as usual on Google Colab.

As we can see, transforming the data to its first 250 independent components did not capture all the necessary variability in the data. This has resulted in the degradation of the classification results for this method. We can conclude that ICA is not suitable for this dataset.

It was also observed that the time taken to find the best independent features was longer than for PCA. However, it should be noted that different methods vary in results according to the input data. Even though ICA was not suitable for this dataset, it still is a potent method for dimensionality reduction that should be in the repertoire of a data scientist.

From this exercise, you may come up with a few questions:

- How do you think we can improve the classification results using ICA?
- Increasing the number of components results in a marginal increase in the accuracy metrics.
- Are there any other side effects because of the strategy adopted to improve the results?

Increasing the number of components also results in a longer training time for the logistic regression model.

FACTOR ANALYSIS

Factor analysis is a technique that achieves dimensionality reduction by grouping variables that are highly correlated. Let's look at an example from our context of predicting advertisements.

In our dataset, there could be many features that describe the geometry (the size and shape of an image in the ad) of the images on a web page. These features can be correlated because they refer to specific characteristics of an image.

Similarly, there could be many features that describe the anchor text or phrases occurring in a URL, which are highly correlated. Factor analysis looks at correlated groups such as these from the data and then groups them into latent factors. Therefore, if there are 10 raw features describing the geometry of an image, factor analysis will group them into one feature that characterizes the geometry of an image. Each of these groups is called factors. As many correlated features are combined to form a group, the resulting number of features will be much smaller in comparison with the original dimensions of the dataset.

Let's now see how factor analysis can be implemented as a technique for dimensionality reduction.

EXERCISE 14.06: DIMENSIONALITY REDUCTION USING FACTOR ANALYSIS

In this exercise, we will fit a logistic regression model after reducing the original dimensions to some key factors and then observe the performance of the model.

The following steps will help you complete this exercise:

1. Open a new Colab notebook file.
2. Implement the same initial steps from *Exercise 14.01*, *Loading and Cleaning the Dataset*, up until scaling the dataset using the **minmaxscaler()** function:

```
filename = 'https://raw.githubusercontent.com'\
           '/PacktWorkshops/The-Data-Science-Workshop'\
           '/master/Chapter14/Dataset/ad.data'

import pandas as pd
adData = pd.read_csv(filename,sep=",",header = None,\
                     error_bad_lines=False)

X = adData.loc[:,0:1557]
Y = adData[1558]

import numpy as np
for i in range(0,3):
    X[i] = X[i].str.replace("?", 'NaN')\
           .values.astype(float)
```

```
for i in range(3,1557):
    X[i] = X[i].replace("?", 'NaN')\
              .values.astype(float)
for i in range(0,1557):
    X[i] = X[i].fillna(X[i].mean())

from sklearn import preprocessing
minmaxScaler = preprocessing.MinMaxScaler()
X_tran = pd.DataFrame(minmaxScaler.fit_transform(X))
```

3. Let's now augment the dataset artificially to a factor of **50**. Augmenting the dataset to factors that are higher than **50** will result in the notebook crashing because of a lack of memory. This is implemented using the following code snippet:

```
# Creating a high dimension data set
X_hd = pd.DataFrame(pd.np.tile(X_tran, (1, 50)))

print(X_hd.shape)
```

   You should get the following output:

```
(3279, 77900)
```

4. Let's split the high-dimensional dataset into train and test sets:

```
from sklearn.model_selection import train_test_split
# Splitting the data into train and test sets
X_train, X_test, y_train, y_test = train_test_split\
                                   (X_hd, Y, test_size=0.3,\
                                    random_state=123)
```

5. An important step in factor analysis is defining the number of factors in a dataset. This step is achieved through experimentation. In our case, we will arbitrarily assume that there are **20** factors. This is implemented as follows:

```
# Defining the number of factors
from sklearn.decomposition import FactorAnalysis
fa = FactorAnalysis(n_components = 20,\
                    random_state=123)
```

   The number of factors is defined through the **n_components** argument. We also define a random state for reproducibility.

6. Once the factor method is defined, we will fit the method on the training set and also transform the training set to get a new training set with the required number of factors. We will also note the time it takes to fit the required number of factors:

```
"""
Fitting the Factor analysis method and
transforming the training set
"""
import time
t0 = time.time()
X_fac=fa.fit_transform(X_train)
t1 = time.time()
print("Factor analysis fitting time:", \
      round(t1-t0, 3), "s")
```

   In the code, the **`.fit()`** function is used to fit on the training set, and the **`transform()`** method is used to get a new training set with the required number of factors.

   You should get the following output:

```
Factor analysis fitting time: 130.688 s
```

   Factor analysis is also a compute-intensive method. This is the reason that only 20 factors were selected. We can see that it has taken **`130.688`** seconds for **`20`** factors.

7. We now transform the test set with the same number of factors:

```
# Transforming the test set
X_test_fac=fa.transform(X_test)
```

8. Let's verify the shapes of the train and test sets before transformation and after transformation:

```
"""
Printing the shape of train and test sets
before and after transformation
"""

print("original shape of Training set:   ", \
      X_train.shape)
print("original shape of Test set:   ", \
```

```
        X_test.shape)
print("Transformed shape of training set:", \
        X_fac.shape)
print("Transformed shape of test set:", \
        X_test_fac.shape)
```

You should get the following output:

```
original shape of Training set:    (2295, 77900)
original shape of Test set:    (984, 77900)
Transformed shape of training set: (2295, 20)
Transformed shape of test set: (984, 20)
```

Figure 14.32: Original and transformed dataset values

You can see that both the training and test sets have been reduced to **20** factors each.

9. Let's now fit the logistic regression model on the transformed dataset and note the time it takes to fit the model:

```
# Fitting a Logistic Regression Model

from sklearn.linear_model import LogisticRegression
import time
facModel = LogisticRegression()
t0 = time.time()
facModel.fit(X_fac, y_train)
t1 = time.time()
```

10. Print the total time:

```
print("Total training time:", round(t1-t0, 3), "s")
```

You should get the following output:

```
Total training time: 0.028 s
```

We can see that the time it has taken to fit the logistic regression model is comparable with other methods.

11. Let's now predict on the test set and print the accuracy metrics:

```
# Predicting with the factor analysis model
pred = facModel.predict(X_test_fac)
print('Accuracy of Logistic regression '\
      'model prediction on test set: {:.2f}'
      .format(facModel.score(X_test_fac, y_test)))
```

You should get the following output:

```
Accuracy of Logistic regression model prediction on test set: 0.92
```

We can see that the factor model has better results than the ICA model, but worse results than the other models.

12. Print the confusion matrix:

```
from sklearn.metrics import confusion_matrix
confusionMatrix = confusion_matrix(y_test, pred)
print(confusionMatrix)
```

You should get the following output:

```
[[ 48  78]
 [  0 858]]
```

Figure 14.33: Resulting confusion matrix

We can see that the factor model has done a better job at classifying the ads than the ICA model. However, there is still a high number of false positives.

13. Print the classification report:

```
from sklearn.metrics import classification_report

# Getting the Classification_report
print(classification_report(y_test, pred))
```

You should get the following output:

```
              precision    recall  f1-score   support

         ad.       1.00      0.38      0.55       126
      nonad.       0.92      1.00      0.96       858

    accuracy                           0.92       984
   macro avg       0.96      0.69      0.75       984
weighted avg       0.93      0.92      0.90       984
```

Figure 14.34: Resulting classification report

> **NOTE**
>
> To access the source code for this specific section, please refer to https://packt.live/32b9SNk.
>
> This section does not currently have an online interactive example, but can be run as usual on Google Colab.

As we can see in the results, by reducing the variables to just 20 factors, we were able to get a decent classification result. Even though there is degradation on the result, we still have a manageable number of features, which will be able to scale well on any algorithm. The balance between the accuracy measures and the ability to manage features needs to be explored through greater experimentation.

How do you think we can improve the classification results for factor analysis?

Well, increasing the number of components results in an increase in the accuracy metrics.

COMPARING DIFFERENT DIMENSIONALITY REDUCTION TECHNIQUES

Now that we have learned different dimensionality reduction techniques, let's apply all of these techniques to a new dataset that we will create from the existing ads dataset.

We will randomly sample some data points from a known distribution and then add these random samples to the existing dataset to create a new dataset. Let's carry out an experiment to see how a new dataset can be created from an existing dataset.

We import the necessary libraries:

```
import pandas as pd
import numpy as np
```

Next, we create a dummy data frame.

We will use a small dataset with two rows and three columns for this example. We use the **`pd.np.array()`** function to create a data frame:

```
# Creating a simple data frame
df = pd.np.array([[1, 2, 3], [4, 5, 6]])
print(df.shape)
df
```

You should get the following output:

```
(2, 3)
array([[1, 2, 3],
       [4, 5, 6]])
```

Figure 14.35: Sample data frame

What we will do next is sample some data points with the same shape as the data frame we created.

Let's sample some data points from a normal distribution that has mean **0** and standard deviation of **`0.1`**. We touched briefly on normal distributions in *Chapter 3, Binary Classification.* A normal distribution has two parameters. The first one is the mean, which is the average of all the data in the distribution, and the second one is standard deviation, which is a measure of how spread out the data points are.

By assuming a mean and standard deviation, we will be able to draw samples from a normal distribution using the **np.random.normal()** Python function. The arguments that we have to give for this function are the mean, the standard deviation, and the shape of the new dataset.

Let's see how this is implemented in code:

```
# Defining the mean and standard deviation
mu, sigma = 0, 0.1
# Generating random sample
noise = np.random.normal(mu, sigma, [2,3])
noise.shape
```

You should get the following output:

```
(2, 3)
```

As we can see, we give the mean (**mu**), standard deviation (**sigma**), and the shape of the data frame **[2,3]** to generate the new random samples.

Print the sampled data frame:

```
# Sampled data frame
noise
```

You will get something like the following output:

```
array([[-0.07175021, -0.21135372,  0.10258917],
       [ 0.03737542,  0.00045449, -0.04866098]])
```

The next step is to add the original data frame and the sampled data frame to get the new dataset:

```
# Creating a new data set by adding sampled data frame
df_new = df + noise
df_new
```

You should get something like the following output:

```
array([[0.92824979, 1.78864628, 3.10258917],
       [4.03737542, 5.00045449, 5.95133902]])
```

Having seen how to create a new dataset, let's use this knowledge in the next activity.

ACTIVITY 14.02: COMPARISON OF DIMENSIONALITY REDUCTION TECHNIQUES ON THE ENHANCED ADS DATASET

You have learned different dimensionality reduction techniques. You want to determine which is the best technique among them for a dataset you will create.

Hint: In this activity, we will use the different techniques that you have used in all the exercises so far. You will also create a new dataset as we did in the previous section.

The steps to complete this activity are as follows:

1. Open a new Colab notebook.
2. Normalize the original ads data and derive the transformed independent variable, **`X_tran`**.
3. Create a high-dimensional dataset by replicating the columns twice using the **`pd.np.tile()`** function.
4. Create random samples from a normal distribution with mean = 0 and standard deviation = 0.1. Make the new dataset with the same shape as the high-dimensional dataset created in *step 3*.
5. Add the high dimensional dataset and the random samples to get the new dataset.
6. Split the dataset into train and test sets.
7. Implement backward elimination with the following steps:

   Implement the backward elimination step using the **`RFE()`** function.

   Use logistic regression as the model and select the best **`300`** features.

   Fit the **`RFE()`** function on the training set and measure the time it takes to fit the RFE model on the training set.

   Transform the train and test sets with the RFE model.

   Fit a logistic regression model on the transformed training set.

   Predict on the test set and print the accuracy score, confusion matrix, and classification report.

8. Implement the forward selection technique with the following steps:

   Define the number of features using the **`SelectKBest()`** function. Select the best **`300`** features.

   Fit the forward selection on the training set using the **`.fit()`** function and note the time taken for the fit.

   Transform both the training and test sets using the **`.transform()`** function.

   Fit a logistic regression model on the transformed training set.

   Predict on the transformed test set and print the accuracy, confusion matrix, and classification report.

9. Implement PCA:

   Define the principal components using the **`PCA()`** function. Use 300 components.

   Fit **`PCA()`** on the training set. Note the time.

   Transform both the training set and test set to get the respective number of components for these datasets using the **`.transform()`** function.

   Fit a logistic regression model on the transformed training set.

   Predict on the transformed test set and print the accuracy, confusion matrix, and classification report.

10. Implement ICA:

    Define independent components using the **`FastICA()`** function using **`300`** components.

    Fit the independent components on the training set and transform the training set. Note the time for the implementation.

    Transform the test set to get the respective number of components for these datasets using the **`.transform()`** function.

    Fit a logistic regression model on the transformed training set.

    Predict on the transformed test set and print the accuracy, confusion matrix, and classification report.

11. Implement factor analysis:

    Define the number of factors using the **`FactorAnalysis()`** function and **`30`** factors.

    Fit the factors on the training set and transform the training set. Note the time for the implementation.

    Transform the test set to get the respective number of components for these datasets using the **`.transform()`** function.

    Fit a logistic regression model on the transformed training set.

    Predict on the transformed test set and print the accuracy, confusion matrix, and classification report.

12. Compare the outputs of all the methods.

Expected Output:

An example summary table of the results is as follows:

Method	**Dimension Reduction Time (seconds)**	**Model Fitting Time**	**Accuracy**	**Rank of the Method**
Backward Elimination	2,392.68	0.085	97%	4
Forward Selection	0.098	0.114	97%	1
PCA	2.843	0.138	97%	2
ICA	27.562	0.046	87%	5
Factor Analysis	3.802	0.023	96%	3

Figure 14.36: Summary output of all the reduction techniques

> **NOTE**
>
> The solution to the activity can be found here: https://packt.live/2GbJloz.

In this activity, we implemented five different methods of dimensionality reduction with a new dataset that we created from the internet ads dataset.

From the tabulated results, we can see that three methods (backward elimination, forward selection, and PCA) have got the same accuracy scores. Therefore, the selection criteria for the best method should be based on the time taken to get the reduced dimension. With these criteria, the forward selection method is the best method, followed by PCA.

For the third place, we should strike a balance between accuracy and the time taken for dimensionality reduction. We can see that factor analysis and backward elimination have very close accuracy scores, 96% and 97% respectively. However, the time taken for backward elimination is quite large compared to factor analysis. Therefore, we should weigh our considerations toward factor analysis as the third best, even though the accuracy is marginally lower than backward elimination. The last spot should go to ICA because the accuracy is far lower than all the other methods.

SUMMARY

In this chapter, we have learned about various techniques for dimensionality reduction. Let's summarize what we have learned in this chapter.

At the beginning of the chapter, we were introduced to the challenges inherent with some of the modern-day datasets in terms of scalability. To further learn about these challenges, we downloaded the Internet Advertisement dataset and did an activity where we witnessed the scalability challenges posed by a large dataset. In the activity, we artificially created a large dataset and fit a logistic regression model to it.

In the subsequent sections, we were introduced to five different methods of dimensionality reduction.

Backward feature elimination worked on the principle of eliminating features one by one until no major degradation of accuracy measures occurred. This method is computationally intensive, but we got better results than the benchmark model.

Forward feature selection goes in the opposite direction as backward elimination and selects one feature at a time to get the best set of features we predetermined. This method is also computationally intensive. We also found out that this method had marginally lower accuracy.

Principal component analysis (**PCA**) aims at finding components that are orthogonal to each other and that best explain the variability of the data. We had better results with PCA than we got from the benchmark model.

Independent component analysis (**ICA**) is similar to PCA; however, it differs in terms of the approach to the selection of components. ICA looks for independent components from the dataset. We saw that ICA achieved one of the worst results in our context.

Factor analysis was all about finding factors or groups of correlated features that best described the data. We achieved much better results than ICA with factor analysis.

The aim of this chapter was to equip you with a set of techniques that help in scenarios when the scalability of models was challenging. The key to getting good results is to understand which method to use in which scenario. This could be achieved with lots of hands-on practice and experimentation with many large datasets.

Having learned a set of tools to manage scalability in this chapter, we will move on to the next chapter, which addresses the problem of boosting performance. In the next chapter, you will be introduced to a technique called ensemble learning. This technique will help to boost the performance of your machine learning models.

15

ENSEMBLE LEARNING

OVERVIEW

By the end of this chapter, you will be able to describe ensemble learning and apply different ensemble learning techniques to your dataset. You will also be able to fit a dataset on a model and analyze the results after ensemble learning.

In this chapter, we will be using the credit card application dataset, where we will try to predict whether a credit card application will be approved.

INTRODUCTION

In the previous chapter, we learned various techniques, such as the backward elimination technique, factor analysis, and so on, that helped us to deal with high-dimensional datasets.

In this chapter, we will further enhance our repertoire of skills with another set of techniques, called **ensemble learning**, in which we will be dealing with different ensemble learning techniques such as the following:

- Averaging
- Weighted averaging
- Max voting
- Bagging
- Boosting
- Blending

ENSEMBLE LEARNING

Ensemble learning, as the name denotes, is a method that combines several machine learning models to generate a superior model, thereby decreasing variability/variance and bias, and boosting performance.

Before we explore what ensemble learning is, let's look at the concepts of bias and variance with the help of the classical bias-variance quadrant, as shown here:

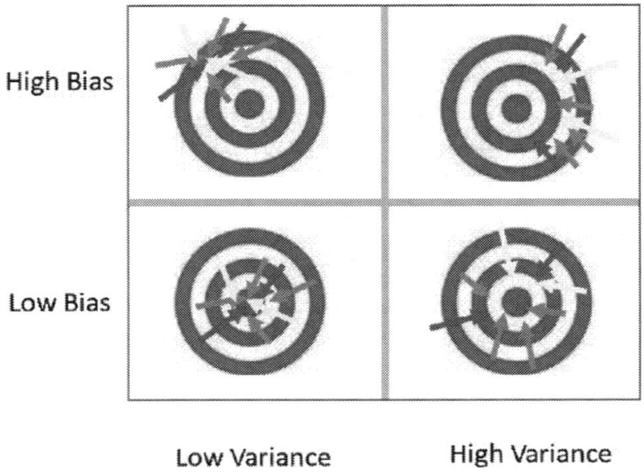

Figure 15.1: Bias-variance quadrant

VARIANCE

Variance is the measure of how spread out data is. In the context of machine learning, models with high variance imply that the predictions generated on the same test set will differ considerably when different training sets are used to fit the model. The underlying reason for high variability could be attributed to the model being attuned to specific nuances of training data rather than generalizing the relationship between input and output. Ideally, we want every machine learning model to have low variance.

BIAS

Bias is the difference between the ground truth and the average value of our predictions. A low bias will indicate that the predictions are very close to the actual values. A high bias implies that the model has oversimplified the relationship between the inputs and outputs, leading to high error rates on test sets, which again is an undesirable outcome.

Figure 15.1 helps us to visualize the trade-off between bias and variance. The top-left corner is the depiction of a scenario where the bias is high, and the variance is low. The top-right quadrant displays a scenario where both bias and variance are high. From the figure, we can see that when the bias is high, it is further away from the truth, which in this case, is the *bull's eye*. The presence of variance is manifested as whether the arrows are spread out or congregated in one spot.

Ensemble models combine many weaker models that differ in variance and bias, thereby creating a better model, outperforming the individual weaker models. Ensemble models exemplify the adage *the wisdom of the crowds*. In this chapter, we will learn about different ensemble techniques, which can be classified into two types, that is, simple and advanced techniques:

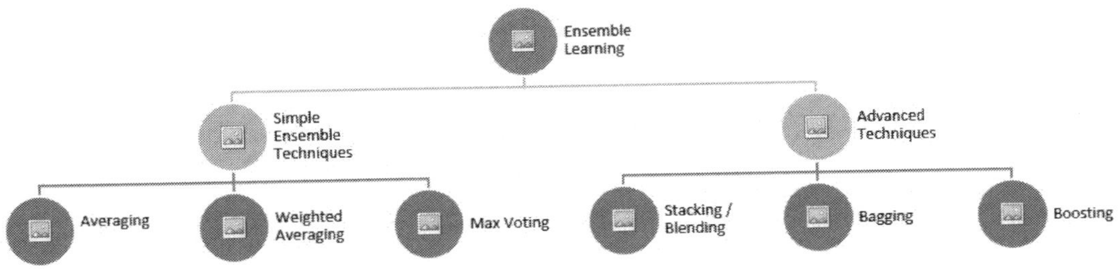

Figure 15.2: Different ensemble learning methods

BUSINESS CONTEXT

You are working in the credit card division of your bank. The operations head of your company has requested your help in determining whether a customer is creditworthy or not. You have been provided with credit card operations data.

This dataset contains credit card applications with around 15 variables. The variables are a mix of continuous and categorical data pertaining to credit card operations. The label for the dataset is a flag, which indicates whether the application has been approved or not.

You want to fit some benchmark models and try some ensemble learning methods on the dataset to address the problem and come up with a tool for predicting whether or not a given customer should be approved for their credit application.

EXERCISE 15.01: LOADING, EXPLORING, AND CLEANING THE DATA

In this exercise, we will download the credit card dataset, load it into our Colab notebook, and perform a few basic explorations. In addition, we will also clean the dataset to remove unwanted characters.

> **NOTE**
>
> The dataset that we will be using in this exercise was sourced from the UCI Machine Learning Repository: https://packt.live/39NCgZ2. You can download the dataset from our GitHub at https://packt.live/3018OdD.

The following steps will help you to complete this exercise:

1. Open a new Colab notebook file.
2. Now, import **pandas** into your Colab notebook:

```
import pandas as pd
```

3. Next, set the path of the GitHub repository where **crx.data** is uploaded, as mentioned in the following code snippet:

```
#Load data from the GitHub repository
filename = 'https://raw.githubusercontent.com'\
           '/PacktWorkshops/The-Data-Science-Workshop'\
           '/master/Chapter15/Dataset/crx.data'
```

4. Read the file using the **pd.read_csv()** function from the **pandas** data frame:

```
credData = pd.read_csv(filename,sep= ",",\
                       header = None,\
                       na_values =  "?")
credData.head()
```

The **pd.read_csv()** function's arguments are the filename as a string and the limit separator of a CSV file, which is **,**.

> **NOTE**
>
> There are no headers for the dataset; we specifically mention this using the **header = None** command.

We replace the missing values represented as **?** in the dataset as **na** values using the **na_values = "?"** argument. This replacement is for ease of further processing.

After reading the file, print the data frame using the **.head()** function. You should get the following output:

	0	1	2	3	4	5	6	7	8	9	10	11	12	13	14	15
0	b	30.83	0.000	u	g	w	v	1.25	t	t	1	f	g	202.0	0	+
1	a	58.67	4.460	u	g	q	h	3.04	t	t	6	f	g	43.0	560	+
2	a	24.50	0.500	u	g	q	h	1.50	t	f	0	f	g	280.0	824	+
3	b	27.83	1.540	u	g	w	v	3.75	t	t	5	t	g	100.0	3	+
4	b	20.17	5.625	u	g	w	v	1.71	t	f	0	f	s	120.0	0	+

Figure 15.3: Loading data into the Colab notebook

5. Change the classes to **1** and **0**.

   If you notice in the dataset, the classes represented in column **15** are special characters: **+** for approved and **–** for not approved. You need to change this to numerical values of **1** for approved and **0** for not approved, as shown in the following code snippet:

```
# Changing the Classes to 1 & 0
credData.loc[credData[15] == '+' , 15] = 1
credData.loc[credData[15] == '-' , 15] = 0
credData.head()
```

   You should get the following output:

	0	1	2	3	4	5	6	7	8	9	10	11	12	13	14	15
0	b	30.83	0.000	u	g	w	v	1.25	t	t	1	f	g	202.0	0	1
1	a	58.67	4.460	u	g	q	h	3.04	t	t	6	f	g	43.0	560	1
2	a	24.50	0.500	u	g	q	h	1.50	t	f	0	f	g	280.0	824	1
3	b	27.83	1.540	u	g	w	v	3.75	t	t	5	t	g	100.0	3	1
4	b	20.17	5.625	u	g	w	v	1.71	t	f	0	f	s	120.0	0	1

Figure 15.4: Data frame after replacing special characters

   In the preceding code snippet, **.loc()** was used to locate the fifteenth column and replace the **+** and **–** values with **1** and **0**, respectively.

6. Find the number of **null** values in the dataset.

   We'll now find the number of **null** values in each of the features using the **.isnull()** function. The **.sum()** function sums up all such null values across each of the columns in the dataset.

   This is represented in the following code snippet:

```
# Finding number of null values in the data set
credData.isnull().sum()
```

You should get the following output:

```
0      12
1      12
2       0
3       6
4       6
5       9
6       9
7       0
8       0
9       0
10      0
11      0
12      0
13     13
14      0
15      0
dtype: int64
```

Figure 15.5: Summarizing null values in the dataset

As seen from the preceding output, there are many columns with **`null`** values.

7. Now, print the shape and data types of each column:

```
# Printing Shape and data types
print('Shape of raw data set',credData.shape)
print('Data types of data set',credData.dtypes)
```

You should get the following output:

```
Shape of raw data set (690, 16)
Data types of data set 0       object
1      float64
2      float64
3       object
4       object
5       object
6       object
7      float64
8       object
9       object
10       int64
11      object
12      object
13     float64
14       int64
15       int64
dtype: object
```

Figure 15.6: Shape and data types of each column

8. Remove the rows with **na** values.

   In order to clean the dataset, let's remove all the rows with **na** values using the **.dropna()** function with the following code snippet:

```
# Dropping all the rows with na values
newcred = credData.dropna(axis = 0)
newcred.shape
```

   You should get the following output:

```
(653, 16)
```

   As you can see, around 37 rows that, which had **na** values, were removed. In the code snippet, we define **axis = 0** in order to denote that the dropping of **na** values should be done along the rows.

9. Verify that no **null** values exist:

```
# Verifying no null values exist
newcred.isnull().sum()
```

You should get the following output:

```
0     0
1     0
2     0
3     0
4     0
5     0
6     0
7     0
8     0
9     0
10    0
11    0
12    0
13    0
14    0
15    0
dtype: int64
```

Figure 15.7: Verifying that no null values are present

10. Next, make dummy values from the categorical variables.

    As you can see from the data types, there are many variables with categorical values. These have to be converted to dummy values using the **pd.get_dummies()** function. This is done using the following code snippet:

```
"""
Separating the categorical variables to
make dummy variables
"""
credCat = pd.get_dummies(newcred[[0,3,4,5,6,8,9,11,12]])
```

11. Separate the numerical variables.

    We will also be separating the numerical variables from the original dataset to concatenate them with the dummy variables. This step is done as follows:

```
# Separating the numerical variables
credNum = newcred[[1,2,7,10,13,14]]
```

> **NOTE**
>
> You can view these new DataFrames by running the commands **`credCat`** and **`credNum`**.

12. Create the **`X`** and **`y`** variables. The dummy variables and the numerical variables will now be concatenated to form the **`X`** variable. The **`y`** variable will be created separately by taking the labels of the dataset. Let's see these steps in action in the following code snippet:

```
"""
Making the X variable which is a concatenation
of categorical and numerical data
"""

X = pd.concat([credCat,credNum],axis = 1)
print(X.shape)

# Separating the label as y variable
y = pd.Series(newcred[15], dtype="int")
print(y.shape)
```

    You should get the following output:

```
(653, 46)
(653,)
```

13. Normalize the dataset using the **`MinMaxScaler()`** function:

```
# Normalizing the data sets
# Import library function
from sklearn import preprocessing
# Creating the scaling function
```

```
minmaxScaler = preprocessing.MinMaxScaler()
# Transforming with the scaler function
X_tran = pd.DataFrame(minmaxScaler.fit_transform(X))
```

14. Split the dataset into training and test sets.

    As the final step of data preparation, we will now split the dataset into training and test sets using the **train_test_split()** function:

```
from sklearn.model_selection import train_test_split
# Splitting the data into train and test sets
X_train, X_test, y_train, y_test = train_test_split\
                                   (X_tran, y, test_size=0.3,\
                                    random_state=123)
```

> **NOTE**
>
> To access the source code for this specific section, please refer to https://packt.live/31hM3od.
>
> You can also run this example online at https://packt.live/3glWdZf.

We now have the required dataset ready for further actions. As always, let's start off by fitting a benchmark model using logistic regression on the cleaned dataset. This will be achieved in the next activity.

ACTIVITY 15.01: FITTING A LOGISTIC REGRESSION MODEL ON CREDIT CARD DATA

You have just cleaned the dataset that you received to predict the creditworthiness of your customers. Before applying ensemble learning methods, you want to fit a benchmark model on the dataset.

Perform the following steps to complete this activity:

1. Open a new Colab notebook.
2. Implement all the appropriate steps from *Exercise 15.01, Loading, Exploring, and Cleaning the Data*, until you have split the dataset into training and test sets.
3. Fit a logistic regression model on the training set.
4. Get the predictions on the test set.

5. Print the confusion matrix and classification report for the benchmark model.

   You should get an output similar to the following after fitting the logistic regression model on the dataset:

```
[[93 14]
 [ 8 81]]
              precision    recall  f1-score   support

           0       0.92      0.87      0.89       107
           1       0.85      0.91      0.88        89

    accuracy                           0.89       196
   macro avg       0.89      0.89      0.89       196
weighted avg       0.89      0.89      0.89       196
```

Figure 15.8: Expected output after fitting the logistic regression model

> **NOTE**
>
> Please note that you will not get exact values as output due to variability in the prediction process.
>
> The solution to this activity can be found here: https://packt.live/2GbJloz.

In this activity, we created a benchmark model for comparison with subsequent models.

As you can see from the output, we achieved an accuracy level of **0.89** with the benchmark model.

Now that we have fit a benchmark model, we will explore different methods of ensemble learning in the next section, starting with simple methods.

SIMPLE METHODS FOR ENSEMBLE LEARNING

As defined earlier in the chapter, ensemble learning is all about combining the strengths of individual models to get a superior model. In this section, we will explore some simple techniques such as the following:

- Averaging
- Weighted averaging
- Max voting

Let's take a look at each of them in turn.

AVERAGING

Averaging is a naïve way of doing ensemble learning; however, it is extremely useful too. The basic idea behind this technique is to take the predictions of multiple individual models and then average the predictions to generate a final prediction. The assumption is that by averaging the predictions of different individual learners, we eliminate the errors made by individual learners, thereby generating a model superior to the base model. One prerequisite to make averaging work is to have the predictions of the base models be uncorrelated. This would mean that the individual models should not make the same kinds of errors. The diversity of the models is a critical aspect to ensure uncorrelated errors.

When implementing the averaging technique, there are some nuances in predictions that need to be taken care of. When predicting, so far, we have been using the **`predict()`** function. As you might know by now, the **`predict()`** function outputs the class that has the highest probability. For example, in our benchmark model, when we predicted on the test set, we got an output of either '1' or '0' for each of the test examples. There is also another way to make predictions, which is by generating the probability of each class. If we were to output the probability of each class for our benchmark model, we would get two outputs for each example corresponding to the probability for each class. This is demonstrated in an example prediction in the following table:

Example	**Class: '1'**	**Class: '0'**
Test set example 1	0.902	0.098
Test set example 2	0.401	0.559
Test set example 3	0.732	0.268

Figure 15.9: An example prediction

From the preceding example, we can see that each test example has two outputs corresponding to the probabilities of each class. So, for the first example, the prediction would be class '1' as the probability for class **`1`** (**`0.902`**) is higher than class **`0`** (**`0.098`**). The respective predictions for example **`2`** and **`3`** would be class **`0`** and class **`1`** respectively.

When we generate an ensemble by averaging method, we generate the probability of each class instead of the class predictions. The probability of each class is predicted using a separate function called **`predict_proba()`**. We will see the implementation of the averaging method in *Exercise 15.02, Ensemble Model Using the Averaging Technique*.

EXERCISE 15.02: ENSEMBLE MODEL USING THE AVERAGING TECHNIQUE

In this exercise, we will implement an ensemble model using the averaging technique. The base models that we will use for this exercise are the logistic regression model, which we used as our benchmark model, and the KNN and random forest models, which were introduced in *Chapter 4, Multiclass Classification with RandomForest*, and *Chapter 8, Hyperparameter Tuning*:

1. Open a new Colab notebook.
2. Execute all the appropriate steps from *Exercise 15.01, Loading, Exploring, and Cleaning the Data*, to split the dataset into train and test sets.
3. Let's define the three base models. Import the selected classifiers, which we will use as base models:

```
from sklearn.linear_model import LogisticRegression
from sklearn.neighbors import KNeighborsClassifier
from sklearn.ensemble import RandomForestClassifier

model1 = LogisticRegression(random_state=123)
model2 = KNeighborsClassifier(n_neighbors=5)
model3 = RandomForestClassifier(n_estimators=500)
```

4. Fit all three models on the training set:

```
# Fitting all three models on the training data
model1.fit(X_train,y_train)
model2.fit(X_train,y_train)
model3.fit(X_train,y_train)
```

5. We will now predict the probabilities of each model using the **predict_proba()** function:

```
"""
Predicting probabilities of each model
on the test set
"""
pred1=model1.predict_proba(X_test)
pred2=model2.predict_proba(X_test)
pred3=model3.predict_proba(X_test)
```

6. Average the predictions generated from all of the three models:

```
"""
Calculating the ensemble prediction by
averaging three base model predictions
"""
ensemblepred=(pred1+pred2+pred3)/3
```

7. Display the first four rows of the ensemble prediction array:

```
# Displaying first 4 rows of the ensemble predictions
ensemblepred[0:4,:]
```

You should get an output similar to the following:

```
array([[0.90646696, 0.09353304],
       [0.96005012, 0.03994988],
       [0.18882019, 0.81117981],
       [0.05134285, 0.94865715]])
```

Figure 15.10: First four rows of ensemble predictions

As you can see from the preceding output, we have two probabilities for each example corresponding to each class.

8. Print the order of each class from the prediction output. As you can see from *Step 6*, the prediction output has two columns corresponding to each class. In order to find the order of the class prediction, we use a method called **.classes_**. This is implemented in the following code snippet:

```
# Printing the order of classes for each model
print(model1.classes_)
print(model2.classes_)
print(model3.classes_)
```

You should get the following output:

```
[0 1]
[0 1]
[0 1]
```

Figure 15.11: Order of classes

9. We now have to get the final predictions for each example from the output probabilities. The final prediction will be the class with the highest probability. To get the class with the highest probability, we use the **numpy** function, **.argmax()**. This is executed as follows:

```
import numpy as np
pred = np.argmax(ensemblepred,axis = 1)
pred
```

From the preceding code, **axis = 1** means that we need to find the index of the maximum value across the columns.

You should get the following output:

```
array([0, 0, 1, 1, 0, 1, 1, 1, 1, 1, 0, 0, 0, 0, 0, 0, 0, 1, 1, 0, 0, 0,
       0, 1, 0, 0, 0, 0, 0, 1, 1, 0, 1, 0, 0, 1, 1, 0, 1, 0, 0, 0, 0, 0,
       1, 0, 1, 0, 1, 0, 1, 1, 1, 1, 1, 0, 1, 0, 0, 1, 1, 0, 1, 1, 1, 0,
       0, 1, 0, 1, 1, 1, 1, 1, 1, 1, 1, 0, 1, 1, 0, 1, 1, 1, 0, 1, 0, 0,
       0, 1, 0, 0, 1, 0, 0, 0, 1, 0, 1, 0, 0, 1, 0, 1, 0, 0, 1, 0, 0, 0,
       1, 0, 0, 0, 0, 0, 1, 0, 1, 1, 0, 0, 1, 0, 0, 1, 0, 0, 1, 0, 0, 1,
       0, 0, 1, 1, 0, 1, 1, 1, 1, 0, 1, 0, 1, 0, 0, 0, 0, 0, 0, 0, 1, 1,
       1, 0, 1, 1, 1, 0, 1, 0, 0, 0, 1, 1, 1, 0, 0, 0, 1, 0, 1, 0, 0, 0,
       1, 1, 1, 1, 1, 1, 0, 0, 1, 1, 0, 0, 0, 0, 1, 0, 0, 1, 0, 1])
```

Figure 15.12: Array output

10. Generate the confusion matrix for the predictions:

```
# Generating confusion matrix
from sklearn.metrics import confusion_matrix
confusionMatrix = confusion_matrix(y_test, pred)
print(confusionMatrix)
```

You should get an output similar to the following:

```
[[97 10]
 [ 8 81]]
```

Figure 15.13: Confusion matrix

11. Generate a classification report:

```
# Generating classification report
from sklearn.metrics import classification_report
print(classification_report(y_test, pred))
```

You should get an output similar to the following:

```
              precision    recall  f1-score   support

           0       0.92      0.91      0.92       107
           1       0.89      0.91      0.90        89

    accuracy                           0.91       196
   macro avg       0.91      0.91      0.91       196
weighted avg       0.91      0.91      0.91       196
```

Figure 15.14: Classification report

> **NOTE**
>
> To access the source code for this specific section, please refer to https://packt.live/31aLa0w.
>
> You can also run this example online at https://packt.live/31hMpex.

In this exercise, we implemented the averaging technique for ensemble learning. As you can see from the classification report, we managed to improve the accuracy rate from **0.89**, which was achieved with the benchmark model, to **0.91** by averaging. However, it should be noted that ensemble methods are not guaranteed to improve the results in all cases. There could be instances where no improvement in performance would be observed.

Let's also look at the results from the business context of credit card applications. An accuracy of **91%** means that out of the **196** cases in the test set, we were correctly able to predict whether a customer is creditworthy in **91%** of those cases. It would also be interesting to look at the recall value of class **0**, which is **91%**. In this case, we correctly identified unworthy customers in **91%** of the cases. It is also an area of concern that the balance of **9%** of unworthy customers have been wrongly identified as creditworthy, which is, in fact, a risk to the credit card division. Ideally, we would want to increase the recall value of the non-worthy customers if we want to reduce the risk to the credit card division.

On the other hand, there is also an issue of maximizing a business opportunity with the correct predictions of creditworthy customers (**1**). We have seen that **91%** of creditworthy customers out of a total of **107** were correctly predicted, which is a positive outcome. The balance of **9%** of creditworthy customers would be a lost business opportunity.

Fine-tuning models is a balancing act, which a data scientist has to be cognizant about. A data scientist has to act according to the preferences of the business. If the business is risk-averse and would prefer to forego business opportunities, then the models will have to be tuned to increase the recall value of the non-worthy customers. On the other hand, if the business is aggressive and would like to go for growth, then the preferred route would be to improve the recall value of creditworthy customers. At the end of the day, fine-tuning models is a balancing act based on business realities.

WEIGHTED AVERAGING

Weighted averaging is an extension of the averaging method that we saw earlier. The major difference in both of these approaches is in the way the combined predictions are generated. In the weighted averaging method, we assign weights to each model's predictions and then generate the combined predictions. The weights are assigned based on our judgment of which model would be the most influential in the ensemble. These weights, which are initially assigned arbitrarily, have to be evolved after a lot of experimentation. To start off, we assume some weights and then iterate with different weights for each model to verify whether we get any improvements in the performance. Let's implement the weighted averaging method in the upcoming exercise.

EXERCISE 15.03: ENSEMBLE MODEL USING THE WEIGHTED AVERAGING TECHNIQUE

In this exercise, we will implement an ensemble model using the weighted averaging technique. We will use the same base models, logistic regression, KNN, and random forest, which were used in *Exercise 15.02, Ensemble Model Using the Averaging Technique*:

1. Open a new Colab notebook.

2. Execute all the steps from *Exercise 15.02, Ensemble Model Using the Averaging Technique*, up until predicting the probabilities of the three models.

3. Take the weighted average of the predictions. In the weighted averaging method, weights are assigned arbitrarily based on our judgment of each of the predictions. This is done as follows:

```
"""
Calculating the ensemble prediction by applying
weights for each prediction
"""
ensemblepred=(pred1 *0.60 + pred2 * 0.20 + pred3 * 0.20)
```

Please note that the weights are assigned in such a way that the sum of all weights becomes **1** (**0.6 + 0.2 + 0.2 = 1**).

4. Display the first four rows of the ensemble prediction array:

```
# Displaying first 4 rows of the ensemble predictions
ensemblepred[0:4,:]
```

You should get an output similar to the following:

```
array([[0.92164053, 0.07835947],
       [0.94769021, 0.05230979],
       [0.14187634, 0.85812366],
       [0.09121714, 0.90878286]])
```

Figure 15.15: Array output for ensemble prediction

As you can see from the output, we have two probabilities for each example corresponding to each class.

5. Print the order of each class from the prediction output:

```
# Printing the order of classes for each model
print(model1.classes_)
print(model2.classes_)
print(model3.classes_)
```

You should get the following output:

```
[0 1]
[0 1]
[0 1]
```

Figure 15.16: Order of class from prediction output

6. Calculate the final predictions from the probabilities.

We now have to get the final predictions for each example from the output probabilities using the **np.argmax()** function:

```
import numpy as np
pred = np.argmax(ensemblepred,axis = 1)
pred
```

You should get an output similar to the following:

```
array([0, 0, 1, 1, 0, 1, 1, 1, 1, 1, 0, 1, 0, 0, 0, 0, 0, 1, 1, 0, 0, 0,
       0, 1, 0, 0, 0, 0, 0, 1, 1, 0, 1, 0, 0, 1, 1, 0, 1, 0, 0, 0, 0, 0,
       1, 0, 1, 0, 1, 0, 1, 1, 1, 1, 1, 0, 1, 0, 0, 1, 1, 0, 1, 1, 1, 0,
       0, 1, 0, 1, 1, 1, 1, 1, 1, 1, 1, 0, 1, 1, 0, 1, 1, 1, 0, 1, 0, 1,
       0, 1, 0, 0, 1, 0, 0, 0, 1, 0, 1, 0, 0, 1, 0, 1, 0, 0, 1, 0, 0, 0,
       1, 0, 0, 0, 0, 0, 1, 0, 1, 1, 1, 0, 1, 0, 0, 1, 0, 1, 1, 0, 0, 1,
       0, 0, 1, 1, 0, 1, 1, 1, 1, 0, 1, 0, 1, 0, 0, 0, 0, 0, 0, 0, 1, 1,
       1, 0, 1, 1, 1, 0, 1, 0, 0, 0, 1, 1, 1, 0, 0, 0, 1, 0, 1, 0, 0, 0,
       1, 1, 1, 1, 1, 1, 0, 0, 1, 1, 0, 0, 0, 0, 1, 0, 0, 1, 0, 1])
```

Figure 15.17: Array for final predictions

7. Generate the confusion matrix for the predictions:

```
# Generating confusion matrix
from sklearn.metrics import confusion_matrix
confusionMatrix = confusion_matrix(y_test, pred)
print(confusionMatrix)
```

You should get an output similar to the following:

```
[[94 13]
 [ 8 81]]
```

Figure 15.18: Confusion matrix

8. Generating a classification report:

```
# Generating classification report
from sklearn.metrics import classification_report
print(classification_report(y_test, pred))
```

You should get an output similar to the following:

```
              precision    recall  f1-score   support

           0       0.92      0.88      0.90       107
           1       0.86      0.91      0.89        89

    accuracy                           0.89       196
   macro avg       0.89      0.89      0.89       196
weighted avg       0.89      0.89      0.89       196
```

Figure 15.19: Classification report

NOTE

To access the source code for this specific section, please refer to https://packt.live/2CINUc5.

You can also run this example online at https://packt.live/2YfrTZK.

ITERATION 2 WITH DIFFERENT WEIGHTS

From the first iteration, we saw that we got accuracy of **89%**. This metric is a reflection of the weights that we applied in the first iteration. Let's try to change the weights and see what effect it has on the metrics. The process of trying out various weights is based on our judgment of the dataset and the distribution of data. Let's say we feel that the data distribution is more linear, and therefore we decide to increase the weight for the linear regression model and decrease the weights of the other two models. Let's now try the new combination of weights in *iteration 2*:

1. Take the weighted average of the predictions.

   In this iteration, we increase the weight of logistic regression prediction from **0.6** to **0.7** and decrease the other two from **0.2** to **0.15**:

```
"""
Calculating the ensemble prediction by applying
weights for each prediction
"""
ensemblepred=(pred1 *0.70+pred2 * 0.15+pred3 * 0.15)
```

2. Calculate the final predictions from the probabilities.

   We now have to get the final predictions for each example from the output probabilities using the **np.argmax()** function:

```
# Generating predictions from probabilities
import numpy as np
pred = np.argmax(ensemblepred,axis = 1)
```

3. Generate the confusion matrix for the predictions:

```
# Generating confusion matrix
from sklearn.metrics import confusion_matrix
confusionMatrix = confusion_matrix(y_test, pred)
print(confusionMatrix)
```

You should get an output similar to the following:

```
[[94 13]
 [ 7 82]]
```

Figure 15.20: Confusion matrix

4. Generate a classification report:

```
# Generating classification report
from sklearn.metrics import classification_report
print(classification_report(y_test, pred))
```

You should get an output similar to the following:

	precision	recall	f1-score	support
0	0.93	0.88	0.90	107
1	0.86	0.92	0.89	89
accuracy			0.90	196
macro avg	0.90	0.90	0.90	196
weighted avg	0.90	0.90	0.90	196

Figure 15.21: Classification report

In this exercise, we implemented the weighted averaging technique for ensemble learning. We did two iterations with the weights. We saw that in the second iteration, where we increased the weight of the logistic regression prediction from **0.6** to **0.7**, the accuracy actually improved from **0.89** to **0.90**. This is a validation of our assumption about the prominence of the logistic regression model in the ensemble. To check whether there is more room for improvement, we should again change the weights, just like we did in iteration **2**, and then validate against the metrics. We should continue these iterations until there is no further improvement noticed in the metrics.

Comparing it with the metrics from the averaging method, we can see that the accuracy level has gone down from **0.91** to **0.90**. However, the recall value of class **1** has gone up from **0.91** to **0.92**, and the corresponding value for class **0** has gone down from **0.91** to **0.88**. It could be that the weights that we applied have resulted in a marginal degradation of the results from what we got from the averaging method.

Looking at the results from a business perspective, we can see that with the increase in the recall value of class `1`, the card division is getting more creditworthy customers. However, this has come at the cost of increasing the risk with more unworthy customers, with **`12%`** (**`100% - 88%`**) being tagged as creditworthy customers.

MAX VOTING

The max voting method works on the principle of majority rule. In this method, the opinion of the majority rules the roost. In this technique, individual models, or, in ensemble learning jargon, individual learners, are fit on the training set and their predictions are then generated on the test set. Each individual learner's prediction is considered to be a vote. On the test set, whichever class gets the maximum vote is the ultimate winner. Let's demonstrate this with a toy example.

Let's say we have three individual learners who learned on the training set. Each of them generates their predictions on the test set, which is tabulated in the following table. The predictions are either for class '1' or class '0':

Test Example	Prediction of learner 1	Prediction of learner 2	Prediction of learner 3	Final Prediction
Example 1	1	1	1	1
Example 2	1	0	0	0
Example 3	1	1	0	1
Example 4	0	1	0	0

Figure 15.22: Predictions for learners

In the preceding example, we can see that for **`Example 1`** and **`Example 3`**, the majority vote is for class '1,' and for the other two examples, the majority of the vote is for class '0'. The final predictions are based on which class gets the majority vote. This method of voting, where we output a class, is called "hard " voting.

When implementing the max voting method using the **`scikit-learn`** library, we use a special function called **`VotingClassifier()`**. We provide individual learners as input to **`VotingClassifier`** to create the ensemble model. This ensemble model is then used to fit the training set and then is finally used to predict on the test sets. We will explore the dynamics of max voting in *Exercise 15.04, Ensemble Model Using Max Voting*.

EXERCISE 15.04: ENSEMBLE MODEL USING MAX VOTING

In this exercise, we will implement an ensemble model using the max voting technique. The individual learners we will select are similar to the ones that we chose in the previous exercises, that is, logistic regression, KNN, and random forest:

1. Open a new Colab notebook.
2. Execute all the steps from *Exercise 15.01*, *Loading, Exploring, and Cleaning the Data*, up until the splitting of the dataset into train and test sets.
3. We will now import the selected classifiers, which we will use as the individual learners:

```
"""
Defining the voting classifier and three
individual learners
"""
from sklearn.ensemble import VotingClassifier
from sklearn.linear_model import LogisticRegression
from sklearn.neighbors import KNeighborsClassifier
from sklearn.ensemble import RandomForestClassifier
# Defining the models
model1 = LogisticRegression(random_state=123)
model2 = KNeighborsClassifier(n_neighbors=5)
model3 = RandomForestClassifier(n_estimators=500)
```

4. Having defined the individual learners, we can now construct the ensemble model using the **VotingClassifier()** function. This is implemented by the following code snippet:

```
# Defining the ensemble model using VotingClassifier
model = VotingClassifier(estimators=[('lr', model1),\
                         ('knn', model2),('rf', model3)],\
                          voting= 'hard')
```

As you can see from the code snippet, the individual learners are given as input using the **estimators** argument. Estimators take each of the defined individual learners along with the string value to denote which model it is. For example, **lr** denotes logistic regression. Also, note that the voting is "hard, " which means that the output will be class labels and not probabilities.

5. Fit the training set on the ensemble model:

```
# Fitting the model on the training set
model.fit(X_train,y_train)
```

6. Print the accuracy scores after training:

```
"""
Predicting accuracy on the test set using
.score() function
"""
model.score(X_test,y_test)
```

You should get an output similar to the following:

```
0.9081632653061225
```

7. Generate the predictions from the ensemble model on the test set:

```
# Generating the predictions on the test set
preds = model.predict(X_test)
```

8. Generate the confusion matrix for the predictions:

```
# Printing the confusion matrix
from sklearn.metrics import confusion_matrix
# Confusion matrix for the test set
print(confusion_matrix(y_test, preds))
```

You should get an output similar to the following:

```
[[96 11]
 [ 7 82]]
```

Figure 15.23: Confusion matrix

9. Generate the classification report:

```
# Printing the classification report
from sklearn.metrics import classification_report
print(classification_report(y_test, preds))
```

You should get an output similar to the following:

```
              precision    recall  f1-score   support

           0       0.93      0.90      0.91       107
           1       0.88      0.92      0.90        89

    accuracy                           0.91       196
   macro avg       0.91      0.91      0.91       196
weighted avg       0.91      0.91      0.91       196
```

Figure 15.24: Classification report

> **NOTE**
>
> To access the source code for this specific section, please refer to https://packt.live/3aESLr6.
>
> You can also run this example online at https://packt.live/31cL7RJ.

In this exercise, we implemented the max voting technique for ensemble learning. As you can see from the classification report, the results are similar to what we got from the averaging method (**0.91**). From a business context, we can see that this result is more balanced. The recall value for worthy customers is high, at **92%**; however, this has come at the cost of more risk by having more unworthy customers. The percentage of unworthy customers is around **10%** in this case (**100%** - **90%**).

ADVANCED TECHNIQUES FOR ENSEMBLE LEARNING

Having learned simple techniques for ensemble learning, let's now explore some advanced techniques. Among the advanced techniques, we will be dealing with three different kinds of ensemble learning:

- Bagging
- Boosting
- Stacking/blending

Before we deal with each of them, there are some basic dynamics of these advanced ensemble learning techniques that need to be deciphered. As described at the beginning of the chapter, the essence of ensemble learning is in combining individual models to form a superior model. There are some subtle nuances in the way the superior model is generated in the advanced techniques. In these techniques, the individual models or learners generate predictions and those predictions are used to form the final predictions. The individual models or learners, which generate the first set of predictions, are called **base learners** or **base estimators** and the model, which is a combination of the predictions of the base learners, is called the **meta learner** or **meta estimator**. The way in which the meta learners learn from the base learners differs for each of the advanced techniques. Let's understand each of the advanced techniques in detail.

BAGGING

Bagging is a pseudonym for **B**ootstrap **Agg**regat**ing**. Before we explain how bagging works, let's describe what bootstrapping is. Bootstrapping has its etymological origins in the phrase, *Pulling oneself up by one's bootstrap*. The essence of this phrase is to make the best use of the available resources. In the statistical context, bootstrapping entails taking samples from the available dataset by replacement. Let's look at this concept with a toy example.

Suppose we have a dataset consisting of 10 numbers from 1 to 10. We now need to create 4 different datasets of 10 each from the available dataset. How do we do this? This is where the concept of bootstrapping comes in handy. In this method, we take samples from the available dataset one by one and then replace the number we took before taking the next sample. We continue with this until we get a sample with the number of data points we need.

As we are replacing each number after it is selected, there is a chance that we might have more than one of a given data point in a sample. This is explained by the following figure:

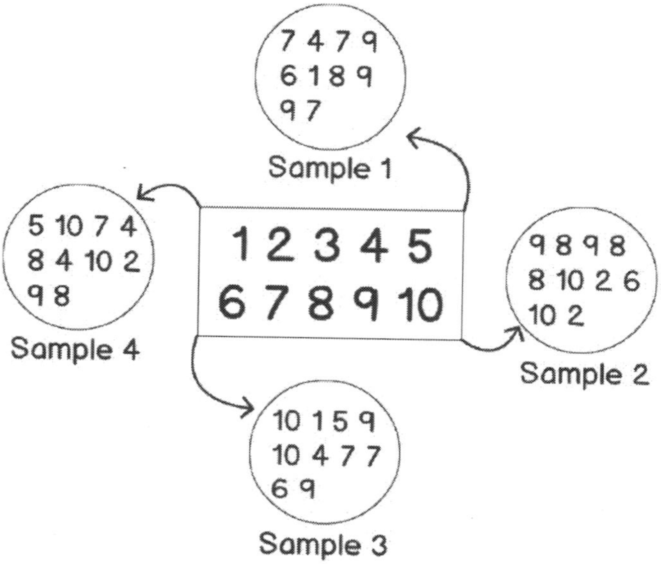

Figure 15.25: Bootstrapping

Now that we have understood bootstrapping, let's apply this concept to a machine learning context. Earlier in the chapter, we discussed that ensemble learning helps in reducing the variance of predictions. One way that variance could be reduced is by averaging out the predictions from multiple learners. In bagging, multiple subsets of the data are created using bootstrapping. On each of these subsets of data, a base learner is fitted and the predictions generated. These predictions from all the base learners are then averaged to get the meta learner or the final predictions.

When implementing bagging, we use a function called **`BaggingClassifier()`**, which is available in the **`Scikit learn`** library. Some of the important arguments that are provided when creating an ensemble model include the following:

- **`base_estimator`**: This argument is to define the base estimator to be used.
- **`n_estimator`**: This argument defines the number of base estimators that will be used in the ensemble.
- **`max_samples`**: The maximum size of the bootstrapped sample for fitting the base estimator is defined using this argument. This is represented as a proportion (0.8, 0.7, and so on).

- **`max_features`**: When fitting multiple individual learners, it has been found that randomly selecting the features to be used in each dataset results in superior performance. The **`max_features`** argument indicates the number of features to be used. For example, if there were 10 features in the dataset and the **`max_features`** argument was to be defined as 0.8, then only 8 (0.8 x 10) features would be used to fit a model using the base learner.

Let's explore ensemble learning with bagging in *Exercise 15.05, Ensemble Learning Using Bagging*.

EXERCISE 15.05: ENSEMBLE LEARNING USING BAGGING

In this exercise, we will implement an ensemble model using bagging. The individual learner we will select will be random forest:

1. Open a new Colab notebook.

2. Execute all the steps from *Exercise 15.01, Loading, Exploring, and Cleaning the Data*, up until the splitting of the dataset into train and test sets.

3. Define the base learner, which will be a random forest classifier:

```
# Defining the base learner
from sklearn.ensemble import RandomForestClassifier
bl1 = RandomForestClassifier(random_state=123)
```

4. Having defined the individual learner, we can now construct the ensemble model using the **`BaggingClassifier()`** function. This is implemented by the following code snippet:

```
# Creating the bagging meta learner
from sklearn.ensemble import BaggingClassifier
baggingLearner = \
BaggingClassifier(base_estimator=bl1, n_estimators=10, \
                  max_samples=0.8, max_features=0.7)
```

   The arguments that we have given are arbitrary values. The optimal values have to be identified using experimentation.

5. Fit the training set on the ensemble model:

```
# Fitting the model using the meta learner
model = baggingLearner.fit(X_train, y_train)
```

6. Generate the predictions from the ensemble model on the test set:

```
# Predicting on the test set using the model
pred = model.predict(X_test)
```

7. Generate a confusion matrix for the predictions:

```
# Printing the confusion matrix
from sklearn.metrics import confusion_matrix
print(confusion_matrix(y_test, pred))
```

You should get an output similar to the following:

```
[[99  8]
 [12 77]]
```

Figure 15.26: Confusion matrix

8. Generate the classification report:

```
# Printing the classification report
from sklearn.metrics import classification_report
print(classification_report(y_test, pred))
```

You should get an output similar to the following:

```
              precision    recall  f1-score   support

           0       0.89      0.93      0.91       107
           1       0.91      0.87      0.89        89

    accuracy                           0.90       196
   macro avg       0.90      0.90      0.90       196
weighted avg       0.90      0.90      0.90       196
```

Figure 15.27: Classification report

> **NOTE**
>
> To access the source code for this specific section, please refer to https://packt.live/3iYcHZ3.
>
> You can also run this example online at https://packt.live/3hfRCbZ.

In this exercise, we implemented ensemble learning using bagging. As you can see from the classification report, we have a slightly lower result (**0.90**) than what we got from the averaging and max voting methods (**0.91**). However, looking at the results from a business perspective, we can see some big swings in the recall values for both of the classes. We see that the recall value of creditworthy customers is around 87%. That means that there is around **13%** of lost opportunities. We can also see that the risks in terms of unworthy customers being identified are also being reduced. The recall value for identifying unworthy customers is around 93%, which means that only around 7% of the unworthy customers are wrongly classified as creditworthy. So, for a business that is more risk-averse, it is recommended that you use this model.

BOOSTING

The bagging technique, which we discussed in the last section, can be termed as a parallel learning technique. This means that each base learner is fit independently of the other and their predictions are aggregated. Unlike the bagging method, boosting works in a sequential manner. It works on the principle of correcting the prediction errors of each base learner. The base learners are fit sequentially one after the other. A base learner tries to correct the error generated by the previous learner and this process continues until a superior meta learner is created. The steps involved in the boosting technique are as follows:

1. A base learner is fit on a subset of the dataset.
2. Once the model is fit, predictions are made on the entire dataset.
3. The errors in the predictions are identified by comparing them with the actual labels.
4. Those examples that generated the wrong predictions are given larger weights.
5. Another base learner is fit on the dataset where the weights of the wrongly predicted examples in the previous step are altered.
6. This base learner tries to correct the errors of the earlier model and gives their predictions.
7. *Steps 4*, *5*, and *6* are repeated until a strong meta learner is generated.

When implementing the boosting technique, one method we can use is **AdaBoostClassifier()** in scikit-learn. Like the bagging estimator, some of the important arguments for the **AdaBoostClassifier()** method are **base_estimator** and **n_estimators**. We will now implement the boosting algorithm in *Exercise 15.06, Ensemble Learning Using Boosting*.

EXERCISE 15.06: ENSEMBLE LEARNING USING BOOSTING

In this exercise, we will implement an ensemble model using boosting. The individual learner we will select will be the logistic regression model. The steps for implementing this algorithm are very similar to the bagging algorithm:

1. Open a new Colab notebook file.
2. Execute all of the steps from *Exercise 15.01*, *Loading, Exploring, and Cleaning the Data*, up until the splitting of the dataset into train and test sets.
3. Define the base learner, which will be a logistic regression classifier:

```
# Defining the base learner
from sklearn.linear_model import LogisticRegression
bl1 = LogisticRegression(random_state=123)
```

4. Having defined the individual learner, we can now construct the ensemble model using the **AdaBoostClassifier()** function. This is implemented by the following code snippet:

```
# Define the boosting meta learner
from sklearn.ensemble import AdaBoostClassifier
boosting = AdaBoostClassifier(base_estimator=bl1, \
                              n_estimators=200)
```

   The arguments that we have given are arbitrary values. The optimal values have to be identified using experimentation.

5. Fit the training set on the ensemble model:

```
# Fitting the model on the training set
model = boosting.fit(X_train, y_train)
```

6. Generate the predictions from the ensemble model on the test set:

```
# Getting the predictions from the boosting model
pred = model.predict(X_test)
```

7. Generate a confusion matrix for the predictions:

```
# Printing the confusion matrix
from sklearn.metrics import confusion_matrix
print(confusion_matrix(y_test, pred))
```

You should get a similar output to the following:

```
[[96 11]
 [ 8 81]]
```

Figure 15.28: Confusion matrix

8. Generate the classification report:

```
# Printing the classification report
from sklearn.metrics import classification_report
print(classification_report(y_test, pred))
```

You should get an output similar to the following:

```
              precision    recall  f1-score   support

           0       0.92      0.90      0.91       107
           1       0.88      0.91      0.90        89

    accuracy                           0.90       196
   macro avg       0.90      0.90      0.90       196
weighted avg       0.90      0.90      0.90       196
```

Figure 15.29: Classification report

> **NOTE**
>
> To access the source code for this specific section, please refer to https://packt.live/3iUas96.
>
> You can also run this example online at https://packt.live/2EkkW2J.

In this exercise, we implemented the ensemble learning model using boosting. As you can see from the classification report, we got very similar results (0.90) to the bagging method, which we implemented in the previous exercise. From a business context, the results are more balanced compared to the results that we got for the bagging method (the recall values of 0.93 and 0.87). Here, we can see that the recall value of the unworthy customers (90%) and that of creditworthy customers (91%) are quite close to each other, which indicates a very balanced result.

STACKING

Stacking, in principle, works in a similar way to bagging and boosting in that it combines base learners to form a meta learner. However, the approach for getting the meta learners from the base learners differs substantially in stacking. In stacking, the meta learner is fit on the predictions made by the base learners. The stacking algorithm can be explained as follows:

1. The training set is split into multiple parts, say, five parts.
2. A base learner (say, KNN) is fitted on four parts of the training set and then predicted on the fifth set. This process continues until the base learner predicts on each of the five parts of the training set. All the predictions, which are so generated, are collated to get the predictions for the complete training set.
3. The same base learner is then used to generate predictions on the test set as well.
4. *Steps 2* and *3* are then repeated with a different base learner (say, random forest).
5. Next enters a new model, which acts as the meta learner (say, logistic regression).
6. The meta learner is fit on the predictions generated on the training set by the base learners.
7. Once the meta learner is fit on the training set, the same model is used to predict on the predictions generated on the test set by the base learners.

All these processes are explained pictorially as follows:

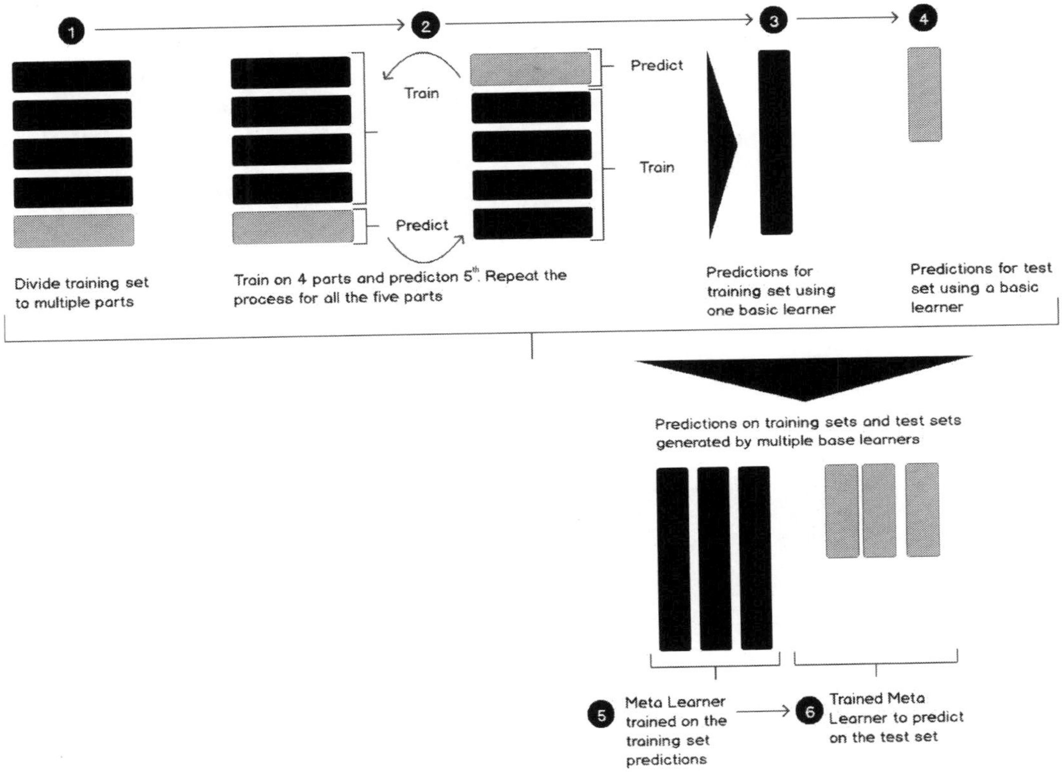

Figure 15.30: Process of stacking

The implementation of stacking is done through a function called **`StackingClassifier()`**. This is available from a package called **`mlxtend`**. The various arguments for this function are the models that we assign as base learners and the model assigned as a meta learner. The implementation of the stacking technique is executed in *Exercise 15.07, Ensemble Learning Using Stacking*.

EXERCISE 15.07: ENSEMBLE LEARNING USING STACKING

In this exercise, we will implement an ensemble model using stacking. The individual learners we will use are KNN and random forest. Our meta learner will be logistic regression:

1. Open a new Colab notebook.
2. Execute all of the steps from *Exercise 15.01*, *Loading, Exploring, and Cleaning the Data*, up until the splitting of the dataset into train and test sets.
3. Import the base learners and the meta learner. In this implementation, we will be using two base learners (KNN and random forest). The meta learner will be logistic regression:

```
# Importing the meta learner and base learners
from sklearn.linear_model import LogisticRegression
from sklearn.neighbors import KNeighborsClassifier
from sklearn.ensemble import RandomForestClassifier

bl1 = KNeighborsClassifier(n_neighbors=5)
bl2 = RandomForestClassifier(random_state=123)
ml = LogisticRegression(random_state=123)
```

4. Once the base learners and meta learner are defined, we will proceed to create the stacking classifier:

```
# Creating the stacking classifier
from mlxtend.classifier import StackingClassifier
stackclf = StackingClassifier(classifiers=[bl1, bl2],\
                              meta_classifier=ml)
```

   The arguments that we have been given are the two base learners and the meta learner.

5. Fit the training set on the ensemble model:

```
# Fitting the model on the training set
model = stackclf.fit(X_train, y_train)
```

6. Generate the predictions from the ensemble model on the test set:

```
# Generating predictions on test set
pred = model.predict(X_test)
```

7. Generate the classification report:

```
# Printing the classification report
from sklearn.metrics import classification_report
print(classification_report(y_test, pred))
```

You should get a similar output to the following:

```
              precision    recall  f1-score   support

           0       0.88      0.92      0.89       107
           1       0.89      0.84      0.87        89

    accuracy                           0.88       196
   macro avg       0.88      0.88      0.88       196
weighted avg       0.88      0.88      0.88       196
```

Figure 15.31: Classification report

8. Generate a confusion matrix for the predictions:

```
# Printing the confusion matrix
from sklearn.metrics import confusion_matrix
print(confusion_matrix(y_test, pred))
```

You should get a similar output to the following:

```
[[98  9]
 [14 75]]
```

Figure 15.32: Confusion matrix

> **NOTE**
>
> To access the source code for this specific section, please refer to https://packt.live/31dZRjy.
>
> You can also run this example online at https://packt.live/2Fwsdgf.

In this exercise, we implemented the ensemble learning model using stacking. As you can see from the classification report, we did not get any improvements over the benchmark model using the stacking classifier. The possible reasons for this could range from the choice of base learners and meta learners that we used to the size of the dataset. It should be noted that not all ensemble learners will be the desired silver bullet. There will be many instances where many advanced methods will fail to improve performance. This exercise proved to be one such instance. However, the secret recipe for getting the most optimal method, which boosts performance, is intense experimentation. That is what will yield results. After all, in machine learning, there are no free lunches.

From a business context, the results have huge implications from a revenue perspective as a large number of creditworthy customers, **`16%`** (**`100%`** - **`84%`**), have been tagged as unworthy. The risk side of recall is quite good with a higher percentage (**`92%`**) of unworthy customers identified.

So far, we have seen three advanced techniques for ensemble learning. Let's now apply all of these techniques to the credit card dataset and then pick the best method. We will do this in *Activity 15.02, Ensemble Model Using the Averaging Technique*.

ACTIVITY 15.02: COMPARISON OF ADVANCED ENSEMBLE TECHNIQUES

Scenario: You have tried the benchmark model on the credit card dataset and have got some benchmark metrics. Having learned some advanced ensemble techniques, you want to determine which technique to use for the credit card approval dataset.

In this activity, you will use all three advanced techniques and compare the results before selecting your final technique.

The steps are as follows:

1. Open a new Colab notebook.
2. Implement all steps from *Exercise 15.01, Loading, Exploring, and Cleaning the Data,* up until the splitting of the dataset into train and test sets.
3. Implement the bagging technique with the base learner as the logistic regression model. In the bagging classifier, define **`n_estimators = 15`**, **`max_samples = 0.7`**, and **`max_features = 0.8`**. Fit the model on the training set, generate the predictions, and print the confusion matrix and the classification report.

4. Implement boosting with random forest as the base learner. In the **AdaBoostClassifier**, define **n_estimators = 300**. Fit the model on the training set, generate the predictions, and print the confusion matrix and classification report.

5. Implement the stacking technique. Make the KNN and logistic regression models base learners and random forest a meta learner. Fit the model on the training set, generate the predictions, and print the confusion matrix and classification report.

6. Compare the results across all three techniques and select the best technique.

7. Output: You should get an output similar to the following for all three methods. Please note you will not get exact values as output due to variability in the prediction process.

   The output for bagging would be as follows:

```
[[93 14]
 [ 6 83]]

              precision    recall  f1-score   support

           0       0.94      0.87      0.90       107
           1       0.86      0.93      0.89        89

    accuracy                           0.90       196
   macro avg       0.90      0.90      0.90       196
weighted avg       0.90      0.90      0.90       196
```

Figure 15.33: Output for bagging

The output for boosting would be as follows:

```
[[97 10]
 [ 8 81]]
              precision    recall  f1-score   support

           0       0.92      0.91      0.92       107
           1       0.89      0.91      0.90        89

    accuracy                           0.91       196
   macro avg       0.91      0.91      0.91       196
weighted avg       0.91      0.91      0.91       196
```

Figure 15.34: Output for boosting

The output for stacking would be as follows:

```
[[99  8]
 [18 71]]
              precision    recall  f1-score   support

           0       0.85      0.93      0.88       107
           1       0.90      0.80      0.85        89

    accuracy                           0.87       196
   macro avg       0.87      0.86      0.86       196
weighted avg       0.87      0.87      0.87       196
```

Figure 15.35: Output for stacking

> **NOTE**
>
> The solution to this activity can be found here: https://packt.live/2GbJloz.

In this activity, we implemented all three advanced ensemble techniques on the credit card dataset. Based on the metrics, we found that boosting (**0.91**) has better results than bagging (**0.90**) and stacking (**0.87**). We, therefore, select the boosting algorithm to boost the performance of our models. From a business perspective, the boosting algorithm has generated more balanced results where the recall value of both creditworthy and not creditworthy customers (91%) is similar.

SUMMARY

In this chapter, we learned about various techniques of ensemble learning. Let's summarize our learning in this chapter.

At the beginning of the chapter, we were introduced to the concepts of variance and bias and we learned that ensemble learning is a technique that aims to combine individual models to create a superior model, thereby reducing variance and bias and improving performance. To further explore different techniques of ensemble learning, we downloaded the credit card approval dataset. We also fitted a benchmark model using logistic regression.

In the subsequent sections, we were introduced to six different techniques of ensemble learning; three of them being simple techniques and the remaining three being advanced techniques. The averaging method creates an ensemble by combining the predictions of base learners and averaging the prediction probabilities. We were able to get better results than the benchmark model using this technique. The weighted averaging method is similar to the averaging method. The difference is in the way the predictions are combined. In this method, arbitrary weights are applied to the predictions of individual learners to get the final prediction. Max voting is a technique that arrives at final predictions based on the votes of the majority of the base learners.

Ensemble learning with bagging leverages bootstrapping techniques. The base learners are fitted on bootstrapped datasets and the results are aggregated to get the meta learner. Boosting is a sequential learner, which works on the principle of error correction of the base learners. We found that boosting techniques produced some superior results for our context. We used the stacking technique to generate the final predictions by learning from the output of the predictions by the base learners.

The objective of this chapter was to equip you with a repertoire of skills aimed at boosting the performance of your machine learning models. However, it should be noted that there are no silver bullets among machine learning techniques. Not all techniques will work in all scenarios. The secret sauce, which will help you on your journey to being a good data scientist, is the rigor of experimentation with different techniques, use cases, and datasets.

Having learned a set of tools aimed at boosting performance, you are now well prepared to apply these on a range of real-world projects. This chapter marks the end of the book and is a good opportunity for you to reflect on all the skills you have learned in working your way through the different chapters. However, there are still three bonus chapters available to you in the free online interactive edition of this Workshop. You can access this via the following link: https://packt.live/2sSKX3D.

INDEX

A

addata: 686-688, 697, 699, 707, 716-717, 723, 729
aggfunc: 200, 207
altair: 94-95, 98, 100, 136, 201-204, 208, 212, 215, 218-219, 225-226, 234-235, 238-239, 242, 250-251, 253, 256, 447, 452, 457-458, 461, 465, 467, 469, 471, 474-475, 486, 518-522, 524-525, 527-528, 532-533, 618, 639
amazon: 601
argmax: 758, 761, 763
astype: 110, 435, 564, 566, 568, 570, 593, 604, 689-690, 699, 707, 717, 724, 729-730
atom-type: 273

B

backmodel: 700
baldata: 663-664
bankcorr: 119
bankdata: 87-88, 94-95, 97, 100, 103-107, 109-113, 115, 118, 122, 136-138, 649-651
barplot: 353-355
binary: 6, 81, 83, 85, 128, 145, 148, 186, 260, 264, 286, 291, 293-294, 297, 299, 303, 311, 316, 318, 344, 413, 438, 445, 552, 582-583, 600, 629, 648-650, 654-655, 677, 685, 691, 694, 735
bivariate: 41, 58, 81
boosting: 741, 744, 768, 773-774, 776, 781-784
bootstrap: 769
boxplot: 530-532, 537-543, 545
boxplots: 530, 533, 543, 546

C

catprop: 98, 108, 114
chromatin: 559
churnmodel: 678
contour: 400
corrmatrix: 55
crisp-dm: 492-493, 546

D

database: 18, 20, 42, 326, 601, 643, 696
datetime: 496, 528, 563, 603, 622-624, 627, 630-631, 644
denmark: 506
dimension: 269-270, 400, 694, 697, 700, 708, 717, 724, 730, 740
downstream: 115, 125, 128
dropna: 51, 59, 505, 508, 584, 750
drop-out: 447, 458, 467, 474, 482, 484-485
dtypes: 115, 137, 496, 502, 507, 514, 543, 562-564, 567, 569-570, 589, 593, 622, 627-628, 688, 749
dummies: 137-138, 142, 288-289, 316, 343, 348, 358, 364, 651, 677, 751

E

encoding: 289, 343-344, 349, 358, 364, 438, 566
entropy: 434, 439, 455
errors: 77, 268, 286, 573, 576, 686, 755, 773

F

facmodel: 732-733
figsize: 60, 62
fillna: 586-587, 590-593, 691, 699, 707, 717, 724, 730
five-fold: 335, 338, 343
framework: 79
f-string: 8
f-test: 80
f-value: 80

G

gaussian: 121, 126, 130, 256
groupby: 95, 97, 100-101, 104, 106-107, 113, 632-635, 639, 641

H

heatmap: 48, 56-57
histogram: 90, 122-123, 427, 524-527, 533-537, 545

I

intercept: 46, 65, 68, 70, 74, 130, 395
invoiceday: 604-608
invoiceno: 496, 498-500, 522, 552, 554-557, 564-565
iterator: 335

J

joblib: 312, 314-315

K

kernel: 395, 413, 415, 418
key-value: 11-12, 23
k-fold: 334, 342, 415, 428
kmeans: 194, 196-197, 204-206, 211, 213, 215-216, 218-219, 223-226, 228-229, 232, 235, 248, 250-252, 256
k-nearest: 31, 81, 126, 393

L

linspace: 422, 426

M

mlxtend: 464-465, 467, 777-778
msmote: 667-668, 673-676, 678, 680
mssubclass: 517, 567-568
mszoning: 508

N

ncolumn: 508, 515
ndarray: 268-270
nearest: 130, 222, 232, 396
netflix: 148
n-fold: 334
nunique: 504, 508, 610, 612, 617-618

O

offset: 624-625
one-hot: 289, 364, 438
openml: 155, 163, 168, 174, 181
outliers: 90, 190, 214, 248-249, 491, 511-512, 516, 521, 530-532, 534-535, 542, 546, 575
overfit: 153, 171, 177, 184, 186, 261, 322, 356, 368, 391
overkill: 566
overlap: 122
override: 397
oversample: 667, 669, 673

P

pandas: 1-2, 18-27, 38-39, 41, 44, 49, 51, 53, 57, 59, 65, 72, 81, 87-88, 94-95, 100, 103, 109, 118, 136, 149-150, 154-155, 163, 168, 174, 181, 185, 194-195, 199-200, 204-207, 215-216, 219, 225-226, 231, 235-237, 239-240, 250, 256, 262, 273-274, 276-278, 281-282, 287, 289, 304, 313, 316, 326-327, 337, 347-348, 357, 363, 369, 379, 412-413, 416-417, 428, 431, 435, 438, 446-447, 456, 458, 465, 467, 471, 474-475, 482-483, 486, 494-498, 500-508, 510-515, 519,

533, 550-552, 554, 557-558, 562-567, 572-573, 575, 577, 579, 582, 584, 586-588, 592, 599, 601-604, 606, 609-610, 615, 618, 620, 622-624, 626, 632-633, 635, 637, 639, 645, 649, 660, 663, 677, 686-687, 691, 693, 697, 699, 707, 716, 723, 729, 735, 746-747
pcamodel: 721
perceptron: 130
p-value: 79-80
pyplot: 49, 59, 91, 119-120, 122-123, 308-309, 420, 425, 713, 718
pytorch: 2

Q

quadrant: 744-745
quartile: 530

R

randint: 434, 439
rangeindex: 328
regplot: 60, 62-63
render: 301-302, 411
re-train: 252
rfemodel: 703-704

S

seaborn: 44, 49-50, 59-60, 62, 201, 518
security: 45, 668
segmenting: 256
sensor: 150
separator: 26, 87, 282, 686, 747
server: 685
sigmoid: 131
simulation: 447
skewed: 121, 648, 654
skiprows: 25-27, 304
sklearn: 28, 31-32, 34, 36-39, 50, 59, 65, 72, 110, 125, 137, 140-141, 150-151, 153, 156-157, 161, 163, 168, 172, 174, 179, 181, 185, 194, 196-198, 201, 204, 206, 215, 218-219, 225-226, 235, 245-247, 250, 256, 260, 262, 273, 277, 281, 287, 291-292, 294-302, 304, 311-314, 325-327, 335, 339, 342, 344, 347, 349, 359, 365, 369, 379, 395-396, 400, 404, 409, 414, 424, 430, 433-434, 445, 447, 455, 458, 464, 467, 471, 474-478, 482-483, 486, 649, 652-653, 663-665, 671-672, 675, 692, 699-700, 702, 704-705, 707-708, 710-711, 714, 717-718, 720-722, 724, 726-727, 730, 732-733, 752-753, 756, 758, 762-764, 766-767, 771-772, 774-775, 778-779
stackclf: 778
stochastic: 140, 680
stockcode: 496, 498, 522-523, 552, 554-557, 572-574, 633-636, 638
subplot: 119-120
subset: 138, 179, 195, 231, 395, 552, 554, 557, 574-575, 579, 581, 583-584, 773
sub-tree: 455

T

tableau: 202
taxstats: 194, 204, 215, 226, 236, 250, 609, 611
tensorflow: 2
test-set: 410, 416, 428
timedelta: 625
trade-off: 745
traindata: 660-662
train-test: 55
tree-based: 31, 454-455, 463, 487
t-test: 80

tuning: 81, 151, 154, 162, 168, 174, 181, 186, 351, 362-363, 368, 391, 393-396, 398-399, 403-404, 409, 414, 424-425, 428, 430, 432-433, 440, 756
tuples: 283, 371, 382
t-values: 67, 75, 80

U

usecols: 195, 204, 215, 226, 236, 250

V

varimp: 456-457, 460-461, 465-466, 469
vector: 125-126, 130, 268-271, 323, 350, 393, 413-415

Z

z-score: 245, 247, 250, 254

Made in the USA
Las Vegas, NV
18 February 2021

18110553R00453